THEATRE/ THEORY/ THEATRE

THEATRE/
THEORY /
THEATRE

THE MAJOR CRITICAL TEXTS
from Aristotle and Zeami
to Soyinka and Havel

Edited with introductions by
Daniel Gerould

APPLAUSE
NEW YORK • LONDON

THEATRE /THEORY /THEATRE
The Major Critical Texts from Aristotle and Zeami to Soyinka and Havel
© Copyright 2000 Daniel Gerould (ed.)
ISBN 1-55783-309-5 (Cloth)

Printed in Canada.

Library of Congress Cataloging-in-Publication Data

Library of Congress Number 99-068319

British Library Catalogue in Publication Data
A catalogue record for this book is available from the British Library

APPLAUSE BOOKS

1841 Broadway
Suite 1100
New York, New York 10023
Phone: (212) 765-7880
FAX: (212) 765-7875

Combined Book Services Ltd.
Units I/K Paddock Wood Dist. Ctr.
Paddock Wood,
Tonbridge Kent TN12 6UU
Phone 0189 283-7171
FAX   0189 283-7272

CONTENTS

FOREWORD

The aim of this collection is to present in a single volume of not more than 500 pages essential theorists and theories of theatre. What is innovative about the anthology is its scope and its emphasis. As we navigate the turn of the century and enter a new millennium, our perspective on the development of theatre and the theories that have shaped it is more inclusive that ever before. *Natya* in Sanskrit means both theatre and drama, and in the *Natyasastra*, one of the earliest and greatest theoretical works, both are considered together. Drama and theatre can no longer be studied in isolation one from the other, nor can Western theatre be separated from Eastern. The ideal of a world literature (first advanced by Goethe at another turn of the century) has evolved from earlier concepts of national literatures and is particularly applicable to theatrical theory.

Theatrical activity has traditionally been central to the life of the community and nation. The theory of the theatre is a reflection of politics and of international relations. It is shaped by attitudes to authority and power, the status quo and social change. The politics of theatrical theory is accordingly the focus of my introduction.

A simple set of principles has guided me in putting together this anthology. My goal has been to chart a main course through what for many readers is unknown territory and to provide a clear road map for the journey. I have chosen basic texts by the major artists, poets, playwrights, and philosophers who have shaped the ongoing theoretical debate about the nature and function of theatre. Wherever possible I have given complete essays and coherent, consecutive selections, rather than highly edited snippets. With longer works and the voluminous *Natyasastra* and *Commentary on The Poetics of Aristotle* by Castelvetro, this was not feasible. Brackets containing three periods [...] indicate that there has been an omission.

Because such a comprehensive anthology must cover many centuries, inevitable constraints of length have made it impossible to establish a beachhead on the rugged and highly contested terrain of contemporary Anglo-American academic theory. Recent theoretical approaches to theatre within the academy, addressed to a specialized readership and written in a professional jargon, belong in a seperate volume. Such a valuable collection could aptly supplement the basic texts found in *Theatre / Theory / Theatre*, which are designed not as a final resting place, but rather the point of departure.

Constraints of length also precluded the inclusion of footnotes elucidating the rich fabric of quotations and allusions to authors, works, ideas, and events embedded in each of the selections. Hundreds and hundreds of such notes would be required to documents adequately the incredibly diverse and dense tissue of references to be found in the forty-one texts by thirty-seven theorists. Such scholarly apparatus would make *Theatre / Theory / Theatre* half as a long again and change the nature of the collection. Instead of annotated versions requiring constant interruption to consult notes at the bottom of the page, the anthology presents texts to be read, savored, and pondered.

The translations are a mixture of old and new. For the sake of clarity, I have made a few corrections and minor revisions in several of the non-contemporary translations. Sometimes a version from the same period as the original captures the spirit of an older work, as is the case with the anonymous eighteenth-century rendering of Rousseau's *Letter to D'Alembert*. Verse translations are essential for the poetry of Horace and Lope de Vega. John Conington's mid-nineteenth century version of the *Ars Poetica* in heroic couplets, recalling Alexander Pope, gives Horace the right jaunty and witty tone, and Marvin Carlson's new rhymed version of *The New Art of Writing Plays* captures for the first time in English Lope de Vega's irony and ambivalence.

Many friends and colleagues have helped me first in the conception and then in the realization of this anthology; among them Jarka Burian, Harry Carlson, Marvin Carlson, Alma Law, Jim Leverett, Benito Ortolani, Joanne Pottlitzer, Eszter Szalczer, Michel Vinaver, Stanley Waren, and Glenn Young deserve special mention. I also wish to acknowledge the dedicated work of Marla Carlson, Lars Myers, Richard Niles, and Alissa Roost, my students in the Ph.D. Program in Theatre at the Graduate School of the City University of New York who assisted me in preparing the manuscript.

New York   Daniel Gerould
August 1999

INTRODUCTION:
THE POLITICS OF THEATRE THEORY

A Pocketful of Theory

On September 9, 1920 the twenty-two-year-old Bertolt Brecht noted in his diary, "A person with only one theory is lost. He must have several, four, many! He must stuff his pockets with them as if they were newspapers, always the latest, one can live nicely among theories, one can be snugly housed among theories. If one is to get on, one needs to know that there are lots of theories."

Theories are a way of making one's presence felt, and the more new-fangled and varied the better—Brecht recognized these truths early in his career and no other twentieth-century theatre artist has had his pockets better stuffed. But Brecht has not been alone. Artists as diverse as Zeami, Lope de Vega, Corneille, Dryden, Goethe, Hugo, Craig, and Meyerhold, to mention just a few, likewise saw the need of theory to justify practice, and in the process of self-explication they offered a speculative view of the art of theatre past, present, and future.

This collection brings together some of the major theories with which theatre artists—playwrights, poets, actors, and directors (and their counterparts among scholars and philosophers)—have stuffed their pockets and prepared for the fray. For these polemicists, theory has been a means of both defense and aggression, leading to conquest and the wielding of power (if only, in some cases, posthumously). Hence the profusion of competing systems.

Risks and Dangers of Theorizing

Theatre theory is systematic generalizing, or discourse, about the nature and function of the stage, the composition and performance of plays, and the art of the actor, director, and designer. Some theorists speculate about the role of theatre in relation to audience, society and state. Others consider how the stage can best represent humankind's existence on earth, battle with demons, and afterlife in heaven or hell. From Aristotle to Boal, Soyinka, and Havel, many theatrical theorists have been engaged in politics. And there are those—Bharata, Zeami, Mickiewicz, and Artaud come to mind—who have been hailed as seers, prophets, holy fools or madmen, saints, even deities. Given the sacred origins of the stage and the sometime status of the theatre as a temple, it is hardly surprising that theoreticians often play the role of magus.

The involvement of theatre theorists in the organized life of society is only natural. Theatre is the most public of the arts, and for centuries the stage has been an institution close to the seats of power and patronage and subject to state control. Rules and regulations affecting plays in performance inevitably have political dimensions.

Because of the unusual ability of "live" performance to excite and incite audiences, those theorizing about the functions of this communal art must contend with the question of how to channel the unruly passions aroused in the spectators and for what purpose. Theorists of theatre are inevitably cast as authorities whose role it is to impose a cohesive—and sometimes coercive—view of culture on others. Opposing visions clash as proponents of new theories challenge the authority of predecessors and rivals.

Theorists may view theatre as a place of riot and excess or as a site of civic festivity and ritual. In the beginning Plato denounced the popular mania for the stage as "theatocracy" and condemned its appeal to base human emotions as an invitation to mob rule. Then his pupil Aristotle came to the defense of theatre, showing how the natural impulse to imitate could, in proper dramatic form, become educational and therapeutic in its effects.

Across the ages an ongoing dialogue takes place among theorists—the backward-glancing and the forward-looking—who uphold or challenge the reigning values of their age. Aristotle's *Poetics* was grounded on the drama of a past time—fifth-century Greece—hence its "prophetic hindsight," whereas Mickiewicz and Artaud with inspired foresight took aim at an impossible theatre of the future.

Theory—descriptive, prescriptive, or prophetic—may inhibit or liberate, generate tensions or unloose repressed energies. By aligning themselves with dominant parties or regimes, theatre theorists become defenders of *de facto* authority. Or, by using theatre as an instrument of opposition, they seize upon its revolutionary potential to strike a blow against conformity and undermine existing social structures. Theorizing about theatre is sure to put whoever attempts it in the midst of ideological controversy.

For example, the cause of nationalism and anti-imperialism has found a powerful voice in theatre theory. By opposing the imposition of an alien aesthetic, theatre theorists have affirmed their country's right to its own indigenous traditions. As dramaturg (i.e. theoretician) at the Hamburg National Theatre, Lessing "rent asunder the authority of the French canon" (in the words of Thomas Mann). His call for liberation from the yoke of foreign cultural domination led Germany toward political unification. From eighteenth-century German reclamation of native roots to twentieth-century Czech rebellion against Soviet-enforced socialist realism, theatre theory has played a significant role in battles for national cultural identity.

In *The Sociology of the Theatre* Jean Duvignaud argues that theatrical performance (i.e. the interplay between stage and spectator) by its very nature is "a revolt against the established order" because it reflects desires still seeking definition and poses questions to which there are as yet no available answers, thus opening vistas on the future rather than consolidating the present. Theatre theory, on the contrary, usually attempts to socialize the raw power of performance and rationalize its impact. To be acceptable to society and its civilizing institutions, theatre's anarchic impulses must be transformed into—or at least disguised as—constructive forces amenable to control.

For if, as Duvignaud argues, the theatrical spectacle is ultimately subversive in its relation to the status quo, theorists often find themselves posed precariously between conformity and dissent, forced to play the role of accommodating mediators who, by their conciliatory speculations, justify practices that appear dangerous to the cultural establishment serving as patron to playwrights and theatre artists. Such was the plight of the aging Corneille trammeled by the court classicism of French absolute monarchy; such was the dilemma of the later Brecht confronted by the socialist realism of Communist orthodoxy. Was Jesuitical theorizing a cunning ruse, the inevitable and legitimate adaptation to circumstances, or was it abject submission to totalitarianism?

Theatre theorists sometimes play for high stakes. In the dangerous world of state tyranny, the "wrong" theory could land one in jail or on the scaffold. Becoming involved in the politics of theatrical theory has entailed risks, threatening to life and liberty. Censorship, persecution, excommunication, exile, imprisonment, even death might be the consequences. Aristotle, Zeami, Castelvetro, Mickiewicz, Rousseau, Diderot, Schiller, Mme de Staël, Hugo, Zola, Strindberg, Maeterlinck, Brecht, and Artaud fled, went into self-exile, were arrested, jailed or condemned in absentia—if not because of their theatrical speculations, at least on account of their roles as authorities seeking to influence the public by their theories. Some escaped with their lives like Castelvetro and Brecht, others were driven into exile like Mme de Staël and Zeami. Meyerhold was tortured and executed, Artaud forcibly incarcerated, Boal arrested, tortured, and forced into exile, Soyinka and Havel repeatedly jailed.

Theatre/Theory or Theory/Theatre?

Theatre theory has its roots in spectatorship. Observation of plays and players usually provides the impetus for theorizing. It may be potent discontent with the current state of affairs that impels visionaries like Mickiewicz and Artaud to condemn the stage of the present and dream of a radically different theatre of the future. Or, on the contrary, it may be a contemporary production or solo performance that reveals previously unforeseen possibilities and leads to theoretical discoveries in the realm of acting or stagecraft.

Sometimes we can pinpoint exact moments—a particular theatrical event or performer seen on such and such a day—that were instrumental in the genesis of theory. For example, Diderot based his *Paradox of Acting* on the conclusions he drew from witnessing Garrick's chameleon-like virtuosity during the English actor's second visit to Paris in October, 1764. Garrick's impromptu solo performance, in which he changed his face dozens of times in a matter of minutes, confirmed Diderot in the view that self-command and intensive study of roles, not empathy, made performers like Mlle Clairon geniuses.

Marinetti's frequenting the Parisian Cirque Medrano with Apollinaire and Picasso in 1914 lead to the formulation of his Variety Theatre Manifesto. Discovery of the Balinese dancers at the Colonial Exposition in Paris in the summer of 1931 helped Artaud realize his own ideas about ritual theatre. Brecht's theory of the alienation effect took shape after he saw an acting demonstration by the Chinese actor Mei Lan-fang in Moscow in the spring of 1935.

In other cases theory originates from an attempt to synthesize an entire lifetime of experience in the theatre. In the vast one-thousand-page treatise *Nātyasástra* the mysterious Bharata (godhead of Indian theatre) and subsequent editors appear to have catalogued and systematized the total practice of the Sanskrit stage, as Aristotle had done far less completely for the Greek drama of an age preceding his own by almost a century. In secret writings not intended for public view, Zeami set out to transmit theories, based on his own experience as well as that of his father, to family members working in the theatre generations later. On the contrary, Brecht wished to make available to the world at large the conclusions he had drawn from a "scientific" study of his own stage practice as well as of the drama and theatre of all times.

This much seems incontrovertible: theatre theory arises from creative contacts with the stage made by those given to speculation, codification, and legislation about the art of the drama. But even if theory has its sources in the experience of performance, does it follow that theory then influences subsequent theatrical practice?

In *A History of Modern Criticism* René Wellek maintains that although it is "something that many literary historians are reluctant to recognize," there is such a "deep gulf between theory and practice throughout the history of literature" that criticism can best be treated as an autonomous and self-contained discipline without relation to the actual practice of writing poetry, drama, and fiction.

In the case of the applied art, theatre, however, there appears to be no necessary disjunction between performance and theory. On the contrary, theatre seems theory-ridden; it has often been created according to the rules, conceived to illustrate manifestoes, copied from theoretical models and formulas. Theatres are founded to test or exemplify a theory. And theorists themselves are often performers of their own speculations, embodying abstract ideas in theatrical form by means of words and gestures.

Theorists as Performers: Spectatorship and Theatricality

Theatre theory is, I believe, less of an abstraction and more of a show than is generally recognized. This drama comes alive when we consider the public dimensions and politics of theory as well as the spectatorship and theatricality of theorists.

In brief introductions to the individual authors, I try to tell what the theorists saw when they attended the theatre and how they were seen—by others and themselves. The appearance of theorists is not irrelevant to their thinking or to the reception of their thoughts. Sidney, Rousseau, and Artaud are striking instances of the extent to which a theorist's authority is histrionic.

Rather than provide thumbnail sketches of authors' life, works, and views (readily available in reference books), I offer instead an anatomy of the theorist's attachments to the theatre, including play-going habits, predilections and prejudices, as well as dramatic style and bearing—in a word, what was theatrical about the theorist.

"Our most purely intellectual ideas," Diderot writes in *The Letter on the Blind*, "result from the structure of our bodies." I have rehearsed the theorists' physical appearances and personal eccentricities, as revealed in portraits and pictures, eyewitness accounts, and anecdotes, readily allowing that these images are often self-created, multiple and subject to revisions. Intensely concerned with outer show, theatre theorists use gesture, face, and dress as projections of a persona (or personae).

Theatre theory is predicated on personal theatricality as well as passionate spectatorship. Each theorist is both a theatregoer and fabricator of a histrionic self. Theorists usually "perform" as lecturers, promulgating their doctrines through public appearances and tours. The lecture is a special "theoretical" performance seen and heard for its style and verve as well as for its ideas.

As an art form, theatrical theory is inherently dramatic. The earliest polemic against mimesis, Plato's *Republic*, is mimetic in form. *The Art of Poetry*, Horace's longest and best composition, erodes boundaries between genres by turning theory into great poetry. Dryden's *Essay of Dramatic Poesy*, which takes the form of an elegant conversation among four friends on a barge floating down the Thames debating the relative merits of ancients and moderns, French and English, Shakespeare and the present age, is a more satisfying performance than the author's plays.

In the case of Futurist manifestoes, the theoretical treatises publicly declaimed by Marinetti and his cohorts at Futurist evenings were their most striking works of art. Artaud enacted the plague that he wished the theatre to be in his theoretical lectures. His greatest performance, in which he played himself as tragic scapegoat, was his final lecture at the Vieux Colombier in 1946. In recent times, the theoretical writings of Corneille and of Brecht have been put on stage as autonomous dramas.

Theatrical theory naturally assumes the form of a dialogue—with predecessors, enemies, friends, students, and above all with oneself. "Even when we are, or at least think ourselves alone," writes Friedrich Schlegel in *The Philosophy of Language*, "we still think as two, and are constrained as it were to recognize our inmost profoundest being as essentially dramatic."

The theorist's physical presence can be the stamp of authority for the validity of ideas. A double of theatrical performance, theatre theory has its own character types, plots, and props. Appearance, dress, and style of wearing one's hair are accessories to the theoretical performance. By means of facial expression, gestures, and costume the theorist sets forth propositions, much as the actor establishes character.

As dramaturg for the Hamburg National Theatre Lessing donned the traditional powdered wig. To mount his attack on Molière and the classical theatre, Rousseau wore his own hair. Gesturing through the flames, Artaud displayed his ravaged features as the ultimate expression of his apocalyptic vision of a theatre of cruelty. Brecht's carefully tailored shabby suit, his proletarian cap, and expensively plain steel-rimmed glasses served to convey the concept of the alienation effect.

Because theatrical theorists think dramaturgically and understand the nature of illusion, they know—better than others—how appearances are subject to manipulation. Their biographies are legends expounded by the authors themselves, their images conscious self-creations, their portraits and photographs exhibits in an ever-changing gallery.

"Everything profound loves a mask," Nietzsche declared. Like actors, theatrical theorists wear many masks and adopt shifting personae to present their ideas. They are adepts at metamorphosis. The disunity of the self evident in such ephemeral poses raises questions of identity central to their theoretical inquiries.

Protean Selves

Theorists—constant playgoers even when their only stage is in the mind—are endowed with powerful histrionic personalities and strong attractions to the feigned and the seeming. Wrestling with their own penchant for impersonation, some theorists, like St. Augustine, renounce the stage, others, like Rousseau, denounce it and propose a "healthy" alternative, while reformers, like Gordon Craig, strive to rid it of actors, whom they see as the culprits responsible for the theatre's malignant deceptiveness.

Because all find the symptoms of mercurial instability within themselves, theatre theorists are well equipped to explain the fascination of the stage's mutability and endless play of insubstantial shadows. In attempting to justify the theatre, theorists are forced to confront their own Protean natures and examine the transformational tendencies of the histrionic personality. In *The Antitheatrical Prejudice*, Jonas Barish examines the overwhelmingly negative response to the art of theatrical illusion that characterizes the moral stance of most writers and theorists. Rare indeed are those who, like Marinetti and Meyerhold, celebrate the actor's changeability, variety, and powers of metamorphosis; rather these signs of inconstancy are usually seen as the very traits that have made the actor the emblem of inauthenticity and lost identity. For these reasons, theatre theorists like Maeterlinck and Craig prefer puppets to human actors whose "accidental" qualities of perpetual metamorphosis they wish to banish from the stage.

Mutability is at the heart of the debate on the immorality of the stage. To the Latin Church Fathers, Elizabethan Puritans, and seventeenth-century French Jansenists, theatre is nothing but a tissue of falsehoods begotten by the Father of Lies. Because the pleasures afforded by theatrical performance are so seductive, political and religious ideologues view the stage as a place of danger whose threats to public order must be contained. "All great amusements are dangerous to the Christian," writes Pascal in his *Pensées*, "but among all those which the world has invented there is none to be more feared than the theatre. It is a representation of the passions so natural and so delicate that it excites them and gives birth to them."

Defenders of the theatre must argue that the stage, rather than inciting harmful passions, presents instructive and truthful representations of reality. But does the stage represent the reality? Here we confront a recurring issue—perhaps the central issue—in the history of theatre theory. The problem of mimesis, which serves as the spine holding together the theoretical writings in this anthology, is the subject of the speculations that follow.

Mimesis and Its Enemies

The relation of art and life is a perennial concern of aesthetics. The traditional idea that drama is a representation of reality may, in the eyes of romanticists, avant-gardists, and poststructuralists, be the most banal and naive assumption, but the concept of mimesis, or imitation, has been at the center of controversy in the theoretical discourse about theatre stretching from Aristotle to the present. Because of the powerful impact of "live" performance (with "real" people performing "real" actions on stage) on audiences, mimetic and anti-mimetic theories continue to dominate theatrical discourse.

At different times and places mimesis has been seen as a reactionary concept, aesthetically and politically, or as a daring revolutionary doctrine. It has been both a bastion of tradition to be overthrown and a rallying cry for innovation. In Plato's *Republic*, the earliest document for theatrical theory, mimesis comes under attack as epistemologically false and morally dangerous. Those, like Aristotle, who come to the defense of mimesis must respond to these charges and demonstrate how potentially subversive or debasing emotions may be curbed or redirected toward higher goals.

Aristotle

For Aristotle, the concept of mimesis includes both strict imitation of nature and a more general perfecting of what nature has left unfinished without the need to reproduce anything that actually exists. The embellishing or perfecting of nature advocated by Aristotle becomes the doctrine of *la Belle Nature* in French seventeenth-century aesthetics.

Aristotle's master plan of politics provides a benign role for theatre. The end or final cause of tragedy is the pleasure given by imitation. Containment of the contagious effect of tragic passion is brought about through catharsis which purges souls that might grow intoxicated on represented desire. But as Richard McKeon points out, drama in the *Poetics* is considered largely in its own terms without reference to its social, moral, or religious premises or purposes. Paying scant attention to audience or performance, Aristotle assumes a generic reader/spectator sharing his standards and capable of appreciating excellence in drama through a study of the artistic medium, the forms suited to expression in that medium, and the manner of such expression.

Horace: Imitation of Culture, Not Nature

The rhetorical school that flourished after Aristotle shifted the emphasis of poetics from the internal construction of a work to the effect produced on audiences. A second meaning of imitation—the imitation of other artists and works of art—came to replace the Aristotelian conception of mimesis. In his awareness that artists imitate culture, not nature, and that writing grows out of other writing, Horace reveals a "modern" sensibility and sophisticated understanding of the creative process. He also pays close attention to the role of commerce and money in the cultural production and reception of poetry, asking practical questions such as: who buys what and for how much.

In *The Art of Poetry* (or "Letter to the Pisos") the Roman poet recommends to two would-be writers the imitation of Greek models, while arguing that language, which is constantly evolving and changing, must be updated. Originality consists in the manipulation of artistic convention and in the recasting of the familiar in new modes of expression. The dependence of Latin culture on Greek arts and letters favors intertextuality. For Horace the craft of poetry is a matter of hard work and ceaseless revision. Writing must never be pandering to the masses or amateurish self-indulgence. But more than a disciplined artisan, the poet is a moral law-giver and civilizer.

Horace's many brief *dicta* (such as *in medias res* and *dulce et utile*) are proffered conversationally and non-dogmatically as witty bits of advice. Only centuries later, in the Renaissance, would they become proverbial and prescriptive definitions of major critical issues. While upholding propriety and decorum as common sense guideposts to success, the Roman author advocated adroit juggling with tradition rather than blind adherence to rules. By a clever blend of daring and conformity the state-sponsored poet Horace managed to occupy a privileged position in a dangerous world of tyranny under Augustus. No wonder that Horace was regarded by ambitious young Renaissance court artists as mentor and model, or that he was Brecht's favorite poet in his later years.

Recognizing that in his own time audiences preferred animal shows to standard theatrical entertainment, Horace proposed reinstating the satyr play, an old genre not practiced by the Romans. With close ties to the primitive Dionysian festival and to rural Latin rites and floral games, the satyr play as interpreted by Horace forecasts Guarini's theory of pastoral tragicomedy.

Monsters

Despite his promotion of the satyr play, Horace's concept of mimesis excludes the monstrous and the fantastic. As cautionary examples the Roman poet opens *The Art of Poetry* with descriptions of hybrid monstrosities—human head on horse's neck and woman's torso with fish's tail—that violate the laws of uniformity and identity upon which his classical aesthetics are based.

In all ages ghosts, monsters, and the insane make terrifying entrances and exits on the stages of the world, including the Greek and Roman. The supernatural and abnormal explain much of the popular appeal of drama, but these are horrors that most theorists prefer to ignore (although in arguing against the cognitive value of mimesis Plato stressed the role of Eros, demonic possession, and madness in the creation of poetry). Aristotle tried to control the irrational and keep the uncanny and horrible at bay (by keeping most manifestations offstage), but at the same time the author of the *Poetics* admitted that "a touch of madness" may help the poet compose. And Horace brings *The Art of Poetry* to a close with a portrait of the hirsute mad poet who pisses on his father's grave. But only Artaud will openly avow that he is in search of monsters.

"Raging Demon-Hearted Demons" — *Imitation and Nō Drama*

Because Aristotle's *Poetics* made mimesis a cornerstone of the Western tradition of theatrical theory, we tend to overlook the fact that imitation is also a central concept in Sanskrit aesthetics and plays a prominent role in classical theories of Chinese and Japanese theatres.

For example, Nō drama is mimetic in its acting traditions and representation of diverse and colorful character types. "Imitation is a foremost principle in our art," Zeami stated in his first treatise *Fūshikaden*. Within the total Nō performance, mimesis occupies a complex position that depends on the type of play and subject as well as the school of performers, and it undergoes changes as the art evolved over the centuries.

In other words, mimesis is not the defining mode of Nō, but rather one available means of theatrical presentation that may be used in different dosages. Whereas for Aristotle music, dance, and spectacle were subordinate aspects of mimesis, for Zeami imitation is an essential element of theatre on a par with song and dance, the two arts of Nō. The degree of imitation varies according to the class of those imitated. Unlike court ladies, men of lowly occupation should not be imitated in any meticulous fashion.

After his father's death Zeami moved away from the predominantly mimetic acting style that Kan'ami favored toward abstraction and interiority. In Zeami's later treatises, *yūgen*, an elegant and mysterious veiled beauty, gains preeminence as an aesthetic ideal over literal role playing or *monomane* (imitation).

Zeami developed a paradoxical theory of opposites, derived from Zen Buddhist metaphysics, that undermined from within the decorum of character types. He sought for a sublimity that lay beyond physical appearance. Instead of doddering and feeble, the aged should be played in the sprightly, youthful manner that an old person would like to assume. The popular crowd-pleasing jealous Nō demon should no longer be revealed as a violent, raging, demon-hearted fiend, but rather as someone profoundly melancholy.

Inner, not outer nature, became the object of mimesis. Zeami wished to represent the spirit rather than visible action, realizing that the true master actor can captivate audiences by doing nothing, not even moving. At the height of his art the imitator is united with the thing imitated. In the art of imitation a stage of non-imitation is reached when the actor enters the thing imitated and becomes the character. Empathic identification leads the spectators—aristocrats and commoners alike—to a state of trance.

"Our art," Zeami maintained, "is based on the desires of our audience," which are different not only for each generation but which vary according to the time and place of performance. Successful performance of Nō depends on the level of the play, the skill of the performers, the discernment of the audience, the nature of playing area, and the occasion itself. Imitation, which had been the centerpiece of Kan'ami's stage practice, came to occupy a smaller and smaller place in Zeami's later theoretical writings. When Zeami was writing these treatises between 1418 and 1424, Aristotle's *Poetics* and mimesis were still unknown in Europe.

Renaissance Rediscovery of Imitation

The doctrine of mimesis, self-evident in classical antiquity, had first been attenuated by Neoplatonism, then all but forgotten during the Medieval period. Christian art made its goal the glorification of God, not the representation of life on earth. Tertullian, Augustine, and other Church Fathers, reviving Plato's denunciations of theatrical representation, attacked the stage as an instrument of Satan.

After the rediscovery of Aristotle in the fifteenth century, imitation of nature became a revolutionary new doctrine for Renaissance painters and poets. It held sway as the dominant theory of art until the late eighteenth century. The subject imitated the object, it was claimed, according to laws of nature first discovered by the Greeks and Romans. Antiquity as a model at first proved liberating. Renaissance reformulations of classical mimesis were a source of innovation and renewal in the theatre of the Renaissance.

A new cultural epoch began when works of art were once again viewed as representations of reality, initiating an unbroken chain of critical discourse on theatre stretching from the Italian interpreters of Aristotle's *Poetics* through Corneille and d'Aubignac to Dryden and Johnson. Verisimilitude, truth to nature, likeness to the thing represented—these were the new criteria for excellence. In painting mimesis now meant direct imitation of the external world. In drama the imitation of nature was accomplished largely at second-hand via cultural artifacts. In keeping with Horace's injunctions, erudite Renaissance poets imitated Greek models made accessible through Roman imitations by Plautus, Terence, and Seneca. Popular dramatists reworked ("imitated") legends, tales, and historical anecdotes that had appeared in romances and chronicles or in the dramas of earlier playwrights.

Of all the Italian Renaissance theatre theorists, Lodovico Castelvetro was by far the most idiosyncratic and influential. In his learned one-thousand page commentary on the *Poetics* the Italian scholar felt free to disagree with Aristotle on almost every central issue. Castelvetro imagines a theatre, quite unlike any that actually existed in Renaissance Italy, whose sole purpose is the entertainment, not the instruction, of an audience composed of "the rude multitude."

Poetry and historiography are virtually indistinguishable in Castelvetro's sweeping revision of Aristotle's *Poetics*. Tragedy, the Italian theorist informs us, must present the "magnificent actions of royal personages" such as are known to the audience from the news of the day and contemporary history. Castelvetro's royal personage was dynamic and proud, he "intensely wanted what he wanted," he did not endure injury patiently, he was naturally immoderate, he followed his instincts without apology, he was temperamentally more inclined to go to war than to law, and he was most likely capable of "killing both strangers and relatives." Castelvetro's description of the imperious, violent Renaissance tragic hero seems drawn directly from "nature"—i.e. the rulers of the time.

In Renaissance theory the marvelous becomes a major source of artistic pleasure no longer to be denied sensation-loving audiences. For uncultivated but demanding spectators, Castelvetro argues that strict mimesis in spatial and temporal matters must be maintained if the performance is to be believable. Although the word itself is never once used in his long treatise, the concept of unity is central to Castelvetro's propagation of strict verisimilitude. In striking contrast to Aristotle, the Italian theorist considers unity of action, which would inhibit the variety of incidents favored by audiences, far less important to the credibility of the performance than the unities of time and place.

At the same time Castelvetro points out that the spectators, quite conscious of the illusion, recognize the poet's artfulness in condensing the dramatic action in such narrow confines. Thus the audience's admiration of the playwright's efforts in overcoming the difficulties of observing the unities is an additional source of aesthetic pleasure. Since copying earlier authors would not entail any real effort worthy of admiration, Castelvetro discourages writers from imitating the ancients. The playwright must always display personal inventiveness, in historical subjects choosing little known episodes that can be freely developed.

In the Renaissance understanding of mimesis the concept of verisimilitude went hand in hand with the highest degree of artifice. From Castelvetro the doctrine of the three unities as integral to mimesis spread to France where it became a reigning dogma.

In the *Compendium of Tragicomic Poetry* defending his play, *Il Pastor Fido*, Guarini offered the most complete theoretical justification for Renaissance pastoral tragicomedy, which had already been the subject of critical debate for almost half a century.

Arguing that the end of poetry is solely amusement now that the Christian religion takes care of moral education, Guarini continued the separation of *delectare* and *docere* begun by Castelvetro and proposed a new aesthetic for the creation of a complex modern genre containing seemingly contradictory elements of both tragedy and comedy, but by ridding tragedy of savagery and comedy of lewdness achieving its own unity. Within a single work mimesis could now encompass characters from opposite ends of the social scale and the serious and comic actions appropriate to their stations. The function of this blend is to purge the audience of melancholy.

Sidney's version of mimesis is a heady mixture of the Aristotelian, Horatian, and Neoplatonic concepts to which the British poet was exposed during his travels in Italy and which he then introduced to England as the latest continental critical theory. For Sidney the poet is above all a *vates* or *magus*, whose absolute powers of the imagination permit him as a divine maker to create fabulous creatures such as have never existed.

Rejecting the "realist" mimesis of the "meaner sort of painters" who simply reproduce what is, Sidney celebrates artistic freedom and the joy of creativity—except in the case of drama. Under the influence of Italian theory about the unities, he rejects the native English tradition, even though his own poetics favors unbridled diversity and variety. While embracing the medieval romance tradition in his courtly entertainments for Elizabeth, the cosmopolitan humanist Sidney condemns the popular theatre derived from the medieval cycles and moralities when it comes to playwriting. What he objects to in "mongrel tragicomedy" is its naïveté and lack of self-conscious artistry. That a powerful new drama could grow out of these crude popular roots would have seemed inconceivable to the elegant court poet.

It was Sidney's friend, the heretical thinker and playwright Giordano Bruno who expressed the most radical Renaissance view of mimesis. Disdaining even to write a theoretical discourse, he condemned imitation as the servile unimaginative copying of those who had not enough genius to invent for themselves. Bruno was burned at the stake as a heretic.

The prolific and immensely successful Lope de Vega found a more oblique way to confront the pressures of classical theory that was making its presence felt throughout Europe. The Spanish poet made up an academy and addressed a verse treatise to its imaginary members, in which he paid lip service to the tenets sanctioned by antiquity, lamenting that he could not follow them, but was forced to compromise his principles by the entertainment-hungry Spanish mob for whom he wrote his plays.

French Classicism

Mimesis became the servant of monarchy in mid-seventeenth-century France when Cardinal Richelieu undertook the institutionalizing of a state-sponsored theatre. As interpreted by the theorists at the newly established French Academy, imitation became the repetition of formulas derived from the ancients.

In *The Whole Art of the Stage*, the abbé d'Aubignac, Richelieu's chief theoretician (although not a member of the Academy), rehabilitates the theatre—until then shunned by polite society for its scandalous reputation—as an innocent form of entertainment and proves the profession of actor to be compatible with the precepts of Christianity. D'Aubignac presents all the arguments for state support and control of the arts that will be used in the centuries to follow. The stage serves the glory of the ruler, contributes to the country's international prestige, and makes citizens forget internal problems and seditious thoughts.

Although he stressed the political function of mimesis and hoped—vainly—to become the salaried commissioner of state theatres, the abbé, himself a playwright, was intensely interested in contemporary stage practice and audience taste. For d'Aubignac and the entire French seventeenth century, the poetics of theatre was a branch of the art of oratory. Dramatic action was expressed almost exclusively by the word, hence the overwhelmingly verbal nature of classicist theatre. The playwright must keep the action simple so that audiences understand the play quickly and easily. The public and its beliefs and opinions were crucial in determining *vraisemblance* (probability) and *bienséance* (propriety), the key concepts of French classicist rhetoric of the theatre. Corneille, d'Aubignac's principal French example, was frequently cited for violating these rules, but the abbé was enough of a practical man of the theatre to recognize that Corneille compensated for his technical failings by the expressive power of his representations of strong emotion.

In his three *Discourses* of 1660, Corneille, looking back over a successful career of thirty years as a professional playwright, defended himself against the pedants and learned theoreticians who in the name of orthodoxy had tried to clip the wings of his inventiveness. Critics sometimes referred to Corneille as a disciple of d'Aubignac and the abbé himself even accused the dramatist of stealing his ideas, but although as playwright he capitulated to the pedants after the *Cid* controversy, in his theoretical writings Corneille advanced heretical views and struck back at his tormenters (without ever mentioning d'Aubignac's name).

Scorning the "mediocre goodness" of Aristotle's ideal tragic hero, Corneille sought sublimity in extremely virtuous or extremely evil characters who, placed in exceptional circumstances, displayed greatness of soul. The appropriate tragic emotion, the author of the *Cid* argued, was wonder or admiration, not pity and fear. While accepting the concept of mimesis, the playwright undertakes major revisions in the traditional understanding of its function.

Most daringly, Corneille declared himself an opponent of probability—the cornerstone of classicist conformity—preferring incredible situations ("great subjects") whose authenticity was guaranteed by history or tradition. In the face of repressive demands for strict adherence to the unities and *vraisemblance*, the playwright called for a margin of creative freedom, trusting the audience's imagination to do the rest. The beleaguered playwright defended his departures from classical precedent, saying he had done his best to reconcile "ancient rules and modern pleasures." Knowing the rules, Corneille asserted, was not sufficient qualification for writing a successful play, and the only goal of dramatic art was to please the audience.

Li Yu: A Chinese Rationalist

An almost exact contemporary of Corneille, and Dryden's elder by twenty years, Li Yu was like his European counterparts a playwright as well as a theorist. But Li was also a manager, producer, and director of his own traveling troupe of actresses.

Before Li, most theoretical writing on Chinese theatre considered drama simply as a branch of poetry and directed its attention to the songs and words. Li's theory, based on his own experience as a practical man of the theatre and on his observation of the work of his predecessors, was the first comprehensive study of the theatre as an autonomous art and the most thorough and systematic discussion in Chinese until modern times. Addressed to novice playwrights and prospective owners of private dramatic troupes, Li's *Casual Expressions of Idle Feelings* upset traditional priorities by placing speech on a par with song and arguing for a rationally organized plot.

Adopting an aggressive pro-mimetic stand, Li maintained that the proper concern of drama is everyday reality and that the fundamental law of playwriting is to make each work new. He advocated the revision of old dramatic masterpieces to bring them up-to-date by giving them a living language.

At a time when actors and actresses were held in low esteem, and playwrights suffered from social stigma, Li argued for the worth of the theatre and its artists and strove to give drama a coherent and credible form. Because drama is performed before a mixed audience of the educated and the uneducated, Li insisted that the presentation must be immediately intelligible. He stressed unity of plot centering around a single protagonist and one central event, resulting in a tight-knit structure that does not exclude the unpredictable and surprising so necessary to hold the audience's attention. Li's contention that the events must appear probable and convincing to the audience and that the dialogue should consist of the appropriate language befitting the social station of each character corresponds to seventeenth-century French neoclassical concerns with *vraisemblance* and decorum, no matter how different these concepts prove to be in actual practice in such different cultural contexts.

Dryden

Unlike Corneille, whose example he follows in composing theoretical treatises to justify his own practice, Dryden—always pliant—had little difficulty conforming to the reigning political and aesthetic norms of his age, which were in any case considerably less absolute than those at the French court, where totalitarian statecraft demanded totalitarian stagecraft.

In the *Essay of Dramatic Poesy*, Dryden opened the debate on mimesis and theatrical form to the general public. Designed to appeal to well-bred theatregoers and readers rather than contentious scholars, the *Essay* is a lively dialogue among four different speakers written in an immediately intelligible conversational style. At this early point in a long and productive life, the poet sought to establish his career as a playwright by "creating" an audience. The dramatic form of the essay gave the protean Dryden, always open to opposing arguments, an opportunity to try out contrasting viewpoints without being narrowly partisan or confined to a single position.

Yet at the same time the *Essay* is overtly nationalistic and political, affirming Dryden's allegiance to modernity and the British state. Although he favors more variety than the French allow, Dryden recognizes unity of action as a corollary of political centralism and authority. Secondary plots must be subsidiary to the main action upholding a single protagonist, just as all subjects must be subservient to one ruler.

Dryden's concept of mimesis as a heightened version of reality ("nature wrought up to a higher pitch") is a continuation of the French *Belle Nature* and its idealizing and generalizing tendencies. But although he recognizes a universal nature that is one and the same at all times and places, Dryden sees that the genius of an age and nation determines its taste—Shakespeare appeals to English audiences more than do the Greek dramatists. By taking into account the temporal and geographical context, Dryden introduces historical relativism into his analysis of mimesis. This comparative method enables the playwright to justify violence, bloodshed, and battles on the Restoration stage as a native tradition springing from popular British taste.

For Dr. Johnson as for Dryden, Shakespeare was great because of the truth to nature of his characters. In praising Shakespeare as a portrayer of general, not individual, nature, Johnson was a consummate classicist. But in the same "Preface to Shakespeare," the great dictionary maker demolished whatever arguments remained to buttress the tottering neoclassical unities of time and place. In the process Johnson went to the opposite extreme, denying that any illusion was ever created in the theatre. Hostile to actors and unversed in stage practice, the nearly blind Dr. Johnson felt a play read was no different from a play seen. Superstitiously terrified of ghosts and apparitions, the editor of Shakespeare wished to stay in full possession of his critical reasoning faculties at all times and maintained that neither spectators or actors projected themselves into the action portrayed onstage. The last great authority to pontificate confidently about the imitation of general nature, Dr. Johnson soon became the very symbol of dull, unfeeling rationalism to the coming generations of anti-mimeticists.

Three Continental Reformers

During the course of the eighteenth century challenges to the dominance of French classicist theatre produced many revisionist theories of mimesis. Most notably, Diderot, Rousseau, and Lessing—versatile thinkers given to speculation on painting, poetry, and music—turned their dissatisfaction with old formulas into a commitment to cultural innovation in the performing arts.

For Rousseau, modern theatre was an inherently empty and vicious institution and a cause of financial extravagance and misuse of time. While granting that existing theatres could serve a useful purpose in corrupt societies by forestalling worse evils, the Swiss philosopher was determined to prevent the establishment of a stage in his native Geneva. In its stead he proposed a communal festive drama with neither actors or spectators, only equal participants in an idyllic ritual.

In quest of an authentic self that would remain forever constant, Rousseau, like Plato and the Christian moralists, fulminates against theatrical mimesis as false seeming and brands the actor a charlatan and prostitute. To the elitist closed world of court theatre with its shameful images of servitude and inequality, the author of *The Social Contract* opposes an outdoor civic ceremony serving to unite all people. Rousseau's influential theory became the inspiration for festivals of the French Revolution, American civic pageants, Soviet mass spectacles, and other forms of participatory "people's theatre." Liquidating the separation of actors and spectators has been the dream of many later theorists.

Diderot, on the contrary, considered the stage the very best teacher of morality because of its ability to move audiences deeply. Despite their recent estrangement, Diderot and Rousseau had long been close friends and still shared many beliefs. Both were convinced of the contemporary theatre's mediocrity and of the growing irrelevance of the classic French repertory. Both were prejudiced against performers for the supposed immorality of their lives. Both admired the ancient Greek theatre for the vast size of its democratic auditorium, its teaching of civic virtue, and its powerful moral effect on audiences.

To replace dead neoclassical traditions and conventions, Diderot advocated a new intermediate genre between tragedy and comedy: the *drame bourgeois* in prose or serious drama of private life depicting social conditions and the various professions. Recognizing that movement and picture were more effective than words in touching hearts and teaching lessons, Diderot urged that the relentless talk of French classicist theatre give way to pantomime, gesture, tableau, even silence. With his concept of the fourth wall (which would eventually become a cornerstone of late nineteenth-century realism), Diderot promoted an illusionistic version of mimesis that was designed to serve sentimental didacticism rather than an objective and truthful portrayal of life. In the *drame* staging had to be lifelike to elicit maximum audience empathy. Yet, paradoxically, the actor was to be unmoved—a cold and disciplined artist capable of mimicking observed, not felt emotions.

A follower and translator of Diderot, Lessing supported the cause of serious domestic drama, which he attempted to give Aristotelian legitimacy. Full of reverence for the *Poetics* (which he held to be "as infallible as the elements of Euclid"), the German dramaturg condemned Corneille as both theorist and playwright for his many heretical misinterpretations of Aristotle, which for years had provided a false model for German drama.

The politics of Lessing's endorsement of Aristotelian mimesis had as its goal the establishment of a national theatre that would unite Germans linguistically and culturally. To reestablish connection with the native German popular tradition, the dramaturg thought it desirable to return to the medieval Faust legend and to repeal the banishment of the popular clown Hanswurst by the Frenchifying neoclassicist Gottsched.

For the author of *The Hamburg Dramaturgy*, the superiority of drama over all other literary genres lies in its use of natural, not arbitrary signs. Lessing's belief in theodicy—the revelation of God's justice in human affairs—informs his sense of the high moral purpose of theatre.

Eighteenth-century theorists, like Diderot and Lessing, approached the theatre as social philosophers intent on reform of the stage in the interests of the moral instruction. The generations of romantic poets that followed had a far more radical program of renewal.

Romantic Revolt

Romantic theory, while embracing the theatre as an ideal place of communion with the people, rejected the nineteenth-century playhouse as it actually existed and proposed instead a visionary drama that could be realized only in the future once an imaginative new stagecraft, drawing upon opera and popular melodrama, had come into being.

Anticipating by more than a century and a half the arguments of structuralists and poststructuralists about language, German romantic theorists challenged the representational model and turned mimesis on its head. Art does not imitate nature, they proclaimed, but creates living works; the subject constitutes, rather than reflects, the object. The Enlightenment with its smug glorification of reason was actually a darkening of the imagination.

August Wilhelm Schlegel regarded Dr. Johnson, who had extolled Shakespeare's "truth to nature," as a baneful authority to be overthrown. For Schlegel, each work for the stage was an autonomous world true only to its own laws where the creator reigns supreme. Ludwig Tieck promulgated a poetics of parody and self-referentiality, while Friedrich Schlegel maintained that literature was only about literature. Novalis asserted that "No one knows the essential thing about language, that it is only concerned with itself." For a short period mimesis was forced underground by romantic ideology.

"The poetry of the ancients was that of enjoyment, and ours is that of desire," observed August Schlegel, whose prestigious lectures exerted immense influence. Art for the romantic theorist reflected the mind's creativity and the indwelling spirit of the imagination.

The romantic artist, freed from the represented object, produced self-created illusion that at any point could be self-destroyed. These tensions between self-creation and self-destruction eventuated in romantic irony. Only such an ambivalent attitude could capture the contradictory totality of experience.

In the face of the world's disharmony and chaos, romantic irony gave voice to a yearning (*Sehnsucht*) for the infinite. This "truly transcendental buffoonery" (that Hegel condemned as frivolous) turned art into a self-conscious game. "Even in the most popular forms, such as the theatre," August Schlegel insisted, "we demand irony; we demand that the events, the characters, in short, the whole game of life really be conceived and represented as a game."

Deprived of a fixed identity and aware of being alone in an infinite universe, the creator became engaged in an impossible self-mocking quest for wholeness. And if the artistic self was divided, the work of art could not help but be fragmentary.

The Poetics of the Fragment

In opposition to Hegel's all-embracing master plan of a rational world order that assured humankind's forward march through history to ultimate perfectibility (a belief in progress taken over *in toto* by Marxists), the brothers Schlegel proposed a poetics of incompletion and desire.

For several centuries the concept of dramatic unity had been a pillar of all theories that sanctioned theatre as a cultural institution enhancing the power of the sovereign state. Now for the first time a rebellious aesthetics of disunity emerged to complete the shattering of a once firm edifice.

Arguments about the unities always touched on questions of power and authority. Both Aristotle and Horace considered the concept of unity central to their doctrine of imitation because a homogeneous view of reality served to make representation possible. For Aristotle, the unity of a work was organic, founded upon a biological analogy between artistic creation and living growth, while for Horace, unity of effect was achieved by the craftsman's mastery of the medium.

From the Renaissance to the early seventeenth century, pressures for dramatic unity were akin to *raisons d'état* for consolidating rather than dispersing political power. In the times of Corneille and Dryden, strict dramatic unity proclaimed by scholars as a *sine qua non* seemed the reflection of the recently won triumphs of monarchy and absolutism.

By the mid-eighteenth century the unities of time and place had already lost critical standing. But it was not until the romantic period that the last and most enduring of the internal unities, unity of action, came under serious attack (although in practice variety had often gained the upper hand in Renaissance drama). Instead of the wholeness and oneness of dramatic action previously deemed indispensable, the most farsighted romantic theorists proposed an aesthetics of the fragment and incompletion.

When creativity itself becomes the material of creation, artistic activity, or "process," replaces the finished product of an art work as the goal. The ideal of a rationally structured beginning, middle, and end gives way to the dream logic of the fragment which, more than the perfect work, approaches the secret of the universe. Unending becoming, not being, is that secret.

In creating a forward looking aesthetics of the fragment, the Schlegel brothers recognized that artists are attracted to the chaos of existence at the center of a seemingly ordered universe from which marvelous new births are called forth by the spirit of primal love. Ready to let chaos loose again, the romantics acknowledge the monsters that the Renaissance had enjoyed but kept under strict control—in the epic or in minor genres and popular subliterary forms.

The fragment or short unsupported pronouncement—in the aphorisms of the German romantics (and, later, of Nietzsche)—becomes a razor-sharp instrument of criticism. In the twentieth century the aesthetics of the fragment will be adopted by André Breton and the surrealists, Antonin Artaud, and Heiner Müller.

While still clinging to unity of action, the French romantic theorists eventually adopted the northern alternative to the classical south. Mme de Staël was the first to promote a nationalist aesthetic that favored the local and particular rather than the timelessly beautiful, seeing literature as the product of geography, climate, and historical period. Hugo argued that the grotesque, monstrous, and deformed are infinitely richer sources of art than the monotonous beauty of harmonious proportions.

With the demise of the old internal unities, new external unities came into prominence. In an attempt to mold social consciousness through theatre, the exiled Mickiewicz—lecturing as a performing theoretician—addressed all classes of society, seeking a unity of spectators conceived as the "nation" that he hoped to awaken to political action on a vast scale. To increase the stage's ability to arouse the people, the Polish poet also called for a unity of all the arts—music, opera, popular melodrama, panoramas, architecture—to create a total theatre anticipating Wagner's *Gesamtkunstwerk*.

Barriers between the arts must fall. "We should strive to bring the arts closer together and search for bridges from one to the other," August Schlegel urged. "Statues will come alive to become perhaps paintings; paintings will become poems; poems will become music; and who knows, perhaps solemn religious music will rise up again as a temple in the sky."

The Case of Naturalism

With the triumph of science, industry, and technology in nineteenth-century France, the imitation of nature returned as a dominant ideology. Zola claimed that realism was no radical departure from tradition, but rather the ultimate destination toward which all previous artistic practice and theory had been moving for over three centuries. But to the outraged custodians of propriety, Zola's "scientific" naturalism, which seemed to wallow in the most sordid aspects of late nineteenth-century civilization, was a revolutionary doctrine that challenged the very foundations of society.

Friend and champion of the Impressionist painters, Zola praised their close observation of contemporary reality and precise rendition of all its details according to the objective laws of nature. Abstract metaphysical man, the novelist boasted, had at last been routed by physiological man subject to the influences of heredity and environment.

By bringing the theatre, the last citadel of convention, into direct contact with real life, Zola hoped to rid the stage of its ameliorative lies, prettified sentiments, and false playhouse morality. The brutal facts of modern life were simply to be shown, analyzed, and made intelligible without any moralizing. The goal of naturalist mimesis was truth, not pleasure or instruction.

"The imagination no longer has a function," Zola proclaimed, "We no longer select, we do not idealize." To make the illusion total, representation had to be rigorously objective. No concessions were to be offered the spectators, whose presence in the darkened auditorium must be ignored and whose prejudices disregarded. Above all, "sympathetic characters"—designed to mollify audiences and guide their responses—must be forever banished. The naturalist author should reign supreme, impartial as a scientist and implacable as a god toward an ignorant public denied any activity in the creation of the work.

While acknowledging that theatre as artifice required special techniques of condensation and perspective, Zola believed that the representation of reality in drama should be as unstructured and untheatrical—i.e. as close to life and as far from art—as possible. Opposed to formal concerns, Zola recognized no autonomous theatricality and made few suggestions for innovations in dramatic technique beyond proposing that real settings be exactly reproduced and everyday language faithfully transcribed and spoken. Naively assuming the existence of a single reality scientifically knowable and objectively reproducible in either novel or drama, Zola denied the theatre a poetics of its own and made it an appendage of his theory of fiction.

Although it was a misbegotten creed in its confusion of art with science, naturalism liberated the stage from restrictive rules more completely than had any previous version of mimesis. In his vast ambition to encompass the totality of the real and render it exactly, Zola rode rough shod over all the proprieties and moral constraints of traditional decorum, thereby opening up vast areas of previously tabooed experience, chiefly sexual, for serious as well as sensational theatrical exploitation. Naturalist playwrights became muck-raking investigative reporters probing social sores and exploring new dramatic terrains.

But illusionistic naturalism, which began as a provocative mimetic attack on social hypocrisy, was soon accepted in attenuated forms as the most accessible dramatic mode by the bourgeois theatre of commerce and subsequently by the totalitarian fascist right and communist left for the glorification of their repressive systems.

The theoretical attack on naturalism began shortly after the movement itself. Both traditionally-minded opponents and renegade former disciples turned symbolists were quick to point out that, for all his hatred of obslete conventions, Zola failed to realize that realism itself was only a convention, no closer to ontological reality than any other artistic style. There was no single uniform reality waiting to be recorded. Abandoning crude sociological or reportorial quests for the truth, partisans of later, more flexible realisms were obliged to take the personal and subjective into account.

In the "Preface to *Miss Julie*" (called a "naturalistic tragedy" by the author), Strindberg provided a richly detailed manifesto for naturalism in the theatre that went far beyond Zola's simplistic conception. The Swedish playwright-theorist recognized that memory and imagination shape human perceptions. Elsewhere condemning petty photographic realism of the everyday (drawing "a piece of nature in a natural way"), the author of *The Father* proclaimed himself a proponent of "great naturalism" which presents titanic battles between natural forces. Strindberg's theory of mimesis was capacious enough to include fragmented character, aleatoric action, dream states and random dialogue.

Nietzsche and the Return of Myth

In 1872, as naturalism was gaining force in both France and Germany, Nietzsche wrote *The Birth of Tragedy*, a dazzling mix of scholarship, art, and philosophy that explored the origins of theatre in the timeless metaphysics of the dialectics (unlike Hegel's, not leading to a synthesis) between Apollonian and Dionysian. Radically anti-mimetic in scorning faithful reproduction of the lives of ordinary individuals, Nietzsche drew prophetic conclusions from Greek tragedy for the theatre of his own time. Instead of putting the spectator on stage in a mask of reality, as Euripides had done, the German philosopher argued that the audience should be transformed into a chorus of satyrs participating in a sacred rite. Tragedy was rooted neither in imitation nor in action, but in myth and ritual.

For the author of *The Birth of Tragedy*, Aristotle's grave misunderstanding was in believing the tragic emotions to be depressive feelings of pity and fear. Tragedy, on the contrary, was a stimulant celebrating the desires of an intensified life, not a tranquilizer as his early master Schopenhauer had thought. In contemporary theatre Nietzsche discovered this primeval tragic spirit first in Wagner's music dramas, then in Bizet's *Carmen*.

Symbolist and Avant-Garde Rejection of Mimesis

In the form of realism and naturalism, mimesis—the basis of traditional theatre theory—has been attacked by almost all innovative artistic and intellectual movements from the beginnings of modernism to the postmodern present. The turn-of-the-century symbolists and twentieth-century avant-gardists (Futurists, Expressionists, Constructivists) joined the battle against realist mimesis as the entrenched aesthetic of the bourgeois establishment and offered alternative styles in abstraction, discontinuity, disruption, and indeterminacy.

Looking through and beyond manifestations of outer reality, the Neoplatonic Maeterlinck asked that each spectator be placed in a state of creative reverie before a vague, polyvalent *mise en scène* liberating to the imagination by what was *not* shown. Maeterlinck's theory of the tragical in daily life called for a static theatre expressive of the soul in repose touched by the mysteries.

Like most turn-of-the-century theorists, Yeats and Craig included, the Belgian playwright was openly hostile to the profession of the actor. Burdened with the accidental and the particular, the clumsy human performer had the unfortunate habit of intruding between the spectator and the eternal spectacle that induces dreaming. Seeking ways to eliminate the mimetic weight of performers, the symbolist theorists called for the "depersonalized actor"—rarefied, dematerialized, spiritualized—who could be a celebrant in the holy theatre.

An unrelenting opponent of the slavish copying of nature, Craig argued that performers must stop impersonating and pretending if the theatre was to be saved from irreversible degeneration. Citing Plato on the evils of mimesis, the son of Ellen Terry and former actor with Henry Irving held that actors imparted the weaknesses they imitated to audiences. Craig planned to replace human performers with the *Übermarionette*, huge oversized puppets that he had constructed in semi-secrecy for use in special scenarios.

Rather than living beings, the British designer-theorist preferred the dead, for whom corporeal actors were not qualified to speak, but who could be eloquently represented by shadows, wax figures, mannequins, or puppets—all inherently immortal. Like Mickiewicz and later Tadeusz Kantor, Craig believed that the theatre opens communications with the spirits of ancestors.

In the restlessly innovative period in Russian theatre before the Revolution of 1917, Meyerhold—both as practitioner and theorist—led the assault on realist mimesis through the "cult of the mask," which meant for him a return to the popular traditions of the Medieval and Renaissance fairgrounds of Western Europe. Meyerhold himself identified passionately with Pierrot and all his examples come from France and Italy, not the native Russian fairground of Petrushka.

Like the *cabotins* and *commedia* artists of the past, the modern "mask" must display perfect physical mastery of the body. Gesture and movement alone give the performer chameleonic powers to reveal diversity of character beneath the comedian's expressionless visage. The grotesque, mixing opposites and suddenly shifting planes of reality, was Meyerhold's favored means of conveying the inscrutable and drawing spectators into the riddle.

For the Russian director, the relations of actor and audience must undergo a radical transformation. "We intend the audience not merely to observe," Meyerhold maintained, "but to participate in a corporate creative act." Thanks to the fairground performer and grotesque style, the theatre can be reinvested with "enchantment."

The most violent rejection of mimesis came from the Italian Futurists who repudiated the past for the sake of a new aesthetic of speed and noise. Taking the variety show as a model, Marinetti and his band of iconoclasts set out to destroy the concept of serious art with capital "A" through a series of shock effects, treating their own creations as something ephemeral to be rapidly consumed and discarded. Without a ponderous tradition or learned authorities, music hall and circus were free to be constantly new. Instead of an imitation of life, the variety show presented dazzling displays of invention, mechanical contrivance, and technical skill. Alogicality and nonlinearity shattered the spatial coherence of the playing area, opening multiple perspectives on a series of stunts taking place at the same time. By adopting the circus poetics of variety and simultaneity instead of the traditional dramatic values of unity and sequentiality, Marinetti (although later allied with Fascism) endorsed diversity and disorder, not totalitarian oneness.

The most theatrical of the avant-gardes, the Futurist movement engaged in deliberate buffoonery to amuse jaded spectators and make them forget the monotony of their everyday lives. Modern techniques of advertising, entrepreneurship, and political propaganda were for the first time used systematically to attract the public to a new art form.

Like music hall, Futurist theatre broke down the separation of performers and audience. Marinetti and his Futurist performers aspired to the precision and mastery of clowns, acrobats, and record-setting athletes. Through aggression, violent sensations, and assaults on the nerves, spectators were brought riotously into the action. Futurist evenings featuring the declamation of manifestoes ended in brawls, spontaneous or staged, in which the audience attacked performers or vice versa.

"Art, in fact, can be nothing but violence, cruelty, and injustice," Marinetti declared. By applying Futurist principles to the stage, Marinetti brought the theatre into the twentieth century, making it reflect the staccato rhythms of the modern metropolis, its electrification and glaring lights, its overpowering din and mechanized motion.

Mid-twentieth-century theatre was dominated by the theories of Artaud and Brecht, two contrasting temperaments and ideologues born at the end of the nineteenth century and nurtured in the modernist era of Symbolism, Futurism, and Expressionism.

Artaud: Resacralization of Theatre

Artaud wished to return the theatre to its ritual origins and restore its sacral functions. The author of *The Theatre and Its Double* felt the "most urgent revolution to accomplish lay in a kind of regression." The stage, he maintained, should disclose a mythic world peopled by "monsters of the primitive imagination seen through the primitive mind."

For Artaud, art did not imitate life because there was an absolute identity of art and life. Performance was direct self-representation and therefore a unique event, not a reproducible version of something else. Thus theatre was the double of no everyday reality, but of a true way of living beyond the grasp of speech.

Given its own autonomy, a theatrical language of gesture, movement, and sound would cease to be referential and become a magical incantation capable of creating its own reality, as Artaud discovered from the Balinese dance theatre which he saw in 1931. To reach the metaphysical through the physical, the theatre of cruelty made the concrete reality of the body its primary means of expression.

Identification of audience with performer was central to Artaud's belief in the theatre's overwhelming power to produce a visceral effect. Through the body of the actor, spectators could be put into a contagious state of trance. Artaud found the notion of theatre as the plague in *The City of God*, which he was reading as he wrote *The Theatre and Its Double*. By wrenching Saint Augustine's term of malediction to unexpected uses, the French poet-theorist glorified the infectious nature of violent tragic passions as a redemptive force. Artaud created a new language of blows and screams.

Soyinka's Metaphysics of the Irreducible and the Chthonic Realm

Contemporary mythic theory can achieve new life when it is derived from a living tradition of ritual theatre. In his 1976 Cambridge lectures, "Myth, Literature, and the Africa," Soyinka explores the ritual origins of drama, drawing parallels between Yoruba and Greek patterns of tragedy. The playwright's theory of African aesthetics is derived from the Ogun Festival and Mysteries, which provide the major source of mythological archetypes for Yoruba drama. In his hubris Ogun, God of iron, war, and creative fire, challenges the reigning order and undergoes sacrificial suffering in order to restore communal prosperity. The stage symbolically represents earth and cosmos. Repeating Ogun's sacrifice, the tragic human actor confronts the dangerous realm of transformation and forges a new identity in an encounter with infinity. Disruptions are a prelude to returning harmony.

The African worldview with its belief in spirits presupposes the co-existence of three realms: the world of the living, the world of the dead, and the world of the unborn. Individual experience parallels the experience of the deity; the relationship of deities to the living parallels the relationship of ancestors and the unborn to the living. The dead influence the living and determine who among the unborn should visit the living. The fourth stage, which makes possible the tragic hero's transformation, is a mediatory world, or area of transition between worlds. Soyinka calls it "the chthonic realm" of really dark forces and dark spirits that serves as the staging ground for cosmic monsters. Because the traditional Egungun masquerade, upon which Soyinka bases his theory, dramatizes the movement of transition between these worlds, the use of the mask itself is sufficient to call up the worldview.

The Egungun masquerade is a cult devoted to ancestors that is celebrated at annual festivals to mark the solidarity of the community with its dead. The spirits of the ancestors return to bless or berate the living. The all-male members of the Egungun society carry the ancestral masks and parade through the town, creating a spectacle that is a mixture of carnival, ballet, and satirical revue. The masqueraders enters into communion with the dead in a trance-like state of possession by ancestors that results in voice transformation.

Brecht: Rehabilitation of Mimesis

In sharp contrast to Artaud's theatre of cruelty and other radical departures from mimesis by the early twentieth-century avant-gardes, Brecht in the 1930s and 40s rehabilitated the imitation of reality through a "scientific" study of theatrical representation that revealed it to be a complex process involving all the elements of performance—text, actors, staging, audience—rather than a reductive one-to-one correspondence between drama and life, as in naturalism.

In his theory of epic theatre (polemically labeled anti-Aristotelian) Brecht proposed an episodic form of narrative drama, mimetic in conception, that incorporated techniques of distancing (derived from Chinese acting and Russian formalist notions of "estrangement") in order to provoke a critical response, rather than empathy, toward the characters on stage. The aim was to give spectators an understanding of social environment necessary to effect changes and remake the world.

Brecht set out to demystify the "enchantment" advocated by theorists from Nietzsche through Craig, Meyerhold, and the symbolists to Artaud. In the theatre of dreams, where according to Brecht art functions as a drug, spectators are lulled into passivity conducive to accepting things as they are.

In epic theatre, on the contrary, audiences, stimulated to active thought through the pleasures of contradiction, are made aware of the alternative possibilities. Instead of impersonating a character, the actor in epic theatre demonstrates his role, disclosing by the "gestus of showing" how the social reality represented has been constituted and how it could be reconstituted in other forms.

From the exclusively social viewpoint of epic theatre, monsters of the subconscious and irrational cannot be directly confronted. Dark forces are tamed through constructive reason enabling spectators to grasp the possibility of remodeling society. Since Marxism offers the sole scientific understanding of reality, dialectical materialism and the theory of class struggle are the principles by which the modeling can be effected.

In reconciling the demands of poetry with Marxism, Brecht adopted an ambiguous stance toward realist mimesis. On the one hand, he scorned the murky metaphysics of modernism and the avant-gardes (with its plurality of enigmatic subjective realities), and on the other he avoided the shallow optimistic formulas of socialist realism. Although Brecht's epic theatre posited objective social reality (knowable through dialectical materialism), the cognitive means of theatrical revelation were skeptical, playful, and irreverent. Rather than the positive accomplishments of the proletariat, the negative aspects of capitalist reality were revealed through the oblique devices of legend, fable, parable, and chronicle.

In opposition to the Wagnerian integrated work of art (*Gesamtkunstwerk*) designed to produce total hypnotic illusion, Brecht's epic theatre sought to disunify the spectacle and set the different theatrical means of dialogue, gesture, and music one against the other in mutual alienation as critical commentary on the action. Drawing upon his skills as playwright, poet, actor, director, and musician, Brecht created a complex new theoretical model for mid-twentieth-century mimesis with overt political intentions. While often ignoring its underlying realist foundations, left-leaning theatrical avant-gardists have adopted aspects of Brecht's theory as an aesthetic of social activism and change. Bourgeois artists and audiences in the Western theatre of commerce, against which Brecht formulated his theory, have also embraced epic theatre and learned to adapt the alienation effect for their own purposes.

Shaw's Constructive Comedy

Many years before Brecht proposed the alienation effect and distanciation of the spectator, Bernard Shaw, by his own boast a cold-hearted spectator and therefore an ideal theatre critic, opposed the sort of "all-out" acting designed to make the audience shed torrents of tears over the woes of suffering heroines. He detested pity and hoped to rid the world of it, because he did not wish there to be anything to pity. Wallowing in the misfortunes of others was an impediment to finding the causes of human unhappiness and eradicating them.

Instead of a drama of pity and fear productive of pleasurable emotional binges, Shaw proposed a detoxifying theatre that would stimulate thought. His aim was to reforge the audience. By laughing at the false and remediable ideas of the spectators, he hoped to lead them to think critically. Shaw saw the evolution of nineteenth-century drama as resulting in a tough-minded post-Ibsen tragicomedy that could attack society and its ills in the person of the audience. Brecht admired Shaw, sending him greetings on his seventieth birthday.

Proliferation of "Theory" in the Poststructuralist Era: A Parenthesis

New perspectives on literature and the arts opened during the last quarter of the twentieth century. Something disturbing to the equilibrium called "theory" appeared in the academy in the late 1960s, opening the floodgates to upstart disciplines that subjected previous study of the humanities to radical revision. Traditional scholars, outraged at the questioning of their most deeply held beliefs, have been pushed into a rear guard defense of humanist values. Not only were the conclusions of their "objective" scholarship challenged, but the very premises of "objectivity" were called into doubt.

Most of this "theory" has been of a general philosophical and literary nature rather than of a specifically theatrical application, although Jacques Derrida has written provocatively of Artaud, and Ronald Barthes in the 1950s and 60s did considerable theorizing in his writings on Brecht for *Le Théâtre Populaire*.

Of this explosion of "theory" in the academy during the past quarter century, it would not be unjust to say that the profusion has been greater than the variety. The common use of the singular generic "theory" is symptomatic. Rather than many conflicting theories of dissimilar provenance, there has been one broad flowing stream fed by several tributaries. The primary sources, all located on French soil, are Lacan's psychoanalysis, Derrida's deconstruction, and Foucault's sociology of power.

Pandora's box sprang open, but what flew out was all of one kind. "Theory" proved to be a series of variation on poststructuralist themes. The basic values of Western culture were subjected to a thorough-going linguistic critique exposing the ideological biases of what had been taken for eternal truths. There followed neo-Marxist and neo-Freudian unmaskings of "hegemonic" civilizations and repressive thought-systems masquerading paternalistically as objective norms. Resolutely anti-authoritarian, the demystifiers nonetheless cite their own authorities—Lacan, Derrida, Foucault, Barthes—almost as piously as Marx and Lenin were once cited by the orthodox left.

Although not specifically theatrical, "theory" has implications for all the humanities, including the performing arts. By questioning formerly sacrosanct assumptions about genius, the canon of masterpieces, and the disinterested timelessness of art, the poststructuralists have forced a fundamental rethinking of issues. We are now alerted to the proposition that every critical position is a form of special pleading with its own inner contradictions and self-serving presuppositions waiting to be exposed. No longer must we passively accept what is handed down from on high, but have the right to intervene and make our own counter propositions. After all, the revisionists argue, it is the reader or receiver who creates the meaning. The best texts are interrogative texts that refuse to adopt any single point of view and invite our active collaboration in constructing a critique from within. No special deference is due authors who are not the autonomous creators they once claimed to be, but simply stitches in an endless intertextual web. Egalitarian in their belief in the ability of everyone—and not just a few exceptional individuals—to theorize, the poststructuralists have broken down barriers and opened doors, for which we should be grateful.

"Theory" benefited from the vigorous resuscitation of Marxism and Freudianism that took place in French intellectual life in the 1950s and 60s. These two essentially nineteenth-century doctrines after hardening into rigid dogmas had already seen their claims to scientific validity challenged and were becoming discredited in actual practice as effective politics or therapy. Revamped for poststructuralist goals, they proved to be effective critical weapons. Although they no longer worked in the real world, they acquired new life in the realms of the imagination. These doctrines reemerged as cornerstones for sweeping theoretical revision of older, more traditional critical presuppositions.

Poststructuralists have found the very notion that literature is—or ever could be—"a representation of life" a naive, false, and reactionary idea. Mimesis is perceived as an instrument for subordinating literature to "reality" which is nothing more than the dominant linguistic constructs that are given the value of truth and knowledge at any point in Western literature. Language does not have the ability to apprehend reality. The apprehension of external reality is only an illusion. Words and things go separate ways; one cannot imitate the other.

The animus against mimesis has been particularly strong among the poststructuralist left because in its realist guises the doctrine of imitation calls for the representation of things as they are, not as they might or should be. Unable to reveal contradictions because it cannot stand outside the object, realism has often been accused of being an essentially conservative artistic form based on familiarity and readily recognizable stereotypes rather than creating objects of desire.

Aristotle has been held responsible for the dominance of theatrical illusionism with its characters soliciting empathetic identification and rational plots depicting the inevitability of things as they are, all leading spectators to passive submission to the status quo and acceptance of reigning stereotypes. Taken as the norm, the mimesis of realism (whether capitalist or socialist) functions as a conspiracy to impose a single version of reality and deny alternative perspectives the right to exist. The Aristotelian and neoclassical concept of oneness thus becomes a unitary tyranny used to enforce an orthodox perception of one reality supportive of the dominant ideology. Against the law and order of identity, the poststructuralists argue, the forces of difference and desire (already let out of the bottle by the romantic theorists) can produce alternative readings of reality. In their theories, two postmodern writers, Boal and Havel, address the issues of uniformity and diversity in theatre under "posttotalitarianism" (the word is Havel's).

After Brecht—Postmodern Theories of Political Theatre: Boal and Havel

Although Boal's Theatre of the Oppressed and Havel's Absurd Theatre addressed different audiences and grew out of opposed systems of persecution (capitalist and communist), both theories result from the authors' personal experiences of injustice and persecution and reflect a postmodern sensibility characteristic of those who came of age during the cold war. They share the same fundamental conception of the function of the stage.

Boal and Havel reject answers from on high, insist on taking responsibility for one's actions, and seek to give power to the powerless. They consider theatre an interpersonal experience for overcoming alienation and purging fears, not a place of ideological instruction. To transform society, the individual first must change. For a passive mimeticism sanctioning the self-perpetuation of systems in power, they substitute an active egalitarian involvement of spectators. Boal and Havel put theatre to the service of politics—but in strikingly different ways.

Drawing inspiration from Brazilian carnival as well as from Brecht, Boal turned the alienation effect into forms of direct audience participation leveling barriers between art and life, illusion and reality, performer and spectator.

According to *The Theatre of the Oppressed*, Aristotelian catharsis occurred when spectators, believing in a timeless human nature above epochs and classes, identified with a tragic protagonist's fated suffering and lost their own desire to change society. By undermining the hypnotic stage illusion that puts the audience into a trance, Boal like Brecht sought to cut off spectator identification with character that perpetuated acceptance of the status quo as inevitable. But whereas Brecht's epic theatre sought only to arouse critical thinking in audiences through distancing toward a mimetic spectacle on stage, Boal's Forum, Invisible Theatre, and Joker allowed spectators to collaborate with actors in exploring choices and acting out alternatives.

Havel's theory differs most radically from Boal's in its refusal to offer any constructive alternatives. Kafka, not Brecht, is the model for the Czech playwright. The cornerstone of Havel's theory is the absurd: humankind's ridiculousness and loss of identity in the face of anonymous, impersonal and inhuman power under any oppressive system capitalist or communist.

Drawing inspiration from many different arts both high and low, including Czech cabaret and 1920s avant-garde, modern jazz and rock, and theatre of the absurd, Havel carved his theory out of his communal experiences as spectator, stagehand, dramaturg, and playwright in the small Prague theatres of the 1960s where there was neither teacher nor doctrine, but all activities and understandings were shared.

For the Czech playwright, theatre is above all a special cultural site in a repressive society, a "suspect" and "disreputable" meeting place where performers and spectators enjoy conspiratorial togetherness and achieve social self-awareness (or interexistentiality). By hearing truths spoken that cannot be said elsewhere, audiences begin to free themselves from fear. Havel redefined spectatorship, making the spectators his collaborators. Catharsis constitutes both an existential and a social awakening co-created by audience and performer.

Because sociality is the essential characteristic of theatre, performance—as an interpersonal event utterly distinct from reading a play—seems threatening to totalitarian systems of control. In the eternal struggle between the entropic will to make things uniform and the creative will to cultivate uniqueness, theatre defends the self and its diversity, vital energy, and unpredictability against the dullness of inert regimes wielding impersonal and inhuman power.

Havel's absurd theatre disavowed any claim to be lifelike, jettisoning mimetic narrative, character, and illusion in favor of the freedom of pure humor and fantasy. Performers remained performers, playing with each other and with the audience. As action shifted from stage to auditorium, spectators constructed meaning from its very absence. Denied answers or alternatives in the face of the absurd, each was compelled to assume existential responsibility for one's own individual truth. Only apolitical political theatre uninfected with ideology, Havel argued, is capable of producing fundamental social change.

Paradoxically, whereas Brecht and Boal considered theatre a weapon against oppression only when it offered spectators constructive possibilities for change, for Havel the recognition of hopelessness was genuinely liberating. Living under a regime where feelings of despair and futility were forbidden and where "building a better future" was the official ideology dinned into one's head in relentlessly optimistic slogans, Havel saw open acknowledgement of the absurd as a powerful voice for truth.

Does theatre theory reflect a whole human life and engage one's physical being? Cunning and crafty, Brecht avoided choices that could put at risk his privileges and ability to amass the bourgeois comforts for which he exploited friends and lovers. In going to jail repeatedly, Havel, like Boal and Soyinka, lived his theory of existential responsibility for one's own truth. It was Havel's non-ideological theory of absurd theatre that helped to topple the stagnant entropic regimes of Eastern Europe, refuting Brecht's contention that "for art to be apolitical means only to ally itself with the ruling group."

In November, 1989 theatre became life in Czechoslovakia. The velvet revolution, directed from the theatres of Prague, was a vast *theatrum mundi* or carnival—"the most momentous fusion of theatre and society in the history of world theatre." And Havel's transformation from political prisoner to head of state was the apex of theatrical transformation, lacking all probability—in keeping with the author's theory of the absurd.

ARISTOTLE

ARISTOTLE (384-322 BC), when he gave his lectures on poetry in the afternoon, was always meticulously attired. "His personal appearance was foppish, not to say eccentric," according to Diogenes Laertius in his *Lives of the Philosophers*. "He was balding, spindle-shanked, and had small eyes. Perhaps in an effort to compensate for these disadvantages, he wore dandified clothes, cut and curled his hair in an affected manner, and spoke with a lisp. Numerous rings sparkled on his fingers."

Aristotle's unpublished course on poetics, as part of the program of instruction at his Academy, was available for consultation by his students. Although the treatise was addressed to students interested in the nature of poetry rather than in the art of writing for the stage, Aristotle was a pioneer in scientific research on Greek theatre. Trained in medicine, biology, and botany, the philosopher applied his boundless intellectual curiosity and empirical cast of mind to the study of theatre history.

All that we know about the records of Greek theatrical performances comes from Aristotle's collection of *Didascaliae* (now lost except for fragments), based on the entries about the Athenian dramatic contests that he consulted in the city archives. Aristotle collected the first great library of antiquity, which contained a large number of plays. On a study of these specimens and the inferences he drew from them, Aristotle based his theory of theatre.

Aristotle was not only an observant theatregoer, but also a collector and reader of play texts. He read many plays—now lost—by the great fifth-century dramatists, but he was also influenced by the dramatic production of his own day. Tragedies began to be written to be read as well as to be performed; there was a new reading public for tragedies.

Aristotle lived in the century after the great Athenian dramatists. Euripides had died twenty years before the philosopher was born, and Aeschylus eighty. Aristotle was thus more distant from the three outstanding fifth-century Greek tragedians than Dryden from the "race of giants" that preceded him: Shakespeare, Fletcher, and Jonson. If, as is likely, Aristotle composed the *Poetics* toward the end of his career, it appeared one hundred years after *Oedipus* and *Antigone*. Derived largely from past models, the philosopher's specifications for the tragedy were backward looking rather than oriented to the future.

Yet Aristotle inevitably saw the "classical" tragedy of Aeschylus, Sophocles, and Euripides through fourth-century eyes. The philosopher viewed ancient fifth-century theatre in the light of the modern stage practice that he knew. Although he most frequently singles out for praise classical tragedies (which were periodically revived at festivals), Aristotle also cites examples from the new plays by fourth-century tragedians like Theodectes, Carcinus, and Astydamas. It is the dramatic technique of these works that interests Aristotle.

The philosopher discusses the elements common to tragedy of both the fifth and fourth centuries. Because for Aristotle what is distinctive to tragedy are those features originating in fifth-century practice that have best survived in the drama of his own day, he devotes most of his attention to plot construction. He has far less to say on those aspects of classical tragedy that have lost importance in the fourth century: the chorus, its poetry, the moral stature of the tragic heroes, and their relations to gods.

Tragedy became self-conscious, concerned with its own technique and form rather than with its former substance as religious ritual. Tragic dimensions were replaced by complex and ingenious plots full of spectacular scenic effects and inventive *coups de théâtre*. In a theatrical context where tragedy that excited audiences by means of suspense and surprise was highly valued, Aristotle's high opinion of *Iphigenia in Tauris* and neglect of Aeschylus become intelligible.

The fourth century was an age of great actors and virtuoso acting. Prizes were introduced for acting as well as for playwriting. Poets wrote their plays as occasions for actors, who won more public adulation than dramatists. Aristotle reacted against the dominance of acting and spectacle at the same time that he was influenced by the new modes of playwriting.

THE POETICS (4th c. B.C.)

1. [***The poetic arts distinguished by their means.***] Our subject being Poetry, I propose to speak not only of the art in general but also of its species and their respective capacities; of the structure of plot required for a good poem; of the number and nature of the constituent parts of a poem; and likewise of any other matters in the same line of inquiry. Let us follow the natural order and begin with the primary facts. Epic poetry and Tragedy, as also Comedy, Dithyrambic poetry, and most flute playing and lyre playing, are all, viewed as a whole, modes of imitation. But at the same time they differ from one another in three ways, either by a difference of kind in their means, or by differences in the objects, or in the manner of their imitations.

I. Just as color and form are used as means by some, who (whether by art or constant practice) imitate and portray many things by their aid, and the voice is used by others; so also in the above-mentioned group of arts, the means with them as a whole are rhythm, language, and harmony—used, however, either singly or in certain combinations. A combination of harmony and rhythm alone is the means in flute playing and lyre playing, and any other arts there may be of the same description, e.g., imitative piping. Rhythm alone, without harmony, is the means in the dancer's imitations; for even he, by the rhythms of his attitudes, may represent men's characters, as well as what they do and suffer. There is further an art which imitates by language alone, without harmony, in prose or in verse, and if in verse, either in some one or in a plurality of meters. This form of imitation is to this day without a name. We have no common name for a mime of Sophron or Xenarchus and a Socratic Conversation; and we should still be without one even if the imitation in the two instances were in trimeters or elegiacs or some other kind of verse—though it is the way with people to tack on "poet" to the name of a meter, and talk of elegiac poets and epic poets thinking that they call them poets not by reason of the imitative nature of their work, but indiscriminately by reason of the meter they write in. Even if a theory of medicine or physical philosophy be put forth in a metrical form, it is usual to describe the writer in this way; Homer and Empedocles, however, have really nothing in common apart from their meter; so that, if the one is to be called a poet, the other should be

From Aristotle, *On the Art of Poetry*, trans. Ingram Bywater.
Oxford: Clarendon, 1920.

termed a physicist rather than a poet. We should be in the same position also, if the imitation in these instances were in all the meters, like the *Centaur* (a rhapsody in a medley of all meters) of Chaeremon; and Chaeremon one has to recognize as a poet. So much, then, as to these arts. There are, lastly, certain other arts, which combine all the means enumerated, rhythm, melody, and verse, e.g., Dithyrambic and Nomic poetry, Tragedy and Comedy; with this difference, however, that the three kinds of means are in some of them all employed together, and in others brought in separately, one after the other. These elements of difference in the above arts I term the means of their imitation.

2. [*The poetic arts distinguished by their objects.*] II. The objects the imitator represents are actions, with agents who are necessarily either good men or bad—the diversities of human character being nearly always derivative from this primary distinction, since the line between virtue and vice is one dividing the whole of mankind. It follows, therefore, that the agents represented must be either above our own level of goodness, or beneath it, or just such as we are; in the same way as, with the painters, the personages of Polygnotus are better than we are, those of Pauson worse, and those of Dionysius just like ourselves. It is clear that each of the above-mentioned arts will admit of these differences and that it will become a separate art by representing objects with this point of difference. Even in dancing, flute playing, and lyre playing such diversities are possible; and they are also possible in the nameless art that uses language, prose or verse without harmony, as its means; Homer's personages, for instance, are better than we are; Cleophon's are on our own level; and those of Hegemon of Thasos, the first writer of parodies, and Nicochares, the author of the *Diliad*, are beneath it. The same is true of the Dithyramb and the Nome: the personages may be presented in them with the difference exemplified in the … of … and Argas, and in the Cyclopses of Timotheus and Philoxenus. This difference it is that distinguishes Tragedy and Comedy also; the one would make its personages worse, and the other better, than the men of the present day.

3. [*The poetic arts distinguished by the manner of their imitations.*] III. A third difference in these arts is in the manner in which each kind of object is represented. Given both the same means and the same kind of object for imitation, one may either (1) speak at one moment in narrative and at another in an assumed character, as Homer does; or (2) one may remain the same throughout, without any such change; or (3) the imitators may represent the whole story dramatically, as though they were actually doing the things described.

As we said at the beginning, therefore, the differences in the imitation of these arts come under three heads, their means, their objects, and their manner.

So that as an imitator Sophocles will be on one side akin to Homer, both portraying good men; and on another to Aristophanes, since both present their personages as acting and doing. This in fact, according to some, is the reason for plays being termed dramas, because in a play the personages act the story. Hence too both Tragedy and Comedy are claimed by the Dorians as their discoveries; Comedy by the Megarians—by those in Greece as having arisen when Megara became a democracy, and by the Sicilian Megarians on the ground that the poet Epicharmus was of their country, and a good deal earlier than Chionides and Magnes; even Tragedy also is claimed by certain of the Peloponnesian Dorians. In support of this claim they point to the words "comedy" and "drama." Their word for the outlying hamlets, they say, is *comae*, whereas Athenians call them *demes*—thus assuming that comedians got the name not from their *comoe* or revels, but from their strolling from hamlet to hamlet, lack of appreciation keeping them out of the city. Their word also for "to act," they say, is *dran*, whereas Athenians use *prattein*. So much, then, as to the number and nature of the points of difference in the imitation of these arts.

    4. [*Origin and development of poetry and its kinds*.] It is clear that the general origin of poetry was due to two causes, each of them part of human nature. Imitation is natural to man from childhood, one of his advantages over the lower animals being this, that he is the most imitative creature in the world, and learns at first by imitation. And it is also natural for all to delight in works of imitation. The truth of this second point is shown by experience: though the objects themselves may be painful to see, we delight to view the most realistic representations of them in art, the forms for example of the lowest animals and of dead bodies. The explanation is to be found in a further fact: to be learning something is the greatest of pleasures not only to the philosopher but also to the rest of mankind, however small their capacity for it, the reason of the delight in seeing the picture is that one is at the same time learning—gathering the meaning of things, e.g., that the man there is so-and-so; for if one has not seen the thing before, one's pleasure will not be in the picture as an imitation of it, but will be due to the execution or coloring or some similar cause. Imitation, then, being natural to us—as also the sense of harmony and rhythm, the meters being obviously species of rhythms—it was through their original aptitude, and by a series of improvements for the most part gradual on their first efforts, that they created poetry out of their improvisations.

    Poetry, however, soon broke up into two kinds according to the differences of character in the individual poets; for the graver among them would represent noble actions, and those of noble personages; and the meaner sort the actions of the ignoble. The latter class produced invectives at first, just as others did hymns and panegyrics. We know of no such poem by any of the pre-Homeric poets, though there were probably many such writers among them; instances, however, may be found from Homer downwards, e.g., his *Margites*, and the similar poems of others. In this poetry of invective its natural fitness brought an iambic meter into use; hence our present term "iambic," because it was the meter of their "iambs" or invectives against one another. The result was that the old poets became some of them writers of heroic and others of iambic verse. Homer's position, however, is peculiar: just as he was in the serious style the poet of poets, standing alone not only through the literary excellence, but also through the dramatic character of his imitations, so too he was the first to outline for us the general forms of Comedy by producing not a dramatic invective, but a dramatic picture of the Ridiculous; his *Margites* in fact stands in the same relation to our comedies as the *Iliad* and *Odyssey* to our tragedies. As soon, however, as Tragedy and Comedy appeared in the field, those naturally drawn to the one line of poetry became writers of comedies instead of iambs, and those naturally drawn to the other, writers of tragedies instead of epics, because these new modes of art were grander and of more esteem than the old.

If it be asked whether Tragedy is now all that it need be in its formative elements, to consider that, and decide it theoretically and in relation to the theatres, is a matter for another inquiry.

It certainly began in improvisations—as did also Comedy; the one originating with the authors of the Dithyramb, the other with those of the phallic songs, which still survive as institutions in many of our cities. And its advance after that was little by little, through their improving on whatever they had before them at each stage. It was in fact only after a long series of changes that the movement of Tragedy stopped on its attaining to its natural form. (1) The number of actors was first increased to two by Aeschylus, who curtailed the business of the Chorus, and made the dialogue, or spoken portion, take the leading part in the play. (2) A third actor and scenery were due to Sophocles. (3) Tragedy acquired also its magnitude. Discarding short stories and a ludicrous diction, through its passing out of its satyric stage, it assumed, though only at a late point in its progress, a tone of dignity; and its meter changed then from trochaic to iambic. The reason for their original use of the trochaic tetrameter was that their poetry was satyric and more connected with dancing than it now is. As soon, however, as a spoken part came in, nature herself found the appropriate meter. The iambic, we know, is the most speakable of meters, as is shown by the fact that we very often fall into it in conversation, whereas we rarely talk hexameters, and only when we depart from the speaking tone of voice. (4) Another change was a plurality of episodes or acts. As for the remaining matters, the superadded embellishments and the account of their introduction, these must be taken as said, as it would probably be a long piece of work to go through the details.

5. [*Comic and epic poetry*.] As for Comedy, it is (as has been observed) an imitation of men worse than the average; worse, however, not as regards any and every sort of fault, but only as regards one particular kind, the Ridiculous, which is a species of the Ugly. The Ridiculous may be defined as a mistake or deformity not productive of pain or harm to others; the mask, for instance, that excites laughter, is something ugly and distorted without causing pain.

Though the successive changes in Tragedy and their authors are not unknown, we cannot say the same of Comedy; its early stages passed unnoticed, because it was not as yet taken up in a serious way. It was only at a late point in its progress that a chorus of comedians was officially granted by the archon; they used to be mere volunteers. It had also already certain definite forms at the time when the record of those termed comic poets begins. Who it was who supplied it with masks, or prologues, or a plurality of actors and the like, has remained unknown. The invented Fable, or Plot, however, originated in Sicily with Epicharmus and Phormis; of Athenian poets Crates was the first to drop the Comedy of invective and frame stories of a general and non-personal nature, in other words, Fables or Plots.

Epic poetry, then, has been seen to agree with Tragedy to this extent, that of being an imitation of serious subjects in a grand kind of verse. It differs from it, however, (1) in that it is in one kind of verse and in narrative form; and (2) in its length—which is due to its action having no fixed limit of time, whereas Tragedy endeavors to keep as far as possible within a single circuit of the sun, or something near that. This, I say, is another point of difference between them, though at first the practice in this respect was just the same in tragedies as in epic poems. They differ also (3) in their constituents, some being common to both and others peculiar to Tragedy—hence a judge of good and bad in Tragedy is a judge of that in epic poetry also. All the parts of an epic are included in Tragedy; but those of Tragedy are not all of them to be found in the Epic.

6. [*Definition and analysis of tragedy.*] Reserving hexameter poetry and Comedy for consideration hereafter, let us proceed now to the discussion of Tragedy; before doing so, however, we must gather up the definition resulting from what has been said. A tragedy, then, is the imitation of an action that is serious and also, as having magnitude, complete in itself; in language with pleasurable accessories, each kind brought in separately in the parts of the work; in a dramatic, not in a narrative form; with incidents arousing pity and fear, wherewith to accomplish its catharsis of such emotions. Here by "language with pleasurable accessories" I mean that with rhythm and harmony or song superadded; and by "the kinds separately" I mean that some portions are worked out with verse only, and others in turn with song.

I. As they act the stories, it follows that in the first place the Spectacle (or stage appearance of the actors) must be some part of the whole; and in the second

Melody and Diction, these two being the means of their imitation. Here by "Diction" I mean merely this, the composition of the verses; and by "Melody," what is too completely understood to require explanation. But further: the subject represented also is an action; and the action involves agents, who must necessarily have their distinctive qualities both of character and thought, since it is from these that we ascribe certain qualities to their actions. There are in the natural order of things, therefore, two causes, Thought and Character, of their actions, and consequently of their success or failure in their lives. Now the action (that which was done) is represented in the play by the Fable or Plot. The Fable, in our present sense of the term, is simply this, the combination of the incidents, or things done in the story; whereas Character is what makes us ascribe certain moral qualities to the agents; and Thought is shown in all they say when proving a particular point or, it may be, enunciating a general truth. There are six parts consequently of every tragedy, as a whole (that is) of such or such quality, viz., a Fable or Plot, Characters, Diction, Thought, Spectacle, and Melody; two of them arising from the means, one from the manner, and three from the objects of the dramatic imitation; and there is nothing else besides these six. Of these, its formative elements, then, not a few of the dramatists have made due use, as every play, one may say, admits of Spectacle, Character, Fable, Diction, Melody, and Thought.

II. The most important of the six is the combination of the incidents of the story. Tragedy is essentially an imitation not of persons but of action and life, of happiness and misery. All human happiness or misery takes the form of action; the end for which we live is a certain kind of activity, not a quality. Character gives us qualities, but it is in our actions—what we do—that we are happy or the reverse. In a play accordingly they do not act in order to portray the Characters; they include the Characters for the sake of the action. So that it is the action in it, i.e., its Fable or Plot, that is the end and purpose of the tragedy; and the end is everywhere the chief thing. Besides this, a tragedy is impossible without action, but there may be one without Character. The tragedies of most of the moderns are characterless—a defect common among poets of all kinds, and with its counterpart in painting in Zeuxis as compared with Polygnotus; for whereas the latter is strong in character, the work of Zeuxis is devoid of it. And again: one may string together a series of characteristic speeches of the utmost finish as regards Diction and Thought, and yet fail to produce the true tragic effect; but one will have much better success with a tragedy which, however inferior in these respects, has a Plot, a combination of incidents, in it. And again: the most powerful elements of attraction in Tragedy, the Peripeties and Discoveries, are parts of the Plot. A further proof is in the fact that beginners succeed earlier with the Diction and Characters than with the construction of a story; and the same may be said of nearly all the early dramatists. We maintain, therefore, that the first essential, the life and soul, so to speak, of Tragedy is the Plot; and that the Characters come second—compare the parallel in painting, where the most beautiful colors laid on without order will not give one the same pleasure as a simple black-and-white sketch of a portrait. We maintain that Tragedy is primarily an imitation of action, and that it is mainly for the sake of the action that it imitates the personal agents. Third comes the element of Thought, i.e., the power of saying whatever can be said, or what is appropriate to the occasion. This is what, in the speeches in Tragedy, falls under the arts of Politics and Rhetoric; for the older poets make their personages discourse like statesmen, and the modern like rhetoricians. One must not confuse it with Character. Character in a play is that which reveals the moral purpose of the agents, i.e., the sort of thing they seek or avoid, where that is not obvious—hence there is no room for Character in a speech on a purely indifferent subject. Thought, on the other hand, is shown in all they say when proving or disproving some particular point, or enunciating some universal proposition. Fourth among the literary elements is the Diction of the personages, i.e., as before explained, the expression of their thoughts in words, which is practically the same thing with verse as with prose. As for the two remaining parts, the Melody is the greatest of the pleasurable accessories of Tragedy. The Spectacle, though an attraction, is the least artistic of all the parts, and has least to do with the art of poetry. The tragic effect is quite possible without a public performance and actors; and besides, the getting-up of the Spectacle is more a matter for the costumier than the poet.

7. [*Tragedy: arrangement and length of the play.*] Having thus distinguished the parts, let us now consider the proper construction of the Fable or Plot, as that is at once the first and the most important thing in Tragedy. We have laid it down that a tragedy is an imitation of an action that is complete in itself, as a whole of some magnitude; for a whole may be of no magnitude to speak of. Now a whole is that which has beginning, middle, and end. A beginning is that which is not itself necessarily after anything else, and which has naturally something else after it; an end is that which is naturally after something itself, either as its necessary or usual consequent, and with nothing else after it; and a middle, that which is by nature after one thing and has also another after it. A well-constructed Plot, therefore, cannot either begin or end at any point one likes; beginning and end in it must be of the forms just described. Again: to be beautiful, a living creature, and every whole made up of parts, must not only present a certain order in its arrangement of parts, but also be of a certain definite magnitude. Beauty is a matter of size and order, and therefore impossible either (1) in a very minute creature, since our perception becomes indistinct as it approaches instantaneity; or (2) in a creature of vast size—one, say, 1000 miles long—as in that case, instead of the object being seen all at once, the unity and wholeness of it is lost to the beholder. Just in the same way, then, as a beautiful whole made up of parts, or

a beautiful living creature, must be of some size, but a size to be taken in by the eye, so a story or Plot must be of some length, but of a length to be taken in by the memory. As for the limit of its length, so far as that is relative to public performances and spectators, it does not fall within the theory of poetry. If they had to perform a hundred tragedies, they would be timed by water clocks, as they are said to have been at one period. The limit, however, set by the actual nature of the thing is this: the longer the story, consistently with its being comprehensible as a whole, the finer it is by reason of its magnitude. As a rough general formula, "a length which allows of the hero passing by a series of probable or necessary stages from misfortune to happiness, or from happiness to misfortune," may suffice as a limit for the magnitude of the story.

   8. [*Tragedy: unity of action.*] The Unity of a Plot does not consist, as some suppose, in its having one man as its subject. An infinity of things befall that one man, some of which it is impossible to reduce to unity; and in like manner there are many actions of one man which cannot be made to form one action. One sees, therefore, the mistake of all the poets who have written a *Heracleid*, a *Theseid*, or similar poems; they suppose that, because Heracles was one man, the story also of Heracles must be one story. Homer, however, evidently understood this point quite well whether by art or instinct, just in the same way as he excels the rest in every other respect. In writing an *Odyssey*, he did not make the poem cover all that ever befell his hero—it befell him, for instance, to get wounded on Parnassus and also to feign madness at the time of the call to arms, but the two incidents had no necessary or probable connection with one another—instead of doing that, he took as the subject of the *Odyssey*, as also of the *Iliad*, an action with a Unity of the kind we are describing. The truth is that, just as in the other imitative arts one imitation is always of one thing, so in poetry the story, as an imitation of action, must represent one action, a complete whole, with its several incidents so closely connected that the transposal or withdrawal of any one of them will disjoin and dislocate the whole. For that which makes no perceptible difference by its presence or absence is no real part of the whole.

   9. [*Tragedy: the probable and universal.*] From what we have said it will be seen that the poet's function is to describe, not the thing that has happened, but a kind of thing that might happen, i.e., what is possible as being probable or necessary. The distinction between historian and poet is not in the one writing prose and the other verse—you might put the work of Herodotus into verse, and it would still be a species of history; it consists really in this, that the one describes the thing that has been, and the other a kind of thing that might be. Hence poetry is something more philosophic and of graver import than history, since its statements are of the nature rather of universals, whereas those of history are singulars. By a universal statement I mean one as to what such or such a kind of man will probably or necessarily say or do—

which is the aim of poetry, though it affixes proper names to the characters, by a singular statement, one as to what, say, Alcibiades did or had done to him. In Comedy this has become clear by this time; it is only when their plot is already made up of probable incidents that they give it a basis of proper names, choosing for the purpose any names that may occur to them, instead of writing like the old iambic poets about particular persons. In Tragedy, however, they still adhere to the historic names; and for this reason: what convinces is the possible; now whereas we are not yet sure as to the possibility of that which has not happened, that which has happened is manifestly possible, else it would not have come to pass. Nevertheless even in Tragedy there are some plays with but one or two known names in them, the rest being inventions, and there are some without a single known name, e.g., Agathon's *Antheus*, in which both incidents and names are of the poet's invention; and it is no less delightful on that account. So that one must not aim at a rigid adherence to the traditional stories on which tragedies are based. It would be absurd, in fact, to do so, as even the known stories are only known to a few, though they are a delight none the less to all.

It is evident from the above that the poet must be more the poet of his Stories or Plots than of his verses, inasmuch as he is a poet by virtue of the imitative element in his work, and, it is actions that he imitates. And if he should come to take a subject from actual history, he is none the less a poet for that; since some historic occurrences may very well be in the probable and possible order of things; and it is in that aspect of them that he is their poet.

Of simple Plots and actions the episodic are the worst. I call a Plot episodic when there is neither probability nor necessity in the sequence of its episodes. Actions of this sort bad poets construct through their own fault, and good ones on account of the players. His work being for public performance, a good poet often stretches out a Plot beyond its capabilities, and is thus obliged to twist the sequence of incident.

Tragedy, however, is an imitation not only of a complete action, but also of incidents arousing pity and fear. Such incidents have the very greatest effect on the mind when they occur unexpectedly and at the same time in consequence of one another; there is more of the marvelous in them then than if they happened of themselves or by mere chance. Even matters of chance seem most marvelous if there is an appearance of design as it were in them; as for instance the statue of Mitys at Argos killed the author of Mitys' death by falling down on him when a looker-on at a public spectacle; for incidents like that we think to be not without a meaning. A Plot, therefore, of this sort is necessarily finer than others.

*10. [**Tragedy: simple and complex plots.**]* Plots are either simple or complex, since the actions they represent are naturally of this twofold description. The action, proceeding in the way defined, as one continuous whole, I call simple, when the change in the hero's fortunes takes place without

Peripety or Discovery; and complex, when it involves one or the other, or both. These should each of them arise out of the structure of the Plot itself, so as to be the consequence, necessary or probable, of the antecedents. There is a great difference between a thing happening *propter hoc* and *post hoc*.

11. [Tragedy: peripety, discovery, and suffering.] A Peripety is the change of the kind described from one state of things within the play to its opposite, and that too in the way we are saying, in the probable or necessary sequence of events; as it is for instance in *Oedipus:* here the opposite state of things is produced by the Messenger, who, coming to gladden Oedipus and to remove his fears as to his mother, reveals the secret of his birth. And in *Lynceus:* just as he is being led off for execution, with Danaus at his side to put him to death, the incidents preceding this bring it about that he is saved and Danaus put to death. A Discovery is, as the very word implies, a change from ignorance to knowledge, and thus to either love or hate, in the personages marked for good or evil fortune. The finest form of Discovery is one attended by Peripeties, like that which goes with the Discovery in *Oedipus.* There are no doubt other forms of it; what we have said may happen in a way in reference to inanimate things, even things of a very casual kind; and it is also possible to discover whether some one has done or not done something. But the form most directly connected with the Plot and the action of the piece is the first-mentioned. This, with a Peripety, will arouse either pity or fear—actions of that nature being what Tragedy is assumed to represent; and it will also serve to bring about the happy or unhappy ending. The Discovery, then, being of persons, it may be that of one party only to the other, the latter being already known; or both the parties may have to discover themselves. Iphigenia, for instance, was discovered to Orestes by sending the letter; and another Discovery was required to reveal him to Iphigenia.

Two parts of the Plot, then, Peripety and Discovery, are on matters of this sort. A third part is Suffering; which we may define as an action of a destructive or painful nature, such as murders on the stage, tortures, woundings, and the like. The other two have been already explained.

12. [The quantitative parts of a tragedy.] The parts of Tragedy to be treated as formative elements in the whole were mentioned in a previous Chapter [6]. From the point of view, however, of its quantity, i.e., the separate sections into which it is divided, a tragedy has the following parts: Prologue, Episode, Exode, and a choral portion, distinguished into Parode and Stasimon; these two are common to all tragedies, whereas songs from the stage and *Commoe* are only found in some. The Prologue is all that precedes the Parode of the chorus; an Episode all that comes in between two whole choral songs; the Exode all that follows after the last choral song. In the choral portion the Parode is the whole first statement of the chorus; a Stasimon, a song of the chorus without anapaests or trochees; a *Commos*, a lamentation sung by chorus and actor in concert. The parts of Tragedy to be used as formative elements in the whole we have already mentioned; the above are its parts from the point of view of its quantity, or the separate sections into which it is divided.

13. [***The tragic hero.***] The next points after what we have said above will be these: (1) What is the poet to aim at, and what is he to avoid, in constructing his Plots? and (2) What are the conditions on which the tragic effect depends?

We assume that, for the finest form of Tragedy, the Plot must be not simple but complex; and further, that it must imitate actions arousing fear and pity, since that is the distinctive function of this kind of imitation. It follows, therefore, that there are three forms of Plot to be avoided. (1) A good man must not be seen passing from happiness to misery, or (2) a bad man from misery to happiness. The first situation is not fear inspiring or piteous, but simply odious to us. The second is the most untragic that can be; it has no one of the requisites of Tragedy; it does not appeal either to the human feeling in us, or to our pity, or to our fears. Nor, on the other hand, should (3) an extremely bad man be seen falling from happiness into misery. Such a story may arouse the human feeling in us, but it will not move us to either pity or fear; pity is occasioned by undeserved misfortune, and fear by that of one like ourselves; so that there will be nothing either piteous or fear inspiring in the situation. There remains, then, the intermediate kind of personage, a man not pre-eminently virtuous and just, whose misfortune, however, is brought upon him not by vice and depravity but by some error of judgment, of the number of those in the enjoyment of great reputation and prosperity; e.g., Oedipus, Thyestes, and the men of note of similar families. The perfect Plot, accordingly, must have a single, and not (as some tell us) a double issue; the change in the hero's fortunes must be not from misery to happiness, but on the contrary from happiness to misery; and the cause of it must lie not in any depravity, but in some great error on his part; the man himself being either such as we have described, or better, not worse, than that. Fact also confirms our theory. Though the poets began by accepting any tragic story that came to hand, in these days the finest tragedies are always on the story of some few houses, on that of Alcmeon, Oedipus, Orestes, Meleager, Thyestes, Telephus, or any others that may have been involved, as either agents or sufferers, in some deed of horror. The theoretically best tragedy, then, has a Plot of this description. The critics, therefore, are wrong who blame Euripides for taking this line in his tragedies, and giving many of them an unhappy ending. It is, as we have said, the right line to take. The best proof is this: on the stage, and in the public performances, such plays, properly worked out, are seen to be the most truly tragic; and Euripides, even if his execution be faulty in every other point, is seen to be nevertheless the most tragic certainly of the dramatists. After this comes the construction of Plot which some rank first, one with a double story (like the *Odyssey)* and an opposite issue for the good and the bad personages. It is ranked as first only through the weakness of the audiences; the poets merely follow their public, writing as its wishes dictate. But the pleasure here is not that of Tragedy. It belongs rather to Comedy, where the bitterest enemies in the piece (e.g., Orestes and Aegisthus) walk off good friends at the end, with no slaying of any one by any one.

14. [*The tragic deed.*] The tragic fear and pity may be aroused by the Spectacle; but they may also be aroused by the very structure and incidents of the play—which is the better way and shows the better poet. The Plot in fact should be so framed that, even without seeing the things take place, he who simply hears the account of them shall be filled with horror and pity at the incidents, which is just the effect that the mere recital of the story in *Oedipus* would have on one. To produce this same effect by means of the Spectacle is less artistic, and requires extraneous aid. Those, however, who make use of the Spectacle to put before us that which is merely monstrous and not productive of fear, are wholly out of touch with Tragedy; not every kind of pleasure should be required of a tragedy, but only its own proper pleasure.

The tragic pleasure is that of pity and fear, and the poet has to produce it by a work of imitation; it is clear, therefore, that the causes should be included in the incidents of his story. Let us see, then, what kinds of incident strike one as horrible, or rather as piteous. In a deed of this description the parties must necessarily be either friends, or enemies, or indifferent to one another. Now when enemy does it on enemy, there is nothing to move us to pity either in his doing or in his meditating the deed, except so far as the actual pain of the sufferer is concerned; and the same is true when the parties are indifferent to one another. Whenever the tragic deed, however, is done within the family—when murder or the like is done or meditated by brother on brother, by son on father, by mother on son, or son on mother—these are the situations the poet should seek after. The traditional stories, accordingly, must be kept as they are, e.g., the murder of Clytaemnestra by Orestes and of Eriphyle by Alcmeon. At the same time even with these there is something left to the poet himself; it is for him to devise the right way of treating them. Let us explain more clearly what we mean by "the right way." The deed of horror may be done by the doer knowingly and consciously, as in the old poets, and in Medea's murder of her children in Euripides. Or he may do it, but in ignorance of his relationship, and discover that afterwards, as does the Oedipus in Sophocles. Here the deed is outside the play; but it may be within it, like the act of the Alcmeon in Astydamas, or that of the Telegonus in *Ulysses Wounded.* A third possibility is for one meditating some deadly injury to another, in ignorance of his relationship, to make the discovery in time to draw back.

These exhaust the possibilities, since the deed must necessarily be either done or not done, and either knowingly or unknowingly.

The worst situation is when the personage is with full knowledge on the point of doing the deed, and leaves it undone. It is odious and also (through the absence of suffering) untragic; hence it is that no one is made to act thus except in some few instances, e.g., Haemon and Creon in *Antigone*. Next after this comes the actual perpetration of the deed meditated. A better situation than that, however, is for the deed to be done in ignorance, and the relationship discovered afterwards since there is nothing odious in it, and the Discovery will serve to astound us. But the best of all is the last; what we have in *Cresphontes*, for example, where Merope, on the point of slaying her son, recognizes him in time; in *Iphigenia*, where sister and brother are in a like position; and in *Helle*, where the son recognizes his mother, when on the point of giving her up to her enemy.

This will explain why our tragedies are restricted (as we said just now) to such a small number of families. It was accident rather than art that led the poets in quest of subjects to embody this kind of incident in their Plots. They are still obliged, accordingly, to have recourse to the families in which such horrors have occurred. On the construction of the Plot, and the kind of Plot required for Tragedy, enough has now been said.

15. [***The character of the tragic personages.***] In the Characters there are four points to aim at. First and foremost, that they shall be good. There will be an element of character in the play, if (as has been observed) what a personage says or does reveals a certain moral purpose; and a good element of character, if the purpose so revealed is good. Such goodness is possible in every type of personage, even in a woman or a slave, though the one is perhaps an inferior, and the other a wholly worthless being. The second point is to make them appropriate. The Character before us may be, say, manly; but it is not appropriate in a female Character to be manly, or clever. The third is to make them like the reality, which is not the same as their being good and appropriate, in our sense of the term. The fourth is to make them consistent and the same throughout; even if inconsistency be part of the man before one for imitation as presenting that form of character, he should still be consistently inconsistent. We have an instance of baseness of character, not required for the story, in the Menelaus in *Orestes;* of the incongruous and unbefitting in the lamentation of Ulysses in *Scylla*, and in the (clever) speech of Melanippe; and of inconsistency in *Iphigenia at Aulis*, where Iphigenia the suppliant is utterly unlike the later Iphigenia. The right thing, however, is in the Characters just as in the incidents of the play to endeavor always after the necessary or the probable; so that whenever such-and-such a personage says or does such-and-such a thing, it shall be the necessary or probable outcome of his character; and whenever this incident follows on that it shall be either the necessary or the probable consequence of it. From this one sees (to digress for a moment) that the Denouement also should arise out of the plot itself, and not depend on a stage artifice, as in *Medea,* or in the story of the (arrested) departure of the Greeks in the *Iliad.* The artifice must be reserved for matters outside the play—for past events beyond human knowledge, or events yet to come, which require to be foretold or announced, since it is the privilege of the Gods to know everything. There should be nothing improbable among the actual incidents. If it be unavoidable, however, it should be outside the tragedy, like the improbability in the *Oedipus* of Sophocles. But to return to the Characters. As Tragedy is an imitation of personages better than the ordinary man, we in our way should follow the example of good portrait painters, who reproduce the distinctive features of a man, and at the same time, without losing the likeness, make him handsomer than he is. The poet in like manner, in portraying men quick or slow to anger, or with similar infirmities of character, must know how to represent them as such, and at the same time as good men, as Agathon and Homer have represented Achilles.

All these rules one must keep in mind throughout, and, further, those also for such points of stage effect as directly depend on the art of the poet, since in these too one may often make mistakes. Enough, however, has been said on the subject in one of our published writings.

    *16. [**The various forms of discovery.**]* Discovery in general has been explained already. As for the species of Discovery, the first to be noted is (1) the least artistic form of it, of which the poets make most use through mere lack of invention, Discovery by signs or marks. Of these signs some are congenital, like the "lance-head which the Earth-born have on them," or "stars," such as Carcinus brings in his *Thyestes;* others acquired after birth—these latter being either marks on the body, e.g., scars, or external tokens, like necklaces, or (to take another sort of instance) the ark in the Discovery in *Tyro.* Even these, however, admit of two uses, a better and a worse; the scar of Ulysses is an instance; the Discovery of him through it is made in one way by the nurse and in another by the swineherds. A Discovery using signs as a means of assurance is less artistic, as indeed are all such as imply reflection; whereas one bringing them in all of a sudden, as in the *Bath-story,* is of a better order. Next after these are (2) Discoveries made directly by the poet; which are inartistic for that very reason; e.g. Orestes' Discovery of himself in *Iphigenia:* whereas his sister reveals who she is by the letter, Orestes is made to say himself what the poet rather than the story demands. This, therefore, is not far removed from the first-mentioned fault, since he might have presented certain tokens as well. Another instance is the "shuttle's voice" in the *Tereus* of Sophocles. (3) A third species is Discovery through memory, from a man's consciousness being awakened by something seen. Thus in *The Cyprioe* of Dicaeogenes, the sight of the picture makes the man burst into tears; and in the *Tale of Alcinous*, hearing the harper Ulysses is reminded of the past and weeps; the Discovery of them being the result. (4) A fourth kind is Discovery through reasoning; e.g., in *The Choephoroe:* "One like me is here; there is no one like me but Orestes; he, therefore, must be here." Or that which Polyidus the Sophist suggested for *Iphigenia;* since it was natural for Orestes to reflect: "My sister was sacrificed, and I am to be sacrificed like her." Or that in the *Tydeus* of Theodectes: "I came to find a son, and am to die myself." Or that in *The Phinidae:* on seeing the place the women inferred their fate, that they were to die there, since they had also been exposed there. (5) There is, too, a composite Discovery arising from bad reasoning on the side of the other party. An instance of it is in *Ulysses the False Messenger:* he said he should know the bow—which he had not seen; but to suppose from that that he would know it again (as though he had once seen it) was bad reasoning. (6) The best of all Discoveries, however, is that arising from the incidents themselves, when the great surprise comes about through a probable incident like that in the *Oedipus* of Sophocles; and also in *Iphigenia;* for it was not improbable that she should wish to have a letter taken home. These last are the only Discoveries independent of the artifice of signs and necklaces. Next after them come Discoveries through reasoning.

17. [*Additional rules for the construction of a play.*] At the time when he is constructing his Plots, and engaged on the Diction in which they are worked out, the poet should remember (1) to put the actual scenes as far as possible before his eyes. In this way, seeing everything with the vividness of an eyewitness as it were, he will devise what is appropriate, and be least likely to overlook incongruities. This is shown by what was censured in Carcinus, the return of Amphiaraus from the sanctuary; it would have passed unnoticed, if it had not been actually seen by the audience; but on the stage his play failed, the incongruity of the incident offending the spectators. (2) As far as may be, too, the poet should even act his story with the very gestures of his personages. Given the same natural qualifications, he who feels the emotions to be described will be the most convincing; distress and anger, for instance, are portrayed most truthfully by one who is feeling them at the moment. Hence it is that poetry demands a man with a special gift for it, or else one with a touch of madness in him; the former can easily assume the required mood, and the latter may be actually beside himself with emotion. (3) His story, again, whether already made or of his own making, he should first simplify and reduce to a universal form, before proceeding to lengthen it out by the insertion of episodes. The following will show how the universal element in *Iphigenia*, for instance, may be viewed: A certain maiden having been offered in sacrifice, and spirited away from her sacrificers into another land, where the

custom was to sacrifice all strangers to the Goddess, she was made there the priestess of this rite. Long after that the brother of the priestess happened to come; the fact, however, of the oracle having for a certain reason bidden him go thither, and his object in going, are outside the Plot of the play. On his coming he was arrested, and about to be sacrificed, when he revealed who he was—either as Euripides puts it, or (as suggested by Polyidus) by the not improbable exclamation, "So I too am doomed to be sacrificed, as my sister was"; and the disclosure led to his salvation. This done, the next thing, after the proper names have been fixed as a basis for the story, is to work in episodes or accessory incidents. One must mind, however, that the episodes are appropriate, like the fit of madness in Orestes, which led to his arrest, and the purifying, which brought about his salvation. In plays, then, the episodes are short; in epic poetry they serve to lengthen out the poem. The argument of the *Odyssey* is not a long one. A certain man has been abroad many years; Poseidon is ever on the watch for him, and he is all alone. Matters at home too have come to this, that his substance is being wasted and his son's death plotted by suitors to his wife. Then he arrives there himself after his grievous sufferings; reveals himself, and falls on his enemies; and the end is his salvation and their death. This being all that is proper to the *Odyssey*, everything else in it is episode.

   18. [*Additional rules for the construction of a play.*] (4) There is a further point to be borne in mind. Every tragedy is in part Complication and in part Denouement; the incidents before the opening scene, and often certain also of those within the play, forming the Complication; and the rest the Denouement. By Complication I mean all from the beginning of the story to the point just before the change in the hero's fortunes; by Denouement, all from the beginning of the change to the end. In the *Lynceus* of Theodectes, for instance, the Complication includes, together with the presupposed incidents, the seizure of the child and that in turn of the parents; and the Denouement all from the indictment for the murder to the end. Now it is right, when one speaks of a tragedy as the same or not the same as another, to do so on the ground before all else of their Plot, i.e., as having the same or not the same Complication and Denouement. Yet there are many dramatists who, after a good Complication, fail in the Denouement. But it is necessary for both points of construction to be always duly mastered. (5) There are four distinct species of Tragedy—that being the number of the constituents also that have been mentioned: first, the complex Tragedy, which is all Peripety and Discovery; second, the Tragedy of suffering, e.g., the *Ajaxes* and *Ixions*; third, the Tragedy of character, e.g., *The Phthiotides* and *Peleus*. The fourth constituent is that of "Spectacle," exemplified in *The Phorcides*, in *Prometheus*, and in all plays with the scene laid in the nether world. The poet's aim, then,

should be to combine every element of interest, if possible, or else the more important and the major part of them. This is now especially necessary owing to the unfair criticism to which the poet is subjected in these days. Just because there have been poets before him strong in the several species of tragedy, the critics now expect the one man to surpass that which was the strong point of each one of his predecessors. (6) One should also remember what has been said more than once, and not write a tragedy on an epic body of incident (i.e., one with a plurality of stories in it), by attempting to dramatize, for instance, the entire story of the *Iliad*. In the epic owing to its scale every part is treated at proper length; with a drama, however, on the same story the result is very disappointing. This is shown by the fact that all who have dramatized the fall of Ilium in its entirety, and not part by part, like Euripides, or the whole of the Niobe story, instead of a portion, like Aeschylus, either fail utterly or have but ill success on the stage; for that and that alone was enough to ruin even a play by Agathon. Yet in their Peripeties, as also in their simple plots, the poets I mean show wonderful skill in aiming at the kind of effect they desire—a tragic situation that arouses the human feeling in one, like the clever villain (e.g., Sisyphus) deceived, or the brave wrongdoer worsted. This is probable, however, only in Agathon's sense, when he speaks of the probability of even improbabilities coming to pass. (7) The Chorus too should be regarded as one of the actors; it should be an integral part of the whole, and take a share in the action— that which it has in Sophocles, rather than in Euripides. With the later poets, however, the songs in a play of theirs have no more to do with the Plot of that than of any other tragedy. Hence it is that they are now singing intercalary pieces, a practice first introduced by Agathon. And yet what real difference is there between singing such intercalary pieces, and attempting to fit in a speech, or even a whole act, from one play into another?

19. [*The thought of the tragic personages.*] The Plot and Characters having been discussed, it remains to consider the Diction and Thought. As for the Thought, we may assume what is said of it in our Art of Rhetoric, as it belongs more properly to that department of inquiry. The Thought of the personages is shown in everything to be effected by their language—in every effort to prove or disprove, to arouse emotion (pity, fear, anger, and the like), or to maximize or minimize things. It is clear, also, that their mental procedure must be on the same lines in their actions likewise, whenever they wish them to arouse pity or horror, or to have a look of importance or probability. The only difference is that with the act the impression has to be made without explanation; whereas with the spoken word it has to be produced by the speaker, and result from his language. What, indeed, would be the good of the speaker, if things appeared in the required light even apart from anything he says?

As regards the Diction, one subject for inquiry under this head is the turns given to the language when spoken; e.g., the difference between command and prayer, simple statement and threat, question and answer, and so forth. The theory of such matters, however, belongs to Elocution and the professors of that art. Whether the poet knows these things or not, his art as a poet is never seriously criticized on that account. What fault can one see in Homer's "Sing of the wrath, Goddess"?—which Protagoras has criticized as being a command where a prayer was meant, since to bid one do or not do, he tells us, is a command. Let us pass over this, then, as appertaining to another art, and not to that of poetry. [...]

23. [*The epic must preserve unity of action.*] As for the poetry which merely narrates, or imitates by means of versified language (without action), it is evident that it has several points in common with Tragedy.

I. The construction of its stories should clearly be like that in a drama; they should be based on a single action, one that is a complete whole in itself, with a beginning, middle, and end, so as to enable the work to produce its own proper pleasure with all the organic unity of a living creature. Nor should one suppose that there is anything like them in our usual histories. A history has to deal not with one action, but with one period and all that happened in that to one or more persons, however disconnected the several events may have been. Just as two events may take place at the same time, e.g., the sea fight off Salamis and the battle with the Carthaginians in Sicily, without converging to the same end, so too of two consecutive events one may sometimes come after the other with no one end as their common issue. Nevertheless most of our epic poets, one may say, ignore the distinction.

Herein, then, to repeat what we have said before, we have a further proof of Homer's marvelous superiority to the rest. He did not attempt to deal even with the Trojan war in its entirety, though it was a whole with a definite beginning and end—through a feeling apparently that it was too long a story to be taken in in one view, or if not that, too complicated from the variety of incident in it. As it is, he has singled out one section of the whole; many of the other incidents, however, he brings in as episodes, using the Catalogue of the Ships, for instance, and other episodes to relieve the uniformity of his narrative. As for the other epic poets, they treat of one man, or one period; or else of an action which, although one, has a multiplicity of parts in it. This last is what the authors of the *Cypria* and *Little Iliad* have done. And the result is that, whereas the *Iliad* or *Odyssey* supplies materials for only one, or at most two tragedies, the *Cypria* does that for several and the *Little Iliad* for more than eight: for an *Adjudgement of Arms*, a *Philoctetes*, a *Neoptolemus*, a *Eurypylus*, a *Ulysses as Beggar*, a *Laconian Women*, a *Fall of Ilium*, and a *Departure of the Fleet;* as also a *Sinon*, and a *Women of Troy.*

24. [*Comparison of epic and tragedy.*] II. Besides this, Epic poetry must divide into the same species as Tragedy; it must be either simple or complex, a story of character or one of suffering. Its parts, too, with the exception of Song and Spectacle, must be the same, as it requires Peripeties, Discoveries, and scenes of suffering just like Tragedy. Lastly, the Thought and Diction in it must be good in their way. All these elements appear in Homer first, and he has made due use of them. His two poems are each examples of construction, the *Iliad* simple and a story of suffering, the *Odyssey* complex (there is Discovery throughout it) and a story of character. And they are more than this, since in Diction and Thought too they surpass all other poems.

There is, however, a difference in the Epic as compared with Tragedy, (1) in its length, and (2) in its meter. (1) As to its length, the limit already suggested will suffice: it must be possible for the beginning and end of the work to be taken in in one view—a condition which will be fulfilled if the poem be shorter than the old epics, and about as long as the series of tragedies offered for one hearing. For the extension of its length epic poetry has a special advantage, of which it makes large use. In a play one cannot represent an action with a number of parts going on simultaneously; one is limited to the part on the stage and connected with the actors. Whereas in epic poetry the narrative form makes it possible for one to describe a number of simultaneous incidents; and these, if germane to the subject, increase the body of the poem. This then is a gain to the Epic, tending to give it grandeur, and also variety of interest and room for episodes of diverse kinds. Uniformity of incident by the satiety it soon creates is apt to ruin tragedies on the stage. (2) As for its meter, the heroic has been assigned it from experience; were any one to attempt a narrative poem in some one, or in several, of the other meters, the incongruity of the thing would be apparent. The heroic in fact is the gravest and weightiest of meters—which is what makes it more tolerant than the rest of strange words and metaphors, that also being a point in which the narrative form of poetry goes beyond all others. The iambic and trochaic, on the other hand, are meters of movement, the one representing that of life and action, the other that of the dance. Still more unnatural would it appear, if one were to write an epic in a medley of meters, as Chaeremon did. Hence it is that no one has ever written a long story in any but heroic verse; nature herself, as we have said, teaches us to select the meter appropriate to such a story.

Homer, admirable as he is in every other respect, is especially so in this, that he alone among epic poets is not unaware of the part to be played by the poet himself in the poem. The poet should say very little in *propria persona*, as he is no imitator when doing that. Whereas the other poets are perpetually coming forward in person, and say but little, and that only here and there, as imitators, Homer after a brief preface brings in forthwith a man, a woman, or some other Character—no one of them characterless, but each with distinctive characteristics.

The marvelous is certainly required in Tragedy. The Epic, however, affords more opening for the improbable, the chief factor in the marvelous, because in it the agents are not visibly before one. The scene of the pursuit of

Hector would be ridiculous on the stage—the Greeks halting instead of pursuing him, and Achilles shaking his head to stop them; but in the poem the absurdity is overlooked. The marvelous, however, is a cause of pleasure, as is shown by the fact that we all tell a story with additions, in the belief that we are doing our hearers a pleasure.

Homer more than any other has taught the rest of us the art of framing lies in the right way. I mean the use of paralogism. Whenever, if A is or happens, a consequent, B, is or happens, men's notion is that, if the B is, the A also is—but that is a false conclusion. Accordingly, if A is untrue, but there is something else, B, that on the assumption of its truth follows as its consequent, the right thing then is to add on the B. Just because we know the truth of the consequent, we are in our own minds led on to the erroneous inference of the truth of the antecedent. Here is an instance, from the *Bath-story* in the *Odyssey*.

A likely impossibility is always preferable to an unconvincing possibility. The story should never be made up of improbable incidents; there should be nothing of the sort in it. If, however, such incidents are unavoidable, they should be outside the piece, like the hero's ignorance in *Oedipus* of the circumstances of Laius' death; not within it, like the report of the Pythian games in *Electra*, or the man's having come to Mysia from Tegea without uttering a word on the way, in *The Mysians*. So that it is ridiculous to say that one's Plot would have been spoilt without them, since it is fundamentally wrong to make up such Plots. If the poet has taken such a Plot, however, and one sees that he might have put it in a more probable form, he is guilty of absurdity as well as a fault of art. Even in the *Odyssey* the improbabilities in the setting ashore of Ulysses would be clearly intolerable in the hands of an inferior poet. As it is, the poet conceals them, his other excellences veiling their absurdity. Elaborate Diction, however, is required only in places where there is no action, and no Character or Thought to be revealed. Where there is Character or Thought, on the other hand, an over-ornate Diction tends to obscure them.

25. [***Possible criticisms of an epic or tragedy.***] As regards Problems and their Solutions, one may see the number and nature of the assumptions on which they proceed by viewing the matter in the following way. (1) The poet being an imitator just like the painter or other maker of likenesses, he must necessarily in all instances represent things in one or other of three aspects, either as they were or are, or as they are said or thought to be or to have been, or as they ought to be. (2) All this he does in language, with an admixture, it may be, of strange words and metaphors, as also of the various modified forms of words, since the use of these is conceded in poetry. (3) It is to be remembered, too, that there is not the same kind of correctness in poetry as in politics, or indeed any other art. There is, however, within the limits of poetry itself a possibility of two kinds of error, the one directly, the other only accidentally connected with the art. If the poet meant to describe the thing correctly, and failed through lack of power of expression, his art itself is at fault. But if it was through his having meant to describe it in some incorrect way (e.g., to make the horse in movement have both right legs thrown forward) that the technical error (one in a matter of, say, medicine or some other special science), or impossibilities of whatever kind they may be, have got into his description, his error in that case is not in the essentials of the poetic art. These, therefore, must be the premises of the Solutions in answer to the criticisms involved in the Problems.

I. As to the criticisms relating to the poet's art itself. Any impossibilities there may be in his descriptions of things are faults. But from another point of view they are justifiable, if they serve the end of poetry itself—if (to assume what we have said of that end) they make the effect of either that very portion of the work or some other portion more astounding. The Pursuit of Hector is an instance in point. If, however, the poetic end might have been as well or better attained without sacrifice of technical correctness in such matters, the impossibility is not to be justified, since the description should be, if it can, entirely free from error. One may ask, too, whether the error is in a matter directly or only accidentally connected with the poetic art; since it is a lesser error in an artist not to know, for instance, that the hind has no horns, than to produce an unrecognizable picture of one.

II. If the poet's description be criticized as not true to fact, one may urge perhaps that the object ought to be as described—an answer like that of Sophocles, who said that he drew men as they ought to be, and Euripides as they were. If the description, however, be neither true nor of the thing as it ought to be, the answer must be then, that it is in accordance with opinion. The tales about Gods, for instance, may be as wrong as Xenophanes thinks, neither true nor the better thing to say; but they are certainly in accordance with opinion. Of other statements in poetry one may perhaps say, not that they are better than the truth, but that the fact was so at the time—e.g., the description of the arms: "their spears stood upright, butt end upon the ground;" for that was the usual way of fixing them then, as it is still with the Illyrians. As for the question whether something said or done in a poem is morally right or not, in dealing with that one should consider not only the intrinsic quality of the actual word or deed, but also the person who says or does it, the person to whom he says or does it, the time, the means, and the motive of the agent—whether he does it to attain a greater good, or to avoid a greater evil. [...]

Speaking generally, one has to justify (1) the Impossible by reference to the requirements of poetry, or to the better, or to opinion. For the purposes of poetry a convincing impossibility is preferable to an unconvincing possibility; and if men such as Zeuxis depicted be impossible, the answer is that it is better they should be like that, as the artist ought to improve on his model. (2) The Improbable one has to justify either by showing it to be in accordance with opinion, or by urging that at times it is not improbable; for there is a probability of things happening also against probability. (3) The contradictions found in the poet's language one should first test as one does an opponent's confutation in a dialectical argument, so as to see whether he means the same thing, in the same relation, and in the same sense, before admitting that he has contradicted either something he has said himself or what a man of sound sense assumes as true. But there is no possible apology for improbability of Plot or depravity of character, when they are not necessary and no use is made of them, like the improbability in the appearance of Aegeus in *Medea* and the baseness of Menelaus in *Orestes*.

The objections, then, of critics start with faults of five kinds. The allegation is always that something is either (1) impossible, (2) improbable, (3) corrupting, (4) contradictory, or (5) against technical correctness. The answers to these objections must be sought under one or other of the above-mentioned heads, which are twelve in number.

26. [*Tragedy artistically superior to epic poetry.*] The question may be raised whether the epic or the tragic is the higher form of imitation. It may be argued that, if the less vulgar is the higher, and the less vulgar is always that which addresses the better public, an art addressing any and every one is of a very vulgar order. It is a belief that their public cannot see the meaning, unless they add something themselves, that causes the perpetual movements of the performers—bad flute players, for instance, rolling about, if quoit throwing is to be represented, and pulling at the conductor, if Scylla is the subject of the piece. Tragedy, then, is said to be an art of this order—to be in fact just what the later actors were in the eyes of their predecessors; for Mynniscus used to call Callippides "the ape," because he thought he so overacted his parts; and a similar view was taken of Pindarus also. All Tragedy, however, is said to stand to the Epic as the newer to the older school of actors. The one, accordingly, is said to address a cultivated audience, which does not need the accompaniment of gesture; the other, an uncultivated one. If, therefore, Tragedy is a vulgar art, it must clearly be lower than the Epic.

The answer to this is twofold. In the first place, one may urge (1) that the censure does not touch the art of the dramatic poet, but only that of his interpreter; for it is quite possible to overdo the gesturing even in an epic recital, as did Sosistratus, and in a singing contest, as did Mnasitheus of Opus. (2) That one should not condemn all movement, unless one means to condemn even the dance, but only that of ignoble people—which is the point of the criticism passed on Callippides and in the present day on others, that their women are not like gentlewomen. (3) That Tragedy may produce its effect even without movement or action in just the same way as Epic poetry, for from the mere reading of a play its quality may be seen. So that, if it be superior in all other respects, this element of inferiority is no necessary part of it.

In the second place, one must remember (1) that Tragedy has everything that the Epic has (even the epic meter being admissible), together with a not inconsiderable addition in the shape of the Music (a very real factor in the pleasure of the drama) and the Spectacle. (2) That its reality of presentation is felt in the play as read, as well as in the play as acted. (3) That the tragic imitation requires less space for the attainment of its end; which is a great advantage, since the more concentrated effect is more pleasurable than one with a large admixture of time to dilute it—consider the *Oedipus* of Sophocles, for instance, and the effect of expanding it into the number of lines of the *Iliad*. (4) That there is less unity in the imitation of the epic poets, as is proved by the fact that any one work of theirs supplies matter for several tragedies; the result being that, if they take what is really a single story, it seems curt when briefly told, and thin and waterish when on the scale of length usual with their verse. In saying that there is less unity in an epic, I mean an epic made up of a plurality of actions, in the same way as the *Iliad* and *Odyssey* have many such parts, each one of them in itself of some magnitude; yet the structure of the two Homeric poems is as perfect as can be, and the action in them is as nearly as possible one action. If, then, Tragedy is superior in these respects, and also, besides these, in its poetic effect (since the two forms of poetry should give us, not any or every pleasure, but the very special kind we have mentioned), it is clear that, as attaining the poetic effect better than the Epic, it will be the higher form of art.

So much for Tragedy and Epic poetry—for these two arts in general and their species; the number and nature of their constituent parts; the causes of success and failure in them; the Objections of the critics, and the Solutions in answer to them.

HORACE

HORACE (85-8 BC) was a fat little arriviste, the son of a freedman (former slave) who rose to wealth and prominence in a dangerous society by allying himself with the state and its highest authorities. He enjoyed the patronage of Maecenas, who gave him a villa in the Sabine hills, and the favor of Augustus, who made him a privileged poet at the imperial court. Horace received a commission to write and perform the Centennial Hymn at Augustus's great *Ludi Saeculare* (Secular Games) in 17 B.C. Paid to celebrate the glory of his benefactor, the poet directed the singing of his hymn by huge choruses to musical accompaniment before an audience of thousands.

Although Horace was a poet, not a playwright, *The Art of Poetry* is chiefly about drama. A friend of the tragic poet Varius Rufus, author of the tragedy *Thyestes*, Horace was a discriminating theatregoer of fastidious predilections, who found Plautus crude and overrated. From other verse epistles, satires, and odes, we know that Horace detested the vulgar mob and deplored the poor taste of "unlearned and foolish spectators" who called for a bear or boxers. The mob delighted not in the ears (intended for nobler messages), but in the "uncertain eyes and their vain amusements." Elephants, captive kings, squadrons of horsemen, and model ships were among the extravagant crowd-pleasing Roman spectacles that aroused Horace's bemused exasperation.

The poet's poet, he extolled technique and professionalism and ridiculed the inspiration vaunted by self-proclaimed geniuses of amateur standing. Horace's theory was forward-looking and dynamic, full of provocative insights, casually tossed off, about the interrelations of the arts and their dependence on perpetual change in language and society. Educated in both Rome and Athens, Latin and Greek, the poet was attuned to the interplay of civilizations and the imitation of cultural models. Nonetheless, he claimed that Rome possessed an indigenous dramatic tradition that had developed from certain religious ceremonies and from the ritual abuse—Fescennine verses—which accompanied them.

Not surprisingly, Horace—master craftsman, upstart, and self-made man close to the seats of power and patronage—was the favorite of the Renaissance courtier poets boldly seeking to get ahead through their wits and talents in a world of treachery and deceit. Ben Jonson, the first English poet laureate, translated *The Art of Poetry*, and even Queen Elizabeth was working on an English version.

THE ART OF POETRY (1st c. B.C.)

Suppose some painter, as a *tour de force*,
Should couple head of man with neck of horse,
Invest them both with feathers, 'stead of hair,
And tack on limbs picked up from here and there,
So that the figure, when complete, should show
A maid above, a hideous fish below:
Should you be favored with a private view,
You'd laugh, my friends, I know, and rightly too.
Yet trust me, Pisos, not less strange would look,
To a discerning eye, the foolish book
Where dreamlike forms in sick delirium blend,
And nought is of a piece from end to end.
"Poets and painters (you know the plea)
Have always been allowed their fancy free."
I own it; 'tis a fair excuse to plead;
By turns we claim it, and by turns concede;
But 'twill not screen the unnatural and absurd,
Unions of lamb with tiger, snake with bird.
When poets would be lofty, they commence
With purple patch of cheap magnificence:
Of Dian's altar and her grove we read,
Or rapid streams meandering through the mead;
Or grand descriptions of the river Rhine,
Or watery bow, will take up many a line.
All in their way good things, but not just now:
You're happy at a cypress, we'll allow;
But what of that? you're painting by command
A shipwrecked sailor, striking out for land:
That crockery was a jar when you began;
It ends a pitcher: you an artist, man!
Make what you will, in short, so, when 'tis done,

From Horace, *Satires, Epistles, and Ars Poetica*, trans. John Conington.
London: G. Bell and Sons, 1922.

'Tis but consistent, simple, one.
Ye worthy trio! we poor sons of song
Oft find 'tis fancied right that leads us wrong.
I prove obscure in trying to be terse;
Attempts at ease emasculate my verse;
Who aims at grandeur into bombast falls;
Who fears to stretch his pinions creeps and crawls;
Who hopes by strange variety to please
Puts dolphins among forests, boars in seas.
Thus zeal to 'scape from error, if unchecked
By sense of art, creates a new defect.
Fix on some casual sculptor; he shall know
How to give nails their sharpness, hair its flow;
Yet he shall fail, because he lacks the soul
To comprehend and reproduce the whole.
I'd not be he: the blackest hair and eye
Lose all their beauty with the nose awry.
Good authors, take a brother bard's advice:
Ponder your subject o'er not once nor twice,
And oft and oft consider, if the weight
You hope to lift be or be not too great.
Let but our theme be equal to our powers,
Choice language, clear arrangement, both are ours.
Would you be told how best your pearls to thread?
Why, say just now what should just now be said,
But put off other matter for to-day,
To introduce it later by the way.
In words again be cautious and select,
And duly pick out this, and that reject.
High praise and honor to the bard is due
Whose dexterous setting makes an old word new.
Nay more, should some recondite subject need
Fresh signs to make it clear to those who read,
A power of issuing terms till now unused,
If claimed with modesty, is ne'er refused.
New words will find acceptance, if they flow
Forth from the Greek, with just a twist or so.
But why should Rome capriciously forbid
Our bards from doing what their fathers did?
Or why should Plautus and Caecilius gain
What Virgil or what Varius asks in vain?
Nay, I myself, if with my scanty wit
I coin a word or two, why grudge me it,
When Ennius and old Cato boldly flung

Their terms broadcast, and amplified our tongue?
To utter words stamped current by the mill
Has always been thought right and always will.
When forests shed their foliage in fall,
The earliest born still drops the first of all:
So fades the elder race of words, and so
The younger generations bloom and grow.
Death claims humanity and human things,
Aye, e'en "imperial works and worthy kings":
What though the ocean, girdled by the shore,
Gives shelter to the ships it tossed before?
What though the marsh, once waste and watery, now
Feeds neighbor towns, and groans beneath the plow?
What though the river, late the corn-field's dread,
Rolls fruit and blessing down its altered bed?
Man's works must perish: how should words evade
The general doom, and flourish undecayed?
Yes, words long faded may again revive,
And words may fade now blooming and alive,
If usage wills it so, to whom belongs
The rule, the law, the government of tongues.
For meters, Homer shows you how to write
Heroic deeds and incidents of fight.
Complaint was once the Elegiac's theme;
From thence 'twas used to sing of love's young dream:
But who that dainty measure first put out,
Grammarians differ, and 'tis still in doubt.
Archilochus, inspired by fiery rage,
Called forth Iambics: now they tread the stage
In buskin or in sock, conduct discourse,
Lead action on, and awe the mob perforce.
The glorious gods, the gods' heroic seed,
The conquering boxer, the victorious steed,
The joys of wine, the lover's fond desire,
Such themes the Muse appropriates to the lyre.
Why hail me poet, if I fail to seize
The shades of style, its fixed proprieties?
Why should false shame compel me to endure
An ignorance which common pains would cure?
A comic subject steadily declines
To be related in high tragic lines.
The Thyestean feast no less disdains
The vulgar vehicle of comic strains.
Each has its place allotted; each is bound

To keep it, nor invade its neighbor's ground.
Yet Comedy sometimes will raise her note:
See Chremes, how he swells his angry throat!
And when a tragic hero tells his woes,
The terms he chooses are akin to prose.
Peleus or Telephus, suppose him poor
Or driven to exile, talks in tropes no more;
His yard-long words desert him, when he tries
To draw forth tears from sympathetic eyes.
Mere grace is not enough: a poem should thrill
The hearer's soul, and move it at its will.
Smiles are contagious; so are tears; to see
Another sobbing, brings a sob from me.
No, no, good Peleus; set the example, pray,
And weep yourself; then weep perhaps I may:
But if no sorrow in your speech appear,
I nod or laugh; I cannot squeeze a tear.
Words follow looks: wry faces are expressed
By wailing, scowls by bluster, smiles by jest,
Grave airs by saws, and so of all the rest.
For nature forms our spirits to receive
Each bent that outward circumstance can give:
She kindles pleasure, bids resentment glow,
Or bows the soul to earth in hopeless woe;
Then, as the tide of feeling waxes strong,
She vents it through her conduit-pipe, the tongue.
Unless the speaker's words and fortune suit,
All Rome will join to jeer him, horse and foot.
Gods should not talk like heroes, nor again
Impetuous youth like grave and reverend men;
Lady and nurse a different language crave,
Sons of the soil and rovers o'er the wave;
Assyrian, Colchian, Theban, Argive, each
Has his own style, his proper cast of speech.
In painting characters, follow tradition,
Or in inventing, be consistent,
If great Achilles figure in the scene,
Make him impatient, fiery, ruthless, keen;
All laws, all covenants let him still disown,
And test his quarrel by the sword alone.
Make Medea all revenge and scorn,
Ino still sad, Ixion still forsworn,
Io a wanderer still, Orestes still forlorn.
If you would be original, and seek

To frame some character ne'er seen in Greek,
See it be wrought on one consistent plan,
And end the same creation it began.
'Tis hard, I grant, to treat a subject known
And hackneyed so that it may look one's own;
Far better turn the Iliad to a play
And carve out acts and scenes the readiest way,
Than alter facts and characters, and tell
In a strange form the tale men know so well.
But, with some few precautions, you may set
Your private mark on public chattels yet:
Avoid careering and careering still
In the old round, like carthorse in a mill;
Nor, bound too closely to the Grecian Muse,
Translate the words whose soul you should transfuse,
Nor act the copyist's part, and work in chains
Which, once put on by rashness, shame retains.
Don't open like the older epics, with a burst:
"Troy's war and Priam's fate are here rehearsed."
What's coming, pray, that thus he winds his horn?
The mountain labors, and a mouse is born.
Far better he who enters at his ease,
Nor takes your breath with empty flourishes:
"Sing, Muse, the man who, after Troy was burned,
Saw divers cities, and their manners learned."
Not smoke from fire his object is to bring,
But fire from smoke, a very different thing;
Yet has he dazzling miracles in store,
Cyclops, and Laestrygons, and fifty more.
He sings not, he, of Diomed's return,
Starting from Meleager's funeral urn,
Nor when he tells the Trojan story, begs
Attention first for Leda and her eggs.
He hurries to the climax, lets you fall
Where facts crowd thick, as though you knew them all,
And what he judges will not turn to gold
Beneath his touch, he passes by untold.
And all this glamour, all this glorious dream,
Truth blent with fiction in one motley scheme,
He so contrives, that, when 'tis o'er, you see
Beginning, middle, end alike agree.
Now listen, dramatists, and I will tell
What I expect, and all the world as well.
If you would have your auditors to stay

Till curtain-rise and plaudit end the play,
Observe each age's temper, and impart
To each the grace and finish of your art.
Note first the boy who just knows how to talk
And feels his feet beneath him in his walk:
He likes his young companions, loves a game,
Soon vexed, soon soothed, and not two hours the same.
The beardless youth, at last from tutor freed,
Loves playing-field and tennis, dog and steed:
Pliant as wax to those who lead him wrong,
But all impatience with a faithful tongue;
Imprudent, lavish, hankering for the moon,
He takes things up and lays them down as soon.
His nature revolutionized, the man
Makes friends and money when and how he can:
Keen-eyed and cool, though on ambition bent,
He shuns all acts of which he may repent.
Gray hairs have many evils: without end
The old man gathers what he dares not spend,
While, as for action, do he what he will,
'Tis all half-hearted, spiritless, and chill:
Inert, irresolute, his neck he cranes
Into the future, grumbles, and complains,
Extols his own young years with peevish praise,
But rates and censures these degenerate days.
Years, as they come, bring blessings in their train;
Years, as they go, take blessings back again:
Yet haste or chance may blink the obvious truth,
Make youth discourse like age, and age like youth:
Attention fixed on life alone can teach
The traits and adjuncts which pertain to each.
Sometimes an action on the stage is shown,
Sometimes 'tis done elsewhere, and there made known.
A thing when heard, remember, strikes less keen
On the spectator's mind than when 'tis seen.
Yet 'twere not well in public to display
A business best transacted far away,
And much may be secluded from the eye
For well-graced tongues to tell of by and by.
Medea must not shed her children's blood,
Nor savage Atreus cook man's flesh for food,
Nor Philomel turn bird or Cadmus snake,
With people looking on and wide awake.
If scenes like these before my eyes be thrust,

They shock belief and generate disgust.
Would you your play should prosper and endure?
Then let it have five acts, nor more nor fewer.
Bring in no god save as a last resource,
Nor make four speakers join in the discourse.
An actor's part the chorus should sustain
And do their best to get the plot in train:
And whatsoe'er between the acts they chant
Should all be apt, appropriate, relevant.
Still let them give sage counsel, back the good,
Temper wrath, and cool impetuous blood,
Praise the spare meal that pleases but not sates,
Justice, and law, and peace with unbarred gates,
Conceal all secrets, and the gods implore
To crush the proud and elevate the poor.
Not trumpet-tongued, as now, nor brass-belayed,
The flute was used to lend the chorus aid:
Simple and slight and moderately loud,
It charmed the ears of not too large a crowd,
Which, frugal, rustic, primitive, severe,
Flocked in those early days to see and hear.
Then, when the city gained increase of land,
And wider walls its waxing greatness spanned,
When the good Genius, frolicsome and gay,
Was soothed at festivals with cups by day,
Change spread to scenic measures: breadth, and ease
And freedom unrestrained were found in these:
For what (said men) should jovial rustic, placed
At random 'mid his betters, know of taste?
So graceful dance went hand in hand with song,
And robes of kingly splendor trailed along:
So by the side of music words upgrew,
And eloquence came rolling, prompt and new:
Shrewd in things mundane, wise in things divine,
Its voice was like the voice of Delphi's shrine.
The aspiring bard who served the tragic muse,
A paltry goat the summit of his views,
Soon brought in Satyrs from the woods, and tried
If grave and gay could flourish side by side,
That the spectator, feasted to his fill,
Noisy and drunk, might ne'ertheless sit still.
Yet, though loud laugh and frolic jest commend
Your Satyr folk, and mirth and morals blend,
Let not your heroes doff their robes of red

To talk low language in a homely shed,
Nor, in their fear of crawling, mount too high,
Catching at clouds and aiming at the sky.
The Muse, when bidden to be gay,
Like matron dancing on a festal day,
Deals not in idle banter, nor consorts
Without reserve with Satyrs and their sports.
In plays like these I would not deal alone
In words and phrases trite and too well known,
Nor, stooping from the tragic height, drop down
To the low level of buffoon and clown,
As though pert Davus, or the saucy jade
Who sacks the gold and jeers the gull she made,
Were like Silenus, who, though quaint and odd,
Is yet the guide and tutor of a god.
A hackneyed subject I would take and treat
So deftly, all should hope to do the feat,
Then, having strained and struggled, should concede
To do the feat were difficult indeed.
So much may order and arrangement do
To make the cheap seem choice, the threadbare new.
Your rustic Fauns, methinks, should have a care
Lest people deem them bred in city air;
Should shun the cant of exquisites, and shun
Coarse ribaldry no less and blackguard fun.
For those who have a father or a horse
Or an estate will take offense of course,
Nor think they're bound in duty to admire
What gratifies the pea and chestnut buyer.
The Iambic foot is briefly thus defined:
Two syllables, a short with long behind:
Repeat it six times o'er, so quick its beat,
'Tis trimeter, three measures for six feet:
At first it ran straight on; but, years ago,
Its hearers begged that it would move more slow;
On which it took, with a good-natured air,
Stout spondees in, its native rights to share,
Yet so that none should ask it to resign
The sixth, fourth, second places in the line.
But search through Accius' trimeters, or those
Which Ennius took such pleasure to compose,
You'll rarely find it: on the boards they groan,
Laden with spondees, like a cart with stone,

And brand our tragedy with want of skill
Or want of labor, call it which you will.
What then? false rhythm few judges can detect,
And Roman bards of course are all correct.
What shall a poet do? make rules his sport,
And dash through thick and thin, through long and short?
Or pick his steps, endeavor to walk clean,
And fancy every mud-stain will be seen?
What good were that, if though I mind my ways
And shun all blame, I do not merit praise?
My friends, make Greece your model when you write,
And turn her volumes over day and night.
"But Plautus pleased our sires, the good old folks;
They praised his numbers, and they praised his jokes."
They did: 'twas mighty tolerant in them
To praise where wisdom would perhaps condemn;
That is, if you and I and our compeers
Can trust our tastes, our fingers, and our ears,
Know polished wit from horseplay, and can tell
What verses do, and what do not, run well.
Thespis began the drama: rumor says
In traveling carts he carried round his plays,
Where actors, smeared with lees, before the throng
Performed their parts with gesture and with song.
Then Aeschylus brought in the mask and pall,
Put buskins on his men to make them tall,
Turned boards into a platform, not too great,
And taught high monologue and grand debate.
The Old Comedy had next its turn,
Nor small the glory it contrived to earn:
But freedom passed into unbridled spite,
And law was soon invoked to set things right:
Law spoke: the chorus lost the power to sting,
And (shame to say) thenceforth refused to sing.
Our poets have tried all things; nor do they
Deserve least praise, who follow their own way,
And tell in comedy or history-piece
Some story of home growth, not drawn from Greece.
Nor would the land we love be now more strong
In warrior's prowess than in poet's song,
Did not her bards with one consent decline
The tedious task, to alter and refine.
Dear Pisos! as you prize old Numa's blood,
Set down that work, and that alone, as good,
Which, blurred and blotted, checked and counter-checked,

Has stood all tests, and issued forth correct.
Because Democritus thinks fit to say,
That wretched art to genius must give way,
Stands at the gate of Helicon, and guards
Its precinct against all but crazy bards,
Our poets keep long nails and untrimmed hair,
Much in solitude, shunning baths.
For things are come to this; the merest dunce,
So but he choose, may start up bard at once,
Whose head, too hot for hellebore to cool,
Was ne'er submitted to a barber's tool.
What ails me now, to dose myself each spring?
Else had I been a very swan to sing.
Well, never mind: mine be the whetstone's lot,
Which makes steel sharp, though cut itself will not.
Although no writer, I may yet impart
To writing folk the precepts of their art,
Whence come its stores, what trains and forms a bard,
And how a work is made, and how 'tis marred.
Of writing well, be sure, the secret lies
In wisdom: therefore study to be wise.
The page of Plato may suggest the thought,
Which found, the words will come as soon as sought.
The man who once has learned to comprehend
His duty to his country and his friend,
The love that parent, brother, guest may claim,
The judge's, senator's, or general's aim,
That man, when need occurs, will soon invent
For every part its proper sentiment.
Look too to life and manners, as they lie
Before you: these will living words supply.
A play, devoid of beauty, strength, and art,
So but the thoughts and morals suit each part,
Will catch men's minds and rivet them when caught
More than the clink of verses without thought.
To Greece, fair Greece, ambitious but of praise,
The Muse gave ready wit, and rounded phrase.
Our Roman youth, by puzzling days and nights,
Bring down a shilling to a hundred mites.
Come, young Albinus, tell us, if you take
A penny from a sixpence, what 'twill make.
Fivepence. Good boy! you'll come to wealth one day.
Now add a penny. Sevenpence, he will say.
O, when this cankering rust, this greed of gain,
Has touched the soul and wrought into its grain,

What hope that poets will produce such lines
As cedar-oil embalms and cypress shrines?
A bard will wish to teach or to please,
Or, as a tertium quid, do both of these.
Whene'er you lecture, be concise: the soul
Takes in short maxims, and retains them whole:
But pour in water when the vessel's filled,
It simply dribbles over and is spilled.
Keep near to truth in a fictitious piece,
Nor treat belief as matter of caprice.
If on a child you make a vampire sup,
It must not be alive when she's ripped up.
Our elders see an uninstructive strain;
Young lordlings treat grave verse with tall disdain:
But he who, mixing grave and gay, can teach
And yet give pleasure, gains a vote from each:
His works enrich the vendor, cross the sea,
And hand the author down to late posterity
Some faults may claim forgiveness: for the lyre
Not always gives the note that we desire;
We ask a flat; a sharp is its reply;
And the best bow will sometimes shoot awry.
But when I meet with beauties thickly sown,
A blot or two I readily condone,
Such as may trickle from a careless pen,
Or pass unwatched: for authors are but men.
What then? the copyist who keeps stumbling still
At the same word had best lay down his quill
The harp-player, who forever wounds the ear
With the same discord, makes the audience jeer:
So the poor dolt who's often in the wrong
I rank with Choerilus, the dunce of song,
Who, should he ever "deviate into sense,"
Moves but fresh laughter at his own expense:
While e'en good Homer may deserve a tap,
If, as he does, he drop his head and nap.
Yet, when a work is long, 'twere somewhat hard
To blame a drowsy moment in a bard.
Some poems, like some paintings, take the eye
Best at a distance, some when looked at nigh.
One loves the shade; one would be seen in light,
And boldly challenges the keenest sight:
One pleases straightway; one, when it has passed
Ten times before the mind, will please at last.

Hope of the Pisos! trained by such a sire,
And wise yourself, small schooling you require;
Yet take this lesson home; some things admit
A moderate point of merit, e'en in wit.
There's yonder counselor; he cannot reach
Messala's stately altitudes of speech,
He cannot plumb Cascellius' depth of lore,
Yet he's employed, and makes a decent score:
But gods, and men, and booksellers agree
To place their ban on middling poetry.
At a great feast an ill-toned instrument,
A sour conserve, or an unfragrant scent
Offends the taste: 'tis reason that it should;
We do without such things, or have them good:
Just so with verse; you seek but to delight;
If by an inch you fail, you fail outright.
He who knows naught of games abstains from all,
Nor tries his hand at quoit, or hoop, or ball,
Lest the thronged circle, witnessing the play,
Should laugh outright, with none to say them nay:
He who knows naught of verses needs must try
To write them ne'ertheless. "Why not?" men cry:
"Free, gently born, unblemished and correct,
His means a knight's, what more can folks expect?"
But you, my friend, at least have sense and grace;
You will not fly in queen Minerva's face
In action or in word. Suppose some day
You should take courage and compose a lay,
Entrust it first to Maecius' critical ears,
Your sire's and mine, and keep it back nine years.
What's kept at home you cancel by a stroke:
What's sent abroad you never can revoke.
Orpheus, the priest and harper, pure and good,
Weaned savage tribes from deeds and feasts of blood,
Whence he was said to tame the monsters of the wood.
Amphion too, men said, at his desire
Moved massy stones, obedient to the lyre,
And Thebes arose. 'Twas wisdom's province then
To judge 'twixt states and subjects, gods and men,
Check vagrant lust, give rules to wedded folk,
Build cities up, engrave a code in oak.
So came great honor and abundant praise,
As to the gods, to poets and their lays.
Then Homer and Tyrtaeus, armed with song,
Made manly spirits for the combat strong:

Verse taught life's duties, showed the future clear,
And won a monarch's favor through his ear:
Verse gave relief from labor, and supplied
Light mirth for holiday and festal tide.
Then blush not for the lyre: Apollo sings
In unison with her who sweeps its strings.
But here occurs a question some men start,
If good verse comes from nature or from art.
For me, I cannot see how native wit
Can e'er dispense with art, or art with it.
Set them to pull together, they're agreed,
And each supplies what each is found to need.
The youth who runs for prizes wisely trains,
Bears cold and heat, is patient and abstains:
The flute-player at a festival, before
He plays in public, has to learn his lore.
Not so our bardlings: they come bouncing in—
"I'm your true poet: let them laugh that win:
Plague take the last! although I ne'er was taught,
Is that a cause for owning I know naught?"
As puffing auctioneers collect a throng,
Rich poets bribe false friends to hear their song:
Who can resist the lord of so much rent,
Of so much money at so much per cent?
He may give a grand regale,
Act as a poor man's counsel or his bail,
Blest though he be, his wealth will cloud his view,
Nor suffer him to know false friends from true.
Don't ask a man whose feelings overflow
For kindness that you've shown or mean to show
To listen to your verse: each line you read,
He'll cry, "Good! bravo! exquisite indeed!"
He'll change his color, let his eyes run o'er
With tears of joy, dance, beat upon the floor.
Hired mourners at a funeral say and do
A little more than they whose grief is true:
'Tis just so here: false flattery displays
More show of sympathy than honest praise.
'Tis said when kings a would-be friend will try,
With wine they rack him and with bumpers ply:
If you write poems, look beyond the skin
Of the smooth fox, and search the heart within.
Read verses to Quintilius, he would say,
"I don't like this and that: improve it, pray":

Tell him you found it hopeless to correct;
You'd tried it twice or thrice without effect
He'd calmly bid you make the three times four,
And take the unlicked cub in hand once more.
But if you chose to vindicate the crime,
Not mend it, he would waste no further time,
But let you live, untroubled by advice,
Sole tenant of your own fool's paradise.
A wise and faithful counselor will blame
Weak verses, note the rough, condemn the lame,
Retrench luxuriance, make obscureness plain,
Cross-question this, bid that be writ again:
A second Aristarch, he will not ask,
"Why for such trifles take my friend to task?"
Such trifles bring to serious grief ere long
A hapless bard, once flattered and led wrong.
See the mad poet! another, though sick
Of itch or jaundice, moon-struck, fanatic,
Was never half so dangerous: men whose mind is sound
Avoid him; fools pursue him, children hound.
Suppose, while spluttering verses, head on high,
Like fowler watching blackbirds in the sky,
He falls into a pit; though loud he shout
"Help, neighbors, help!" let no man pull him out:
Should some one seem disposed a rope to fling,
I will strike in with, "Pray do no such thing:
I'll warrant you he meant it," and relate
His brother bard Empedocles's fate,
Who, wishing to be thought a god, poor fool,
Leapt down hot Aetna's crater, calm and cool.
"Leave poets free to perish as they will:
Save them by violence, you as good as kill.
'Tis not his first attempt: if saved to-day,
He's sure to die in some outrageous way.
Beside, none knows the reason why this curse
Was sent on him, this love of making verse,
By what offense heaven's anger he incurred,
A grave defiled, a sacred boundary stirred:
So much is plain, he's mad: like bear that beats
His prison down and ranges through the streets,
This terrible reciter puts to flight
The learned and unlearned left and right:
Let him catch one, he reads to him till he kills,
As leeches stick till they have sucked their fills."

BHARATA

BHARATA is the most complete and yet the most elusive of theatre theorists, whose identity—and dates and place of birth and death—are lost in the mists of legend. He is the most legendary of theorists and the most directly tied to actual theatrical practice, the most exalted and the most practical, both a god and a stage manager.

Theatre was created when the world passed from the Golden Age to the Silver Age. The celestial *Nāṭyaśāstra*, or holy book of dramaturgy, was brought from heaven to earth for benefit of people as the fifth Veda or sacred text.

The author of the *Nāṭyaśāstra* was divinely inspired by Brahma, the god of creation. Seeing the need for a noble form of diversion in a world of mortals given over to sensual pleasures and jealousy, anger, desire, and greed, Brahma summoned the great sage Bharata and his 100 sons, appointed them the first actors, and taught them the arts of the theatre. The first performance was to represent the defeat of the demons by the gods. The drama, with its origins in ritual, is always performed on consecrated ground, and the theatre structure itself must be sanctified to keep away the evil spirits who plague actors.

Theatre has often been theorized as originating in a struggle of diabolic forces. Augustine, Tertullian, and the early Christian church fathers saw the theatre solely as the work of demons and therefore an evil to be abhorred. Sanskrit theory discovered the wisdom of encompassing one's enemies and making the demonic element part of the theatrical event. Brahma summoned the demons, explaining that no class can be excluded from the theatre, not even one's diabolical enemies. In its goal of educating and entertaining, the all-inclusive Sanskrit theatre rejects no subject—except death, which always takes place offstage and is never mentioned directly. The defeat of the demons is celebrated not as the extinction of one's enemies but as their transformation.

Because he was the father of actors, Bharata has come to mean "actor" in general as an occupational group. Traditionally Bharata is said to have ascended to heaven, where he oversees the daily theatrical productions acted by celestial spirits for the gods. At the same time in the legends evidence of prejudice and discrimination against actors is also apparent. Bharata and his sons were cursed by the respected sages who took offense at being caricatured by actors. On the verge of suicide, the desperate and outcast actors were granted royal patronage by Kings in order to preserve their art from extinction. Actors may be divine in origin, but respectable society has never accepted them.

Bharata presents a complete poetics of the theatre addressed to playwrights, directors, and actors, consolidating and codifying in infinite detail the various traditions in dance, mime, and drama. It is a vast handbook telling how the desired reactions can be produced in the audience. Success is measured by causing the spectators to weep, shout, and have their hair stand on end (horripilation).

The *Nātyaśāstra* sometimes resembles a cook book in telling how to mix aesthetic flavors and combine tastes—*rasa*—in a Sanskrit culinary theatre. At other times it resembles an Indian love manual in its specifications of the erotic inclinations of different male and female character types. No theorist is more concerned with the creative spirit of sexuality than Bharata. But at the same time he insists that decorum be observed. Families attend the theatre together; nothing shown on the stage should make any member of the audience blush.

NĀṬYAŚĀSTRA

1. [*Origin of Nāṭyaśāstra.*] Once Ātreya and other sages came to Bharata, the great scholar and expert on Nāṭya (= drama + dance + music). It was holiday time. Bharata who had finished his daily ablutions was sitting in the midst of his sons. Joining the group, the sages asked Bharata in all politeness about the Nāṭyaveda he had composed, "It is said to be well composed and equal to Vedas," they said, "could you tell us how you came to write it and for whom? What are the subsidiary subjects? What about its authoritativeness? How is it to be applied?"

Bharata, in reply to their curiosity, said "Nāṭya was created by Brahma. I shall tell that story. Listen to me in all humility and attention."

"Long, long, very long ago," said Bharata, "People of this world of pain and pleasure, goaded by greed and avarice, and jealousy and anger, took to uncivilized ways of life. The world was then inhabited by gods and demons. Various lords were ruling. It was the gods among them who, led by Mahendra, approached God Brahma and requested him thus: "'Please give us something which would not only teach us but be pleasing both to eyes and ears. True, the Vedas are there but some like the Śūdras are prohibited from listening to and learning from them. Why not create for us a fifth Veda which would be accessible to all the castes?'"

Brahma agreed. Dismissing the petitioners, he meditated in solitude and finally decided to compose a fifth Veda incorporating all the arts and sciences and enlightening too. This he did by taking words from Ṛgveda, music from Sāmaveda, movements and make-up from Yajurveda, and emotional acting from Ātharvanaveda. Then he called Indra and others and said, "Here is the Nāṭyaveda. Let the gods practice it. It requires persons who are smart, intelligent, observant and self-controlled." [...]

Then Brahma said: "I have created the Nāṭyaveda to show good and bad actions and feelings of both the gods and yourselves. It is the representation of the entire three worlds and not only of the gods or of yourselves. Now Dharma, now Artha, now Kāma, humor or fights, greed or killing; right for the people going wrong; enjoyment for those who are pleasure-seekers;

From Bharata Muni, *Nāṭyaśāstra*, trans. Adya Rangacharya.
Bangalore: Ibh Prakashama, 1986.

restraint of the ill-behaved or tolerance of the well-behaved; putting courage into cowards or the exploits of the brave; knowledge for the unknowing or the wisdom of the wise; enjoyments of the rich or fortitude of the grief-stricken; money for those who want to make a living and stability to disturbed minds: Nāṭya is the representation of the ways of the world involving these various emotions and differing circumstances. It gives you peace, entertainment and happiness, as well as beneficial advice based on the actions of high, low and middle people. It brings rest and peace to persons afflicted by sorrow or fatigue or grief of helplessness. There is no art, no knowledge, no yoga, no action that is not found in Nāṭya."

Then he asked the gods to perform a sacrifice on the stage according to proper rites by reciting mantras, offering *bali* and food and drinks. "Never start a show without worshipping the stage." [...]

2. [*Choice of site and foundation.*] The Producer should first consider the locality, then decide about the measurements, and select a site accordingly. It should be on a level, firm and hard ground; the soil must be black, not white. It should be cleared by a plough of bone-pieces, skulls, wooden pieces, grass, roots etc. And then it should be measured out. [...]

[*Walls and pillars.*] After laying the foundation on an auspicious day at a convenient moment, the raising of walls should commence. When that is finished, pillars must be raised on an auspicious day and at an auspicious moment on a star-day. The priest, under strict discipline, should fast for three nights and at sun-rise on the fourth morning he should start the work. [...]

6. [*Rasa.*] Let me begin with the explanation of Rasa first, because there is no Nāṭya without Rasa.

Rasa is the cumulative result of stimulus, involuntary reaction and voluntary reaction. For example, just as when various condiments and sauces and herbs and other materials are mixed, a taste (different from the individual tastes of the compounds) is felt, or when the mixing of materials like molasses with other materials produces six kinds of tastes, so also along with the different Bhāvas (emotions) the "eight fundamental emotions" become a Rasa or taste.

But what is this thing called *Rasa?* Here is the reply. Because it is enjoyably tasted, it is called *Rasa.* How does the enjoyment come? Persons who eat prepared food mixed with different condiments and sauces, if they are sensitive, enjoy the different tastes and then feel pleasure; likewise, sensitive spectators, after enjoying the various emotions expressed by the actors through words, gestures and feelings feel pleasure. This final feeling by the spectators is here explained as *Rasas* of Nāṭya.

[*Relation between Rasa and Bhāva.*] A question is asked here. Are the *Bhāvas* produced by *Rasas*, or *Rasas* produced by *Bhāvas* [emotions]? Some are of the opinion that their relation is symbiotic. That however is not correct. It can be clearly seen that *Rasa* is produced from *Bhāvas* and not vice versa.

Here are the verses in support of the above.

1) Theatre-producers say that a *Bhāva* is called as such because it leads to a *Rasa* arising out of various kinds of acting.

2) Many materials of different kinds produce a distinctive flavor; likewise, a flavor is produced by the *Bhāvas* through acting.

3) There is no *Rasa* (Flavor) without a *Bhāva* and there is no *Bhāva* without *Rasa*. Through acting, mutually they lead to a distinct result.

4) Condiments and herbs (i.e. vegetables) render food tasty; so is the mutual relation between *Bhāvas* and *Rasas*.

5) Out of a seed grows a tree, out of a tree a flower, out of a flower a fruit, so *Rasa* is the seed of all *Bhāvas*.

[***Origin, color and deities of Rasas***.] Now we shall describe the origin, the color and the deities of the *Rasas*. The source (i.e. basic) *Rasas* are four: viz. the Erotic, Heroic, Terror, and Disgust. Further, Humor is derived from the Erotic, Compassion and Pathos from Terror, Wonder or the Magical from Heroics, and Dread from Disgust. Humor results when Love (the Erotic) is parodied, a terrible thing or situation produces pity, a heroic deed appears marvelous, and anything disgusting or repulsive produces fright. [...]

8. [*Acting of the subordinate parts of the body*.]

[***The eyes***.] First, from the point of view of the look of the eyes, the author mentions thirty-six varieties. Of these, eight convey eight Rasas, the next eight express the eight fundamental emotions, and the remaining twenty the other Bhāvas. The eight fundamental emotions are what the actor feels as demanded by the character and the context; so the look for love is described as affectionate. The acting for this is a sweet or graceful inviting look with tears of glistening joy. Now this look has to convey a *Rasa*, viz. the erotic or romantic sentiment, to the audience. For that purpose, not only the eyebrows are contracted but the eyes look sidelong. [...]

Raised brows, sidelong glances, distended eyes, unwinking look, closed and half-closed eyelids, looking down the nose, drooping brows, contracted eye-corners, laughing look, contemptuous look, thoughtful look— these are the looks which give us the different thirty-six looks. Roving pupils, steady pupils, moist pupils, winking and unwinking eyelids, contracted eyelids, raised eyebrows, lowered eyebrows, contracted eyebrows and knitted eyebrows—all these change the look. In this way, the author had described a total of thirty-six looks and given a name to each of them.

[***The nose***.] Here it is the nostrils which determine the expression of grief, impatience, strong smell, fragrance, laughter, contempt, etc. They might be quivering slightly, flinched, drawn back, breathing, distended, an normal. So the author distinguishes six varieties. [...]

20. [*Ten kinds of plays.*]

[*Nāṭaka.*] That which has as its theme a well-known story, a well-known hero of exalted nature, which concerns the story of a royal sage and his family, in which there are superhuman elements, which speaks of the various aspects of glory, grandeur and success of love-affairs and which has acts and prologues is a Nāṭaka. In a Nāṭaka there is the story of kings, various Rasas and emotions and sorrows and pleasures.

The seed or the beginning must develop from act to act in a Nāṭaka. Aṅka, or act, is the usual word which is so called because, connected with sentiments and emotions and according to certain rules, the story develops from part to part. An act is that in which an episode is complete, but not the beginning which should still cling to it. In an act, the direct exploits of the Hero with various ups and downs must be drawn out. An act must contain more than one Rasa (arising out of the words and acts) of the hero, the Queen, the attendants, the religious leaders, the ministers, the merchant and so on.

A Nāṭaka or a Prakaraṇa, must have five to ten acts. At the end of an act all the characters must exit.

Anger, grief, pronouncement of curse, flight or panic, marriages and miracles must be directly shown in the act.

Battle, loss of a kingdom, death, siege of a city should not be referred to in the act but in the Interludes.

Neither in an act, nor in an Interlude, nor in a Nāṭaka nor a Prakaraṇa, should there be killing of a hero.

Death or conclusion of peace or capture (of the hero) must be suggested in the Interlude by various acts.

An act should cover events of a single day. [...]

In a Nāṭaka or a Prakaraṇa there should not be a crowd of characters. There could be four or five necessary ones.

Chariots, elephants, horses, aerial chariots are not to be brought on the stage. Either by shape or costume or by distinctive gestures and movements, actors should represent them. Or their models, like those of weapons, may be made. This applies to mountains also.

If, for any reason, a regiment of an army is to be brought in, this may be represented by four or six actors. In the case of kings, there should be a very small number of servants, attendants, horses, etc. and their movements also may be few or for a short distance, since, in a play, all the detailed splendor of kingship need not be shown. In a play, the actions must be like the tip of a cow's tail—the significant and high emotions coming at the end. (It is the tip that is used as a fan.) Similarly, it is in the end that the Rasa of the play, out of the various emotions, must emerge. [...]

23. [*Costumes and make-up.*]

[*Make-up for different characters.*] One should paint the body according to the region, custom and age of the character. [...]

Gods and others, snakes and the other animals, mountains, rivers, some weapons—all these are treated as living human beings for the sake of

Drama. Human beings who dwell on the seven continents are to be painted in the color of burnished gold. And even in Jambūdvïpa, except the North and the Kuru regions, all others dwelling in the other regions must be given the complexion of burnished gold. In Bhadrāśva the people have white complexion, in Ketumāla blue, but pale red everywhere else.

The Bhūtas will be of many colors; they may be dwarfs with ugly (deformed) faces, and even with faces of a boar, a ram, a buffalo, or a deer.

Now I shall tell you the color of people in Bhārata-Varsa. Kings should be of pale red or dark blue or lotus colored. Persons who are happy should also be given pale red complexion. Those who do vile deeds, or are possessed by evil spirits, or diseased or engaged in miseries or of inferior birth, should be not fair. Sages must always be given the color of a plum and also sages practicing penance. If necessary, or if the author feels like it, color may be varied, but in accordance with region, custom and age. [...]

[*Beards and mustaches.*] After painting the face and parts of the body as above, one should set about providing beard (and mustache) according to region, profession and work. To suit various ages and conditions four kinds of beards much be provided, viz. white, black, mixed (or grey) and bushy. Beards of sages, religious mendicants, ministers and religious leaders must be white; those of persons of unfulfilled vows, of people in sorrow, or ascetics and of people in calamities should be black; those of celestial persons, of Kings and princes and officers of Kings, or gallants and persons proud of their youth, must be mixed; and the beards of sages and ascetics and persons observing a long-time vow, and of those seeking and bent on vengeance, must be bushy. This is about the beards.

[*Costumes for different occasions.*] Now I shall speak of costumes proper for different occasions. Costumes are of three kinds: clean or pure or white; of mixed colors or middling clean, etc.; and soiled.

While going to the temples or observing a vow or during an auspicious occasion, at marriage ceremonies and also while carrying out a religious duty, men and women should wear clean costumes. [...]

Intoxicated persons, lunatics, travelers, those in calamity should wear soiled clothes.

Even among the three varieties, an expert producer should observe the quality of the cloth (i. e. soiled, more soiled, etc.) [...]

Those employed in harems should wear clothes made of pieces of dark red cloth. Those born in a good family, women in special conditions should have appropriate costume. Warriors should wear costumes convenient for fighting and should have armor, different weapons, and bow and arrows. The costume of the King must always be multicolored except when he is engaged in a rite to ward off an evil star, for which he should wear white. [...]

24. [*Basic representation.*]

[*Desire, the source of all.*] Almost all feelings have their source in Kāma, desire. This desire is varied, e.g. desire for justice, for wealth, etc.

The union of a man and a woman is a proper union. It may end either in happiness or sorrow. Many a time, even in misery, it is observed to cause happiness. When this union leads to a sexual act, that is called Love. In this world, everyone craves happiness, and women, though they have various natures, are the source of that happiness. [...]

[*Erotic behavior.*] In a drama, achievement of love is of two sorts; one inner, i.e. within the rules of social propriety, and the other, external, i. e. outside the normal ways of society. In a drama love affairs of Kings are inner; but external is a love affair with courtesans and that should be treated in a Prakaraṇa.

There are three kinds of women with whom a love affair is possible: a woman of good family; a courtesan; and a mixture of the two, viz. a woman who is pure.

Kings should have love affairs only with a woman of good family and not with a courtesan; but they can do so if the woman is a divine courtesan. Other (i.e. common) people can have love affairs with courtesans. The courting of a virgin is the same as that of one of a high family; the same applies to courtesans also.

In the case of men and women of high, low or middling status, the sex-desire is aroused by many causes; i.e. hearing, seeing, physical beauty, graceful gestures and sweet words. Therefore, a man or a woman in love should closely observe the signs and indications. [...]

[*Acting of these heroines.*] The four heroines whose lovers are absent should express their condition by anxiety, sighs, lassitude, talking with their female friends, referring to their lot, weakness, depression, tears, anger, throwing off the ornaments, rubbing their hands, sorrow and weeping.

A woman with her husband (lover) under her control should have brilliant and beautiful costumes, her face beaming with joy and looking extremely beautiful.

Whether a courtesan, or a lady of noble birth, or a maid servant, a heroine who is going to meet her beloved in a tryst should act as follows:

If a courtesan, she must deck herself with various ornaments, and, in the company of her servants, must walk slowly. If a highborn lady, she should cover herself with a veil and walk timidly and with downcast eyes in a lurking manner. If a maid servant, she should walk with uneven steps, eyes beaming with joy, gesturing and babbling under the influence of intoxication.

If the lover is in bed and asleep, she should awaken him in the following manner. A high born lady should awaken him with the sound of her ornaments, a courtesan by her scents, and a maid servant by fanning him with her clothes.

[*Union of lovers.*] When, either out of fear or anger, the woman is not willing, the lover should try to consummate the union under some pretexts. A man not getting his beloved for union will not be in the control of love; but once he achieves the union, he is doubly delighted. At the time of the union, there should be graceful gestures, sweet words and sportive behavior between the lovers who are looking at each other with loving eyes. A woman also should prepare for the union which would give pleasure and wait for her lover to come. She should keep in readiness for her lover scents and flowers and scented pieces of cloth and also make herself up. At the time of the union, too many ornaments are not advised; but jingling ones, like girdles and anklets, may be retained. [...]

25. [*Men and women.*]

[**Certain prohibitions when showing the erotic on stage.**] There should be no sleeping on the stage; under some pretext the act must be brought to a close. If the context requires it and one has to sleep, either alone or with someone else, then kissing, embracing, any other private acts, biting the lips (of one another), marks of nails (on the woman's breasts), loosening the front knot, crushing the lips or breasts should not be shown on the stage. Nor should eating, or sporting in water, or anything which makes the audience blush be shown. For a drama is seen by a father, a son, a daughter-in-law, a mother-in-law (all sitting together); so these must be avoided. In a drama, words must be pleasant to hear, not harsh, they must be sweet, not cruel; they must convey good advice. [...]

26. [*Acting–miscellaneous.*] There are some particulars about expression through gestures, which have not been mentioned. They could be called "Expression of miscellaneous ideas or things."

[**Gestures for natural phenomena.**] For example, morning and evening, day and night, seasons and dark clouds, wide expanse of water, the different quarters, the big stars and many such things which are far and wide and fixed (i.e. permanent) may be indicated by the hands in the Swastika gesture and on one side, and head raised and eyes looking up (or in the distance). With the same gestures of hands and head but eyes looking down, anything on the ground may be indicated.

To indicate moonlight, happiness, air, taste and smell, gestures used for touch and horripilation may be employed. Hot ground and heat of the sun may be indicated by movements suggesting search for a shady place. By covering one's head and face by a cloth dust, storm and smoke could be indicated.

Looking up with half-shut eyes, the midday sun is indicated. Similarly, sunrise and sunset may also be indicated by suggesting depth (of the ocean, out of which the sun is supposed to rise and into which to sink).

[*Indicating anything pleasant or unpleasant.*] Anything pleasant or happy is indicated by touching the limbs, by a rising of the hairs on the body; anything harsh and unpleasant also by similar gestures but by contracting the body as well. When one is to express or indicate important and noble objects (or persons), one must have grace and strength in one's gestures. [...]

[*Gestures for seasons.*] With all the limbs relaxed, suggesting that all quarters are clear and conveying that various flowers can be seen, autumn is conveyed; and winter by contracting the body, by seeking the sun or fire or warmth (in the case of superior and middling characters) and by chattering teeth and sneezing and shaking the head (in the case of inferior characters, and in some cases, even by superior characters); severe winter by gestures of touch, suggesting a chilly wind or drinking wine; spring by gestures of rejoicing, enjoying in festival occasions and blossoming of various flowers; summer by suggesting the heat of the ground, movements of fanning and wiping of sweat; and rainy season by the appropriate flowers, grass and the presence of peacocks.

Seasons, as a rule, are to be indicated by the appropriate (i.e. seasonal) marks, activity, costumes, etc. And the other thing is, seasons and other such experiences are a pleasure to one in happy circumstances but a pain when miserable. So in acting one should remember one's circumstances, then the cause of a particular experience and then know the automatic responses to it. (e.g. Spring to a lover in the company of his beloved is one thing, but to one separated from her is exactly the opposite.) [...]

27. [*Success of the productions.*] Now I shall speak to you about the success in connection with production; for, the production of drama is, above all, intended to be successful. Success which results from acting, emotion and gestures and which depends on different Rasas and Bhāvas is of two kinds: human and divine (i.e. depending on factors outside human control).

[*Human success.*] This depends on various factors, physical and verbal. Success is indicated vocally by a gentle smile, smile, loud laughter, remarks or exclamations like "good," "wonderful," "alas," loud applause, etc.

The physical indications are: "hair standing on end,'" "jumping in the seat," "throwing garlands and rings on the stage," etc.

When actors create humor by a *double entendre*, spectators should receive it with a gentle smile. [...]

When the humor, or the words suggesting it are not clear, then the audience should just part its lips in a half-smile.

Humor produced by the pranks of the jester or by some other artifice should be received with loud laughter.

Any act of virtue done in an excellent way should be received by exclamations of "good." Similarly, when surprised or greatly pleased, one naturally exclaims "how wonderful." But for pathetic things or acts, the audience should exclaim "Alas!" When there is something astonishing, it should be received by vociferous applause. At words of condemnation, or when the actor acts a "thrill," i.e., his hair standing on end, or when there are retorts and replies making one curious, the audience should applaud. At brilliant passages in the play or when there are scenes of cutting or breaking or fighting or some such commotion, the audience should applaud by rising from their seats and with tears of appreciation. [...]

[*Competitions.*] This is applicable particularly to competitions. During a competition, faults due to factors outside should not be considered. But other successes and faults may be noted down. The one whose faults are few and successes more should be awarded the victory flag by the king. In cases of an equal number of successes i.e. points of success, the one whom the king chooses as the victor should get the flag. The experts should be seated at a distance of twelve hastas. [...]

35. [*Distribution of roles.*]

[*Manner of entry and impersonation.*] When one enters the stage, it should always be with the make-up of the character he is playing and not in his natural character.

Just as a man gives up his nature and his body and assumes those of another, so an actor, if he is clever, says, "I am not I, but I am *He*," and then takes up the style of the other's (i.e. character's) speech, gait and gestures.

[*Three ways of impersonation.*] The relation between the actor and the character he plays can be described in three ways; fitting, unfitting and suitable.

When a woman plays a female role and a man plays a male role, and there is no age-disparity between the actor and the role he plays, the casting may be called fitting; but when a child plays an old man's role and vice versa it is called unfitting casting. When a man assumes a female role and vice versa it is called suitable, provided other factors like age, limbs are also suitable.

[*Suitability of women for roles.*] Singing and dancing must be given to women because their voice is naturally sweet and their gestures and movements naturally graceful. Grace of body and movements and sweetness of voice in a man should be considered as an exception. The roles not only of women but of gods and men who are delicate must be played by women. A Director should not give any instructions to an actress when she is playing a female role; but if she plays a male role he should instruct her. [...]

[*Impersonation of a king.*] It may be asked how can an actor, with a few accessories, express the qualities of a king? Why not? He has been painted, he has been decked with ornaments; with all this, if he walks with dignity, he could feel he owns the whole earth. (Why a king behaves like that we do not know.) But if a king behaves like an actor, an actor can behave like a

King. [...]

[*Qualities of a director.*] Now I shall describe the qualities a Director should possess. He should know everything about *Nāṭyaśāstra*; he should be an expert in four kinds of musical instruments; he should know not only about polity, the various Śāstras, but also know about the non-vedic practices; he should have full knowledge of courtesans and their ways, about the Kāmaśastra, about Rasas and Bhāvas, about the various arts and crafts, about poetics, about astronomy and the science of wealth; he should know about the people, he should be able to read, understand and explain and even give instructions about the Śāstras; he should be a man of good memory, keen intelligence, patient, liberal, firm, not susceptible to anger and illness, truthful, impartial, honest and not amenable to flattery.

ZEAMI

ZEAMI (1363-1443), the greatest Asian theorist, is a figure of mystery. A master of transformation, he was known at different times in his life as Oniyasha, Fujiwaka, Motokiyo, Kiyomoto, Shio, Zea, Zeshi, Zeamidabutsu, but never referred to himself as Zeami, an honorific name given him posthumously. No portrait of him exists, only a mask he may have worn on stage. He wrote a secret doctrine, concealed from the public and passed down by confidential transmission within the family, generation by generation, to a single individual. Like Craig and Artaud, the Japanese playwright-theorist feared having his ideas stolen.

By the nineteenth century he had fallen into obscurity. Only with the discovery and publication of all his treatises in the twentieth century did Zeami gain pre-eminent status as a theorist of Nō. European interest in his work contributed to his growing celebrity. Translated into French, his treatises were read aloud by Barrault and Vilar at the Odéon.

As a twelve-year-old child actor in his father Kan'ami's provincial troupe, Zeami's dramatic beauty and charm were such that the seventeen-year-old Shōgun Yoshimitsu fell in love with the boy on first seeing him perform and became his patron, making Nō a court entertainment subject to aristocratic taste. The Shōgun's infatuation scandalized the court because actors, who came from the lowest classes in society, were regarded as beggars and thieves. But to gain favor with the Shōgun, the aristocrats followed suit and gave Zeami expensive presents.

Zeami had begun appearing on stage when he was six; by the time he was twelve he was attending and commenting perceptively on performances by all the great actors from rival companies. When his father died, Zeami at twenty-two assumed the leadership of the Kanze troupe. In 1400 he wrote *Fūshikaden* (also called *Kadensho*)—"A Treatise on the Transmission of the Flower"—the first such work in Japan and more a reflection of his father Zan'ami's teachings on technique than his own mature theory. The aesthetics of the flower stressed the importance of novelty, consideration of the psychology of audience, and respect for the taste of both the elite and the common people. The "flower" was reflected in the spectators' gaze. Although music and dance were constituent elements, imitation (*monomane*) or mimicry remained central to the early popular Nō.

In his later treatises summarizing his own personal experience as a writer and performer, Zeami introduced a new aesthetic vocabulary that indicated his movement away from mimesis to abstraction. As a writer and performer, Zeami specialized in the phantasmal (*mugen*) Nō with its obsessive ghosts and emotionally disoriented sensibilities.

In his old age Zeami fell from favor for a combination of political and aesthetic reasons, being first forbidden to perform at Imperial Palace, and then at the age of seventy-two banished to Sado Island. The new Shōgun Yoshimori preferred the lively, colorful, mimetic Nō that went back to his father's days. Zeami's nephew was appointed head of the troupe.

Adversity made Zeami lose his public and forced him to confront the abyss. He put his art above all and consecrated himself to his studies. The artist's task was, above all, to perfect his art and transmit it to future generations.

ON THE ART OF THE NŌ DRAMA
(15th c.)

Teachings on Style and the Flower (Fūshikaden)

Chapter 7: A Separate Secret Teaching.

In this secret teaching, I wish to explain how to understand of what the Flower consists. First of all, one must understand the conception that, just as a flower can be observed blooming in nature, the flower can be used as well as a metaphor for all things in the *nō*.

When speaking of flowers, in all their myriad varieties, it can be said that they will bloom at their appointed time during the four seasons; and because they always seem fresh and novel when they bloom at that appointed season, they are highly appreciated. In performing *sarugaku* as well, when this art appears novel to the spectators, they will be moved to find it attractive. Flower, charm and novelty: all three of these partake of the same essence. There is no flower that remains and whose petals do not scatter. And just because the petals scatter, then, when the flower blooms again, it will seem fresh and novel. An understanding of the principle of the Flower explains why in the *nō* there does not exist that stagnation that results from the monotony of any single means of expression. As the *nō* does not always remain the same, various new aesthetic qualities can be emphasized, bringing a sense of novelty.

However, one note of caution is necessary. When one speaks of "novelty," the term does not necessarily refer to some means of artistic expression that never existed before. After thoroughly mastering all the various principles that have been set down in these *Teachings on Style and the Flower*, an actor, thinking to perform a play, can show as the occasion demands the various arts that he has mastered. To cite again the example of flowers, among all growing things, there are no special flowers that bloom out of their appointed seasons. In the same way, if an actor masters the various elements of *nō* that he has learned to remember, he can show his art, basing it on taste of the moment and the kind of plays that his audiences appreciate. His performance can thus be compared to looking at a flower that blooms at the proper time. The con-

From *On the Art of the Nō Drama: The Major Treatises of Zeami*, trans. J. Thomas Rimer and Yamazaki Masakazu. Princeton, N.J.: Princeton University Press, 1984.

cept of a flower suggests a seed grown from a flower of years before. The *nō*, too, includes artistic elements seen before; but if all aspects of our art are practiced to the utmost, a considerable span of time will be required before they are exhausted. Seen after a lapse of time, elements of our art look fresh again. Then, too, the taste of audiences differs, and as interest in chanting, movement, and Role Playing varies, no artistic elements can be neglected. Thus an actor who has mastered every aspect of his art can be said to hold within him the seeds of flowers that bloom in all seasons, from the plum blossoms of early spring to the chrysanthemums of the fall. As he possesses all the Flowers, he can perform in response to any expectation on any occasion. Yet if an actor has not mastered various aspects of his art, there will be occasions when he will invariably lose his Flower. For example, suppose that the flowers of the spring are finished and the occasion has come when it seems appropriate to admire the summer grasses. If an actor can only show his audience the spring flowers, how can it be said that he matches himself to the flower of the season? From this example, my point should be clear.

A real flower is the one that seems novel to the imagination of the spectator. This is what I meant when I wrote earlier that only after an actor "will have practiced assiduously and mastered the various necessary techniques will he be able to grasp the principle of the Flower that does not fade." Indeed, the Flower is not something special unto itself. The Flower represents a mastery of technique and thorough practice, achieved in order to create a feeling of novelty. When I wrote "the flower blooms from the imagination; the seed represents merely the various skills of our art," I had the same principle in mind.

In the section on demon roles in the chapter on Role Playing, I also wrote that an actor who strives only to play demon roles will never come to understand what is really of interest about them. An actor who has mastered every technique and occasionally plays a demon role, will create the Flower, because his portrayal of the role will be unusual and so will be of interest to his audiences. On the other hand, an actor who thinks to play only demon roles and possesses no other art may appear to perform his part well, but there will be no sensation of novelty, and those who observe him will experience no Flower. I wrote that a good performance of a demon role was "like a flower blooming in the rocks," because the only appropriate style of acting for such roles calls for strength, fierceness, and a frightening manner. This particular art represents the rocks. And the Flower? It comes when an actor gifted with Grace and who can play in a variety of styles performs a demon role, contrary to the public's expectations, and so creates a real sense of novelty. This is the Flower. On the other hand, an actor who only thinks to play demon roles possesses merely the rock, but not the Flower.

A certain secret teaching on details of performance reveals the following: chanting, dance, gesture, expressive movements—all of these require the same spirit of novelty. On an occasion when the audience believes that a performance will consist of the same movement and chanting as usual, they imagine that they know what to expect. An actor can carry out his performance in a different fashion, however, so that for example, even if the play being performed maintains fundamentally the same appearance, he will attempt to play his role in such a way that he infuses it with a more delicate level of feeling than before; or, in the case of his chanting, even though he changes nothing, he will use anew all his old arts, color the music and his voice in a skillful manner, using a level of concentration he has never felt before, and show exceptional care. If such a successful performance is achieved, those who see it and hear it will find it more novel than usual and they will praise it. This effect is surely what constitutes the feeling of novelty felt by the audience.

So it is that even when the usual play is chanted and the same gestures are involved, a fine actor will bring something novel to the performance. An unskilled performer, even if he does remember all the proper musical notations, will not approach them with any original conceptions. A gifted performer is one who will truly grasp the essence of the "inner music." This "inner music" is the Flower that lies behind the chant itself. Even for players of equally great ability, with the same Flower, the player who has studied his art to its furthest reaches will come to know the Flower that lies within the Flower. In general, the melody is fixed in the chant, but the "inner music" can only be captured by a gifted performer. In the dance as well, the various patterns can be learned, but the emotions engendered from them come from the performer.

In the art of Role Playing, there is a level at which imitation is no longer sought. When every technique of Role Playing is mastered and the actor has truly become the subject of his impersonation, then the reason for the desire to imitate can no longer exist. Then, if the actor seeks to enjoy his own performance to its fullest extent, how can the Flower not be present? For example, in imitating an old man, the psyche of a truly gifted player will become altogether like that of a real old man, who, perhaps, dresses himself up for some procession or temple entertainment, thinking to dance and make music himself. Now since the actor has already himself assumed the personality of an old man, he actually "becomes" the old man and can have no wish to imitate one. Rather, he will think only of the part he, the old man, will play in the entertainment.

According to the teaching about creating the Flower when playing the role of an old person, it is important, first of all, to make no attempt merely to imitate the external attributes of old persons. When speaking in general of dance and movement, it can be assumed that these will be performed in time to the rhythm of the music, and that the stamping of the feet, the motions of the hands, and the actor's gestures and movements will be attuned to that mutual rhythm. In the case of an old person, however, when the beat sounds from the *taiko*, the chant, or the *tsutsumi*, his feet will be just a bit slow in responding, and his gestures and movements as well will follow an instant after. Such movements surely represent the best way to show the character of an old person. Keeping this concern in mind, the role must otherwise be performed with the kind of expansiveness that an old man would wish to show. It can be said that, above all else, an old person wants to appear young. Yet he can do nothing about the fact that his limbs are heavy and he is hard of hearing, so that, although he may still be quick of spirit, his physical movements cannot keep pace. Knowing this principle represents true Role Playing. One should basically play the role in a youthful manner such as that which an old person would wish to assume. In this way the actor can show through his performance the envy the old feel for the young. An elderly person, no matter how youthfully he wishes to dance, will not, in principle, be able to keep up with the beat of the music. Here, for the spectator, the sense of novelty comes from the fact that an old person dances like a young one. This is a flower blooming on an ancient tree.

An actor must absorb all styles of acting. An actor who can manage all styles of expression will require a certain time before he can perform them all, and he will thus be able to create a continuous impression of novelty. One who has truly grasped the various styles can summon up his art to color them and expand upon them a hundredfold. And actor should plan to repeat himself only once in a three- to five-year period, so as to create a sense of novelty for his audiences. This technique will give an actor a great sense of ease. In addition, during the course of the year, the actor must keep in mind the plays appropriate to each season. Also, in a sequential performance of *sarugaku* that extends over several days, the various styles of acting must be alternated and colored not only on each day but throughout the whole program. Thus if one concentrates naturally on all aspects of our art, from the most fundamental principles to the smallest details, there will be no danger of losing the Flower throughout one's career.

Then too it has been said that, more important than learning the myriad styles of expression, an actor must not forget the Flower that he has established at various phases of his career. These various Flowers, past and future, make up the various elements of one's acting style. By "past and future" I mean that the various styles that an actor has naturally mastered at various times, such as his presence as a child actor, his art as a young adult, and his elaborate skill as a mature actor, as well as his technique as an older performer, should all form a part of his art. Sometimes it should appear as though his performance were that of a child, sometimes of a youth; then again, on occasion like that of an actor at the height of his power, or again, like an actor who has in his maturity thoroughly mastered his art. In other words, the actor must perform so that it appears as though he were not the same person in each role. That is, he must hold to the idea that, within his accomplishment at any given time, there must lie an art ranging from that of a child to that of an old man. So it is that one can speak of a Flower drawn from past and future.

However, no one has ever seen or heard of such a supremely gifted artist from the beginnings of our art down to the present day. Perhaps only my father Kan'ami, during the vigor of his youth, played in the kind of polished style capable of giving his spectators that kind of satisfaction, or so I have heard. I myself witnessed his performances when he was about forty, and I have no doubt about it. In performing the play *Jinen Koji*, when he played one particular scene on a dais, people who saw him at the time were convinced that he had the appearance of a youth of sixteen or seventeen: such was his reputation. As many said that this was true, and as I myself witnessed his performances, I can say that he really did achieve this level of excellence. Yet how rare is the actor who, in this way, can learn as a youth the styles of acting he would later use, and who, as a mature artist, never manages to forget the styles he mastered as a youth. I have never seen or heard of another.

Again, an actor must never forget the aspects of his art that he has learned from his beginnings as an actor, so that, in response to varying circumstances, he may make use of them. If a young artist studies the style appropriate for an older actor, and if a mature actor retains the art of his vigorous period, will each not be able to create a sensation of novelty in his spectators? So it is that, as a performer grows more skillful, he will surely lose the seed that produces the Flower if he should abandon the styles of acting that he has already mastered. If those various Flowers have not themselves produced seed, they will represent nothing more than a broken branch of flowers. But if there is a seed, then a flower will form in consonance with every season as it arises. To repeat again, an actor must never forget what he has learned as a young performer. Quite ordinarily he hears it said of a young actor that "he has quickly risen to high accomplishment," or, "he already seems mature," while it is said of an older actor that "he seems youthful." Such remarks illustrate the importance of novelty. If an actor embellishes the basic styles, he can color them a hundredfold. Then, if an actor can incorporate into his accomplishments at any given moment all the past and future aspects of his art, then what a flowering that would represent.

When performing *nō* there are endless matters that must be kept in mind. For example, when an actor plans to express the emotion of anger, he must not fail to retain a tender heart. Such is his only means to prevent his acting from developing roughness, no matter what sort of anger is expressed. To appear angry while possessing a tender heart gives rise to the principle of novelty. On the other hand, in a performance requiring Grace, an actor must not forget to remain strong. Thus all aspects of his performance—dance, movement, Role Playing—will be genuine and lifelike.

Then too, there are various concerns in connection with using the actor's body on the stage. When he moves himself about in a powerful way, he must stamp his foot in a gentle way. And when he stamps his feet strongly, he must hold the upper part of his body quiet. This matter is difficult to describe in words. It is better to learn this directly from a teacher. (This technique is explained in more detail in a section of the *Kashū*.)

Over and above this, it is important to know that a Flower blooms by maintaining secrecy. It is said that "when there are secrets, the Flower exists; but without secrets, the Flower does not exist." Understanding this distinction is the most crucial aspect of the Flower. Indeed, concerning all things, and in any aspect of artistic endeavor, each family maintains its secrets, since those secrets are what make its art effective. However, when these so-called secret things are revealed openly, they often appear to be nothing special. Those who say that there is nothing to such secrets, however, have not yet grasped the principle of the efficacy of such teachings. For example, even in terms of what I have written here, should everyone come to know that the principle of novelty represents the nature of the Flower, then the spectators coming to watch a performance would expect just this quality. Before such an audience, even if the performance did contain something novel, those who watched could not be disposed to accept it as such. The Flower of the actor is possible precisely because the audience does not know where that Flower may be located. The spectators merely know that they are seeing something unexpected and quite skillfully performed, but they cannot recognize the Flower as such. Thus the technique can represent the Flower of the actor. The Flower provides the means to give rise to a sensation of the unexpected in the hearts of the audience.

To give an example from the military arts, a skillful commander will, through his plans and stratagems, find an unexpected means to conquer a powerful enemy. Indeed, in such a case, has not the loser been vanquished because he has been taken in by the use of this principle of novelty? In all things, in all arts, there is the element of achieving victory in a contest. As for the strategy itself, once the affair is over, and once the loser realizes the scheme that has been used against him, he will be more careful afterwards. After all, he lost because he did not know the means used against him at the time. Thus, I want to pass this matter along as one important secret teaching to our family. Knowing this, the following will be clear as well. It is not enough to keep from revealing a secret; an actor must not let others know that he is one who even knows a secret. For if others know his heart, then his opponents will not remain careless but will be circumspect and so will be on guard against their enemy. On the other hand, if their caution is not aroused, then he will easily win over them. And is it not by making use of this principle of novelty that he can put the others off their guard and so defeat them? Thus, in our house, by refusing to tell others of our secret teaching, we will be the lifelong possessors of the Flower. When there are secrets, the Flower exists; without secrets, the Flower does not exist.

You must also know the Law of Cause and Effect with respect to the Flower. This principle holds great significance for our art. Indeed, in all things, the Law of Cause and Effect is in operation. In the case of *nō*, the skills an actor has gained since his early days constitute the Cause. To master the *nō* and achieve distinction represent the Effect. Thus if an actor is negligent in practice, which is the Cause, the proper Effect will be difficult to bring about. This is a principle an actor must truly take to heart.

Then too, an actor must pay due heed to the movements of fortune. He must understand the idea that, if blossoms have been profuse in times past, there may be none this season. Time can be divided up into moments of good luck and bad luck. Thus with regard to the *nō* as well, when there is a period of good luck, then there must inevitably follow a period of bad. Such is the inevitable process of Cause and Effect.

If an actor really understands this principle, then when it comes to a performance that he feels is not such an important one, he need not commit himself so completely to winning the contest; therefore, he should not overextend his efforts. He will not be too concerned about losing and, holding back some of his skill, he will perform with a certain restraint. His audience, thinking that this is all he has to offer, may lose interest. Yet for a really important performance, he will summon up all his skills, and, choosing a play that shows off his special strengths, he will put forth all his energies and so move and surprise those who watch him. Thus, in a really important contest, he will doubtless gain a victory. Such is the vital efficacy of novelty. And so, after a bad period, the Law of Cause and Effect brings about good in the end.

For example, on the occasion of a three-day series of performances, an actor may be expected to perform perhaps three times. On the first day, he should not overextend his energies and should hold himself back; but, when he believes that he knows which is the crucial day for him, he should expend every effort to perform a good play that shows off his special talents. Even in the course of a single day's performance, when participating in a contest, the moment may come when the actor faces a period of bad luck. At this moment, he should perform with restraint, so that at the moment when the luck of the opposing troupe turns from good to bad, he can himself press forward with a fine play. On such an occasion, if his performance goes well, he will surely win the day.

In the matter of good luck and bad luck, in every contest there inevitably comes a time when the performance becomes more colorful and more relaxed, and so the situation improves. An actor should look on this moment as one of good luck. In the case of a contest that continues on for a considerable time, then luck will of its own accord change hands again and again from one side to the other. It is written that "both the god of victory and the god of defeat are always present to decide the outcome of any contest. Such is a crucial secret in the military arts." Therefore, in a contest of *nō*, if the opponent is doing well, the actor must realize that the god of victory dwells on the enemy's side and be awed accordingly. However, these gods decide the Cause and Effect for only a short time, so that fortune switches again and again from one side to the other; thus, if an actor is convinced that his turn will come, he will be able to perform with confidence. Such is the Law of Cause and Effect in performance. An actor must never be remiss in pondering over this truth. Remember the expression "to him who believes accrues virtue."

If the matter is examined thoroughly, however, it can be said that, after all, the Law of Cause and Effect or a good or bad occasion can be reduced to the matter of novelty or a lack of novelty. If a spectator sees the same actor in the same play for two days in succession, what he found effective the day before will now seem uninteresting. This is because the spectator has a memory of something novel, which, since he does not find it again on the second day, makes him feel the performance is unsatisfactory. Later, however, on another occasion, he will go to the play with the memory of an unsatisfactory performance, and as he will now discover something new, he will find the performance successful.

Thus, when an artist masters our art to the highest degree, he finds that the Flower as such does not exist as a separate entity. When all the secret mysteries of the nō have been penetrated, it can be seen that Flower exists only to the extent that the actor has a firm self-understanding of the principle of novelty in all things. As the sutra says, "good and bad alike are undifferentiated; wickedness and righteousness are the same." It is not true that, fundamentally, there is nothing fixed concerning good or bad? Rather, depending on the occasion, what is useful is good, and what is not useful is bad. Our art depends on the taste of the audience at a particular time and place and will be produced in response to the general taste of the time. Such is the Flower that is truly useful. Here, one kind of performance is appreciated; there, another sort of acting is welcomed. The Flower thus must differ depending on the spirit of the audience. Which of those Flowers then represents the true one? The nature of the Flower truly depends on the occasion on which it will be employed.

This separate secret teaching concerning the art of the nō is crucial to our family and should be passed down to only one person in each generation. For example, even where the rightful heir is concerned, should he be without the proper abilities, this teaching must not be given to him. It is written that "a house does not mean merely lineage. Carrying on the line correctly defines a house. Succession is not a question of being born into a family, but of a real grasp of the art." This teaching can provide the means to come to truly master that exquisite Flower that permits the understanding of a myriad virtues.

I have previously passed along these teachings to my younger brother Shirō, and I have given them as well to Mototsugu, who is also a gifted player. They should only be passed on as an important secret.

Ōe 25 [1418] the first day of the 6th month.   (signed) Ze

A Mirror Held to the Flower (Kakyō)

Chapter 14. Connecting All the Arts through One Intensity of Mind.

It is often commented on by audiences that "many times a performance is effective when the actor does nothing." Such an accomplishment results from the actor's greatest, most secret skill. From the techniques involved in the Two Basic Arts down to all the gestures and the various kinds of Role Playing, all such skills are based on the abilities found in the actor's body. Thus to speak of an actor "doing nothing" actually signifies that interval which exists between two physical actions. When one examines why this interval "when nothing happens" may seem so fascinating, it is surely because of the fact that, at the bottom, the artist never relaxes his inner tension. At the moment when the dance has stopped, or the chant has ceased, or indeed at any of those intervals that can occur during a performance of a role, or, indeed, during any pause or interval, the actor must never abandon his concentration but must keep his consciousness of that inner tension. It is this sense of inner concentration that manifests itself to the audience and makes the moment enjoyable.

However, it is wrong to allow an audience to observe the actor's inner state of control directly. If the spectators manage to witness this, such concentration will merely become another ordinary skill or action, and the feeling in the audience that "nothing is happening" will disappear.

The actor must rise to a selfless level of art, imbued with a concentration that transcends his own consciousness, so that he can bind together the moments before and after that instant when "nothing happens." Such a process constitutes that inner force that can be termed "connecting all the arts through one intensity of mind."

"Indeed, when we come to face death, our life might be likened to a puppet on a cart [decorated for a great festival]. As soon as one string is cut, the creature crumbles and fades." Such is the image given of the existence of man, caught in the perpetual flow of life and death. This constructed puppet, on a cart, shows various aspects of himself but cannot come to life of itself. It represents a deed performed by moving strings. At the moment when the strings are cut, the figure falls and crumbles. *Sarugaku* too is an art that makes use of just such artifice. What supports these illusions and gives them life is the intensity of mind of the actor. Yet the existence of this intensity must not be shown directly to the audience. Should they see it, it would be as though they could see the strings of a puppet. Let me repeat again: the actor must make his spirit the strings, and without letting his audience become aware of them, he will draw together the forces of his art. In that way, true life will reside in his *nō*.

In general, such attitudes need not be limited to the moments involved in actual performance. Morning and night alike, and in all the activities of daily life, an actor must never abandon his concentration, and he must retain his resolve. Thus, if without ever slackening, he manages to increase his skill, his art of the *nō* will grow ever greater. This particular point represents one of the most secret of all the teachings concerning our art. However, in actual rehearsal, there must be within this concentration some variations of tension and relaxation.

LODOVICO CASTELVETRO

Lodovico **CASTELVETRO (1505-1571)**, the last great Renaissance translator and interpreter of Aristotle's *Poetics*, was a surly pedant, a snarling polemicist, and a proclaimed public enemy. Accused of murder and object of an assassination attempt, the Italian theorist became a man on the run. A heretic in religion and art, Castelvetro saw the first edition of his *Poetics* put on the Index of Prohibited Books and all copies burned. Arrested by the Inquisition, the scholar escaped by night from Rome and fled the country, living the rest of his life in exile. The second expurgated edition of his *Poetics* appeared with numerous passages blacked out, but because the censor's ink has faded, the heretical passages may easily be read. When the house where he lived in Lyons caught fire, Castelvetro cried, "*The Poetics! The Poetics!* Save me my *Poetics!*"

No Renaissance theorist was more influential or more widely attacked. In his commentary, the Italian scholar makes no attempt to explicate the *Poetics*, but rather advances his own views that flatly contradict Aristotle.

Castelvetro ridicules the idea that the poet must be divinely inspired or a madman. The process of creation is coolly rational. Unlike the purely literary conceptions of most Renaissance theorists, Castelvetro's theory of drama was based entirely upon the assumption of stage representation. All the essentials of dramatic literature are determined by the exigencies of the stage. Castelvetro insisted on the need for strict adherence to the rule of a single time and place of representation if the drama were to seem believable to the rude multitude. Unity of action is less important because Renaissance audiences favor diversity and the miraculous.

Dispensing with the Horatian notion of teaching and delighting, Castelvetro declares that the sole end of art is pleasure. What pleases mass audiences is the marvelous. Since unsophisticated audiences are impressed by the amount of labor involved, difficulty overcome becomes one of the criteria of art. Because to copy from another does not involve any labor, the ancients should not be imitated. The humanist Castelvetro reaches strangely antihumanist conclusions.

THE POETICS OF ARISTOTLE (1570)

1. [*Poetry is delightful.*] The poet's function is after consideration to give a semblance of truth to the happenings that come upon men through fortune, and by means of this semblance to give delight to his readers; he should leave the discovery of the truth hidden in natural or accidental things to the philosopher and the scientist, who have their own way of pleasing or giving profit which is very remote from that of the poet. Besides, there is another reason more manifest to sense why the matter of the sciences and the arts cannot be the subject of poetry; poetry has been discovered solely to delight and to recreate, I say to delight and to recreate the minds of the crude multitude and the common people, who do not understand the reasons and the divisions and the arguments, subtle and far from the practice of ordinary men, which the philosophers use in investigating the truth of things, and professional men in their labors. It is not proper that a listener, when anyone addresses him, should feel irritation and displeasure, for it naturally annoys us excessively when anyone speaks to us in such a way that we are unable to understand him. [...].

2. [*Poetry is for the common people.*] Now because poetry has been discovered, as I say, to delight and recreate the common people, it should have as its subject those things that can be understood by the common people and when understood can make them happy. These are things that happen every day and that are spoken of among the people, and that resemble historical accounts and the latest reports about the world. For this reason we affirm, with respect to matter, that poetry is the similitude or resemblance of history; this matter, because it only resembles the truth, not merely renders its inventor glorious, and makes and constitutes him a poet, but delights more than does the history of things that have happened. [...] Because, then, the matter of the sciences and the arts is not understood by the people, not merely should it be avoided and shunned as the subject of a poem, but care must also be taken that no part of these arts and sciences is used in any part of the poem. In this matter Lucan and Dante in his *Comedy* have especially sinned without any necessity, for these poets by means of astrology show the seasons of the year and the hours

From Allan H. Gilbert, *Literary Criticism: Plato to Dryden*, trans. Allan H. Gilbert. Detroit: Wayne State, 1962.

of the day and the night. Homer and Virgil in his *Aeneid* never fell into this error. I cannot do other than wonder somewhat at Quintilian, who thinks that no one can understand the poets well who is not versed in the art of astronomy and instructed in philosophy

3. [*Dramatic verisimilitude.*] Because of the difficulty of representing actions and making them verisimilar, dramas do not present on the stage murders and other things that it is difficult to present with dignity, and it is proper that they should be done off stage and then narrated by a messenger. Still they are different because the narrative is able to relate in a few hours many things that happened in many hours, and to relate in many hours a few things that happened in a few hours. But the dramatic method, which spends as many hours in representing things as was taken by the actions themselves, is able to do none of these things; thence it comes about that tragedy and comedy, which are members of the dramatic class, cannot last longer than the time allowed by the convenience of the audience, nor represent more things than those which come about in the space of time that the comedies and the tragedies themselves require. And as I say, there must always be regard to the ease of the people, for after some hours the people have to leave the theater because the human necessities for eating, drinking, sleeping, and other things. [...]

6. [*The purging power of tragedy.*] Since it appeared to Plato that tragedy through the example of the tragic persons might injure the citizens and lower their moral tone, making them vile, cowardly, and full of pity, he did not wish tragedy to be presented in his republic, for he thought, if the people heard and saw men of high reputation do and say the things they do on the stage, that the too compassionate, the timorous, and the vile would console themselves, and pardon in themselves their softness of mind and fear of pusillanimity, for they would see that they have companions among the great, such as kings, and would learn to allow themselves to be carried farther than is fitting by such passions. But Aristotle, in order that men should not believe on the authority of Plato that he himself, when writing on tragedy, had set out to present an art injurious to the citizens and likely to contaminate their morals, in a few words rejects what Plato says, affirming that tragedy has just the opposite effect, that is, that with its example and its frequent representation it changes the spectators from vile to magnanimous, from fearful to firm, and from over-pitying to strict, for it is the opinion of Aristotle that continual experience with things worthy of pity, fear, and baseness does not make men too pitying, nor fearful, nor vile, because tragedy by means of the aforesaid passions, terror and pity, purges and drives out of the heart of men the passions that have been mentioned. [...]

Then tragedy, which represents to us similar actions, and makes us see them and hear them much more frequently than we would see them or hear them without tragedy, causes fear and compassion to diminish in us, since we have to divide the effect of this passion among many diverse actions. The clearest proof of this comes before our eyes in a time of pestilence, for at the beginning, when three or four persons die, we are moved with pity and terror, but when we see hundreds and thousands die, the emotion of pity and horror ceases in us. [...]

[*Poetry not primarily moral.*] If the plot is the end of tragedy, and consequently of every sort of poem, for the plot holds the same place in every sort of poem as in tragedy—if the plot is final and not a thing accessory to the morals of the agents, but on the contrary the morals do not hold the final place and are accessory to the plot, it follows that many authors of high reputation for letters among the ancients and the moderns, among whom is even Julius Caesar Scaliger, have greatly erred, for they think the intention of good poets, like Homer and Virgil in their most famous works, the *Iliad*, the *Odyssey*, and the *Aeneid*, has been to depict and show to the world, let us say, a general portrayed in the most excellent manner that is possible, or a valorous leader, or a wise man, and their nature, and like absurdities. For if this is true the moral habits of characters would not have been chosen by poets to second the action as Aristotle says, but the action would have been chosen to second the characteristics. [...]

8. [*Unity of plot.*] Aristotle [...] firmly requires that the action making up the plot should be one and relate to one person only, and if there are more actions than one, that one should depend on the other. He brings forward no reason or proof for this except the example of the tragic poets and Homer, who in composing their plots have used a single action by one person. But it can easily be understood that in tragedy and in comedy the plot contains one action or two which because of their interdependence can be reputed one, and more often of one person than of one family, not because the plot is not fitted to contain more actions but because the space of time of twelve hours at most in which the action is presented and the limitation of the space in which it is acted do not permit a multitude of actions or even the actions of one family, nor indeed the complete presentation of one action, if it is somewhat long. This is the principal and necessary reason why the plot of tragedy and comedy ought to be one, that is, ought to contain one action of a single person or of two that through their dependence may be thought as one. [...]

9. [*Tragedy and epic deal with kings.*] In the plot of tragedy and of the epic there are necessarily to be found occurrences that happen to have taken place in the life of a particular man, and are known in outline, as for example, Orestes accompanied by Pylades his friend, and aided by him and by Electra his sister, kills Clytemnestra his mother, but no one knows in detail and exactly the ways he took and the methods he used in accomplishing this murder.

Now the reason is manifest, and so clearly manifest that it can be spoken of as proved, because it is fitting that the plot of a tragedy and of an epic should accept such actual events as are common to it and to the truth of history. For the plot of the two kinds of poem mentioned should contain action not human alone but also magnificent and royal. And if it ought to contain action by a prince, the conclusion follows that it contains action that has happened and is certain, and that concerns a ruler who has been and who is known to have been, since we cannot imagine a king who has not been nor attribute to him any act, and so far as he has been and is known to have been, we cannot attribute to him an act that has not really happened. [...] For kings are known through fame or through history and equally their notable acts are known, and to introduce new names of kings and to attribute to them new actions is to contradict history and fame, and to sin against the manifest truth, a much greater sin in the composition of the plot than to sin in verisimilitude. Therefore the plots of all tragedies and all epics are and should be composed of happenings that can be called historical, though Aristotle had a different opinion. [...] But these incidents should not be set forth by history or fame except briefly and generally, in order that the poet may be able to perform his function and show his ability in finding the ways and particular methods through which the aforesaid incidents were accomplished. For if the ways and special methods through which these incidents were brought to completion were also known, there would be no matter fitted for the plot and it would not pertain to the poet but to the historian. Nor withal should we allow anyone to form the opinion that it is easier to compose the plot of a tragedy or of an epic than of a comedy, because in the plots of the first two the poet does not find out everything for himself as he does in comedy. [...]

[*Comedy is the poet's invention*.] Now to compose the plot of a comedy the poet searches out with his own powers a happening in its universal and particular aspects, and because everything is invented by him and no part is given to actual events or to history, he gives names to the persons as it pleases him and is able to do it with no inconvenience and in a reasonable way. He is able to shape a happening he has invented in all its parts, and therefore it should concern a private person of whom and of the things that have happened to him no one has any recollection, nor will they be given to the memory of the future through history or fame. Hence he who forms a complete and new experience of private persons and gives them names as he pleases cannot be rebuked by history or fame as falsifier. And, if he wishes to be thought a poet in the true meaning of the word, that is an inventor, he ought to invent everything, because since the private material makes it easy for him, he is able to do it. But no one should think that he who composes the plot of the comedy has license to make up for himself new cities that he has imagined, or rivers or mountains or kingdoms or customs or laws, or to change the course of the things of nature, making it snow in summer and putting harvest in the winter, and the like, for it befits him to follow history and truth, if in forming his plot it happens that he needs such things, just as it equally befits him who forms the fable of a tragedy or of an epic. [...]

[*The marvelous.*] There is presented here the sixth thing required of the plot that it may be beautiful, namely that it should be marvelous, since it is said in the definition of tragedy that it should be not merely an imitation of an action that is magnificent, perfect, etc., but also an imitation of things terrible and worthy of compassion. And because these things are terrible and excite compassion chiefly by means of the marvelous, it is not well to omit speaking of the marvelous, which generates and increases terror and compassion, in order that there may be full knowledge of terror and compassion as principal parts of the action or of the fable of the tragedy. But before we undertake the exposition of the words of the text of Aristotle, it appears that three things must be discussed. The first is, what is the true end of tragedy or of the plot of a tragedy? and at the same time, what is the true end of comedy or of the plot of a comedy? Then of what sort is the person peculiarly suited to tragedy and to the plot of tragedy and what are his characteristics? And finally, what sort of astonishing event can make the action more terrible and more fitted to arouse compassion? If we can make these things clear, the words of Aristotle will be clearly and plainly explained to us. [...]

[*The end of tragedy.*] So, commencing with the first thing laid down, I say that the end of tragedy or of the plot of tragedy is gladness or sadness but not every gladness or sadness, in order that the gladness and the sadness connected with the end of tragedy may not be confounded with the gladness or the sadness that are the ends of comedy or of the plot of comedy, as will be said. The gladness of the end of tragedy, then, consists in and is restricted to the escape by oneself or by persons dear to one from death or from sad life or from the loss of royal station. On the other hand, its sadness consists in and is limited to the coming on oneself or on persons dear to one of death or of a life of sorrow or of the loss of regal position. And these two are its appropriate ends.

[*The end of comedy.*] The end of comedy, as I say, in like manner is gladness or sadness, but not the same gladness or sadness which we say pertains to tragedy. For the gladness which is the end of comedy consists in the covering up of some disgrace that has been brought on oneself or some person dear to one, or in the cessation of some shame which others did not think could cease, or in the recovery of a person or a precious possession that has been lost, or in the fulfilling of amorous desire. But the sadness of comedy consists in and is limited to the reception by oneself or persons dear to one of some disgrace or shame of a moderate sort, or in damage to property not very serious, or in the hindering of the enjoyment of the person loved, and in such things. These are the two ends proper to comedy.

[*The persons of tragedy.*] But it can be asked why tragedy or the plot of tragedy does not receive or cannot receive that gladness or sadness for its end that comedy receives, and why on the other hand comedy or the plot of comedy does not receive or is not able to receive that gladness or sadness for its end that tragedy receives. To this question we can answer that the persons of tragedy are of one sort and those of comedy of another. Those of tragedy are royal and have greater souls and are proud and have a strong desire for what they desire, and, if injury is done to them or they think it is going to be done to them, they do not run to the magistrates to make complaint of that injury nor do they bear it patiently, but they make a law for themselves according as their passions speak to them and kill for vengeance those who are distant and those united to them by blood, and in their desperation not merely those united to them by blood but sometimes themselves. To such persons, when they are put in a royal position, which is thought the summit of human felicity, and have the power to revenge themselves for any outrages done to them, injuries or insults of a moderate sort are not done, nor do they suffer or have done to them injuries in property of a trivial sort. Nor is their happiness increased by marriages or fulfillment of amorous desires, for they live, it can be truly said, in perpetual marriages and in continual amorous satisfactions to such an extent that if they are to be happy it is needful that they be removed from felicity, or at least that they fall into manifest peril which it is happiness to escape from, and to make sadness arise it is necessary that they fall into misery or into a low state with a spectacular plunge.

[*The persons of comedy*.] But the persons of comedy are of poor spirit and inclined to obey the magistrates and to live under the laws and to endure injuries and damage and to run to the officers of the law and to beg that by means of the statutes their honor may be restored to them or the damage they have suffered made good. They do not make laws unto themselves nor rush into murders of relatives or of themselves or of others for the reasons for which kings rush into them. And because they are in a poor and humble state it is not necessary, to make happiness come to them, that their felicity should abandon them, since it can increase through many steps and through some moderate happening, such as a wedding that is desired and similar things. On the other side, moderate injury and disgrace can produce melancholy in them. And these are the reasons why the happy and sad ends of tragedy are different from the happy and sad ends of comedy. [...]

[*Political influence on dramatic subjects*.] And if it should be asked why it is not possible to introduce into comedy a private person who in a prosperous course of events will become a king, since we know through history that some from a lowly private condition have been elevated to kingship, I say first of all such a story would be a subject not for comedy, but for tragedy, nor would it be possible reasonably to imagine such a plot, but it would be fitting to take it from history, for the reasons that have been given. Then a drama on that theme would not delight nor be pleasing if it were acted in a state with a popular government where people live in equality, for those who love liberty and wish to maintain it do not wish examples to be set before the citizens of private persons who have occupied the lordship over them. And it would be much less delightful and pleasing if represented in a state governed by a king, where the people live under the rule of one man, for a king is very jealous of his royal condition, and is careful about putting before the humble and before individuals examples that may arouse and direct their spirit toward innovations and a change of rulers. On the contrary, because the king knows that the common people delight in and enjoy the evil fortunes of the great, they do not ever have tragedies produced in public. Tragedies never appear on the stage except among people who are subject to no individual ruler. [...]

[*Summary of tragic qualities.*] The end of a tragedy is then, either happy or sad, and since when it has a happy end a regal person must of necessity fall into great peril, it generates fear and compassion along with the gladness which, because of the peril mingled with it, it is not without sadness, as one may say, though to a greater extent it may generate similar passions with its final sadness. Then the end of the fable of the tragedy is gladness and sadness produced as we have said. [...]

13. [*Tragedy exists for pleasure, not for utility.*] Now whether it is true or false that tragedy can have no other material than the terrifying or the piteous, I will not now speak further on it. But it surely appears to me that this has not been proved by Aristotle by means of the things he has said up to now, even though he presupposes that they are proved. Since he has set out to contradict Plato, who had said that tragedy was injurious to the morals of the people, he does not wish to approve any other sort of tragedy than that which according to him is of value in giving the people good morals and purging with fear and compassion those passions and driving them from the minds of the people in the manner we have mentioned above. Aristotle was so intent on this that he did not take care not to contradict himself and the things he had said before. If it is true that poetry was invented chiefly for the sake of pleasure and not for the sake of utility, as he has shown when he speaks of the origin of poetry in general, why does he hold that in tragedy, which is one part of poetry, utility should chiefly be sought? Why is not pleasure chiefly sought for without any regard for utility? Either Aristotle should pay no attention to utility or he should at least pay so little that he would not reject all the other kinds of tragedy which do not have it, and he should limit utility to one kind alone, namely the bringing about of the purgation of terror and compassion. And nonetheless, if utility is to be considered, it would be possible to present other kinds of tragedy, as, for example, those that contain the changes of good men from misery into happiness, or the change of the wicked from felicity into misery, in order that the people may be assured by the examples that are presented, and confirm themselves in the holy belief that God takes care of the world and exercises special providence over his own, defending them and confounding their enemies and his. [...]

23. [*Delight, the end of tragedy.*] Those who hold that poetry was invented chiefly for the sake of giving benefit, or to give benefit and delight together, should beware of opposing the authority of Aristotle, who here and elsewhere does not seem to assign any other end than delight; if indeed he consents to some profit, he grants it incidentally, as in the purgation of terror and compassion by means of tragedy. [...]

24. [*The realism of tragedy.*] Now in order to understand full what is being talked about, one must remember that Aristotle said above that there were two measures of tragedy, one obvious to the senses and external, which he thought did not pertain to art, and was measured by the clock, and the other intellectual and internal, and comprehended with the mind; the latter is the end of the process of passing from misery into felicity or from felicity into misery. The termination which is obvious to the senses and is measured with the clock cannot endure more than one course of the sun over the earth for the reasons that were spoken of above; this termination, though it is not that of art, as Aristotle says, yet properly is determined by and receives its measure from the time of the intellectual limit, since the two measures cannot be diverse in relation to time. As we said above, in presenting before spectators in tragedy an action that passes from misery to happiness or from happiness to misery, as much time is spent as is occupied in the actual occurrence of the same action in reality or in imagination.

SIR PHILIP SIDNEY

Sir Philip SIDNEY (1554-1586), the epitome of Elizabethan chivalry, was said to be "extremely beautiful," with hair of a dark amber color. But, according to Ben Jonson, "Sidney was no pleasant man in countenance, his face being spoiled with pimples" due to measles and smallpox contracted at the age of six.

His interest in theatre began at Shrewsbury School where the acting of comedies was part of the curriculum for older boys. Annual outdoor staging of morality plays took place in "The Quarry," a large natural arena seating 10,000. At Oxford he saw English Latin tragedies staged and met their authors.

Sidney was a public entertainer deeply involved in the theatrical culture of his times and susceptible to the Elizabethan obsession with self-dramatization. Famous as a jouster and deviser of courtly spectacles, the handsome young poet participated in festive entertainments and equestrian events for the Queen, writing texts himself, as well as contriving the emblems painted on the pasteboard shields used for tilting.

After three years of traveling on the continent (where he picked up the latest theory from Italy), Sidney returned to England in 1575 to take a public role in the "princely pleasures" at the court of Elizabeth. That year he accompanied the Queen on the royal progress to Kenilworth, a small town not far from Stratford, at which the eleven-year-old Shakespeare might have been in the audience to see the principal shows, *The Delivery of the Lady of the Lake* and *Arion on a Dolphin's Back*.

Sidney succeeded his father as "Cup-Bearer to the Queen" (poorly paid and little status), in which capacity he wrote pastoral masques, such as *The Lady of May* (whose pedantic schoolmaster Rombus may have inspired Shakespeare's Holofernes in *Love's Labour's Lost*) performed for her Majesty as she walked in the grove at Wanstead Garden. The Queen, a gifted actress and improviser, was expected to make a spontaneous response in verse to the hyperbolic flattery.

In 1581 Sidney devised and participated in the lavish *Triumph of the*

Four Foster Children of Desire, which featured costly machinery, sumptuous costumes and armor, caparisoned horses, and spectacular effects. The triumph was shown before the Queen and 400 French Ambassadors for the treaty of marriage between Elizabeth and the Duke of Anjou, heir apparent to the French throne. Sidney, who opposed the marriage, gave the entertainment a political message that made clear the Duke's pretensions to the virgin Queen were unwelcome and in vain.

The royal gallery at the end of the tilt-yard was transformed into the Fortress of Perfect Beauty. The four challengers, who call themselves the Four Foster Children of Desire (one of whom was played by Philip Sidney), besiege the Fortress before each day's tilting. The siege engine, moving to the sound of hidden music, shoots scented powders and cannonades of perfumes at the Castle, while flowers and other fancies are flung from scaling ladders. The Four Foster Children finally realize that they have overreached themselves and make their submission—through a boy bearing an olive-branch—to Perfect Beauty, the unconquerable occupant of the Fortress, played to perfection by Elizabeth herself.

In 1585 Sidney planned to go to America with Sir Francis Drake, but instead he was sent with his uncle Leicester to Holland to defend the Protestant cause against Spain. The famous clowns, William Kempe and Richard Tarleton, went along on the expedition as members of Leicester's Men.

In September 1586 Sidney was wounded in an insignificant skirmish. After 26 days of suffering from the festering wound, during which time the poet composed a song about the wound, entitled *La cuisse rompue*, and caused it to be sung to him, Sir Philip (knighted only three years earlier) died at the age of 32 massively in debt (his father-in-law bankrupted himself to pay it off). Despite extraordinary talent, Sidney's dazzling career had never taken off.

THE DEFENSE OF POESY (1583)

And first, truly to all them that professing learning inveigh against poetry may justly be objected that they go very near to ungratefulness, to seek to deface that which, in the noblest nations and languages that are known, hath been the first light-giver to ignorance, and first nurse, whose milk by little and little enabled them to feed afterwards of tougher knowledges. [...]

This did so notably show itself that the philosophers of Greece durst not a long time appear to the world but under the masks of poets. [...] And truly even Plato whosoever well considereth shall find that in the body of his work, though the inside and strength were philosophy, the skin as it were and beauty depended most of poetry; for all stands upon dialogues, wherein he feigns many honest burgesses of Athens speak of such matters, that if they had been set on the rack they would never have confessed them. [...]

And even historiographers (although their lips sound of things done, and verity be written in their foreheads) have been glad to borrow both fashion and perchance weight of the poets. [...] So that truly neither philosopher nor historiographer could at the first have entered into the gates of popular judgments, if they had not taken a great passport of poetry, which in all nations at this day where learning flourisheth not is plain to be seen; in all which they have some feeling of poetry.

In Turkey, besides their law-giving divines they have no other writers but poets. In our neighbor country Ireland, where truly learning goes very bare, yet are their poets held in a devout reverence. Even among the most barbarous and simple Indians where no writing is, yet have they their poets, who make and sing songs, which they call *areytos*, both of their ancestors' deeds and praises of their gods—a sufficient probability that, if ever learning come among them, it must be by having their hard dull wits softened and sharpened with the sweet delights of poetry. For until they find a pleasure in the exercise of the mind, great promises of much knowledge will little persuade them that know not the fruits of knowledge. In Wales, the true remnant of the ancient Britons, as there are good authorities to show the long time they had poets, which they called bards, so through all the conquests of Romans, Saxons,

From Philip Sidney, *The Defense of Poesy*, ed. Albert S. Cook. Boston: Ginn and Co., 1890.

Danes, and Normans, some of whom did seek to ruin all memory of learning from among them, yet do their poets even to this day last; so as it is not more notable in soon beginning than in long continuing.

But since the authors of most of our sciences were the Romans, and before them the Greeks, let us a little stand upon their authorities, but even so far as to see what names they have given unto this now scorned skill. Among the Romans a poet was called *vates*, which is as much as a diviner, foreseer, or prophet. [...]

But let us see how the Greeks have named it, and how they deemed of it. The Greeks named him poet, which name hath, as the most excellent, gone through other languages. It cometh of this word *poiein*, which is *to make*; wherein I know not whether by luck or wisdom, we Englishmen have met with the Greeks in calling him a maker; which name, how high and incomparable a title it is, I had rather were known by marking the scope of other sciences than by any partial allegation.

There is no art delivered unto mankind that hath not the works of nature for his principal object, without which they could not consist, and on which they so depend as they become actors and players, as it were, of what nature will have set forth. So doth the astronomer look upon the stars, and by that he seeth, set down what order nature hath taken therein. So doth the geometrician and arithmetician in their diverse sorts of quantities. So doth the musician in times tell you which by nature agree, which not. The natural philosopher thereon hath his name, and the moral philosopher standeth upon the natural virtues, vices, or passions of man; and "follow Nature" (saith he) "therein, and thou shalt not err." The lawyer saith what men have determined; the historian what men have done. The grammarian speaketh only of the rules of speech; and the rhetorician and logician, considering what in nature will soonest prove and persuade thereon, give artificial rules, which still are compassed within the circle of a question according to the proposed matter. The physician weigheth the nature of man's body, and the nature of things helpful or hurtful unto it. And the metaphysic, though it be in the second and abstract notions, and therefore be counted supernatural, yet doth he indeed build upon the depth of nature. Only the poet, disdaining to be tied to any such subjection, lifted up with the vigor of his own invention, doth grow in effect into another nature, in making things either better than nature bringeth forth, or, quite anew, forms such as never were in nature, as the heroes, demigods, cyclops, chimeras, furies, and such like; so as he goeth hand in hand with nature, not enclosed within the narrow warrant of her gifts but freely ranging within the zodiac of his own wit. Nature never set forth the earth in so rich tapestry as divers poets have done, neither with so pleasant rivers, fruitful trees, sweet-smelling flowers, nor whatsoever else may make the too much loved earth more lovely. Her world is brazen, the poets only deliver a golden. [...]

Neither let it be deemed too saucy a comparison to balance the highest point of man's wit with the efficacy of nature; but rather give right honor to the heavenly maker of that maker, who, having made man to his own likeness, set him beyond and over all the works of that second nature; which in nothing he showeth so much as in poetry, when with the force of a divine breath he bringeth things forth far surpassing her doings. [...]

[...] Poesy therefore is an art of imitation, for so Aristotle termeth it in his word *mimesis*, that is to say, a representing, counterfeiting, or figuring forth—to speak metaphorically, a speaking picture, with this end, to teach and delight. Of this have been three general kinds.

The chief, both in antiquity and excellency, were they that did imitate the inconceivable excellencies of God. Such were David in his Psalms; Solomon in his Song of Songs, in his Ecclesiastes, and Proverbs; Moses and Deborah in their Hymns; and the writer of Job. [...]

The second kind is of them that deal with matter philosophical: either moral, as Tyrtaeus, Phocylides, and Cato; or natural, as Lucretius and Virgil's *Georgics*; or astronomical, as Manilius and Pontanus; or historical, as Lucan. [...]

For these third be they which most properly do imitate to teach and delight, and to imitate borrow nothing of what is, hath been, or shall be; but range, only reined with learned discretion, into the divine consideration of what may be and should be. These be they that, as the first and most noble sort may justly be termed *vates*, so these are waited on in the excellentest languages and best understandings, with the fore-described name of poets; for these, indeed, do merely make to imitate, and imitate both to delight and teach, and delight to move men to take that goodness in hand, which without delight they would fly as from a stranger. [...]

The philosopher therefore and the historian are they which would win the goal, the one by precept, the other by example. But both, not having both, do both halt. For the philosopher, setting down with thorny arguments the bare rule, is so hard of utterance and so misty to be conceived, that one that hath no other guide but him shall wade in him till he be old before he shall find sufficient cause to be honest. For his knowledge standeth so upon the abstract and general that happy is that man who may understand him, and more happy that can apply what he doth understand. On the other side, the historian, wanting the precept, is so tied not to what should be but to what is, to the particular truth of things and not to the general reason of things, that his example draweth no necessary consequence, and therefore a less fruitful doctrine.

Now doth the peerless poet perform both; for whatsoever the philosopher saith should be done, he gives a perfect picture of it in some one by whom he presupposeth it was done; so as he coupleth the general notion with the particular example. [...]

For conclusion, I say the philosopher teacheth, but he teacheth obscurely, so as the learned only can understand him; that is to say, he teacheth them that are already taught. But the poet is the food for the tenderest stomachs, the poet is indeed the right popular philosopher. [...]

So then the best of the historian is subject to the poet; for whatsoever action, or faction, whatsoever counsel, policy, or war stratagem the historian is bound to recite, that may the poet, if he list, with his imitation make his own, beautifying it both for further teaching, and more delighting, as it please him, having all, from Dante's heaven to his hell, under the authority of his pen. [...]

If evil men come to the stage, they ever go out (as the tragedy writer answered to one that misliked the show of such persons) so manacled as they little animate folks to follow them. But history, being captived to the truth of a foolish world, is many times a terror from well doing, and an encouragement to unbridled wickedness. [...]

No, perchance it is the comic, whom naughty play-makers and stage-keepers have justly made odious. To the arguments of abuse I will after answer. Only thus much now is to be said, that the comedy is an imitation of the common errors of our life, which he representeth in the most ridiculous and scornful sort that may be, so as it is impossible that any beholder can be content to be such a one. Now, as in geometry the oblique must be known as well as the right, and in arithmetic the odd as well as the even, so in the actions of our life who seeth not the filthiness of evil wanteth a great foil to perceive the beauty of virtue. This doth the comedy handle so in our private and domestical matters, as with hearing it we get as it were an experience, what is to be looked for of a niggardly Demea, of a crafty Davus, of a flattering Gnatho, of a vainglorious Thraso; and not only to know what effects are to be expected, but to know who be such, by the signifying badge given them by the comedian. And little reason hath any man to say that men learn evil by seeing it so set out; since, as I said before, there is no man living but, by the force truth hath in nature, no sooner seeth these men play their parts, but wisheth them in *pistrinum*; although perchance the sack of his own faults lie so behind his back that he seeth not himself dance the same measure; whereto yet nothing can more open his eyes than to see his own actions contemptibly set forth.

So that the right use of comedy will (I think) by nobody be blamed; and much less of the high and excellent tragedy, that openeth the greatest wounds, and showeth forth the ulcers that are covered with tissue, that maketh kings fear to be tyrants, and tyrants manifest their tyrannical humors; that with stirring the affects of admiration and commiseration teacheth the uncertainty of this world, and upon how weak foundations gilden roofs are builded, that maketh us know,

Qui sceptra saevus duro imperio regit,
Timet timentes, metus in auctorem redit.

But how much it can move, Plutarch yieldeth a notable testimony of the abominable tyrant Alexander Pheraeus, from whose eyes a tragedy, well made and represented, drew abundance of tears, who without all pity had murdered infinite numbers, and some of his own blood, so as he that was not ashamed to make matters for tragedies yet could not resist the sweet violence of a tragedy. And if it wrought no further good in him, it was that he, in despite of himself, withdrew himself from hearkening to that which might mollify his hardened heart. But it is not the tragedy they do mislike; for it were too absurd to cast out so excellent a representation of whatsoever is most worthy to be learned. [...]

Now then go we to the most important imputations laid to the poor poets. For aught I can yet learn, they are these. First, that there being many other more fruitful knowledges, a man might better spend his time in them than in this. Secondly, that it is the mother of lies. Thirdly, that it is the nurse of abuse, infecting us with many pestilent desires, with a siren's sweetness drawing the mind to the serpent's tale of sinful fancies (and herein especially comedies give the largest field to err, as Chaucer saith), how both in other nations and in ours, before poets did soften us we were full of courage, given to martial exercises, the pillars of manlike liberty, and not lulled asleep in shady idleness with poets' pastimes. And lastly and chiefly, they cry out with open mouth, as if they had overshot Robin Hood, that Plato banished them out of his commonwealth. Truly, this is much, if there be much truth in it.

First to the first, that a man might better spend his time is a reason indeed, but it doth, as they say, but *petere principium*, for if it be, as I affirm, that no learning is so good as that which teacheth and moveth to virtue, and that none can both teach and move thereto so much as poesy, then is the conclusion manifest that ink and paper cannot be to a more profitable purpose employed. And certainly though a man should grant their first assumption, it should follow (methinks) very unwillingly, that good is not good because better is better. But I still and utterly deny that there is sprung out of earth a more fruitful knowledge.

To the second therefore, that they should be the principal liars, I answer paradoxically, but truly I think truly, that of all writers under the sun the poet is the least liar and, though he would, as a poet can scarcely be a liar. The astronomer with his cousin the geometrician can hardly escape, when they take upon them to measure the height of the stars. How often, think you, do the physicians lie, when they aver things good for sicknesses, which afterwards send Charon a great number of souls drowned in a potion before they come to his ferry? And no less of the rest which take upon them to affirm. Now, for the poet, he nothing affirms and therefore never lieth. For as I take it, to lie is to affirm that to be true which is false. So as the other artists, and especially the historian, affirming many things, can in the cloudy knowledge of mankind hardly escape from many lies. But the poet, as I said before, never affirmeth. The poet never maketh any circles about your imagination, to conjure you to believe for true what he writes. He citeth not authorities of other histories, but even for his entry calleth the sweet Muses to inspire into him a good invention; in troth, not laboring to tell you what is or is not but what should or should not be. And therefore, though he recount things not true, yet because he telleth them not for true, he lieth not, without we will say that Nathan lied in his speech, before alleged, to David; which as a wicked man durst scarce say, so think I none so simple would say that Aesop lied in the tales of his beasts; for who thinks that Aesop wrote it for actually true were well worthy to have his name chronicled among the beasts he writeth of. What child is there that coming to a play and seeing *Thebes* written in great letters upon an old door doth believe that it is Thebes? If then a man can arrive to the child's age, to know that the poets' persons and doings are but pictures what should be and not stories what have been, they will never give the lie to things not affirmatively but allegorically and figuratively written. And therefore as in history, looking for truth, they may go away full fraught with falsehood, so in poesy, looking but for fiction, they shall use the narration but as an imaginative ground-plot of a profitable invention. [...]

But now indeed my burthen is great, that Plato's name is laid upon me, whom I must confess of all philosophers I have ever esteemed most worthy of reverence, and with good reason, since of all philosophers he is the most poetical. Yet if he will defile the fountain out of which his flowing streams have proceeded, let us boldly examine with what reasons he did it. [...] Plato found fault that the poets of his time filled the world with wrong opinions of the gods, making light tales of that unspotted essence; and therefore would not have the youth depraved with such opinions. [...] And a man need go no further than to Plato himself to know his meaning, who in his Dialogue called *Ion* giveth high and rightly divine commendation unto poetry. So as Plato, banishing the abuse, not the thing, not banishing it but giving due honor to it, shall be our patron and not our adversary. [...]

Our tragedies and comedies not without cause cried out against, observing rules neither of honest civility nor skillful poetry, excepting *Gorboduc* (again, I say, of those that I have seen), which notwithstanding, as it is full of stately speeches and well-sounding phrases, climbing to the height of Seneca's style, and as full of notable morality, which it doth most delightfully teach, and so obtain the very end of poesy, yet in truth it is very defectious in the circumstances, which grieves me, because it might not remain as an exact model of all tragedies. For it is faulty both in place and time, the two necessary companions of all corporal actions. For where the stage should always represent but one place, and the uttermost time presupposed in it should be, both by Aristotle's precept and common reason, but one day, there is both many days and many places, inartificially imagined. But if it be so in *Gorboduc*, how much more in all the rest, where you shall have Asia of the one side and

Afric of the other, and so many other under-kingdoms, that the player, when he comes in, must ever begin with telling where he is, or else the tale will not be conceived? Now ye shall have three ladies walk to gather flowers, and then we must believe the stage to be a garden. By and by we hear news of shipwreck in the same place, and then we are to blame if we accept it not for a rock. Upon the back of that comes out a hideous monster, with fire and smoke, and then the miserable beholders are bound to take it for a cave. While in the meantime two armies fly in, represented with four swords and bucklers, and then what hard heart will not receive it for a pitched field? Now of time they are much more liberal, for ordinary it is that two young princes fall in love. After many traverses, she is got with child, delivered of a fair boy; he is lost, groweth a man, falleth in love, and is ready to get another child; and all this in two hours' space; which how absurd it is in sense, even sense may imagine, and art hath taught, and all ancient examples justified, and at this day, the ordinary players in Italy will not err in. Yet will some bring in an example of *Eunuchus* in Terence, that containeth matter of two days, yet far short of twenty years. True it is, and so was it to be played in two days, and so fitted to the time it set forth. And though Plautus have in one place done amiss, let us hit with him, and not miss with him. But they will say, How then shall we set forth a story, which contains both many places and many times? And do they not know that a tragedy is tied to the laws of poesy, and not of history; not bound to follow the story, but having liberty either to feign a quite new matter or to frame the history to the most tragical conveniency? Again, many things may be told which cannot be showed, if they know the difference betwixt reporting and representing. As for example, I may speak (though I am here) of Peru, and in speech digress from that to the description of Calicut; but in action I cannot represent it without Pacolet's horse. And so was the manner the ancients took, by some *Nuntius* to recount things done in former time or other place. Lastly, if they will represent an history, they must not (as Horace saith) begin *ab ovo*, but they must come to the principal point of that one action which they will represent. By example this will be best expressed. I have a story of young Polydorus, delivered for safety's sake, with great riches, by his father Priam to Polymnestor, king of Thrace, in the Trojan war time. He, after some years, hearing the overthrow of Priam, for to make the treasure his own, murdereth the child. The body of the child is taken up by Hecuba. She, the same day, findeth a slight to be revenged most cruelly of the tyrant. Where now would one of our tragedy writers begin, but with the delivery of the child? Then should he sail over to Thrace, and so spend I know not how many years, and travel numbers of places. But where doth Euripides? Even with the finding of the body, leaving the rest to be told by the spirit of Polydorus. This needs no further to be enlarged; the dullest wit may conceive it.

But besides these gross absurdities, how all their plays be neither right tragedies nor right comedies, mingling kings and clowns, not because the matter so carrieth it, but thrust in the clown by head and shoulders to play a part in majestical matters, with neither decency nor discretion, so as neither the admiration and commiseration nor the right sportfulness is by their mongrel tragicomedy obtained. I know Apuleius did somewhat so, but that is a thing recounted with space of time, not represented in one moment, and I know the ancients have one or two examples of tragicomedies, as Plautus hath *Amphitryo*. But if we mark them well we shall find that they never, or very daintily, match hornpipes and funerals. So falleth it out that, having indeed no right comedy, in that comical part of our tragedy we have nothing but scurrility unworthy of any chaste ears, or some extreme show of doltishness, indeed fit to lift up a loud laughter, and nothing else; where the whole tract of a comedy should be full of delight, as the tragedy should be still maintained in a well-raised admiration.

But our comedians think there is no delight without laughter; which is very wrong, for though laughter may come with delight, yet cometh it not of delight, as though delight should be the cause of laughter; but well may one thing breed both together. Nay rather in themselves they have, as it were, a kind of contrariety; for delight we scarcely do but in things that have a conveniency to ourselves or to the general nature; laughter almost ever cometh of things most disproportioned to ourselves and nature. Delight hath a joy in it, either permanent or present. Laughter hath only a scornful tickling. For example, we are ravished with delight to see a fair woman, and yet are far from being moved to laughter. We laugh at deformed creatures, wherein certainly we cannot delight. We delight in good chances, we laugh at mischances; we delight to hear the happiness of our friends and country, at which he were worthy to be laughed at that would laugh. We shall, contrarily, laugh sometimes to find a matter quite mistaken and go down the hill against the bias, in the mouth of some such men as for the respect of them one shall be heartily sorry, yet he cannot choose but laugh, and so is rather pained than delighted with laughter. Yet deny I not but that they may go well together. For as in Alexander's picture well set out we delight without laughter, and in twenty mad antics we laugh without delight, so in Hercules, painted with his great beard and furious countenance, in woman's attire, spinning at Omphale's commandment, it breeds both delight and laughter. For the representing of so strange a power in love procures delight; and the scornfulness of the action stirreth laughter. But I speak to this purpose, that all the end of the comical part be not upon such scornful matters as stir laughter only, but mix with it that delightful teaching which is the end of poesy. And the great fault even in that point of laughter, and forbidden plainly by Aristotle, is that they stir laughter in sinful things, which are rather execrable than ridiculous; or in miserable, which are rather to be pitied than scorned. For what is it to make folks gape at a wretched beggar or a beggarly clown; or against law of hospitality to jest at strangers, because they speak not English so well as we do? What do we learn? since it is certain

Nil habet infelix paupertas durius in se,
Quam quod ridiculos homines facit.

But rather a busy loving courtier, a heartless threatening Thraso, a self-wise-seeming schoolmaster, a wry transformed traveler—these if we saw walk in stage names, which we play naturally, therein were delightful laughter, and teaching delightfulness; as in the other, the tragedies of Buchanan do justly bring forth a divine admiration. But I have lavished out too many words of this play matter. I do it because, as they are excelling parts of poesy, so is there none so much used in England, and none can be more pitifully abused; which, like an unmannerly daughter showing a bad education, causeth her mother Poesy's honesty to be called in question. [...]

GIAMBATTISTA GUARINI

Giambattista **GUARINI** (1538-1612), a professor of rhetoric at the scholarly and refined court at Ferrara, underwent a series of metamorphoses that caused him to lead a masquerade existence. "Ours is an age of appearances," he lamented, "and one goes a-masquerading all the year." He became a politician and diplomat in the service of Alfonso II, traveling about all the courts of Italy and sent as ambassador to Rome, Turin, and Poland. When Tasso went mad and was confined in prison, Alfonso commanded Guarini to be court poet, threatening him with a similar fate if he refused to serve him.

"I strove to transform myself into another man," Guarini explained, "and, like a play actor, to reassume the character, manners, and emotions of a past period. Mature in age, I forced myself to appear young; exchanged my melancholy for gaiety; affected loves I did not feel; turned my wisdom into folly, and, in a word, passed from philosopher to poet." Involved in unending lawsuits and family quarrels, the poet grew embittered and contentious in his pursuit of worldly success and wealth. His later years were a prolonged nightmarish imbroglio.

His pastoral tragicomedy *Il Pastor Fido* was the greatest hit of the late sixteenth century, going through forty editions and inspiring many performances and imitations (among others, 550 madrigals by 100 composers), although it may have been staged only once in the author's lifetime. Its sentimental and seductive sensuality was condemned as causing the ruin of many families and reputations. Cardinal Bellarmino told Guarini that he had done as much harm to Christendom by *Il Pastor Fido* as Luther and Calvin had by their heresies. The play stirred controversy, being attacked by strict Aristotelians for its irregularities and defended by the author even before it was published. Guarini's *Compendium* is the climax of a long and heated debate on tragicomedy, starting with Giraldi's *Treatise on the Composition of Comedies and Tragedies* (1554). The genre and the theorizing about it show intense critical self-consciousness about the creation of a new genre not found in antiquity. In the definitive edition of 1602, the notes at the end of each scene of *Il Pastor Fido*, which rationalize and justify every detail, constitute a text longer than the play itself. "Poetry has been my pastime, never my profession," Guarini confessed.

As an amateur court playwright, Guarini condemned the flourishing rival, *commedia dell'arte*, as crass commercialism that degraded the ancient art of comedy. Its mercenary professional comedians were no better than the vagabond buffoons and jugglers of mountebank entertainment. The mixture of high and low, tragic and comic, in the *commedia* was a contamination, not a harmonious union. Guarini cites Terence as the classical model for his own hybrid genre of tragicomedy, whose image is the hermaphrodite blending male and female.

THE COMPENDIUM OF TRAGICOMIC POETRY (1599)

[*Types of plot.*] Tragicomedy is not made up of two entire plots, one of which is perfect tragedy and the other a perfect comedy, connected in such a way that they can be disjoined without doing injury to either. Nor should anyone think that it is a tragic story vitiated with the lowliness of comedy or a comic fable contaminated with the deaths of tragedy, for neither of these would be a proper component; for he who makes a tragicomedy does not intend to compose separately either a tragedy or a comedy, but from the two a third thing that will be perfect of its kind and may take from the others the parts that with most verisimilitude can stand together.

[*Components common to tragedy and comedy.*] Tragedy shares with comedy presentation on the stage, and all the rest of the apparatus, rhythm, harmony, limited time, dramatic plot, probability, recognition and reversal. I mean that each makes use of the same things, though in the method of use there is some difference between them. [...] And I have no doubt that he who would think of making one of them pass entire into the confines of the other, and of using in tragedy what belongs to comedy alone, or *vice versa*, would produce an unseemly and monstrous story. But the point is that one should see whether these specific differences cause so much opposition that it is in no way possible to form a third species that can be a legitimate and reasonable poem.

[*Comic characters in tragedy.*] In tragedy these differences are the character of high rank, the serious action, terror and commiseration. In comedy they are private character and affairs, laughter, and witty speeches. As to the first, I confess, and admit it is the doctrine of Aristotle, that characters of high rank are fitting to tragedy, and those of humble station are suited to comedy; but I deny that it is contrary to nature and to poetic art in general that persons great, and those not great should be introduced in one plot. What tragedy has there ever been that did not have many more servants and other persons of similar station than men of great consequence? Who unfastens the admirably tied knot in the *Oedipus* of Sophocles? Not the king, not the queen, not Creon, not Tiresias, but two servants, guardians of herds. Then it is not

From Allan H. Gilbert, *Literary Criticism: Plato to Dryden*, trans. Allan H. Gilbert. Detroit: Wayne State, 1962.

contrary to the nature of the stage that there should be united in a play persons of high rank and those of low station, not merely under the name of a mixed poem, such as is tragicomedy, but also under that of pure tragedy, and comedy as well, if Aristophanes is alluded to, who mixes men and gods, citizens and countrymen, and even brings in beasts and clouds to speak in his plays.

[*Grave and light are to be reconciled.*] With respect to actions that are great and not great, I cannot see for what reason it is unfitting that they should appear in one same plot, not entirely tragic, if they are inserted with judgement. Can it not be that amusing events intervene between serious actions? Are they not many times the cause of bringing perils to a happy conclusion? But then, do princes always act majestically? Do they not at times deal with private affairs? Assuredly they do. Why, then, cannot a character of high importance be presented on the stage at a time when he is not dealing with important matters? Certainly Euripides did this in his *Cyclops*, where he mixed grave danger for the life of Odysseus, a tragic character, with the drunkenness of the Cyclops, which is a comic action. And among the Latins, Plautus did the same thing in the *Amphitryo*, mingling the laughter and the jests of Mercury with persons of importance, not merely Amphitryo, but the king of the gods. It is, then, not unreasonable that in one story for the stage there can be at the same time persons of high rank and those not of high rank.

[*Pity and laughter not inharmonious.*] The same can be said of commiseration and laughter, qualities of which one is tragic and the other comic. [...] I do not say that there can be happiness and sorrow in the same story, but there can be pity with laughter. Thus all the sum of this contradiction is seen to be reduced to a single difference, that is, the terrible, which can never occur except in a tragic plot, nor can any comedy ever be mixed with it, since terror is never introduced except by means of serious and mournful dramas; where it is found, there is never any room for laughter and sport. [...]

[*Nature joins diverse things.*] Speaking first of nature, are not the horse and the ass two distinct species? Certainly, and yet of the two is made a third, the mule, which is neither one or the other. [...]

[*Tragic and comic elements that cohere.*] He who composes tragicomedy takes from tragedy its great persons but not its great actions, its verisimilar plot but not its true one, its movement of the feelings but not its disturbance of them, its pleasure but not its sadness, its danger but not its death; from comedy it takes laughter that is not excessive, modest amusement, feigned difficulty, happy reversal, and above all the comic order, of which we shall speak in its place. [...]

[*Tragicomedy the highest form.*] But it would be possible here to raise a new question, namely, what actually is such a mixture as tragicomedy? I answer that it is the mingling of tragic and comic pleasure, which does not allow hearers to fall into excessive tragic melancholy or comic relaxation. [...]

[*The end of tragicomedy*.] Now if we concede that tragicomedy is a reasonable mixture, what does it attempt to do? what end has it? does it wish laughter or tears? for the two cannot be done at once. Then what does it do first? what next? what is of less importance? what of chief importance? what is subaltern? To such questions one can hardly give answers without first determining what the end of tragedy is and what the end of comedy. [...]

[*The ends of comedy*.] Beginning with comedy, its instrumental end is to imitate those actions of private men which by their deficiency move us to laughter; this is Aristotle's notion. But the architectonic end is not mentioned in his extant writings, for we lack the discussion of comedy in that treatise of his called the *Poetics*, though it may be supposed that there he gave an end for comedy as he did for tragedy. But from the instrumental end we are able to conjecture what he would assign as the architectonic end, since this is the exemplar which the artist sets before himself. [...] It purges melancholy, an emotion so injurious that often it leads a man to grow mad and to inflict death on himself. [...] As a breeze is wont to drive away the thickened air, comedy by moving us to laughter shakes off that gloomy and foggy humor, generated in us by too much mental concentration, which often renders us slow and obtuse in our activities. For this reason comedy represents only private persons, with defects evoking laughter, mocks, sports, intrigues of little importance, covering but a short time and ending happily. Such is the architectonic end of comedy.

[*The ends of tragedy*.] But tragedy, on the other hand, calls back the relaxed and wandering soul; it has, therefore, ends wholly diverse, both of them demonstrated by Aristotle in the *Poetics*, where he defines tragedy, more fortunate in this matter than comedy. One end is the imitation of some horrible and pitiable action, and this is the instrumental; the other is the purgation of terror and compassion, the architectonic end. [...]

[*The function of tragedy to purge, not to teach*.] A tragedy is a story and does not have as its function the teaching of virtue, but that its function is to purge—so far as a story can—those two perturbations of the spirit which are an obstacle to fortitude, which in all human actions is so noble and necessary a virtue.

[*Tragicomedy does not purge pity and terror*.] Though tragicomedy, like the others, has two ends, the instrumental, which is the form resulting from the imitation of tragic and comic affairs mixed together, and the architectonic, which is to purge the mind from the evil affection of melancholy, an end which is wholly comic and wholly simple, yet I say that tragicomedy can be connected in no way with tragedy. [...] But the instrumental end can be a mixed one, since tragedy has many parts which, when the terrible is removed, have with the other comic parts the power of producing comic pleasure. Therefore, since Aristotle concedes pleasure in tragedy, pleasure is easily reconciled with pleasure. And what is tragic pleasure? The imitation of serious actions of persons of rank with new and unexpected accidents. Now if terror is removed and the work is reduced to pleasure alone, a new story and new names may be feigned and all may be made harmonious with laughter; the delight in the imitation will remain, which will be tragic in possibility but not in fact. [...] There is a great difference between the two types; for one, with its simple narrative, does not wish to purge; but the other, with its gravity, and its stage setting, with harmony, numbers, magnificent and sumptuous diction and other tragic sights and devices, wishes to excite the terrible and piteous, in order to purge them. This is the reason why, when Aristotle says that stories with sad endings are especially tragic, he thinks it well to add "when they are well handled," meaning that all dramas do not produce a tragic effect, but merely those accompanied by all the other parts that belong with them. Tragic pleasure consists, then, in the imitation of horrible and pitiable actions, which in itself, according to Aristotle, is delightful. But that is not enough; it is also necessary that the other parts also be of similar sort, if the end of purging is to be attained; otherwise it will be a tragedy only equivocally, that is, outside the terms of the definition given by the Philosopher. If a poet wishes to make use of any subject in such a way as not to purge terror, he must temper it with laughter and other comic qualities in such a manner that, though it is by nature terrible and pitiable, yet it has not the power of producing either terror or compassion, and much less of purging them, but remains with the single virtue of delighting by imitating.[...]

[*Purgation no longer needed.*] Tragic sights delight, but then they leave at the end a great sadness in the spirit, and that is what has purgative effect. Hence, to many the tragic poem is not pleasing in nature, since all do not have need of what purges. And just as the age changes, habits change. [...] And to come to our age, what need have we today to purge terror and pity with tragic sights, since we have the precepts of our most holy religion, which teaches us with the word of the gospel? Hence these horrible and savage spectacles are superfluous, nor does it seem to me that today we should introduce a tragic action for any other reason than to get delight from it.

[*The decay of comedy.*] On the other side comedy has come to be so tedious and is so little valued that if she is not accompanied with the marvels of the intermezzi, there is today no one who can endure her. This is because of mercenary and sordid persons who have contaminated her and reduced her to a vile state, carrying here and there for vile pay that excellent poem which was once accustomed to crown its makers with glory. In order to raise comic poetry from such a state of disgrace, that it may be able to please the unwilling ears of a modern audience, the makers of tragicomedy—following the steps of Menander and Terence, who raised it to dignity graver and more entitled to respect—have undertaken to mingle with the pleasing parts of comedy those parts of tragedy that can suitably accompany comic scenes to such an extent that they strive for the purgation of sadness. [...]

[*Description of tragicomedy.*] But to conclude once for all that which it was my first intention to show, I say that to a question on the end of tragicomedy I shall answer that it is to imitate with the resources of the stage an action that is feigned and in which are mingled all the tragic and comic parts that can coexist in verisimilitude and decorum, properly arranged in a single dramatic form, with the end of purging with pleasure the sadness of the hearers. This is done in such a way that the imitation, which is the instrumental end, is that which is mixed, and represents a mingling of both tragic and comic events. But the purging, which is the architectonic end, exists only as a single principle, which unites two qualities in one purpose, that of freeing the hearers from melancholy. And as in mixed bodies found in nature, though in these all four of the elements are found in an abated state, as has been said, yet each of them retains a peculiar quality of either one or another of the elements that is dominant and surpasses the others and toward which especially that which is most like it is directed, so in the mixed form of which I speak, though its parts are altogether tragic and comic, it is still not impossible for the plot to have more of one quality than of another, according to the wish of him who composes it, if only he will remain within the bounds that have been mentioned above. The *Amphitryo* of Plautus has more of the comic, the *Cyclops* of Euripides more of the tragic. Yet it is not true that the first or the second is not a tragicomedy, since neither of them has as its end the purging of terror and compassion, for this purgation cannot exist where there is laughter, which disposes the spirits to expand, and not to restrain themselves. [...]

[*The style of tragicomedy*.] The normal and chief style of tragicomedy is the magnificent, which, when accompanied with the grave, becomes the norm of tragedy, but when mingled with the polished, makes the combination fitting to tragicomic poetry. Since it deals with great persons and heroes, humble diction is unfitting, and since it is not concerned with the terrible and the horrible, but rather avoids it, it abandons the grave and employs the sweet, which modifies the greatness and sublimity that is proper to pure tragedy.[...] Now how does the tragicomic poet proceed in giving the right effect to his style? Certainly he will not compose a sentence or a figure in the sublime manner, and a locution and a number in the humble style, but, moderating the gravity of the sentence with those methods that normally make it humble, and in other ways sustaining the humility of some person or subject of which he treats, and using a little of that nobility of speech that is proper to the magnificent style, he proceeds to turn out an idea in harmony with its subject matter, not so grand that it rises to the tragic nor so humble that it approaches the comic.

[*No punishment in tragicomedy*.] Punishment, which in the double form of tragedy comes upon the malefactors, is unfitting to tragicomic poetry, in which according to comic custom, the bad characters are not chastised. [...] Comedy ordinarily desires to give a prosperous end to its worst characters. [...]

FELIX LOPE DE VEGA

Felix LOPE DE VEGA (1562-1635) was in his own lifetime almost as mythical a figure as Bharata. His picture was displayed everywhere, along with the idolatrous verse, "I believe in Lope de Vega all powerful, poet of heaven and earth." "*Es de Lope*" became synonymous for "it's excellent." He was all things to all men.

Tall, thin, swarthy, with a long, hooked nose, he passed his youth dancing, fencing, and borrowing money. As a young libertine in Madrid, Lope consorted principally with actors and actresses and spent much of his time in the *corrales*, attending the Principe or Cruz theatres. Tried and convicted for slandering one of his mistresses, he was sentenced to eight years of exile from Madrid, to which he periodically returned on the sly. He kept a houseful of beloved cats.

When he was ordained as a priest in 1614, Lope shaved off his mustache by order of the bishop. He became a judge of Inquisition and a censor. The Pope made him a member of the Order of Saint John of Jerusalem, and he received an honorary degree of Doctor of Theology.

Written when he was forty seven, Lope's only theoretical work, *Arte nuevo de hacer comedias* (New Art of Writing Plays), consists of 376 lines of ten syllables, unrhymed with occasional couplets. *Arte* refers to the characteristic type of Spanish play and also has the modern meaning of "art" or craft. *Comedia* likewise means the specifically Spanish form of drama that escapes from classical genre categories.

The treatise, Lope tells us, was addressed to the Madrid Academy, a mysterious institution that has defied identification and probably never existed. The verse itself is full of subtle ironies and ambiguities.

Instead of using classical theory to justify his own practice as a playwright, Lope first displays his erudition by citing the rules laid down by the best authorities and then mockingly reproves himself for failing to observe them. It was, he explains, by conforming to the popular Spanish tradition and the demands of the public of his day, not to the precepts of Aristotle and his Renaissance interpreters, that he has become the most popular playwright of his day, author of hundreds of successful plays.

THE NEW ART OF WRITING PLAYS

You ask me, noble spirits, flower of Spain—
Whose famed Academy will surely reign
Supreme, ere long, not only over those
Italian assemblies which rose
By Lake Avernes under Cicero,
But those Athenian gatherings also,
At the Lyceum, owing their renown
To philosophic conclaves like your own—
To tell you what in plays is now allowed
For those whose wish it is to please the crowd.

The subject seems an easy one, it's true,
And easy it would be for those of you
Who've written little, but who've studied more
The art of writing and of all such lore.
For what condemns my efforts at the start
Is that I've always written without art.

Not, thank God, that I didn't know the rules.
I did my course of Grammar in the schools,
Casting my eye on every useful source
Before the sun had ten times run its course,
Leaving the Ram and coming to the Fishes,
Only to find, contrary to my wishes,
That plays today in Spain are not devised
The way that their inventors all advised,
But barbarously our poets their talents waste
Confirming vulgar patrons in their taste.

Playwriting here began in such a way
That he who would artistic rules obey
Will perish without glory or resource,

A new translation by Marvin Carlson © 2000.

For custom is more powerful a force
Than reason or coercion. It is true
That I have sometimes written like those few
Who follow art, but then my eye is caught
By monstrous works, with painted settings fraught,
Where flock the crowds and ladies canonize
By their support such sorry exercise.

So when I have a comedy to write
I lock up with six keys out of my sight
Plautus and Terence, and their precepts too
For fear their cries will even reach me through
Dumb books, for I know truth insists on speaking.
And then I write, for inspiration seeking
Those whose sole aim was winning vulgar praise.
Since after all it is the crowd who pays
Why not consider them when writing plays?

True comedy must its own end embrace
Like every sort of poetry, in this case
To imitate men's action and display
A portrait of the customs of the day.
Poetic imitation all must be
Composed of elements that number three:
Discourse, and pleasant verse, and harmony.
All three of these are also to be found
In tragedy, but comedy is bound
To deal with humble and plebeian themes
While tragedy seeks royal and high extremes.
Now see if in our plays the flaws are great.

They were called *actos*, since they imitate
The actions and the doings of the crowd.
Lope de Rueda was in Spain endowed
With skill in writing *actos* and one may
See still in print his comedies today,
In prose so low in style as to display
Mechanics rude, and stories dealing with
Love coming to the daughter of a smith.

And so the custom holds in many places
To keep the ancient name of *entremeses*
For these old plays where art was still allowed
That show a single action of the crowd

And never place a sovereign on show.
Twas thus the art, because its style was low,
Came to be scorned, and comedies ere long
Added in kings to please the ignorant throng.

In his *Poetics* Aristotle shows,
Though sketchily, how comedy arose,
With Athens and Megara in contention
Which was the first to sponsor this invention.
For Magnetes Athenians made their claim
While Epicarmus Megara would name.
The origins, according to Donatus,
Were ancient sacrifices, and he taught us
As Horace did, to say that Thespis brought us
The first true tragedies, while comedies
Were started off by Aristophanes.

Twas comedy that Homer imitated
Within his *Odyssey*, but he created
The Iliad with tragedy in mind,
In imitation of which I defined
My own *Jerusalem* by epic's name
But added tragic, doing much the same
As all those people who call comedy
The celebrated Dante's trilogy
As Prologist Manetti recognizes.

Now comedy, everyone realizes,
Was silenced for a time, under suspicion.
Twas then that satire first came to fruition.
Its cruelty soon brought it to an end,
And the New Comedy became the favored trend.
First came the chorus, then it was decided
How many characters could be provided.
Although Menander, Terence's descendant,
Despised the chorus as an idle pendant,
Terence observed the precepts with more care.
The style of comedy he'd never dare
Give tragic grandeur, a mistake pernicious,
Which many see in Plautus' works as vicious.
Terence was much more cautious of the laws.

From history the tragic author draws.
Through fictions comic authors seek applause.

Humble in origin, comedy was known
As flat of foot, its actors could be shown
Without cothurni or the tragic scene.
Many comedic genres there have been—
Atellan farces, mimes, and the *togatas*,
Also the tavern plays, and *palliatas* —
Which then as now were various in approach.

Poets with Attic elegance would reproach
In comedy both vice and evil living,
And the Athenians were always giving
Prizes alike for comic poets and planners.
Thus Tully called these plays mirrors of manners,
And also living images of truth,
The very highest accolade, in sooth.
So comedy matched history in renown.
See then if it deserves so rich a crown!
But I perceive, by all your weary looks,
That this is merely translating old books
And boring you with scholarly distraction.
Believe me, I had reason for my action.
I must recall this ancient lore again
In order to be able to explain
The art of writing plays today in Spain.
Here everything is done in art's despite
And if I were to tell you how to write
Today, my own experience must season
My discourse, not the ancient laws or reason
And certainly not art, which truth reflects—
A truth the ignorant multitude rejects.

If, my wise friends, it is for art you're zealous,
Read Udine's learned doctor, Robortellus
On Aristotle and especially
In what he writes concerning comedy,
For writings have appeared in such profusion
That everything today is in confusion.
If you wish my opinion on the plays
Most popular today and on the ways
The crowd and laws it fosters now support
Vile chimeras and monsters of that sort—
I must obey, forgive but understand me,
Whoever has the power to command me.
Gilding the errors of the public taste

I'll tell you in what mode I'd have them placed,
The only path for art today it seems
Is that midway between the two extremes.

Select your subject and don't be dismayed—
Forgive these rules—if kings must be portrayed.
Though as for that I understand our lord
Philip the Prudent, King of Spain, deplored
Seeing a king in them, either because
He thought it went against artistic laws
Or did not want authority on show
Before an audience so mean and low.
This but repeats Old Comedy's depictions.
Plautus brought even gods into his fictions
As Jupiter in his *Amphitrion*.
God knows I don't approve such goings-on
Since Plutarch, as Menander he discussed
Showed for Old Comedy no small disgust.
But since so far from art our era strays
Betraying it in Spain a thousand ways
Let learned doctors here avert their gaze.
Tragedy mixed throughout with comedy
Terence with Seneca—although this be
Another minotaur or Pasiphaë,
One section serious, another slight,
Such varied mixtures lead to much delight.
For this let nature our example be
Gaining much beauty in variety.

Be sure that in your fable you've employed
One single action, by all means avoid
The episodic, that is, draw the line
At all those things outside the main design.
And yet be sure that nothing you delete
That is required to make the whole complete.
No use advising that your action run,
As Aristotle wished, within one sun,
But our respect for him we surely lose
When tragedy's sententious style we fuse
With meaner comedy's more humble fable.

Take up as little time as you are able
Unless to history you have aspired
In which some years of time may be required.

If you require a character to take
A lengthy journey, utilize the break
Between the acts. If this offend,
Those who do not approve should not attend.
Oh, many in these days gain satisfaction
Seeing in one fictitious day an action
Requiring years, although they realize
No actual day could see such enterprise.
But since we can expect a Spaniard's rage
If in two hours' traffic on the stage
He's not presented everything in mumming
From Genesis until the Second Coming
I think it best to recognize his need,
And offer him whatever will succeed.

The subject chosen, write in prose, dividing
The story into three acts, coinciding
If possible, with real unbroken days.
That clever author, Captain Verués,
Made comedies in three acts, that before
Had crawled, as babies do, upon four,
Since comedies were also infants then.
And I myself, when I was twelve or ten
Scrawled on four sheets of paper four-act plays,
An act on every page, and in those days
An *entremesa* filled each entre'acte.
Now there may be but one, and that in fact
A dance, for dance to comedy is fitted
As even Aristotle has admitted.
And Athenaes, Plato, Xenophon
Speak of it, though the latter frown upon
Indecorous dancing, like those parodies
Of ancient choruses by Callipedes.

The matter being split into two parts,
Be sure to carry through from where it starts
Until the action end, and don't untie
Your plot until the final scene is nigh.
Hold back your ending. If the crowd expects it
They'll turn their backs, while heading for the exit,
On what they watched for hours when they feel
That you have nothing further to reveal.
Silence on stage should rarely be allowed,
For when no one is speaking, then the crowd

Grows restless and the story slows its pace.
Avoiding this defect adds art and grace.

Begin then, in plain language phrase your matter,
Avoiding odd conceits or clever patter
On family doings, which is what the chatter
Of your few characters will represent.
But if you have a character who's meant
To give advice, persuade, or turn aside,
Then rhetoric and wit may be applied.
Here truth is given its due, for we depart
From common speech and utilize more art
In seeking to condemn or to persuade.
Aristides, the rhetorician, laid
A charge on comic language to be
Pure, clear, and flexible, adding that we
Find this in common speech, which differs quite
From that found in society polite,
Where sonorous discourse is cultivated
And language is adorned and elevated.

Do not drag in quotations nor offend
With words flamboyant, for if you intend
To imitate real speech, don't put before us
The discourse of Pancaya or Metaurus,
Or hippogriffs, or centaurs, or the like.
Whenever kings are speaking, try to strike
A note of royal gravity, for the sage,
Sententious modesty befitting age.
Describe young lovers with those passions proved
So those who listen will be deeply moved.
Soliloquies should be, for he who writes them
A way to transform whoever recites them,
And changing him change everyone who came.
He may pose questions, answering the same,
And in his plaints, let him invite no blame
By giving women less than due respect.
The ladies naturally we would expect
To be in character. If they change their dress,
Let it be seemly done, for I confess,
The crowd is always pleased by male disguise.

Impossibilities avoid, your duty lies
Only in seeking truthful imitation.

Don't let your lackey speak above his station
Nor, as we've seen in certain foreign plays,
Express conceits. Whatever someone says
He should not contradict what he has spoken,
I mean forget. Sophocles, by this token
Erred when Oedipus doesn't understand
That Laius was destroyed by his own hand.
Each scene with wit and epigram conclude,
Expressed in verse, with elegance imbued,
So that the one entrusted with the ending
Will not arouse disgust in those attending.

In your first act set forth your matter, leaving
Until the second act the interweaving
Of deeds, so by the middle of the third
The end of all may still not be inferred.
Deceive anticipation, thus you may
Let understanding follow when you stray
Quite far from what was promised at the start.
Use prudence, never let your verse depart
From what will suit your subject matter best.
Complaints should be in *décimas* expressed.
Sonnets are good for those in expectation,
Romances are best suited for relation
Of actions, though *octavas* have more lustre.
For grave events, the tercets you should muster
And *redondillas* for the heart's concerns.
Figures of rhetoric one never spurns
Such as repeating or anadiplosis
And, at the start of lines this figure closes,
Anaphora in various permutations,
Ironies and such-like manifestations,
Apostrophies, queries, and exclamations.

To make your public by the truth deceived
Is a device that has been well received.
It's always found in Miguel Sánchez' plays,
An innovation meriting high praise.
Equivocation and uncertainty
Arising from the ambiguous will be
Forever popular, since crowds delight
In thinking only they perceive aright.
Best are those plots where honor has a part,
These stir profoundly every hearer's heart.

Also show virtuous action, for tis known
That everyone loves virtue to be shown.

Thus if an actor should the role attempt
Of traitor, he arouses such contempt
No one will sell him what he wants to buy,
And everywhere he goes, the people fly,
But he who's loyal is honored and invited,
Not even by the highest is he slighted.
They seek him, to regale and to acclaim.

Four pages for each act should be your aim,
For twelve best suit the patience and also
The time of those who come to see the show.
Don't be too clear in satire, for you know
Greek and Italian dramas were forbidden
In which the satire was not sagely hidden.
Don't prick too deep, if anyone you blame,
For this will garner neither praise nor fame.
Some precepts, though by ancient art neglected,
As aphorisms yet should be respected,
Though we have little space to treat them now.
Virtuvius tells stage directors how
Three kinds of scenes are managed, Maximus,
Horace in his epistles, Critinus,
And others give details on such things as these—
Backdrops, false marble, houses, huts, and trees.
On costume Julius Pollux is the source
For all we need to know, although of course
In Spain today there are presented plays
Containing the most barbarous displays—
Turks wearing Christian collars, Roman knights
Dressed in tight breeches—these are common sights.

Not one of these should any designate
More barbarous than myself, who dares to state
Precepts in art's defense, even while knowing
I don't resist the vulgar current's flowing.
For this England and France call me untaught.
What can I do, for I have now begot
Four hundred eighty-three dramatic pieces,
A sum this week's new offering increases,
And all of these but six, I must admit,
The gravest sins against the art commit.

And yet, at last, I must defend my plays
While knowing they are flawed in many ways

Because their vogue depended on these flaws
For sometimes something charms the taste because
It is in fact contrary to the laws.

Humanae cur sit speculum comoedia vitae
Quaeve ferat iuveni commoda, quaeve seni
Quid praeter lepidosque sales, excultaque verba,
Et genus eloquii purius inde petas,
Quae gravia in mediis ocurrant lusibus, et quae
Iucundis passim seria mexta iocis,
Quam sint fallaces serui, quam improba semper,
Fraudeque et omnigenis foemina plena dolis,
Quam miser, infelix, stultus, et ineptus amator,
Quam vix succedant, quae bene coepta putes. *

Then listen carefully and do not fear
For art, since comedy is of that sphere
That, when one listens, everything comes clear.

* *Here is an approximate translation of the Latin passage:*

How comedy reflects our human state
How well both young and old she represents
What else can matter with such grace relate
With cultivated words and eloquence
How charmingly she mixes matters light
With grave concerns, the serious with jest,
How traitors are exposed and put to flight
And scheming women's strategies confessed.
How silly courses simple lovers run
And how things may end ill, though well begun.

FRANÇOIS HÉDELIN, abbé D'AUBIGNAC

François Hédelin, abbé D'AUBIGNAC (1604-1676) was theatrical advisor to Cardinal Richelieu and unofficial minister of culture who formulated the state policy declaring the stage an instrument of government, a reflection of national glory, and an innocent amusement useful for keeping subjects docile and content. Himself a playwright, the abbé wrote the first handbook on how to write for the theatre and by his precepts laid the groundwork for the French classical doctrine.

In love with drama but shocked by the disreputable nature of early seventeenth-century French theatre, d'Aubignac worked as a reformer determined to rid the stage of its crudeness and improbabilities and transform it into a civilized art fit for the best society. He proposed that all plays should be submitted to an official censor before performance. Countering charges of immorality made against the stage by conservative churchmen, d'Aubignac sought to raise the profession of actor to the level of respectability and make the theatre the centerpiece of French cultural life in the second half of the seventeenth century. By a royal decree of 1641 the actor was rehabilitated (except for farceurs and Italian comedians), absolved from charge of infamy, and no longer barred from assuming public office and entering religious orders.

Although not published until 1657, the abbé began *La Pratique du Théâtre* (The Whole Art of the Stage) in 1640 when he was commissioned by Richelieu to write a treatise on playwriting. More interested in actual stage practice than in abstract dramatic theory, d'Aubignac prefers empirical observations to general maxims. To establish his credentials, the self-taught abbé cites Aristotle some 60 times and gives 150 examples from Greek tragedy, but shows little interest in the authority of the Ancients, which he feels should not outweigh reason and good sense. At a time when classical Greek tragedy was only read, not performed on the French stage, the abbé studied the ancient dramatic texts so as to discover how they were actually staged.

D'Aubignac expressly states that he wishes to present new ideas and say something different. Accused by Corneille of simply paraphrasing Aristotle, the abbé actually insists on novelty; all his original reflections are on the acting of the performers, the staging and setting, and the response of the audience in seventeenth-century France. The abbé bases his observations on the theatrical practices that evolved between 1635 and 1645 in the plays that he admires by Corneille, Scudéry, Mairet, Tristan, and Du Ryer. D'Aubignac provides 120 examples from the theatre of his own time, of which 40 come from Corneille, his true model for tragedy and tragicomedy (a genre that he does not condemn). Later the abbé quarreled with Corneille and in a revised edition of *La Pratique* planned to cut his extravagant praise of the author of *Le Cid* as a master of the stage above all contemporaries and equal to the ancients.

According to d'Aubignac, a play must conform to the public sensibility of its own time and place. Taste and the rules of propriety are determined by "the customs and manners, as well as opinions of the spectators." What the audience finds believable and acceptable, is the ultimate criterion. In opposition to Corneille's baroque aesthetics of astonishment, the abbé favors economy and structural unity, natural sentiments and simplicity of action.

Although highly esteemed in the seventeenth century by critics and by playwrights like Racine, d'Aubignac's treatise later fell into disrepute as pedantry. An eloquent defender of the stage as a cornerstone of state cultural policy and a pioneer in the technique of playwriting, the abbé helped shape the *grand siècle* of Corneille, Molière, and Racine.

THE WHOLE ART OF THE STAGE (1657)

Book the Third, Chapter the First: Of the actors or persons to be brought upon the stage, and what the poet is to observe about them.

I do not design here to instruct the players, but the poet, who will find in this chapter some observations for the better disposing of the dramatic poem, as to the persons that are to appear upon the stage.

But before we begin them, it will not be amiss to observe to the reader a thing which will make us make a wish in favor of our stage, when we reflect upon the magnificency of the representation of the ancients, which is, that in many places of their poems, where we see but one actor named, he did not appear alone upon the stage; but on the contrary, when it was a prince, or princess, or some person of eminent quality, he was followed by a very great retinue, suitable to his dignity; sometimes of courtiers, sometimes of soldiers, and always of persons proper to the subject of the play: nay, a rich citizen appeared with a great many servants, and a public courtesan, if she were of free condition, and mistress of her own actions, had always a great many maids and servants about her; and in short, persons of quality were always accompanied, except some particular reason required they should be alone, which may be easily perceived by the verses, or the nature of the action. [...]

And to begin, it has been often asked how many actors may be brought on at once, speaking and acting upon the stage, in the same scene. Some have confined us to three, taking their rule from Horace's *Art of Poetry*; but experience is the best judge in these cases; and Horace, I believe, is not so well understood as he should be. Tis true, that the stage having attained to have three actors in the time of Sophocles, who brought dramatic poetry to its perfection; the Greeks seldom bring any more than three actors at a time upon the stage, if there be a fourth, he generally is silent; and indeed a scene is not ill filled when three chief actors are discoursing at once upon the scene. But the answer to this question depends not so much upon the number of persons, as upon the order of confusion that would follow if too many were speaking in the same scene; and therefore I am of opinion, that the poet may bring on as many as he pleases, provided neither their number, nor their discourses do

From Abbé d'Aubignac, *The Whole Art of the Stage*, translator anonymous. London: William Cadman, 1684.

confound the spectator's attention; and there will be no confusion if the actors' names, and their concerns be so known as to give a true understanding of what is in the action: three actors indeed seldom bring any confusion, because there is no spectator so simple, but he can easily distinguish their words and designs; but still the poet must consider what necessity he lies under: for if his subject requires that four or five should appear and discourse in the same scene, if he performs it with distinction, and without obscurity, I don't believe anybody will say he goes against the rules, there being nothing there against probability. The examples of this are frequent in the comic poets, both Greek and Latin; and as for Horace, his advice is only that the poet does not bring a fourth person upon the stage as to embarrass or confound the business in hand, or perplex the discourse of the other three.

Our second observation is that the poet must bring no actor upon the stage that is not known to the spectators as soon as he appears, and that not only as to his name and person, but also as to the sentiments he brings upon the stage, else the spectator will be puzzled, and the poet's fine discourse will be lost, because the audience will not know how to apply them; and I have seen often 20 or 30 noble verses thrown away because the spectator knew not him that spoke them, nor how to apply them. The ancients never failed in this, to which the choruses were a great help to them; for they never leaving the stage, generally as soon as a new actor came on they named him with some expression of fear, also astonishment or joy, according as the subject required but if he were a stranger, and unknown to the chorus, then he named himself, giving some account of his good or bad fortune, or some confidant of his declared it without affectation, either by pitying him, or seeming to be concerned for the doubtful success of his enterprise.

As for us who have no choruses, we must, instead of them, make some of those actors speak who are already upon the stage, and known; and if we open an act with persons unknown, they must themselves declare their condition, or some of their followers must by the by, and without affectation insinuate it; but if it be necessary that an actor should be incognito both as to his name and quality, in order to his being known with more pleasure towards the end of the play, then the spectators must at least know that he is incognito; and in a word all confusion must be avoided, and it will be well if the spectators conceive something in general concerning the interests of this new actor; not indeed so far as to discover or prevent an incident, but as much as is necessary to facilitate their easier comprehending all that is to be said afterwards.

The third observation is, that the actors do always come on, and go off the scene with some probable reason, which makes it more proper for them to do so than otherwise, and yet that must not be done grossly, but by nice and natural pretexts. For any art that discovers itself too much, loses its grace; and yet it is not necessary that the reason which makes actors go on and off should always take effect; quite contrary, the less things succeed according to their first appearance, the more pleasing and surprising they are. Tis one of the beauties of the stage, that things cross one another, and so produce unforeseen events; and when an actor is upon the stage, his good or bad fortune is in the poet's hands, though the reason that brought him on be not at all conformable to what he meets with there.

As for the practice of this rule, I must desire our poets to have recourse to the ancients, and to observe with what art they govern themselves; for the reading of one poem of theirs, particularly of Sophocles, will give them more light in this matter, that all the allegations with which I might swell this treatise.

The fourth observation is about a dispute which I have often been witness to, which is, whether or no in the same act the same actor may appear more than once. First, to answer this question right, it is necessary to distinguish the plays; for in a comedy, the subject whereof is taken from the meaner sort of people, it would not be amiss that the persons concerned should appear more than once in an act, because they are people whose business is not weighty, their actions quick, and the manner of their life unquiet, and their intrigues, most of them happening in the neighborhood, so that they need but a little time to go and come; but in tragedy where they are most commonly kings and princes; where their manner of living is very different, the actions all full of gravity and weight, it does not appear easy nor reasonable to make them appear more than once in an act; for their intrigues are generally with persons remote, their designs great, and which are not to be brought to pass but by slow means, and with great circumspection, so the more time is regularly required to move all the springs of their affairs.

Secondly, in both these sorts of poems, one must consider the condition of the person, for in a slave or servant it would be nothing to see him often in an act, but it would be something strange in a man or woman of quality, if some extraordinary reason did not oblige them to precipitate their action.

Thirdly, we are to consider how far an actor went, and if the thing he went about required much time: or if he had some reason to return so soon; for the place he went to being near, and having but a short business, and being obliged to return immediately, all these are circumstances which may bring an actor upon the stage twice in an act, without offending against the rules. Plautus does it very ingeniously in many of his comedies, but I know of no example of it in any tragedy of the ancients. Monsieur Corneille indeed in his *Horatius* brings his hero twice on in the same act, because he went but from the hall of his palace to his father's chamber, to take his leave of him before he engaged in the combat between the six brothers. But for my part, I should counsel the poet to do it as little as possible, and with great circumspection; for, methinks, it is a little indecent to see a person of quality go and come so suddenly, and act with so much appearance of precipitation.

The fifth observation is about a thing which the ancients never failed in, and the modern writers often have, which is, to bring their principal actors on, upon the opening of the stage, and indeed with a great deal of reason, because their persons being considered as the principal subject of all the adventures of the play, and as the center to which all the other lines are to be drawn, the spectators desire to see them at first, and all that is said or done before their arrival gives them more impatience than pleasure, and is often reckoned for nothing: and besides they often take the first actor of quality for the hero of the play, and when they are undeceived, find themselves in confusion and perplexed; therefore those authors who bring not on their actor till the third or fourth act, are much to blame, for that causes in the audience so much impatience and uncertainty, that it is afterwards very hard to satisfy them; not but that in some occasions one may luckily defer the bringing on a chief actor for a while, but then that must give some extraordinary grace to the play, and be ordered so, as not to confound the spectators' application.

The sixth observation is, that the chief actors ought to appear as often, and stay as long as possible upon the stage; first, because they are always the best actors, and so satisfy most; then they are the best clothed, and so please the spectators, who are taken with their dress; and lastly, because they have the finest things to say, and the noblest passions to show; in which, to say truth consists the greatest charm of the stage; and besides, the whole event being to turn upon them, the spectator rejoices and grieves with them, fears and hopes as they do, and always has some inward concern according to the present state of their affairs. This makes me not approve of Seneca, who in a play where Agamemnon is the chief hero, and is killed, makes him say not above two and twenty verses in all. The best advice I can give the poet in this matter, is not to have anything told by way of narrative, which may be any ways decently performed by the chief actors themselves; but if the subject cannot suffer that the chief actors should appear in every act, he must endeavor that that act where they do not appear, be filled with some great circumstance of the story, and that the second parts may repair the want of the first by some noble and majestic adventure, else it is certain the play will pall and languish.

The seventh and last observation of this chapter is particular enough, and it may be at first will not be relished by all our poets; but I desire them to examine it in the practice, before they judge of it here upon the paper. To explain myself rightly, we must observe, that where an actor appears first upon the stage, he may come on in one of these three dispositions, either in a moderate, calm temper, or in a violent passion, or in a disposition something moved, but not raised to the high pitch of transport; and that may be called a half-passion. Now in the first case an actor may easily acquit himself, for it comes so near our natural temper, that few fail to personate it well. In the second case likewise of violent transport, good actors seldom fail to represent it well, because experience has taught them how far their voice and action is to be strained in such a case; but as it is much easier go from one extremity to another, than to stop with discretion in the middle; so the actors, though they can easily represent these two sentiments directly opposite, they do not always succeed when they are to come upon the stage with the sentiment of a half-passion, which passes a little our natural tranquility, and yet rises not to the extremest violence; and the reason is, that not being stirred of themselves, and yet not daring to rise to the highest pitch of violence, tis hard for them to find that just temper to enter into this half passion; from hence it comes, that they often provoke the laughter of the audience, by delivering with an ill grace, and unconcernedly, that which requires some emotion, or appearing over-alarmed at that which does not in its nature so highly affect the spectators. Therefore my observation to the poet is, that he first put some moderate words in his actor's mouth, before he raises him to the half-passion, that he may grow warm by little and little, and that his voice may rise by degrees, and all his gestures acquire more and more motion with his discourse; and as for the actor, I will tell him what in this case I have seen Mondory, the best actor of our days do, which was, that in these occasions having taken a turn or two upon the stage and with some posture suitable to his part, as lifting up his hands and eyes, or the like; having begun to move himself, he brought himself to the true point of a half-passion, and so came sensibly out of the natural state of indifferency in which he came on upon the stage; withal, retaining his motions so as they should not go too far. All this will be better understood by both poets and actors, if they please to make some reflections at rehearsals, and have the comedians' own opinions who are best judges, having often experienced this, and other methods of performing a half-passion.

PIERRE CORNEILLE

Pierre CORNEILLE (1606-1684) was a tall, big-boned, brusque, melancholy man, common in appearance, unkempt and slovenly, with a large nose, sharp features, and eyes full of fire. A bourgeois lawyer from Normandy and a devoted husband and father, he disliked the stylish Parisian court where, as the most successful playwright of the day, his attendance was obligatory. He spoke French poorly, with a strong Normand accent and bad diction, and read his own works forcefully but without any grace or charm. Of a proud, independent nature, he was inflexible in his integrity.

A brilliant pupil of Latin at the Jesuits, he developed at a young age lasting admiration for the heroic figures and great events of Roman history. By temperament he was well suited to portray stoic virtue, but unable to thread his way through the maze of court intrigue.

The first in France to set a high value on the profession of dramatist, Corneille insisted on respect for his works and his talent, selling his plays to the actors at steep prices, and using his younger brother Thomas as press agent and publicist. The playwright edited his own works diligently, checking the proofs and correcting typos. In his library he displayed the many foreign translations of *Le Cid*.

During the nine-month controversy following the unprecedented success of *Le Cid*, Corneille answered the erudite theoreticians who attacked him from the point of view of a theatre professional who rejected the tyranny of the probable for the sake of exciting plots. The playwright preferred incredible situations whose authenticity, guaranteed by history or tradition, compels the spectator's belief. In his theory of catharsis, either of the tragic emotions—pity or fear alone—was sufficient.

Corneille faced the problem of how to be a dramatist in an absolutist state where the arts had to be brought under control. In the authoritarian realm of the Sun King, totalitarian statecraft demanded obedience at the expense of class and family loyalties and called for an equally totalitarian stagecraft. Corneille the playwright revised his plays to conform more completely to the emerging classical doctrine, but in the three *Discourses* that served as prefaces to the three volumes of his collected plays, Corneille the theoretician set out to prove that as the most successful dramatist in France he understood playwriting better than the learned scholars.

"I like following the rules," he had written earlier, "but, far from being their slave, I relax or tighten them up as my subject demands, and I even make no bones about breaking the rule regarding the duration of the plot when it bears so harshly on the work as to be incompatible with the finer points of the events described. To know the rules is one thing; to possess the secret of taming them adroitly and harnessing them to our stage is a very different one. And, to make a play a success, it is, I suggest, not enough these days merely to have read up Aristotle and Horace."

OF THE THREE UNITIES OF ACTION, TIME, AND PLACE (1660)

The two preceding discourses and the critical examination of the plays which my first two volumes contain have furnished me so many opportunities to explain my thoughts on these matters that there would be little left for me to say if I absolutely forbade myself to repeat.

I hold then, as I have already said, that in comedy, unity of action consists in the unity of plot or the obstacle to the plans of the principal actors, and in tragedy in the unity of peril, whether the hero falls victim to it or escapes. It is not that I claim that several perils cannot be allowed in the latter or several plots or obstacles in the former, provided that one passes necessarily from one to the other; for then escape from the first peril does not make the action complete since the escape leads to another danger; and the resolution of one plot does not put the actors at rest since they are confounded afresh in another. My memory does not furnish me any ancient examples of this multiplicity of perils linked each to each without the destruction of the unity of action; but I have noted independent double action as a defect in *Horace* and in *Théodore*, for it is not necessary that the first kill his sister upon gaining his victory nor that the other give herself up to martyrdom after having escaped prostitution; and if the death of Polyxène and that of Astyanax in Seneca's *Trojan Women* do not produce the same irregularity I am very much mistaken.

In the second place, the term unity of action does not mean that tragedy should show only one action on the stage. The one which the poet chooses for his subject must have a beginning, a middle, and an end; and not only are these three parts separate actions which find their conclusion in the principal one, but, moreover, each of them may contain several others with the same subordination. There must be only one complete action, which leaves the mind of the spectator serene; but that action can become complete only through several others which are less perfect and which, by serving as preparation, keep the spectator in a pleasant suspense. This is what must be contrived at the end of each act in order to give continuity to the action. It is not necessary that we know exactly what the actors are doing in the intervals

From *The Continental Model*, ed. Scott Elledge, trans. Donald Schier.
Ithaca: Cornell University Press, 1970.

which separate the acts, nor even that they contribute to the action when they do not appear on the stage; but it is necessary that each act leave us in the expectation of something which is to take place in the following one.

If you asked me what Cléopâtre is doing in *Rodogune* between the time when she leaves her two sons in the second act until she rejoins Antiochus in the fourth, I should be unable to tell you, and I do not feel obliged to account for her; but the end of this second act prepares us to see an amicable effort by the two brothers to rule and to hide Rodogune from the venomous hatred of their mother. The effect of this is seen in the third act, whose ending prepares us again to see another effort by Antiochus to win back these two enemies one after the other and for what Séleucus does in the fourth, which compels that unnatural mother [Cleopatra] to resolve upon what she tries to accomplish in the fifth, whose outcome we await with suspense.

In *Le Menteur* the actors presumably make use of the whole interval between the third and fourth acts to sleep; their rest, however, does not impede the continuity of the action between those two acts because the third does not contain a complete event. Dorante ends it with his plan to seek ways to win back the trust of Lucrèce, and at the very beginning of the next he appears so as to be able to talk to one of her servants and to her, should she show herself.

When I say that it is not necessary to account for what the actors do when they are not on stage, I do not mean that it is not sometimes very useful to give such an accounting, but only that one is not forced to do it, and that one ought to take the trouble to do so only when what happens behind the scenes is necessary for the understanding of what is to take place before the spectators. Thus I say nothing of what Cléopâtre did between the second and the fourth acts, because during all that time she can have done nothing important as regards the principal action which I am preparing for; but I point out in the very first lines of the fifth act that she has used the interval between these latter two for the killing of Séleucus, because that death is part of the action. This is what leads me to state that the poet is not required to show all the particular actions which bring about the principal one; he must choose to show those which are the most advantageous, whether by the beauty of the spectacle or by the brilliance or violence of the passions they produce, or by some other attraction which is connected with them, and to hide the others behind the scenes while informing the spectator of them by a narration or by some other artistic device; above all, he must remember that they must all be so closely connected that the last are produced by the preceding and that all have their source in the protasis which ought to conclude the first act. This rule, which I have established in my first *Discourse*, although it is new and contrary to the usage of the ancients, is founded on two passages of Aristotle. Here is the first of them: "There is a great difference," he says, "between events which succeed each other and those which occur because of others."

The Moors come into the *Cid* after the death of the Count and not because of the death of the Count; and the fisherman comes into *Don Sanche* after Charles is suspected of being the Prince of Aragon and not because he is suspected of it; thus both are to be criticized. The second passage is even more specific and says precisely "that everything that happens in tragedy must arise necessarily or probably from what has gone before."

The linking of the scenes which unites all the individual actions of each act and of which I have spoken in criticizing *La Suivante* is a great beauty in a poem and one which serves to shape continuity of action through continuity of presentation; but, in the end, it is only a beauty and not a rule. The ancients did not always abide by it although most of their acts have but two or three scenes. This made things much simpler for them than for us, who often put as many as nine or ten scenes into each act. I shall cite only two examples of the scorn with which they treated this principle: one is from Sophocles, in *Ajax*, whose monologue before he kills himself has no connection with the preceding scene; the other is from the third act of Terence's *The Eunuch*, where Antipho's soliloquy has no connection with Chremes and Pythias who leave the stage when he enters. The scholars of our century, who have taken the ancients for models in the tragedies they have left us, have even more neglected that linking than did the ancients, and one need only glance at the plays of Buchanan, Grotius, and Heinsius, of which I spoke in the discussion of *Polyeucte*, to agree on that point. We have so far accustomed our audiences to this careful linking that they cannot now witness a detached scene without considering it a defect; the eye and even the ear are outraged by it even before the mind has been able to reflect upon it. The fourth act of *Cinna* falls below the others through this flaw; and what formerly was not a rule has become one now through the assiduousness of our practice.

I have spoken of three sorts of linkings in the discussion of *La Suivante*: I have shown myself averse to those of sound, indulgent to those of sight, favorable to those of presence and speech; but in these latter I have confused two things which ought to be separated. Links of presence and speech both have, no doubt, all the excellence imaginable; but there are links of speech without presence and of presence without speech which do not reach the same level of excellence. An actor who speaks to another from a hiding-place without showing himself forms a link of speech without presence which is always effective; but that rarely happens. A man who remains on stage merely to hear what will be said by those whom he sees making their entrance forms a link of presence without speech; this is often clumsy and falls into mere pretense, being contrived more to accede to this new convention which is becoming a precept than for any need dictated by the plot of the play. Thus, in the third act of *Pompée*, Achorée, after having informed Charmion of the reception Caesar gave to the king when he presented to him the head of that hero, remains on the stage where he sees the two of them come together merely to hear what they will say and report it to Cléopâtre. Ammon does the same thing in the fourth act of *Andromède* for the benefit of Phinée, who retires when he sees the king and all his court arriving. Characters who become mute connect rather badly scenes in which they play little part and in which they count for nothing. It is another matter when they hide in order to find out some important secret from those who are speaking and who think they are not overheard, for then the interest which they have in what is being said, added to a reasonable curiosity to find out what they cannot learn in any other way, gives them an important part in the action despite their silence; but in these two examples Ammon and Achorée lend so cold a presence to the scenes they overhear that, to be perfectly frank, whatever feigned reason I give them to serve as pretext for their action, they remain there only to connect the scenes with those that precede, so easily can both plays dispense with what they do.

Although the action of the dramatic poem must have its unity, one must consider both its parts: the complication and the resolution. "The complication is composed," according to Aristotle, "in part of what has happened off stage before the beginning of the action which is there described, and in part from what happens on stage; the rest belongs to the resolution. The change of fortune forms the separation of these two parts. Everything which precedes it is in the first part, and this change, with what follows it, concerns the other." The complication depends entirely upon the choice and industrious imagination of the poet and no rule can be given for it, except that in it he ought to order all things according to probability or necessity, a point which I have discussed in the second *Discourse*; to this I add one piece of advice, which is that he involve himself as little as possible with things which have happened before the action he is presenting. Such narrations are annoying, usually because they are not expected, and they disturb the mind of the spectator, who is obliged to burden his memory with what has happened ten or twelve years before in order to understand what he is about to see; but narrations which describe things which happen and take place behind the scenes once the action has started always produce a better effect because they are awaited with some curiosity and are a part of the action which is being shown. One of the reasons why so many illustrious critics favor *Cinna* above anything else I have done is that it contains no narration of the past, the one Cinna makes in describing his plot to Emilie being rather an ornament which tickles the mind of the spectators than a necessary marshaling of the details they must know and impress upon their memories for the understanding of what is to come. Emilie informs them adequately in the first two scenes that he is conspiring against Augustus in her favor, and if Cinna merely told her that the plotters are ready for the following day he would advance the action just as much as by the hundred lines he uses to tell both what he said to them and the way in which they received his words. There are plots which begin at the very birth of the hero like that of *Héraclius*, but these great efforts of the imagination demand an extraordinary attention of the spectator and often keep him from taking a real pleasure in the first performances, so much do they weary him.

In the resolution I find two things to avoid: the mere change of intention and the machine. Not much skill is required to finish a poem when he who has served as the obstacle to the plans of the principal actors for four acts desists in the fifth without being constrained to do so by any remarkable event; I have spoken of this in the first *Discourse* and I shall add nothing to that here. The machine requires no more skill when it is used only to bring down a god who straightens everything out when the actors are unable to do so. It is thus that Apollo functions in the *Orestes*: this prince and his friend Pylades, accused by Tyndarus and Menelaus of the death of Clytemnestra and condemned after prosecution by them, seize Helen and Hermione; they kill, or think they kill the first, and threaten to do so the same with the other if the sentence pronounced against them is not revoked. To smooth out these difficulties Euripides seeks nothing subtler than to bring Apollo down from heaven, and he, by absolute authority, orders that Orestes marry Hermione and Pylades Electra; and lest the death of Helen prove an obstacle to this, it being improbable that Hermione would marry Orestes since he had just killed her mother, Apollo informs them that she is not dead, that he has protected her from their blows and carried her off to heaven at the moment when they thought they were killing her. This use of the machine is entirely irrelevant, being founded in no way on the rest of the play, and makes a faulty resolution. But I find a little too harsh the opinion of Aristotle, who puts on the same level the chariot Medea uses to flee from Corinth after the vengeance she has taken on Creon. It seems to me there is a sufficient basis for this in the fact that she has been made a magician and that actions of hers as far surpassing natural forces as that one have been mentioned in the play. After what she did for Jason at Colchis and after she had made his father Aeson young again following his return, and after she had attached invisible fire to the gift she gave to Creusa, the flying chariot is not improbable and the poem has no need of other preparation for that extraordinary effect. Seneca gives it preparation by this line which Medea speaks to her nurse:

Tuum quoque ipsa corpus hinc mecum aveham;

and I by this one which she speaks to Aegeus:

I shall follow you tomorrow by a new road.

Thus the condemnation of Euripides, who took no precautions, may be just and yet not fall on Seneca or on me; and I have no need to contradict Aristotle in order to justify myself on this point.

From the action I turn to the acts, each of which ought to contain a portion of it, but not so equal a portion that more is not reserved for the last than for the others and less given to the first than to the others. Indeed, in the first act one may do no more than depict the moral nature of the characters and mark off how far they have got in the story which is to be presented. Aristotle does not prescribe the number of the acts; Horace limits it to five; and although he prohibits having fewer, the Spaniards are obstinate enough to stop at three and the Italians often do the same thing. The Greeks used to separate the acts by the chanting of the chorus, and since I think it reasonable to believe that in some of their poems they made it chant more than four times, I should not want to say they never exceeded five. This way of distinguishing the acts was less handy than ours, for either they paid attention to what the chorus was chanting or they did not; if they did, the mind of the spectators was too tense and had no time in which to rest; if they did not, attention was too much dissipated by the length of the chant, and when a new act began, an effort of memory was needed to recall to the imagination what had been witnessed and at what point the action had been interrupted. Our orchestra presents neither of these two inconveniences; the mind of the spectator relaxes while the music is playing and even reflects on what he has seen, to praise it or to find fault with it depending on whether he has been pleased or displeased; and the short time the orchestra is allowed to play leaves his impressions so fresh that when the actors return he does not need to make an effort to recall and resume his attention.

The number of scenes in each act has never been prescribed by rule, but since the whole act must have a certain number of lines which make its length proportionate to that of the others, one may include it in more or fewer scenes depending on whether they are long or short to fill up the time which the whole act is to consume. One ought, if possible, to account for the entrance and exit of each actor; I consider this rule indispensable, especially for the exit, and think there is nothing so clumsy as an actor who leaves the stage merely because he has no more lines to speak.

I should not be so rigorous for the entrances. The audience expects the actor, and although the setting represents the room or the study of whoever is speaking, yet he cannot make his appearance there unless he comes out from behind the tapestry, and it is not always easy to give a reason for what he has just done in town before returning home, since sometimes it is even probable that he has not gone out at all. I have never seen anybody take offense at seeing Emilie begin *Cinna* without saying why she has come to her room; she is presumed to be there before the play begins, and it is only stage necessity which makes her appear from behind the scenes to come there. Thus I should willingly dispense from the rigors of the rule the first scene of each act but not the others, because once an actor is on the stage anyone who enters must have a reason to speak to him or, at least, must profit from the opportunity to do so when it offers. Above all, when an actor enters twice in one act, in comedy or in tragedy, he must either lead one to expect that he will soon return when he leaves the first time, like Horace in the second act and Julie in the third act of

Horace, or explain on returning why he has come back so soon.

Aristotle wishes the well-made tragedy to be beautiful and capable of pleasing without the aid of actors and quite aside from performance. So that the reader may more easily experience that pleasure, his mind, like that of the spectator, must not be hindered, because the effort he is obliged to make to conceive and to imagine the play for himself lessens the satisfaction which he will get from it. Therefore, I should be of the opinion that the poet ought to take great care to indicate in the margin the less important actions which do not merit being included in the lines, and which might even mar the dignity of the verse if the author lowered himself to express them. The actor easily fills this need on the stage, but in a book one would often be reduced to guessing and sometimes one might even guess wrong, unless one were informed in this way of these little things. I admit that this is not the practice of the ancients; but you must also allow me that because they did not do it they have left us many obscurities in their poems which only masters of dramatic art can explain; even so, I am not sure they succeed as often as they think they do. If we forced ourselves to follow the method of the ancients completely, we should make no distinction between acts and scenes because the Greeks did not. This failure on their part is often the reason that I do not know how many acts there are in their plays, nor whether at the end of an act the player withdraws so as to allow the chorus to chant, or whether he remains on stage without any action while the chorus is chanting, because neither they nor their interpreters have deigned to give us a word of indication in the margin.

We have another special reason for not neglecting that helpful little device as they did: this is that printing puts our plays in the hands of actors who tour the provinces and whom we can thus inform of what they ought to do, for they would do some very odd things if we did not help them by these notes. They would find themselves in great difficulty at the fifth act of plays that end happily, where we bring together all the actors on the stage (a thing which the ancients did not do); they would often say to one what is meant for another, especially when the same actor must speak to three or four people one after the other. When there is a whispered command to make, like Cléopâtre's to Laonice which sends her to seek poison, an aside would be necessary to express this in verse if we were to do without the marginal indications, and that seems to me much more intolerable than the notes, which give us the real and only way, following the opinion of Aristotle, of making the tragedy as beautiful in the reading as in performance, by making it easy for the reader to imagine what the stage presents to the view of the spectators.

The rule of the unity of time is founded on this statement of Aristotle "that the tragedy ought to enclose the duration of its action in one journey of the sun or try not to go much beyond it." These words gave rise to a famous dispute as to whether they ought to be understood as meaning a natural day of twenty-four hours or an artificial day of twelve; each of the two opinions has important partisans, and, for myself, I find that there are subjects so difficult to limit to such a short time that not only should I grant the twenty-four full hours but I should make use of the license which the philosopher gives to exceed them a little and should push the total without scruple as far as thirty. There is a legal maxim which says that we should broaden the mercies and narrow the rigors of the law, *odia restringenda, favores ampliandi*; and I find that an author is hampered enough by this constraint which forced some of the ancients to the very edge of the impossible. Euripides, in *The Suppliants*, makes Theseus leave Athens with an army, fight a battle beneath the walls of Thebes, which was ten or twelve leagues away, and return victorious in the following act; and between his departure and the arrival of the messenger who comes to tell the story of his victory, the chorus has only thirty-six lines to speak. That makes good use of such a short time. Aeschylus makes Agamemnon come back from Troy with even greater speed. He had agreed with Clytemnestra, his wife, that as soon as the city was taken he would inform her by signal fires built on the intervening mountains, of which the second would be lighted as soon as the first was seen, the third at the sight of the second, and so on; by this means she was to learn the great news the same night. However, scarcely had she learned it from the signal fires when Agamemnon arrives, whose ship, although battered by a storm, if memory serves, must have traveled as fast as the eye could see the lights. *The Cid* and *Pompée*, where the action is a little precipitate, are far from taking so much license; and if they force ordinary probability in some way, at least they do not go as far as such impossibilities.

Many argue against this rule, which they call tyrannical, and they would be right if it were founded only on the authority of Aristotle; but what should make it acceptable is the fact that common sense supports it. The dramatic poem is an imitation, or rather a portrait of human actions, and it is beyond doubt that portraits gain in excellence in proportion as they resemble the original more closely. A performance lasts two hours and would resemble reality perfectly if the action it presented required no more for its actual occurrence. Let us then not settle on twelve or twenty-four hours, but let us compress the action of the poem into the shortest possible period, so that the performance may more closely resemble reality and thus be more nearly perfect. Let us give, if that is possible, to the one no more than the two hours which the other fills. I do not think that *Rodogune* requires much more, and perhaps two hours would be enough for *Cinna*. If we cannot confine the action within the two hours, let us take four, six, or ten, but let us not go much beyond twenty-four for fear of falling into lawlessness and of so far reducing the scale of the portrait that it no longer has its proportionate dimensions and is nothing but imperfection.

Most of all, I should like to leave the matter of duration to the imagination of the spectators and never make definite the time the action requires unless the subject needs this precision, but especially not when probability is a little forced, as in the *Cid*, because precision serves only to make the crowded action obvious to the spectator. Even when no violence is done to a poem by the necessity of obeying this rule, why must one state at the beginning that the sun is rising, that it is noon at the third act, and that the sun is setting at the end of the last act? This is only an obtrusive affectation; it is enough to establish the possibility of the thing in the time one gives to it and that one be able to determine the time easily if one wishes to pay attention to it, but without being compelled to concern oneself with the matter. Even in those actions which take no longer than the performance it would be clumsy to point out that a half hour has elapsed between the beginning of one act and the beginning of the next.

I repeat what I have said elsewhere, that when we take a longer time, as, for instance, ten hours, I should prefer that the eight extra be used up in the time between the acts and that each act should have as its share only as much time as performance requires especially when all scenes are closely linked together. I think, however, that the fifth act, by special privilege, has the right to accelerate time so that the part of the action which it presents may use up more time than is necessary for performance. The reason for this is that the spectator is by then impatient to see the end, and when the outcome depends on actors who are off stage, all the dialogue given to those who are on stage awaiting news of the others drags and action seems to halt. There is no doubt that from the point where Phocas exits in the fifth act of *Héraclius* until Amyntas enters to relate the manner of his death, more time is needed for what happens off stage than for the speaking of the lines in which Héraclius, Martian, and Pulchérie complain of their misfortune. Prusias and Flaminius, in the fifth act of *Nicomède*, do not have the time they would need to meet at sea, take counsel with each other, and return to the defense of the queen; and the Cid has not enough time to fight a duel with Don Sanche during the conversations of the Infanta with Léonor and of Chimène with Elvire. I was aware of this and yet have had no scruples about this acceleration of which, perhaps, one might find several examples among the ancients, but the laziness of which I have spoken will force me to rest content with this one, which is from the *Andria* of Terence. Simo slips his son Pamphilus into the house of Glycerium in order to get the old man, Crito, to come out and to clear up with him the question of the birth of his mistress, who happens to be the daughter of Chremes. Pamphilus enters the house, speaks to Crito, asks him for the favor and returns with him; and during this exit, this request, and this re-entry, Simo and Chremes, who remain on stage, speak only one line each, which could not possibly give Pamphilus more than time enough to ask where Crito is, certainly not enough to talk with him and to explain to him the reasons for which he should reveal what he knows about the birth of the unknown girl.

When the conclusion of the action depends on actors who have not left the stage and about whom no one is awaiting news, as in *Cinna* and

Rodogune, the fifth act has no need of this privilege because then all the action takes place in plain sight, as does not happen when part of it occurs off stage after the beginning of the act. The other acts do not merit the same freedom. If there is not time enough to bring back an actor who has made his exit, or to indicate what he has done since that exit, the accounting can be postponed to the following act; and the music, which separates the two acts, may use up as much time as is necessary; but in the fifth act no postponement is possible: attention is exhausted and the end must come quickly.

I cannot forget that although we must reduce the whole tragic action to one day, we can nevertheless make known by a narration or in some other more artful way what the hero of the tragedy has been doing for several years, because there are plays in which the crux of the plot lies in an obscurity of birth which must be brought to light, as in *Oedipus*. I shall not say again that the less one burdens oneself with past actions, the more favorable the spectator will be, because of the lesser degree of trouble he is given when everything takes place in the present and no demands are made on his memory except for what he has seen; but I cannot forget that the choice of a day both illustrious and long-awaited is a great ornament to a poem. The opportunity for this does not always present itself, and in all that I have written until now you will find only four of that kind: the day in *Horace* when two nations are to decide the question of supremacy of empire by a battle; and the ones in *Rodogune*, *Andromède*, and *Don Sanche*. In *Rodogune* it is a day chosen by two sovereigns for the signature of a treaty of peace between the hostile crowns, for a complete reconciliation of the two rival governments through a marriage, and for the elucidation of a more than twenty-year-old secret concerning the right of succession of one of the twin princes on which the fate of the kingdom depends, as does the outcome of both their loves. The days in *Andromède* and *Don Sanche* are not of lesser importance, but, as I have just said, such opportunities do not often present themselves, and in the rest of my works I have been able to choose days remarkable only for what chance makes happen on them and not by the use to which public arrangements destined them long ago.

As for the unity of place, I find no rule concerning it in either Aristotle or Horace. This is what leads many people to believe that this rule was established only as a consequence of the unity of one day, and leads them to imagine that one can stretch the unity of place to cover the points to which a man may go and return in twenty-four hours. This opinion is a little too free, and if one made an actor travel post-haste, the two sides of the theater might represent Paris and Rouen. I could wish, so that the spectator is not at all disturbed, that what is performed before him in two hours might actually be able to take place in two hours, and that what he is shown in a stage setting which does not change might be limited to a room or a hall depending on a choice made beforehand; but often that is so awkward, if not impossible, that one must necessarily find some way to enlarge the place as also the time of the action. I have shown exact unity of place in *Horace*, *Polyeucte*, and *Pompée*, but for that it was necessary to present either only one woman, as in *Polyeucte*; or to arrange that the two who are presented are such close friends and have such closely related interests that they can be always together, as in *Horace*; or that they may react as in *Pompée* where the stress of natural curiosity drives Cléopâtre from her apartments in the second act and Cornélie in the fifth; and both enter the great hall of the king's palace in anticipation of the news they are expecting. The same thing is not true of *Rodogune*: Cléopâtre and she have interests which are too divergent to permit them to express their most secret thoughts in the same place. I might say of that play what I have said of *Cinna*, where, in general, everything happens in Rome and, in particular, half of the action takes place in the quarters of Auguste and half of it in Emilie's apartments. Following that arrangement, the first act of this tragedy would be laid in Rodogune's antechamber, the second, in Cléopâtre's apartments, the third, in Rodogune's; but if the fourth act can begin in Rodogune's apartments it cannot finish there, and what Cléopâtre says to her two sons one after the other would be badly out of place there. The fifth act needs a throne room where a great crowd can be gathered. The same problem is found in *Héraclius*. The first act could very well take place in Phocas's quarters, the second, in Léontine's apartments; but if the third begins in Pulchérie's rooms, it cannot end there, and it is outside the bounds of probability that Phocas should discuss the death of her brother in Pulchérie's apartments.

The ancients, who made their kings speak in a public square, easily kept a rigorous unity of place in their tragedies. Sophocles, however, did not observe it in his *Ajax*, when the hero leaves the stage to find a lonely place in which to kill himself and does so in full view of the people; this easily leads to the conclusion that the place where he kills himself is not the one he has been seen to leave, since he left it only to choose another.

We do not take the same liberty of drawing kings and princesses from their apartments, and since often the difference and the opposition on the part of those who are lodged in the same palace do not allow them to take others into their confidence or to disclose their secrets in the same room, we must seek some other compromise about unity of place if we want to keep it intact in our poems; otherwise we should have to decide against many plays which we see succeeding brilliantly.

I hold, then, that we ought to seek exact unity as much as possible, but as this unity does not suit every kind of subject, I should be very willing to concede that a whole city has unity of place. Not that I should want the stage to represent the whole city, that would be somewhat too large, but only two or three particular places enclosed within its walls. Thus the scene of *Cinna* does not leave Rome, passing from the apartments of Auguste to the house of Emilie. *Le Menteur* takes place in the Tuileries and in the Place Royale at

Paris, and *La Suite* shows us the prison and Mélisse's house at Lyons. *The Cid* increases even more the number of particular places without leaving Seville; and since the close linking of scenes is not observed in that play, the stage in the first act is supposed to represent Chimène's house, the Infante's apartments in the king's palace, and the public square; the second adds to these the king's chamber. No doubt there is some excess in this freedom. In order to rectify in some way this multiplication of places when it is inevitable, I should wish two things done: first, that the scene should never change in a given act but only between the acts, as is done in the first three acts of *Cinna*; the other, that these two places should not need different stage settings and that neither of the two should ever be named, but only the general place which includes them both, as Paris, Rome, Lyons, Constantinople, and so forth. This would help to deceive the spectator, who, seeing nothing that would indicate the difference in the places, would not notice the change, unless it was maliciously and critically pointed out, a thing which few are capable of doing, most spectators being warmly intent upon the action which they see on the stage. The pleasure they take in it is the reason why they do not seek out its imperfections lest they lose their taste for it; and they admit such an imperfection only when forced, when it is too obvious, as in *Le Menteur* and *La Suite*, where the different settings force them to recognize the multiplicity of places in spite of themselves.

But since people of opposing interests cannot with verisimilitude unfold their secrets in the same place, and since they are sometimes introduced into the same act through the linking of scenes which the unity of place necessarily produces, one must find some means to make it compatible with the contradiction which rigorous probability finds in it, and consider how to preserve the fourth act of *Rodogune* and the third of *Héraclius*, in both of which I have already pointed out the contradiction which lies in having enemies speak in the same place. Jurists allow legal fictions, and I should like, following their example, to introduce theatrical fictions by which one could establish a theatrical place which would not be Cléopâtre's chamber nor Rodogune's, in the play of that name, nor that of Phocas, of Léontine or of Pulchérie in *Héraclius*, but a room contiguous to all these other apartments, to which I should attribute these two privileges: first, that each of those who speaks in it is presumed to enjoy the same secrecy there as if he were in his own room; and second, that whereas in the usual arrangement it is sometimes proper for those who are on stage to go off, in order to speak privately with others in their rooms, these latter might meet the former on stage without shocking convention, so as to preserve both the unity of place and the linking of scenes. Thus Rodogune, in the first act, encounters Laonice, whom she must send for so as to speak with her; and, in the fourth act, Cléopâtre encounters Antiochus on the very spot where he has just moved Rodogune to pity, even though in utter verisimilitude the prince ought to seek out his mother in her own room since she hates the princess too much to come to speak to him in Rodogune's, which, following the first scene, would be the locus of the whole act, if one did not introduce that compromise which I have mentioned into the rigorous unity of place.

Many of my plays will be at fault in the unity of place if this compromise is not accepted, for I shall abide by it always in the future when I am not able to satisfy the ultimate rigor of the rule. I have been able to reduce only three plays, *Horace*, *Polyeucte*, and *Pompée*, to the requirements of the rule. If I am too indulgent with myself as far as the others are concerned, I shall be even more so for those which may succeed on the stage through some appearance of regularity. It is easy for critics to be severe; but if they were to give ten or a dozen plays to the public, they might perhaps slacken the rules more than I do, as soon as they have recognized through experience what constraint their precision brings about and how many beautiful things it banishes from our stage. However that may be, these are my opinions, or if you prefer, my heresies concerning the principal points of the dramatic art, and I do not know how better to make the ancient rules agree with modern pleasures. I do not doubt that one might easily find better ways of doing that, and I shall be ready to accept them when they have been put into practice as successfully as, by common consent, mine have been.

JOHN DRYDEN

John DRYDEN (1631-1700) was short and plump, "of a fresh color, and a down look—and not very conversible," according to Alexander Pope. Like his spokesman Neander in *An Essay of Dramatic Poesy*, Dryden represented the new man from a new class for a new age: the professional writer who associates primarily with other literary figures and is not regarded by polite society as "very genteel," although he aspires to that condition.

Lacking a title or fortune, Dryden had to earn his living by his pen. By nature a supporter of *de facto* authority, he readily adapted to the shifting taste and temper of his age and was always in accord with his times, accommodating in politics and in poetic fashions.

In Restoration England playwriting was the most lucrative art and the surest road to fame. So Dryden chose to make his way in the world through the theatre. Because his plays pleased the king and the court, he was appointed Poet Laureate in 1668 (the year he published *An Essay of Dramatic Poesy*). Enjoying royal favor, but finding himself irregularly paid and infrequently employed, the new laureate sought profitable financial arrangements with London theatres. For ten years three of Dryden's plays were premiered each season at the Theatre Royal by the King's Company with which he had an exclusive contract. In return, the author became a shareholder, receiving one and a quarter shares (as did the three principal actors).

But his life as a playwright embroiled Dryden in controversy and vituperative quarrels. He was frequently attacked in pamphlets and on the stage in a malicious satire, *The Rehearsal*. A nasty dispute with his brother-in-law Sir Robert Howard on theatrical matters finally led to physical violence; late one night in a dark alley, the playwright was waylaid and beaten by three masked thugs.

Longing to be free of the drudgery of playwriting, Dryden had an ambivalent, often hostile attitude towards the theatre. Stage performance, he felt, impeded an audience's ability to understand ideas and appreciate language. "'Tis my ambition to be read," the playwright admitted, "that I am sure is the most lasting and the nobler design." Sharing his literary colleagues' bias against spectacle as an appeal to the senses, not the imagination, he rejected Italian *commedia* and condemned plays that featured animals, thunder and lightning, and "machines." Towards the end of his career Dryden was happy to renounce the theatre forever and concentrate on work that he preferred: the writing of poetry and essays.

But in the summer of 1665 when Dryden and his wife fled plague-stricken London for the countryside taking along only a few books, the theatres had been re-opened for only a few years and there were exciting new critical ideas from France to be debated. There in a quiet rustic setting Dryden went fishing and wrote theory (*An Essay of Dramatic Poesy*), paraphrasing and quoting directly from Corneille's *Prefaces* that lay open on the desk. Never having been to France, Dryden knew the French dramatist's plays not from theatre, but from the study.

In *An Essay of Dramatic Poesy*, Dryden created a new kind of theoretical work addressed to a cultivated audience of non-specialists and written in an urbane conversational prose that avoided the technical jargon and arrogant long-windedness of bickering pedants. The dialogue form allowed the author not to commit himself to any single point of view, but to debate the key issues of ancient versus modern, French versus English, and blank verse versus rhyme.

By taking into account the historical and social context in which works of art arose, Dryden discovered the idea of national and cultural relativism and introduced the comparative method into English literary criticism.

"The genius of each age is different," he argued; "Shakespeare and Fletcher have written to the genius of the age and nation in which they lived; for though nature is the same in all places, and reason too the same, yet the climate, the age, the disposition of the people, to which a poet writes, may be so different, that what pleased the Greeks would not satisfy an English audience." One must write for one's own audience was Dryden's pragmatic conclusion.

AN ESSAY OF DRAMATIC POESY (1668)

[...] Lisideius concluded in this manner; and Neander, after a little pause, thus answered him:

"I shall grant Lisideius, without much dispute, a great part of what he has urged against us; for I acknowledge that the French contrive their plots more regularly and observe the laws of comedy and decorum of the stage (to speak generally) with more exactness than the English. Farther, I deny not but he has taxed us justly in some irregularities of ours which he has mentioned; yet, after all, I am of opinion that neither our faults nor their virtues are considerable enough to place them above us.

"For the lively imitation of nature being in the definition of a play, those which best fulfill that law ought to be esteemed superior to the others. Tis true, those beauties of the French poesy are such as will raise perfection higher where it is, but are not sufficient to give it where it is not; they are indeed the beauties of a statue but not of a man, because not animated with the soul of poesy, which is imitation of humor and passions; and this Lisideius himself or any other, however biased to their party, cannot but acknowledge, if he will either compare the humors of our comedies or the characters of our serious plays with theirs. He who will look upon theirs which have been written till these last ten years, or thereabouts, will find it a hard matter to pick out two or three passable humors amongst them. Corneille himself their arch-poet, what has he produced except *The Liar?* and you know how it was cried up in France; but when it came upon the English stage, though well translated and that part of Dorant acted to so much advantage as I am confident it never received in its own country, the most favorable to it would not put it in competition with many of Fletcher's or Ben Jonson's. In the rest of Corneille's comedies you have little humor; he tells you himself his way is first to show two lovers in good intelligence with each other; in the working up of the play to embroil them by some mistake and in the latter end to clear it and reconcile them.

"But of late years Molière, the younger Corneille, Quinault, and some others have been imitating afar off the quick turns and graces of the English

From *The Works of John Dryden*, Vol. II.
Edinburgh: William Patterson, 1883.

stage. They have mixed their serious plays with mirth, like our tragicomedies, since the death of Cardinal Richelieu; which Lisideius and many others not observing have commended that in them for a virtue which they themselves no longer practice. Most of their new plays are, like some of ours, derived from the Spanish novels. There is scarce one of them without a veil, and a trusty Diego who drolls much after the rate of *The Adventures*. But their humors, if I may grace them with that name, are so thin-sown that never above one of them comes up in any play. I dare take upon me to find more variety of them in some one play of Ben Jonson's than in all theirs together; as he who has seen *The Alchemist*, *The Silent Woman*, or *Bartholomew Fair* cannot but acknowledge with me.

"I grant the French have performed what was possible on the ground-work of the Spanish plays; what was pleasant before, they have made regular; but there is not above one good play to be writ on all those plots; they are too much alike to please often; which we need not the experience of our own stage to justify. As for their new way of mingling mirth with serious plot, I do not, with Lisideius, condemn the thing, though I cannot approve their manner of doing it. He tells us we cannot so speedily recollect ourselves after a scene of great passion and concernment as to pass to another of mirth and humor and to enjoy it with any relish; but why should he imagine the soul of man more heavy than his senses? Does not the eye pass from an unpleasant object to a pleasant in a much shorter time than is required to this? and does not the unpleasantness of the first commend the beauty of the latter? The old rule of logic might have convinced him that contraries, when placed near, set off each other. A continued gravity keeps the spirit too much bent; we must refresh it sometimes, as we bait in a journey that we may go on with greater ease. A scene of mirth, mixed with tragedy, has the same effect upon us which our music has between the acts; which we find a relief to us from the best plots and language of the stage, if the discourses have been long. I must therefore have stronger arguments ere I am convinced that compassion and mirth in the same subject destroy each other; and in the meantime cannot but conclude, to the honor of our nation, that we have invented, increased, and perfected a more pleasant way of writing for the stage than was ever known to the ancients or moderns of any nation, which is tragi-comedy.

"And this leads me to wonder why Lisideius and many others should cry up the barrenness of the French plots above the variety and copiousness of the English. Their plots are single; they carry on one design which is pushed forward by all the actors, every scene in the play contributing and moving towards it. Our plays, besides the main design, have under-plots or by-concernments of less considerable persons and intrigues, which are carried on with the motion of the main plot: as they say the orb of the fixed stars and those of the planets, though they have motions of their own, are whirled about by the motion of the *primum mobile*, in which they are contained. That similitude expresses much of the English stage; for if contrary motions may be found in nature to agree, if a planet can go east and west at the same time—one way by virtue of his own motion, the other by the force of the first mover—it will not be difficult to imagine how the under-plot, which is only different, not contrary to the great design, may naturally be conducted along with it.

"Eugenius has already shown us, from the confession of the French poets, that the unity of action is sufficiently preserved if all the imperfect actions of the play are conducing to the main design; but when those petty intrigues of a play are so ill ordered that they have no coherence with the other, I must grant that Lisideius has reason to tax that want of due connection; for co-ordination in a play is as dangerous and unnatural as in a state. In the meantime he must acknowledge our variety, if well ordered, will afford a greater pleasure to the audience.

"As for his other argument, that by pursuing one single theme they gain an advantage to express and work up the passions, I wish any example he could bring from them would make it good; for I confess their verses are to me the coldest I have ever read. Neither, indeed, is it possible for them, in the way they take, so to express passion as that the effects of it should appear in the concernment of an audience, their speeches being so many declamations which tire us with the length; so that instead of persuading us to grieve for their imaginary heroes, we are concerned for our own trouble, as we are in tedious visits of bad company; we are in pain till they are gone. [. . .] But to speak generally, it cannot be denied that short speeches and replies are more apt to move the passions and beget concernment in us than the other; for it is unnatural for any one in a gust of passion to speak long together, or for another in the same condition to suffer him without interruption. Grief and passion are like floods raised in little brooks by a sudden rain; they are quickly up; and if the concernment be poured unexpectedly in upon us, it overflows us; but a long sober shower gives them leisure to run out as they came in, without troubling the ordinary current. As for comedy, repartee is one of its chiefest graces; the greatest pleasure of the audience is a chase of wit, kept up on both sides and swiftly managed. And this our forefathers, if not we, have had in Fletcher's plays to a much higher degree of perfection than the French poets can reasonably hope to reach.

"There is another part of Lisideius's discourse in which he has rather excused our neighbors than commended them; that is, for aiming only to make one person considerable in their plays. 'Tis very true what he has urged, that one character in all plays, even without the poet's care, will have advantage of all the others, and that the design of the whole drama will chiefly depend on it. But this hinders not that there may be more shining characters in the play, many persons of a second magnitude, nay, some so very near, so almost equal to the first that greatness may be opposed to greatness and all the persons be made considerable, not only by their quality but their action. 'Tis evident that the more the persons are, the greater will be the variety of the plot. If then the parts are managed so regularly that the beauty of the whole be kept entire and that the variety become not a perplexed and confused mass of accidents, you will find it infinitely pleasing to be led in a labyrinth of design where you see some of your way before you, yet discern not the end till you arrive at it. And that all this is practicable I can produce for examples many of our English plays, *The Maid's Tragedy*, *The Alchemist*, *The Silent Woman*; I was going to have named *The Fox*, but that the unity of design seems not exactly observed in it, for there appear two actions in the play, the first naturally ending with the fourth act, the second forced from it in the fifth; which yet is the less to be condemned in him because the disguise of Volpone, though it suited not with his character as a crafty or covetous person, agreed well enough with that of a voluptuary; and by it the poet gained the end at which he aimed, the punishment of vice and the reward of virtue, both which that disguise produced. So that to judge equally of it, it was an excellent fifth act but not so naturally proceeding from the former

"But to leave this and pass to the latter part of Lisideius's discourse, which concerns relations: I must acknowledge with him that the French have reason to hide that part of the action which would occasion too much tumult on the stage, and to choose rather to have it made known by narration to the audience. Farther, I think it very convenient, for the reasons he has given, that all incredible actions were removed; but whether custom has so insinuated itself into our countrymen or nature has so formed them to fierceness, I know not; but they will scarcely suffer combats and other objects of horror to be taken from them. And indeed, the indecency of tumults is all which can be objected against fighting; for why may not our imagination as well suffer itself to be deluded with the probability of it as with any other thing in the play? For my part, I can with as great ease persuade myself that the blows are given in good earnest, as I can that they who strike them are kings or princes or those persons which they represent. For objects of incredibility, I would be satisfied from Lisideius whether we have any so removed from all appearance of truth as are those of Corneille's *Andromède*, a play which has been frequented the most of any he has writ. If the Perseus, or the son of an heathen god, the Pegasus, and the Monster were not capable to choke a strong belief, let him blame any representation of ours hereafter. Those indeed were objects of delight; yet the reason is the same as to the probability, for he makes it not a ballet or masque but a play, which is to resemble truth. But for death, that it ought not to be represented, I have, besides the arguments alleged by Lisideius, the authority of Ben Jonson, who has forborne it in his tragedies, for both the death of Sejanus and Catiline are related; though in the latter I cannot but observe one irregularity of that great poet: he has removed the scene in the same act from Rome to Catiline's army, and from thence again to

Rome; and besides, has allowed a very inconsiderable time after Catiline's speech for the striking of the battle and the return of Petreius, who is to relate the event of it to the senate; which I should not animadvert on him, who was otherwise a painful observer of [...] the *decorum* of the stage, if he had not used extreme severity in his judgment on the incomparable Shakespeare for the same fault. To conclude on this subject of relations; if we are to be blamed for showing too much of the action, the French are as faulty for discovering too little of it; a mean betwixt both should be observed by every judicious writer, so as the audience may neither be left unsatisfied by not seeing what is beautiful, or shocked by beholding what is either incredible or undecent.

"I hope I have already proved in this discourse that though we are not altogether so punctual as the French in observing the laws of comedy, yet our errors are so few and little and those things wherein we excel them so considerable that we ought of right to be preferred before them. But what will Lisideius say if they themselves acknowledge they are too strictly bounded by those laws for which he has blamed the English? I will allege Corneille's words as I find them in the end of his Discourse of the Three Unities: *Il est facile aux spéculatifs d'être sévères etc.*" 'Tis easy for speculative persons to judge severely; but if they would produce to public view ten or twelve pieces of this nature, they would perhaps give more latitude to the rules than I have done, when by experience they had known how much we are limited and constrained by them and how many beauties of the stage they banished from it." To illustrate a little what he has said: by their servile observations of the unities of time and place and integrity of scenes, they have brought on themselves that dearth of plot and narrowness of imagination which may be observed in all their plays. How many beautiful accidents might naturally happen in two or three days which cannot arrive with any probability in the compass of twenty-four hours? There is time to be allowed also for maturity of design, which amongst great and prudent persons such as are often represented in tragedy cannot, with any likelihood of truth, be brought to pass at so short a warning. Farther, by tying themselves strictly to the unity of place and unbroken scenes, they are forced many times to omit some beauties which cannot be shown where the act began; but might, if the scene were interrupted and the stage cleared for the persons to enter in another place; and therefore the French poets are often forced upon absurdities; for if the act begins in a chamber, all the persons in the play must have some business or other to come thither or else they are not to be shown that act; and sometimes their characters are very unfitting to appear there. As suppose it were the king's bed-chamber; yet the meanest man in the tragedy must come and dispatch his business there rather than in the lobby or courtyard (which is fitter for him), for fear the stage should be cleared and the scenes broken. Many times they fall by it in a greater inconvenience; for they keep their scenes unbroken and yet change the place, as in one of their newest plays where the act begins in the street. There a gentleman is to meet his friend; he sees him with his man, coming out from his father's house; they talk together, and the first goes out; the second, who is a lover, has made an appointment with his mistress; she appears at the window, and then we are to imagine the scene lies under it. This gentleman is called away and leaves his servant with his mistress; presently her father is heard from within; the young lady is afraid the serving-man should be discovered and thrusts him into a place of safety, which is supposed to be her closet. After this the father enters to the daughter, and now the scene is in a house, for he is seeking from one room to another for this poor Philipin, or French Diego, who is heard from within, drolling and breaking many a miserable conceit on the subject of his sad condition. In this ridiculous manner the play goes forward, the stage being never empty all the while; so that the street, the window, the houses, and the closet are made to walk about and the persons to stand still. Now what, I beseech you, is more easy than to write a regular French play, or more difficult than to write an irregular English one, like those of Fletcher, or of Shakespeare?

"If they content themselves, as Corneille did, with some flat design which, like an ill riddle, is found out ere it be half proposed, such plots we can make every way regular, as easily as they; but whenever they endeavor to rise to any quick turns and counterturns of plot, as some of them have attempted since Corneille's plays have been less in vogue, you see they write as irregularly as we, though they cover it more speciously. Hence the reason is perspicuous why no French plays, when translated, have or ever can succeed on the English stage. For if you consider the plots, our own are fuller of variety; if the writing, ours are more quick and fuller of spirit; and therefore 'tis a strange mistake in those who decry the way of writing plays in verse, as if the English therein imitated the French. We have borrowed nothing from them; our plots are weaved in English looms; we endeavor therein to follow the variety and greatness of characters which are derived to us from Shakespeare and Fletcher; the copiousness and well-knitting of the intrigues we have from Jonson; and for the verse itself we have English precedents of elder date than any of Corneille's plays. Not to name our old comedies before Shakespeare, which were all writ in verse of six feet or Alexandrines, such as the French now use, I can show in Shakespeare many scenes of rhyme together, and the like in Ben Jonson's tragedies; in *Catiline* and *Sejanus* sometimes thirty or forty lines—I mean besides the chorus or the monologues; which, by the way, showed Ben no enemy to this way of writing, especially if you read his *Sad Shepherd*, which goes sometimes on rhyme, sometimes on blank verse, like an horse who eases himself on trot and amble. You find him likewise commending Fletcher's pastoral of *The Faithful Shepherdess*, which is for the most part rhyme, though not refined to that purity to which it hath since been brought. And these examples are enough to clear us from a servile imitation of the French.

"But to return whence I have digressed, I dare boldly affirm these two things of the English drama: First, that we have many plays of ours as regular as any of theirs, and which besides have more variety of plot and characters; and secondly, that in most of the irregular plays of Shakespeare or Fletcher (for Ben Jonson's are for the most part regular) there is a more masculine fancy and greater spirit in the writing than there is in any of the French. I could produce, even in Shakespeare's and Fletcher's works some plays which are almost exactly formed, as *The Merry Wives of Windsor*, and *The Scornful Lady*; but because (generally speaking) Shakespeare, who writ first, did not perfectly observe the laws of comedy and Fletcher, who came nearer to perfection, yet through carelessness made many faults, I will take the pattern of a perfect play from Ben Jonson, who was a careful and learned observer of the dramatic laws, and from all his comedies I shall select *The Silent Woman*, of which I will make a short examen, according to those rules which the French observe."

As Neander was beginning to examine *The Silent Woman*, Eugenius, earnestly regarding him: "I beseech you, Neander," said he, "gratify the company and me in particular so far as, before you speak of the play, to give us a character of the author; and tell us frankly your opinion, whether you do not think all writers, both French and English, ought to give place to him." "I fear," replied Neander," that in obeying your commands I shall draw some envy on myself. Besides, in performing them, it will be first necessary to speak somewhat of Shakespeare and Fletcher, his rivals in poesy; and one of them in my opinion at least his equal, perhaps his superior.

"To begin, then, with Shakespeare. He was the man who of all modern and perhaps ancient poets had the largest and most comprehensive soul. All the images of nature were still present to him, and he drew them not laboriously but luckily; when he describes anything, you more than see it, you feel it too. Those who accuse him to have wanted learning give him the greater commendation; he was naturally learned; he needed not the spectacles of books to read nature; he looked inwards and found her there. I cannot say he is everywhere alike; were he so, I should do him injury to compare him with the greatest of mankind. He is many times flat, insipid; his comic wit degenerating into clenches, his serious swelling into bombast. But he is always great when some great occasion is presented to him; no man can say he ever had a fit subject for his wit and did not then raise himself as high above the rest of poets,

Quantum lenta solent inter viburna cupressi.

The consideration of this made Mr. Hales of Eton say that there was no subject of which any poet ever writ but he would produce it much better done in Shakespeare; and however others are now generally preferred before him, yet the age wherein he lived, which had contemporaries with him Fletcher and Jonson, never equaled them to him in their esteem; and in the last king's court, when Ben's reputation was at highest, Sir John Suckling and with him the greater part of the courtiers set our Shakespeare far above him.

"Beaumont and Fletcher, of whom I am next to speak, had, with the advantage of Shakespeare's wit, which was their precedent, great natural gifts improved by study, Beaumont especially being so accurate a judge of plays that Ben Jonson, while he lived, submitted all his writings to his censure, and 'tis thought used his judgment in correcting, if not contriving, all his plots. What value he had for him appears by the verses he writ to him; and therefore I need speak no farther of it. The first play that brought Fletcher and him in esteem was their *Philaster*, for before that they had written two or three very unsuccessfully, as the like is reported of Ben Jonson before he writ *Every Man in His Humor*. Their plots were generally more regular than Shakespeare's, especially those which were made before Beaumont's death, and they understood and imitated the conversation of gentlemen much better, whose wild debaucheries and quickness of wit in repartees no poet before them could paint as they have done. Humor, which Ben Jonson derived from particular persons, they made it not their business to describe; they represented all the passions very lively, but above all love. I am apt to believe the English language in them arrived to its highest perfection; what words have since been taken in are rather superfluous than ornamental. Their plays are now the most pleasant and frequent entertainments of the stage, two of theirs being acted through the year for one of Shakespeare's or Jonson's; the reason is because there is a certain gaiety in their comedies and pathos in their more serious plays which suits generally with all men's humors. Shakespeare's language is likewise a little obsolete, and Ben Jonson's wit comes short of theirs.

"As for Jonson, to whose character I am now arrived, if we look upon him while he was himself (for his last plays were but his dotages), I think him the most learned and judicious writer which any theater ever had. He was a most severe judge of himself as well as others. One cannot say he wanted wit, but rather that he was frugal of it. In his works you find little to retrench or alter. Wit and language and humor also in some measure we had before him; but something of art was wanting to the drama till he came. He managed his strength to more advantage than any who preceded him. You seldom find him making love in any of his scenes, or endeavoring to move the passions; his genius was too sullen and saturnine to do it gracefully, especially when he knew he came after those who had performed both to such a height. Humor was his proper sphere; and in that he was delighted most to represent mechanic people. He was deeply conversant in the ancients, both Greek and Latin, and he borrowed boldly from them; there is scarce a poet or historian among the Roman authors of those times whom he has not translated in *Sejanus* and *Catiline*. But he has done his robberies so openly that one may see he fears not to be taxed by any law. He invades authors like a monarch; and what would be theft in other poets is only victory in him. With the spoils of these writers he so represents old Rome to us, in its rites, ceremonies, and customs, that if one of their poets had written either of his tragedies, we had seen less of it than in him. If there was any fault in his language, 'twas that he weaved it too closely and laboriously, in his comedies especially; perhaps too, he did a little too much Romanize our tongue, leaving the words which he translated almost as much Latin as he found them; wherein, though he learnedly followed their language, he did not enough comply with the idiom of ours. If I would compare him with Shakespeare, I must acknowledge him the more correct poet but Shakespeare the greater wit. Shakespeare was the Homer or father of our dramatic poets; Jonson was the Virgil, the pattern of elaborate writing; I admire him, but I love Shakespeare. To conclude of him; as he has given us the most correct plays, so in the precepts which he has laid down in his *Discoveries* we have as many and profitable rules for perfecting the stage as any wherewith the French can furnish us." [...]

LI YU

LI YU (1611-1680) went by many names, calling himself "The leaf-hatted old man on the lake," "The old man with the bamboo rain-hat," and "The fisherman of the lake." Li had a dozen or more personae—as poet, novelist, essayist, pornographer, inventor, garden designer, conversationalist, comedian, publisher, bookseller, and as playwright, manager, producer, and director for his own company of actresses, with whom he toured throughout China.

By the mid-seventeenth century China had entered into an era of aggressive profit-making and pleasure-seeking that fostered a new eating culture, the wearing of extravagant clothes, and the growth of an entertainment industry.

The product of this new age of materialism, rationalism, and skepticism, Li Yu represented a modern breed of professional writer. As a highly educated entrepreneur and business man, he knew how to join commerce to art and dared criticize the great literary playwrights of the past and advance a novel theory of theatre to justify his own innovative practices.

From the start Li Yu has been a controversial figure, attacked for his crass hucksterism and dismissed as a roaming stage impresario preying on wealthy patrons, from whom he begged money in wheedling letters predicting his imminent starvation. The Confucian code condemned as acquisitive business ventures like Li's troupe of sing-song girls, and prejudice against the theatrical profession kept such a popular entertainer from being accepted as a serious writer and even led to his works being proscribed in later periods.

Although trained in classical poetry and prose, Li could not pass the requisite examinations for an academic or government career. Caught in the social turmoil and warfare during the Manchu conquest (as the Qing Dynasty replaced the Ming), the writer was forced to abandon his home and flee for his life. His townhouse, library, and writings were burned.

Having neither inherited fortune nor bureaucratic position, he was obliged to earn his own living, but proved incapable of subsisting within his means, displaying a weakness for elegant houses, fancy clothes, and extravagant entertaining. He became a printer and started a publishing house and quality bookstore, called the Mustard Seed Garden after his diminutive hill-top home in Nanking. The sale of exquisite editions produced a steady income, but the main source of the money he needed to support his large household of over forty wives, concubines, children, and servants came from performances by his singing girls for high-ranking officials and patrons of wealth and culture who maintained private theatres in their homes. At the height of his popularity, the elite competed to host Li Yu and give him rewards.

The company came into being accidentally as a household troupe when two of Li's teenage concubines, given him as gifts, asked to be taught singing and dancing. Ch'iao appeared in the principal female roles, and Wang played the male leads, delighting her master with her transvestite costumes. Li wrote new plays for the girls and reworked the classics, maintaining that old plays like beautiful women need new clothes to keep them interesting. His other concubines joined the theatrical study group that at first performed only for family, friends, and small invited audiences. Quick to profit from the family troupe, Li embarked on extended tours throughout China in 1667, but both his stars died young at only eighteen. Grief-stricken, Li wrote a combined biography of the two girls who had been his joy and inspiration.

In his actor training, Li stressed the need for the performers, who came from poor and often illiterate families, to understand the meaning of the songs they sang. He taught the girls by demonstrating how they should sing and move himself.

Li's ideas on stagecraft and stage management and his theories of playwriting and acting grew directly out of his theatrical practice as director and producer. An analysis of the author's own domestic pleasures and pursuits (until then the private self had not been considered a worthy subject) unified by his multifaceted persona, *Casual Expression of Idle Feelings* contains 300 essays on the composition and writing of plays, theatrical production, women and beauty, houses and gardens, furniture and objets d'art, food and drink, flowers and trees, and health and pleasure. Designed for a broad readership, *Casual Expression* is written in a new, less formal style, closer to the vernacular and similar in tone to the artist's conversations with his rich and powerful patrons.

Living in an age of science, Li wrote botanical treatises on flowers and trees, promoted technological discoveries that could contribute to people's well-being in their daily lives, and held revolutionary views about the uses of psychotherapy for self-fulfillment and gratification of hidden desires. Because of his belief in the practical values of drama for increasing human happiness, Li placed his comments on playwriting, actor training, and theatre management in a "how to" compendium that includes advice on cooking, clothing, home furnishing, hobbies, bird-watching, grooming, cosmetics, and hairstyles for women, as well as tips on sexual fulfillment as the greatest source of satisfaction. Like the proper methods of cooking rice, the rules of playwriting and stage management belong to the arts of living designed to increase humankind's pleasures. A book about how to get the most out of life, *Casual Expression of Idle Feelings* contains proposals for new household conveniences and domestic utensils that Li has invented, such as his heated armchair for winter and porcelain cooling bench for summer.

CASUAL EXPRESSIONS OF IDLE FEELINGS (1671)

On Playwriting

Playwriting has been considered as the least important of literary skills, ranking just slightly higher than hobbies like horse-racing, sword-fighting, wine-tasting or gambling. [...] I say a skill is a skill, big or small, and it should be valued by a person's proficiency at it. If you are really good at what you do, you can make a name for yourself. [...] The writing of drama not only has made writers famous, but it has even attracted some former emperors, and because of their skill in this literary genre their names and statecraft have been remembered by posterity. Let history speak for itself: writers like Gao Zecheng and Wang Shifu were noted scholars of the Yuan Dynasty, but their fame rests primarily on their plays. Had the first not written *The Lute* and the second *The West Chamber*, who would remember their names today? It is *The Lute* and *The West Chamber* that have kept their names alive. Tang Xianzu, a genius of the Ming Dynasty, is noted for his poetry, essays, and correspondence, but he is a household name today not because of those works but because of his play *The Return of the Soul* [another title of *The Peony Pavilion*]. Had he not penned the play, Tang would not have been remembered. Each dynasty has been outstanding in one particular type of literary genre, as indicated by the tried but true phrases: "Han History," "Tang Poetry," "Song Prose," and "Yuan Drama." Were it not for the tremendous output of plays, including *The Lute* and *The West Chamber*, the memory of the Yuan, which was intrinsically wanting in any other achievements, would have quickly faded and certainly would not have stood a chance of being esteemed by the learned along with the three other great dynasties. A dynasty's position in history rests on the plays that it produced. Therefore, while different from other genres, the art of playwriting is not a minor skill but ranks high, along with history, biography, poetry, and prose.

The central brain. What is the central brain of a play? It is nothing but the germ from which the author develops the work. In a play there are many characters, but they all have supporting roles in relation to the single

A new translation by Faye C. Fei and William H. Sun © 2000.

leading character from whom the play originates. It is this character's experience of life's vicissitudes that unites the play from beginning to end; everything else, no matter how sensational, colorful, or complex, is there merely as an accompaniment. A play not only germinates from a single character, it comes from one single inciting incident related to that character. Taken together, this character and this incident make up the central brain of the play. Only when this character and this incident are truly extraordinary can the play be worthy of passing from generation to generation, resulting in the eternal life of the character, the incident, and the author. [...]

Many of today's playwrights know how to write about one all-important character, but they often do not know how to write starting from one inciting incident. They enumerate the character's deeds one by one, as though they were spreading pieces of gold and jade all over the place. As individual pieces they are all fine, but they do not make a good full-length play, because they are loose pearls without a string, a house without a beam. When the author does not know where to begin, naturally the audience does not know what to follow. No wonder theatre lovers have drifted away! Many writers make this mistake. Now that I have pointed it out, I hope the number will get smaller and smaller.

Unity and wit. Unity and wit (*jiqu*) are two indispensable qualities in drama. The former is the internal spirit of drama, the latter is its external manifestation. Lacking these two qualities, a play is like a clay man or a clay horse, possessing only the shape of a living form without the breathing spirit—clearly the result of a playwright's inferior craftsmanship. Such a playwright pads out his play line by line, forcing his audience to remember the play section by section. If the audience becomes in the least inattentive, it will be impossible to recall what the previous song or scene was about. Watching the second act, the audience will have no idea what is likely to happen in the next act. A play put together in such a disconnected and disunified manner is a waste of time both for the writer and the spectators, who suffer pain from straining their eyes and ears. Eliminate disunity, eliminate pedantic and affected ways.

When I use the word unity, I do not simply mean that one scene follows another or that a single actor plays one character. Rather I mean that the action of the play should be unified, coherent, and as interconnected as the veins are by the blood that flows through them. Even seemingly unrelated incidents should have hidden connections to the main action that gradually become evident, just as the fibers of the lotus root remain intricately interconnected even though it has been snapped in half. Unity is essential.

When I say use wit and eliminate pedantry and affectation, I am not just talking about romantic love stories. The same principle also applies to subject matter concerning loyalty, filial piety, moral integrity, and righteousness, or dealing with the emotions of grief, pain, sorrow, and enmity. Wit refers to the ability to challenge authority, to do the unexpected, to make people laugh through their tears. [...]

It takes a special gift to be a playwright. If someone is not endowed with this gift, he simply is not suited to be a playwright no matter how hard he tries. It is really not hard to tell if someone is gifted or not. You will know by observing how this person speaks and writes. If his conversation is not pedantic, he will show his inventiveness in one or two sentences out of every ten; if his writing is not wooden, he will have one or two paragraphs that are truly inspired in every essay. If he is also endowed with great imagination, then this person is suited to write plays. If one is not born with such a gift, he is far better off doing something other than trying to write plays. [...]

Beware of the superficial. Drama is the most complex form of writing. There are so many different things to attend to, such as, for example, creating distinct characters who come to life on the stage and developing credible situations and actions. I feel that the ability to handle "emotion" (*qing*) and the ability to handle "scene" (*jing*) constitute the two most important challenges for a playwright. Emotion is what is felt in each character's heart, whereas a scene is what is observed by everyone in the external world. One comes from the inside, the other comes from the outside. It is easy to depict a scene, but it is difficult to describe emotions. These two things are as far apart as heaven and earth. A person's emotions are his alone. Zhang San [Tom] feels differently than Li Si [Dick], and therefore their emotions must be described differently. The external scenes, however, are shared by many. In describing spring and summer, a playwright needs only to distinguish them from autumn and winter. Gifted playwrights naturally devote themselves more to the hard work of conveying inner emotions and less to the easy job of describing external scenes. Those who excel in depicting mountain-and-river excursion scenes will only succeed partially if they cannot handle the emotions of each of their characters.

The truth of language. Of all literary endeavors, playwriting is the most heroic, most magnificent, and most satisfying, and it even does wonders for one's physical well-being. Without this genre, the gifted and talented would feel stifled, the brave and the gallant would feel trapped. I was born into turmoil and accompanied by hardship from childhood to old age. Worries and anxieties temporarily leave me only when I write plays. On those occasions, I feel not only that I am ridding myself of my grievances, but also that I am secretly becoming the happiest man between heaven and earth, reveling in so much luxury and glory that what is desired in real life all seems paltry compared to the illusions I create. If I fancy being a mandarin, I am gloriously promoted to the top at once. If I desire to leave office and live like a recluse, in a wink I am transported to the wooded mountains. [...]

Writing in other literary genres, you can make an allegory only through various implicit means. If you have ten points of grievance, you can express only three or four directly. If you have eight buckets of talent, you can only pour out two or three. If you are just a bit unconventional and unhampered in expressing yourself, you are considered lacking in proper Confucian composure, accused of being reckless and frivolous, thus ruining your chance of having your work reach every household. To write a play, on the contrary, is to say what you mean to say and to say all you want to say. The worst enemy for a playwright is the implicit and restraint.

To speak without inhibition is not as easy as it sounds. Language is the expression of the feelings of the heart. If you are to speak for a character, you must first reveal the feelings of the character you are going to portray. And how can you put yourself in someone else's shoes without experiencing his dreams and obsessions? I put myself in my character's shoes and try to feel and think like him when I write the words for him to speak. I do this not only for upright characters, but also for wicked characters. Thus a virtuous character should speak like a virtuous character, and a vicious character should use language that reveals the evil thoughts he harbors.

In short, all the subtleties of human emotion and thought should be evident in the kind of language that a character uses. The words should ring true and be unique to the character. Do not use stereotypes or generalizations. Follow the lead of the narrative of *On the Water's Edge* and Wu Daozi's paintings, which are the best in this respect. Once a play is written in that way, it will certainly become popular even if you do not intended it to.

On Performance

The only reason for writing a play is to have it performed on the stage, and here success or failure depends on many factors. [...]

Understanding the play. The meaning and feeling of the arias should come across in the singing. Meaning comes from the plot, the action of the play. Having understood the plot and its meaning, a performer can then sing the words with conviction: a question is a question, an answer is an answer; a sad person looks distraught; a happy person seems exuberant, not vice versa. Moreover, there are all kinds of nuances in the use of the voice that affect the meaning and the feeling of a play. Nowadays, all an actor does in preparing to perform a play is to read it and then to sing it, no understanding actually being required. Some actors can perform the same play all day long for months, or even all their lives, and still not understand what or whom they are singing about. They only sing with their mouths, without using their minds. An aria that comes straight from the mouth, but is not reflected in the facial expressions or body movements, deprives the play of its meaning and feeling. Like children reciting the classics by rote, it is forced and unnatural. Even if the melody and rhythm are extremely precise and the elocution absolutely clear, such a performance is not of the highest quality, only second-rate or worse.

Any actor wishing to perform a play well must ask a good teacher to explain its meanings clearly. If the teacher is not clear, ask the author or a good scholar for help. Start singing the words only after clarifying what they mean. While performing, concentrate on the spirit of the play throughout and strive for maximum truth and naturalness

Coaching speech. Almost all acting coaches and their students agree that learning to sing arias is difficult and learning to speak dialogue is easy. It seems that if you can read dialogue fluently, you can speak it well too. As for an aria, you have to read the lyrics fluently and sing it dozens of times before you can really sing it well. Therefore it seems obvious that singing is much more difficult than speaking. I, however, do not think this is true. Singing is difficult, but also easy. Speaking is easy, but also difficult. To know that speaking is difficult will actually make it easier, whereas to assume that speaking is easy will make it more difficult. In singing an aria, the pitches, tones, and rhythms have fixed rules for one to follow, because they are written precisely in the scores and taught strictly by teachers. Once accustomed to these rules through standard training, the performer will naturally do things the right way. But in delivering a spoken passage, the pitches, tones, and rhythms are not governed by fixed rules. One can imitate teachers, who, unfortunately, most likely learned the speeches only haphazardly on their own when they themselves were neophytes. So how can they teach their students properly? Vagueness vaguely taught becomes a vicious circle. The proper ways of delivering dialogue are not clearly explicated. No wonder people assume that speaking fluently is good enough and quite easy. As far as I can tell in the Pear Gardens [academy of acting], at least twenty to thirty percent of the performers are good singers but only one or two percent of the performers are good speakers. The one or two percent are good at delivering speeches not because they themselves are actually knowledgeable, but because their teachers are well grounded. The choice of a good teacher is crucial. [...]

Getting rid of senseless old clichés. There are countless clichés in the theatre, some of which are very odd. It is particularly ridiculous that some extremely trite and vulgar devices are imitated by thousands of theatre people, becoming fixed conventions. If it is ludicrous to try to look beautiful by imitating West Shi's famous melancholy countenance, it is even more absurd to copy East Shi's infamous frown. Theatre depends on novelty and freshness to keep from being predictable to the audience. If every actor performs in the same way and everything looks the same, the audience does not need to see the performance to know the play. When clichés are used, the suspenseful scenes will not arouse suspense, nor will the touching scenes move the audience. Some long established comic routines can still make people laugh, but the laughter comes from the recognition of the expected, seen before in other plays, not the pleasure of seeing the novel or unexpected.

Recently costumes in the theatre have become extravagant and ostentatious. Generally speaking, it seems unreasonable to ask for frugality and modesty in a business which is meant to dazzle and entertain. What is peculiar, however, is that women's dancing costumes which are supposed to be light and soft have become as bulky and hard as suits of armor—they boast of wide and thick shoulder pads, double-layered dresses with additional gold embroidery and silk brocade, and "modesty" shields for the back and front of the lower body. This is sheer madness.

Costumes should be light and soft, easily flowing with the moving body. As for the embroidery on costumes, only two patterns are appropriate: the phoenix and birds for the upper part, and white and rosy clouds for the lower part—the well-established "clouds-and-feathers costume." Any mixing with gaudy colors or ornaments is not acceptable. I am making no innovation here; I am simply trying to restore a good and sound tradition.

On Training

Literacy and artistry. To acquire artistry one must acquire literacy first. It is not that one should learn the difficult subject first so that what comes next becomes easy; it is rather that mastering the easier subject will help one tackle the more difficult later on. Everything under heaven has a key that opens it. What is this key? It is literacy and reason. One key usually opens only one door, yet the key of literacy and reason can open thousands of doors. It is because every profession between heaven and earth has its key in literacy and reason. I advocate this idea not only for the women I am training. In fact, it is applicable to everyone—scholars, farmers, workers, merchants, and so on.

It may already seem rather simplistic to think that the two words, "literacy" and "reason," can solve all the problems in the great big world. But I still wish to point out that one of the two words is more fundamental than the other. People acquire literacy not for its own sake, but as a step toward reason. Once a person enters the door of reason, the key of literacy can be put aside. There are countless numbers of trades and professions under heaven, and the ability to understand reason is the key to every one of them. To acquire artistry or skill is easy for those who understand reason and very hard for those who do not; the disparity is comparable to that between heaven and earth. And if one is illiterate or does not read, how can one understand reason? That is why to acquire artistry, one must first acquire literacy. To help female performers understand poetry, one must ask them to read a lot. Once an actress has read so much that she sounds as if poetry naturally rolls off her tongue, the poetic mood and emotion will spontaneously come through. The development of both her wit and reason depends on the quality of the poetry that she reads.

Singing and dancing. In the old days, the masters of song and dance taught their girls singing and dancing not for its own sake, but to help enhance their vocal abilities and natural gracefulness. Singing helps to cultivate a sweet and clear voice. Once having learned to sing well, the actress, even when speaking casually, will sound like a mesmerizing nightingale—there is music and song in the spoken words. Dancing helps to train a graceful and flexible body. Once having learned to dance well, the actress, even when walking or turning casually, will move like dancing willows and smiling flowers—there is grace and movement in the movement itself.

I have said that the way a woman carries herself is something she is born with, not something she can learn. Then why am I talking about studying *tai* [manner, attitude, posture, carriage, or bearing]? Because there is a difference between manners in real life and those on the stage. A girl at home conducts herself freely and naturally, but on the stage her bearing only seems natural, but is actually carefully controlled. This is the result of study and training.

Everybody knows that a *sheng* (male character type) has a *sheng*'s prescribed manners, a *dan* (female character type) has a *dan*'s prescribed manners, and so do the other stock character types. While it is the same for the male performers, here I am mainly talking about female performers. When a male performer impersonates a woman character, he has to accentuate his transformation, manners and all, or else he could not pretend to be a woman. When a female performer plays a woman character, it is very important for her not to be artificial, but instead natural and subtle; otherwise she would be like a man playing a woman. Someone may ask: how can a female performer be artificial when she is playing a woman? This person does not know that often when a female performer goes on stage, she self-consciously assumes a reserved and dignified manner. While she sees herself as being reserved and dignified, the audience sees her as being artificial. She must be asked to forget that she is acting on the stage and to imagine that she is at home going about her usual business. Only in this way can she avoid being artificial. If it takes some doing for a female performer to play a woman character well, it is even harder for her to play a male character, particularly the minor male character types such as an old man or a clown. It is not hard to play those male types in situations where the character is sitting, lying in bed, or happily chatting away. What is hard is when the action requires that the male character move about or cry big tears. Female performers cannot take strides because of their bound feet, and they cannot look wan and sallow because of their pretty young faces. The old saying goes: "One playing a dragon should look like a dragon, and one playing a tiger should look like a tiger." But rather than having people laugh at her because outwardly she does not resemble the male character type she is playing, a female performer should try to get closer to her character inwardly. If she puts herself in her character's shoes and lives the part, the female performer will win praises because she embodies his spirit and expresses his emotions truthfully and accurately.

DENIS DIDEROT

Denis DIDEROT (1713-1784), thickset and powerful in frame, was built like a sedan chair porter. He had a big inquisitive nose, bright chestnut-brown eyes, and an open, tolerant smile. He dressed simply in a plain, middle-class black suit and wore a bob-tailed wig, which he often whisked off, revealing a high-domed head.

A connoisseur of his own physical appearance, Diderot enjoyed sitting for painters and sculptors. Because his face was never the same from one moment to the next, he proved to be a difficult subject for the artists who tried to represent him. He complained that Michel Van Loo's flattering portrait of 1767 made him look like a simpering coquette: "Very alive. Catches the sitter's gentleness and his vitality. But too young, the head too small. A feminine prettiness, ogling, smiling, delicate, fastidious, pouting … The look of a Secretary of State, not of a philosopher… It is not me."

Diderot, a professional art critic, was adept at painting his own self-portrait in words. "I had a large brow, very lively eyes, rather massive features, a head altogether in the style of an ancient orator's, with a bonhomie verging on the stupid and the rusticity of a bygone age." In a single day, he said he displayed a hundred different physiognomies: serene, sad, contemplative, tender, violent and impassioned. His social and cultural identities were equally protean. "It is really bizarre the variety of roles I play in this world." He could never limit himself to doing one thing at a time or holding only one opinion. He was in a state of constant struggle with himself, battling to control his own overly sensitive temperament.

Sociable in the extreme, Diderot craved companionship and opportunities to talk. He spoke at high speed, his voice now vehement, now falling to a whisper for effect. Despite a weakness for divagations, his conversation was always lively, full of sudden ejaculations, dramatic pauses, and copious gestures. It was a pantomime. A master conversationalist, he cast much of his fiction and even his philosophical writing directly in the form of dramatic dialogue.

As a young pupil educated by the Jesuits, Diderot saw the classics in school performances and undoubtedly played in them himself. He knew the famous French dramatic monologues by heart and hoped to become a playwright himself. But by the time he was thirty he had stopped going to the theatre on a regular basis and in fifteen years since 1743 he confessed that he had perhaps been to the theatre no more than ten times, finding the falsity of everything that takes place on stage so deadly. He pointed out that French theatres, which at the beginning of the century had been unruly but lively places of popular entertainment, had grown as respectable, orderly, and quiet as churches, with the result that they lost all their vitality.

Diderot sought strong emotion in the theatre, just as in painting he took delight in violent and tumultuous scenes depicting tortures and the horrors of the plague. Identifying with Socrates and admiring Philoctetes, he found the ultimate expression of emotion in the simplicity and profundity of Greek life and art.

In seeking to replace the anemic neoclassical drama of his time with a powerful new genre of domestic drama, Diderot drew upon his knowledge of the other arts—particularly painting—for inspiration. The moral tableaux of Diderot's friend Jean-Baptiste Greuze, painter of sentimental genre scenes, served as models.

Although he had seen Garrick at the time of his first appearance in Paris in 1751, it was not until his meeting with the British actor in 1764 that Diderot's ideas on acting crystallized. Garrick claimed that there was no emotional effect in the theatre that he could not produce solely by facial expression and physical gesture. Garrick's remarkable transformational abilities convinced Diderot of the paradox of acting: the unmoved performer moves the audience most. He found in Mlle Clairon of the Comédie Française the traits of absolute discipline and control that he now thought constituted the height of art.

Diderot only saw Garrick performing exercises and virtuoso stunts in a drawing room, never in a complete role on stage. From the Englishman's mastery of technique Diderot concluded that great acting required no sensibility. Garrick was to have commented on Diderot's manuscript (not published until 1830), but failed to do so. Diderot, however, would have been surprised to learn Garrick's private opinion that Mlle Clairon's acting suffered from a severe lack of sensibility.

CONVERSATIONS ON *THE NATURAL SON* (1757)

Second Conversation

DORVAL: There is too much talking in our plays; consequently, our actors do not act enough. We have lost an art whose effectiveness was well known to the Ancients. At one time, mime plays depicted all conditions of men—kings, heroes, tyrants, the rich, the poor, city dwellers, and country folk—selecting from every rank the trait that was peculiar to it and from every action its most striking aspect [...]

What this scene also made me see is that there are moments that should be left almost entirely to the actor. It is his right to use the text of the scene as he sees fit, to repeat certain words, to return to certain ideas, to cut out some, and to add others. In cantabile, the composer will allow a great singer freedom to exercise his own taste and talent; he will be satisfied to provide no more than the principal intervals of a bel canto. And the poet should do likewise when he knows his actor well. What is it that moves us when we see a man animated by some great passion? Is it his words? Sometimes. But what never fails to stir us is cries, inarticulate words, a broken voice, a group of monosyllables with pauses in between, a murmur, impossible to describe, deep in the throat or between the teeth. As the violence of the emotion cuts off the breath and fills the mind with perturbation, so the syllables of words become disjunct, and the man jumps from one idea to another; he initiates a great many different lines of thought but does not finish any of them; and though there are a few sentiments he succeeds in expressing during the onset of his passion, and to which he returns again and again, the rest is merely a sequence of confused and feeble noises, of fading sounds, of stifled cries—all things about which the actor knows far more than the poet. The voice, the tone, the gestures, the stage movements—these are what belong to the actor. And these are the things that strike us, especially in the portrayal of great passions. It is the actor who provides the written text with energy. It is he who conveys to our ears the force and the truth of a character's words. [...]

From Denis Diderot, *Selected Writings*, ed. Lester Crocker, trans. Derek Coltman. N.Y.: Macmillan, 1966.

MYSELF: Then you think your play would not be successful on the stage?

DORVAL: There would be difficulties. It would mean either cutting out certain sections of the text or else changing our methods of staging plays.

MYSELF: What do you mean by changing our methods of staging plays?

DORVAL: I mean clearing all those things off the stage itself that are at present making such a small area even smaller still; introducing scenery; being able to present different stage pictures from the ones we've been looking at for the past hundred years; and, in short, transporting Clairville's drawing room to the theater just as it is. [...]

What a moment of terror and pity is that when we hear the prayer and the groans of the unfortunate Orestes as they pierce through the shrieks and frightful gestures of the cruel beings who are hunting him down! Could we execute such a scene on our stages? No, for we can present only single actions, whereas in nature there are almost always several occurring simultaneously, and the concomitant representation of these, each action lending force to the others, would produce terrible effects in us. Then we should tremble indeed at the thought of going to the theater—and yet be unable to prevent ourselves from going. Then at last, instead of all the petty, passing emotions, the lukewarm applause, the scanty tears with which our present-day poets content themselves, they might topple people's minds, bring confusion and fear into their souls, and we should see the prodigies of ancient tragedy, so possible and so little credited, renew themselves in our time. In order to show themselves again, they are only waiting for a man of genius to appear who is able to mingle mime with speech, combine a spoken scene with a silent one, and take advantage of the moment when they come together, especially of that instant, whether it be frightening or comic, when we see, as we always would, that the two scenes are on the point of merging. After the Eumenides have done their savage dance upon the stage, they move on into the sanctuary where the guilty Orestes has taken refuge, and the two scenes become one.

MYSELF: Two scenes at once, alternately mimed and spoken. I understand what you mean. But wouldn't it be confusing?

DORVAL: A mimed scene is a tableau—an animated decor. When we go to the opera, does the pleasure of looking detract from the pleasure of what we hear?

MYSELF: No ... I meant is that the way we should interpret the information that has come down to us about the ancient drama, the accounts of how they used speech and music and mime, sometimes all together and sometimes separately?

DORVAL: Sometimes, but a discussion of that would take us too far. Let us stick to our subject. Let us consider what might possibly be done today in this respect, and let us take an example from ordinary domestic life.

A father has lost his son in a duel. It is night. A servant who saw the fight has come to bring the news. He goes into the unhappy father's room, where the latter is asleep. He walks up and down. The noise of his footsteps wakes the father, who then asks who it is in his room. "It's me, sir," the servant answers, in a voice that betrays his emotions. "Well! What's the matter?" "Nothing." "Nothing the matter?" "No, sir." "That's not true. You're trembling, you're turning your head away, you're avoiding my eyes. Now tell me what's the matter. I want to know. Speak! I order you to speak!" "I tell you there's nothing the matter, sir," the servant says again, weeping as he speaks. "Ah, you miserable wretch," the father cries, leaping from the bed where he has been lying, "you are deceiving me. Some great misfortune has occurred. . . . Is my wife dead?" "No, sir." "My daughter?" "No, sir." "It is my son, then?" The servant doesn't reply; the father realizes what this silence means; he throws himself onto the floor, he fills the room with his grief-stricken cries. He does, he says everything that despair would suggest to a father who has lost an only son, his family's sole hope for the future.

The same servant runs to tell the mother. She too is asleep. She is awakened by the sound of her bed curtains being pulled violently aside. "What's the matter?" she asks. "Madame, the greatest possible misfortune. Now is the moment to show yourself a Christian. You no longer have a son." "Oh, God!" the heartbroken mother cries. And then, unhooking the crucifix from above her bed, she folds it in her arms and fastens her lips upon it; her eyes are streaming with tears, and with those tears she sprinkles her God, nailed on his cross.

The tableau of a religious woman...

Meanwhile, the son's body having been carried into the father's room, a scene of despair has been taking place there simultaneously with the mother's mimed expression of piety in hers.

You see how mime and speech move alternately from place to place. That is what we should substitute for our asides. But the moment for combining the two scenes is approaching. The mother, led by the servant, moves toward her husband's room... And imagine the feelings of the spectator as she does so. ...The eyes of a mother are about to fall upon her husband, her son's father, stretched out upon the young man's corpse! But by now she has crossed the space between the two sets. Agonized laments have reached her ears. She has seen. She recoils violently, then all the strength drains out of her, and she falls senseless into the arms of the servant who is escorting her. Soon her throat will fill with sobs. *Tum verae voces.*

There is very little speech in this action. But a man of genius, when faced with the task of filling up these empty spaces, will scatter no more than a few monosyllables here and there; he will throw in an exclamation in one place, the beginning of a sentence in another, but he will rarely allow himself an entirely coherent speech, no matter how short.

That would be true tragedy; but if we are to create such a genre, we need new authors, new actors, a new theater, and perhaps a new race of spectators.

MYSELF: What! You want to put all those things into a tragedy? A bed, a mother and a father both lying asleep, a crucifix, a corpse, two scenes with speech and mime alternating between them! But what about the conventions?

DORVAL: Ah, those cruel conventions, how decorous, and how petty they make our plays!

"And so," Dorval added, with a composure that amazed me, "you think that what I have suggested is no longer possible?"

MYSELF: No, I don't think we shall ever progress as far as that.

DORVAL: Then all is lost! [...]

At this point Dorval exclaimed, "O you [Voltaire] who still possess all the fire of your genius at an age when others have nothing left but cold reason, why can I not be at your side to scourge you forward like one of the Eumenides? I would give you no peace. You would write it for us, this work. [...] And then, in disappearing from among us, you would not leave us still repining for a genre that you had the power to create."

MYSELF: And what will you call this new genre?

DORVAL: Domestic middle-class tragedy. The English have *The London Merchant* and *The Gamester*, their prose tragedies. And Shakespeare's tragedies are half in verse, half in prose. The first poet who made us laugh with prose introduced prose into comedy. The first poet who makes us weep with prose will have introduced prose into tragedy.

But in art, as in nature, everything is linked; if we approach nearer to the truth in one way, then we shall find other ways of approach opening up to us as well. Then we shall see those natural situations portrayed upon the stage that propriety, ever the enemy of genius and sublime effects, has outlawed from it. I shall never tire of shouting to our fellow countrymen: Truth! Nature! The Ancients! Sophocles! *Philoctetes!* For Sophocles, in his play about Philoctetes, showed him, lying at the entrance to his cave, dressed in tattered rags. He writhed on the ground, racked by a fit of pain; he gave vent to yells, he made inarticulate noises. The setting was primitive; the action unfurled without the help of machinery. Real clothes, real speech, and a simple and natural plot. Our taste would be quite corrupt if such a spectacle did not affect us more than that of a richly dressed man, tricked out in finery. [...]

Third Conversation

After a few general remarks on the way events occur in real life and the way they are imitated on the stage, he said to me:

DORVAL: We can divide every moral matter into a middle and two extremes. It appears then, since every dramatic action is a moral matter, that there should exist a central genre and two extreme genres. We already have the last two; they are comedy and tragedy. But man is not always in a state of grief or joy. Therefore there must be a point that bisects the distance between the comic genre and the tragic genre. [...]

How would you classify this particular play, then? [Terence's *Hecyra*] Is it comedy? There isn't a funny line in it. Tragedy? There is no point at which it arouses terror or pity or any of the great passions. Yet it holds the interest; and any dramatic composition, even though it contains no laughable absurdity, no perils to make us shudder, will always hold the interest if the poet adopts the tone that we ourselves use in serious matters and if the action evolves through a series of perplexities and hindrances. And since such actions are the ones most commonly met with in real life, it seems to me that the genre taking these as its object will be the most useful and the most comprehensive. I shall term this the serious genre.

Once this genre has been established, there will be no rank in society and no important actions in life that we cannot relegate to some part of the dramatic system.

Would you like to enlarge this system to its greatest possible extent? Would you like to see it include truth as well as fantasy, the world of the imagination as well as the world of reality? Then add burlesque below comedy and the supernatural above tragedy.

MYSELF: I understand what you mean: burlesque...comedy...serious drama...tragedy...supernatural drama.

DORVAL: It is the advantage of the serious genre, being placed midway between the other two, that it can draw its resources from both above and below itself. This is not true of the tragic and comic genres. All the nuances available to comedy are comprised in the region between itself and the serious genre, and all those available to tragedy between the serious genre and the tragic genre. [...]

If you need to be convinced of the danger that lies in crossing the barrier nature has placed between the genres, then push things to excess: take two widely separated genres, such as tragedy and burlesque, and put them together; the result will be a scene in which a grave senator indulges in the vilest debauchery at the feet of a courtesan being immediately succeeded by another in which a band of conspirators discusses its plans for destroying a republic.

[...] The subject [in the serious genre] should be important, the plot simple, domestic, and close to everyday life.

I want to see no valets in serious drama. Right-thinking people do not admit valets to a knowledge of their affairs, and the scenes will be the more interesting for taking place entirely between masters. If a valet speaks on the stage as he does in real life, he is tedious; if he speaks in any other way, he is false.

The nuances borrowed from the comic genre must never be too strong. If they are, the work will make us laugh and cry, and it will lack both unity of interest and unity of tone.

The serious genre contains soliloquies. From this, I conclude that it is nearer to tragedy than to comedy; for in comedy, soliloquies are infrequent and always short.

The moral content of a serious drama should be general and strong.

[...] A great deal of attention should be paid to mime. All *coups de théâtre* whose effect is momentary should be eliminated, and tableaux invented in their stead. [...]

But, above all, remember that there is no general principle: there is not one of the rules I have just set forth that could not successfully be infringed by a man of genius. [...]

MYSELF: But what material will it use, this serious kind of comedy that you look upon as a new branch of dramatic literature? There are only a dozen or so clearly defined and truly comic types in the whole of human nature.

DORVAL: I agree.

MYSELF: The minor differences observable in men's characters can never be used to such good effect as clear-cut humors.

DORVAL: Again I agree. But do you know what follows from that? It follows that we should no longer be portraying characters, properly speaking, in our plays, but rank or station. Up till now, character has always been the main object of comedy, and station only accessory. Now the social function must become its principal object, and character merely accessory. The entire plot used to be built from the character. Generally speaking, we tried to find a set of circumstances that would bring it out, then linked those circumstances together. But it is social station—its duties, its advantages, and its difficulties—that should serve as the basis of our plays. In my opinion, this is a more fruitful, more comprehensive, and more useful source of material than mere characters. A character need only be slightly exaggerated for the spectator to be able to say to himself, "I'm not like that." But he cannot deceive himself in this way when it is his social function that is being portrayed before him; he cannot fail to recognize his duties. He is compelled to apply what he hears to himself.

MYSELF: It seems to me that some of these subjects have already been treated.

DORVAL: No, they haven't. Make no mistake about that.

MYSELF: But we have financiers in our plays, don't we?

DORVAL: Certainly we do. But the social role of the financier has never been explored.

MYSELF: It would be difficult to cite a play without a father in it.

DORVAL: True, but the father as a social function has not been done. I would like you to consider, in a word, whether the various social functions, their duties, their disadvantages, and their dangers, have ever been depicted on the stage; whether they have ever formed the basis for the plots and moral arguments of our plays; and whether these same duties, advantages, disadvantages, and dangers do not daily provide us with the spectacle of men enmeshed in the most complicated situations.

MYSELF: So you want us to enact the man of letters, the philosopher, the merchant, the judge, the lawyer, the politician, the citizen, the magistrate, the financier, the great lord, the estate manager.

DORVAL: Yes, all those plus the fundamental family relationships: what it means to be a father, a husband, a sister, or a brother. A father! What a subject that is in an age such as ours, when no one seems to have the slightest idea of what it means to be the father of a family!

Remember that new social roles are coming into being every day. Remember that there is possibly nothing we know less about than social functions, and nothing that should interest us more. We each of us have our own place in society, but we all have to deal with men of every other station.

Social station! Think how many important details such a source will yield! How many public and domestic themes! How many unknown truths! How many fresh situations! Are there not the same contrasts between social roles as between characters? Will the writer have any difficulty in producing conflicts between them?

Though these subjects do not belong to the serious genre alone. They can be made comic or tragic, too, according to the talents of the man who takes possession of them.

Such are the vicissitudes of comic faults and vices that I believe a new *Misanthrope* could be written every fifty years. And isn't the same thing true of many other basic characters? [...]

THE PARADOX OF ACTING (1773-8)

THE FIRST. [...] But the important point on which your author and I are entirely at variance concerns the main qualities necessary to a great actor. In my view he must have a good deal of judgment. He must have in himself an unmoved and disinterested onlooker. He must have, consequently, penetration and no sensibility; the art of mimicking everything, or, which comes to the same thing, the same aptitude for every sort of character and part.

THE SECOND. No sensibility?

THE FIRST. None. [...] If the actor were overcome by feeling, how could he play the same part twice running with the same spirit and success? Full of fire at the first performance, he would be worn out and cold as marble at the third. But when the actor is an attentive mimic and thoughtful disciple of nature, then the first time he comes on the stage as Augustus, Cinna, Orosmanes, Agamemnon, or Mahomet, faithful copying himself and the effects he has arrived at, and constantly observing human nature, he will so prevail that his acting, far from losing in force, will gather strength with the new observations he will make from time to time. He will increase or moderate his effects, and you will be more and more pleased with him. If he is himself while he is playing, how is he to stop being himself? If he wants to stop being himself, how is he to catch just the point where he is to stay his hand?

What confirms me in this view is the uneven acting of actors who play from the heart. From them you must expect no unity. Their playing is alternately strong and feeble, fiery and cold, dull and sublime. Tomorrow they will miss the point they have excelled in today; and to make up for it will excel in some passage where last time they failed. On the other hand, the actor who plays from reflection, from the study of human nature, from constant imitation of some ideal model, from imagination, from memory, will be one and the same at all performances, will be always at his best mark; he has considered, combined, learnt and arranged the whole thing in his head; his diction is neither monotonous nor dissonant. His passion has a definite course—it has bursts, and it has reactions; it has a beginning, a middle, and an end. The accents are the same, the positions are the same, the movements are the same;

From Denis Diderot, *The Paradox of Acting*, trans. Walter Herries Pollock. London: Chatto & Windus, 1883.

if there is any difference between two performances, the latter is generally the better. He will be invariable; a looking-glass, as it were, ready to reflect realities, and to reflect them ever with the same precision, the same strength, and the same truth. Like the poet he will dip forever into the inexhaustible treasure-house of nature, instead of coming very soon to an end of his own poor resources.

What acting was ever more perfect than Clairon's? Yet if you follow her work and study it, you will find that at the sixth performance of a given part she has every detail of her acting by heart, just as much as every word of her part. Doubtless she has constructed a model for herself, and to conform to this model has been her first thought; doubtless she has chosen for her purpose the highest, the greatest, the most perfect model she could conceive. This model, however, which she has borrowed from history, or which her imagination has created like a great phantom, is not herself. Were it indeed bounded by her own dimensions, how paltry, how feeble her playing would be! When, by dint of hard work, she has got as near as she can to this idea, the thing is done; to hold her ground is a mere matter of memory and practice. [...]

And pray, why should the actor be different from the poet, the painter, the orator, the musician? It is not in the transport of the first outburst that characteristic traits come out; it is in moments of stillness and self-command; in moments entirely unexpected. Who can tell whence these traits have their being? They are a sort of inspiration. They come when the man of genius is hovering between nature and his sketch of it, and keeping a watchful eye on both. The beauties of inspiration, the chance hits of which his work is full, and of which the sudden appearance startles himself, have an importance, a success, a sureness very different from that belonging to the first fling. Cool reflection must bring the delirium of enthusiasm to its bearings.

The extravagant creature who loses his self-control has no hold on us; this is an advantage reserved for the man who is self-controlled. The great poets, especially the great dramatic poets, keep a keen watch on what is going on, both in the physical and the moral world.

THE SECOND. Which are one and the same.

THE FIRST. They seize on everything that strikes them; they make, as it were, a collection of such things. And from these collections, made all unconsciously, issue the grandest achievements of their work. Fiery, extravagant, sensitive men are forever on stage; they give the performance, but they get nothing out of it. They are the models according to which the man of genius makes his copies. Great poets, great actors, and, I may add, all great imitators of nature, in whatever art, beings gifted with fine imagination, with broad judgment, with exquisite tact, with a sure touch of taste, are the least sensitive of all creatures. They are too apt for too many things, too busy with observing, considering, and imitating, to have their innermost beings deeply affect-

ed. I see them always with their portfolios spread on their knees and their pen-
cils in their hands.

It is we who feel; it is they who watch, study, and give us the results.
And then ... well, why should I not say it? Sensibility is hardly the distinguishing mark of a great genius. He will have, let us say, an abstract love of
justice, but he will not be moved to temper it with mercy. It is the head, not
the heart, which works in and for him. Let some unforeseen opportunity arise,
the man of sensibility will lose it; he will never be a great king, a great minister, a great commander, a great advocate, a great physician. Fill the theatre
auditorium with these cry-babies, but don't put any of them on the stage. [...]

Even if these truths were conclusively proved, great actors would not
acknowledge them; it is their secret. Middling actors or novices are sure to
contradict you flatly; and of some others it may be said that they believe they
feel, just as it has been said of the superstitious that they believe they believe;
and that without faith in the one case and without sensibility in the other there
is no salvation.

This is all very well, you may reply; but what of these touching and
sorrowful accents that are drawn from the very depth of a mother's heart and
that shake her whole being? Are these not the result of true feeling? are those
not inspired by despair? Most certainly not. The proof is that they are in
meter; that they are part of a system of declamation; that, raised or lowered by
the twentieth part of a quarter of a tone, they would ring false; that they are
subject to a law of unity; that, as in harmony, they are arranged in chords and
in discords; that long study is needed to satisfy all the requisite conditions; that
they are elements necessary to the solving of a given problem; that, to hit the
right mark once, they have been practiced a hundred times; and that, despite
all this practice, they are yet found wanting. [...]

The actor's whole talent depends not, as you think, upon feeling, but
upon rendering so exactly the outer signs of feeling that you fall into the trap.
He has rehearsed to himself every note of his passion. He has learnt before a
mirror every particle of his despair. He knows exactly when he must produce
his handkerchief and shed tears; and you will see him weep at the word, at the
syllable, he has chosen, not a second sooner or later. The broken voice, the
half-uttered words, the stifled or prolonged notes of agony, the trembling
limbs, the faintings, the bursts of fury—all this is pure mimicry, lessons carefully learned, the grimacing of sorrow, the magnificent aping which the actor
remembers long after his first study of it, of which he was perfectly conscious
when he first put it before the public, and which leaves him, luckily for the
poet, the spectator, and himself, a full freedom of mind. Like other gymnastics, it taxes only his bodily strength. He puts off the sock or the buskin; his
voice is gone; he is extremely tired; he changes his clothes, or he goes to bed;
and he feels neither trouble, nor sorrow, nor depression, nor weariness of soul.
All these emotions he has given to you. The actor is tired, you are sad; he has

had exertion without feeling, you feeling without exertion. Were it otherwise the actor's lot would be most wretched on earth; but he is not the character he represents; he plays it, and plays it so well that you think he is the character; the illusion is all on your side; he knows well enough that he is not the character. [...]

Reflect a little as to what, in the language of the theatre, is *being true*. Is it showing things as they are in nature? Certainly not. Were it so, the true would be the commonplace. What, then, is truth on the stage? It is the conformity of action, diction, face, voice, movement, and gesture, to an ideal model imagined by the poet, and frequently exaggerated by the actor. This is the strange part of it. This model not only influences the tone, it alters the actor's very gait and bearing. And so it is that the actor in private and the actor on the stage are two characters so different that one can scarce recognize one in the other. The first time I saw Mlle Clairon in her own house I exclaimed, quite spontaneously, "Ah, mademoiselle, I thought you were at least a head taller!" [...]

Is it at the moment when you have just lost your friend or your mistress that you will begin composing a poem on her death? No! woe to him who at such a moment delights in his talent. It is when the storm of sorrow is over, when the extreme of sensibility is dulled, when the event is far behind us, when the soul is calm, that one remembers one's eclipsed happiness, that one is capable of appreciating one's loss, that memory and imagination unite, one to retrace, the other to accentuate, the delights of a past time: then it is that one regains self-possession and expression. One writes of one's falling tears, but they do not fall while one is hunting a strong epithet that always escapes one; one writes of one's falling tears, but they do not fall while one is employed in polishing one's verse; or if the tears do flow the pen drops from the hand; one falls to feeling, and one ceases writing. [...]

One is one's self by nature; one becomes some one else by imitation; the heart one imagines for oneself is not the heart one has. What, then, is true talent? That of knowing well the outer symptoms of the soul we borrow, of addressing ourselves to the sensations of those who hear us and see us, of deceiving them by the imitation of these symptoms, by an imitation which magnifies everything in their imagination, and which becomes the measure of their judgment. [...]

He, then, who best knows and best conveys these outer signs, according to the best conceived ideal model, is the greatest actor.

JEAN-JACQUES ROUSSEAU

Jean-Jacques ROUSSEAU (1712-1778), a masterful self-publicist, developed special ways of wearing his hair and dressing in order to draw attention to himself. His defiance of the social conventions became reflected in his appearance. "I began my reformation with my dress," he explained. "I gave up gold lace and white stockings and wore a round wig. I gave up my sword and sold my watch." His "signature" article of clothing now was his Armenian kaftan.

Even when he let his hair grow and his beard become rough, Rousseau looked distinguished. He had a large head on a small body, an oval face, intense black eyes, and an expression that was vivacious and engaging. Aware of his own protean nature and constantly changing exterior, he was critical of the many pictures painted of him, liking only a pastel portrait of 1753 that showed an intelligent, sensitive young face, with dark sparkling eyes, and a pleasing half-smile.

Rousseau never lost his Swiss accent, and in society, where he was ill at ease, he often stammered and stuttered, although he was naturally voluble. With his close friend Diderot, Rousseau discussed the need for cultural innovation in the arts, while they played chess (Rousseau usually won).

A playwright, amateur actor, and passionate theatre lover, Rousseau supported himself throughout most of his life by music—as teacher of singing, copyist, composer, performer, critic, and theorist. When the French Academy rejected his idea for a new system of musical notation based on numbers, he replied with a disputatious book that challenged its authority.

Dependent on private music lessons to survive, Rousseau could afford playgoing only twice a week. Dreaming of a theatrical career, he showed his comedy, *Narcissus*, to Marivaux, who tried unsuccessfully to get the play performed at the Théâtre des Italiens.

In his *Letter on French Music*, Rousseau argued that French was a profoundly unmusical language. In 200 entries on musical subjects for Diderot's *Encyclopedia*, Rousseau, a self-taught amateur, attacked the official, state-sponsored French opera (represented by Jean Philippe Rameau) as academic, authoritarian, and stultifying, promoting instead popular Italian *opera buffa*, whose simple tuneful arias anyone could sing. His advocacy of spontaneous melody over artful harmony helped start a culture war between the supporters of Italian and French opera. When musicians at the Paris Opera burned Rousseau in effigy and rescinded his free pass, he continued attending performances accompanied by a bodyguard.

In 1752 Rousseau—inspired by Pergolesi's *La Serva padrona* (The Servant as Mistress)—wrote *Le Devin du village* (The Village Soothsayer), a pastoral drama of love between a shepherd and shepherdess that changed the course of French music by introducing the lyrical expression of feeling. Devoid of the usual artificial theatricality of French opera, *Le Devin* celebrates in a simple style the purity of heart of uncorrupted human nature.

Sophisticated Parisians loved it. Submitted anonymously, Rousseau's musical drama was quickly accepted by the Paris Opera, but the King insisted the premiere be given at court. Rousseau was taken to Fontainebleau in the royal carriage for the dress rehearsal and attended the premiere unshaven and dressed in his old clothes. Unable to sit still for long because of a urinary disorder, he fled from court unceremoniously.

Enchanted by *Le Devin*, Madame Pompadour and Louis XV, who did not like music, kept singing the arias, and lords and ladies of the court staged a second performance in which they played the shepherds and shepherdesses themselves. A great hit at the Paris Opera, Rousseau's opera stayed in the repertory for many years and opened the way for Gluck and Mozart, whose early *Bastien und Bastienne* is directly based on *Le Devin*.

Rousseau turned down the offer of a royal pension, preferring the humble trade of copyist, but he often charmed fashionable Parisian salons by singing airs from *Le Devin* to his own accompaniment on harpsichord. Back in Geneva, where public theatres were forbidden, Rousseau worked on a prose tragedy and never stopped praising Molière. Granting that "there can be a very good play on a subject which has no utility, such as the *Oedipus* of Sophocles," he still did not insist that the theatre always serve a moral goal.

D'Alembert's article on Geneva in Diderot's *Encyclopedia* lamenting the absence of a theatre in his native city made Rousseau change his mind. As an offended citizen, he defended Swiss simplicity against attempts to corrupt it by so-called "advanced societies."

According to Rousseau, the greatest virtue is to be oneself, the greatest vice to be any other. Geneva must stay Geneva.

AN EPISTLE
FROM J. J. ROUSSEAU, CITIZEN OF
GENEVA TO MR. D'ALEMBERT (1758)

[...] I hasten now to the discussion of a question less grave and serious; but which is important enough to deserve our consideration; and which I shall examine the more willingly, as it is more immediately within my own province: this is the project of establishing a public theatre in Geneva. I shall not trouble you with my conjectures concerning the motives that might induce you to recommend an institution so contrary to the political maxims of our republic. Whatever might be your reasons to propose it, I have only to do with ours for rejecting it; with regard to yourself, therefore, I shall only take the liberty to say that you are certainly the first philosopher that ever encouraged a free people, of a small city and a poor state, to burden themselves with theatrical entertainments.

I see a number of questions to be discussed in that which you seem to have so easily resolved: for instance, whether such entertainments are in themselves salutary or pernicious, whether they are compatible with a people's morals, or with the austerity of manners necessary to a republic, whether they should be permitted in any small city, whether the profession of a comedian be consistent with probity, whether the actresses can possibly be as prudent as other women, whether even good laws are sufficient to restrain the abuse that might arise from them, whether such laws would be observed, and many others. Everything is at present problematical with us regarding the actual effects of a theatre, because the disputes it occasions, are discussed only between the ecclesiastics and the laity; and each party places them in the light of their own peculiar prejudices. These researches, Sir, are not unworthy of your pen. For my part, without taking upon me to engage in them, I shall content myself in this essay with endeavoring to throw only such light on the subject which you have made necessary. At the same time, I hope you will reflect that in frankly giving my opinion, as you have done yours, I discharge my duty to my country, and that if I lie under a mistake at least my error cannot be injurious to anyone.

On the first view of theatrical institutions, we see they are intended principally for amusement; and if it be true that people must have amusement,

From *The Miscellaneous Works of Mr. J. J. Rousseau*, Vol. III, translator anonymous. London: T. Beckett and P.A. De Hout, 1767.

you must admit that they are lawful only in proportion as they are necessary; while every useless entertainment is an evil, particularly to a being whose life is so short and whose time is so precious.

The state of man has its pleasures, which are derived from his nature, and arise from his occupations, his connections and his necessities; and as these pleasures are most agreeable to uncorrupted, innocent minds, they render all others in a manner useless. A father, a son, a husband, a citizen, lie under obligations of so pleasing and interesting a nature that they can want no amusement more agreeable than the discharge of them. The proper employment of our time increases its value, while the better it is employed, the less we have to spare. Thus we find that the habit of labor renders idleness tiresome, and that a good conscience deprives us of all taste for frivolous pleasures. But it is the being dissatisfied with ourselves; it is the weight of indolence; it is the loss of taste for simple and natural pleasures, that gives occasion to the expediency of artificial entertainments. I do not like to see the heart set upon theatrical amusements, as if it was uneasy or unhappy within itself. The answer of the barbarian to a person who had been extolling the magnificence of the circus and the games instituted at Rome was dictated by nature itself. Have the Romans, said that honest creature, no wives or children? The barbarian was in the right. People imagine themselves to be in company at the theatre, but it is there that everybody is alone. We repair thither to forget our relations, our friends, our neighbors; to interest ourselves in fabulous representations, to mourn over the imaginary misfortunes of the dead, or to laugh at the expense of the living. But I should have perceived that this is not the language of the present age. Let us endeavor, therefore, to assume one that will be better understood.

To inquire whether public amusements are good or bad in themselves is a question too vague and indeterminate: it would be to examine into a relation before we had fixed the terms of it. They are made for the people, and it is only from their effects on the people that we are to determine their real good or bad qualities. There may be an almost infinite variety of such entertainments; and there is a like variety in the manners, constitutions and character of different people. I allow that man is everywhere the same; but when he is variously modified by religion, government, laws, customs, prejudices, and climates, he becomes so different from himself that the question no longer is what is proper for mankind in general, but what is proper for him in such a particular age and country. Hence it is that the dramatic pieces of Menander, calculated for the Athenian stage, were ill-suited for that of Rome. Hence the combats of the gladiators, which under the republican government animated the people with courage and a love of glory, only served under the emperors to render the populace brutal, bloodthirsty and cruel. The very same objects exhibited under different circumstances taught the people at one time to despise their own lives, and at another to sport with the lives of others.

With respect to the species of public amusements, it is necessarily determined by the particular pleasure they afford the spectators and not by their public utility. If any utility can be derived from them, it is so much the better; but their principal intent is to please, and provided the people are amused, this end is sufficiently answered. This circumstance alone will ever prevent such institutions from having all the advantages they are capable of; and those persons must be egregiously mistaken who form an idea of their perfection so inconsistent with practice that they would thereby necessarily disgust those whom they were intended to instruct. Hence arises the difference of public entertainments, according to the tastes of different nations.

A people of an intrepid, saturnine and cruel disposition would be fond of perilous and murdering exhibitions, exemplifying valor and resolution; a people ferocious and fiery would be for bloodshed and battles; a voluptuous people for music and dancing; a polite nation for shows of love and gallantry; and a light and frivolous people for those of pleasantry and ridicule. *Trahit sua quemque voluptas.*

It is necessary, in order to please them, that their public entertainments should favor their several dispositions, whereas they ought in reason to moderate them.

The stage in general presents us with a picture of the human passions, the original of which is in the heart; but if the poet were not careful to flatter these passions, the spectators would soon be offended, as they would not like to see themselves in such a light as must render them contemptible. If he draws some characters in odious colors, it is such only as are not general and which are naturally odious. And in this, the poet does nothing more than adopt the public opinion, while even these disgustful passions are always employed to recommend others, more agreeable to the spectators without being more lawful. Reason is the only thing that is useless on the stage. The character of a man without passions, or who should keep them always under command, would be totally uninteresting, and it has been already observed that a stoic in a tragedy would be an insupportable personage and in comedy would at best only make one laugh.

Let us not ascribe to the theatre, therefore, the power of changing sentiments and manners, when it can only pursue and embellish them. A dramatic writer who should oppose the general taste of the public would soon be left to write only for himself. When Molière corrected the comic drama, he attacked only ridiculous modes and characters; but in doing this, he indulged the public taste, as did also Corneille. It was the old French stage that began to displease this taste because, while the nation improved in politeness, the stage still retained its primitive barbarism.

It is for the same reason that, as the general taste is so greatly altered since their times, the very best pieces of these two authors, if now first brought on the stage, would infallibly be damned. The connoisseurs may admire them as much as they please; the public admire them rather because they are ashamed to do otherwise than from any real beauties they discover in them. It is said, indeed, that a good piece can never miscarry; truly, I believe it, but this is because a really good piece is never disgusting to the manners of the times. There cannot be the least doubt that the very best tragedy of Sophocles would be totally damned in our theatres. It is impossible for us to put ourselves in the place of people to whom we bear no sort of resemblance.

Every author who undertakes to describe foreign manners is very careful, however, to accommodate his piece to ours. It would be impossible for him to succeed without this caution; and even the success of it often depends on causes very different from those to which it is imputed by a superficial observer. When Harlequin-Savage is so well received by the spectators, can it be thought to proceed from the liking which they have for the sense and simplicity of such a character, or that any one of them has an inclination to resemble him! Quite the contrary. The piece humors the general taste, which is to be fond of novelties; and nothing can be newer to a Parisian audience than a picture of nature. It is their very aversion to things which are usual and common that sometimes induces them to return to the most simple.

It follows from the first of these observations that the general effect of a theatrical entertainment is to enforce the national character, to augment the natural inclinations, and to give a new energy to all the passions of a people.

In this sense it should seem that, as this effect is confined to the heightening, and does not extend to the altering of established manners, the comedy would be salutary for the virtuous and bad for the vicious. In the first case, however, it still remains to be determined whether the passions when too much heightened do not degenerate into vices. I know that dramatic poesy pretends to the contrary, and to purge the passions while it excites them; but I do not readily comprehend this kind of purgation. Can it be that, in order to grow temperate and prudent, we must first be made intemperate and foolish?

"Oh no! It is not that," say the partisans of the theatre. "Tragedy, indeed, pretends that we are to be moved by all the passions it describes; but it does not always require that we should be affected in the same manner as a person really under the tormenting influence of passion. Its aim, on the contrary, is most frequently to excite sentiments very different from those which actuate the persons of the drama."

They further tell us that, although the poets sometimes make an ill use of their power over the heart, in order to influence the audience in favor of a bad character; this error ought to be imputed to ignorance, or to the depravity of the artist, not to the art. They tell us, in short, that a faithful representation of the passions, and the anxieties attending them, alone suffices to make us avoid them with all possible solicitude.

Let us but consult our own hearts, however, at the end of a tragedy, and we shall be convinced of the insufficiency and insincerity of such pleas. Do the emotions, the trouble, the compassion, we feel during the piece, and even some time after it is over, show any disposition to surmount and regulate our passions? Are those lively and affecting impressions which grow habitual and are so often reiterated proper to moderate our passions and affections in cases of necessity? Why should the sense of pain arising from the passions efface that of pleasure and transport arising from the same source, and which the authors take care to heighten as much as possible in order to render their performance agreeable? Are not all the passions known sisters, one of which only is sufficient to excite a thousand? And do not we know that to oppose the one to the other is only the way to render the heart more susceptible of them all? The only instrument which serves to purge them is reason, and I have already said that reason has no effect on the stage. It is certain that we do not partake of the feelings or affections of all the characters; for their interests being opposed, the poet must so contrive it as to induce us to give the preference to one of the parties; otherwise we shall not interest ourselves in any; but he is so far from choosing, to this end, the passions he would make us love that he is compelled to make choice of those we already prefer. What I have said of the species of plays ought also to be understood of the passions and interests that prevail in them.

At London a play interests the audience if calculated to make them hate the French; at Tunis the prevailing passion is for piracy; at Messina for revenge; at Goa for the honor of burning a Jew. Let an author go against these maxims and, though he may write a very good play, he will find nobody will come to see it. In such a case also, he would be charged with ignorance, and that very justly, for having neglected the very first principle of his art which serves as a basis to all the rest—that is, to please. Thus the stage purges the passions we have not and irritates those we have. Is not this a medicine admirably administered?

A concurrence of general and particular causes will therefore always hinder theatrical exhibitions from attaining that perfection they are capable of and from producing those good effects one might expect from them. But were we even to suppose this perfection as great as possible, and the people as well disposed as one could desire, their effects would still be next kin to nothing for want of means to render them sensible. I know but of three kinds of instruments by means of which the manners of a people are to be acted on: the power of the laws, the influence of opinion, and the allurements of pleasure. Now the laws have no access to the stage where the least restraint would give pain instead of amusement. The authority of opinion depends on it as little; for instead of the theatre's giving laws to the public, it receives them from it; and with regard to the pleasure we find there, its only effect is to make us the more often return thither.

We shall see if there can be any other. The stage, it is said, if directed as it may and ought to be, would serve to render virtue amiable and vice odious. Well, and what then? Were not honest men respected and knaves detested before there were any comedies? And are they less so in places where there are not theatrical entertainments? The stage serves to render virtue amiable. A great matter truly, to effect what nature and reason had done before! Bad men are rendered odious on the stage. Pray, are they less so in society when they are known to be such? Is it very certain that this odium is to be imputed to the art of the writer rather than to the affections of which he represents them guilty? Is it very certain that the simple relation of those crimes would fill us with less indignation than arises from all the glowing colors in which he has described them? If all his art consists in exhibiting malefactors in order to render them hateful to us, I see nothing so very admirable in such art; and we have of these too many real examples in real life to need having any recourse to the fictitious ones of the drama. Shall I venture to add another suspicion that suggests itself? I much doubt whether any person to whom one should simply relate the crimes of Phaedra and Medea before he saw the play would not abhor them much more at the beginning of the first act than at the end of the representation; and if so, what must we think of the so much boasted effects of the theatre?

I should be glad to see it clearly and concisely demonstrated how the drama can produce sentiments in us that we had not before in our minds, and cause us to judge of moral entities otherwise than we judge of them within ourselves. Believe me, these mighty pretensions, if examined into, will be all found to be insignificant and puerile. If the beauty of virtue were the work of art, it would have been long since defaced! As to myself, let me be treated as a bad man for saying that mankind were born good, I care not, as I think I have fully proved it. The source of our love for virtue, and our hatred to vice, is seated within ourselves and is not to be found in the play. No art can produce it, although it may take advantage of it. The love of the beautiful is a sentiment as natural to the human heart as that of self-love. It does not spring from any arrangement or disposition of the scenes; the writer does not carry it to the theatre, he finds it there; and it is by flattering this purity of sentiment he is enabled to draw forth those tears which sometimes flow from the audience.

Conceive the theatre to be as perfect as you will; where is the man who, on going thither the first time, does not go previously convinced of the truth of what is inculcated there and already prejudiced in favor of those characters which are rendered amiable? But this is not the point in dispute; it is to act in conformity with our principles and to imitate those we esteem. The heart of man is always upright respecting what does not immediately regard his own personal interest. Thus we ever take the side of justice in quarrels of which we are merely spectators and feel a high indignation at every baseness from which we can derive no personal advantage; but when our own interest is concerned, our sentiments are presently corrupted, and it is in this case only that we prefer the evil which is useful to us to the good which we should otherwise naturally approve. Is it not a necessary effect inseparable from the con-stitution of things that a bad man shall possess a twofold advantage in all his actions, one arising from his own injustice, and the other from the probity of others? Could he possibly enter into a more advantageous treaty than to engage the whole world to be honest except himself so that everyone should behave justly towards him and he unjustly towards everybody? He loves virtue without doubt, but it is the virtue of other people because he hopes to profit by it; he does not choose to practice it himself because it would be hurtful to his interest. What does he go to see and hear therefore at the theatre? Exactly what he would be glad to meet with everywhere: lectures of moral virtue for the public, out of which number he is himself excepted, and examples of men sacrificing everything to their duty, while he himself is bound by none.

I hear it said that tragedy excites to pity by means of terror, but what is this pity? A transitory and fruitless emotion which lasts no longer than the illusion producing it, the remains of natural feeling presently stifled by the passions—in a word, only a barren compassion indulging itself in a few tears, but never productive of any act of humanity. Thus did the bloodthirsty Sulla weep at the recital of all those misfortunes which he himself did not inflict. Thus did Alexander, the tyrant of Pherae, hide himself in the theatre that he might not be seen to sigh with Priam and Andromache, although he could hear without emotion the cries of the unhappy wretches who were daily butchered at his commands.

If the observation of Diogenes Laertius be true that the heart is more affected by imaginary than by real evils, if theatrical representations some-times cause us to shed more tears than would flow from the actual appearance of the objects represented, it is less, according to the Abbé du Bos, because the emotion is weaker and does not amount to grief than because it is pure and without any alloy of concern for ourselves. In shedding tears at fictitious mis-fortunes, we discharge all the duties humanity requires of us on such occasions without any further inconvenience to ourselves; whereas when persons are under real miseries, humanity requires something more; it requires us to afford them assistance, relief and consolation, which would be making us par-take of their affections and involve us at least in solicitudes, from which our natural indolence would willingly exempt us. Hence it may be said that the human heart is selfish and afraid of being hurt by feeling for others.

But on the whole, when a man goes to a play in order to admire the heroic actions of fabulous characters and to weep at imaginary misfortunes, what more can be expected of him? Is he not perfectly satisfied with himself? Does he not even boast of his sensibility? Does he not acquit himself of every-thing he owes to virtue by doing honor to its appearance on the stage? What would we have of him more? Would you have him practice it himself? He has no part to play; he is no comedian.

The more I reflect on this matter, the more I find that whatever is represented on the stage is so far from being brought home to us that it is rather removed to a greater distance. When I see the play *Le Comte d'Essex* [by Thomas Corneille], the reign of Queen Elizabeth is in my apprehension thrown two centuries back. And if an event that happened yesterday were to be represented on the stage, I should conceive it to have happened at least in the time of Molière. The theatre has rules, maxims and morals, as well as dress, peculiar to itself, of which we very naturally and justly observe nothing of all this is proper for us; and indeed should think it as ridiculous to adopt the virtues of dramatic heroes as to strut about in costume or to talk in verse. Of all those sublime sentiments and brilliant maxims, therefore, that are so emphatically extolled in the theatre, it is plain they are calculated only for the stage, representing virtue as a pretty theatrical amusement, the practice of which it would be mighty absurd to think of carrying into life. Thus the most advantageous impression of the best tragedies is to reduce the duties and obligations of life to a few transitory affections, fruitless and ineffectual, just as some polite people conceive they have done an act of charity in bestowing a mere verbal blessing on a poor object as they pass by.

It is true that the stage might be made to assume a plainer appearance and that the language and modes of the theatre might be more accommodated to real life. But manners are described only, not corrected, by such means; for deformity is never shocking to those who are in like manner deformed. And yet should we attempt to correct them by aggravating the description into caricature, we should depart from nature, the picture would have no resemblance and be of no effect. Exaggeration does not make objects odious so much as it makes them ridiculous; whence results this great inconvenience that we are so afraid of ridicule that vice no longer strikes us with horror; and yet we cannot cure the former without encouraging the latter. You will ask perhaps why this opposition should be thought so necessary? Why, Sir, because men of probity never laugh at the vicious, but heartily despise them, nor is there anything in the world less pleasant or risible than the just indignation of virtue. Ridicule is, on the other hand, the favorite weapon of vice. With this it assails the veneration due to virtue till even the very sense of it is in time extinguished in the human breast.

Thus are we compelled to renounce that false idea of perfection which is imputed to dramatic entertainments as calculated for public utility. It is an error, says a certain grave writer [Muralt], to expect that in plays we should see the true relations of things, the poet seeking only, in general, to adapt them to the public taste. In comedy he diminishes everything and sinks it below the standard of nature; in tragedy he is inflated into heroism and rises as far above humanity as he was before below it. Thus in the theatre all is disproportionate, and we constantly see characters on the stage that are to be met with nowhere else. So certain indeed is this disproportion that Aristotle in his *Poetics* lays it down as a rule: *Comedia enim deteriores, tragedia meliores quam nunc funt imitari conantur* [for comedy aims at imitating men worse, and tragedy men better, than those of today]. This is undoubtedly a well-intended imitation that proposes for its object what has no existence, to the neglect of the mean between deficiency and excess, which really does exist, as if it were entirely useless! But of what consequence is the exactness of the imitation, if the illusion succeeds? The point is to excite the curiosity of the people. Dramatic productions, like all other masterpieces of human wit, have no other end than public applause. When the author meets with this applause, and the actors share in it, the end of the whole is answered, and they never trouble themselves further about the matter. Now if it have no good effect, it must have a bad one, and as this is not at all doubtful, the question seems to be determined. [...]

Having given this slight sketch of the nature and situation of the place, we will suppose that a theatre was erected at a small expense on the top of a mountain and in the midst of the habitations we have been speaking of, with the view of affording a decent entertainment for a people constantly employed and able to support the expense. Let us suppose further that these people should contract a liking for such entertainment, and then let us inquire what would be the result of such an institution. The first inconvenience that presents itself is that the occupation of these people ceasing to be their amusement, as soon as they have got another, they will be disgusted with the former; hence their industry will not furnish them with their former leisure, nor with the same inventions. Besides there will be every day so much time lost by all those who go to the play, who will hardly return immediately to their work with their heads full of what they have been seeing at the theatre, and of which they will continue to talk and ruminate. Hence will arise a decrease of labor, the first ill consequence.

However little they pay at entrance, it must still be something. Here is an expense they have not been at before. They must pay also for their wives and children when they take them thither, as of course they sometimes will. Add to this that a man cannot go to a public assembly in his working dress; he will hence be obliged to put on his Sunday clothes, to change his linen, and to be shaved and powdered more frequently, all of which will cost him both money and time. Here we have an increase of expenses, the second ill consequence.

An additional expense and diminished labor must have some means of indemnification. This will be found only in the price of labor, which of course will raise the price of their commodities. The traders, disgusted at this rise, will leave these mountaineers and provide themselves with the like commodities from their neighbors, who without being grown less industrious, should have no theatre and therefore would not have the same reason to raise the price of their goods. Hence decrease of trade, a third ill consequence.

In bad weather the roads are impassable, but the comedians must live in all weathers; their representation therefore must not be interrupted. The playhouse must of course then be accessible at all seasons. In the winter, roads must be opened through the snow; possibly they will be paved, and, God forgive us, perhaps lighted. Here arises a public expense, and consequently there must be a tax laid upon individuals to discharge it. Hence the establishment of taxes, a fourth ill consequence.

The wives of our mountaineers, going first to see and afterwards to be seen, must be dressed up, and that with marks of distinction. The squire's lady will not be seen at a play in the same attire as the wife of a schoolmaster, while the latter will endeavor to make as good an appearance as the former. Hence will soon arise an emulation in dress which will ruin their husbands and perhaps infect them with the same spirit, while every expedient will be thought of to evade the restraint of sumptuary laws. Hence the introduction of luxury, a fifth ill consequence.

What follows is easy to be conceived. Without placing to account, therefore, the other inconveniences which I already have, or hereafter shall mention, without examining into the nature of theatrical entertainments or the morality of their effects, I confine myself entirely to the articles of labor and profit; and I conceive I have proved, by a simple deduction of consequences, how a people who live easy and happy while they owe that ease and happiness to their industry hasten their own destruction when they exchange reality for appearance and precipitate themselves into luxury.

By the way, you are not to object that my supposition is chimerical. I lay it down as such, endeavoring only to render its inevitable consequences more or less perceptible. A few circumstances excepted, there are other mountaineers besides those I have described and the example is, *mutatis mutandis*, very generally applicable.

Thus, were it even true that theatrical entertainments are not bad in themselves, we are yet to enquire whether they may not become so with regard to any particular people for whom they are intended. In some places they may be useful to attract foreigners, to increase the circulation of specie, to afford encouragement to artists, to diversify modes of dress, to amuse the rich or those who aspire to become so, to render them less hurtful to society, to divert the poorer sort from thinking on their misery, to make them forget the demerit of their chiefs by attending to that of dancers, to maintain a kind of taste when real virtue is no more, to hide the deformity of vice with the varnish of decorum, and in a word, to prevent a corruption of manners from degenerating into flagrant licentiousness. In other places, however, they would tend to suppress the love of labor, to discourage industry, to ruin individuals, to infect them with idleness, to set them looking out for means of subsistence without working, to render the common people indolent and mean, to divert their attention from those public and private concerns which ought to employ their thoughts, to turn prudence into ridicule, to substitute a theatrical jargon in the place of virtue, to place all their morality in metaphysics, to convert sober citizens into rattling wits, their modest wives into fine ladies, and their daughters into amorous coquettes. The general effect would be the same on all men, but men thus perverted would be more or less proper for their situation and country. In becoming equal, the bad would be gainers, but the good would be still greater losers; both of them would contract a taste for indolence and effeminacy, which would deprive the one of great virtues and preserve the other from attempting great crimes.

From these new reflections we may infer a consequence directly contrary to that which I drew from the former, namely that when a people are corrupted, playhouses are good for them, and that when the people are uncorrupted, playhouses are bad. It should seem, therefore, that these two contrary effects counteracting each other, dramatic entertainments should be found indifferent to all. But there is this difference that the effect which enforces both the good and the evil is deduced from the spirit and tendency of the particular performance itself; it is subject, like them, to a thousand modifications that reduce it in a manner to nothing, whereas that effect which converts the good into evil and the evil into good results from the very institution itself and is a constant and real effect which is daily renewed and must in the end prevail. [...]

What then is the so highly boasted talent of a comedian? It is the art of dissimulation, of assuming a foreign character, and of appearing different to what he really is, of flying into a passion without cause and of saying what he does not think as naturally as if he really did, in a word, of forgetting himself to personate others. What is the profession of a comedian? A trade, in which a man publicly exhibits himself with a mercenary design, a trade in which he submits to insults and affronts from people who think they purchase a right to offer them when they please, a trade, in short, by which he exposes his person, carriage and demeanor to public sale. I appeal to every ingenuous mind whether he does not think this traffic has something in it extremely base and servile. Tell me, ye philosophers who affect to be above all vulgar prejudices, would you support the shame of being meanly metamorphosed into kings and obliged to play a part so different from your own, exposing your majestical personages to the rude shouts of the populace? What kind of spirit, then, is it in reality that a comedian imbibes from his profession? A mixture of meanness, falsehood and ridiculous pride which fits him for acting every kind of character except the noblest of all, that of man, which he throws aside.

I know that the profession of a comedian is not like that of a cheat who endeavors to impose on you; he does not indeed pretend that you should take him for the person represented, or that you should suppose him really actuated by the passions whose appearance he imitates. I am sensible, also, that in giving this imitation for what it really is he renders it perfectly innocent. I do not directly charge him therefore with being an impostor, but with his making it the business of his life to cultivate the arts of deception and with acquiring habits that, however innocent they may be on the stage, must everywhere else be subservient to vice. Will these fellows, so gaily dressed and so well practiced in gallantry, never make use of their arts to seduce young females? Will those cunning valets, who display such a volubility of tongue and dexterity of hand on the stage, never exert those abilities elsewhere? Will they never take a purse from an extravagant son or from an avaricious father for that of Léander or Argan? It will be found throughout the world that the temptation of doing ill increases with the facility of executing it so that it is necessary comedians should be more virtuous than other men, if they are not more corrupt.

It may be objected to this that the orator and preacher expose their persons in public as well as the comedian. But there is a very great difference between them. When the orator displays himself, it is to plead in somebody's behalf, and not to exhibit himself as a show. He represents no fictitious character, but plays his own proper part and speaks in his own name. He says, or at least ought to say, no more than he really thinks. The man and the character being one and the same, he is in his own place and in the case of every other citizen who discharges the duties of his station. But a comedian on the stage, displaying only the sentiments of others, says nothing but what he is directed, frequently representing even an imaginary being, so that the man is lost, as it were, in the hero; and in this state of oblivion, if any vestige of him is discoverable, it is only to be made the jest of the spectators. What shall I say of those who seem afraid of appearing too respectable in their own persons and therefore debase themselves so far as to act in characters what they would be very sorry really to resemble? It is undoubtedly a melancholy circumstance to see such a number of bad men in the world pass for honest people, but can anything be more base and odious than to see an honest comedian act the part of a villain and displaying all his art to inculcate such criminal maxims as in his heart he abhors. […]

Such, Sir, are the reflections I had to make and to lay before you and the public in relation to a question which you thought proper to discuss under an article, which was in my opinion quite foreign to the purpose. But though my arguments should be in fact less solid than they appear to me and therefore insufficient to counterbalance yours, you must yet agree with me that in so small a state as the republic of Geneva all innovations must be dangerous and that they should never be made without very cogent reasons. Now I should be glad to know the urgent motives of this. What are those disorders which should oblige us to have recourse to so dangerous an expedient? Are we undone if we do not adopt this measure? Is our city so extensive that it is impossible for our state to subsist any longer without theatrical entertainments? Will you say that it tolerates worse? Even such as are shocking to good taste as well as morality? But there is a very wide difference between the bare exhibition of vice and a direct attack on virtue, the latter depending not so much on the nature of the entertainment as on the impression made by it. In this sense, what affinity or connection is there between a few temporary drolls at a fair and the constant amusements of an established theatre, between the buffoonery of a mountebank and the regular exhibitions of the drama, between dirty booths erected to divert the populace a day or two and a decent theatre where genteel people expect to be instructed? One kind of these amusements is of no consequence, being forgotten the next day, while the other is an object of great importance, meriting the whole attention of government. It is permitted to amuse children in all countries, and everyone that has a mind to it may be a child when he pleases without any great inconvenience. If such diversions are tasteless, so much the better, the people will be the sooner tired of them; if they are gross and indelicate, they will be the less seductive. Vice seldom gains ground by transgressing the bounds of modesty, but generally by distinguishing itself under a decent appearance; and with regard to obscenity, it is certainly more impolite than it is immoral. It is for this reason that the most corrupt nations are always the most scrupulous and refined in their language and expressions. Was it ever perceived that the entertainments exhibited in fairs and market-places had much effect on the minds of those young people who went to see them? This is expected only from the polished conversation of the stage; and it would be a great deal better for a young girl to see a hundred drolls at a fair than to be once present at the representation of the *Oracle* [comedy by Saint-Foix].

Not but that I own with regard to myself that I should be glad we could do without even these drolls, and that all of us, great and small, could learn to derive our pleasures and duties from ourselves and our station in life. But it does not follow that because we ought to banish our mountebanks and puppet shows, we should introduce a company of comedians. You have in your own country an example of the city of Marseilles having stood out long against the like innovation, opposing even the repeated orders of the ministry in its favor, hence plainly showing it still preserved the memory and breathed the spirit of its ancient liberty. What a striking instance is this to a city still in possession of its liberty!

Above all things, however, we should never think of forming an establishment of this kind in the way of essay and with a view to its suppression when found to be attended with inconveniences, for these are not so easily removed as the object that gives rise to them. These effects will remain when the cause is no more, and indeed no sooner begin to be felt than they are already past remedy. When our taste and manners are once corrupted, they will not be so easily reformed, but our pleasures, our innocent pleasures, will lose their charms; the theatre will make us dislike them forever. Distraction from business once become necessary, we shall not know how to fill up our vacant hours, which will render us burdensome to ourselves; the comedians will leave us in a state of listlessness, which will be a pledge of their return and compel us to recall them or to do still worse. We shall do ill to erect a theatre; we shall do ill in suffering it to subsist when erected; we shall do ill to pull it down again; in short, after the first error, do what we will, it must be wrong.

Must there be, then, no public shows or entertainments in a republican state? There should be a great many. It was in republics they were first instituted, and it is in them they are celebrated with the genuine air of festivity. What people does it more become to have frequent meetings, to engage in parties of pleasure and diversion than those who have so many reasons for loving each other and for continuing united? We have many of these festivals already, and I should be delighted if we had more. But let us not adopt these exclusive entertainments which keep a small number of people shut up in a gloomy cavern, there to sit for hours motionless, silent and inactive, within partitions, iron-spikes, and files of soldiery, the disagreeable badges of slavery and inequality. No, my happy countrymen, such are not your festivals! It is in the open air, in the face of heaven, you ought to meet and indulge yourselves in the enjoyment of your own happiness. Your pleasures should be neither venal nor effeminate, unpoisoned by interest or constraint; but free and generous like ourselves, the sun should enliven your innocent spectacles with his meridian beams, while you yourselves would form one of the noblest sights they ever enlightened.

But what will be the objects exhibited at these spectacles? What will there be to be seen there? Nothing, if you will. When liberty is to be found in the midst of plenty, there is the seat of human happiness. Raise a maypole with a chaplet of flowers in the middle of a plain; call the people about it, and their assembly will become a festival. But you may still do better; the spectators themselves may be made actors; they may be made to see and reciprocally love themselves in each other to the end that all may be more intimately united. I need not refer to the games of ancient Greece; there are others more modern still subsisting and which subsist even among us. We have our annual reviews, public prizes, and contests in firing small arms, in the management of artillery, and in the art of sailing, in all which those who excel are crowned kings of the day. We cannot have too many institutions so useful and agreeable; the number of such kings cannot hurt us. Why should we not take the same measures to render ourselves healthy and active as we do to learn the exercise of arms? Does the Republic stand in less need of artisans than soldiers? Why should we not adopt the plan of military rewards and found other gymnastic prizes for running, wrestling, throwing quoits, and other bodily exercises? Why do not we animate our watermen to exert themselves for wagers on the lake? Can there possibly be a finer sight in the world than to see some hundreds of boats, elegantly equipped, floating on that spacious basin and setting off at a given signal, to seize a flag hoisted as a mark and to be brought off by the victor in triumph when he returns to claim the prize? All such kind of entertainments are no more expensive than people please to make them, while the concourse alone renders them sufficiently magnificent. It is necessary, however, to have been present at our exercises of this kind to form an idea of the avidity which the Genevans seem to take in them. They appear to be no longer the same people: they are no more those methodical economists, those formal casuists that weigh even pleasantry itself in the balance of reason. Everyone is cheerful, gay and complacent; his heart is at these seasons to be read in his eyes, as it speaks at all others from his lips; he endeavors to communicate his satisfaction to everyone he sees, inviting, pressing, and contending with him in the zeal of good-fellowship and civility. All the several companies form themselves into one, and everything is made common among them. It is almost indifferent at what table you sit down, and the whole would be a complete image of a Spartan entertainment if it were not so profuse. Even this profusion itself, however, has its propriety; the aspect of abundance heightens that of liberty which produces it. [...]

SAMUEL JOHNSON

Samuel JOHNSON (1709-1784) was a sickly weak-eyed child given to odd gesticulations and convulsive fits and starts that shook his entire frame. He grew into a huge, ungainly monstrosity. Nearly six feet tall, large-boned, broad-shouldered, and thick-necked, he walked bent over almost double. His face was rugged, pitted, and scrofula-scarred, and he eventually lost the sight of one of his wild, staring eyes which were light blue in color. Slovenly in dress, he wore a rough suit of rusty-looking brown cloth and a little old shriveled unpowdered wig, which was much too small for his oversized head.

Johnson's devoted biographer Boswell has described the extraordinary show that his hero put on when making his famous literary judgments.

"While talking or even musing as he sat in his chair, he commonly held his head to one side towards his right shoulder, and shook it in a tremulous manner, moving his body backwards and forwards, and rubbing his left knee in the same direction, with the palm of his hand. In the intervals of articulating he made various sounds with his mouth, sometimes as if ruminating, or what is called chewing the cud, sometimes giving half a whistle, sometimes making his tongue play backwards from the roof of his mouth, as if clucking like a hen, and sometimes protruding it against his upper gums in front, as if pronouncing quickly under his breath, too, too, too ... Generally when he had concluded a period in the course of a dispute, by which time he was a good deal exhausted by violence and vociferation, he used to blow out his breath like a Whale."

As a youth, Johnson had seen the strolling players, but his real experience of theatre was as a reader of Shakespeare. It is doubtful he ever saw many plays well performed. After spending years studying the text as an editor, Johnson came to see Shakespeare as a poet, not a player. During the last twenty-five years of his life, unable to see or hear well, Johnson attended the theatre only infrequently. He knew nothing about painting or any of the other arts that contribute to theatrical performances.

Johnson was totally ignorant of the practical side of the stage, had a low view of the theatrical profession, and disparaged actors as mere entertainers, although as a clever mimic in conversation, he had the talent that he despised in performers. An actor, he said, is "a fellow who claps a hump on his back, and a lump on his leg, and cries, 'I am Richard III.'" He resented the huge success and vast fortune of his former friend and pupil Garrick whom he called "a player—a showman—a fellow who exhibits himself for a shilling." A great admirer of the *fantoccini* in London, Johnson considered a performance of *Macbeth* by puppets as satisfactory as when played by human actors.

Skeptical of the ability of actors to create any sense of make-believe, Johnson opposed the theory of dramatic illusion. He had his own personal reasons for resisting the powers of delusion and the horrors of tragedy. Ever since he had been terrified by the ghost on first reading *Hamlet* as a boy of nine, he suffered from an obsessive dread of madness and the irrational. Prone to depression and fearful of his own dreams, Johnson insisted on sanity and order in art as a defense against a self-tormented, melancholy inner nature.

Only in his secret diary did he reveal his dark and anguished thoughts. There Johnson created his own theatre of the irrational, disclosing that he gave a pair of manacles to his admiring friend, Mrs. Thrail, and implored her to lock him up and beat him if he ever gave way to raging despair.

Set in a remote place, far removed from common life, Johnson's sole attempt at drama, *Irene*, a stiff, stylized tragedy performed nine times by Garrick, was totally deficient in what he extolled in Shakespeare—a just representation of general nature. Johnson was an idiosyncratic neoclassicist, proclaiming truth to life as the sole criterion of excellence.

For the romantics, he was the very antithesis of poetry, absolutely incapable of understanding the great poet whom he edited.

For his admirers, he represents the heroic triumph of reason and sanity over adversity. "What I loved," Peter Hall said of Johnson, "was his commonsense understanding of Shakespeare, with no antiquarian or romantic nonsense, and his huge capacity for life."

PREFACE TO SHAKESPEARE (1765)

That praises are without reason lavished on the dead, and that the honors due only to excellence are paid to antiquity, is a complaint likely to be always continued by those, who, being able to add nothing to truth, hope for eminence from the heresies of paradox; or those, who, being forced by disappointment upon consolatory expedients, are willing to hope from posterity what the present age refuses, and flatter themselves that the regard which is yet denied by envy, will be at last bestowed by time.

Antiquity, like every other quality that attracts the notice of mankind, has undoubtedly votaries that reverence it, not from reason, but from prejudice. Some seem to admire indiscriminately whatever has been long presented, without considering that time has sometimes co-operated with chance; all perhaps are more willing to honor past than present excellence; and the mind contemplates genius through the shades of age, as the eye surveys the sun through artificial opacity. The great contention of criticism is to find the faults of the moderns, and the beauties of the ancients. While an author is yet living we estimate his powers by his worst performance, and when he is dead, we rate them by his best.

To works, however, of which the excellence is not absolute and definite, but gradual and comparative; to works not raised upon principles demonstrative and scientific, but appealing wholly to observation and experience, no other test can be applied than length of duration and continuance of esteem. What mankind have long possessed they have often examined and compared; and if they persist to value the possession, it is because frequent comparisons have confirmed opinion in its favor. As among the works of nature no man can properly call a river deep, or a mountain high, without the knowledge of many mountains, and many rivers; so in the productions of genius, nothing can be styled excellent till it has been compared with other works of the same kind. Demonstration immediately displays its power, and has nothing to hope or fear from the flux of years; but works tentative and experimental must be estimated by their proportion to the general and collective ability of man, as it is discovered in a long succession of endeavors. Of the first building that was raised, it might be with certainty determined that it was round or square; but

From *The Works of Samuel Johnson*, Vol II.
N.Y.: Harper & Brothers, 1851.

whether it was spacious or lofty must have been referred to time. The Pythagorean scale of numbers was at once discovered to be perfect; but the poems of Homer we yet know not to transcend the common limits of human intelligence, but by remarking, that nation after nation, and century after century, has been able to do little more than transpose his incidents, new-name his characters, and paraphrase his sentiments.

The reverence due to writings that have long subsisted arises therefore not from any credulous confidence in the superior wisdom of past ages, or gloomy persuasion of the degeneracy of mankind, but is the consequence of acknowledged and indubitable positions, that what has been longest known has been most considered, and what is most considered is best understood.

The Poet, of whose works I have undertaken the revision, may now begin to assume the dignity of an ancient, and claim the privilege of established fame and prescriptive veneration. He has long outlived his century, the term commonly fixed as the test of literary merit. Whatever advantages he might once derive from personal allusions, local customs, or temporary opinions, have for many years been lost; and every topic of merriment, or motive of sorrow, which the modes of artificial life afforded him, now only obscure the scenes which they once illuminated. The effects of favor and competition are at an end, the tradition of his friendships and his enmities has perished; his works support no opinion with arguments, nor supply any faction with invectives; they can neither indulge vanity nor gratify malignity; but are read without any other reason than the desire of pleasure, and are therefore praised only as pleasure is obtained; yet, thus unassisted by interest or passion, they have past through variations of taste and changes of manners, and, as they devolved from one generation to another have received new honors at every transmission.

But because human judgment, though it be gradually gaining upon certainty, never becomes infallible; and approbation, though long continued, may yet be only the approbation of prejudice or fashion; it is proper to inquire, by what peculiarities of excellence Shakespeare has gained and kept the favor of his countrymen.

Nothing can please many, and please long, but just representations of general nature. Particular manners can be known to few, and therefore few only can judge how nearly they are copied. The irregular combinations of fanciful invention may delight a-while, by that novelty of which the common satiety of life sends us all in quest; but the pleasures of sudden wonder are soon exhausted, and the mind can only repose on the stability of truth.

Shakespeare is above all writers, at least above all modern writers, the poet of nature; the poet that holds up to his readers a faithful mirror of manners and of life. His characters are not modified by the customs of particular places, unpracticed by the rest of the world; by the peculiarities of studies or professions, which can operate but upon small numbers; or by the accidents of transient fashions or temporary opinions: they are the genuine progeny of common humanity, such as the world will always supply, and observation will always find. His persons act and speak by the influence of those general passions and principles by which all minds are agitated, and the whole system of life is continued in motion. In the writings of other poets a character is too often an individual; in those of Shakespeare it is commonly a species.

It is from this wide extension of design that so much instruction is derived. It is this which fills the plays of Shakespeare with practical axioms and domestic wisdom. It was said of Euripides, that every verse was a precept; and it may be said of Shakespeare, that from his works may be collected a system of civil and economical prudence. Yet his real power is not shown in the splendor of particular passages, but by the progress of his fable, and the tenor of his dialogue; and he that tries to recommend him by select quotations, will succeed like the pedant in *Hierocles*, who, when he offered his house to sale, carried a brick in his pocket as a specimen.

It will not easily be imagined how much Shakespeare excels in accommodating his sentiments to real life, but by comparing him with other authors. It was observed of the ancient schools of declamation, that the more diligently they were frequented, the more was the student disqualified for the world, because he found nothing there which he should ever meet in any other place. The same remark may be applied to every stage but that of Shakespeare. The theatre, when it is under any other direction, is peopled by such characters as were never seen, conversing in a language which was never heard, upon topics which will never rise in the commerce of mankind. But the dialogue of this author is often so evidently determined by the incident which produces it, and is pursued with so much ease and simplicity, that it seems scarcely to claim the merit of fiction, but to have been gleaned by diligent selection out of common conversation, and common occurrences.

Upon every other stage the universal agent is love, by whose power all good and evil is distributed, and every action quickened or retarded. To bring a lover, a lady and a rival into the fable; to entangle them in contradictory obligations, perplex them with oppositions of interest, and harass them with violence of desires inconsistent with each other; to make them meet in rapture and part in agony; to fill their mouths with hyperbolical joy and outrageous sorrow; to distress them as nothing human ever was distressed; to deliver them as nothing human ever was delivered; is the business of a modern dramatist. For this probability is violated, life is misrepresented, and language is depraved. But love is only one of many passions; and as it has no great influence upon the sum of life, it has little operation in the dramas of a poet, who caught his ideas from the living world, and exhibited only what he saw before him. He knew, that any other passion, as it was regular or exorbitant, was a cause of happiness or calamity.

Characters thus ample and general were not easily discriminated and preserved, yet perhaps no poet ever kept his personages more distinct from each other. I will not say with Pope, that every speech may be assigned to the proper speaker, because many speeches there are which have nothing characteristical; but perhaps, though some may be equally adapted to every person, it will be difficult to find any that can be properly transferred from the present possessor to another claimant. The choice is right, when there is reason for choice.

Other dramatists can only gain attention by hyperbolical or aggravated characters, by fabulous and unexampled excellence or depravity, as the writers of barbarous romances invigorated the reader by a giant and a dwarf; and he that should form his expectations of human affairs from the play, or from the tale, would be equally deceived. Shakespeare has no heroes; his scenes are occupied only by men, who act and speak as the reader thinks that he should himself have spoken or acted on the same occasion: even where the agency is supernatural the dialogue is level with life. Other writers disguise the most natural passions and most frequent incidents; so that he who contemplates them in the book will not know them in the world: Shakespeare approximates the remote, and familiarizes the wonderful; the event which he represents will not happen, but if it were possible, its effects would probably be such as he has assigned; and it may be said, that he has not only shown human nature as it acts in real exigencies, but as it would be found in trials, to which it cannot be exposed.

This therefore is the praise of Shakespeare, that his drama is the mirror of life; that he who has mazed his imagination, in following the phantoms which other writers raise up before him, may here be cured of his delirious ecstasies, by reading human sentiments in human language, by scenes from which a hermit may estimate the transactions of the world, and a confessor predict the progress of the passions.

His adherence to general nature has exposed him to the censure of critics, who form their judgments upon narrow principles. Dennis and Rhymer think his Romans not sufficiently Roman; and Voltaire censures his kings as not completely royal. Dennis is offended, that Menenius, a senator of Rome, should play the buffoon; and Voltaire perhaps thinks decency violated when the Danish Usurper is represented as a drunkard. But Shakespeare always makes nature predominate over accident; and if he preserves the essential character, is not very careful of distinctions superinduced and adventitious. His story requires Romans or kings, but he thinks only on men. He knew that Rome, like every other city, had men of all dispositions; and wanting a buffoon, he went into the senate-house for that which the senate-house would certainly have afforded him. He was inclined to show an usurper and a murderer not only odious but despicable, he therefore added a drunkenness to his other qualities, knowing that kings love wine like other men, and that wine exerts its natural power upon kings. These are the petty cavils of petty minds;

a poet overlooks the casual distinction of country and condition; as a painter, satisfied with the figure, neglects the drapery.

The censure which he has incurred by mixing comic and tragic scenes, as it extends to all his works, deserves more consideration. Let the fact be first stated, and then examined.

Shakespeare's plays are not in the rigorous and critical sense either tragedies or comedies, but compositions of a distinct kind; exhibiting the real state of sublunary nature, which partakes of good and evil, joy and sorrow, mingled with endless variety of proportion and innumerable modes of combination; and expressing the course of the world, in which the loss of one is the gain of another; in which, at the same time, the reveler is hasting to his wine, and the mourner burying his friend; in which the malignity of one is sometimes defeated by the frolic of another; and many mischiefs and many benefits are done and hindered without design.

Out of this chaos of mingled purposes and casualties the ancient poets, according to the laws which custom had prescribed, selected some the crimes of men, and some their absurdities; some the momentous vicissitudes of life, and some the lighter occurrences; some the terrors of distress, and some the gaieties of prosperity. Thus rose the two modes of imitation, known by the names of tragedy and comedy, compositions intended to promote different ends by contrary means, and considered as so little allied, that I do not recollect among the Greeks or Romans a single writer who attempted both.

Shakespeare has united the powers of exciting laughter and sorrow not only in one mind, but in one composition. Almost all his plays are divided between serious and ludicrous characters, and, in the successive evolutions of the design, sometimes produce seriousness and sorrow, and sometimes levity and laughter.

That this is a practice contrary to the rules of criticism will be readily allowed; but there is always an appeal open from criticism to nature. The end of writing is to instruct; the end of poetry is to instruct by pleasing. That the mingled drama may convey all the instruction of tragedy or comedy cannot be denied, because it includes both in its alterations of exhibition and approaches nearer than either to the appearance of life, by showing how great machinations and slender designs may promote or obviate one another, and the high and the low co-operate in the general system by unavoidable concatenation.

It is objected, that by this change of scenes the passions are interrupted in their progression, and that the principal event, being not advanced by a due gradation of preparatory incidents, wants at last the power to move, which constitutes the perfection of dramatic poetry. This reasoning is so specious, that it is received as true even by those who in daily experience feel it to be false. The interchanges of mingled scenes seldom fail to produce the intended vicissitudes of passion. Fiction cannot move so much, but that the attention may be easily transferred; and though it must be allowed that pleasing melancholy be sometimes interrupted by unwelcome levity, yet let it be considered likewise, that melancholy is often not pleasing, and that the disturbance of one man may be the relief of another; that different auditors have different habitudes; and that, upon the whole, all pleasure consists in variety.

The players, who in their edition divided our author's works into comedies, histories, and tragedies, seem not to have distinguished the three kinds by any very exact or definite ideas.

Any action which ended happily to the principal persons, however serious or distressful through its intermediate incidents, in their opinion, constituted a comedy. This idea of a comedy continued long amongst us; and plays were written, which, by changing the catastrophe, were tragedies today, and comedies tomorrow.

Tragedy was not in those times a poem of more general dignity or elevation than comedy; it required only a calamitous conclusion, with which the common criticism of that age was satisfied, whatever lighter pleasure it afforded in its progress.

History was a series of actions, with no other than chronological succession, independent of each other, and without any tendency to introduce or regulate the conclusion. It is not always very nicely distinguished from tragedy. There is not much nearer approach to unity of action in the tragedy of *Antony and Cleopatra*, than in the history of *Richard II*. But a history might be continued through many plays; as it had no plan, it had no limits.

Through all these denominations of the drama, Shakespeare's mode of composition is the same; an interchange of seriousness and merriment, by which the mind is softened at one time, and, exhilarated at another. But whatever be his purpose, whether to gladden or depress, or to conduct the story, without vehemence or emotion through tracts of easy and familiar dialogue, he never fails to attain his purpose; as he commands us, we laugh or mourn or sit silent with quiet expectation, in tranquillity without indifference.

When Shakespeare's plan is understood, most of the criticisms of Rhymer and Voltaire vanish away. The play of *Hamlet* is opened, without impropriety, by two sentinels; Iago bellows at Brabantio's window, without injury to the scheme of the play, though in terms which a modern audience would not easily endure; the character of Polonius is seasonable and useful; and the Grave-diggers themselves may be heard with applause.

Shakespeare engaged in dramatic poetry with the world open before him; the rules of the ancients were yet known to few; but public judgment was unformed; he had no example of such fame as might force him upon imitation, nor critics of such authority as might restrain his extravagance: he therefore indulged his natural disposition, and his disposition, as Rhymer has remarked, led him to comedy. In tragedy he often writes, with great appearance of toil and study, what is written at last with little felicity; but in his comic scenes, he seems to produce without labor what no labor can improve. In tragedy he is always struggling after some occasion to be comic; but in comedy he seems to repose, or to luxuriate, as in a mode of thinking congenial to his nature. In his tragic scenes there is always something wanting, but his comedy often surpasses expectation or desire. His comedy pleases by the thoughts and the language and his tragedy for the greater part by incident and action. His tragedy seems to be skill, his comedy to be instinct.

The force of his comic scenes has suffered little diminution from the changes made by a century and a half, in manners or in words. As his personages act upon principles arising from genuine passion, very little modified by particular forms, their pleasures and vexations are communicable to all times and to all places; they are natural, and therefore durable; the adventitious peculiarities of personal habits, are only superficial dies, bright and pleasing for a little while, yet soon fading to a dim tinct, without any remains of former luster; but the discriminations of true passion are the colors of nature; they pervade the whole mass, and can only perish with the body that exhibits them. The accidental compositions of heterogeneous modes are dissolved by the chance which combined them; but the uniform simplicity of primitive qualities neither admits increase, nor suffers decay. The sand heaped by one flood is scattered by another, but the rock always continues in its place. The stream of time, which is continually washing the dissoluble fabrics of other poets, passes without injury by the adamant of Shakespeare.

If there be, what I believe there is, in every nation, a style which never becomes obsolete, a certain mode of phraseology so consonant and congenial to the analogy and principles of its respective language as to remain settled and unaltered; this style is probably to be sought in the common intercourse of life, among those who speak only to be understood, without ambition of elegance. The polite are always catching modish innovations, and the learned depart from established forms of speech, in hope of finding or making better; those who wish for distinction forsake the vulgar, when the vulgar is right; but there is a conversation above grossness and below refinement, where propriety resides, and where this poet seems to have gathered his comic dialogue. He is therefore more agreeable to the ears of the present age than any other author equally remote, and among his other excellencies deserves to be studied as one of the original masters of our language.

These observations are to be considered not as unexceptionally constant, but as containing general and predominant truth. Shakespeare's familiar dialogue is affirmed to be smooth and clear, yet not wholly without ruggedness or difficulty; as a country maybe eminently fruitful, though it has spots unfit for cultivation: his characters are praised as natural, though their sentiments are sometimes forced, and their actions improbable; as the earth upon the whole is spherical, though its surface is varied with protuberances and cavities.

Shakespeare with his excellencies has likewise faults, and faults sufficient to obscure and overwhelm any other merit. I shall show them in the proportion in which they appear to me, without envious malignity or superstitious veneration. No question can be more innocently discussed than a dead poet's pretensions to renown; and little regard is due to that bigotry which sets candor higher than truth.

His first defect is that to which may be imputed most of the evil in books or in men. He sacrifices virtue to convenience, and is so much more careful to please than to instruct, that he seems to write without any moral purpose. From his writings indeed a system of social duty may be selected, for he that thinks reasonably must think morally; but his precepts and axioms drop casually from him; he makes no just distribution of good or evil, nor is always careful to show in the virtuous a disapprobation of the wicked; he carries his persons indifferently through right and wrong, and at the close dismisses them without further care, and leaves their examples to operate by chance. This fault the barbarity of his age cannot extenuate; for it is always a writer's duty to make the world better, and justice is a virtue independent of time or place.

The plots are often so loosely formed, that a very slight consideration may improve them, and so carelessly pursued, that he seems not always fully to comprehend his own design. He omits opportunities of instructing or delighting which the train of his story seems to force upon him, and apparently rejects those exhibitions which would be more affecting, for the sake of those which are more easy.

It may be observed, that in many of his plays the latter part is evidently neglected. When he found himself near the end of his work, and, in view of his reward, he shortened the labor to snatch the profit. He therefore remits his efforts where he should most vigorously exert them, and his catastrophe is improbably produced or imperfectly represented.

He had no regard to distinction of time or place, but gives to one age or nation, without scruple, the customs, institutions, and opinions of another, at the expense not only of likelihood, but of possibility. These faults Pope has endeavored, with more zeal than judgment, to transfer to his imagined interpolators. We need not wonder to find Hector quoting Aristotle, when we see the loves of Theseus and Hippolyta combined with the Gothic mythology of fairies. Shakespeare, indeed, was not the only violator of chronology, for in the same age Sidney, who wanted not the advantages of learning, has, in his *Arcadia*, confounded the pastoral with the feudal times, the days of innocence, quiet and security, with those of turbulence, violence, and adventure.

In his comic scenes he is seldom very successful, when he engages his characters in reciprocations of smartness and contests of sarcasm; their jests are commonly gross, and their pleasantry licentious; neither his gentlemen nor his ladies have much delicacy, nor are sufficiently distinguished from his clowns by any appearance of refined manners. Whether he represented the real conversation of his time is not easy to determine; the reign of Elizabeth is commonly supposed to have been a time of stateliness, formality and reserve; yet perhaps the relaxations of that severity were not very elegant. There must, however, have been always some modes of gaiety preferable to others, and a writer ought to choose the best.

In tragedy his performance seems constantly to be worse, as his labor is more. The effusions of passion which exigency forces out are for the most part striking and energetic; but whenever he solicits his invention, or strains his faculties, the offspring of his throes is tumor, meanness, tediousness, and obscurity.

In narration he affects a disproportionate pomp of diction, and a wearisome train of circumlocution, and tells the incident imperfectly in many words, which might have been more plainly delivered in few. Narration in dramatic poetry is naturally tedious, as it is unanimated and inactive, and obstructs the progress of the action; it should therefore always be rapid, and enlivened by frequent interruption. Shakespeare found it an encumbrance, and instead of lightening it by brevity, endeavored to recommend it by dignity and splendor.

His declamations or set speeches are commonly cold and weak for his power was the power of nature; when he endeavored, like other tragic writers, to catch opportunities of amplification, and instead of inquiring what the occasion demanded, to show how much his stores of knowledge could supply, he seldom escaped without the pity or resentment of his reader.

It is incident to him to be now and then entangled with an unwieldy sentiment, which he cannot well express, and will not reject; he struggles with it a while, and if it continues stubborn, comprises it in words such as occur, and leaves it to be disentangled and evolved by those who have more leisure to bestow upon it.

Not that always where the language is intricate the thought is subtle, or the image always great where the line is bulky; the equality of words to things is very often neglected, and trivial sentiments and vulgar ideas disappoint the attention, to which they are recommended by sonorous epithets and swelling figures.

But the admirers of this great poet have never less reason to indulge their hopes of supreme excellence, than when he seems fully resolved to sink them in dejection, and mollify them with tender emotions by the fall of greatness, the danger of innocence, or the crosses of love. He is not long soft and pathetic without some idle conceit, or contemptible equivocation. He no sooner begins to move, than he counteracts himself; and terror and pity, as they are rising in the mind, are checked and blasted by sudden frigidity.

A quibble is to Shakespeare, what luminous vapors are to the traveler: he follows it at all adventures; it is sure to lead him out of his way, and sure to engulf him in the mire. It has some malignant power over his mind, and its fascinations are irresistible. Whatever be the dignity or profundity of his disquisition, whether he be enlarging knowledge or exalting affection, whether he be amusing attention with incidents, or enchaining it in suspense, let but a quibble spring up before him, and he leaves his work unfinished. A quibble is the golden apple for which he will always turn aside from his career, or stoop from his elevation. A quibble, poor and barren as it is, gave him such delight, that he was content to purchase it, by the sacrifice of reason, propriety and truth. A quibble was to him the fatal Cleopatra for which he lost the world, and was content to lose it.

It will be thought strange, that, in enumerating the defects of his writer, I have not yet mentioned his neglect of the unities; his violation of those laws which have been instituted and established by the joint authority of poets and critics.

For his other deviations from the art of writing I resign him to critical justice, without making any other demand in his favor, than that which must be indulged to all human excellence: that his virtues be rated with his failings: but, from the censure which this irregularity may bring upon him, I shall, with due reverence to that learning which I must oppose, adventure to try how I can defend him.

His histories, being neither tragedies nor comedies are not subject to any of their laws; nothing more is necessary to all the praise which they expect, than that the changes of action be so prepared as to be understood, that the incidents be various and affecting, and the characters consistent, natural, and distinct. No other unity is intended, and therefore none is to be sought.

In his other works he has well enough preserved the unity of action. He has not, indeed, an intrigue regularly perplexed and regularly unraveled: he does not endeavor to hide his design only to discover it, for this is seldom the order of real events, and Shakespeare is the poet of nature: but his plan has commonly what Aristotle requires, a beginning, a middle, and an end; one event is concatenated with another, and the conclusion follows by easy consequence. There are perhaps some incidents that might be spared, as in other poets there is much talk that only fills up time upon the stage; but the general system makes gradual advances, and the end of the play is the end of expectation.

To the unities of time and place he has shown no regard; and perhaps a nearer view of the principles on which they stand will diminish their value, and withdraw from them the veneration which, from the time of Corneille, they have very generally received, by discovering that they have given more trouble to the poet, than pleasure to the auditor.

The necessity of observing the unities of time and place arises from the supposed necessity of making the drama credible. The critics hold it impossible, that an action of months or years can be possibly believed to pass in three hours; or that the spectator can suppose himself to sit in a theatre, while ambassadors go and return between distant kings, while armies are levied and towns besieged, while an exile wanders and returns, or till he whom they saw courting his mistress, shall lament the untimely fall of his son. The mind revolts from evident falsehood, and fiction loses its force when it departs from the resemblance of reality.

From the narrow limitation of time necessarily arises the contraction of place. The spectator, who knows that he saw the first acts at Alexandria, cannot suppose that he sees the next at Rome, at a distance to which not the dragons of Medea could, in so short a time, have transported him; he knows with certainty that he has not changed his place, and he knows that place cannot change itself; that what was a house cannot become a plain; that what was Thebes can never be Persepolis.

Such is the triumphant language with which a critic exults over the misery of an irregular poet, and exults commonly without resistance or reply. It is time therefore to tell him by the authority of Shakespeare, that he assumes, as an unquestionable principle, a position, which, while his breath is forming it into words, his understanding pronounces to be false. It is false, that any representation is mistaken for reality; that any dramatic fable in its materiality was ever credible, or, for a single moment, was ever credited.

The objection arising from the impossibility of passing the first hour at Alexandria, and the next at Rome, supposes, that when the play opens, the spectator really imagines himself at Alexandria, and believes that his walk to the theatre has been a voyage to Egypt, and that he lives in the days of Antony and Cleopatra. Surely he that imagines this may imagine more. He that can take the stage at one time for the palace of the Ptolemies, may take it in half an hour for the promontory of Actium. Delusion, if delusion be admitted, has no certain limitation; if the spectator can be once persuaded, that his old acquaintances are Alexander and Caesar, that a room illuminated with candles is the plain of Pharsalia, or the bank of Granicus, he is in a state of elevation above the reach of reason, or of truth, and from the heights of empyrean poetry, may despise the circumscriptions of terrestrial nature. There is no reason why a mind thus wandering in ecstasy should count the clock, or why an hour should not be a century in that calenture of the brains that can make the stage a field.

The truth is, that the spectators are always in their senses, and know, from the first act to the last, that the stage is only a stage, and that the players are only players. They came to hear a certain number of lines recited with just gesture and elegant modulation. The lines relate to some action, and an action must be in some place; but the different actions that complete a story may be in places very remote from each other; and where is the absurdity of allowing that space to represent first Athens, and then Sicily, which was always known to be neither Sicily nor Athens, but a modern theatre?

By supposition, as place is introduced, times may be extended; the time required by the fable elapses for the most part between the acts; for, of so much of the action as is represented, the real and poetical duration is the same. If, in the first act, preparations for war against Mithridates are represented to be made in Rome, the event of the war may, without absurdity, be represented, in the catastrophe, as happening in Pontus; we know that there is neither war, nor preparation for war; we know that we are neither in Rome nor Pontus; that neither Mithridates nor Lucullus are before us. The drama exhibits successive imitations of successive actions; and why may not the second imitation represent an action that happened years after the first, if it be so connected with it, that nothing but time can be supposed to intervene? Time is, of all modes of existence, most obsequious to the imagination; a lapse of years is as easily conceived as a passage of hours. In contemplation we easily contract the time of real actions, and therefore willingly permit it to be contracted when we only see their imitation.

It will be asked, how the drama moves, if it is not credited. It is credited with all the credit due to a drama. It is credited, whenever it moves, as a just picture of a real original; as representing to the auditor what he would himself feel, if he were to do or suffer what is there feigned to be suffered or to be done. The reflection that strikes the heart is not, that the evils before us are real evils, but that they are evils to which we ourselves may be exposed. If there be any fallacy, it is not that we fancy the players, but that we fancy ourselves unhappy for a moment; but we rather lament the possibility than suppose the presence of misery, as a mother weeps over her babe, when she remembers that death may take it from her. The delight of tragedy proceeds from our consciousness of fiction; if we thought murders and treasons real, they would please no more.

Imitations produce pain or pleasure, not because they are mistaken for realities, but because they bring realities to mind. When the imagination is recreated by a painted landscape, the trees are not supposed capable to give us shade, or the fountains coolness; but we consider, how we should be pleased with such fountains playing beside us, and such woods waving over us. We are agitated in reading the history of Henry V, yet no man takes his book for the field of Agencourt. A dramatic exhibition is a book recited with concomitants that increase or diminish its effect. Familiar comedy is often more powerful in the theatre, than on the page; imperial tragedy is always less. The humor of Petruchio may be heightened by grimace; but what voice or what gesture can hope to add dignity or force to the soliloquy of Cato.

A play read, affects the mind like a play acted. It is therefore evident, that the action is not supposed to be real; and it follows, that between the acts a longer or shorter time may be allowed to pass, and that no more account of space or duration is to be taken by the auditor of a drama, than by the reader of a narrative, before whom may pass in an hour the life of a hero, or the revolutions of an empire.

Whether Shakespeare knew the unities, and rejected them by design, or deviated from them by happy ignorance, it is, I think, impossible to decide, and useless to inquire. We may reasonably suppose, that when he rose to notice, he did not want the counsels and admonitions of scholars and critics, and that he at last deliberately persisted in a practice, which he might have begun by chance. As nothing is essential to the fable, but unity of action, and as the unities of time and place arise evidently from false assumptions, and, by circumscribing the extent of the drama, lessen its variety, I cannot think it much to be lamented, that they were not known by him, or not observed: nor, if such another poet could arise, should I very vehemently reproach him, that his first act passed at Venice, and his next in Cyprus. Such violations of rules merely positive, become the comprehensive genius of Shakespeare, and such censures are suitable to the minute and slender criticism of Voltaire. [...]

Yet when I speak thus slightly of dramatic rules, I cannot but recollect how much wit and learning may be produced against me; before such authorities I am afraid to stand, not that I think the present question one of those that are to be decided by mere authority, but because it is to be suspected, that these precepts have not been so easily received but for better reasons than I have yet been able to find. The result of my inquiries, in which it would be ludicrous to boast of impartiality, is, that the unities of time and place are not essential to a just drama, that though they may sometimes conduce to pleasure, they are always to be sacrificed to the nobler beauties of variety and instruction; and that a play, written with nice observation of critical rules, is to be contemplated as an elaborate curiosity, as the product of superfluous and ostentatious art, by which is shown, rather what is possible, than what is necessary.

He that, without diminution of any other excellence, shall preserve all the unities unbroken, deserves the like applause with the architect, who shall display all the orders of architecture in a citadel, without any deduction from its strength, but the principal beauty of a citadel is to exclude the enemy; and the greatest graces of play, are to copy nature and instruct life.

Perhaps what I have here not dogmatically but deliberately written may recall the principles of the drama to a new examination. I am almost frightened at my own temerity; and when I estimate the fame and the strength of those that maintain the contrary opinion, I am ready to sink down in reverential silence; as Aeneas withdrew from the defense of Troy, when he saw Neptune shaking the wall, and Juno heading the besiegers.

Those whom my arguments cannot persuade to give their approbation to the judgment of Shakespeare, will easily, if they consider the condition of his life, make some allowance for his ignorance.

Every man's performances, to be rightly estimated, must be compared with the state of the age in which he lived, and with his own particular opportunities; and though to the reader a book be not worse or better for the circumstances of the author, yet as there is always a silent reference of human works to human abilities, and as the inquiry, how far man may extend his designs, or how high he may rate his native force, is of far greater dignity than in what rank we shall place any particular performance, curiosity is always busy to discover the instruments, as well as to survey the workmanship, to know how much is to be ascribed to original powers, and how much to casual and adventitious help. The palaces of Peru or Mexico were certainly mean and incommodious habitations, if compared to the houses of European monarchs; yet who could forbear to view them with astonishment, who remembered that they were built without the use of iron?

The English nation, in the time of Shakespeare, was yet struggling to emerge from barbarity. The philology of Italy had been transplanted hither in the reign of Henry VIII; and the learned languages had been successfully cultivated by Lilly, Linacer, and More; by Pole, Cheke, and Gardiner; and afterwards by Smith, Clerk, Haddon, and Ascham. Greek was now taught to boys in the principal schools; and those who united elegance with learning, read, with great diligence, the Italian and Spanish poets. But literature was yet confined to professed scholars, or to men and women of high rank. The public was gross and dark; and to be able to read and write, was an accomplishment still valued for its rarity.

Nations, like individuals, have their infancy. A people newly awakened to literary curiosity, being yet unacquainted with the true state of things, knows not how to judge of that which is proposed as its resemblance. Whatever is remote from common appearances is always welcome to vulgar, as to childish credulity; and of a country unenlightened by learning, the whole people is the vulgar. The study of those who then aspired to plebeian learning was laid out upon adventures, giants, dragons, and enchantments. *The Death of Arthur* was the favorite volume. [...]

His plots, whether historical or fabulous, are always crowded with incidents, by which the attention of a rude people was more easily caught than by sentiment or argumentation; and such is the power of the marvelous even over those who despise it, that every man finds his mind more strongly seized by the tragedies of Shakespeare than of any other writer; others please us by particular speeches, but he always makes us anxious for the event, and has perhaps excelled all but Homer in securing the first purpose of a writer, by exciting restless and unquenchable curiosity and compelling him that reads his work to read it through.

The shows and bustle with which his plays abound have the same original. As knowledge advances, pleasure passes from the eye to the ear, but returns, as it declines, from the ear to the eye. Those to whom our author's labors were exhibited had more skill in pomps or processions than in poetical language, and perhaps wanted some visible and discriminated events, as comments on the dialogue. He knew how he should most please; and whether his practice is more agreeable to nature, or whether his example has prejudiced the nation, we still find that on our stage something must be done as well as said, and inactive declamation is very coldly heard, however musical or elegant, passionate or sublime.

Voltaire expresses his wonder, that our author's extravagances are endured by a nation, which has seen the tragedy of *Cato*. Let him be answered, that Addison speaks the language of poets, and Shakespeare, of men. We find in *Cato* innumerable beauties which enamor us of its author, but we see nothing that acquaints us with human sentiments or human actions; we place it with the fairest and the noblest progeny which judgment propagates by conjunction with learning, but *Othello* is the vigorous and vivacious offspring of observation impregnated by genius. *Cato* affords a splendid exhibition of artificial and fictitious manners, and delivers just and noble sentiments, in diction easy, elevated and harmonious, but its hopes and fears communicate no vibration to the heart; the composition refers us only to the writer; we pronounce the name of *Cato*, but we think on Addison.

The work of a correct and regular writer is a garden accurately formed and diligently planted, varied with shades, and scented with flowers; the composition of Shakespeare is a forest, in which oaks extend their branches, and pines tower in the air, interspersed with weeds and brambles, and sometimes giving shelter to myrtles and to roses; filling the eye with awful pomp, and gratifying the mind with endless diversity. Other poets display cabinets of precious rarities, minutely finished, wrought into shape, and polished into brightness. Shakespeare opens a mine which contains gold and diamonds in unexhaustible plenty, though clouded by incrustations, debased by impurities, and mingled with a mass of meaner minerals. [...]

GOTTHOLD EPHRAIM LESSING

Gotthold Ephraim LESSING (1729-1781), the "most honest theoretician" according to Goethe, was of medium height, comely and well-built with broad shoulders and blue eyes. He wore a dark red frock coat and a high powdered wig. Unusually obliging and convivial, he liked good talk and lively arguments in congenial tavern settings.

Son of a Lutheran pastor, Lessing was sent to the University of Leipzig to study theology, but took more interest in cards, dancing, fencing, and the theatre, to which he was introduced by a freethinking cousin. News that their son was consorting with actors and atheists scandalized the pastor and wife, who brought the boy home briefly by sending word his mother was dying, but, discovering the trick, young Gotthold went straight back to his theatre friends and started writing comedies in imitation of Plautus. He read Diderot's licentious oriental tale, *The Indiscreet Jewels*, and was impressed with its attack on French classical tragedy, which he later translated in *The Hamburg Dramaturgy*.

After the Carolina Neuber troupe, which had performed his first play, *The Young Scholar*, left town, the nineteen-year-old Lessing, who had stood surety for their debts, had to flee to escape jail. He became a freelance journalist in Berlin, living from hand to mouth by writing drama criticism, publishing plays, starting several theatre periodicals, and doing translating (including Dryden's *Essay of Dramatic Poesy*), sometimes interpreting for a visiting celebrity like Voltaire.

In *Letters on Literature* Lessing attacked the pompous theatrical reformer Gottsched for ignoring German national taste and frustrating the natural development of German theatre. The Faust story, which as a child he would have seen in the form of a puppet play, was particularly attractive to Lessing who identified with the hero's insatiable pursuit of knowledge.

After a five-year hiatus in theatrical activity (in which he wrote *Laocoon* on the boundaries of literature and painting), Lessing was invited in 1767 by a group of businessmen to come to Hamburg as resident playwright, critic, and literary manager of the first German national theatre during its opening season. He auctioned off his own library in order to start a publishing firm that could bring out the *Hamburg Dramaturgy* as a bi-weekly publication. Lessing hoped to serve as an educator, improving the taste of the audience and raising the level of performance.

Symptomatic of the problems of theatre ever since, the Hamburg project failed because of jealous bickering among the actors, meddling by the patrons, and lack of public support. Lessing, who lost all his money when the publishing venture collapsed, became disillusioned with the idea of cultural revival through drama and regretted ever having become involved in an attempt to found a German National Theatre.

The new dramaturg was given no part in the choice of the repertory, which consisted of mediocre and forgotten contemporary plays. Lessing admired and praised the natural acting of Konrad Ekhof, a leading actor of the troupe and follower of Garrick's realism. But after the twentieth-fifth number of the *Hamburg Dramaturgy*, the dramaturg was no longer allowed to discuss the actual performances because of protests by infuriated actors and actresses.

Whenever possible Lessing alluded to plays from the classical Greek, Spanish, and English theatres, urging Germans to get to know Shakespeare—whom he knew from reading—but none of these works was represented in the Hamburg repertory. The true classical tradition had been lost, Lessing argued, because Corneille's theory and practice provided a bad example, continued by Voltaire and docilely imitated by inferior German dramatists. His own comedy, *Minna von Barnhelm*, proved to be the most popular work at the National Theatre.

As the *Hamburg Dramaturgy* progressed, Lessing's discussions became more abstract, literary, and theoretical, detached from the daily life of the theatre. The final sections, devoted to Aristotle's *Poetics*, are the playwright's reflections on the nature and function of drama.

A practical innovator experimenting with new forms in comedy tragedy, and domestic drama, Lessing was a theoretical conservative, urging a return to the true principles of Aristotle. He promoted contemporary bourgeois realism, to which he strove to give Aristotelian legitimacy, by translating two of Diderot's plays and their accompanying theoretical essays. His own domestic tragedy, *Miss Sara Sampsom*, preceded Diderot's plays.

After the Hamburg fiasco, Lessing did not work in theatre again, declining offers from Vienna and Mannheim to serve as dramaturg under court patronage.

Lessing never wrote a systematic treatise on dramatic theory. He was less concerned with drawing conclusions than with revealing his own thought processes and thereby stimulating the reader to think. According to Goethe, "Lessing was reported to have said that, if God would give him truth, he would decline the gift, and prefer the labor of seeking it for himself."

HAMBURG DRAMATURGY (1767-9)

No. 14. Domestic tragedies found a very thorough defender in the person of the French art critic who first made *Miss Sara Sampson* known to his nation. As a rule the French rarely approve anything of which they have not a model among themselves.

The names of princes and heroes can lend pomp and majesty to a play, but they contribute nothing to our emotion. The misfortunes of those whose circumstances most resemble our own, must naturally penetrate most deeply into our hearts, and if we pity kings, we pity them as human beings, not as kings. Though their position often renders their misfortunes more important, it does not make them more interesting. Whole nations may be involved in them, but our sympathy requires an individual object and a state is far too much an abstract conception to touch our feelings. [...]

No. 19. [...] Now Aristotle has long ago decided how far the tragic poet need regard historical accuracy: not farther than it resembles a well-constructed fable wherewith he can combine his intentions. He does not make use of an event because it really happened, but because it happened in such a manner as he will scarcely be able to invent more fitly for his present purpose. If he finds this fitness in a true case, then the true case is welcome; but to search through history books does not reward his labor. And how many know what has happened? If we only admit the possibility that something can happen from the fact that it has happened, what prevents us from deeming an entirely fictitious fable a really authentic occurrence, of which we have never heard before? What is the first thing that makes a history probable? Is it not its internal probability? And is it not a matter of indifference whether this probability be confirmed by no witnesses or traditions, or by such as have never come within our knowledge? It is assumed quite without reason, that it is one of the objects of the stage, to keep alive the memory of great men. For that we have history and not the stage. From the stage we are not to learn what such and such an individual man has done, but what every man of a certain character would do under certain given circumstances. The object of tragedy is more philosophical than the object of history, and it is degrading to her true digni-

From G.E. Lessing, *Selected Prose Works*, trans. Helen Zimmern. London: George Bell and Sons, 1879.

ty to employ her as a mere panegyric of famous men or to misuse her to feed national pride..

No. 45. [...] What good does it do the poet, that the particular actions that occur in every act would not require much more time for their real occurrence than is occupied by the representation of each act; and that this time, including what is absorbed between the acts, would not nearly require a complete revolution of the sun; has he therefore regarded the unity of time? He has fulfilled the words of the rule, but not their spirit. For what he lets happen in one day, can be done in one day it is true, but no sane mortal would do it in one day. Physical unity of time is not sufficient, the moral unity must also be considered, whose neglect is felt by every one, while the neglect of the other, though it generally involves an impossibility, is yet not so generally offensive because this impossibility can remain unknown to many. If, for instance, in a play a person must travel from one place to another and this journey alone would require more than a day, the fault is only observed by those who know the distance of the locality. Not everybody knows geographical distances, while everybody can feel in themselves for what actions they would allow themselves one day, for what several. The poet therefore who does not know how to preserve physical unity of time except at the expense of moral unity, who does not hesitate to sacrifice the one to the other, consults his own interests badly and sacrifices the essential to the accidental.

No. 46. It is one thing to circumvent the rules, another to observe them. The French do the former, the latter was only understood by the ancients.

Unity of action was the first dramatic law of the ancients; unity of time and place were mere consequences of the former which they would scarcely have observed more strictly than exigency required had not the combination with the chorus arisen. For since their actions required the presence of a large body of people and this concourse always remained the same, who could go no further from their dwellings nor remain absent longer than it is customary to do from mere curiosity, they were almost obliged to make the scene of action one and the same spot and confine the time to one and the same day. They submitted *bonâ fide* to this restriction; but with a suppleness of understanding such that in seven cases out of nine they gained more than they lost thereby. For they used this restriction as a reason for simplifying the action and to cut away all that was superfluous, and thus, reduced to essentials, it became only the ideal of an action which was developed most felicitously in this form which required the least addition from circumstances of time and place.

The French on the contrary, who found no charms in true unity of action, who had been spoilt by the wild intrigues of the Spanish school, before they had learnt to know Greek simplicity, regarded the unity of time and place

not as consequences of unity of action, but as circumstances absolutely needful to the representation of an action, to which they must therefore adapt their
richer and more complicated actions with all the severity required in the use
of a chorus, which, however, they had totally abolished. When they found,
however, how difficult, nay at times how impossible this was, they made a
truce with the tyrannical rules against which they had not the courage to rebel.
Instead of a single place, they introduced an uncertain place, under which we
could imagine now this, now that spot; enough if the places combined were
not too far apart and none required special scenery, so that the same scenery
could fit the one about as well as the other. Instead of the unity of a day they
substituted unity of duration, and a certain period during which no one spoke
of sunrise or sunset, or went to bed, or at least did not go to bed more than
once, however much might occur in this space, they allowed to pass as a day.

Now no one would have objected to this, for unquestionably even
thus excellent plays can be made, and the proverb says: cut the wood where it
is thinnest. But I must also allow my neighbor the same privilege. I must not
always show him the thickest part, and cry, "There you must cut! That is
where I cut!" Thus the French critics all exclaim, especially when they speak
of the dramatic works of the English. What a to-do they then make of regularity, that regularity which they have made so easy to themselves! But I am
weary of dwelling on this point!

As far as I am concerned Voltaire's and Maffei's *Merope* may extend
over eight days and the scene may be laid in seven places in Greece! if only
they had the beauties to make me forget these pedantries!

No. 59. Many hold pompous and tragic to be much the same thing.
Not only many of the readers but many of the poets themselves. What! their
heroes are to talk like ordinary mortals! What sort of heroes would those be?
Ampullae et sesquipedalia verba, sentences and bubbles and words a yard long,
this constitutes for them the true tone of tragedy.

Diderot says, "We have not omitted anything that could spoil the
drama from its very foundations." (Observe that he speaks especially of his
countrymen.) "We have retained the whole splendid versification of the
ancients that is really only suited to a language of very measured quantities
and very marked accents, for very large stages and for a declamation fitted to
music and accompanied with instruments. But its simplicity in plot and conversation and the truth of its pictures we have abandoned."

Diderot might have added another reason why we cannot throughout
take the old tragedies for our pattern. There all the personages speak and con-
verse in a free public place, in presence of an inquisitive multitude. They must
therefore nearly always speak with reserve and due regard to their dignity;
they cannot give vent to their thoughts and feelings in the first words that
come, they must weigh and choose them. But we moderns, who have abol-

ished the chorus, who generally leave our personages between four walls, what reason have we to let them employ such choice stilted rhetorical speech notwithstanding? Nobody hears it except those whom they permit to hear it; nobody speaks to them but people who are involved in the action, who are therefore themselves affected and have neither desire nor leisure to control expressions. This was only to be feared from the chorus who never acted, however much they might be involved in the play, and always rather judged the acting personages than took a real part in their fate. It is as useless to invoke the high rank of the personages; aristocratic persons have learned how to express themselves better than the common man, but they do not affect incessantly to express themselves better than he. Least of all in moments of passion; since every passion has its own eloquence, is alone inspired by nature, is learnt in no school and is understood by the most uneducated as well as by the most polished.

There never can be feeling with a stilted, chosen, pompous language. It is not born of feeling, it cannot evoke it. But feeling agrees with the simplest, commonest, plainest words and expressions. [...]

No. 79. Now to return to our Richard [Christian Felix Weisse's *Richard III*]. Richard arouses in us as little fear as pity; neither fear in the misused application of that term for the sudden surprise of pity, nor in the real meaning of Aristotle of a wholesome fear lest a similar misfortune befall us. For if he awakened this fear, he would also excite our pity as certainly as he would on the other hand excite our fear if we in the least deemed him worthy of our pity. But he is such an abominable rascal, such an incarnate devil, in whom we cannot find the least trait resembling ourselves, that I firmly believe if he were delivered over to all the tortures of hell before our very eyes we should not have the smallest pity for him, nor the least fear that such punishments could be in store for ourselves, if they are the inevitable consequences of such crimes. Now finally what is the misfortune, the punishment that befalls him? After being obliged to witness him committing frightful crimes, we hear that he died sword in hand. When the queen is told this the poet makes her say "This is something." I could never refrain from saying to myself; no this is nothing! many a good king died thus defending his crown against a powerful rebel. Richard dies like a man on the battlefield of honor, and such a death is to indemnify me for the displeasure I felt throughout the play at the triumph of his crimes. [...] Do not the queen, Elizabeth, the princes excite this pity?

To avoid all verbal disputes, I say yes. But what strange, harsh sensation [...] we experience at sight of misfortunes of wholly good, wholly innocent persons; and are not the queen, Elizabeth, and the princes such persons? What have they done? How have they drawn it down upon themselves that they are in the clutches of this monster? Is it their fault that they have a bet-

ter right to the throne than he? How about the little moaning victims who can
scarcely distinguish right from left; who will deny that they deserve our whole
sorrow? But is this sorrow that causes me to think with a shudder of the destiny of these people, with a shudder to which a murmur against Providence is
added which is followed afar by despair; is this sorrow? I will not ask—pity?
but call it as we may, is it that meant to be excited by an imitative art?

Let no one say history evokes it, that it is founded upon something
that really occurred. That really occurred? Granted; then it has its good reason in the external and infinite connection of all things. In this connection all
is wisdom and goodness which appears to us blind fate and cruelty in these few
links picked out by the poet. Out of these few links he ought to make a whole,
rounded in itself, that is fully explained out of itself, where no difficulty arises, a solution of which is not found in his plan and which we are therefore
forced to seek outside of it in the general plan of all things. The whole of this
earthly creator should be a mere outline of the whole of the eternal Creator,
should accustom us to the thought that as in Him all things are resolved for
the best so also it will be here; and the poet forgets his most noble calling
when he forces into a narrow circle the incomprehensible ways of Providence
and advisedly awakens our shudder thereat. O spare us ye that have our hearts
in your power! To what end these sad emotions?—to teach us submission?
Cool reason alone could teach us this and if the teachings of reason are to have
any hold on us, if we for all our submission are to retain confidence and joyful courage, it is most necessary that we should be reminded as little as possible of the perplexing instances of such unmerited terrible fates. Away with
them from the stage, away with them if it might be from all books. Now if not
one of the personages in Richard possesses the necessary qualities which they
ought to have were this work a real tragedy, how has it nevertheless come to
be considered an interesting play by our public? If it excites neither pity nor
fear, what does it effect? It must produce some effect, and it does, and if it does
produce an effect, is it not indifferent whether it produces this kind or that? If
it occupies the spectators, if it amuses them what more do we want? Must they
needs be amused and occupied according to the rules of Aristotle?

This does not sound unreasonable but there is an answer to it. Even if *Richard*
is no tragedy, it remains a dramatic poem, even if it lacks the beauties of
tragedy it may yet have other beauties: poetical expressions, metaphors,
tirades, bold sentiments, the spirited dialogue, fortunate situations for the
actor to display the whole compass of his voice, the whole strength of his pan-
tomimic art, etc.

Of these beauties *Richard* has many, and also has some others that are
more nearly related to the genuine beauties of tragedy.

Richard is an abominable villain, but even the exercise of our disgust,
especially upon imitation, is not wholly without its pleasures. Even the monstrous in crime participates in the emotions awakened in us by sublimity and
audacity; everything that Richard does is horrible, but all these horrors are

committed for a purpose; Richard has a plan, and wherever we perceive a plan our curiosity is excited and we willingly wait to see whether and how it will be executed; we so love anything that has an aim that it affords us pleasure quite regardless of the morality of this aim.

We wish that Richard should attain his aim and we wish that he should not attain it. If he attains it, we are spared displeasure at means uselessly employed, if he does not attain it, then so much blood has been shed in vain, and since it has once been shed we would rather it had not been shed for the sake of pastime. On the other hand this attainment would be the triumph of malignity and there is nothing we less like to hear. The aim interested us as an aim to be attained but as soon as it is attained we only see in it all its abominable features and we wish it had not been attained. This wish we foresee and we shudder at the accomplishment of his aim.

We love the good personages of the play, such a tender vivacious mother, sisters and brothers who live for each other; such objects always please us, always excite our sweetest and most sympathetic emotions wherever we encounter them. To see them suffering innocently is harsh and not adapted to awaken emotions conducive to our peace and improvement, but still it does evoke emotions.

Thus the play occupies us throughout and pleases us by this occupation of our mental powers. This is true; only the inference is not true that is thought to be drawn from it, namely, that we should therefore be satisfied with the play.

The poet may have done much and yet have accomplished nothing. It is not enough that his work has an effect upon us, it must have that effect upon us which belongs to its species, and it must have that above all others. The lack of that can be in no wise replaced by other effects, especially if the species is of that importance, value and difficulty that all trouble and exertions would be in vain if it produced nothing but such effects as could be attained by an easier species requiring less preparation. We must not set machines in motion to raise a bundle of straw; I must not blast what I can turn over with my foot; I must not set fire to a funeral pile in order to burn a gnat.

No. 80. To what end the hard work of dramatic form? Why build a theatre, disguise men and women, torture their memories, invite the whole town to assemble at one place if I intend to produce nothing more with my work and its representation, than some of those emotions that would be produced as well by any good story that every one could read by his chimney-corner at home? The dramatic form is the only one by which pity and fear can be excited, at least in no other form can these passions be excited to such a degree. Nevertheless it is preferred to excite all others rather than these;— nevertheless it is preferred to employ it for any purpose but this, for which it is so especially adapted.

The public will put up with it; this is well, and yet not well. One has no special longing for the board at which one always has to put up with something.

It is well known how intent the Greek and Roman people were upon their theatres; especially the former on their tragic spectacles. Compared with this, how indifferent, how cold is our people towards the theatre! Whence this difference if it does not arise from the fact that the Greeks felt themselves animated by their stage with such intense, such extraordinary emotions, that they could hardly await the moment to experience them again and again, whereas we are conscious of such weak impressions from our stage that we rarely deem it worth time and money to attain them. We most of us go to the theatre from idle curiosity, from fashion, from ennui, to see people, from desire to see and be seen, and only a few, and those few very seldom, go from any other motive.

I say we, our people, our stage, but I do not mean the Germans only. We Germans confess openly enough that we do not as yet possess a theatre. What many of our critics who join in this confession and are great admirers of the French theatre think when they make it I cannot say, but I know well what I think. I think that not alone we Germans, but also that those who boast of having had a theatre for a hundred years, ay, who boast of having the best theatre in all Europe, even the French have as yet no theatre, certainly no tragic one. The impressions produced by French tragedy are so shallow, so cold.

No. 81. Of the two it is Corneille who has done the greatest harm and exercised the most pernicious influence on these tragedians. Racine only seduced by his example. Corneille by his examples and doctrines together, the latter especially, which were accepted as oracles by the whole nation (excepting one or two pedants, a Hédelin, a Dacier who however did not know themselves what they desired) and followed by all succeeding poets. I would venture to prove bit by bit that these doctrines could produce nothing but the most shallow, vapid and untragical stuff.

The rules of Aristotle are all calculated to produce the greatest tragic effect. What does Corneille do with them? He brings them forward falsely and inaccurately and because he still finds them too severe, he endeavors with one and the other to introduce *quelques modérations, quelques favorable interprétations* and thus weakens and disfigures, misinterprets and frustrates every rule, and why? *pour n'être pas obligé de condamner beaucoup de poëmes que nous avons vu réussir sur nos théâtres*; an excellent reason!

I will rapidly mention the chief points, some of them I have touched on already but for the sake of connection I must mention them again.

1. Aristotle says tragedy is to excite pity and fear, Corneille says, oh, yes, but as it happens, both together are not always necessary, we can be contented with one of them, now pity without fear, another time fear without pity.

Else where should I be, I the great Corneille with my Rodrigue and my Chimène? These good children awaken pity, very great pity, but scarcely fear. And again where should I be with my Cleopatra, my Prusias, and my Phocas? Who can have pity on these wretches? but they create fear. So Corneille believed and the French believed it after him.

2. Aristotle says tragedy should excite pity and fear, both, be it understood, by means of one and the same person. Corneille says: if it so happens very good. It is not however absolutely necessary and we may employ two different persons to produce these two sensations as I have done in my *Rodogune*. This is what Corneille did and the French do after him.

3. Aristotle says by means of the pity and fear excited in us by tragedy our pity and our fear and all that is connected with them are to be purified. Corneille knows nothing of all this and imagines that Aristotle wished to say tragedy excites our pity in order to awaken our fear, in order to purify by this fear the passions which had drawn down misfortunes upon the person we commiserate. I will say nothing of the value of this aim, enough that it is not Aristotle's and that since Corneille gave to his tragedies quite another aim they necessarily became works totally different from those when Aristotle had abstracted his theories, they needs became tragedies which were no true tragedies. And such not only his but all French tragedies became because their authors did not think of the aim of Aristotle, but the aim of Corneille.

Nos. 101, 102, 103, and 104. When a year and a day ago some good folk in this place conceived the idea of trying whether something more could not be done for the German theatre, than could be done under the management of a so-called director, I do not know how it was that they thought of me and dreamed that I could be useful to such an undertaking.

I am neither actor nor poet.

It is true that I have sometimes had the honor of being taken for the latter, but only because I have been misunderstood. It is not right to draw such liberal inferences from the few dramatic attempts I have ventured. Not every one who takes up a brush and lays on colors is a painter. The earliest of my attempts were made at that time of life when we are but too apt to regard inclination and facility as genius. What is tolerable in my later attempts is due, as I am well aware, simply and solely to criticism. I do not feel within myself the living spring that works itself out of its native strength and breaks forth out of its own strength into such rich, fresh, clear streams. I must force everything out of myself by pressure and pipes. I should be poor, cold, shortsighted if I had not learnt in a measure to borrow foreign treasures, to warm myself at foreign fires and to strengthen my eyes by the glasses of art. I am therefore always ashamed or annoyed when I hear or read anything in disparagement of criticism. It is said to suppress genius, and I flattered myself that I had gained from it something very nearly approaching to genius. I am a lame man who cannot possibly be edified by abuse of his crutch.

At last they hit upon a plan to use that in me which makes me such a slow, or as my more energetic friends deem, such a lazy workman; criticism. And thus arose the idea of these papers.

It pleased me, this idea. It reminded me of the Didaskalia of the Greeks, i.e., of the short notices of the kind which even Aristotle thought it worth while to write on the plays of the Greek stage.

But it is possible to study until one has studied oneself deep into error. What therefore assures me that this has not happened to me, that I do not mistake the essence of dramatic art is this, that I acknowledge it exactly as Aristotle abstracted it from the countless masterpieces of the Greek stage. I have my own thoughts about the origin and foundation of this philosopher's poetics which I could not bring forward here without prolixity. I do not however hesitate to acknowledge (even if I should therefore be laughed to scorn in these enlightened times) that I consider the work as infallible as the Elements of Euclid. Its foundations are as clear and definite, only certainly not as comprehensible and therefore more exposed to misconstruction. Especially in respect to tragedy, as that concerning which time would pretty well permit everything to us, I would venture to prove incontrovertibly, that it cannot depart a step from the plumbline of Aristotle, without departing so far from its own perfection.

In this conviction I set myself the task of judging in detail some of the most celebrated models of the French stage. For this stage is said to be formed quite in accordance with the rules of Aristotle, and it has been particularly attempted to persuade us Germans that only by these rules have the French attained to the degree of perfection from which they can look down on all the stages of modern peoples. We have long so firmly believed this, that with our poets, to imitate the French was regarded as much as to work according to the rules of the ancients.

Nevertheless this prejudice could not eternally stand against our feelings. These were fortunately roused from their slumbers by some English plays, and we at last experienced that tragedy was capable of another quite different effect from that accorded by Corneille and Racine. But, dazzled by this sudden ray of truth, we rebounded to the edge of another prejudice. Certain rules with which the French had made us acquainted, were too obviously lacking to the English plays. What did we conclude thence? This, that without these rules the aim of tragedy could be attained, ay, that these rules were even at fault if this aim were less attained.

Now even this deduction might have passed. But with these rules we began to confound all rules, and to pronounce it generally as pedantry to prescribe to genius what it must do or leave alone. In short we were on the point of wantonly throwing away the experience of all past times and rather demanding from the poet that each one should discover the art anew.

I should be vain enough to deem I had done something meritorious for our theatre, if I might believe that I have discovered the only means of checking this fermentation of taste. I may at least flatter myself that I have worked hard against it, since I have had nothing more at heart than to combat the delusion concerning the regularity of the French stage. No nation has more misapprehended the rules of ancient drama than the French. They have adopted as the essential some incidental remarks made by Aristotle about the most fitting external division of drama, and have so enfeebled the essential by all manner of limitations and interpretations, that nothing else could necessarily arise therefrom but works that remained far below the highest effect on which the philosopher had reckoned in his rules.

FRIEDRICH SCHILLER

Friedrich SCHILLER (1759-1805), chronically ill with tuberculosis, had a sunken chest and misshapen legs. Five feet ten and one half inches tall and severely knock-kneed, he walked with the slow gait of a stork. A long thin neck supported a gaunt emaciated face without expression. His pale freckled cheeks, sharp jutting nose, protruding lower lip, and disheveled dark red hair produced a singular impression. The deep-set, "bug" eyes, under inflamed lids, were flabby and tired; the gaze piercing and anxious. His long thin fingers fidgeted with a handkerchief, and a pronounced tic made his head twitch. Yet such was the poet's inner fire that to friends he appeared proud and majestic.

Schiller never lost a strong Swabian accent that made his German seem a dialect. He had a shrieky, hoarse voice and terrible diction; his declamation of his own verse was sheer torture.

While a pupil—and prisoner—at the Karlsschule, the military academy he was forced to attend by the despotic Duke Karl Eugen (as son of the Duke's overseer), the fifteen-year-old Schiller appeared in the title role of Goethe's *Clavigo*, but lacking talent as an actor, he so wildly overplayed his role that he reduced the audience to laughter. There at the court pageants and entertainments the future playwright acquired a taste for Italian opera and the operatic style.

The young poet, who was required to study medicine and become a doctor, went about poorly dressed in an ugly regimental uniform, or in some garish combination of colors: blue frock coat, red scarf, yellow pantaloons, and black stockings.

Shy, antisocial, and reclusive, Schiller sometimes never went out of the house for a whole year. He abhorred visitors. Writing all through the night, he got up at 2 PM the following afternoon exhausted and ate breakfast. Suffering from insomnia, he drank quantities of coffee and tea. Racked by colds and coughs, abdominal cramps and constipation, he remained passionately attached to pipe-smoking and snuff-taking.

Without an independent income, Schiller had to earn his livelihood by writing two dramas annually, even when sick and in such pain that he took to drink.

Schiller's friendship with Goethe began in the summer of 1794, when the former regimental physician was thirty-five and the patrician sage of Weimar was forty-five, and their artistic collaboration lasted until Schiller's death in 1805. The two playwrights developed a perfect understanding in the theatre, but did not share private lives, never abandoning the second person plural form of address in their social intercourse (although they used the intimate *Du* in their literary correspondence about theory). The sane Olympian Goethe did not approve of Schiller's unhealthy way of life and morbid inclinations, appalled by his constant smoking and voicing surprise at discovering that his fellow poet found inspiration for his writing in the smell of rotten apples.

The supremely literary Goethe said, disapprovingly, that Schiller's genius was made for the theatre; he always thought about actors, stage directions, and listeners, not readers. Goethe felt that love of the horrible evident in Schiller's work revealed a streak of violence and cruelty in his nature.

Although both poets had started their playwriting careers as *Sturm-und-Drang* iconoclasts (Schiller had to flee and go into hiding after the stormy premiere of *The Robbers* in Stuttgart), for their productions at the Weimar court theatre the now classicizing Goethe and Schiller reworked all the plays, even their own, to suit the stage, the audience, and their goals of moral education. Schiller made a classically bowdlerized adaptation of *Macbeth* and toned down the extravagant *commedia* elements of Gozzi's *Turandot*.

For Schiller drama served a false purpose when it attempted to create a convincing imitation. The creative process liberates humankind by allowing the spectator to see through sensuous matter and discover the "free working of the mind." In a similar manner Schiller sought to liberate the actors from naturalistic acting by reviving the ancient chorus as an anti-naturalistic device designed to uphold tragedy's ideal ground and poetic freedom (much as Yeats wished to use the Nō chorus).

THE STAGE AS A MORAL INSTITUTION
(1784)

Sulzer has remarked that the stage has arisen from an irresistible long-ing for the new and extraordinary. Man, oppressed by divided cares, and sati-ated with sensual pleasure, felt an emptiness or want. Man, neither altogether satisfied with the senses, nor forever capable of thought, wanted a middle state, a bridge between the two states, bringing them into harmony. Beauty and aesthetics supplied that for him. But a good lawgiver is not satisfied with discovering the bent of his people—he turns it to account as an instrument for higher use; and hence he chose the stage, as giving nourishment to the soul, without straining it, and uniting the noblest education of the head and heart.

The man who first pronounced religion to be the strongest pillar of the state, unconsciously defended the stage, when he said so, in its noblest aspect. The uncertain nature of political events, rendering religion a necessi-ty also demands the stage as a moral force. Laws only prevent disturbances of social life; religion prescribes positive orders sustaining social order. Law only governs actions; religion controls the heart and follows thought to the source.

Laws are flexible and capricious; religion binds forever. If religion has this great sway over man's heart, can it also complete his culture? Separating the political from the divine element in it, religion acts mostly on the senses; she loses her sway if the senses are gone. By what channel does the stage oper-ate? To most men religion vanishes with the loss of her symbols, images, and problems; and yet they are only pictures of the imagination, and insolvable problems. Both laws and religion are strengthened by a union with the stage, where virtue and vice, joy and sorrow, are thoroughly displayed in a truthful and popular way; where a variety of providential problems are solved; where all secrets are unmasked, all artifice ends, and truth alone is the judge, as incorruptible as Rhadamanthus.

Where the influence of civil laws ends that of the stage begins. Where venality and corruption blind and bias justice and judgment, and intimidation perverts its ends, the stage seizes the sword and scales and pronounces a ter-rible verdict on vice. The fields of fancy and of history are open to the stage; great criminals of the past live over again in the drama, and thus benefit an

From Friedrich von Schiller, *Complete Works*, Vol. VIII, translator anonymous.
New York: P. F. Collier & Son, 1902.

indignant posterity. They pass before us as empty shadows of their age, and we heap curses on their memory while we enjoy on the stage the very horror of their crimes. When morality is no more taught, religion no longer received, or laws exist, Medea would still terrify us with her infanticide. The sight of Lady Macbeth, while it makes us shudder, will also make us rejoice in a good conscience, when we see her, the sleepwalker, washing her hands and seeking to destroy the awful smell of murder. Sight is always more powerful to man than description; hence the stage acts more powerfully than morality or law.

But in this the stage only aids justice. A far wider field is really open to it. There are a thousand vices unnoticed by human justice, but condemned by the stage; so, also, a thousand virtues overlooked by man's laws are honored on the stage. It is thus the handmaid of religion and philosophy. From these pure sources it draws its high principles and the exalted teachings, and presents them in a lovely form. The soul swells with noblest emotions when a divine ideal is placed before it. When Augustus offers his forgiving hand to Cinna, the conspirator, and says to him: "Let us be friends, Cinna!" what man at the moment does not feel that he could do the same. Again, when Francis von Sickingen, proceeding to punish a prince and redress a stranger, on turning sees the house, where his wife and children are, in flames, and yet goes on for the sake of his word—how great humanity appears, how small the stern power of fate!

Vice is portrayed on the stage in an equally telling manner. Thus, when old Lear, blind, helpless, childless, is seen knocking in vain at his daughters' doors, and in tempest and night he recounts by telling his woes to the elements, and ends by saying: "I have given you all"—how strongly impressed we feel at the value of filial piety, and how hateful ingratitude seems to us!

The stage does even more than this. It cultivates the ground where religion and law do not think it dignified to stop. Folly often troubles the world as much as crime; and it has been justly said that the heaviest loads often hang suspended by the slightest threads. Tracing actions to their sources, the list of criminals diminish, and we laugh at the long catalogue of fools. In our sex all forms of evil emanate almost entirely from *one* source, and all our excesses are only varied and higher forms of one quality, and that a quality which in the end we smile at and love; and why should not nature have followed this course in the opposite sex too? In man there is only one secret to guard against depravity; that is, to protect his heart against wickedness.

Much of all this is shown up on the stage. It is a mirror to reflect fools and their thousand forms of folly, which are there turned to ridicule. It curbs vice by terror and folly still more effectively by satire and jest. If a comparison be made between tragedy and comedy, guided by experience, we should probably give the palm to the latter as to effects produced. Hatred does not wound the conscience so much as mockery does the pride of man. We are exposed specially to the sting of satire by the very cowardice that shuns terrors. From

sins we are guarded by law and conscience, but the ludicrous is specially punished on the stage. Where we allow a friend to correct our morals, we rarely
forgive a laugh. We may bear heavy judgment on our transgressions, but our
weaknesses and vulgarities must not be criticized by a witness.

The stage alone can do this with impunity, chastising us as the anonymous fool. We can bear this rebuke without a blush, and even gratefully.

But the stage does even more than this. It is a great school of practical wisdom, a guide for civil life, and a key to the mind in all its sinuosities. It
does not, of course, remove egoism and stubbornness in evil ways; for a thousand vices hold up their heads in spite of the stage, and a thousand virtues
make no impression on cold-hearted spectators. Thus, probably, Molière's
Harpagon never altered a usurer's heart, nor did the suicide in *Beverley* save
any one from the gaming table. Nor, again, is it likely that the high roads will
be safer through Karl Moor's untimely end. But, admitting this, and more
than this, still how great is the influence of the stage! It has shown us the vices
and virtues of men with whom we have to live. We are not surprised at their
weaknesses, we are prepared for them. The stage points them out to us, and
their remedy. It drags off the mask from the hypocrite, and betrays the mesh-
es of intrigue. Duplicity and cunning have been forced by it to show their
hideous features in the light of day. Perhaps the dying Sarah may not deter a
single debauchee, nor all the pictures of avenged seduction stop the evil: yet
unguarded innocence has been shown the snares of the corrupter, and taught
to distrust his oaths.

The stage also teaches men to bear the strokes of fortune. Chance and
design have equal sway over life. We have to bow to the former, but we control the latter. It is a great advantage if inexorable facts do not find us unpre-
pared and unexercised, and if our breast has been steeled to bear adversity.
Much human woe is placed before us on the stage. It gives us momentary pain
in the tears we shed for strangers' troubles, but as a compensation it fills us
with a grand new stock of courage and endurance. We are led by it, with the
abandoned Ariadne, through the Isle of Naxos, and we descend the Tower of
Starvation in *Ugolino*; we ascend the terrible scaffold, and we are present at the
awful moment of execution. Things remotely present in thought become palpable realities now. We see the deceived favorite abandoned by the queen.
When about to die, the perfidious Moor is abandoned by his own sophistry.
Eternity reveals the secrets of the unknown through the dead, and the hateful
wretch loses all screen of guilt when the tomb opens to condemn him.

Then the stage teaches us to be more considerate to the unfortunate,
and to judge gently. We can only pronounce on a man when we know his
whole being and circumstances. Theft is a base crime, but tears mingle with
our condemnation, when we read what obliged Edward Ruhberg to do the
horrid deed. Suicide is shocking; but the condemnation of an enraged father,
her love, and the fear of a convent, lead Marianne to drink the cup, and few

would dare to condemn the victim of a dreadful tyranny. Humanity and tolerance have begun to prevail in our time at courts of princes and in courts of law. A large share of this may be due to the influence of the stage in showing man and his secret motives.

The great of the world ought to be especially grateful to the stage, for it is here alone that they hear the truth.

Not only man's mind, but also his intellectual culture, has been promoted by the higher drama. The lofty mind and the ardent patriot have often used the stage to spread enlightenment.

Considering nations and ages, the thinker sees the masses enchained by opinion and cut off by adversity from happiness; truth only lights up a few minds, who perhaps have to acquire it by the trials of a lifetime. How can the wise ruler put these within the reach of his nation?

The thoughtful and the worthier section of the people diffuse the light of wisdom over the masses through the stage. Purer and better principles and motives issue from the stage and circulate through society; the night of barbarism and superstition vanishes. I would mention two glorious fruits of the higher class of dramas. Religious toleration has latterly become universal. Before Nathan the Jew and Saladin the Saracen put us to shame, and showed that resignation to God's will did not depend on a fancied belief of his nature—even before Joseph II contended with the hatred of a narrow piety—the stage had sown seeds of humanity and gentleness: pictures of fanaticism have taught a hatred of intolerance, and Christianity, seeing itself in this awful mirror, washed off its stains. It is to be hoped that the stage will equally combat mistaken systems of education. This is a subject of the first political importance, and yet none is so left to private whims and caprice. The stage might give stirring examples of mistaken education and lead parents to juster, better views of the subject. Many teachers are led astray by false views, and methods are often artificial and fatal.

Opinions about governments and classes might be reformed by the stage. Legislation could thus justify itself by foreign symbols, and silence doubtful aspersions without offense.

Now, if poets would be patriotic they could do much on the stage to forward invention and industry. A standing theatre would be a material advantage to a nation. It would have a great influence on the national temper and mind by helping the nation to agree in opinions and inclinations. The stage alone can do this, because it commands all human knowledge, exhausts all positions, illumines all hearts, unites all classes, and makes its way to the heart and understanding by the most popular channels.

If one feature characterized all dramas; if the poets were allied in aim—that is, if they selected well and from national topics—there would be a national stage, and we should become a nation. It was this that knit the Greeks so strongly together, and this gave to them the all-absorbing interest in the republic and the advancement of humanity.

Another advantage belongs to the stage; one which seems to have become acknowledged even by its censors. Its influence on intellectual and moral culture, which we have till now been advocating, may be doubted; but its very enemies have admitted that it has gained the palm over all other means of amusement. It has been of much higher service here than people are often ready to allow.

Human nature cannot bear to be always on the rack of business, and the charms of sense die out with their gratification. Man, oppressed by appetites, weary of long exertion, thirsts for refined pleasure, or rushes into dissipations that hasten his fall and ruin, and disturb social order. Bacchanal joys, gambling, follies of all sorts to disturb ennui, are unavoidable if the law-giver produces nothing better. A man of public business, who has made noble sacrifices to the state, is apt to pay for them with melancholy, the scholar to become a pedant, and the people brutish without the stage. The stage is an institution combining amusement with instruction, rest with exertion, where no faculty of the mind is overstrained, no pleasure enjoyed at the cost of the whole. When melancholy gnaws the heart, when trouble poisons our solitude, when we are disgusted with the world, and a thousand worries oppress us, or when our energies are destroyed by over-exercise, the stage revives us, we dream of another sphere, we recover ourselves, our torpid nature is roused by noble passions, our blood circulates more healthily. The unhappy man forgets his tears in weeping for another. The happy man is calmed, the secure made provident. Effeminate natures are steeled, savages made man, and, as the supreme triumph of nature, men of all ranks, zones, and conditions, emancipated from the chains of conventionality and fashion, fraternize here in a universal sympathy, forget the world, and come nearer to their heavenly destination. The individual shares in the general ecstasy, and his breast has now only space for an emotion: he is a *man*.

ON THE USE OF THE
CHORUS IN TRAGEDY (1803)

A poetic work must justify itself, and if the fact does not speak, words will not help very much. It might, therefore, be quite properly left to the chorus to be its own advocate, if it were just presented in the right way. But the work of tragic poetry is rounded to a whole only by theatrical presentation. The poet provides the words merely, and music and dance must be added to bring them alive. Hence, as long as this powerful sensory concomitant is lacking, it will seem an extraneous item in the economy of the tragedy, an alien presence and a hindrance which merely interrupts the course of the action, destroys the illusion, and leaves the spectator cold. To do justice to the chorus a transition must be made from the actual stage to an *ideal* one. Yet the same must be done wherever a higher thing is to be attained. What art does not have, it must acquire, and the accidental lack of auxiliary means must not limit the creative imagination of the poet. He sets loftiest things as his goal, he strives for an ideal, and practical art must accommodate itself to the circumstances.

The commonly heard assertion is not true, that the public debases art. The artist debases the public, and in all eras where art declined, it fell because of the artists. The public needs nothing but receptivity, and this it has. Audiences come before the curtain with an undefined longing and with a many-sided capacity. They bring with them a capability for highest things; they take delight in what is sensible and right; and if they have begun to content themselves with the bad, they will assuredly cease to demand the excellent when such is offered to them.

The poet, one hears it objected, may work toward an ideal, the critic may judge according to ideas, but qualified, limited, practical art rests upon needs. The producer wants to subsist, the actor wants to be seen, the spectator wants to be entertained and moved. He seeks pleasure and he is dissatisfied when exertion is expected of him just when he is looking for recreation and entertainment.

But in treating the theatre more seriously no one is trying to spoil the spectator's pleasure, but rather to ennoble it. It is still a fancy, but a poetic one.

From Friedrich von Schiller, *The Bride of Messina, William Tell, Demetrius,* trans. Charles E. Passage. N.Y.: Frederick Ungar, 1967.

All art is devoted to joy, and there is no higher, no more serious endeavor than making human beings happy. That art alone is genuine which provides the highest enjoyment. The highest enjoyment, however, is freedom of the spirit in the vivacious play of all its powers.

From the arts of the imaginative faculties everyone expects a certain liberation from the limitations of reality; he wants to delight in the possible and give free rein to his fancy. The man with the least expectations still wants to forget his business, his everyday life, his individual self; he wants to feel himself in extraordinary situations, to revel in the odd vagaries of chance. If he is of a more serious nature, he wants to find on the stage that moral government of the world which he misses in actual life. Yet he himself knows perfectly well that he is only carrying on a pointless game, that in the last analysis he is only indulging in dreams, and when he comes away again from the stage into the actual world the latter will once again beset him with all its oppressive constriction; he will be the world's victim as before, for that has remained what it was and nothing in him has been altered. Nothing has been gained thereby but a pleasing illusion of the moment, which will vanish upon awakening.

And precisely because only a transitory illusion is the object here, nothing is required but an appearance of truth or the cherished plausibility so willingly substituted for truth.

Genuine art, on the other hand, does not have as its object a mere transitory game. Its serious purpose is not merely to translate the human being into a momentary dream of freedom, but actually to *make* him free. It accomplishes this by awakening a power within him, by using and developing this power to remove to a distance of objectivity the sensory world, which otherwise only weighs us down as raw material and oppresses us as a blind force, to transform the sensory world into a free creation of our spirit, and to control the material world through ideas.

Precisely because genuine art aims at something real and objective, it cannot be satisfied with the mere appearance of truth. Upon truth itself, on the solid bedrock of nature it rears its ideal structure.

But how art can and shall be at once ideal and yet in the profoundest sense real—how it can and shall totally abandon actuality and at the same time conform most exactly to nature—this is what few people understand, this is what makes the view of poetic and plastic works so ambiguous, because the two demands seem to cancel each other completely out in the general opinion.

It usually happens, moreover, that people try to achieve the one at the sacrifice of the other and by so doing miss both. He whom Nature has endowed with a faithful mind and a fervor of sensitivity but denied creative imagination, will be a faithful portrayer of actuality; he will grasp accidental appearances but never grasp the spirit of Nature. He will bring us back the material of the world only, but for that very reason it will not be our work nor the free product of our formative spirit, and hence cannot have the beneficent effect of art, which subsists in freedom. Serious, to be sure, but joyless is the mood with which such an artist or poet sends us away, and we find ourselves painfully thrust back into common and narrow actuality by the very art which was to have set us free. On the other hand, one endowed with a lively fantasy but without soul and character, will not be worried about any truth but will merely play with the world-material, will try merely to surprise us with fantastic and bizarre combinations, and, since his whole activity is only froth and illusion, he will entertain us for the moment but he will not found and construct anything in our spirits. His game, like the other's seriousness, is not poetic. Arbitrary lining up of fantastic pictures one after another is not penetrating into the ideal, and imitative reproduction of actuality is not portrayal of Nature. The two claims contradict each other so little that they are really one and the same, namely that art is true only as it abandons actuality altogether and becomes purely ideal. Nature itself is only an idea of the spirit, an idea which never comes to sensory perception. It lies beneath the veil of phenomena but never emerges itself as a phenomenon. Only to the art of the ideal is it vouchsafed, or rather enjoined as an obligation, to grasp this spirit of the universe and to encompass it within a corporeal form. Art itself cannot bring it to sensory perception, but by its creative force it can bring it to the powers of the imagination and thereby be truer than any actuality and more real than any experience. It follows, then, that the artist cannot use a single element from actuality as he finds it, that his work must be ideal in *all* its parts if it is to have reality as a whole and be in consonance with Nature.

What is true for poetry and art in their totality is also valid for all their genres, and the application of the foregoing may without difficulty be made to tragedy. Here too there has been and still is a long struggle with the vulgar concept of the *natural*, which reduces all poetry and art to naught and destroys them. To plastic art a certain ideality is conceded rather grudgingly, though more for conventional reasons than for essential ones; but from poetry, and particularly from dramatic poetry, people demand *illusion*, which, if it were actually to be produced, would forever be nothing but a sorry imposture. All the externalities in a dramatic representation go counter to this concept: all things are symbols merely of actual things. In the theatre daylight itself is only artificial daylight, architecture is only symbolic architecture, and metrical speech is itself ideal. Yet the action is supposed to be real and the part is supposed to offset the whole. Thus the French, having completely misunderstood the spirit of the ancients, introduced a unity of place and time upon the stage in the most vulgar empirical sense, as though there were a different place from purely ideal space and a different time from the purely consistent line of action.

With the introduction of metrical speech one has already been brought a large step nearer to poetic tragedy. Several lyrical attempts have been successfully realized on the stage, and through their living power poetry has gained many a victory in individual details over the prevailing prejudice. But little is gained by individual details unless the error is dispelled in regard to the whole, and it is not enough to have a thing tolerated as poetic license when it is, after all, the essence of all poetry. The introduction of the chorus would be the final and decisive step—and if it served no other purpose than to declare war openly and honestly on naturalism in art, it would be a living wall that tragedy draws about itself in order to shut itself definitely away from the actual world and preserve for itself its ideal ground and its poetic freedom.

The tragedy of the Greeks developed, as is well known, out of the chorus. But just as it extricated itself from it historically and time-wise, so it can also be said to have risen out of it poetically and spirit-wise, and that without those persistent witnesses and bearers of the action it would have turned into a wholly different sort of poetry. Abolition of the chorus and the contraction of that materially powerful organ into the characterless and tediously recurrent figure of a sorry *confidant* was, then, not so great an improvement of tragedy as the French and their blind adherents imagined.

Ancient tragedy, concerned as it originally was with only gods, heroes, and kings, needed the chorus as a necessary concomitant; it found it in nature, and made use of it because it found it. The actions and fates of the heroes and kings were public in themselves, even more so in that simple, primeval time. Consequently the chorus was more of a natural organ in ancient tragedy and followed from the poetic form of actual life. In modern tragedy it becomes an artificial organ, helping to *bring forth* poetry. The modern poet no longer finds the chorus in nature. He has to create it poetically and introduce it, that is, he has to manipulate an alteration in the story he is treating in order to transpose it back into that childlike time and into that childlike form.

Hence the chorus performs far more essential service for the modern poet than for the ancient one, precisely because it transforms the modern, vulgar world into the ancient poetic one, because it renders useless to him everything that goes counter to poetry and forces him upward toward the simplest, most primeval, and most naive motifs. The palace of the kings is now closed; the judges have retreated from the gates of the city to the interiors of houses; the letter has crowded out the living word; the people themselves, that materially living mass, has become the state—unless it is acting as raw force—and hence has become an abstract principle; and the gods have returned to the bosoms of men. The poet must reopen the palaces, he must once again bring the judges forth beneath the open skies, he must establish the gods anew, he must restore everything that is direct and which has been abolished by the artificial arrangements of actual life, he must cast off all artificial contrivances in man and around man which hinder the manifestation of his inner nature and his original character, just as sculptors cast away modern garments and accept nothing of all external surroundings except what renders visible the highest of forms—human form.

But just as the plastic artist adjusts the fullness of drapery-folds about his figures in order to fill out the spaces of his picture richly and graciously, in order to bind the separate parts firmly together in tranquil masses, in order to invest the human forms ingeniously and at the same time make them manifest, just so the tragic poet interweaves and surrounds his strictly delimited action and the sharp delineations of his characters with a weft of lyrical splendor in which, as in a far-flung purple drapery, the acting personages move free and noble with dignified restraint and lofty serenity.

In a higher organization the substance or elemental matter must no longer be visible; the chemical pigment disappears in the subtle tint of living flesh. Yet the substance too has its own splendor and can be taken up, as such, in an artistic form. Then, however, it must earn its place by life and fullness and by harmony, it must validate the forms it surrounds instead of oppressing them with its weight.

In works of plastic art this is readily understandable to everyone. But the same thing is true of poetry, and of tragic poetry, our present subject. Everything that the mind expresses in general is precisely like that which merely rouses the senses, it is no more than substance and raw material in a poetic work, and where it predominates it will inevitably destroy the poetic quality. For the latter is situated just at the point of indifferentiation of ideal and sensory things. Now man is so constituted that he always wishes to proceed from the particular to the general, and so reflection must also have its place in tragedy. If it is to deserve this place, it must win anew through presentation what it lacks in sensory life. For, when the two elements of poetry, the ideal and the sensory, do not operate in intimate alliance they must operate side by side, or else all poetry comes to naught. If the scales do not perfectly balance, equilibrium can be achieved only by vacillation of the two scales.

This is what the chorus does in tragedy. The chorus is not itself an individual but rather a general concept. This concept is represented by a sensorily powerful mass which impresses the senses by its expansive presence. The chorus abandons the narrow circle of the action to discourse on past and future, distant ages and peoples, the entire range of things human, in order to draw the great conclusions of life and to pronounce the teachings of wisdom. But it does this with the full power of the imagination, with a bold lyric freedom that marches with the pace of gods about the high peaks of human affairs—and it does so to the accompaniment of the entire sensual power of rhythm and of music in tone and gesture.

The chorus, therefore, *purifies* the tragic poem by dissociating reflection from the action and by endowing reflection itself with poetic power through this very dissociation. In the same way the plastic artist transforms the vulgar necessity of clothing into charm and beauty by means of a rich drapery.

But just as the painter finds himself compelled to heighten the color-tone of living matter in order to hold his powerful materials in balance, just so the lyric speech of the chorus obligates the poet to elevate the total language of his poem, relatively speaking, and by so doing to intensify the sensory power of expression in general. Only the chorus justifies the poet in this elevation of tone which fills the ear, stretches the mind, and expands the total spirit. This single giant-form in his picture requires him to put all his figures upon cothurni and thereby confer tragic grandeur upon his painting. If the chorus is dispensed with, the speech of his tragedy must decline overall, or else what is now great and mighty will appear forced and exaggerated. The ancient chorus, if it were once introduced into French tragedy, would expose it in all its insufficiency and destroy it. The same chorus would doubtless bring out the true significance of Shakespearean tragedy.

Just as the chorus brings life to language, so does it bring calm into action—but the beautiful and lofty calm which must be the character of a noble work of art. For the spectator's feelings must retain their freedom even amid the most vehement passion; they must not be the victim of impressions, but rather they must come away serene and clear from the agitations sustained. What common judgment finds objectionable in the chorus, namely, that it dispels the illusion and shatters the emotional power of the effects, is just what serves as its highest recommendation. For it is precisely this blind power of passions that the true artist avoids, it is precisely this illusion that he scorns to arouse. If the blows with which tragedy afflicts our hearts were to follow one upon another uninterruptedly, affliction would prevail over activity. We would be confused amid the subject matter and no longer hover above it. The chorus, by holding the parts separate and by intervening between the passions with its calming observations, gives us back our freedom, which would otherwise be lost in the storm of emotional agitation. The tragic persons likewise have need of this respite, this calm, to collect themselves, for they are not real beings that merely obey the force of the moment and represent mere individuals, but ideal personages and representatives of their class, who pronounce upon the profound in mankind. The presence of the chorus, which, as a judging witness, hears them and restrains the first outbursts of their passion by its intervention, motivates the circumspection with which they act and the dignity with which they speak. In a certain sense they stand on a natural stage because they speak and act before spectators, and by that token they come to speak more becomingly from an artificial stage to an audience.

So much for my authorization to bring the ancient chorus back to the tragic stage. Choruses are, to be sure, also to be found in modern tragedy, but the chorus of Greek tragedy as I have used it here, the chorus of a single, ideal person who bears and accompanies the entire action, is essentially different from those operatic choruses, and when I hear people talking, in connection with Greek tragedy, about choruses instead of about a chorus, I suspect them of not rightly knowing whereof they speak. To the best of my knowledge, the chorus of ancient tragedy has not reappeared upon the stage at any time since its fall.

I have, it is true, divided the chorus in two parts and represented it in conflict with itself, but this is the case only when it participates in the action as a real personage or as a blind mass. As a *chorus* and as an ideal personage it is always at one with itself. I have shifted the settings and had the chorus leave the stage several times; but Aeschylus too, the creator of tragedy, and Sophocles, the supreme master of that art-form, also availed themselves of this liberty.

Another liberty I have permitted myself may be harder to justify. I have represented the Christian religion and Greek mythology as intermingled, and have even suggested Moorish superstition. But the scene of the action is Messina, where these three religions continued to make themselves felt, partly in life, partly in monuments of art, and where they spoke to the senses. Then, too, I regard it as a privilege of poetry to treat the various religions as a collective whole for the powers of the imagination, in which whole everything that bears a unique character or expresses a unique way of feeling, has its place. Beneath the husk of all religions lies religion, the idea of a divinity, and a poet must be allowed to express this in whatever form he finds most convenient and most fitting.

ANNE-LOUISE GERMAINE NECKER, Mme de STAËL

Anne-Louise Germaine Necker, Mme de STAËL (1766-1817) was of medium height, with a swarthy complexion, thick lips, and prominent upturned nose. As a young woman, she wore her ebony hair long and powdered; later she arranged it in ringlets that protruded from a turban. According to the German playwright Zacharias Werner, "her body, while not as slim as a nymph's, is voluptuously beautiful, especially her breasts and neck"—which her flamboyant décolleté dresses prominently displayed. Everyone was struck by her magnificent luminous eyes through which shone a "great, divine soul." Her face, "although not precisely beautiful," was infinitely expressive.

The first modern political dissident, Mme de Staël spent more than ten years of her life in political exile. A Swiss Protestant and daughter of Louis XVI's liberal minister of finance, Jacques Necker, Germaine was brought up in the company of Enlightenment philosophers like Diderot. Although an initial supporter of the French Revolution, she was forced to flee during the Terror and was later exiled by Napoleon from 1803 to 1814 for opposing his imperial conquests and tyrannical rule.

Mme de Staël wrote *De l'Allemagne* (*Germany*) in exile as covert propaganda protesting against the suppression of intellectual freedom in France. The title itself was a provocation that challenged Napoleon's plans to prevent their ever being a homeland where the German spirit could flourish. On the eve of its publication in 1810, Bonaparte condemned the book as "un-French." After gendarmes surrounded the printing plant, the authorities ordered all 10,000 copies seized as pro-German and had them crushed into pulp; the type was broken up by the imperial police to destroy all traces of the book's existence. Schlegel secretly conveyed a set of carefully hidden "missing" proofs to Berne, preserving the manuscript for eventual publication in London in 1813 and Paris in 1814.

As the leader of the resistance to Napoleonic despotism, Germaine soon found herself isolated and subject to persecution in an increasingly hegemonic Europe. "I do not want to hear any more about that miserable woman or her book," Napoleon told his police minister. On her estate in Coppet on Lake Geneva, Germaine was hounded by police spies and under virtual house arrest; threats were made to discourage friends from visiting her, and measures taken to keep her book from being published anywhere in Europe.

In her sweeping manifesto of romantic nationalism, *De l'Allemagne*, Mme de Staël proposed a new Europe of independent cultural and political entities, and in the process she invented the modern German nation-state. "Different nations ought to serve as guides to each other," she declared, arguing for intercultural unity in diversity; "We should do well then, in all foreign countries, to welcome foreign thoughts and foreign sentiments." Germaine's concept of national theatres growing out of the distinctive geography, language, and social life of Europe's different peoples, seemed unpatriotic to the French establishment, but proved to be a revolutionary idea, enlarging the social function of the stage and liberating the creative energies of writers and artists.

Declaring masterpieces to be superfluous, Germaine rebelled against the imitation of classical models (without rejecting classicism) and urged writers to turn to their own native soil and history for inspiration. Mme de Staël devoted a quarter of the original text of *De l'Allemagne* (consisting of 85 chapters running to 1,196 pages) to German theatre, believing that the drama—her preferred form—best reveals national character, manners, morals, law, and religion.

A keen observer of actors and acting, Mme de Staël was a theatrical theorist who was also a performer, playwright, director, producer, and theatre owner. As a child she built a puppet theatre to stage tragedies; she had acting lessons from the celebrated tragedienne Claire Clairon, she was a friend of Talma (whose technique she analyzed brilliantly), and in 1785 she starred in LaHarpe's *Mélanie* in her mother's salon. Wherever she went—Stockholm, London, Vienna, Moscow—she performed her plays in readings and recitations as well as amateur stagings.

During Germaine's visit to Weimar for ten weeks in 1803-4, the Duke arranged to have the court theatre stage a number of Goethe and Schiller revivals for the distinguished French guest. The German playwrights tried in vain to avoid the endless round of dinners and social gatherings, worn out by "her French volubility" and brilliant conversational skills. After Mme de Staël left, Schiller, who was attempting to finish *Wilhelm Tell*, commented, "I feel as if I have just recovered from a severe illness."

In Geneva Germaine rented an apartment and remodeled it into a theatre, where she gave a theatrical season, and on the ground floor of her chateau at Coppet she maintained a small professional stage, where, in the words of the novelist Benjamin Constant, there was a "fury of spectacles," including plays by Racine, Voltaire, and Mme de Staël herself, who starred in them, giving powerful performances as Racine's Hermione and Phèdre. The rest of the cast consisted of her three children and her guests: Constant, Schlegel (who looked after stage design), Sismondi, and Mme Recamier, among others. Germaine staged the world premiere of Werner's famous tragedy of fate, *The Twenty-Fourth of February* in 1809 with the author and Schlegel playing the principal roles (in German) and twenty people in the audience. People came from all over Switzerland to attend these celebrity performances.

OF THE DRAMATIC ART (1810)

The theatre exercises a powerful influence over men; a tragedy which exalts the soul, a comedy which paints manners and characters, acts upon the mind of the people almost like a real event; but in order to obtain any considerable success upon the stage, it is necessary for the poet to have studied the public which he addresses, and the motives, of every description, on which its opinion is founded. The knowledge of mankind is even equally essential to the dramatic author with imagination itself; he must touch sentiments of general interest without losing sight of the particular relations which influence his spectators; a theatrical performance is literature in action, and the genius which it demands is so rare only because it exhibits the astonishing combination of the perfect knowledge of circumstances with poetical inspiration. Nothing then would be more absurd than an attempt to impose on all nations the same dramatic system; when the object is to adapt a universal art to the taste of each particular country, an immortal art to the manners of the passing moment, most important modifications are unavoidable; and from thence proceeds such a diversity of opinions as to what constitutes dramatic talent: in all other branches of literature men agree more easily.

It cannot, I think, be denied, that the French are the most expert nation in the world in the combination of theatrical effects; they bear away the prize from all others, likewise, in the dignity of situations and of tragic style. But, even while we acknowledge this double superiority, we may experience more powerful emotions from less regular works; the conception is often more bold and striking in foreign drama, and often comprehends I know not what power within itself which speaks more intimately to our heart, and touches more nearly those sentiments by which we have been personally affected. [...]

The difference between French and German theatre may be explained by reference to the national characters; but to these natural diversities must be added some points of systematic opposition, of which it is important to ascertain the cause. What I have said already on the subjects of classical and romantic poetry is also applicable to the theatre. The tragedies of

From Mme de Staël, *Germany*, translation anonymous.
N.Y.: Hurd and Houghton, 1871.

mythological foundation are of a distinct nature from the historical. [...]

Those plays of which the subjects are derived from Greece lose nothing by the severity of our dramatic rules; but would we taste, like the English, the pleasure of possessing an historical theatre, of being interested by our past, or touched by our religious feelings, how would it be possible rigidly to conform at once to the three unities, and to that sort of pomp which is become a law of our tragic poetry?

The question of the three unities is one which has been so often agitated that one hardly dares at present to talk of it; but of all the three, there is but one of importance, the unity of action, and the others can never be considered but as subordinate to that. [...]

The French consider the unity of time and place as an indispensable condition of theatrical illusion; foreigners make this illusion consist in the delineation of characters, in the truth of language, and the exact observation of the manners of the age and country which they design to paint. We must properly understand the meaning of this expression, Illusion, when applied to the arts. Since we consent to believe that actors separated from ourselves by a few boards are Greek heroes dead three thousand years ago, it is very certain that what we call illusion is not the imagination that what we behold really exists; a tragedy can only appear to us with the form of truth by means of the emotion which it inspires. Now if, according to the nature of the circumstances represented, the change of place and the supposed prolongation of time add to this emotion, the illusion thereby becomes the more lively. [...]

Historical subjects accommodate themselves still less than those of invention to the conditions imposed upon our writers; that tragic etiquette which is thought necessary in our theatre is frequently opposed to the new beauties of which plays taken from modern history would be susceptible.[...]

The pomp of Alexandrines is a still greater obstacle than even the routine of good taste to any change in the form and substance of the French tragedies; it cannot be said in an Alexandrine verse that one comes in or goes out, that one sleeps or wakes, without seeking some poetical turn by which to express it; and numberless sentiments and effects are banished from the theatre, not by the rules of tragedy, but by the very exigencies of the verse. [...]

To delineate characters, it is necessary to abandon the majestic tone which is exclusively admitted into French tragedy; for it is impossible to make known the faults and qualities of a man, but by presenting him under different aspects: in nature, the vulgar often mixes with the sublime, and sometimes relieves its effect: in short, the true action of a character cannot be presented but in a space of time somewhat considerable, and in twenty-four hours there is no room for anything but a catastrophe. It will perhaps be contended that catastrophes are more suitable to the theatre than the minute shades of character; the emotion excited by the lively passions pleases the greater part of the spectators more than the attention required for the observation of the human heart. The national taste alone can decide upon these different dramatic systems; but it is justice to acknowledge that if foreigners have a different conception of the theatrical art from ourselves, it is neither through ignorance nor barbarism, but in consequence of profound reflections which are worthy of being examined. [...]

If any innovation on the rules of tragedy were risked in France, all the world would immediately cry out, a melodrama! But is it a matter of no importance whatever, to ascertain what it is that causes so many people to be pleased with melodramas? In England, all classes are equally attracted by the plays of Shakespeare. Our finest tragedies in France do not interest the people; under the pretense of a taste too pure and a sentiment too refined to support certain emotions, the art is divided into two branches; the worst plays contain the most touching situations ill expressed, and the finest paint with admirable skill situations often cold, because they are dignified: we possess few tragedies capable of exciting at the same time the imaginations of all ranks of society. [...]

The point is only to know whether in being confined, as at present, to the imitation of our dramatic masterpieces, we shall ever produce any new ones. Nothing in life ought to be stationary; and art is petrified when it refuses to change. Twenty years of revolution have given to the imagination other wants than those which it experienced when the novels of Crébillon painted the love and the manners of his time. Greek subjects are exhausted. [...]

The taste of the age naturally inclines to historical tragedy.

Everything is tragic in the events by which nations are interested; and this immense drama, which the human race has for these six thousand years past been performing, would furnish innumerable subjects for the theatre, if more freedom were allowed to the dramatic art.

AUGUST WILHELM SCHLEGEL

August Wilhelm SCHLEGEL (1767-1845) was short and stocky, with a not particularly attractive face, except for a pair of expressive blue eyes and much long blond hair. Vain, fussy, and hypochondriacal, he was always impeccably dressed and something of a Frenchified dandy. Even in his advanced years, he maintained a rosy complexion, thanks to liberal use of cosmetics according to Goethe, who was no admirer of August Wilhelm or romanticism.

His uncle Johann Elias Schlegel, author of neoclassical tragedies, was an early proponent of Shakespeare in Germany. Although August Wilhelm wrote *Ion*, an adaptation of Euripides staged by Goethe at Weimar in 1802, he is best known for his still performed translations of Shakespeare and for his lectures and books on theatre and literature.

A more systematic but less original thinker than his intuitive younger brother Friedrich, August Wilhelm was an ideal explicator and mediator of new ideas, which he was able to present in an easily assimilable form. He spoke French and English with native fluency and knew Italian, Spanish, and Portuguese as well as old Provençal and Sanskrit. More than anyone else, he popularized the ideas of German romanticism throughout Europe.

After Mme de Staël met August Wilhelm at one of her aesthetic teas in Berlin in 1803, she engaged the writer as a traveling companion and tutor to her son, offering him 12,000 francs a year and her undying friendship. Impecunious, servile, yet prone to affronts, Schlegel accepted, signing the following agreement: "I declare that you have all the rights over me and that I have none over you. Dispose of my person and my life, order, forbid, I will obey you in everything. I aspire to no other happiness than that you would wish to give me; I do not want to possess anything, I want to have everything from your generosity. I should willingly consent to think no more of my celebrity, to dedicate exclusively to your special use whatever talent and knowledge I may have. I am proud of being your property."

During Mme de Staël's political exile, which lasted as long as Napoleon was emperor, Schlegel appeared as a performer in the private theatricals at her Swiss estate. Her pioneering book, *De l'Allemagne*, reflects six years of daily conversations with Schlegel and helped to spread his ideas in France.

In 1807 August Wilhelm already created a sensation by attacking Racine in an article written in French and published in Paris. "My enthusiasm for this subject," he declared, "springs principally from the fact that it will infuriate the readers."

It was in Vienna during the 1808-9 season that Schlegel gave what proved to be his most influential series of lectures: a course on dramatic art and literature from the ancient Greek to the modern German stage. The lectures were published shortly thereafter and soon translated into many languages. An elite audience came from all over Europe to hear the first international star of theatrical theory hold forth in the lecture hall.

Mme de Staël helped Schlegel obtain a license from the Viennese authorities and rent a suitable hall. 200 fashionable subscribers paid 25 florins each. "I had an audience of more than 250," Schlegel boasted, "almost the entire high nobility, many courtiers, ministers of state, generals, eighteen princesses, and many beautiful and witty women."

Because their content was politically charged, Schlegel's lectures had to be submitted in outline to the police in advance. By assaulting the French laws of drama that had been laid down for all of Europe, the German critic was implicitly challenging the Napoleonic cultural hegemony then being extended over all of Europe.

The impression the German theorist made on his audiences has been captured by Heinrich Heine, who as a student in 1819 attended his lectures at the University of Bonn, where Schlegel occupied the chair for Indian studies because of his work on Sanskrit language and literature.

"Mr. A.W. Schlegel wore kid gloves and still dressed completely in the latest Paris fashion; he was still highly perfumed with good society and *eau de mille fleurs*. He was grace and elegance personified.. [...] Besides him stood his servant in the most baronial Schlegel family livery and trimmed the wax candles that were burning in silver candelabras standing on the desk beside a glass of sugar water. [...] His outward appearance did indeed give him a certain distinction. On his puny little head only a few silver hairs still shone, and his body was so thin, so emaciated, so transparent, that he appeared to be all spirit and looked almost like a symbol of spirituality."

August Wilhelm was allergic to the materialistic nineteenth-century. "I loathe the times we live in," he declared, longing to escape into the Middle Ages. He disliked realism, didacticism, common sense, and, particularly, Molière—Goethe said it was because Schlegel knew that he himself was the sort of far-fetched pedant Molière would have ridiculed.

LECTURES ON DRAMATIC ART AND LITERATURE (1809-11)

Lecture XXII

The English and Spanish Drama

In conformity with the plan which we laid down at the first, we shall now proceed to treat of the English and Spanish theatres. We have been, on various occasions, compelled in passing to allude cursorily, sometimes to the one and sometimes to the other, partly for the sake of placing, by means of contrast, many ideas in a clearer light, and partly on account of the influence which these stages have had on the theatres of other countries. Both the English and Spaniards possess a very rich dramatic literature, both have had a number of prolific and highly talented dramatists, among whom even the least admired and celebrated, considered as a whole, display uncommon aptitude for dramatic animation, and insight into the essence of theatrical effect. The history of their theatres has no connection with that of the Italians and French, for they developed themselves wholly out of the abundance of their own intrinsic energy, without any foreign influence: the attempts to bring them back to an imitation of the ancients, or even of the French, have either been attended with no success, or not been made till a late period in the decay of the drama. The formation of these two stages, again, is equally independent of each other; the Spanish poets were altogether unacquainted with the English; and in the older and most important period of the English theatre I could discover no trace of any knowledge of Spanish plays, (though their novels and romances were certainly known,) and it was not till the time of Charles II that translations from Calderón first made their appearance.

So many things among men have been handed down from century to century and from nation to nation, and the human mind is in general so slow to invent, that originality in any department of mental exertion is everywhere a rare phenomenon. We are desirous of seeing the result of the efforts of inventive geniuses when, regardless of what in the same line has elsewhere been carried to a high degree of perfection, they set to work in good earnest

From Augustus William Schlegel, *A Course of Lectures on Dramatic Art and Literature*, trans. John Black. London: Bell & Daldy, 1871.

to invent altogether for themselves; when they lay the foundation of the new edifice on uncovered ground, and draw all the preparations, all the building materials, from their own resources. We participate, in some measure, in the joy of success, when we see them advance rapidly from their first helplessness and need to a finished mastery in their art. The history of the Grecian theatre would afford us this cheering prospect could we witness its rudest beginnings, which were not preserved, for they were not even committed to writing; but it is easy, when we compare together Aeschylus and Sophocles, to form some idea of the preceding period. The Greeks neither inherited nor borrowed their dramatic art from any other people; it was original and native, and for that very reason was it able to produce a living and powerful effect. But it ended with the period when Greeks imitated Greeks; namely, when the Alexandrian poets began learnedly and critically to compose dramas after the model of the great tragic writers. The reverse of this was the case with the Romans: they received the form and substance of their dramas from the Greeks; they never attempted to act according to their own discretion, and to express their own way of thinking; and hence they occupy so insignificant a place in the history of dramatic art. Among the nations of modern Europe, the English and Spaniards alone (for the German stage is but forming), possess as yet a theatre entirely original and national, which, in its own peculiar shape, has arrived at maturity.

Those critics who consider the authority of the ancients as models to be such, that in poetry, as in all the other arts, there can be no safety out of the pale of imitation, affirm, that as the nations in question have not followed this course, they have brought nothing but irregular works on the stage, which, though they may possess occasional passages of splendor and beauty, must yet, as a whole, be for ever reprobated as barbarous, and wanting in form. We have already, in the introductory part of these Lectures, stated our sentiments generally on this way of thinking; but we must now examine the subject somewhat more closely.

If the assertion be well founded, all that distinguishes the works of the greatest English and Spanish dramatists, a Shakespeare and a Calderón, must rank them far below the ancients; they could in no wise be of importance for theory, and would at most appear remarkable, on the assumption that the obstinacy of these nations in refusing to comply with the rules, may have afforded a more ample field to the poets to display their native originality, though at the expense of art. But even this assumption, on a closer examination, appears extremely questionable. The poetic spirit requires to be limited, that it may move with a becoming liberty, within its proper precincts, as has been felt by all nations on the first invention of meter; it must act according to laws derivable from its own essence, otherwise its strength will evaporate in boundless vacuity.

The works of genius cannot therefore be permitted to be without form; but of this there is no danger. However, that we may answer this objection of want of form, we must understand the exact meaning of the term form, since most critics, and more especially those who insist on a stiff regularity, interpret it merely in a mechanical, and not in an organical sense. Form is mechanical when, through external force, it is imparted to any material merely as an accidental addition without reference to its quality; as, for example, when we give a particular shape to a soft mass that it may retain the same after its induration. Organical form, again, is innate; it unfolds itself from within, and acquires its determination contemporaneously with the perfect development of the germ. We everywhere discover such forms in nature throughout the whole range of living powers, from the crystallization of salts and minerals to plants and flowers, and from these again to the human body. In the fine arts, as well as in the domain of nature—the supreme artist, all genuine forms are organical, that is, determined by the quality of the work. In a word, the form is nothing but a significant exterior, the speaking physiognomy of each thing, which, as long as it is not disfigured by any destructive accident, gives a true evidence of its hidden essence.

Hence it is evident that the spirit of poetry, which, though imperishable, migrates, as it were, through different bodies, must, so often as it is newly born in the human race, mold to itself, out of the nutrimental substance of an altered age, a body of a different conformation. The forms vary with the direction taken by the poetical sense; and when we give to the new kinds of poetry the old names, and judge of them according to the ideas conveyed by these names, the application which we make of the authority of classical antiquity is altogether unjustifiable. No one should be tried before a tribunal to which he is not amenable. We may safely admit, that the most of the English and Spanish dramatic works are neither tragedies nor comedies in the sense of the ancients: they are romantic dramas. That the stage of a people who, in its foundation and formation, neither knew nor wished to know anything of foreign models, will possess many peculiarities; and not only deviate from, but even exhibit a striking contrast to, the theatres of other nations who had a common model for imitation before their eyes, is easily supposable, and we should only be astonished were it otherwise. But when in two nations, differing so widely as the English and Spanish, in physical, moral, political, and religious respects, the theatres (which, without being known to each other, arose about the same time,) possess, along with external and internal diversities, the most striking features of affinity, the attention even of the most thoughtless cannot but be turned to this phenomenon; and the conjecture will naturally occur, that the same, or, at least, a kindred principle must have prevailed in the development of both. This comparison, however, of the English and Spanish theatre, in their common contrast with every dramatic literature which has grown up out of an imitation of the ancients, has, so far as we know, never yet been attempted. Could we raise from the dead a countryman, contemporary, and intelligent admirer of Shakespeare, and another of Calderón, and introduce to their acquaintance the works of the poet to which in life they were strangers, they would both, without a doubt, considering the subject rather from a national than a general point of view, enter with difficulty into the above idea, and have many objections to urge against it. But here a reconciling criticism must step in; and this, perhaps, may be best exercised by a German, who is free from the national peculiarities of either Englishmen or Spaniards, yet by inclination friendly to both, and prevented by no jealousy from acknowledging the greatness which has been earlier exhibited in other countries than in his own.

The similarity of the English and Spanish theatres does not consist merely in the bold neglect of the Unities of Place and Time, and in the commixture of comic and tragic elements: that they were unwilling or unable to comply with the rules and with right reason (in the meaning of certain critics these terms are equivalent) may be considered as an evidence of merely negative properties. The ground of the resemblance lies far deeper, in the inmost substance of the fictions, and in the essential relations, through which every deviation of form becomes a true requisite, which, together with its validity, has also its significance. What they have in common with each other is the spirit of the romantic poetry, giving utterance to itself in a dramatic shape. However, to explain ourselves with due precision, the Spanish theatre, in our opinion, down to its decline and fall in the commencement of the eighteenth century, is almost entirely romantic; the English is completely so in Shakespeare alone, its founder and greatest master: in later poets the romantic principle appears more or less degenerated, or is no longer perceivable, although the march of dramatic composition introduced by virtue of it has been, outwardly at least, pretty generally retained. The manner in which the different ways of thinking of the two nations, one a northern and the other a southern, have been expressed; the former endowed with a gloomy, the latter with a glowing imagination; the one nation possessed of a scrutinizing seriousness disposed to withdraw within themselves, the other impelled outwardly by the violence of passion; the mode in which all this has been accomplished will be most satisfactorily explained at the close of this section, when we come to institute a parallel between Shakespeare and Calderón, the only two poets who are entitled to be called great.

Of the origin and essence of the romantic I treated in my first Lecture, and I shall here, therefore, merely briefly mention the subject. The ancient art and poetry rigorously separate things which are dissimilar; the romantic delights in indissoluble mixtures; all contrarieties: nature and art, poetry and prose, seriousness and mirth, recollection and anticipation, spirituality and sensuality, terrestrial and celestial, life and death, are by it blended together in the most intimate combination. As the oldest lawgivers delivered their mandatory instructions and prescriptions in measured melodies; as this is fabulously ascribed to Orpheus, the first softener of the yet untamed race of mortals; in like manner the whole of the ancient poetry and art is, as it were, a *rhythmical nomos* (law), an harmonious promulgation of the permanently established legislation of a world submitted to a beautiful order, and reflecting in itself the eternal images of things. Romantic poetry, on the other hand, is the expression of the secret attraction to a chaos which lies concealed in the very bosom of the ordered universe, and is perpetually striving after new and marvelous births; the life-giving spirit of primal love broods here anew on the face of the waters. The former is more simple, clear, and like to nature in the self-existent perfection of her separate works; the latter, notwithstanding its fragmentary appearance, approaches more to the secret of the universe. For Conception can only comprise each object separately, but nothing in truth can ever exist separately and by itself; Feeling perceives all in all at one and the same time.

Respecting the two species of poetry with which we are here principally occupied, we compared the ancient Tragedy to a group in sculpture: the figures corresponding to the characters, and their grouping to the action; and to these two in both productions of art is the consideration exclusively directed, as being all that is properly exhibited. But the romantic drama must be viewed as a large picture, where not merely figure and motion are exhibited in larger, richer groups, but where even all that surrounds the figures must also be portrayed; where we see not merely the nearest objects, but are indulged with the prospect of a considerable distance; and all this under a magical light, which assists in giving to the impression the particular character desired.

Such a picture must be bounded less perfectly and less distinctly than the group; for it is like a fragment cut out of the optic scene of the world. However the painter, by the setting of his foreground, by throwing the whole of his light into the center, and by other means of fixing the point of view, will learn that he must neither wander beyond the composition, nor omit any thing within it.

In the representation of figure, Painting cannot compete with Sculpture, since the former can only exhibit it by a deception and from a single point of view; but, on the other hand, it communicates more life to its imitations, by colors which in a picture are made to imitate the lightest shades of mental expression in the countenance. The look, which can be given only very imperfectly by Sculpture, enables us to read much deeper in the mind, and to perceive its lightest movements. Its peculiar charm, in short, consists in this, that it enables us to see in bodily objects what is least corporeal, namely, light and air.

The very same description of beauties is peculiar to the romantic drama. It does not (like the Old Tragedy) separate seriousness and the action, in a rigid manner, from among the whole ingredients of life; it embraces at once the whole of the checkered drama of life with all its circumstances; and while it seems only to represent subjects brought accidentally together it satisfies the unconscious requisitions of fancy, buries us in reflections on the inexpressible signification of the objects which we view blended by order, nearness and distance, light and color, into one harmonious whole; and thus lends, as it were, a soul to the prospect before us.

The change of time and of place (supposing its influence on the mind to be included in the picture; and that it comes to the aid of the theatrical perspective, with reference to what is indicated in the distance, or half-concealed by intervening objects); the contrast of sport and earnest (supposing that in degree and kind they bear a proportion to each other); finally, the mixture of the dialogical and the lyrical elements, (by which the poet is enabled, more or less perfectly, to transform his personages into poetical beings): these, in my opinion, are not mere licenses, but true beauties in the romantic drama. In all these points, and in many others also, the English and Spanish works, which are pre-eminently worthy of this title of Romantic, fully resemble each other, however different they may be in other respects.

JOHANN WOLFGANG GOETHE

Johann Wolfgang GOETHE (1749-1832) was five feet nine and one quarter inches in height, trim and finely built. His pale brown eyes were big and bright, his large nose slightly bent, his forehead impressively high. Because of overdevelopment on the left side, there was a curious asymmetry to his longish face. His complexion had been coarsened by small pox. As a young man, Goethe was lean and thin, almost haggard, and prone to illness; he wore his beautiful brown hair fastened behind his neck, letting the thick wavy locks hang down freely. After his stay of two years in Italy from 1786 to 1788, the poet put on weight and inclined to stoutness. He also became more reserved and self-contained. Although myopic, he would not wear his glasses in public and disliked it when others wore theirs. He did not like animals and found Beethoven the man untamed, although he admired his music.

According to Schiller, Goethe's bearing was stiff, as was his walk, but he was lively in conversation and aroused sympathy on account of his expressive eyes, agreeable voice, and "inner goodness." Younger poets who paid homage to the great man in hopes of getting a few words of encouragement were intimidated by his cold, Jovian manner.

Like other theorists, Goethe first became fascinated with the stage as a child when he put on plays in his own puppet theatre. He never abandoned the aesthetic of the marionette theatre. "He who would work for the stage," Goethe declared, "should leave nature in her proper place and take careful heed not to have recourse to anything but what may be performed by children with puppets upon boards and laths, together with sheets of cardboard and linen."

At twenty Goethe wrote a satirical play for marionettes intended for an audience of friends and family, which he later produced on a specially erected puppet stage after he was put in charge of amateur theatrical entertainments at Weimar. He composed another puppet play to celebrate the marriage festivities of Princess Amelia, and it was the old "puppet show" Faust that inspired him to write his own play on the subject.

A gifted actor, Goethe appeared in amateur productions of his own

Triumph of Sensibility and *Iphigenia in Tauris* as well as in Gozzi and Molière. He played *commedia* roles in Weimar before actually seeing the masked performers in Italy.

Goethe served as Artistic Director of the professional Weimar theatre from 1791 to 1817, functioning as a playwright-manager for twenty-six years. For more than a quarter of a century, he concerned himself with every aspect of production, fascinated by the scenic effects attainable through the use of stage design and lighting. But he devoted all his energies to training the actors in an elevated, classical style of performance and to raising the public taste so that the audience could appreciate such refinement.

By the end of the eighteenth century German actors had grown accustomed to a more natural style of delivery, playing to each other rather than to the spectators. But Goethe and Schiller as theatre practitioners at the Weimar court (decades after their own rebellious debuts under the spell of Shakespeare) insisted on pictorial stylization. Elegant recitation, statuesque poses, and prescribed gestures and choreographed movements characterized the Weimar "court theatre" style of acting. The players were encouraged to study the poses of Greek statues and taught to address the audience directly, delivering their lines downstage and speaking the blank verse rhythmically and harmoniously in a pure, dialect-free German, which amounted to an artificial language.

Goethe was the first to create a "director's theatre." Performers had to forgo customary typecasting so that the ensemble could be totally subordinated to the dramatist's conception of the work. Although no longer an actor himself, the poet gave impressive performances at rehearsals to show how each role should be played.

Seeking to enhance the social respectability of the theatre, Goethe used his authority as Privy Councillor to enforce his pedantic and dictatorial "Rules for Actors" which governed all the details of their private lives. Sanctions ranged from fines to imprisonment for any company member who "will go on acting the strolling player and will not understand what it is to be an actor by appointment to the court of Weimar."

In raising German theatre out of the rut of popular entertainment and everyday realism, Goethe had as his goal to provide pleasure of a higher sort. "It is my conviction," he declared, "that the highest purpose of art is to show human forms that are sensuously and aesthetically as significant and beautiful as possible."

But Goethe grew increasingly skeptical of the possibility of elevating public taste. When, tired of his onerous duties, he finally resigned from the Court Theatre directorship, the incident that tipped the scales was the guest appearance of a touring production of Pixérécourt's canine melodrama, *The Forest of Bondy*. Goethe strongly objected to sharing his stage with a dog star, but the Duke was curious to see the performing poodle. Overflow audiences applauded thunderously; Goethe refused to attend.

SHAKESPEARE ONCE AGAIN (1815)

So much has been said about Shakespeare that it would seem nothing
more could be added. And yet it is characteristic of ideas that they stimulate
new ideas. On this occasion, I intend to discuss Shakespeare from more than
one point of view: first as a poet in general, then in comparison to ancient and
contemporary writers, and finally as a playwright. I shall attempt to establish
what effect the imitation of his style has actually had on us, and what effect it
is able to produce. I shall express my agreement with existing opinions by reit-
erating them; my disagreements I shall state briefly and in a positive spirit,
without engaging in polemics. Let me proceed to the first of these items.

I. Shakespeare as a Poet

The highest goal man can achieve is the awareness of his own attitudes and ideas—knowledge of himself which provides him with the means to
gain intimate knowledge of the minds of others. There are people who have
an innate talent for this and who, through experience, develop and refine it for
practical purposes, deriving from it an ability to profit mainly from worldly
matters. The poet too is born with this talent, except that he does not develop it for practical and mundane purposes, but rather for a higher, spiritual,
universal one. By calling Shakespeare one of the greatest poets, we imply that
there were few who perceived the world as he did, few who, by expressing
their visions, allowed the reader to share so fully in their awareness of the
world. Shakespeare makes the world completely transparent for us. All of a
sudden, we find ourselves the confidants of virtue and vice, greatness, pettiness, nobility, and depravation—and all this, and even more, by the simplest
of means. If we try to determine what those means are, it seems at first as if
Shakespeare were appealing to our visual perception. But that is a delusion.
Shakespeare does not write for the eye. Let me attempt to explain what I
mean.

From Johann Wolfgang von Goethe, *Essays on Art and Literature*, ed. John Gearey,
trans. Ellen von Nardroff and Ernest H. von Nardroff. N.Y.: Suhrkamp, 1986.

The eye may be called the most perceptive of our senses, and hence the most effective means of communication. But the inner sense is even more perceptive, and it is to this sense that the word speaks most directly. After all, it is the word that comes to our aid when the object which our eyes perceive is strange and incomprehensible. Shakespeare addresses our inner sense, which immediately activates our creative imagination and brings about a total effect which is inexplicable to us. And that is the cause of the delusion I referred to, the impression that everything is happening right before our eyes. But if we examine Shakespeare's works carefully, we find that they contain much more action conveyed by the word than physical action. He makes things happen which are easily imagined, indeed are better imagined than seen. Hamlet's ghost, Macbeth's witches, many a gruesome scene become meaningful only through the power of the imagination, and this is true of many minor scenes as well. When reading we readily accept such things as a matter of course, whereas during a stage performance we may find them disturbing, even repugnant.

Shakespeare achieves his effects through the living word, and the living word is best conveyed by reading aloud because then the listener is not distracted by either a skillful or an awkward stage presentation. There is no higher or purer pleasure than listening with closed eyes to a naturally expressive voice reciting, not declaiming, a Shakespeare play. We follow the simple thread of the plot and the unfolding events. To be sure, the description of certain characters causes us to form mental images of them, but actually, we are supposed to discover what is happening in the characters' minds through a sequence of words and speeches. All participants seem to have agreed among themselves not to leave us in the dark about anything. Heroes and foot soldiers, gentlemen and slaves, kings and messengers, all conspire to achieve this end. We may even say that minor figures are often more active in this regard than leading ones. Everything that fills the air, unspoken, during a historical event, everything that is lurking in the human heart in moments of great distress—it is all expressed in words. What the mind anxiously represses and conceals is revealed frankly and without inhibition. We experience the truth of life, and we do not know how.

Shakespeare resembles the world spirit in that he permeates the world as it does, and nothing remains hidden from either. But whereas it is the task of the world spirit to keep secrets before, and even after the event, it is the poet's calling to reveal secrets and to take us into his confidence, if not before, then certainly during the event. The depraved man in power, the well-meaning dullard, the passionately involved man, the detached observer—they all wear their hearts on their sleeves, often improbably so. Everyone is eloquent and loquacious, and come what may, the secret must out, even if the stones have to speak! The inanimate world too is eager to hold forth, and all things participate: natural phenomena of heaven, earth and sea, and thunder and lightning. Wild beasts lift their voices, often seemingly as imagery, yet always as part of the revelation.

Even the civilized world must surrender its treasures. Art and science, craft and trade, they all bear gifts. Shakespeare's works are one great bustling fair, and he owes the richness of his wares to his native land.

England is ever present in Shakespeare's works, this land, surrounded by the sea, shrouded in mist and clouds, active in all corners of the earth. The poet lived during a great and important era, and he portrayed its culture, strengths and even weaknesses in a positive spirit. Indeed, he could not have such an effect on us had he not been a true child of his time. No one has more disdain for externals than he; his interest is directed toward man's inner self, and here all human beings are alike. Shakespeare's portrayal of Romans has been called superb. I disagree. His Romans are all Englishmen through and through—but they are human beings, thoroughly human, and may just as well wear the Roman toga as any other costume. Once we have accepted that, we look upon Shakespeare's anachronisms as admirable, for it is precisely his disregard for externals which makes his works so true to life.

I trust these few words will suffice, although they by no means do complete justice to Shakespeare's accomplishments. His friends and admirers will have much more to add. Let me conclude this part with the following observation: It would prove difficult to find another poet whose every work is based on a different idea which pervades the whole drama.

Coriolanus, for example, is permeated by anger at the refusal of the masses to recognize the superiority of able men. In *Julius Caesar*, everything hinges on the idea that able men refuse to accept a leader because they wrongly assume they can rule as a group. *Antony and Cleopatra* says with a thousand tongues that pleasure and action are incompatible. We could continue in this vein and find ever more reasons for admiring Shakespeare.

II. Shakespeare in Comparison to Ancient and Contemporary Writers

What inspires Shakespeare's great mind is the real world. To be sure, he intersperses magical elements throughout his works at appropriate moments, and we do find soothsaying and madness, dreams, premonitions, omens, fairies and gnomes, ghosts, demons and sorcerers. But by no means do these chimera play a major role in his works. Rather, it is the reality of Shakespeare's own world and its vitality which form the broad basis of his writings—hence our impression of their genuineness and concreteness. This has led to the conclusion that Shakespeare is not so much a modern poet, a romantic, as a representative of the "naive" school because his values are rooted in the here and now, and because he hardly ever approaches the realm of romantic yearning, and if he does, only very gingerly.

Nevertheless, upon closer scrutiny we realize that Shakespeare is very much a modern writer, far removed from the ancients. The tremendous gulf separating him from them has nothing to do with literary form—which is really not to the point here—but rather with the essence of his writings, their innermost spirit.

Before I proceed, I wish to emphasize that it is not my intention to present the terminology I use as exhaustive or definitive, nor do I intend to add a new antithesis to those already known to us. The antithesis I am going to discuss is already contained in the existing ones, as we shall see. These antitheses are:

ancient	modern
naive	sentimental
pagan	Christian
heroic	romantic
real	ideal
necessity	freedom
moral obligation (*Sollen*)	desire (*Wollen*)

The greatest and most common torment man may encounter springs from the conflict between moral obligation and desire, but also between moral obligation and its fulfillment, and between desire and its fulfillment. The last two are the cause of so much inner confusion throughout man's life. The superficial confusion that results from casual errors and can be resolved easily and without serious consequences is the source of comic situations. Serious dilemmas, unresolvable or unresolved, produce our tragic moments.

The predominant conflict in ancient literature is the one between moral obligation and its fulfillment, in modern literature between desire and fulfillment. For the moment, let us incorporate them in the other antitheses to see what results. I submit that in both ancient and modern times, sometimes one category, sometimes the other is predominant. However, since no absolute separation can be made between moral obligation and desire in man, it is only logical that both must always exist side by side, although one may be predominant and the other subordinate. Moral obligation is imposed on man: it is a hard master; desire man creates for himself: his will is his heaven. A persistent moral obligation is bothersome, and not being able to fulfill it is frightful; a persistent desire is pleasant, and with a good measure of will power one may even get over the lack of fulfillment. Let us look at card games as a type of literature, since we find these two elements there too. The rules of the game in combination with chance represent obligation, which for the ancients was represented by fate. Desire in combination with the player's skill counteracts obligation. In this respect, I am tempted to call the game of whist ancient. The rules of the game put limitations on chance, even on desire. With a given number of partners and opponents and the cards that have been dealt me I must control a number of unavoidable chance happenings. In other card games, such as ombre, it is just the opposite. There are no limits on my desire and daring because I can revoke my hand, assign different values to my cards, discard some or all of them, count on luck, and even turn the worst hand into a winning one. This type of game closely resembles modern thinking and modern literature.

Ancient tragedy is based on an inescapable moral obligation which can only intensify and gain momentum if it clashes with an opposing desire. Essentially, this is where the frightfulness of the oracles resides, a domain where *Oedipus* reigns supreme. In *Antigone*, however, obligation in the form of duty seems less harsh. Indeed, there are many variants of obligation, but it is always despotic, no matter whether it is embodied by reason, as in moral code or civil law, or by nature, as in the laws of birth, growth and decay, of life and death. We recoil from all these laws, without realizing that they serve the welfare of the whole. Desire, on the other hand, is free, is perceived as free and favors the individual. Therefore desire is insidious, and it took possession of man as soon as he encountered it. Desire is the god of modern times. Having become his worshipers, we are afraid of the opposing force, and that is the reason why our art and our way of thinking will always remain distinct from those of the ancients. Through moral obligation tragedy becomes great and powerful, through desire weak and insignificant. Desire gave rise not to tragedy but to so-called drama, in which desire takes the place of awesome moral obligation. But precisely because desire comes to the aid of our weakness, we feel grateful when in the end, after painful expectation, we receive some pitiful consolation.

If after these preliminary observations we return to Shakespeare, it is with the hope that the reader himself will be conducting his own comparisons and applying my theories. Shakespeare is indeed unique in that he fuses ancient and modern with such exuberance. In his plays, obligation and desire clearly try to counterbalance each other. Both are powerful contestants, yet Shakespeare always sees to it that desire remains at a disadvantage.

Perhaps no other poet has portrayed more magnificently the underlying connection between desire and moral obligation in individuals. As a character with a role in life, the individual is under an obligation, that is, he is constrained, destined for a specific function. Yet as a human being, he has desires; he is unconstrained, and his desires have no specific target. Already at this point, an inner conflict arises, and Shakespeare gives it special emphasis. But then an external conflict is added, a conflict which is often aggravated by the fact that, for various reasons, an unrealizable desire is raised to the level of a compelling obligation. I refer the reader to my earlier discussion of *Hamlet* where I demonstrated this theory. The principle applies broadly in Shakespeare, however. Many of his characters get into predicaments which they are not equipped to handle. Hamlet does so because of the ghost, Macbeth because of the witches, Hecate and the superwitch, his wife, and Brutus because of his friends. Even in *Coriolanus* we find a similar pattern. In short, we may say that the motif of desire that overpowers the individual is characteristically modern. But since Shakespeare permits this desire to originate from without rather than from within, it becomes a type of obligation close to the ancients' concept. All protagonists in ancient literature desire only what is humanly possible, and that is the reason for the beautiful balance between desire, obligation, and fulfillment. However, their sense of obligation tends to strike us as too extreme and unconvincing, and as a result, despite our admiration, we are not deeply affected. A necessity that excludes freedom to some extent, or altogether, no longer appeals to our modern sensibilities. Shakespeare, on the other hand, closely approximates the modern view. To our amazement and joy, he fuses the ancient and the modern by changing necessity to moral necessity. If we want to learn anything from Shakespeare, this should be the subject of study. I do not wish to chide or condemn our modern romantic literature, but I do maintain that it is extolled, unjustifiedly, as the exclusive model to follow and is praised beyond its merits, which obscures and distorts its strong, robust and admirable features. Instead, we should endeavor to reconcile that great and seemingly irreconcilable antithesis of modern and ancient, especially since a great and peerless master—whom we hold in such high regard and often praise without really knowing why—has already wrought the miracle. Of course, Shakespeare enjoyed the advantage of living in a creative age and in a vigorous Protestant country where the madness of bigotry was silent for a while and where, therefore, a true believer in Nature like Shakespeare was free to develop his pure inner self religiously without paying tribute to any organized religion.

The above remarks were written during the summer of 1813, and I ask the reader not to carp and criticize, but rather bear in mind that they represent only one individual's attempt to point out the different ways various poets have tried to reconcile and resolve that immense antithesis which has assumed so many guises. To say more would be superfluous, especially if we consider that since the time this was written, so much has been said about the subject, and so many excellent explanations have been proffered. I refer particularly to Blümner's commendable treatise, "On the Concept of Fate in the Tragedies of Aeschylus," and its excellent review in the supplement of the *Jenaische Literaturzeitung*. I shall now proceed to my third point, which deals directly with German theater and with Schiller's resolution to make it thrive in the future.

III. Shakespeare as Playwright

To the lover of the arts, the enjoyment of any work means savoring it as a whole. That is to say, he submits to its total impact and is imbued by the sense of unity the artist has given it. The critic, on the other hand, must analyze and dissect it because his purpose is to evaluate and judge, to teach and inform. I tried to do justice to this requirement when I discussed Shakespeare first as a poet in general, and then in comparison with ancient and modern writers. Now I wish to proceed to my third and last point, Shakespeare as a playwright.

To be sure, Shakespeare's fame and accomplishments are part of the history of literature. But we are doing an injustice to all playwrights before and after him if we record his achievements exclusively in the history of the theater.

A universally recognized genius may use his talents in a problematic way; not everything the master does is masterful. While Shakespeare's name is an essential part of the history of literature, he is only a peripheral part of the history of the theater. Yet, since he absolutely deserves our admiration as a writer for the theater, we must examine the conditions under which he had to write, but without extolling those conditions as virtues or models.

There are closely related literary forms which in practice are often combined, such as epic, dialog, drama, and stage play. The epic requires oral delivery by one individual to an audience; dialog requires conversation in a closed circle to which an audience is allowed to listen; drama requires conversation supported by action, even if the action is only created by our imagination; a stage play requires all three together and insofar as it also involves our visual sense, it can be effective as long as it presents a locale and characters to which we can relate. In this sense, Shakespeare's works are predominantly drama. His method of revealing what happens in mind and soul captivates the reader. Stage requirements are unimportant to Shakespeare, so he does not pay much attention to them, nor do we as we read. We skip along from locale to locale, our imagination fills in all the episodes he omits, and we are even grateful to him for stimulating our minds in such a rewarding way. By presenting everything in the form of a stage play, Shakespeare facilitates the task of our imagination, for we are more familiar with the "stage that represents the world" than with the world itself. No matter how fantastic the things we read and hear, we still think that they would be effective in the theater, which might explain why so many bad plays have been adapted from popular novels.

However, strictly speaking, nothing is truly suitable to the theater which is not also perceived as symbolic: an important action which anticipates an even more important one. That Shakespeare knew how to achieve this supreme effect is evident in the scene where the heir to the throne takes the crown from the side of his sleeping, dying father, puts it on his own head and struts off. But such symbolic episodes are few, are isolated jewels in the midst of quantities of material which is not suitable for presentation on the stage. As a matter of fact, the stage almost always presents an obstacle to Shakespeare's creativity. His great talent is that of an epitomizer, one who extracts the essence, and since the poet is the very epitomizer of nature, we must acknowledge Shakespeare's great accomplishment in this regard as well. At the same time however—and this reflects well on him—we must reject the notion that the stage is a vehicle worthy of his genius. Yet it is precisely the limitations of the stage which force him to discipline his poetic talent. In adjusting to these constraints, he does not choose specific material for a specific work as some writers do, but rather, he decides on one idea as the central point, and then makes the world and the universe relate to it. His method of condensing events of ancient and modern history enables him to use material from any chronicle, sometimes even following his source verbatim. He does not proceed as conscientiously with tales, as is evident in *Hamlet*. *Romeo and Juliet* is closer to the original, yet he all but destroys its tragic quality by introducing two comic characters, Mercutio and the Nurse, roles which were probably played by two popular actors, the Nurse most likely by a man. Upon close examination of the play's structure, we notice that these two characters and all that relates to them only appear in farcical interludes, which we find objectionable on the stage, since we are accustomed to a logical, consistent way of thinking.

Shakespeare is most impressive when he revises and adapts existing plays. This can be clearly shown in *King John* and *King Lear* by comparing them with the older versions. But even in these instances, Shakespeare is again more poet than playwright.

In conclusion, let me proceed to the solution of the riddle. The imperfections of the English stage in Shakespeare's time have been well established by scholars. There was no demand at all to strive for realism as we know it, which became possible gradually through improvements in machinery and in the art of perspective and costuming. It would be very difficult for us to return to that early, rudimentary stage, for we could not possibly sit in front of a bare scaffolding with simple props which only suggest reality, with a green curtain symbolizing the king's chamber, and a trumpeter who keeps trumpeting at regular intervals, and the like. What present-day audience would tolerate that? Staged under such conditions, Shakespeare's plays were fascinating fairytales, told by a limited number of persons who wore costumes for better effect and characterization and who moved about, entered and exited when necessary. It was left to the spectator to imagine the countryside and the royal court on the barren stage.

Schröder gained the distinction of having introduced Shakespeare's plays to the German stage solely by becoming the epitomizer of Shakespeare the epitomizer! Schröder used only what is effective on the stage and discarded everything else, even some essential things if he thought they would not produce the proper effect on his countrymen or would seem to contradict the spirit of his time. For example, it is true that by excising the first scenes of *King Lear* he destroyed the essence of the play. But he was justified in doing so, for in the first scene, King Lear seems so absurd that in the subsequent parts of the play we cannot altogether condemn his daughters' actions. We feel sorry for the old man, but we do not feel profound pity for him. And that was Schröder's intent: to arouse our pity for Lear and our abhorrence for the daughters who are indeed unnatural but by no means totally culpable.

In the source Shakespeare adapted, this scene produces the most delightful effects later in the play. Lear flees to France, while daughter and son-in-law, succumbing to some romantic whim, set out on a pilgrimage to the seashore and meet the old man, who does not recognize them. Here everything turns sweet, while Shakespeare's penchant for the tragic turns it bitter. A comparison of the two plays is always a source of pleasure for the critical reader.

For many years the misguided notion has been gaining ground in Germany that if Shakespeare's plays are performed on the German stage, not a single word must be omitted even though that may make actors and audience choke. Attempts to put this notion into practice, prompted by an excellent and accurate translation, have resulted in failure everywhere. The serious and repeated efforts in the theater in Weimar are a case in point. If we want to see a truly Shakespearean play, we must return to Schröder's approach. Yet the senseless demand persists: when we perform Shakespeare, we must not omit the slightest detail! Should the proponents of this opinion prevail,

Shakespeare will within a few years disappear from the German stage altogether. However, that would not be as deplorable as it may sound because the reader, in private or in the company of others, would delight in him in an even purer way.

An attempt has been made to adapt *Romeo and Juliet* for the theater in Weimar in accordance with the points discussed at length above. I shall describe the guiding principles of that venture at some future occasion. It will then perhaps become clear why the adaptation was unsuccessful, despite the fact that the staging is by no means difficult, although it must be handled with artistry and care. Similar projects are now in progress, but since persistent endeavors do not always produce immediate results, their impact may not be felt until some time in the future.

ARTHUR SCHOPENHAUER

Arthur **SCHOPENHAUER** (1788-1860) had curly blond hair, steel blue eyes, a high forehead, assertive nose, and heavy-set mouth. His face somewhat resembled Byron's. He dressed in a frock-coat and vest in the style of the romantics. Wagner, who said he looked like a wild cat, hailed Schopenhauer as his master, dedicated the first part of the *Ring* cycle to him, and invited him to Zürich. Schopenhauer much preferred Rossini and declined the invitation.

The fifteen-year-old Schopenhauer became a superbly qualified spectator on a grand tour with his parents in 1803 that took him to all the major theatres of France, England, and Holland. He was an expert on playhouses and inns, of which he visited many hundred. In his travel diaries he recorded his reactions to the plays that he attended daily, noting the quality of the acting and staging, the costumes, sets, and machinery.

In England he saw John Philip Kemble as Hamlet and became an admirer of George Frederick Cook, whom he preferred to Kemble. He was present at the first British melodrama, Holcroft's *A Tale of Mystery* (adapted from Pixérécourt) at Covent Garden, and he never missed a chance to watch ventriloquists and puppet shows. The *Richard III* that he saw at Drury Lane had been so adapted that he protested indignantly he found it scarcely recognizable as Shakespeare's.

In Paris he saw Talma at the Comédie Française in Lemercier's *Agamemnon* and met the great actor backstage. The playwright and theatre theorist Sebastien Mercier showed him Paris and took him to the Pantheon and the Louvre. In his diary young Schopenhauer observed that the French language and actors were well suited to light comedies and comic operas, but that French declamation made their tragedies insufferable. And he also noted that "At the French Theatre they endlessly argued about the unity of time, place, and action, but paid little attention to unity of thought."

By the time he was in his twenties, Schopenhauer was intimately acquainted with the theatres of five nations in their native languages (England, France, Germany, Italy, and Holland). He knew *commedia* and Sanskrit drama as well as the classics and romantics, and he showed a strong interest in popular arts and superstitions. He participated in table-turning séances, believed in animal magnetism, and feared being buried alive. In Italy he attended mask balls, whose imagery he used in describing human history as carnival.

His mother, a celebrated novelist, had a special table in her salon in Weimar for Goethe who dropped in every day and sketched. Young Schopenhauer fell in love with the actress Caroline Jagemann of the great theatre at Weimar in 1813 while visiting his mother, whom he could not stand, although he felt he owed her his intelligence, "the structure of the brain coming from the mother." Schopenhauer took a lively interest in madness which ran in the family (on his father's side) and shared the romantic belief that genius was related to insanity. Poets he considered to be like dreamers and children: "Every genius is a child, from the very reason that he looks out on the world as a strange one."

Schopenhauer frequented the theatre and opera regularly all his life. He preferred modern to ancient tragedy, Shakespeare to Sophocles, Goethe to Euripides, because the moderns portrayed a tragic human condition imbued with a Christian spirit of resignation and renunciation of the world akin to the Buddhist and Indian philosophy he loved. He was moved to tears by a performance of Calderón's *The Constant Prince* he saw in 1809.

In 1820 for his newly inaugurated lectures at the University of Berlin Schopenhauer chose the same hours as those of Hegel, whom he despised. No students came to Schopenhauer's course and he abandoned a university career forever.

The author of *The World as Will and Idea* has been most admired by artists and writers. Tolstoy, Nietzsche, Strindberg, Appia, Svevo, Chaplin, and Beckett have all sworn by the invigorating pessimism of Schopenhauer, who thought that man was descended from the monkey but only in a degenerate version.

THE WORLD AS WILL AND IDEA

(1819/1844)

Tragedy is to be regarded, and is recognized as the summit of poetical art, both on account of the greatness of its effect and the difficulty of its achievement. It is very significant for our whole system, and well worthy of observation, that the end of this highest poetical achievement is the representation of the terrible side of life. The unspeakable pain, the wail of humanity, the triumph of evil, the scornful mastery of chance, and the irretrievable fall of the just and innocent, is here presented to us; and in this lies a significant hint of the nature of the world and of existence. It is the strife of will with itself, which here completely unfolded at the highest grade of its objectivity, comes into fearful prominence. It becomes visible in the suffering of men, which is now introduced, partly through chance and error, which appear as the rulers of the world, personified as fate, on account of their insidiousness, which even reaches the appearance of design; partly it proceeds from man himself, through the self-mortifying efforts of a few, through the wickedness and perversity of most. It is one and the same will that lives and appears in them all, but whose phenomena fight against each other and destroy each other. In one individual it appears powerfully, in another more weakly; in one more subject to reason, and softened by the light of knowledge, in another less so, till at last, in some single case, this knowledge, purified and heightened by suffering itself, reaches the point at which the phenomenon, the veil of Maya, no longer deceives it. It sees through the form of the phenomenon, the *principum individuationis*. The egoism which rests on this perishes with it, so that now the *motives* that were so powerful before have lost their might, and instead of them the complete knowledge of the nature of the world, which has a *quieting* effect on the will, produces resignation, the surrender not merely of life, but of the very will to live. Thus we see in tragedies the noblest men, after long conflict and suffering, at last renounce the ends they have so keenly followed, and all the pleasures of life for ever, or else freely and joyfully surrender life itself. So is it with the steadfast prince of Calderón; with Gretchen in *Faust*; with Hamlet, whom his friend Horatio would willingly follow, but is bade remain a while, and in this harsh world draw his breath in pain, to tell the story of Hamlet, and clear his memory; so also is it with the Maid of

From Arthur Schopenhauer, *The World as Will and Idea*, trans. R.B. Haldane and J. Kemp. London: Trubner & Co. 1883-6.

Orleans, the Bride of Messina; they all die purified by suffering, i.e., after the will to live which was formerly in them is dead. In the *Mohammed* of Voltaire this is actually expressed in the concluding words which the dying Palmira addresses to Mohammed: "The world is for tyrants: live!" On the other hand, the demand for so-called poetical justice rests on entire misconception of the nature of tragedy, and, indeed, of the nature of the world itself. It boldly appears in all its dullness in the criticisms which Dr. Samuel Johnson made on particular plays of Shakespeare, for he very naively laments its entire absence. And its absence is certainly obvious, for in what has Ophelia, Desdemona, or Cordelia offended? But only the dull, optimistic, Protestant-rationalistic, or peculiarly Jewish view of life will make the demand for poetical justice, and find satisfaction in it. The true sense of tragedy is the deeper insight, that it is not his own individual sins that the hero atones for, but original sin, i.e., the crime of existence itself:

> *Pues el delito mayor*
> *Del hombre es haber nacido*
> (For the greatest crime of man
> Is that he was born)

As Calderón exactly expresses it. [...]

I shall allow myself only one remark, more closely concerning the treatment of tragedy. The representation of a great misfortune is alone essential to tragedy. But the many different ways in which this is introduced by the poet may be brought under three specific conceptions. It may happen by means of a character of extraordinary wickedness, touching the utmost limits of possibility, who becomes the author of the misfortune; examples of this kind are Richard III, Iago in *Othello*, Shylock in *The Merchant of Venice*, Franz Moor, Phaedra of Euripides, Creon in the *Antigone*, etc., etc. Secondly, it may happen through blind fate, i.e., chance and error; a true pattern of this kind is the *Oedipus Rex* of Sophocles, the *Trachiniae* also; and in general most of the tragedies of the ancients belong to this class. Among modern tragedies, *Romeo and Juliet*, *Tancred* by Voltaire, and *The Bride of Messina* are examples. Lastly, the misfortune may be brought about by the mere position of the dramatic personae with regard to each other, through their relations; so that there is no need either for a tremendous error or an unheard-of accident, nor yet for a character whose wickedness reaches the limits of human possibility; but characters of ordinary morality, under circumstances such as often occur, are so situated with regard to each other that their position compels them, knowingly and with their eyes open, to do each other the greatest injury, without any one of them being entirely in the wrong. This last kind of tragedy seems to me far to surpass the other two, for it shows us the greatest misfortune, not as an exception, not as something occasioned by rare circumstances or monstrous characters, but as arising easily and of itself out of the actions and characters of men, indeed almost as essential to them, and thus brings it terribly near to us. In the other two kinds we may look on the prodigious fate and the horrible wickedness as terrible powers which certainly threaten us, but only from afar, which we may very well escape without taking refuge in renunciation. But in the last kind of tragedy we see that those powers which destroy happiness and life are such that their path to us also is open at every moment; we see the greatest sufferings brought about by entanglements that our fate might also partake of, and through actions that perhaps we also are capable of performing, and so could not complain of injustice; then shuddering we feel ourselves already in the midst of hell. This last kind of tragedy is also the most difficult of achievement; for the greatest effect has to be produced in it with the least use of means and causes of movement, merely through the position and distribution of the characters; therefore even in many of the best tragedies this difficulty is evaded. Yet one tragedy may be referred to as a perfect model of this kind, a tragedy which in other respects is far surpassed by more than one work of the same great master; it is *Clavigo*. Hamlet belongs to a certain extent to this class, as far as the relation of Hamlet to Laertes and Ophelia is concerned. *Wallenstein* has also this excellence. *Faust* belongs entirely to this class, if we regard the events connected with Gretchen and her brother as the principal action; also the *Cid* of Corneille, only that it lacks the tragic conclusion, while on the contrary the analogous relation of Max to Thecla has it. [...]

The end of the drama in general is to show us in an example what is the nature and existence of man. The sad or the bright side of these can be turned to us in it, or their transitions into each other. But the expression, "nature and existence of man," already contains the germ of the controversy whether the nature, i.e., the character, or the existence, i.e., the fate, the adventures, the action, is the principal thing. Moreover, the two have grown so firmly together that although they can certainly be separated in conception, they cannot be separated in the representation of them. For only the circumstances, the fate, the events, make the character manifest its nature, and only from the character does the action arise from which the events proceed. Certainly, in the representation, the one or the other may be made more prominent; and in this respect the piece which centers in the characters and the piece which centers in the plot are the two extremes.

The common end of the drama and the epic, to exhibit, in significant characters placed in significant situations, the extraordinary actions brought about by both, will be most completely attained by the poet if he first introduces the characters to us in a state of peace, in which merely their general color becomes visible, and allows a motive to enter which produces an action, out of which a new and stronger motive arises, which again calls forth a more significant action, which, in its turn, begets new and even stronger motives, whereby, then, in the time suitable to the form of the poem, the most passionate excitement takes the place of the original peace, and in this now the important actions occur in which the qualities of the characters which have hitherto slumbered are brought clearly to light, together with the course of the world.

Great poets transform themselves into each of the persons to be represented, and speak out of each of them like ventriloquists; now out of the hero, and immediately afterwards out of the young and innocent maiden, with equal truth and naturalness: so Shakespeare and Goethe. Poets of the second rank transform the principal person to be represented into themselves. This is what Byron does; and then the other persons often remain lifeless, as is the case even with the principal persons in the world of mediocre poets.

Our pleasure in tragedy belongs, not to the sense of the beautiful, but to that of the sublime; nay, it is the highest grade of this feeling. For, as at the sight of the sublime in nature we turn away from the interests of the will, in order to be purely perceptive, so in the tragic catastrophe we turn away even from the will to live. In tragedy the terrible side of life is presented to us, the wail of humanity, the reign of chance and error, the fall of the just, the triumph of the wicked; thus the aspect of the world which directly strives against our will is brought before our eyes. At this sight we feel ourselves challenged to turn away our will from life, no longer to will it or love it. But just in this way we become conscious that then there still remains something over to us, which we absolutely cannot know positively, but only negatively, as that which does not will life. As the chord of the seventh demands the fundamental chord; as the color red demands green, and even produces it in the eye; so every tragedy demands an entirely different kind of existence, another world, the knowledge of which can only be given us indirectly just as here by such a demand. In the moment of the tragic catastrophe the conviction becomes more distinct to us than ever that life is a bad dream from which we have to awake. So far the effect of the tragedy is analogous to that of the dynamical sublime, for like this it lifts us above the will and its interests, and puts us in such a mood that we find pleasure in the sight of what tends directly against it. What gives to all tragedy, in whatever form it may appear, the peculiar tendency towards the sublime is the awakening of the knowledge that the world, life, can afford us no true pleasure, and consequently is not worthy of our attachment. In this consists the tragic spirit: it therefore leads to resignation.

I admit that in ancient tragedy this spirit of resignation seldom appears and is expressed directly. Oedipus Colonus certainly dies resigned and willing; yet he is comforted by the revenge on his country. Iphigenia at Aulis is very willing to die; yet it is the thought of the welfare of Greece that comforts her, and occasions the change of her mind, on account of which she willingly accepts the death which at first she sought to avoid by any means.

Cassandra, in the *Agamemnon* of the great Aeschylus, dies willingly; but she also is comforted by the thought of revenge. Hercules, in the *Trachiniae*, submits to necessity, and dies composed, but not resigned. So also the *Hippolytus* of Euripides, in whose case it surprises us that Artemis, who appears to comfort him, promises him temples and fame, but never points him to an existence beyond life, and leaves him in death, as all gods forsake the dying:—in Christianity they come to him; and so also in Brahmanism and Buddhism, although in the latter the gods are really exotic. Thus Hippolytus, like almost all the tragic heroes of the ancients, shows submission to inevitable fate and the inflexible will of the gods, but no surrender of the will to live itself. As the Stoic equanimity is fundamentally distinguished from Christian resignation by the fact that it teaches only patient endurance and composed expectation of unalterably necessary evil, while Christianity teaches renunciation, surrender of the will; so also the tragic heroes of the ancients show resolute subjection under the unavoidable blows of fate, while Christian tragedy, on the contrary shows the surrender of the whole will to live, joyful forsaking of the world in the consciousness of its worthlessness and vanity. But I am also entirely of opinion that modern tragedy stands higher than that of the ancients. Shakespeare is much greater than Sophocles; in comparison with Goethe's Iphigenia one might find that of Euripides almost crude and vulgar. The *Bacchae* of Euripides is a revolting composition in favor of the heathen priests. Many ancient pieces have no tragic tendency at all, like the *Alcestis* and *Iphigenia in Tauris* of Euripides; some have disagreeable, or even disgusting motives, like the *Antigone* and *Philoctetes*. Almost all show the human race under the fearful rule of chance and error, but not the resignation which is occasioned by it, and delivers from it. All because the ancients had not yet attained to the summit and goal of tragedy, or indeed of the view of life itself.

Although, then, the ancients displayed little of the spirit of resignation, the turning away of the will from life, in their tragic heroes themselves, as their frame of mind, yet the peculiar tendency and effect of tragedy remains the awakening of that spirit in the beholder, the calling up of that frame of mind, even though only temporarily. The horrors upon the stage hold up to him the bitterness and worthlessness of life, thus the vanity of all its struggle. The effect of this impression must be that he becomes conscious, if only in obscure feeling, that it is better to tear his heart free from life, to turn his will from it, to love not the world nor life; whereby then in his deepest soul, the consciousness is aroused that for another kind of willing there must also be another existence. For if this were not so, then the tendency of tragedy would not be this rising above all the ends and good things of life, this turning away from it and its seductions, and the turning towards another kind of existence, which already lies in this, although an existence which is for us quite inconceivable. How would it, then, in general, be possible that the exhibition of the most terrible side of life, brought before our eyes in the most glaring light, could act upon us beneficently, and afford us a lofty satisfaction? Fear and sympathy, in the excitement of which Aristotle places the ultimate end of tragedy, certainly do not in themselves belong to the agreeable sensations: therefore they cannot be the end, but only the means. Thus the summons to turn away the will from life remains the true tendency of tragedy, the ultimate end of the intentional exhibition of the suffering of humanity, and is so accordingly even where this resigned exaltation of the mind is not shown in the hero himself, but is merely excited in the spectator by the sight of great, unmerited, nay, even merited suffering. Many of the moderns also are, like the ancients, satisfied with throwing the spectator into the mood which has been described, by the objective representation of human misfortune as a whole; while others exhibit this through the change of the frame of mind of the hero himself, effected by suffering. The former give, as it were, only the premises, and leave the conclusion to the spectator; while the latter give the conclusion, or the moral of the fable, also, as the change of the frame of mind of the hero, and even also as reflection, in the mouth of the chorus, as, for example, Schiller in *The Bride of Messina*: "Life is not the highest good." Let me remark here that the genuine tragic effect of the catastrophe, thus the resignation and exaltation of the mind of the hero which is brought about by it, seldom appears so purely motivated and so distinctly expressed as in the opera of *Norma*, where it comes in the duet, *"Qual cor tradisti, qual cor perdesti,"* in which the change of the will is distinctly indicated by the quietness which is suddenly introduced into the music. In general, this piece—regarded apart altogether from its excellent music, and also from the diction which can only be that of a libretto, and considered only according to its motives and its inner economy—is a highly perfect tragedy, a true pattern of tragic disposition of the motives, tragic progress of the action, and tragic development, together with the effect of these upon the frame of mind of the hero, raising it above the world, and which is then also communicated to the spectator; indeed the effect attained here is the less delusive and the more indicative of the true nature of tragedy that no Christians, nor even Christian ideas, appear in it.

The neglect of the unity of time and place with which the moderns are so often reproached is only a fault when it goes so far that it destroys the unity of the action; for then there only remains the unity of the principal character, as, for example, in Shakespeare's *Henry VIII*. But even the unity of the action does not need to go so far that the same thing is spoken of throughout, as in the French tragedies which in general observe this so strictly that the course of the drama is like a geometrical line without breadth. There it is constantly a case of "Only get on! *Pensez à votre affaire!*" and the thing is expedited and hurried on in a thoroughly business fashion, and no one detains himself with irrelevancies which do not belong to it, or looks to the right or the left. The Shakespearian tragedy, on the other hand, is like a line which has also breadth: it takes time, *exspatiatur*: speeches and even whole scenes occur which do not advance the action, indeed do not properly concern it, by which, however, we get to know the characters or their circumstances more fully, and then understand the action also more thoroughly. This certainly remains the principal thing, yet not so exclusively that we forget that in the last instance what is aimed at is the representation of human nature and existence generally.

The dramatic or epic poet ought to know that he is fate, and should therefore be inexorable, as it is; also that he is the mirror of the human race, and should therefore represent very many bad and sometimes profligate characters, and also many fools, buffoons, and eccentric persons; then also, now and again, a reasonable, a prudent, an honest, or a good man, and only as the rarest exception a truly magnanimous man. In the whole of Homer there is in my opinion no really magnanimous character presented, although many good and honest. In the whole of Shakespeare there may be perhaps a couple of noble, though by no means transcendently noble, characters to be found; perhaps Cordelia, Coriolanus—hardly more; on the other hand, his works swarm with the species indicated above. But Iffland's and Kotzebue's pieces have many magnanimous characters; while Goldoni has done as I recommended above, whereby he shows that he stands higher. On the other hand, Lessing's *Minna von Barnhelm* labors under too much and too universal magnanimity; but so much magnanimity as the one Marquis Posa displays is not to be found in the whole of Goethe's works together. There is, however, a small German piece called *Duty for Duty's Sake* (a title which sounds as if it had been taken from the *Critique of Practical Reason*), which has only three characters, and yet all the three are of most transcendent magnanimity.

The Greeks have taken for their heroes only royal persons; and so also for the most part have the moderns. Certainly not because the rank gives more worth to him who is acting or suffering; and since the whole thing is just to set human passions in play, the relative value of the objects by which this happens is indifferent, and peasant huts achieve as much as kingdoms. Moreover, civic tragedy is by no means to be unconditionally rejected. Persons of great power and consideration are yet the best adapted for tragedy on this account, that the misfortune in which we ought to recognize the fate of humanity must have a sufficient magnitude to appear terrible to the spectator, whoever he may be. [...] Now the circumstances which plunge a citizen family into want and despair are in the eyes of the great or rich, for the most part, very insignificant, and capable of being removed by human assistance, nay, sometimes even by a trifle: such spectators, therefore, cannot be tragically affected by them. On the other hand, the misfortunes of the great and powerful are unconditionally terrible, and also accessible to no help from without; for kings must help themselves by their own power, or fall. To this we have to add that the fall is greatest from a height. Accordingly persons of the rank of citizens lack height to fall from.

If now we have found the tendency and ultimate intention of tragedy to be a turning to resignation, to the denial of the will to live, we shall easily recognize in its opposite, comedy, the incitement to the continued assertion of the will. It is true that even comedy, like every representation of human life, without exception, must bring before our eyes suffering and adversity; but it presents it to us as passing, resolving itself into joy, in general mingled with success, victory, and hopes, which in the end preponderate; moreover, it brings out the inexhaustible material for laughter of which life, and even its adversities themselves are filled, and which under all circumstances ought to keep us in a good humor. Thus it declares, in the result, that life as a whole is thoroughly good, and especially is always amusing. Certainly it must hasten to drop the curtain at the moment of joy, so that we may not see what comes after; while the tragedy, as a rule, so ends that nothing can come after. And moreover, if once we contemplate this burlesque side of life somewhat seriously, as it shows itself in the naive utterances and gestures which trifling embarrassment, personal fear, momentary anger, secret envy, and many similar emotions force upon the forms of the real life that mirrors itself here, forms which deviate considerably from the type of beauty, then from this side also, thus in an unexpected manner, the reflective spectator may become convinced that the existence and action of such beings cannot itself be an end; that, on the contrary, they can only have attained to existence by an error, and that what so exhibits itself is something which had better not be.

VICTOR HUGO

Victor HUGO (1802-1885) throughout his life adopted histrionic poses and created legendary personalities for himself. The officially sanctioned pictures come from his youth, maturity, and old age. The first shows an elegantly dressed, angelic young poet with a high forehead and beautifully shaped thick black hair; the second discloses a lonely political exile perched high on a rock on the isle of Guernsey; while the third depicts a far-seeing visionary elder as a white haired and bearded patriarch resembling one of Michelangelo's prophets. Hugo controlled and manipulated these evolving images and the resulting iconography of the "great man," avoiding any pictures that would reveal the corporeal ravages wrought by time and circumstance on ordinary mortals.

The young poet of the revolutionary "Preface to *Cromwell*" was in fact a smooth-chinned, soberly dressed bourgeois of medium height who took infinite pains over shaving, carefully stropping his razor, warming it for a quarter hour, and washing his face with rose water. While the upper half of his face appeared pure and chaste, his lips and mouth were cruelly sensual. And the old demigod was an insatiable satyr, making love relentlessly day after day to thousands of actresses, society ladies, and chamber maids. Edmond Goncourt detected in the dark bright eyes of this venerable tiger of health and strength "an indefinable expression of evil cunning." Elevated to the peerage in 1876, Hugo attended the senate of the Third Republic dressed like an old carpenter or brick layer.

Like Goethe, Hugo was introduced to theatre through marionettes when he and his brother Eugène were taken to the Luxembourg Gardens to see the "guignol" puppets shows. Soon the boys had a marionette theatre at home where they could perform their own plays. But it was the overwhelming experience of seeing Pixérécourt's *The Ruins of Babylon* in 1810 that decided the youngster to become a playwright. Victor returned to the theatre again and again to see this spectacular melodrama and even wrote an imitation, *Le Château du diable*. Among his other early plays, *Inès de Castro* and *Amy Robsart* were also melodramas inspired by Pixérécourt, whom Hugo never once mentions in any of his prefaces or critical essays, unwilling to acknowledge as an influence such a subliterary hack.

After first toying with the idea of a play about Corneille, viewed as a misunderstood genius persecuted by society and its oppressive rules, Hugo in 1826 completed his five-act drama in verse, *Cromwell*, written expressly for Talma, whose death the same year ruled out any foreseeable production. Hugo gave public readings and thought of shortening his interminable historical drama to a three-act comedy called *When will He Be King ?* It was not until June 28, 1956 that *Cromwell* was first staged in an outdoor production at the Cour Carrée of the Louvre.

More famous than the play, Hugo's "Preface to *Cromwell*" became the manifesto for French romantic drama in its battle against the sclerotic neo-classical rules. The essay was inspired by Shakespeare, as revealed to Hugo and the young generation of French artists in the British production of *Hamlet* by Charles Kemble at the Odéon.

In 1830 the ideas in the "Preface" reached the theatre itself on the occasion of the tumultuous premiere of *Hernani* at the Comédie Française when the young romantics engaged in fisticuffs with their outraged elders. "Bald pates to the guillotine!" screamed one of Hugo's followers at an aging defender of classicism. Hugo hired a claque of 100 to attend the theatre every night and express their enthusiasm; the result was a semi-triumph for roman-ticism. But Hugo's real success came in 1833 at the popular boulevard theatre, la Porte-Saint-Martin, with *Lucrecia Borgia*, starring the great melodrama actor Frédérick Lemaître.

Hugo, who always dreamed of being a director and working with actors, finally got a theatre of his own. In 1838 he opened the Théâtre de la Renaissance for the express purpose of propagating romantic drama, and the first play staged was Hugo's *Ruy Blas*, starring Lemaître. An extraordinarily talented graphic artist with a penchant for the grotesque and fantastic, Hugo took an active interest in stage design, often drawing sketches of sets on his manuscripts. He treated stage space as a mute character and knew how light-ing could produce chiaroscuro effects in an atmosphere of shadowy dark-ness—through the use of angled light, hand-held lanterns, and torch or can-dlelight processions.

Forced to flee France in 1852 for his political opposition to Louis Napoleon's political coup, Hugo spent eighteen years in self-imposed exile on the islands of Jersey and Guernsey in the English channel. There he and his family engaged in strange dramatic dialogues with the dead, practicing table turning and communing with the spirits of Robespierre, Charlotte Corday, Luther, Moses, and Shakespeare, among many others. Hugo scrupulously recorded the conversations at these séances, which revealed to him the prima-cy of the dead over the living and offered proof that this world is only an antichamber to the next. Shakespeare even dictated scenes of a new play that in French is remarkably close stylistically to Hugo's own work.

PREFACE TO *CROMWELL* (1827)

[...] There is, then, a new religion and a new society. From this dual foundation a new poetry inevitably will arise. Previously—we beg your pardon for setting forth a result that the reader himself must have already foreseen in what we stated above—previously, and in a manner similar to that of ancient polytheism and philosophy, the purely epic muse of the ancients had studied nature in only one aspect, mercilessly eliminating everything in the world subject to imitation by art which did not conform to a certain conception of beauty. This conception of beauty was magnificent at first, but, as always happens when something is systematized, in later times became false, trivial, and conventional. Christianity leads poetry to truth. Like it, the modern muse will view things from a higher and broader vantage point. She will see that everything in creation is not humanly *beautiful*, that the ugly exists beside the beautiful, deformity beside gracefulness, the grotesque on the reverse side of the sublime, evil with good, light with shadow. She will ask herself if the narrow and relative reason of the artist should prevail over the infinite, absolute reason of the Creator; if it is for man to correct God; if a mutilated nature will not seem all the more beautiful; if art has the right to duplicate, so to speak, man, life, creation; if things will function better with their muscle and vigor removed; finally, if being incomplete is a function of achieving harmony. That is when, with its gaze fixed on events, both risible and awesome, and under the influence of the spirit of Christian melancholy and philosophical criticism which we described above, poetry will take a giant step, a step which, like the trembling of an earthquake, will alter the whole face of the intellectual world. It will begin to act as nature does, mixing, but not confounding in its creations shadow and light, the grotesque and the sublime, in other words, body and soul, beast and reason. For religion and poetry have always the same starting point. All things are connected.

Thus we see a principle unknown to the ancients, a new subject introduced into poetry. And, as an additional element in a being modifies the entire being, a new form of art evolves. That subject is the grotesque; its form is comedy.

And we ask leave to stress this point; for we have just indicated the

From *Revolution in the Theatre*, ed. and trans. Barry V. Daniels. Westport, Conn.: Greenwood Press, 1983.

characteristic feature, the fundamental difference which, in our opinion, separates modern art from ancient art, present form from past form, or, to use the vaguer but more acceptable terms, *romantic* literature from *classical* literature.

"Finally!" say those men who for some time now have *seen* where we were *heading*. "We have you now. You are caught in the act. Thus you allow the *ugly* as a type for imitation and the *grotesque* as an element of art! What of the graces... what about good taste... Aren't you aware that art ought to correct nature? That it must be ennobled? That it is necessary to be *selective?* Have the ancients ever exhibited the ugly and the grotesque? Have they ever mixed comedy with tragedy? The example of the ancients, gentlemen! Consider Aristotle... and Boileau... and LaHarpe... my word!"

These arguments are, doubtless, sound and, above all, extremely novel. But it is not our place to answer them. We are not constructing a system here—heaven preserve us from systems! We are stating a fact. We act as an historian not as a critic. Little matter whether this fact pleases or displeases; it is a fact—Let us resume, then, and attempt to illustrate that the fruitful union of the grotesque type with the sublime type produces the modern genius—so complex and varied in its forms, so inexhaustible in its creations, and in that, directly opposed to the uniform simplicity of the genius of the ancients. Let us demonstrate that this must be the point of departure to establish the real and radical difference between the two forms of literature.

This does not mean that comedy and the grotesque were completely unknown to the ancients. In fact, such a thing would be impossible. Nothing grows without roots; the germ of the second epoch is always present in the first. In the *Iliad* Thersites and Vulcan provide comedy, one to mortals, the other to gods. There is too much of nature and originality in Greek tragedy for it not to sometimes include the comic. For example, to cite only what immediately comes to mind, the scene between Menelaus and the palace attendant (*Helen*, Act I), and the scene of the Phrygian (*Orestes*, Act IV). Mermen, satyrs, cyclops are grotesques; sirens, furies, fates, harpies are grotesques. Polyphemus is a terrifying, Silenus a buffoonish, grotesque.

But one senses that this part of the art is still in its infancy. The epic, which in this period imposes its form on everything, the epic bears down upon it and stifles it. The grotesque of the ancients is timid and always seeking to hide itself. One senses that it is not on familiar ground because it is not in its natural surroundings. It is hidden as much as possible. Satyrs, mermen and sirens are hardly deformed. The fates and the harpies are rather more hideous in their characters than in their features; the furies are beautiful and called "*eumenides*," that is, "kindly." There is a veil of grandeur or divinity over the other grotesques. Polyphemus is a giant: Midas is a king; Silenus is a god.

Thus comedy is almost imperceptible in the great epic ensemble of antiquity. What is Thespis' wagon compared with Olympian chariots? What are Aristophanes and Plautus beside the Homeric colossi, Aeschylus,

Sophocles, and Euripides? Homer bears them along, as Hercules bore the pygmies, hidden in his lion skin.

In modern thought, however, the grotesque plays an important role. It is found everywhere; on the one hand, it produces the deformed and the horrible; on the other, the comic and buffoonish. It clothes religion with a thousand original superstitions, poetry with a thousand picturesque fancies. It is the grotesque which scatters freely in air, water, earth and fire those myriads of intermediary creatures which we find again living in the popular traditions of the Middle Ages. It is the grotesque which sets in motion in the shadows the horrifying dance of the Witches' Sabbath, which gives Satan horns, goat's hooves, and bat's wings. It is the grotesque, always the grotesque, which places in the Christian Hell those hideous figures that the austere genius of Dante and Milton will evoke, or peoples Hell with those ridiculous figures which inspire the creations of Callot, the burlesque Michaelangelo. If it passes from the unreal world to the real world, it unfolds an inexhaustible supply of parodies of mankind. Its fantasies give birth to Scaramouches, Crispins, Harlequins—grimacing silhouettes of men, types completely unknown to serious-minded antiquity, though they originated in classical Italy. It is the grotesque, finally, which causes Sganarelle to dance about Don Juan, Mephistopheles to slink after Faust, coloring the same play alternately with the imagination of the South and the North.

And how free and frank is its behavior! How boldly it throws into relief all those strange forms that earlier periods in timidity had wrapped in swaddling. Ancient poetry, obliged to provide the lame Vulcan with companions, attempted to disguise deformity so to speak, by developing it on a colossal scale. The modern genius retains this myth of supernatural blacksmiths, but gives it a completely different character which renders it more striking. Giants are changed into dwarfs, cyclopes are turned into gnomes. With similar originality, it replaces the rather banal Lernaean hydra with all the local dragons of our legends—the gargoyle of Rouen, the *gra-ouilli* of Metz, the *chair sallée* of Troyes, the *drée* of Montlhéry, the *tarasque* of Tarascon—monsters of diverse form, given additional character by their baroque names. All these creations draw from their own nature the energetic and significant coloring which antiquity often studiously avoided. Certainly the Greek Eumenides are much less horrible, and consequently, less true, than the witches of *Macbeth*. Pluto is not the Devil.

In our opinion, a very novel book could be written on the place of the grotesque in art. One could demonstrate what powerful effects the moderns obtain from this fruitful type, although it is still ruthlessly condemned by narrow-minded critics in our day. Our subject may soon cause us to note in passing some of the features of this vast picture. We will simply say here that when placed beside the sublime, as a means of contrast, the grotesque, in our opinion, is the richest source that we can open to art. Rubens doubtless understood this when he placed some hideous figure like a court dwarf amid his displays of royal pomp, coronations, and dazzling ceremonials. The universal beauty which the ancients solemnly imparted to everything was not without monotony. The same effect, constantly repeated, can be fatiguing in the end. It is difficult to develop contrast when sublime effect follows sublime effect. Everything can benefit from repose, even the beautiful. On the other hand, the grotesque seems to be a stopping point, a point for comparison, a point of departure, from which one approaches the beautiful with a fresher and keener perception. The salamander sets off the water-nymph; the gnome heightens the effect of the sylph.

And it would be correct to say that contact with the deformed has endowed modern sublimity with something more pure, more grand, more sublime, in short, than the beauty of the ancients; and that is as it should be. When art is consistent in itself, it more surely draws each element to its goal. If the Homeric Elysium is far from possessing the ethereal charm and angelic sweetness of Milton's paradise, it is because beneath Eden lies a hell far more terrible than the Tartarus of the pagans. Do you believe that Francesca da Rimini and Beatrice would be as enchanting in a poet who would not imprison us in the Tower of Hunger and compel us to share in Ugolino's revolting meal? Dante would have less charm, if he had less vigor. Do the fleshy naiads, the robust mermen, the wanton zephyrs, have the diaphanous sinuosity of our water-nymphs and sylphs? Is it not because the modern imagination can picture vampires, ogres, *aulnes*, snake-charmers, ghouls, *brucolaques*, and *espioles* hideously prowling about cemeteries, that it can give its fairies that incorporeal form, that essential purity, so rarely found in pagan nymphs? The antique Venus is beautiful, admirable, no doubt, but what has imparted that slender, vaporous, other-worldly elegance to the figures of Jean Goujon? What has given them that hitherto unfamiliar lifelike character and grandeur, if not the proximity of the rough and powerful sculptures of the Middle Ages?

If the thread of our argument has not been broken for the reader by these necessary digressions—which could be rendered in much greater detail—he has doubtless understood how powerfully the grotesque—that germ of comedy fostered by the modern muse—must have sprouted and grown since its transplanting in a more propitious soil than that of paganism and epic poetry. In effect, in the new poetry, while the sublime represents the soul as it is, purified by Christian morality, the grotesque will play the role of the animal in man. The former type, free from the admixture of all impurities, will have as its domain all that is charming, graceful, and beautiful; it must one day be able to create Juliet, Desdemona, Ophelia. The latter type assumes all that is ridiculous, infirm and ugly. In this partition of mankind and creation, to the latter will fall passions, vices, and crimes; it will be lustful, servile, gluttonous, miserly, perfidious, mischievous, and hypocritical. It will be, in turn, Iago, Tartuffe, Basile; Harpagon, Polonius, Bartholo; Falstaff, Scapin, Figaro.

The beautiful has only one type; the ugly has thousands. The fact is that the beautiful, in human terms, is merely form considered in its simplest aspect, in its most absolute symmetry, in its most perfect harmony with our constitution. Thus it always presents us with a whole which is complete, but limited, as we are. What we call ugly is, on the contrary, a detail of a larger whole which escapes our perception, and which is in harmony, not with mankind, but with all creation. That is why it constantly presents us with new, but incomplete aspects.

It is interesting to study the advent and progress of the grotesque in modern times. At first, it is an invasion, an overflow, an excess; it is a torrent which has burst its banks. At its inception, it passes over the dying tradition of Latin literature, imparts some coloring to Persius, Petronius, Juvenal, and leaves behind *The Golden Ass* of Apuleius. Thence it is diffused through the imagination of the new peoples who are rebuilding Europe. It flows in waves through the work of the fabulists, the chroniclers, and the writers of romances. We see it spread from the South to the North. It flickers through the dreams of the Teutonic nations and, at the same time, breathes life into those admirable Spanish *romanceros*, the veritable Iliad of the age of chivalry. For example, it is what, in the *Roman de la Rose*, portrays the election of a king, an August ceremonial, in the following terms:

> A great villain did they elect,
> The boniest man of them all.

Above all, it imparts its character to that marvelous architecture which, in the Middle Ages, represented all the arts. It fixes its work on the face of cathedrals, frames its hells and purgatories in the ogives of the great doors, portrays them in a blaze of color in stained glass windows, exhibits its monsters and demons on capitals, in friezes, and along the edges of roofs. Its infinite forms are displayed on the modern fronts of houses, on the stone faces of castles, and on the marble facades of palaces. From the arts it passes into manners and, while causing the people to applaud the *graciosos* of comedy, it gives court jesters to kings. Later, in the age of ceremony, it will show us Scarron perched on the edge of Louis XIV's bed. Meanwhile, it decorates coats of arms and traces on the knight's shields the symbolic hieroglyphics of feudalism. From manners it passes into laws; numerous bizarre practices attest to its presence in the institutions of the Middle Ages. In the same way, it caused Thespis to leap from his cart, his face smeared with wine lees, to dance with the legal fraternity on that famous marble table for royal banquets. Finally, having been assimilated into the arts, manners, and laws of the people, it enters the church. In every Catholic city, we see it organize some one of those curious ceremonies, those strange processions, in which religion is accompanied by all varieties of superstition, the sublime is encircled by all forms of the grotesque.

To paint it with a single stroke: such is its verve, its vigor, its creative force, at the dawn of letters, that, from the outset, it casts on the threshold of modern poetry three burlesque Homers: Ariosto in Italy; Cervantes in Spain; Rabelais in France.

It would be excessive to dwell further on the influence of the grotesque in the third civilization. In the epoch called *romantic*, everything attests to its intimate alliance with the beautiful. Even among the most naïve popular legends, we find explained this mystery of modern art and sometimes with an instinctive perception. Antiquity could not have produced *Beauty and the Beast.*

It is true that in the epoch we have been speaking about the predominance of the grotesque over the sublime, in literature, is quite conspicuous. But this is a feverish reaction, a passion for novelty which passes, a first wave which gradually recedes. The type of the beautiful will soon recapture its place and its rights, not excluding the other principle, but prevailing over it. It is time that the grotesque be content with a corner of the picture in Murillo's royal frescoes, in the sacred works of Veronese; to be part of two notable *Last Judgments*, in Michaelangelo's scene of rapine and horror, embellishing the Vatican, in the awesome catastrophes traced by Rubens across the vault of Antwerp cathedral. The moment has come for an equilibrium to be established between these two principles. A man, a poet-king, "*poeta soverano,*" as Dante says of Homer, will settle everything. The two rival geniuses will unite their double flame; and from the flame issues Shakespeare.

We have now reached the poetic summit of modern times. Shakespeare is the *drame*, and the *drame*, which assimilates in the same inspiration the grotesque and the sublime, the fearful and the absurd, tragedy and comedy, the *drame* is characteristic of the third poetic epoch, the literature of the present.

To hastily summarize the facts we have thus far noted, poetry has three ages, each corresponding to an epoch in society: The ode, the epic, the drama. Primitive periods are lyrical, ancient times are epic, modern times are dramatic. The ode sings of eternity, the epic solemnizes history, the *drame* paints life. The characteristic of the first type of poetry is naïveté; the characteristic of the second is simplicity; the characteristic of the third is faithfulness to life. The rhapsodists mark the transition from lyric to epic poets, as do the romancers from epic to dramatic poets. Historians are born with the second epoch; chroniclers and critics with the third. The characters of the ode are colossi: Adam, Cain, Noah; those of the epic poems are giants: Achilles, Atreus, Orestes; those of the *drame* are men: Hamlet, Macbeth, Othello. The ode takes life from the ideal, the epic from the grandiose, the *drame* from the real. Lastly, this threefold poetry flows from three great sources: the Bible, Homer, Shakespeare.

Such then—and we will limit ourselves to drawing only one conclusion—such are the diverse aspects of thought in the different ages of mankind and society. Such are its three faces, in youth, in manhood, and in old age. Whether you examine one specific literature, or all literature, *en masse*, you will always come to the same conclusion: lyric poets precede epic poets, epic poets precede dramatic poets. In France, Malherbe precedes Chapelain, Chapelain precedes Corneille; in ancient Greece, Orpheus precedes Homer, Homer precedes Aeschylus. In the first of all books, Genesis precedes Kings, Kings precedes Job; or to return to the great scale of all poetic ages, outlined above, the Bible precedes the *Iliad*, the *Iliad* precedes Shakespeare.

In effect, society begins by singing its dreams, then narrates its deeds, and finally sets about describing what it thinks. We must note in passing that it is for this last reason that the *drame*, unifying the most opposing qualities, can be at once both full of depth and rich in surface, philosophical and picturesque. [...]

On the day when Christianity said to man: Thou art twofold, thou art made up of two beings, one perishable, the other immortal, one carnal, the other ethereal, one enslaved by appetites, cravings and passions, the other borne aloft on wings of enthusiasm and revery, the former always stooping to earth, its mother, the latter always darting up toward heaven, its fatherland—on that day, the *drame* was created. It is, in fact, anything other than this constant—on every day, for every man—contrast and struggle between two opposing principles which are ever present in life and which dispute possession of man from the cradle to the grave.

The poetry born of Christianity, the poetry of our times, is, therefore, the *drame*. The characteristic of the *drame* is the real: the real results from the completely natural combination of the two types, the sublime and the grotesque, which intersect in the *drame* as they do in life and creation. For true poetry, complete poetry, resides in the harmony of opposites. It is true, then, to proclaim loudly—and it is especially here that the exceptions prove the rule—everything that exists in nature exists in art.

Assuming this point of view in order to judge our petty conventional rules, in order to escape from these pedantic labyrinths, in order to resolve all these trivial problems laboriously constructed around art by the critics of the past two centuries, we are struck by the promptness with which the question of the modern stage is clarified. The drama has but to take a step to free itself from all the webs which the troops of Lilliput placed around it as it slept.

And so let the mindless pedants (one does not exclude the other) maintain that the deformed, the ugly, the grotesque must never be the subject of imitation in art. Our reply to them is that the grotesque is comedy and that comedy is apparently a part of art. Tartuffe is not handsome: Pourceaugnac is not noble; Pourceaugnac and Tartuffe are shining examples of art.

If, driven back from this entrenchment to the second line of their customs-houses, they renew their prohibition on the joining of the grotesque with the sublime, comedy incorporated into tragedy, we prove to them that in the poetry of Christian nations, the first of these two types represents the human animal, the second the soul. These two strains of art, if their branches are kept from intermingling, if they are systematically separated, will produce as fruit, on the one hand, abstractions of vices and follies and, on the other, abstractions of crime, or heroism, and virtue. The two types, thus isolated, and left to themselves, will each go their own way, leaving the real between them, one to its right, the other to its left. From this it follows that after these abstractions there remains something to represent: man; after these tragedies and comedies, something to write: the *drame*.

In the *drame*, at least as it is conceived, if not executed, everything is connected and ordered as in reality. The body plays its part no less than the soul; and men and events, set into motion by this double agent, appear alternately clownish or terrible, and sometimes both at once. Thus, the judge will say: "Off with his head! Let's go to dinner!" Thus, the Roman senate will deliberate over Domitian's turbot. Thus, Socrates, drinking the hemlock and discoursing on the immortal soul and the only God, will interrupt himself to request that a cock be sacrificed to Aesculapius. Thus, Elizabeth will curse and speak Latin. Thus, Richelieu will suffer Joseph the Capuchin, Louis XI his barber, Olivier-le-Diable. Thus, Cromwell will say, "I have Parliament in my purse and the King in my pocket"; or, with the hand that signed the death warrant of Charles I, will smear with ink the face of a regicide who, smiling, hands it to him. Thus, Caesar, riding in his triumphal chariot, will fear his downfall. For men of genius, however great they may be, always have within them the beast which mocks their intelligence. In this, they touch mankind; in this, they are dramatic. "It is but a step from the sublime to the ridiculous," Napoleon said, when he was convinced of being merely a man; and that flame from a fiery soul which illuminates both art and history, that cry of anguish, epitomized the *drame* and life.

It is a striking thing that all these contrasts are encountered in the poets themselves, considered as men. By dint of meditating on existence, of laying bare its bitter irony, of pouring floods of sarcasm and irony on our weaknesses, these men who make us laugh, become profoundly sad. The Democrituses are Heraclituses as well, Beaumarchais was morose, Molière was gloomy, Shakespeare melancholy.

The grotesque, then, is one of the *drame's* supreme beauties. Not merely an expedient, it is often a necessity. Sometimes it appears in homogeneous masses, in entire characters, as Dandin, Prusias, Trissotin, Brid'oison, Juliet's nurse; sometimes marked by terror as Richard III, Bégears, Tartuffe, Mephistopheles; sometimes even in a veil of grace and elegance as Figaro, Osric, Mercutio, Don Juan. It insinuates itself everywhere; for just as the most commonplace have their moments of sublimity, so the most exalted often pay their tribute to the trivial and the ridiculous. Thus, often impalpable, often imperceptible, it is always present on stage, even when it says nothing, even when it is hidden. Thanks to it, there is no monotony. Sometimes it injects laughter, sometimes horror, into tragedy. It will arrange the confrontation of Romeo with the apothecary, the three witches with Macbeth, the grave-diggers with Hamlet. Finally, it can occasionally, without discord, mingle its shrill voice with the most sublime, the most lugubrious, the dreamiest harmonies of the soul.

That is what Shakespeare, this god of the stage, above all others has been able to do in a manner which is unique and which it would be as useless as it would be impossible to imitate. In Shakespeare, as in a trinity, the three characteristic geniuses of the stage, Corneille, Molière, and Beaumarchais, seem united.

We see how quickly the arbitrary distinction of the genres crumbles before reason and taste. No less easily might the alleged rule of the two unities be destroyed. We say two, not *three*, unities, for the unity of action or of the whole, is the only true and well-founded one, and has been exempt from controversy for a long time.

Distinguished contemporaries, French and foreign, have already attacked in practice and theory the fundamental law of the pseudo-Aristotelian code. The battle ought not to be a long one, for the timber of that aged academic hovel was so worm-eaten that it crumbled at the first blow.

The strange thing is that the slaves to convention claim their rule of the two unities is founded on probability, whereas it is precisely the real that destroys it. In effect, what is more improbable and more absurd than that the vestibule, peristyle, or antechamber—the banal settings in which our tragedies are obliged to unfold—where conspirators come, one knows not how, to declaim against the tyrant, and the tyrant to declaim against the conspirators, each in turn, as if they were repeating to each other the bucolic phrase:

Alternis cantemus, amant alterna Camenae.

Where have you seen that type of vestibule or peristyle? What is more contrary, we will not say to truth, as the pedants hold it cheap, but to probability? The result is that everything which is too personalized, too intimate, too localized to take place in the antechamber or at the cross-roads, that is to say, all the drama, takes place in the wings. On stage we see only the elbows of the drama, so to speak; its hands are elsewhere. Instead of scenes, we have narrations, instead of pictures, descriptions. Solemn characters, placed, like the ancient chorus, between us and the drama, come to tell us what happens in the temple, in the palace, or in the public square, until we are tempted to cry out: "Really! Lead us there then! It must be entertaining there. It must be a beautiful sight to see!" To which you reply: "It is possible that it might amuse or interest you, but that is not the question at all: we are guardians of the dignity of the French Melpomene." And there you are!

"But," someone will say, "the rule you repudiate is derived from the Greek theatre." In what do the Greek theatre and drama resemble our drama and our theatre? Besides, we have already demonstrated that the prodigious expanse of the ancient stage enabled it to encompass an entire locality, so that the poet could, according to the demands of the action, transport it at will from one part of the theatre to another, which is very nearly the equivalent of set changes. Odd contradiction! The Greek theatre, restricted as it was to a national and religious end, was freer than ours, whose sole object is the entertainment and, if you wish, the instruction of the spectator. The reason is that the one only obeys laws which are suited to it, while the other struggles to maintain conditions which are perfectly foreign to its essence. One is artistry; the other is artifice.

It is beginning to be understood in our time that exact localization is one of the first elements of reality. The speaking or acting characters are not the only things which impress a faithful representation of the facts on the minds of the spectators. The place where this or that catastrophe occurred becomes a terrible and inseparable witness of it; and the absence of silent characters of this sort would make the greatest scenes of history incomplete in the drama. Would the poet dare assassinate Rizzio anywhere but in Mary Stuart's chamber? stab Henry IV anywhere but in the rue de la Ferronerie, obstructed with drays and carriages? burn Joan of Arc anywhere but in the Old Market? dispatch the Duke of Guise anywhere but in the chateau at Blois where his ambition roused a popular assembly to frenzy? decapitate Charles I and Louis XVI anywhere but in those sinister squares from which Whitehall and the Tuileries can be seen, as if their scaffolds were extensions of the palaces?

Unity of time rests on no firmer foundation than does the unity of place. The action forcibly confined within twenty-four hours is as ridiculous as one confined within a vestibule. Every action has its proper duration as well as its appropriate setting. Administer the same dose of time to all events. Apply the same standard to everything! You would laugh at the cobbler who would put the same shoe on every foot. To cross the unity of time with the unity of place, like the bars of a cage, and to pedantically, on the authority of Aristotle, introduce into it all the deeds, all the actions, all the figures which Providence displays to us in such richness in real life, is to mutilate both men and objects and make history wince. It is better to say that everything dies in the execution; and it is thus that the dogmatic mutilators achieve their usual result: what was alive in the chronicle is dead in the tragedy. That is why so often the cage of the unities contains nothing but a skeleton.

And then, if twenty-four hours can be comprised in two, it would be logical for four hours to contain forty-eight. Thus Shakespeare's unity is not the unity of Corneille. Pity!

But these are the wretched quibbles posed to genius for over two centuries by mediocrity, envy, and routine! Thus has the flight of our greatest poets been limited. Their wings have been clipped with the scissors of the unities. And what has been offered in exchange for these eagle feathers clipped from Corneille and Racine? Campistron.

We imagine that it might be said: "There is something in the too frequent changing of sets which confuses and fatigues the spectator, and which can disturb his concentration. Numerous transitions, from one place to another, or from one time to another time, can necessitate boring expositions. It is also necessary to avoid leaving gaps in the middle of the action which prevent the different parts of the drama from adhering closely to one another, and which, moreover, confuse the spectator because he does not yet possess a clear idea of what there could be in those gaps. . . ." But these are precisely the difficulties art faces. These are the obstacles peculiar to one subject or another, and for which universal laws cannot be found. It is for genius to resolve them, not for *poetics* to evade them.

Finally, to demolish the absurdity of the rule of the two unities, a last argument taken from the very bowels of art would be sufficient in itself. This is the existence of the third unity, the unity of action, the only one that is universally admitted because it results from a fact: neither the human eye nor the human mind can grasp more than one whole at a single time. This unity is as necessary as the other two are useless. It is what characterizes the viewpoint of drama; and for that reason excludes the other two unities. There no more can be three unities in drama than three horizons in a painting. Furthermore, we should beware of confusing unity with simplicity of action. The unity of the whole does not exclude in any way secondary actions on which the principal action may depend. It is only necessary that these parts, wisely subordinated to the whole, always gravitate toward the central action and be grouped around it on different levels or, rather, on the diverse planes of the drama. The unity of action is the law of perspective in the theatre. [...]

Let us speak boldly. The time has come, and it would be strange, if in this epoch, liberty, like light, penetrated everywhere except in that one place most naturally free in the world: the domain of thought. Let us take the hammer to theories, poetics, and systems. Let us tear down that old plasterwork which masks the façade of art! There are neither rules nor models; or, rather, there are no rules other than the general laws of nature, which soar above all art and the special laws of nature which, for each composition, result from the conditions appropriate to its subject. The former are essential, eternal, and do not change; the latter are external, variable, and used only once. The former are the framework which supports the house; the latter are the scaffolding used in its construction and constructed anew for each building. In sum, the former are the skeleton, the latter the clothing, of the *drame*. But these rules are not found in the poetics. Richelet does not suspect their existence. Genius, which divines more than it apprehends, finds for each work the general laws in the general order of things and the special laws in the isolated whole of the subject treated; not in the manner of the chemist who lights his furnace, fans his fire, heats his crucible, analyzes and destroys; but in the manner of a bee, who flies on golden wings, lights on each flower and draws out its honey, without the flower losing any of its splendor or the corolla losing any of its fragrance. The poet—let us insist on this point—should, then, take counsel only from nature, from truth, and from inspiration, which is both truth and nature. "*Quando he*," said Lope de Vega.

> *Quando he de escrivir una comedia,*
> *Encierro los preceptos con seis llaves.*

In effect, to lock up the rules, six keys are none too many. Let the poet be especially wary of imitating anyone, Shakespeare no more than Molière, Schiller no more than Corneille. If true talent were able to renounce its own nature to that degree, and thus put aside its own personal originality, in order to be transformed into something other than itself, it would sacrifice all to this role of Sosia. It is the god who is turned into a valet. We must draw our inspiration from the original sources. It is the same sap, spread throughout the soil, that nurtures all the trees of the forest, so diverse in fruit, shape, and foliage. The true poet is a tree which can be whipped by all the winds and watered by all the dews, who bears his works like fruit, as the fabulist bore his fables. Why attach oneself to a master or graft oneself to a model? Better that one be a bramble or a thistle, nourished by the same soil as the cedar or the palm, than be a fungus or a lichen on these great trees. The bramble lives; the fungus vegetates. Moreover, however great the cedar or the palm, it is not with the nourishment that can be extracted from them that one can become great oneself. A parasite on a giant will appear all the more dwarfish. As mighty as the oak is, it can only produce and nourish the mistletoe.

Let there be no misunderstanding. If some of our poets have achieved greatness, even through imitation, it is because, while modeling their work on ancient forms, they have often heeded the voice of nature and of their own genius: they have been true to themselves in some respect. Their branches may have become entwined with those of a neighboring tree, but their roots were plunged into the soil of art. They were ivy, rather than mistletoe. Then came the second-rank imitators who, possessing neither roots in the soil nor genius, had to limit themselves to imitation. As Charles Nodier noted, "After the Athenian school, the Alexandrian school." Then there was a flood of mediocrity, followed by numerous poetics, so troublesome to talent, but so convenient to mediocrity. It has been said that everything has been done and God has been forbidden to create more Molières and Corneilles. Memory has replaced imagination. Even imagination has been subjected to rules and has been a topic for aphorisms. "Imagination," says LaHarpe, "is in essence only remembering."

Nature then! Nature and truth!—And here, for the purpose of demonstrating that new ideas, far from destroying art, only wish to reconstruct it solidly and soundly, let us try to indicate what is the impassable limit which, in our opinion, separates the reality of art from the reality of nature. It is careless to confuse them as some of the less informed partisans of *romanticism* do. Truth in art could never be considered *absolute* reality, as several writers have claimed. Art cannot produce the thing itself. Let us imagine one of those rash promoters of absolute nature, of nature seen apart from art, at the performance of a romantic play, *The Cid*, for example. "What is that?" he will ask at the first word. "The Cid speaks verse! Speaking verse is not natural."—How do you want him to speak?—"In prose."—So be it. A moment later, he will continue, if he is consistent: "What! The Cid speaks French!"— So what? —"Nature demands that he speak his native language. He must speak Spanish."—We will not understand any of it, but so be it again. Do you believe this to be all? No, for before the tenth Castilian phrase, he ought to be up demanding to know if this Cid who speaks is the true Cid, in flesh and blood? By what right does this actor, named Pierre or Jacques, take the name of the Cid? That is *false.*—There is no reason for him not to demand next that the sun replace the footlights and *real* trees and houses replace those deceitful sets. For, once on this path, logic has you by the throat, and you cannot stop.

You must recognize, or risk seeming absurd, that the domain of art and of nature are entirely distinct. Nature and art are two things; if this were not so, one or the other would not exist. Art, in addition to its ideal aspect, has an earthy and practical aspect. Whatever it may do, it is enclosed between grammar and prosody, between Vaugelas and Richelet. For its most capricious creations, it possesses forms, methods of execution, a complete apparatus to set in motion. For genius, these are delicate instruments, for mediocrities, they are tools.

It seems to us that others have already stated that the *drame* is a mirror in which nature is reflected. But, if this mirror is an ordinary mirror with a smooth, uniform surface, it will only reflect a dull image without depth, faithful, but colorless. It is known that color and light are lost in simple reflections. It is necessary, then, that drama be a concentrating mirror which, far from weakening, gathers and condenses colored rays and transforms a glimmer into a light, a light into a flame. Then only is drama recognized by art.

The theatre is an optical point. All that is found in the world, in history, in life, in man, can and ought to be reflected in it, but under the magic wand of art. Art reads the ages, reads nature, examines the chronicles, schools itself in the representation of actual facts—especially of manners and characters, much less given to doubt and contradiction than facts. Art restores what the annalists have cut, harmonizes what they have assembled, divines their omissions and replaces them, fills their gaps with imagined scenes painted with appropriate colors, and groups together what had been dispersed. Art reactivates the strings of Providence which control the human marionettes, clothes the whole with a form both natural and poetic, and gives it that brilliant and lifelike truthfulness which produces illusion. Art possesses that prestige of reality which arouses the enthusiasm of the spectator, and of the poet first of all, for the poet is sincere. Thus, the aim of art is almost divine: to bring to life again if writing history; to create, if writing poetry.

It is marvelous sight to see that amplitude displayed in the *drame*, in which art powerfully develops nature; a *drame* in which the action moves to its conclusion with a firm and easy air, without diffuseness or constraint, a *drame*, in short, in which the poet clearly fulfills the multiple aim of art: that is, to open a double horizon to the spectator, to illuminate at once the internal and the external in men; the external through discourse and action; the internal through asides and monologues; in a word, to bring together in the same picture the drama of life and the drama of the conscience.

You will perceive that, for this type of work, if the poet must *choose* (and he must), he must choose not the *beautiful*, but the *characteristic*. Not that it is advisable, as they say today, "to paint local color;" that is to say, the addition, after the fact, of some discordant touches here and there to a whole which is otherwise perfectly false and conventional. Local color should not merely be on the *drame's* surface, but at its center, in the very heart of the work, from which it is diffused to the surface itself, naturally and equally, and, so to speak, into every corner of the *drame*, like the sap which rises from the roots to the topmost leaf of a tree. The *drame* should be thoroughly impregnated with this period color; it must in some way be present in the atmosphere of the theatre, so that it is only on entering and leaving the theatre that one is aware of having changed period and atmosphere. If it requires some study and effort to reach that point, so much the better. It is good that the avenues of art are obstructed by those brambles which repulse all but the strong-willed. Moreover, it is that study, seconded by fiery inspiration, which will protect the *drame* from the ordinary, a vice which destroys it. The ordinary is the failing of short-sighted and short-winded poets. For the optic of the theatre, all figures must be reduced to their most salient, their most precise, their most individual traits. Even the vulgar and the trivial must have an intensity. Nothing must be neglected. Like God, the true poet is present everywhere at the same time in his work. Genius resembles the machine which stamps the royal likeness on copper and gold coins alike.

GEORG WILHELM FRIEDRICH HEGEL

Georg Wilhelm Friedrich HEGEL (1770-1831), even as a young student, was known to his classmates as "the old man." On the stout side, his physical clumsiness made him look prematurely aged, and he spoke awkwardly with a broad sing-song Swabian accent. But Georg was always a model pupil, popular with both teachers and peers. Good-natured and gregarious, he liked drinking, snuff-taking, and *double entendre* jokes.

When he was only eight, his teacher gave the dutiful boy a present of eighteen volumes of Shakespeare's works in German translation. His favorite, *The Merry Wives of Windsor*, was the first play to awaken his interest in drama. At an early age Hegel developed a love of Greek tragedy, and he soon became an inveterate theatre-goer and connoisseur of acting.

Unlike many "literary" theorists, the German philosopher believed that the performance of drama was an essential aspect of the genre and thought it necessary to judge a play "as it appears before us on the stage." He even argued that "no play should really be printed but should remain, more or less as the case was in antiquity, in manuscript for the theatre's repertory and get only an extremely insignificant circulation."

In Berlin Hegel regularly attended the theatre after his lectures, and his fine arts courses of 1821-22 drew directly upon what he saw. Whenever he traveled abroad, he visited cathedrals, museums, and exhibitions and went to the opera and ballet. In Vienna in 1824 he discovered Italian opera, taking particular delight in Rossini.

While on vacation in Paris in 1827, Hegel saw Charles Kemble's company in their epoch-making performances of Shakespeare at the Odéon, which inspired Hugo to write "The Preface to *Cromwell*." All the French romantics—Dumas père, Gautier, Berlioz, Hugo—were in the audience along with Hegel, although neither they nor he could have been aware of the coincidence. Due to a stomach disorder (which, not cholera, would eventually kill him), the philosopher missed *Hamlet* on September 11, but saw *Othello* (with Harriet Smithson as Desdemona) on September 18 and *Romeo and Juliet* on September 20. Hegel, who followed every word of the text in a small edition of Shakespeare that he brought with him, was critical of Kemble's style of acting and did not approve of the English actors' excesses, manifested in their losing their minds and "raging about in the most horrid way." Conservative and nostalgic in his taste, he preferred classical restraint to the Romantic cult of feeling.

In the French theatre, Hegel considered Molière the best and especially admired Mlle Mars in *Tartuffe*. "It was not until I saw Mars perform *Tartuffe* that I realized why *Tartuffe* is a comedy. [...] Through her performance the chambermaid becomes a principal character." For him, the French actress embodied the classical ideal of nature perfected by art. Hegel was particularly impressed by Mars at almost 60 playing the eighteen-year-old blind girl in Scribe's *Valérie* at the Comédie-Française in 1827, finding her "supremely moving." He praised Scribe's play, commented on its "deep impact," and wished to meet Mars.

Hegel's Berlin lectures became known throughout Europe. Aesthetics was his most magnetic and popular course, attracting an international following among leading men of the time. Future teachers and professors, as well as Prussian officials, army officers, and privy councillors flocked to the lecture hall. As a world famous celebrity, Hegel put on a good show for visitors, playing the learned professor for all it was worth.

A disciple described Hegel at this time as cadaverously sallow, his brow, cheeks, and mouth furrowed by constant, taciturn thinking. He had large eyes, an introverted gaze, and a noble curved forehead high above a serene chin. Hawking and coughing, his head bent down low, almost crouching, he read his lectures with an earnestness that held his audiences spellbound.

The author of *The Phenomenology of the Mind* loved to socialize, enjoyed good wines, and played cards and the national lottery. His hobby of geology he copied from his friend Goethe. Hegel was an exemplary pater familias and appeared to be infinitely good-natured, except when he flew into rages and vented his hatred for his enemies (principally those in disfavor with the authorities). First a worshiper of Napoleon and then an admirer of the Prussian state, Hegel justified the police system, to which he reported, and used his close association with the government to get rid of his academic rivals. Advancing the view that "anything rational is real, and anything real is rational," Hegel served the state as a perfect public servant glorifying the status quo. "Reason rules the world," he maintained, "therefore world history advances rationally." For Hegel, the state was the highest expression of the world spirit, in every epoch there was one nation of world-historical importance, and history in every case justified the winner.

THE PHILOSOPHY OF FINE ART (1835)

Chapter I: Tragedy as a Dramatic Art

[...] In modern times, considerable discussion has been raised over the significance of the Greek chorus, and the question has been raised incidentally whether it can or ought to be introduced into modern tragedy. In fact, the need of some substantial foundation has been experienced; but critics have found it difficult to prescribe the precise manner in which effect should be given to such a change, because they failed to grasp with sufficient penetration the nature of that in which true tragedy consists and the necessity of the chorus as an essential constituent of all that Greek tragedy implies. Critics have, no doubt, recognized the nature of the chorus to the extent of maintaining that in it we find an attitude of tranquil meditation over the whole, whereas the characters of the action remain within the limits of their particular objects and situations, and, in short, receive in the chorus and its observations a standard of valuation of their characters and actions in much the same way as the public discovers in it, and within the drama itself, an objective representative of its own judgment upon all that is thus represented. In this view we have to this extent the fact rightly conceived, that the chorus is, in truth, there as a substantive and more enlightened intelligence, which warns us from irrelevant oppositions, and reflects upon the genuine issue. But, granting this to be so, it is by no means a wholly disinterested person, at leisure to entertain such thoughts and ethical judgments as it likes as are the spectators, which, uninteresting and tedious on its own account, could only be attached for the sake of such reflections. The chorus is the actual substance of the heroic life and action itself: it is, as contrasted with the particular heroes, the common folk regarded as the fruitful heritage, out of which individuals, much as flowers and towering trees from their native soil, grow and whereby they are conditioned in this life. Consequently, the chorus is peculiarly fitted to a view of life in which the obligations of State legislation and settled religious dogmas do not, as yet, act as a restrictive force in ethical and social development, but where morality only exists in its primitive form of directly animated human life, and it is merely the equilibrium of unmoved life which remains assured in its sta-

From Hegel, *The Philosophy of Fine Art*, Vol. IV, trans. F.P.B. Osmaston. London: G. Bell & Sons, 1920.

bility against the fearful collisions which the antagonistic energies of individual action produce. We are made aware of the fact that an assured asylum of this kind is also a part of our actual existence by the presence of the chorus. It does not, therefore, practically co-operate with the action; it executes by its action no right as against the contending heroes; it merely expresses its judgment as a matter of opinion; it warns, commiserates, or appeals to the divine law, and the ideal forces imminent in the soul, which the imagination grasps in external guise as the sphere of the gods that rule. In this self-expression it is, as we have already seen, lyrical; for it does not act and there are no events for it to narrate in epical form. The content, however, retains at the same time the epic character of substantive universality; and its lyric movement is of such a nature that it can, and in this respect in contrast to the form of the genuine ode, approach at times that of the paean and the dithyramb. We must lay emphatic stress upon this position of the chorus in Greek tragedy. Just as the theatre itself possesses its external ground, its scene and environment, so, too, the chorus, that is the general community, is the spiritual scene; and we may compare it to the architectural temple which surrounds the image of the god, which resembles the heroes in the action. Among ourselves, statues are placed under the open sky without such a background, which also modern tragedy does not require, for the reason that its actions do not depend on this substantive basis, but on the personal volition and personality, no less than the apparently external contingency of events and circumstances.

In this respect it is an entirely false view which regards the chorus as an accidental piece of residuary baggage, a mere remnant from the origins of Greek drama. Of course, it is incontestable that its source is to be traced to the circumstance that, in the festivals of Bacchus, so far as the artistic aspect is concerned, the choral song was of most importance until the introduction and interruption of its course by one reciter, whose relation finally was transformed into and exalted by the real figures of dramatic action. In the blossoming season of tragedy, however, the chorus was not by any means merely retained in honor of this particular phase of the festival and ritual of the god Bacchus; rather it became continuously more elaborate in its beauty and harmonious measures by reason of the fact that its association with the dramatic action is essential and, indeed, so indispensable to it that the decline of tragedy is intimately connected with the degeneration of the choruses, which no longer remain an integral member of the whole, but are degraded to a mere embellishment. In contrast to this, in romantic tragedy, the chorus is neither intrinsically appropriate nor does it appear to have originated from choric songs. On the contrary, the content is here of a type which defeats from the first any attempt to introduce choruses as understood by Greek dramatists. For, even if we go back to the most primitive of those so-called mysteries, morality plays and farces of a similar character, from which the romantic drama issued, we find that these present no action in that original Greek sense of the term, no outbreak, that is, of opposing forces from the undivided consciousness of life and the god-like. To as little extent is the chorus adapted to the conditions of chivalry and the dominion of kings, in so far as, in such cases, the attitude of the folk is one of mere obedience, or it is itself a party, involved together with the interest of its fortune or misfortune in the course of the action. And in general the chorus entirely fails to secure its true position where the main subject-matter consists of particular passions, ends, and characters, or any considerable opportunity is admitted to intrigue.

In contrast to the chorus, the *second* fundamental feature of dramatic composition is that of the *individuals* who act in *conflict* with each other. In Greek tragedy it is not at all the bad will, crime worthlessness, or mere misfortune, stupidity, and the like, which act as an incentive to such collisions, but rather as I have frequently urged, the ethical right to a definite course of action. Abstract evil neither possesses truth in itself, nor does it arouse interest. At the same time, when we attribute ethical traits of characterization to the individuals of the action, these ought not to appear merely as a matter of opinion. It is rather implied in their right or claim that they are actually there as essential on their own account. The hazards of crime, such as are present in modern drama—the useless, or quite as much the so-called noble criminal, with his empty talk about fate, we meet with in the tragedy of ancient literature, rarely, if at all, and for the good reason that the decision and deed depends on the wholly personal aspect of interest and character, upon lust for power, love, honor, or other similar passions, whose justification has its roots exclusively in the particular inclination and individuality. A resolve of this character, whose claims is based upon the content of its object, which it carries into execution in one restricted direction of particularization, violates, under certain circumstances, which are already essentially implied in the actual possibility of conflicts, a further and equally ethical sphere of human volition, which the character thus confronted adheres to, and, by his thus stimulated action, enforces, so that in this way the collision of powers and individuals equally entitled to the ethical claim is completely set up in its movement.

The sphere of this content, although capable of great variety of detail, is not in its essential features very extensive. The principal source of opposition, which Sophocles in particular, in this respect following the lead of Aeschylus, has accepted and worked out in the finest way, is that of the *body politic*, the opposition, that is, between ethical life in its social universality and the family as the natural ground of moral relations. These are the purest forces of tragic representation. It is, in short, the harmony of these spheres and the concordant action within the bounds of their realized content, which constitute the perfected reality of the moral life. In this respect I need only recall to recollection the *Seven before Thebes* of Aeschylus and, as a yet stronger illustration, the *Antigone* of Sophocles. Antigone reverences the ties of blood-relationship, the gods of the nether world. Creon alone recognizes Zeus, the para-mount Power of public life and the commonwealth. We come across a similar conflict in the *Iphigenia in Aulis*, as also in the *Agamemnon*, the *Choephorae*, and *Eumenides* of Aeschylus, and in the *Electra* of Sophocles. Agamemnon, as king and leader of his army, sacrifices his daughter in the interest of the Greek folk and the Trojan expedition. He shatters thereby the bond of love as between himself and his daughter and wife, which Clytemnestra retains in the depths of a mother's heart, and in revenge prepares an ignominious death for her husband on his return. Orestes, their son, respects his mother, but is bound to represent the right of his father, the king, and strikes dead the mother who bore him.

A content of this type retains its force through all times, and its presentation, despite all difference of nationality, vitally arrests our human and artistic sympathies.

Of a more formal type is that second kind of essential collision, an illustration of which in the tragic story of Oedipus the Greek tragedians especially favored. Of this Sophocles has left us the most complete example in his *Oedipus Rex*, and *Oedipus at Colonus*. The problem here is concerned with the claim of alertness in our intelligence, with the nature of the obligation implied in that which a man carries out with a volition fully aware of its acts as contrasted with that which he has done in fact, but unconscious of and with no intention of doing what he had done under the directing providence of the gods. Oedipus slays his father, marries his mother, begets children in this incestuous alliance, and nevertheless is involved in these most terrible of crimes without active participation either in will or knowledge. The point of view of our profounder modern consciousness of right and wrong would be to recognize that crimes of this description, inasmuch as they were neither referable to a personal knowledge or volition, were not deeds for which the true personality of the perpetrator was responsible. The plastic nature of the Greek on the contrary adheres to the bare fact which an individual has achieved, and refuses to face the division implied by the purely ideal attitude of the soul in the self-conscious life on the one hand and the objective significance of the fact accomplished on the other.

For ourselves, to conclude this survey, other collisions, which either in general are related to the universally accepted association of personal action to the Greek conception of Destiny, or in some measure to more exceptional conditions, are comparatively speaking less important.

In all these tragic conflicts, however, we must above all place on one side the false notion of *guilt* or *innocence*. The heroes of tragedy are quite as much under one category as the other. If we accept the idea as valid that a man is guilty only in the case that a choice lay open to him, and he deliberately decided on the course of action which he carried out, then these plastic figures of ancient drama are guiltless. They act in accordance with a specific character, a specific pathos, for the simple reason that they are this character, this pathos. In such a case there is no lack of decision and no choice. The strength of great characters consists precisely in this that they do not choose, but are entirely and absolutely just that which they will and achieve. They are simply themselves, and never anything else, and their greatness consists in that fact. Weakness in action, in other words, wholly consists in the division of the personal self as such from its content, so that character, volition and final purpose do not appear as absolutely one unified growth; and inasmuch as no assured end lives in the soul as the very substance of the particular personality, as the pathos and might of the individual's entire will, he is still able to turn with indecision from this course to that, and his final decision is that of caprice. A wavering attitude of this description is alien to these plastic creations. The bond between the psychological state of mind and the content of the will is for them indissoluble. That which stirs them to action is just in this very pathos which implies an ethical justification and which even in the pathetic aspects of the dialogue, is not enforced in and through the merely personal rhetoric of the heart and the sophistry of passion, but in the equally masculine and cultivated objective presence, in the profound possibilities, the harmony and vitally plastic beauty of which Sophocles was to a superlative degree master. At the same time, however, such a pathos, with its potential resources of collision, brings in its train deeds that are both injurious and wrongful. They have no desire to avoid the blame that results therefrom. On the contrary, it is their fame to have done what they have done. One can in fact urge nothing more intolerable against a hero of this type than by saying that he has acted innocently. It is a point of honor with such great characters that they are guilty. They have no desire to excite pity or our sensibilities. For it is not the substantive, but rather the wholly personal deepening of the individual character, which stirs our individual pain. These securely strong characters, however, coalesce entirely with their essential pathos, and this indivisible accord inspires wonder, but does not excite heart emotions. The drama of Euripides marks the transition to that.

The final result, then, of the development of tragedy conducts us to this issue and only this, namely, that the twofold vindication of the mutually conflicting aspects are no doubt retained, but the *one-sided* mode under which they were maintained is canceled, and the undistributed ideal harmony brings back again that condition of the chorus, which attributes without reserve equal honor to all the gods. The true course of dramatic development consists in the annulment of the *contradictions* viewed as such, in the reconciliation of the forces of human action, which alternately strive to negate each other in their conflict. Only so far is misfortune and suffering not the final issue, but rather the satisfaction of spirit, as for the first time, in virtue of such a conclusion, the necessity of all that particular individual's experience, is able to appear in complete accord with reason, and our emotional attitude is tranquilized on a true ethical basis, rudely shaken by the calamitous result to the heroes, but reconciled in the substantial facts. And it is only in so far as we retain such a view securely that we shall be in a position to understand ancient tragedy. We have to guard ourselves therefore from concluding that a *dénouement* of this type is merely a moral issue conformably to which evil is punished and virtue reward-ed, as indicated by the proverb that "when crime turns to vomit, virtue sits down at table." We have nothing to do here with this wholly personal aspect of a self-reflecting personality and its conception of good and evil, but are concerned with the appearance of the affirmative reconciliation and with the equal validity of both the powers engaged in actual conflict, when the collision actually took place. To as little extent is the necessity of the issue a blind des-tiny, or in other words a purely irrational, unintelligible fate, identified with the classical world by many; rather it is the rationality of destiny, albeit it does not as yet appear as self-conscious Providence, the divine final end of which in conjunction with the world and individuals appears on its own account and for others, depending as it does on just this fact that the highest Power para-mount over particular gods and mankind cannot suffer this, namely, that the forces, which affirm their self-subsistence in modes that are abstract or incom-plete, and thereby overstep the boundary of their warrant, no less than the conflicts which result from them, should retain their self-stability. Fate drives personality back upon its limits, and shatters it, when it has grown overween-ing. An irrational compulsion, however, an innocence of suffering would rather only excite indignation in the soul of the spectator than ethical tran-quility. [...]

First, we have particularly to emphasize the fact, that if it is the one-sidedness of the pathos which constitutes the real basis of collisions this mere-ly amounts to the statement that it is asserted in the action of life, and there-with has become the unique pathos of a particular individual. If this one-sid-edness is to be abrogated then it is this individual which, to the extent that his action is exclusively identified with this isolated pathos, must perforce be stripped and sacrificed. For the individual here is merely this single life, and, if this unity is not secured in its stability on its own account, the individual is shattered.

The most complete form of this development is possible when the individuals engaged in conflict relatively to their concrete or objective life appear in each case essentially involved in one whole, so that they stand fun-damentally under the power of that against which they battle, and conse-quently infringe that, which, conformably to their own essential life, they ought to respect. Antigone, for example, lives under the political authority of Creon; she is herself the daughter of a king and the affianced of Haemon, so that her obedience to the royal prerogative is an obligation. But Creon also, who is on his part father and husband, is under obligation to respect the sacred ties of relationship, and only by breach of this can give an order that is in con-flict with such a sense. In consequence of this we find immanent in the life of both that which each respectively combats, and they are seized and broken by that very bond which is rooted in the compass of their own social existence. Antigone is put to death before she can enjoy what she looks forward to as bride, and Creon too is punished in the fatal end of his son and wife, who commit suicide, the former on account of Antigone's death, and the latter owing to Haemon's. Among all the fine creations of the ancient and the modern world—and I am acquainted with pretty nearly everything in such a class, and one ought to know it, and it is quite possible—the *Antigone* of Sophocles is from this point of view in my judgment the most excellent and satisfying work of art.

The tragic issue does not, however, require in every case as a means of removing both over-emphasized aspects and the equal honor which they respectively claim the downfall of the contestant parties. The *Eumenides* does not end, as we all know, with the death of Orestes, or the destruction of the Eumenides, these avenging spirits of matricide and filial affection, these opponents of Apollo, who seeks to protect unimpaired the worth of and reverence for the family chief and king, the god who had prompted Orestes to slay Clytemnestra, but will have Orestes released from the punishment and honor bestowed on both himself and the Furies. At the same time we cannot fail to see in this adjusted conclusion the nature of the authority which the Greeks attached to their gods when they presented them as mere individuals contending with each other. They appear, in short, to the Athenian of everyday life merely as definite aspects of ethical experience which the principles of morality viewed in their complete and harmonious coherence bind together. The votes of the Areopagus are equal on either side. It is Athene, the goddess, the life of Athens, that is, imagined in its essential unity, who adds the white pebble, who frees Orestes, and at the same time promises altars and a cult to the Eumenides no less than Apollo. As a contrast to this type of objective reconciliation the settlement may be, *secondly*, of a more personal character. In other words, the individual concerned in the action may in the last instance surrender his one-sided point of view. In this betrayal by personality of its essential pathos, however, it cannot fail to appear destitute of character; and this contradicts the masculine integrity of such plastic figures. The individual, therefore, can only submit to a higher Power and its counsel or command, to the effect that while on his own account he adheres to such a pathos, the will is nevertheless broken in its bare obstinacy by a god's authority. In such a case the knot is not loosened, but, as in the case of Philoctetes, it is severed by a *deus ex machina*.

But as a *further* and final class, and one more beautiful than the above rather external mode of resolution we have the reconciliation more properly of the soul itself, in which respect there is, in virtue of the personal significance, a real approach to our modern point of view. The most perfect example of this in ancient drama is to be found in the ever admirable *Oedipus at*

Colonus of Sophocles. The protagonist here has unwittingly slain his father, secured the scepter of Thebes, and the bridal bed of his own mother. He is not rendered unhappy by these unwitting crimes; but the power of divination he has of old possessed makes him realize, despite himself, the darkness of the experience that confronts him, and he becomes fearfully, if indistinctly, aware of what his position is. [...]

Modern tragedy accepts in its own province from the first the principle of subjectivity or self-assertion. It makes, therefore, the personal intimacy of character—the character, that is, which is no purely individual and vital embodiment of ethical forces in the classic sense—its peculiar object and content. It, moreover, makes, in a type of concurrence that is adapted to this end, human actions come into collision through the instrumentality of the external accident of circumstances in the way that a contingency of a similar character is also decisive in its effect on the consequence, or appears to be so decisive. [...]

To start with, we may observe that, however much in romantic tragedy the personal aspect of suffering and passions, in the true meaning of such an attitude, is the focal center, yet, for all that, it is impossible in human activity that the ground basis of definite ends borrowed from the concrete worlds of the family, the State, the Church, and others should be dispensed with. In so far, however, as in the drama under discussion, it is not the substantive content as such in these spheres of life which constitute the main interest of individuals. Such ends are from a certain point of view particularized in a breadth of extension and variety, as also in exceptional modes of presentment, in which it often happens that what is truly essential is only able to force itself on our attention with attenuated strength. And over and above this fact, these ends receive an entirely altered form. In the province of religion, for example, the content which pre-eminently is asserted is no longer the particular ethical powers exhibited imaginatively under the mode of divine individuals, either in their own person or in the pathos of human heroes. It is the history of Christ, or of saints and the like, which is now set before us. In the political community it is mainly the position of kingship, the power of vassal chiefs, the strife of dynasties, or the particular members of one and the same ruling family which forms the content of the varied picture. Nay, if we take a step further we find as the principal subject-matter questions of civic or private right and other relations of a similar character; and, further, we shall find a similar attention paid to features in the family life which were not yet within the reach of ancient drama. And the reason of this is that, inasmuch as in the spheres of life above-mentioned the principle of the personal life in its independence has asserted its claim, novel phases of existence make their inevitable appearance in each one of them, which the modern man claims to set up as the end and directory of his action.

And, from a further point of view in this drama, it is the right of subjectivity, as above defined, absolutely unqualified, which is retained as the dominating content; and for this reason personal love, honor, and the rest make such an exclusive appeal as ends of human action that, while in one direction other relations cannot fail to appear as the purely external background on which these interests of our modern life are set in motion, in another such relations on their own account actively conflict with the requirements of the more individual state of emotion. Of more profound significance still is wrong and crime, even if a particular character does not deliberately and to start with aim at either, yet does not avoid them to attain his original purpose. [...]

Generally speaking, however, in modern tragedy it is not the substantive content of its object in the interest of which men act, and which is maintained as the stimulus of their passion; rather it is the inner experience of their heart and individual emotion, or the particular qualities of their personality, which insist on satisfaction. [...]

In order to emphasize still more distinctly the difference which in this respect obtains between ancient and modern tragedy, I will merely refer the reader to Shakespeare's *Hamlet*. Here we find fundamentally a collision similar to that which is introduced by Aeschylus into his *Choephorae* and that by Sophocles into his *Electra*. For Hamlet's father, too, and the King, as in these Greek plays, has been murdered, and his mother has wedded the murderer. That which, however, in the conception of the Greek dramatists possesses a certain ethical justification—I mean the death of Agamemnon—relatively to his sacrifice of Iphigenia in the contrasted case of Shakespeare's play, can only be viewed as an atrocious crime, of which Hamlet's mother is innocent; so that the son is merely concerned in his vengeance to direct his attention to the fratricidal king, and there is nothing in the latter's character that possesses any real claim to his respect. The real collision, therefore, does not turn on the fact that the son, in giving effect to a rightful sense of vengeance, is himself forced to violate morality, but rather on the particular personality, the inner life of Hamlet, whose noble soul is not steeled to this kind of energetic activity, but, while full of contempt for the world and life, what between making up his mind and attempting to carry into effect or preparing to carry into effect its resolves, is bandied from pillar to post, and finally through his own procrastination and the external course of events meets his own doom.

If we now turn, in close connection with the above conclusions, to our *second* point of fundamental importance in modern tragedy—that is to say, the nature of the characters and their collisions—we may summarily take a point of departure from the following general observations.

The heroes of ancient classical tragedy discover circumstances under which they, so long as they irrefragably adhere to the *one* ethical state of pathos which alone corresponds to their own already formed personality, must infallibly come into conflict with an ethical Power which opposes them and possesses an equal ethical claim to recognition. Romantic characters, on the contrary, are from the first placed within a wide expanse of contingent relations and conditions, within which every sort of action is possible; so that the conflict, to which no doubt the external conditions presupposed supply the occasion, essentially abides within the *character* itself, to which the individuals concerned in their passion give effect, not, however, in the interests of the ethical vindication of the truly substantive claims, but for the simple reason that they are the kind of men they are. Greek heroes also no doubt act in accordance with their particular individuality; but this individuality, as before noted, if we take for our examples the supreme results of ancient tragedy, is itself necessarily identical with an ethical pathos which is substantive. In modern tragedy the peculiar character in its real significance, and to which it as a matter of accident remains constant, whether it happens to grasp after that which on its own account is on moral grounds justifiable or is carried into wrong and crime, forms its resolves under the dictate of personal wishes and necessities, or among other things purely external considerations. In such a case, therefore, though we may have a coalescence between the moral aspect of the object and the character, yet, for all that, such a concurrence does not constitute, and cannot constitute—owing to the divided character of ends, passions, and the life wholly personal to the individual—the *essential* basis and objective condition of the depth and beauty of the tragic drama. [...]

The last of the subjects which we have still to discuss as proposed is the nature of the *tragic issue* which characters in our present drama have to confront, as also the type of tragic *reconciliation* compatible with such a standpoint. In ancient tragedy it is the eternal justice which, as the absolute might of destiny, delivers and restores the harmony of substantive being in its ethical character by its opposition to the particular forces which, in their strain to assert an independent subsistence, come into collision, and which, in virtue of the rational ideality implied in its operations, satisfies us even where we see the downfall of particular men. In so far as a justice of the same kind is present in modern tragedy, it is necessarily, in part, more abstract on account of the closer differentiation of ends and characters, and, in part, of a colder nature and one that is more akin to that of a criminal court, in virtue of the fact that the wrong and crime into which individuals are necessarily carried, in so far as they are intent upon executing their designs, are of a profounder significance. Macbeth, for instance, the elder daughters of Lear and their husbands, the president in *Kabale und Liebe*, Richard III, and many similar examples, on account of their atrocious conduct, only deserve the fate they get. This type of *dénouement* usually is presented under the guise that individuals are crushed by an actual force which they have defied in order to carry out their personal aims. [...]

From another point of view, however, we may see the tragic issue also merely in the light of the effect of unhappy circumstances and external accidents, which might have brought about, quite as readily, a different result and a happy conclusion. From such a point of view we have merely left us the conception that the modern idea of individuality, with its searching definition of character, circumstances, and developments, is handed over essentially to the contingency of the earthly state, and must carry the fateful issues of such finitude. Pure commiseration of this sort is, however, destitute of meaning; and it is nothing less than a frightful kind of external necessity in the particular case where we see the downfall of essentially noble natures in their conflict thus assumed with the mischance of purely external accidents. Such a course of events can insistently arrest our attention; but in the result it can only be horrible, and the demand is direct and irresistible that the external accidents ought to accord with that which is identical with the spiritual nature of such noble characters. Only as thus regarded can we feel ourselves reconciled with the grievous end of Hamlet and Juliet. From a purely external point of view, the death of Hamlet appears as an accident occasioned by his duel with Laertes and the interchange of the daggers. But in the background of Hamlet's soul, death is already present from the first. The sandbank of finite condition will not content his spirit. As the focus of such mourning and weakness, such melancholy, such a loathing of all the conditions of life, we feel from the first that, hemmed within such an environment of horror, he is a lost man, whom the surfeit of the soul has well-nigh already done to death before death itself approaches him from without. The same thing may be observed in the case of Romeo and Juliet. The ground on which these tender blossoms have been planted is alien to their nature; we have no alternative left us but to lament the pathetic transiency of such a beautiful love, which, as some tender rose in the vale of this world of accident, is broken by rude storms and tempests, and the frangible reckonings of noble and well-meaning devices. This pitiful state of our emotions is, however, simply a feeling of reconciliation that is painful, a kind of *unhappy blessedness* in misfortune.

ADAM MICKIEWICZ

Adam MICKIEWICZ (1798-1855) was in his youth considered to be strikingly handsome. Of medium height, he had deep-set blue eyes, long black eyelashes and black eyebrows, a pale olive complexion, and long dark hair combed back from a high forehead. His face was statuesque, yet capable of expressing a wide range of emotions. Thin and elegant in silhouette, Mickiewicz dressed fashionably and meticulously in the black frock-coat, scarf, and vest that was the preferred costume of romantic poets.

As a student at the university in Vilna, Mickiewicz regularly attended the theatre and studied the theory of drama. Like Mme de Staël, he viewed historical drama based on one's own national history as the new dramatic genre for Europe, and he thought that opera with all its dazzling technical resources offered a model for the kind of total theatre that he envisaged, while at the same time admiring the spectacular equestrian shows and battle re-enactments presented at the Parisian Cirque Olympique.

In permanent political exile from his homeland after his arrest by the Tsarist secret police in 1823, Mickiewicz was first sent to Russia where he met Pushkin, moved freely in the best literary circles, and astounded social gatherings by his abilities as an improviser. Paid professionals had made poetic improvisation a popular form of entertainment in Italy in early 1800s, but the Polish writer was the only major European poet to cultivate the art. Maintaining that this God-given gift was evidence of his credentials as a prophet, the charismatic Mickiewicz improvised poetry in Polish and prose in French, sometimes even creating short dramatic scenes. According to eyewitnesses, his face became transformed and his voice grew deeply resonant, arousing fear among the listeners as if the "spirit was talking through him."

In his travels throughout Europe, Mickiewicz, like all aspiring poets, paid an obligatory visit to Goethe in Weimar (where he witnessed a festival production of *Faust I* in honor of the author's eightieth birthday), and he attended some of Hegel's lectures in Berlin, but was horrified at the German philosopher's justification of the existing political order and approval of the dismemberment of Poland by her stronger neighbors. In Rome he went riding in a carriage with James Fenimore Cooper and in Paris introduced Emerson's essays on transcendentalism to the French. His own books had to be smuggled into Poland, where even mention of his name was forbidden by the censor.

When in 1840 Mickiewicz was appointed to the new chair at the Collège de France in Slavic literatures (a subject hitherto untaught in France), he was at forty already world famous as a long suffering poet in exile and opponent of Tsarist tyranny, and the lectures caused much excitement in French intellectual circles. Grown heavy and bloated, his long disheveled hair thick, bushy, and totally gray, and his dress neglected, Mickiewicz now appeared prematurely aged, sitting motionless wrapped in a dark brown coat, but he still had a magnetic effect on audiences. Casting himself in the role of a *vates* or seer, he presented his lectures as a series of inspired improvisations.

Since his gift as an improviser served as an endorsement from on high, Mickiewicz considered it his religious duty not to prepare his lectures in advance. He brought with him only French translations of the literary texts he planned to quote. The night before each lecture, to induce the improvisatory mood, the poet had his wife play Mozart for him on the piano. "Each lecture is like a battle," Mickiewicz maintained, "only God knows how it will turn out." Fighting for his own life and for that of his nation, he declared, "I went to each lecture as to a duel."

The messianic poet scorned the speculations of reason, abstract thinking, and Germanic philosophical systems. "I acted under the prompting of the spirit of my race, the spirit of my nation and, finally, under the influence of that voice in which my conscience recognized the Divine." In accord with such prophetic poetics, Mickiewicz spoke in a state of exaltation and entered into a mystical state of communion with God enabling him to see into the future and communicate with the spirits of the dead.

Sometimes he screamed and sometimes he shrieked. He gave stirring public performances that often received riotous standing ovations from the packed auditorium (that included celebrity visitors like George Sand and Chopin). Mickiewicz's cloudy rhetoric about shaping history and leading his nation into the future made the French authorities uneasy and led the Tsarist secret agents in the auditorium to suspect a revolutionary conspiracy. The poet made use of the mystical symbol of the spark and developed the romantic concept of the vampire (a specifically Slavic form of ancestor worship) as a force for political action.

After receiving alarming police reports, the French Minister of Education quickly awarded Mickiewicz a leave of absence, forcing him to stop his course before the end of the year. The last lecture created a public scandal. Members of the poet's inner circle of believers rose to their feet, their arms held aloft, then fell to the floor sobbing at the master's feet.

Modern Polish theatre has found inspiration in Mickiewicz's call for a return to myth, ritual, and the sacred spectacles of the past, and his theory of the origins of theatre in vampirism—the contact of the living with the spirits of the dead—has been seminal for Kantor and Grotowski (who in 1997 was appointed professor at the Collège de France like his great precursor).

SLAVIC DRAMA (1843)

[...] The *drama* is the most powerful artistic realization of poetry. It almost always announces the end of one era and the beginning of another. In the drama there are two different aspects that must be distinguished: the *creation* and the *execution*. The drama needs a place on the earth: it requires a building and actors; it needs the support of all the arts. In the drama, *poetry is set in motion before the audience.*

I said that the drama almost always announces the end of one era and the beginning of another. Once the thought animating a nation has already found its representatives in reality, once it has already produced heroes, it strives to fix the memory of their deeds in art; it produces drama. This art is destined to awaken, or rather, if we dare put it thus, to compel sluggish souls to action.

At the beginning of each era an inspired word chooses the geniuses to set this epoch in motion; but the masses remain passive for a long time, and then art uses all possible means; it calls upon architecture, music, and even dance to help animate these masses; but if art degenerates into comedy and farce, it eventually disappears. The drama, in the highest and broadest sense of the word, *should unite all the elements of a truly national poetry*, just as the political institution of a nation should express all its political tendencies.

In the choruses of the tragedies of Aeschylus and Sophocles, you find the noble lyric poetry of primitive times, as you find in their dialogue the epic reproduced in the action of the characters of the drama, the Achilles, the Ulysses, and even the gods, whom the people already knew from Homer's stories; here we recognize the germ of the political eloquence which would soon ring out in the public square. Nowhere else has the drama achieved such perfection, or as complete a realization. In the Christian world, the drama begins after the heroic epoch, after the crusades; and we find magnificent instances of it in the *Mysteries*. The entire universe was also represented there, as Christianity conceived it. The theatre showed us *heaven* with its celestial spirits; *earth*, that is to say, the stage, the sphere of human action; and *hell*, represented by the gaping maw of Satan, from which came streaming forth the rep-

From Adam Mickiewicz, *"Lectures on Slavic Literature: Lesson 16 (4 April 1843),"* trans. Daniel Gerould, *TDR* (T111), Fall 1986.

resentatives of evil, evil of all kinds, running the gamut from treachery to buffoonery. But this drama, soon after its initial ventures, began to decline. Gradually the writers, having taken the Greeks and Romans as their model, and having eliminated the Christian heaven and hell, confined the drama to salons and boudoirs, where it has stayed until the present day.

We may assume that Christian drama will still have several further epochs. The mysteries form its true basis. Spanish drama and Shakespearean drama perfected certain aspects of this vast creation. But the French dramatic art of the age of Louis XIV will probably be rejected as an alien episode, as a kind of reaction by paganism to the development of Christian drama.

We must consider here once more the question of the *marvelous*. Previously, when speaking of the epic, we explained that the *marvelous* is not a poetic device introduced to arouse the reader's curiosity or to make a poem more interesting; but that it is an integral part of each great work that has some life to it. The natural scientists tell us that a plant, or any organic form of being, constitutes, in the last analysis, a miracle that cannot be explained. This miracle is the principle of its organic life. The same holds true of poetry. In every poetic work, there is at its very heart this organic and inexplicable life, this mysterious element, known in academic parlance as the marvelous, which, going higher as the dimensions of each work increase, seems to us, in short poetic compositions, like a breath from a higher region, like a vague memory or a premonition of a supernatural world, and, in the epic or the drama, takes the visible form of *a divine being*.

From what we have said, you will see the great difficulty of creating a Slavic drama, a drama which could unite all the elements of the national poetry, for nowhere else have these elements appeared as numerous and as diverse. Such a drama should be lyrical, and it should remind us of the admirable melodies of popular folk songs. It should at the same time enable us to hear the stories whose perfect model we see in the poetry of the Slavs along the Danube, in the poetry of the Serbs, the mountaineers of Montenegro. It should also transport us into the supernatural world.

We now remind you of the varieties of poetic imagination used by different peoples in conceiving of the supernatural world, and of the different ways in which they approach it and communicate with it. We have said that the Celtic race is gifted with *second sight*; and this faculty of second sight dominates in ancient Celtic poetry, and sometimes animates even the popular creations of the most recent eras. We have said that the Germanic people, this race which has so many connections with the Celtic race, has the special gift of *communication with spirits*. Well known are the stories about spirits recorded in pious legends and in tales of hypnotic and magnetic phenomena. The Slavic people have, above all, believed in the existence of what are called *vampires*, and they have even developed a philosophical theory of vampirism. We have already spoken of this earlier. But, from a philosophical standpoint, this belief is nothing other than faith in the individuality of the human spirit, in the individuality of spirits in general, and nowhere is this belief as strong as it is among the Slavic people. That is why no pantheistic theory will ever manage to take root there; the national instinct rebuffs it. We know from history and mythology that the cult of spirits was an important part of Slavic religion: to this very day there is the custom of invoking the dead in Lithuania and elsewhere; and of all the Slavic sacred rites the most important and solemn is the ceremony of calling forth the spirits of the dead. If there are among the people any who, through contact with the educated classes, have neglected the practice of religion, or have totally forgotten their religious instruction, you will not find a single one who has lost faith in the individual existence of spirits after death.

Thus, to create a drama that could be recognized as national by all classes of the Slavic race, by the Slavic people, it is necessary, as I have said, to play upon all the different strings and to cover the entire spectrum from the simple *song* to the *epic*.

Until now, such a drama has not existed. We have not spoken of numerous Polish works to a greater or lesser degree imitated from foreign models; we have also passed over the celebrated seventeenth-century Slavic drama *Ariadna*, by the Croatian Ivan Gundulić, which is only the libretto of an Italian opera; nor will we speak of the dramas of Czech authors, such as the dramas of František Turinsky, *Virginia* and *Angelina*, recently published in Prague, which, despite their stylistic merits, are nothing but half-French, half-Spanish copies. Three works only stand out from this chaos of imitations: Pushkin's *Boris Godunov*; the drama by the Serbian poet Sima Milutinović, entitled *The Tragedy of Obilić* and the Polish drama called *The Undivine Comedy*, by Zygmunt Krasiński.

We have already said a few words about Pushkin's drama: in form, it is an imitation of the dramas of Schiller and Shakespeare. But Pushkin was wrong to confine his drama to the earth. In the prologue he gives us intimations of the action of the supernatural world; but he soon forgets it entirely, and, by the end, the play is nothing more than political intrigue.

Milutinović's drama soars higher; it is a remarkable work, reminding us uncannily of *The Undivine Comedy*. Milutinović strikes only one tone in this drama, that of the Serbian folk song; but he is a master of it, and his style throughout reminds us of that of the rhapsodists of his country. In his preface, he already invokes the spirits of dead ancestors. The scenes of the drama take place both in heaven and on earth; but his supernatural world of angels is patterned after popular Serbian folk imagery. Nothing has been changed, and nothing has been made more elevated; these are images of angels as you know them from the poems we have previously analyzed. The poet has not even made use of the visions that he could have found in the ecclesiastical books of his country. The terrestrial sphere encompasses a great action. Milutinović takes as his subject the sole theme of Serbian poetry, *The Battle of Kosovo Field*. The drama begins in a Serbian castle, moves into the cathedral, and ends in the Turkish camp by the deathbed of Amurat, killed by Obilić, the hero of the drama. Amurat in Milutinović's drama is reminiscent of the character whom you know by the name of Pancras, that frightful enemy of the Slavic past in Krasiński's drama. Amurat also triumphs over the Slav, and, upon conquering the Serbian land, he dies without having time to finish a prophecy which he pronounces while dying.

The Polish drama *The Undivine Comedy* reaches still higher; it is more national and at the same time more Slavic. First of all, the marvelous, the supernatural world, is not simply poetic and popular here, it is also conceived according to ideas that have been developed in our century. Likewise in the earthly sphere the drama treats all the questions agitating the Slavic race; that is why it is not solely a national work; it also introduces a chorus of inferior spirits, an authentic sacred rite for calling forth spirits of dead ancestors, and ends with a prophecy.

But it does not suffice to create the drama; there is now the problem of having it staged. We should not expect to see a Slavic drama realized on the stage in the near future, for no theatre would suffice even to present *The Undivine Comedy*. It could, however, be represented in part, if current theatrical habits in staging drama were abandoned; it would be necessary to bring the poet himself on stage. The narration, which constitutes an extremely important part of this drama, should be recited in public by the poet, and illustrated by *panoramic* images. Finally, heaven and hell could be borrowed from current productions at the Opera. In general, the theatre architecture of today lags far behind the development of drama. In France, the Cirque Olympique is the only theatre suitable for presenting a serious play. There one could stage scenes from the stormy life of heroes, and show the masses who now have such significance in social life.

Probably the Slavic race will have to wait many years before realizing its drama. First it must await the perfecting of the arts that serve the drama— such as architecture, painting, the play of lights, etc.—which appear now as means in panoramas. But the drama should make use of all these means in order to bring to life the history of past times. In the meantime, the Slavic poets who are creating drama must completely forget about the theatre and the stage. This advice must often be repeated for their benefit, because on the one hand the Poles are discouraged not to have a national stage, and on the other the Czechs attach far too great an importance to the creation of their national theatre. They are quite thrilled to have a building, a stage, and settings, which Polish drama now lacks in several provinces. These accessories are certainly necessary, but they are by no means essential. A German author, Tieck, has discussed this question in one of his works: he has demonstrated that the perfecting of settings and of the theatre building, and above all the importance that is attached to such matters, testifies to the decadence of the drama. When the feelings of the poet are not strong enough to carry his entire audience and transport it to imaginary realms; when his word has not sufficient power to adorn the building and to change the settings at each moment; when he needs to ask for help from the designer and machinist, he proves either his own impotence or the extreme degradation of his public. We know that the most fantastic scenes in Shakespeare were played in ramshackle buildings where there would not have been either settings or stage machinery. Several of his plays were presented for the first time in attics. But the magic of the English poet is such that even if we only read him, we see both the lights and the shadows, the spirits and the heroes, and the castles rising from the earth, and the reader ultimately finds himself on stage in the midst of the actors. I repeat that it is very important to meditate on this advice, and that nowadays the poets writing drama should free themselves of such preoccupations, and suppress the desire to see their plays staged.

To conclude I should say that, even in this matter, the poets should imitate the Slavic storytellers, the Slavic peasants. You are aware that no people have as rich or as marvelous fantastic tales, and perhaps there was never an audience as attentive as the group of listeners that surrounds a poor peasant telling his tale in his thatched hut. Like some Greek poets, for example, Aristophanes, like some authors of mysteries, the storyteller almost invariably puts himself into the tale, and thus plays a role in the action of the drama; sometimes he leads us to believe that he has actually taken part in certain works and deeds of his heroes, and in the most marvelous tales he sometimes makes use of very simple means to heighten the attention of his auditors. Those of you who are Poles and Russians undoubtedly know the tale in which the hero searches for the mysterious and fabulous firebird, a kind of phoenix. This bird, having flown over a Slavic land, lets fall a single feather, which the hero picks up; when he brings it home, it gives off such a bright glow that it fills the entire thatched hut with light. At just this very moment, the storyteller has the habit of lighting a few wood shavings, and the glow that they give off makes the audience shudder. In another tale, when he mentions the crystal mountain occupied by fairies who are as much alike as stars, and among whom it was so difficult to choose the one that the hero must find, the peasant suddenly opens a door, and shows his audience the winter sky shining with stars, and the clouds whose fantastic form represents the crystal mountain better than any theatrical setting.

I cite these examples to show you the artistic secret that the peasants, the native poets, possess. They have preserved that most precious quality, that of admiration. According to the French philosopher, Descartes, man differs from the animals only in that he is able to admire. This is the opposite of the views of several ancient philosophers who cited as a proof of superiority the ability to despise everything, *nihil admirari*.

The people possess this ability to admire, so difficult to satisfy without doubt, and it is astonishing that the same peasant, Russian or Polish, who is enchanted so easily by a popular folk tale, admires, it is true—but without being transported, without being enchanted—the palaces, the productions of the architecture and the theatre settings. Above all he admires the word, he admires feelings and thoughts expressed by the word: that is the poetic character of the Slavic people.

We shall conclude by formulating what we have said so far: first, that the Slavic drama, attempted by Pushkin and Milutinović, already surpasses in the case of *The Undivine Comedy* all the European dramas which we know; that this drama reunites several national elements, but that it is not complete, does not yet give an idea of what the Slavic drama must one day be; that we should not expect such a drama to be realized in the near future, that the poets who are called to create it must above all be deeply impressed with the idea that the art of the drama depends neither on architecture, nor on settings, nor on the stage, but that, quite the contrary, these accessories should be inherent in the poetic idea; and that they must above all be scrupulous and reverential in the use that they are called upon to make of the supernatural world.

FRIEDRICH NIETZSCHE

Friedrich NIETZSCHE (1844-1900) made an extremely agreeable impression. Of medium height, slender, erect, with almost black hair and a thick moustache, noble features and harmonious gestures, always impeccably dressed, the philosopher in no way resembled a typical German scholar but rather recalled an Italian or Spanish officer in civilian clothes. Lou Salome, a Russian philosophy student with whom he fell in love, said of her mentor: "It was hard to imagine this figure in the middle of a crowd—he bore the stamp of one who stands apart, alone. Nietzsche's hands were so incomparably beautiful and nobly shaped that one could not help looking at them, and he himself believed that they revealed his spirit. [. . .] He ascribed a similar significance to his unusually small and finely modeled ears, claiming that they were true 'ears for things unheard.'"

Nietzsche liked to be thought a gallant Polish nobleman. In quest of an "anti-self," he invented an aristocratic Slavic forebear, von Nietsky. A perfect gentleman with women, he hated bad manners and slovenliness. Courtliness served to hide his inner feelings. "Everything profound loves a mask," the philosopher declared, his dark eyes looking inward. Seven/eights blind, he was forced to hold his head very close to the page when he read or wrote. His penmanship was so poor that he used an early typewriter, even for his prolific correspondence.

As a schoolboy, young Fritz discovered the drama through Byron's *Manfred* and Schiller's *The Robbers*, but was most deeply moved by *The Death of Empedocles* by Hölderlin, his favorite poet. He himself wrote a six-act tragedy about the Greek philosopher who threw himself into the crater of Mount Etna. At the gymnasium Fritz acted in the yearly school carnival plays, playing one of the mechanicals in *Midsummer Night's Dream*. But he did not recite his lines well and disliked play-acting, which he found alien to his nature. He found attending the theatre so exhilarating that he became an avid reader of stage reviews and a connoisseur of acting. When he transferred from the University of Bonn to the University of Leipzig, he obtained press credentials and went regularly to plays with the young critics.

Born with a love of music, Nietzsche played and sang the songs he began composing as a youngster. A member of the choral society, he took part in mammoth outdoor music festivals. When a group of the students paid a visit to a brothel in Cologne, Fritz remained in the foyer playing the piano.

At sixteen Nietzsche discovered the sheet music for *Tristan* in a piano transcription, later declaring, "I would never have survived my youth without Wagnerian music." Recently appointed professor at the University of Basel, he met Wagner in 1868 and became a regular in the composer's household, where he ran errands for Cosima and served as publicist for Wagnerism and cultural nationalism. Nietzsche, who had reservations about Wagner's music, shared his dreams for a ritual theatre of the future "to be resurrected through the past," and Wagner liked having a professor as his faithful disciple who, he hoped, would write a book about him.

In *The Birth of Tragedy* Nietzsche celebrated *Tristan* as the true revival of the spirit of Greek tragedy. But when he actually went to Bayreuth for first cycle in 1876, the fastidious philosopher was seized with loathing for the wealthy German burghers reeking of tobacco and stale beer and fled in horror. Nietzsche referred to Bayreuth as a "contemptible little German affair," and, appalled by the maestro's paranoiac anti-semitism, called Wagner a histrion, showman, and charlatan. Wagner told Nietzsche to get married or write an opera.

Nietzsche loved the age of Louis XIV and the French drama and acting of the classical period. *The Birth of Tragedy* was backward-looking in that Nietzsche hoped to resurrect the German theatre of his day by going back to ancient roots (as had Wagner). Once freed by his reading of Schopenhauer from the turgid emotional nationalism of the outdoor music festivals, Nietzsche adopted the Heraclitean view of history as an endlessly recurring flux. The world, ungoverned by purpose, was eternal, senseless play. Nietzsche no longer sought to reconcile the differences between culture and the state, but rather to deepen the conflict. Ultimately rejecting Schopenhauer's pessimism as well as the optimism of Hegelian dialectic, the author of *Zarathustra* saw the agonal principle as the mainspring of Hellenic culture. Nietzsche eventually abandoned the discursive essay form, which he had used in his first book, *The Birth of Tragedy*, as a pedagogic tool integrating the reader into a shared culture; instead, he chose the improvisatory discontinuity of the aphorism, which continued the tradition of the romantic fragment.

As he wandered about Switzerland and Italy in search of the ideal climate to soothe his frayed nerves, Nietzsche maintained an interest in contemporary music and theatre. His favorite opera became *Carmen*, which he first heard in November 1881 and went on to see some twenty times in many different productions, fascinated by the dark side of the Bizet-Mérimée drama of passion.

He corresponded with August Strindberg about *The Father*, which he hailed as "a masterpiece of strong-minded psychology" and claimed it was destined to be performed at Antoine's Théâtre Libre (a prediction that never came true). Impressed with the Swedish playwright's French version of *The Father*, Nietzsche asked Strindberg to translate his autobiographical *Ecce Homo* into French.

In his later years the philosopher (who had often pictured himself as Prometheus Bound) wished to be called the lover of Ariadne and began signing his letters as Dionysus, the Phoenix, and the Monster. "I belong to the machines that may fly to pieces," Nietzsche confessed, sensing his own approaching madness.

THE BIRTH OF TRAGEDY
FROM THE SPIRIT OF MUSIC
(1872)

1. We shall do a great deal for the science of aesthetics, once we perceive not merely by logical inference, but with the immediate certainty of intuition, that the continuous development of art is bound up with the *Apollonian* and *Dionysian* duality; just as procreation depends on the duality of the sexes, involving perpetual strife with only periodically intervening reconciliations. The terms Dionysian and Apollonian we borrow from the Greeks, who disclose to the discerning mind the profound mysteries of their view of art, not, to be sure, in concepts, but in the impressively clear figures of their gods. Through Apollo and Dionysus, the two art-deities of the Greeks, we come to recognize that in the Greek world there existed a sharp opposition, in origin and aims, between the Apollonian art of sculpture, and the non-plastic, Dionysian, art of music. These two distinct tendencies run parallel to each other, for the most part openly at variance; and they continually incite each other to new and more powerful births, which perpetuate an antagonism, only superficially reconciled by the common term "Art;" till at last, by a metaphysical miracle of the Hellenic will, they appear coupled with each other, and through this coupling eventually generate the art-product, equally Dionysian and Apollonian, of Attic tragedy.

In order to grasp these two tendencies, let us first conceive of them as the separate art-worlds of *dreams* and *drunkenness*. These physiological phenomena present a contrast analogous to that exiting between the Apollonian and the Dionysian. [...]

This joyful necessity of the dream-experience has been embodied by the Greeks in their Apollo: for Apollo, the god of all plastic energies, is at the same time the soothsaying god. He, who (as the etymology of the name indicates) is the "shining one," the deity of light, is also ruler over the fair appearance of the inner world of fantasy. The higher truth, the perfection of these states in contrast to the incompletely intelligible everyday world, this deep consciousness of nature, healing and helping in sleep and dreams, is at the same time the symbolical analogue of the soothsaying faculty and of the arts generally, which make life possible and worth living. But we must also include in our picture of Apollo that delicate boundary, which the dream-picture must

From Friedrich Nietzsche, *Ecce Homo and The Birth of Tragedy*, trans. Clifton P. Fadiman. N.Y.: The Modern Library, 1927.

not overstep—lest it act pathologically (in which case appearance would impose upon us as a pure reality). We must keep in mind that measured restraint, that freedom from the wilder emotions, that philosophical calm of the sculptor-god. His eye must be "sunlike," as befits his origin; even when his glance is angry and distempered, the sacredness of his beautiful appearance must still be there. And so, in one sense, we might apply to Apollo the words of Schopenhauer when he speaks of the man wrapt in the veil of Maya (*The World as Will and Idea*, I): "Just as in a stormy sea, unbounded in every direction, raising and falling with howling mountainous waves, a sailor sits in a boat and trusts in his frail barque: so in the midst of a world of sorrows the individual sits quietly, supported by and trusting in his *principium individuationis.*" In fact, we might say of Apollo, that in him the unshaken faith in this *principium* and the calm repose of the man wrapt therein receive their sublimest expression; and we might consider Apollo himself as the glorious divine image of the *principium individuationis*, whose gestures and expression tell us of all the joy and wisdom of "appearance," together with its beauty.

In the same work Schopenhauer has depicted for us the terrible *awe* which seizes upon man, when he is suddenly unable to account for the cognitive forms of phenomenon, when the principle of reason, in some of its manifestations, seems to admit of an exception. If we add to this awe the blissful ecstasy which rises from the innermost depths of man, aye, of nature, at this very collapse of the *principium individuationis*, we shall gain an insight into the nature of *Dionysian*, which is brought home to us most intimately perhaps by the analogy of *drunkenness*.

It is either under the influence of the narcotic draught, which we hear of in the songs of all primitive men and peoples, or with the potent coming of spring that penetrates all nature with joy, that these Dionysian emotions awake, which, as they intensify, cause the subjective to vanish into complete self-forgetfulness. [...]

7. We must now avail ourselves of all the principles of art hitherto considered, in order to find our way through the labyrinth, as we must call it, of *the origin of Greek tragedy*. I do not think I am unreasonable in saying that the problem of this origin has as yet not even been seriously stated, not to say solved, however often the ragged tatters of ancient tradition are sewn together in various combinations and torn apart again. This tradition tells us quite unequivocally *that tragedy arose from the tragic chorus*, and was originally only chorus and nothing but chorus; and hence we feel it our duty to look into the heart of this tragic chorus as being the real proto-drama. We shall not let ourselves be at all satisfied with that current art-lingo which makes the chorus the "ideal spectator," or has it represent the people in contrast to the aristocratic elements of the scene. This latter explanation has a sublime sound to many a politician. It insists that the immutable moral law was embodied by the demo-

cratic Athenians in the popular chorus, which always wins out over the passionate excesses and extravagances of kings. This theory may be ever so forcibly suggested by one of Aristotle's observations; still, it has no influence on the original formation of tragedy, inasmuch as the entire antithesis of king and people, and, in general, the whole politico-social sphere, is excluded from the purely religious origins of tragedy. With this in mind, and remembering the well-known classical form of the chorus in Aeschylus and Sophocles, we should even deem it blasphemy to speak here of the anticipation of a "constitutional popular representation." From this blasphemy, however, others have not shrunk. The ancient governments knew of no constitutional representation of the people *in praxi*, and it is to be hoped that they did not "anticipate" it in their tragedy either.

Much more famous than this political interpretation of the chorus is the theory of A. W. Schlegel, who advises us to regard the chorus, in a manner, as the essence and extract of the crowd of spectators—as the "ideal spectator." This view, when compared with the historical tradition that originally tragedy was only chorus, reveals itself for what it is—a crude, unscientific, yet brilliant generalization, which, however, acquires that brilliancy only through its epigrammatic form of expression, the deep Germanic bias in favor of anything called "ideal," and our momentary astonishment. For we are certainly astonished the moment we compare our familiar theatrical public with this chorus, and ask ourselves whether it could ever be possible to idealize something analogous to the Greek tragic chorus out of such a public. We tacitly deny this, and now wonder as much at the boldness of Schlegel's claim as at the totally different nature of the Greek public. For hitherto we had always believed that the true spectator, whoever he may be, must always remain conscious that he was viewing a work of art and not an empirical reality. But the tragic chorus of the Greeks is forced to recognize *real beings* in the figures of the drama. The chorus of the Oceanides really believes that it sees before it the Titan Prometheus, and considers itself as real as the god of the scene. And are we to designate as the highest and purest type of spectator, one who, like the Oceanides, regards Prometheus as real and present in body? Is it characteristic of the ideal spectator to run onto the stage and free the god from his torments? We had always believed in an aesthetic public, we had considered the individual spectator the better qualified the more he was capable of viewing a work of art as art, that is, aesthetically. But now Schlegel tells us that the perfect, ideal spectator does not at all allow the world of the drama to act on him *aesthetically*, but corporeally and empirically. Oh, these Greeks! we sighed; they upset all our aesthetics! . . . But once accustomed to it, we repeated Schlegel's saying whenever the chorus came up for discussion.

Now, the tradition, which is quite explicit here, speaks against Schlegel. The chorus as such, without the stage—the primitive form of tragedy—and the chorus of ideal spectators do not go together. What kind of art would that be in which the spectator does not enter as a separate concept? What kind of art is that whose true form is identical with the "spectator as such"? The spectator without the play is nonsense. We fear that the birth of tragedy is to be explained neither by the high esteem for the moral intelligence of the multitude nor by the concept of the spectator minus the play. We must regard the problem as too deep to be even touched by such superficial generalizing.

An infinitely more valuable insight into the significance of the chorus had already been displayed by Schiller in the celebrated Preface to his *Bride of Messina*, where he regards the chorus as a living barrier which tragedy constructs round herself to cut off her contact with the world of reality, and to preserve her ideal domain and her poetical freedom.

With this, his chief weapon, Schiller combats the ordinary conception of the natural, the illusion usually demanded in dramatic poetry. Although it is true that the stage day is merely artificial, the architecture only symbolical, and the metrical language purely ideal in character, nevertheless an erroneous view still prevails in the main: that we should not excuse these conventions merely on the ground that they constitute a poetical license. Now in reality these "conventions" form the essence of all poetry. The introduction of the chorus, says Schiller, is the decisive step by which war is declared openly and honorably against all naturalism in art.

It would seem that to denigrate this view of the matter our would-be superior age has coined the disdainful catchword "pseudo-idealism." I fear, however, that we, on the other hand, with our present adoration of the natural and the real, have reached the opposite pole of all idealism, namely, in the region of wax-work cabinets. There is an art in these too, as certain novels much in vogue at present evidence: but let us not disturb ourselves at the claim that by any such art the Schiller-Goethian "pseudo-idealism" has been vanquished.

It is indeed an "ideal" domain, as Schiller correctly perceived, in which the Greek satyr chorus, the chorus of primitive tragedy, was wont to dwell. It is a domain raised high above the actual path of mortals. For this chorus the Greek built up the scaffolding of a fictitious *natural state* and on it placed fictitious *natural beings*. On this foundation tragedy developed and so, of course, it could dispense from the beginning with a painstaking portrayal of reality. Yet it is no arbitrary world placed by whim between heaven and earth; rather it is a world with the same reality and credibility that Olympus with its dwellers possessed for the believing Hellene. The satyr, as the Dionysian chorist, lives in a religiously acknowledged reality under the sanction of the myth and the cult. That tragedy should begin with him, that he should be the voice of the Dionysian tragic wisdom, is just as strange a phenomenon for us as the general derivation of tragedy from the chorus.

Perhaps we shall have a point of departure for our inquiry, if I put forward the proposition that the satyr, the fictitious natural being, bears the same relation to the man of culture that Dionysian music does to civilization. Concerning the latter, Richard Wagner says that it is neutralized by music just as lamplight is neutralized by the light of day. Similarly, I believe, the Greek man of culture felt himself neutralized in the presence of the satyric chorus; and this is the most immediate effect of the Dionysian tragedy, that the state and society and, in general, the gulfs between man and man give way to an overwhelming feeling of unity leading back to the very heart of nature. The metaphysical comfort—with which, as I have here intimated, every true tragedy leaves us—that, in spite of the flux of phenomena, life at bottom is indestructibly powerful and pleasurable, appears with objective clarity as the satyr chorus, the chorus of natural beings, who as it were live ineradicably behind every civilization, and who, despite the ceaseless change of generations and the history of nations, remain the same to all eternity.

With this chorus the deep-minded Hellene consoles himself, he who is so singularly constituted for the most sensitive and grievous suffering, he who with a piercing glance has penetrated into the very heart of the terrible destructive processes of so-called universal history, as also into the cruelty of nature, and who is in danger of longing for a Buddhistic negation of the will. Art saves him, and through art life saves him—for herself. [...]

8. The satyr, like the idyllic shepherd of our more recent time, is the offspring of a longing for the Primitive and the Natural; but how firmly and fearlessly the Greek embraced the man of the woods, and how timorously and mawkishly modern man dallied with the flattering picture of a sentimental, flute-playing, soft-mannered shepherd! Nature, as yet unchanged by knowledge, maintaining impregnable barriers to culture—that is what the Greek saw in his satyr who nevertheless was not on this account to be confused with the primitive cave-man. On the contrary, the satyr was the archetype of man, the embodiment of his highest and most intense emotions, the ecstatic reveler enraptured by the proximity of his god, the sympathetic companion in whom is repeated the suffering of the god, wisdom's harbinger speaking from the very heart of nature, emblem of the sexual omnipotence of nature, which the Greek was wont to contemplate with reverence and wonder.

The satyr was something sublime and godlike: it was inevitable that he should appear so, especially to the sad downcast glance of the Dionysian man. Our counterfeit tricked-up shepherd would have repulsed the Dionysian; but on the naked and magnificent characters of nature his eye dwelt with rapt satisfaction. Here the illusion of culture was cast off from the archetype of man; here the true man, the bearded satyr, revealed himself, shouting joyfully to his god. Face to face with him the man of culture shrank to a specious caricature.

Schiller is right also with regard to these beginnings of tragic art: the chorus is a living bulwark against the onslaught of reality, because it—the satyr chorus—portrays existence more truthfully, more essentially, more perfectly than the cultured man who ordinarily considers himself as the sole reality. The sphere of poetry does not lie outside the world like some chimera of the poetic imagination; it seeks to be the very opposite, the unvarnished expression of the truth, and for this very reason it must reject the false finery of the supposed reality of the cultured man.

The contrast between this intrinsic truth of nature and the falsehood of culture, which poses as the only reality, is similar to that existing between the eternal heart of things, the thing-in-itself, and the collective world of phenomena. And just as tragedy, with its metaphysical comfort, points to the eternal life of this kernel of existence, and to the perpetual dissolution of phenomena, so the symbolism of the satyr chorus already expresses figuratively this primal relation between the thing-in-itself and the phenomenon. The idyllic shepherd of the modern man is but a copy of the sum of culture—illusions which he calls nature; the Dionysian Greek desires truth and nature in their most potent form—and so he sees himself metamorphosed into the satyr.

The reveling throng of the votaries of Dionysus rejoices under the spell of such moods and perceptions, the power of which transforms them before their own eyes, so that they imagine they behold themselves as recreated genii of nature, as satyrs. The later constitution of the tragic chorus is the artistic imitation of this natural phenomenon, which of course necessitated a separation of the Dionysian spectators from the enchanted Dionysians. However, we must always remember that the public of the Attic tragedy rediscovered itself in the chorus of the *orchestra*, that there was at bottom no opposition of public and chorus: for all was but one sublime chorus of dancing and singing satyrs, or of such as allowed themselves to be represented by these satyrs.

Schlegel's observation in this sense reveals a deeper significance. The chorus *is* the "ideal spectator" insofar as it is the only *beholder*, the beholder of the visionary world of the scene. A public of spectators, as we know it, was unknown to the Greeks. In their theaters the terraced structure of the theatron rising in concentric arcs enabled everyone to *overlook*, in an actual sense, the entire world of culture around him, and in an overabundance of contemplation to imagine himself one of the chorus.

According to this view, then, we may call the chorus in its primitive stage in early tragedy a self-mirroring of the Dionysian man: a phenomenon which is most clearly exemplified by the process of the actor, who, if he be truly gifted, sees hovering almost tangibly before his eyes the character he is to represent. The satyr chorus is above all a vision of the Dionysian mass, just as the world of the stage is, in turn, a vision of the satyr chorus. The power of this vision is great enough to render the eye dull and insensible to the impression of "reality," to the presence of the cultured men occupying the tiers of seats on every side. The form of the Greek theater reminds one of a lonesome mountain-valley. The architecture of the scene is a luminous cloud-picture and the Bacchants swarming on the mountains behold this picture from the heights—the splendid encirclement in the midst of which is visible the image of Dionysus.

Brought in contact with our learned views of the elementary artistic processes, this artistic proto-phenomenon, here introduced as an explanation of the tragic chorus, is almost shocking; yet nothing can be more certain than that the poet is a poet only insofar as he sees himself surrounded by forms which live and act before him, and into whose innermost being he penetrates. By reason of a peculiar defect in our modern critical faculty, we are inclined to consider the aesthetic proto-phenomenon too complexly, too abstractly.

For the true poet a metaphor is not a figure of speech, but a vicarious image which actually hovers before him in place of a concept. To him a character is not an aggregate composed of a number of particular traits, but an organic person pressing himself upon his attention, and differing from the similar vision of the painter only in the consciousness of its life and action. Why does Homer describe much more vividly than all the other poets? Because he contemplates much more. We talk so abstractly about poetry because we are all bad poets. At bottom, the aesthetic phenomenon is simple: if a man merely has the faculty of seeing perpetual vitality around him, of living continually surrounded by hosts of spirits, he will be a poet. If he but feels the impulse to transform himself and to speak from out of the bodies and souls of others, he will be a dramatist.

The Dionysian excitement is able to inspire a whole mass of men with this artistic faculty of seeing themselves surrounded by such a host of spirits with whom they know themselves to be essentially one. This process of the tragic chorus is the *dramatic* proto-phenomenon: to see yourself transformed before your own eyes, and then to act as if you had actually taken possession of another body and another character. This process stands at the beginning of the development of the drama. Here we have something different from the rhapsodist, who does not unite with his images, but, like the painter, merely views them contemplatively, with detachment. Here we actually have the individual surrendering himself by the fact of his entrance into an alien nature. Moreover, this phenomenon is epidemic in its manifestation: a whole throng experiences this metamorphosis.

Hence it is that the dithyramb is essentially different from every other variety of choric song. The virgins, who, laurel branches in hand, solemnly make their way to the temple of Apollo singing a processional hymn, remain what they are and retain their civic names: but the dithyrambic chorus is a chorus of transformed beings, whose civic past and social position are totally forgotten. They have become the timeless servants of their god, living apart from all the life of the community. Every other kind of choric lyric of the

Hellenes is nothing but an enormous intensification of the Apollonian individual singer: while in the dithyramb we have a community of unconscious actors, who mutually regard themselves as transformed among one another.

This enchantment is the prerequisite for all dramatic art. Under its spell the Dionysian reveler sees himself as a satyr, *and as a satyr he in turn, beholds the god*, that is, in his transformation he sees a new vision outside him as the Apollonian consummation of his own state. With this new vision the drama completes itself.

According to this view, we must understand Greek tragedy as the Dionysian chorus, disburdening itself again and again in an Apollonian image-world. The choric parts, therefore, with which tragedy is interlaced are in a sense the maternal womb of the entire so-called dialogue, that is, of the whole stage-world, of the drama proper. In several successive outbursts this primal basis of tragedy releases this vision of the drama, which is a dream phenomenon throughout, and, as such, epic in character; on the other hand, however, as the objectification of a Dionysian state, it represents not the Apollonian redemption in appearance, but, on the contrary, the dissolution of the individual and his unification with primordial existence. And so the drama becomes the Apollonian embodiment of Dionysian perceptions and influences, and therefore separates itself by a tremendous gap from the epic.

The *chorus* of the Greek tragedy, the symbol of the collectively excited Dionysian mass, thus finds its full explanation in our conception. Accustomed as we were to the function performed by our modern stage chorus, especially an operatic one, we could never comprehend why the tragic chorus of the Greeks should be older, more primitive, indeed, more important than the "action" proper—as has been so plainly declared by the voice of tradition; whereas, furthermore, we could not reconcile with this traditional primacy and primitiveness the fact that the chorus was composed only of humble, attendant beings—indeed, in the beginning, only of goatlike satyrs; and, finally, there remained the riddle of the orchestra in front of the scene. We have at last realized that the scene, together with the action, was fundamentally and originally thought of only as a *vision;* that the only reality is just the chorus, which of itself generates the vision and celebrates it with the entire symbolism of dancing, music and speech. In the vision this chorus beholds its lord and master Dionysus, and so it is forever a chorus that *serves:* it sees how he, the god, suffers and glorifies himself and therefore does not itself *act.* But though its attitude toward the god is throughout the attitude of ministration, this is nevertheless the highest, that is the Dionysian, expression of *Nature* and therefore, like Nature herself in a state of transport, the chorus utters oracles and wise sayings: as *fellow-sufferer* it is at the same time the *sage* who proclaims truth from out the heart of Nature. Thus, then, originates the fantastic figure, seemingly so discordant, of the wise and inspired satyr, who is at the same time "the dumb man" in contrast to the god: who is the image of Nature and her strongest impulses, the very symbol of Nature, and at the same time the *proclaimer* of her art and vision: musician, poet, dancer, and visionary united in one person.

In accordance with this view, and with tradition, *Dionysus*, the proper stage-hero and focus of vision, is in the remotest period of tragedy not at first actually present, but is only so imagined, which means that tragedy is originally only "chorus" and not "drama." Later on the attempt is made to present the god as real and to display the visionary figure together with its aura of splendor before the eyes of all; here the "drama," in the narrow sense of the term, begins. The dithyrambic chorus is now assigned the task of exciting the minds of the audience to such a pitch of Dionysian frenzy, that, when the tragic hero appears on the stage, they do not see in him an unshapely man wearing a mask, but they see a visionary figure, born as it were of their own ecstasy.

Picture Admetus sunk in a profound meditation about his lately departed wife Alcestis, and quite consuming himself in fancied contemplation. Suddenly the veiled figure of a woman, resembling her in form and gait, is led toward him. Picture his sudden trembling anxiety, his excited comparisons, his instinctive conviction—and we shall have a sensation comparable to that with which the Dionysiacally excited spectator saw approaching on the stage, the god with whose sufferings he has already become identified. Involuntarily, he transferred the whole image of the god, fluttering magically before his soul, to this masked figure and resolved its reality as it were into a phantasmal unreality.

This is the Apollonian dream-state in which the world of day is veiled, and a new world, clearer, more intelligible, more vivid and yet more shadowy than the old, is, by a perpetual transformation, born and reborn before our eyes. Accordingly, we recognize in tragedy a complete stylistic opposition: the language, color, flexibility and movement of the dialogue fall apart into two entirely separate realms of expression: into the Dionysian lyrics of the chorus on the one hand, and the Apollonian dream world of the scene on the other. The Apollonian appearances in which Dionysus objectifies himself are no longer "an eternal sea, a changing weave, a glowing life," as is the music of the chorus. They are no longer those forces, merely felt, but not condensed into a picture, by which the inspired votary of Dionysus divines the proximity of his god. Now the clearness and firmness of epic form speak to him from the scene; now Dionysus no longer speaks through forces but as an epic hero, almost in the language of Homer. [...]

10. The tradition is undisputed that Greek tragedy in its earliest form had for its sole theme the sufferings of Dionysus, and that for a long time the only stage hero was Dionysus himself. With equal confidence, however, we can assert that, until Euripides, Dionysus never once ceased to be the tragic

hero; that in fact all the celebrated figures of the Greek stage—Prometheus, Oedipus, etc.—are but masks of this original hero, Dionysus. There is god-head behind all these masks; and that is the one essential cause of the typical "ideality," so often wondered at, of these celebrated characters. I know not who it was maintained that all individuals as such are comic and consequent-ly untragic; whence we might infer that the Greeks in general *could* not endure individuals on the tragic stage. And they really seem to have felt this: as, in general, we may note in the Platonic distinction so deeply rooted in the Hellenic nature, of the "idea" in contrast to the "eidolon," or image.

Using Plato's terms we should have to speak of the tragic figures of the Hellenic stage somewhat as follows: the one truly real Dionysus appears in a variety of forms, in the mask of a fighting hero, and entangled, as it were, in the net of the individual will. In the latter case the visible god talks and acts so as to resemble an erring, striving, suffering individual. That, generally speaking, he *appears* with such epic precision and clarity is the work of the dream-reading Apollo, who through this symbolic appearance interprets to the chorus its Dionysian state. In reality, however, and behind this appearance, the hero is the suffering Dionysus of the mysteries, the god experiencing in himself the agonies of individuation. [...]

12. [...] Let us pause here a moment in order to recall to our minds our own previously described impression of the discordant and incommensu-rable elements in the genius of Aeschylean tragedy. Let us think of our own surprise at the *chorus* and the *tragic hero* of that tragedy, neither of which we could reconcile with our own customs any more than with tradition—till we rediscovered this duality itself as the origin and essence of Greek tragedy, as the expression of two interwoven artistic impulses, *the Apollonian and the Dionysian*.

To separate this primitive and all-powerful Dionysian element from tragedy, and to construct a new and purified form on the basis of an un-Dionysian art, morality, and conception of the world—this is the tendency of Euripides as it now clearly revealed to us.

In the evening of his life, Euripides himself composed a myth in which he urgently propounded to his contemporaries the question as to the value and significance of this tendency. Is the Dionysian entitled to exist at all? Should it not be forcibly uprooted from Hellenic soil? Certainly, the poet tells us, if it were only possible: but the god Dionysus is too powerful; his most intelligent adversary—like Pentheus in the *Bacchae*—is unwittingly enchanted by him, and in this enchantment runs to meet his fate. The judgment of the two old prophets, Cadmus and Tiresias, seems also to be the judgment of the aged poet: that the reflection of the wisest individuals does not overthrow old popular traditions, nor the perpetually self-propagating worship of Dionysus; that in fact it is to our interest to display at the very least a diplomatically cautious interest in the presence of such strange forces—although there is always the possibility that the god may take offense at such lukewarm participation, and eventually transform the diplomat—in this case Cadmus—into a dragon. This is what we are told by a poet who opposed Dionysus with heroic valor throughout a long life—and who finally ended his career with a glorification of his adversary and with suicide, like one staggering from giddiness, who, to escape the horrible vertigo he can no longer endure, casts himself from a tower.

This tragedy—the *Bacchae*—is a protest against the practicability of his own tendency; but alas, it had already been put into practice! The surprising thing had happened: when the poet recanted, his tendency had already conquered. Dionysus had already been scared from the tragic stage, he had been scared by a demonic power speaking through Euripides. For even Euripides was, in a sense, only a mask: the deity that spoke through him was neither Dionysus nor Apollo. It was an altogether newborn demon. And it was called *Socrates*.

Thus we have a new antithesis: the Dionysian and the Socratic—and on that antithesis the art of Greek tragedy was wrecked. [...]

17. [...] In another direction also we see at work the power of this un-Dionysian myth-opposing spirit, when we turn our attention to the prevalence of *character representation* and psychological refinement in tragedy from Sophocles onward. The character must no longer be expanded into an eternal type, but, on the contrary, must develop individually through artistic subordinate traits and shadings, through the nicest precision of all lines, in such a manner that the spectator is in general no longer conscious of the myth, but of the vigorous truth to nature and the artist's imitative power. Here also we observe the victory of the phenomenon over the Universal, and the delight in a unique, almost anatomical preparation; we are already in the atmosphere of a theoretical world, where scientific knowledge is valued more highly than the artistic reflection of a universal law.

The movement in the direction of character delineation proceeds rapidly: while Sophocles still portrays complete characters and employs myth for their refined development, Euripides already draws only prominent individual traits of character, which can express themselves in violent bursts of passion. In the New Attic Comedy, however, there are only masks with *one* expression: frivolous old men, duped panders, and cunning slaves, recurring incessantly. Where now is the mythopoetic spirit of music? What still remains of music is either excitatory or associational music, that is, either a stimulant for dull and faded nerves, or tone-painting. As regards the former, it hardly matters about the text set to it; the heroes and choruses of Euripides are already dissolute enough when once they begin to sing; to what pass must things have come with his impertinent successors?

The new un-Dionysian spirit, however, reveals itself most plainly in the *dénouements* of the new dramas. In the Old Tragedy one could sense at the end that metaphysical comfort without which the delight in tragedy cannot be explained at all. The reconciliating tones from another world sound purest, perhaps, in the *Oedipus at Colonus*. Now that the genius of music has fled from tragedy, tragedy, strictly speaking, is dead: for from what source shall we now draw this metaphysical comfort? The new spirit, therefore, sought for an earthly resolution of the tragic dissonance. The hero, after being sufficiently tortured by fate, earned a well-deserved reward through a splendid marriage or tokens of divine favor. The hero had turned gladiator. On him, after he had been nicely beaten and covered with wounds, freedom was occasionally bestowed. The *deus ex machina* took the place of metaphysical comfort.

I will not say that the tragic world view was everywhere completely destroyed by this intruding un-Dionysian spirit: we only know that it had to flee from art into the underworld as it were, in the degenerate form of a secret cult. Over the widest extent of the Hellenic character, however, there raged the consuming blast of this spirit, which manifests itself in the form of "Greek cheerfulness," which we have already spoken of as a senile, unproductive love of existence. This cheerfulness is the antithesis of the splendid "naïveté" of the earlier Greeks, which, according to the characteristic indicated above, must be conceived as the blossom of the Apollonian culture springing from a dark abyss, as the victory which the Hellenic will, through its mirroring of beauty, obtains over suffering and the wisdom of suffering. [...]

EMILE ZOLA

Emile ZOLA (1840-1902) was, in the words of his mentors, the Goncourt brothers, "at once sturdy and puny," with a sickly, hypersensitive constitution and a melancholy state of mind. "It is strange what a whiner that fat, pot-bellied young fellow is," they exclaimed.

Zola was the subject of a huge variety of portraits and caricatures by painters, engravers, illustrators, and photographers. As a young man, he had coarse dark hair that fell over his forehead and a fringe of a beard running from ear to ear around a mournful little face with soft soulful eyes. Gloomy, haggard, and worried, he looked ten years older than he actually was.

The middle-aged writer became a paunchy, barrel-chested entrepreneur, with a cannonball head, brush cut, full beard and moustache, pouting lips, and a high, heavily lined forehead. By his fifties, Zola was prematurely aged, appearing as the grandfather to his children, with a grizzled beard and moustache, thinning hair receding up a domed forehead, and eyes that had a pensive, visionary look.

Since adolescence Zola had been extremely near-sighted. At first he refused to wear glasses and even later did not wish to be depicted wearing his lorgnette, although in his last years he appeared with pince-nez. As compensation, he was endowed with a highly developed sense of smell and could evoke places through a precise description of their odors. His expressive nose was cleft at the tip and highly mobile like the muzzle of a retriever.

André Antoine, director of the Théâtre Libre, was struck by Zola's "delicate, mobile, astonishingly expressive hands" and the ceaseless animation of his fingers. Plebeian in appearance, he had a "charming voice with the resonance of a silver bell," but was a gauche conversationalist, feeling nervous and constrained in society. A prey to hypochondria and phobias, he was terrified of thunderstorms and could not tolerate constricting clothing. His hands trembled, his heart raced, and, like Rousseau, he felt a compulsive need to urinate, especially when writing, and kept a chamber pot near the desk.

Zola` loved and hated the nineteenth-century French theatre. Throughout his career he attempted to write for the stage and hoped to achieve fame as a playwright. The obsession began at the small theatre in Aix-en-Provence, where he spent his childhood with classmate Paul Cézanne. Zola would skip dinner so as to be first at the door before the box office opened. Over a period of five or six years he saw the entire Parisian repertory and mastered the intricate code of boulevard theatre: how characters must enter and exist, the technique of dramatic *coups*, the need for sympathetic roles, and the "various ways of cheating truth."

Zola deplored the education he received at that "accursed little theatre." As a theorist, he denounced this artificial language of theatrical convention and insisted that the drama should speak in the same natural tongue as the novel, but as a playwright, he never could unlearn the tricks of the trade and even remained convinced they were necessary for success.

First as an art critic Zola attacked the dictatorship of established authority and championed his friend Manet and the Impressionists whose aesthetics of faithfully observed everyday life he endorsed. Then as a theatre critic Zola struck out at well-made playwrights like Dumas fils and Sardou whom he accused of catering to the stupidity and hypocrisy of the audience. Initially Zola attended performances four times a week, but once he acquired a house in the suburbs, a friend attended for him and sent him elaborate notes upon which he based his reviews. Thanks to Turgenev, Zola wrote about the Parisian stage for *The European Herald*, a liberal Russian journal in St Petersburg, where *Naturalism in the Theatre* (1881) appeared before its publication in France.

After Antoine staged an adaptation of his story, *Jacques Damour*, Zola became a supporter of the Théâtre Libre, attending regularly every month. He advised Antoine to stage Ibsen's *Ghosts*, and corresponded with Strindberg about *The Father*, which he admired, despite reservations about the dramatic foreshortening and abstract characters.

Still under the spell of the glamorous Parisian stage, Zola planned to adapt his best-selling novels and accomplish the "great popular revolution" in the theatre he had long dreamed of. Rejecting offers to adapt *L'Assommoir* from famous writers like Sardou, he selected William Busnach, a Jewish stockbroker turned Boulevard playwright, as his collaborative mask. Zola secretly insisted that the adaptation be made into a profitable melodrama, while publicly pretending that Busnach was the sole author to avoid losing face as the aggressive proponent of naturalism in the theatre. The stage version of *L'Assommoir* was a tremendous success, running for 300 performances; two separate touring companies played it in the provinces to packed houses. Zola, who participated in all aspects of production, attending rehearsals, going to premieres, battling critics, and advising directors, became rich from the adaptations of his novels. But "the great popular revolution" never came about.

PREFACE TO *THÉRÈSE RAQUIN* (1873)

It is always dangerous, in my opinion, to make a play from a novel. One of them will inevitably be inferior to the other and the result is often detrimental to both. The world of the theatre differs so widely from that of the novel that, in order to fit his intentions into another mold, the author finds himself forced to distort his intentions, to coarsen and disfigure them and in the process possibly to reveal diffuseness or omissions. It is the bed of Procrustes, the bed of torture, and the result is a mutilated monster. Then, too, an artist must show some consideration for the maidenly feelings of his beloved daughters, no matter whether they be ugly or beautiful and when he has projected them into the world he no longer has the right to subject them to the hazards of another birth.

In bringing *Thérèse Raquin* into the theatre, therefore, I am acting against my own creed. Indeed, I hesitated for a long time and if, at long last, I yielded it was because of a certain state of affairs which will at least serve as attenuating circumstances. To begin with, the critics were extremely severe to the novel when it appeared and they challenged me to make a play from it. They regarded the book as utter filth. They dragged it gaily through the gutter and declared that if such vileness were to be paraded on the stage, the hisses of the audience would extinguish the footlights. I am, by nature, extremely curious. I have no dislike of a good scrap and from that moment I promised myself a fine one. The provocation was there. It would have been childish to yield to this desire merely for the chance of giving the lie to the critics; I had a higher motive. It seemed to me that *Thérèse Raquin* offered a dramatic subject for a project of which I had often dreamed. In it I found a collection of people such as I had been seeking, characters who completely satisfied me, in short the components I required and all ready to be used. That decided me.

I certainly do not wish to boast about my play; it has great faults and no one can be severer to them than myself. If I were the critic, the only thing that would be left standing would be its definite purpose of helping in the theatre the broad movement of truth and experimental knowledge which in the last century has been growing and spreading throughout the whole field of

Trans. Kathleen Boutall. From *From the Modern Repertoire*, Series Three, ed. Eric Bentley. Bloomington: Indiana University Press, 1966.

human intelligence. The impulse has been given by the new scientific methods. Because of them, naturalism has had an effect on criticism and history by submitting man and his works to an exact analysis, taking into account circumstances, environment and physical attributes. Then, too, art and literature have, in their turn, been influenced by this mighty current. Painting has become altogether realistic and our landscape school has killed the historical school. The novel, with its study of groups and individuals, with its flexible form, has gradually absorbed all the various branches of literature as classified by the rhetoricians of old and now covers their whole field. These are facts no one can deny. In the endless progression of new ideas to which mankind has given birth there is now revealed the newborn babe of truth. And that alone is the driving force of the century. Everything progresses and he who wants to go backwards or to escape will be smothered under the dust of all those who are marching forward. That is why I am absolutely convinced that we shall soon see the naturalist movement forced upon the theatre, bringing with it the power of reality, the new life of modern art.

Any innovation in the theatre is an extremely delicate matter and literary revolutions are slow to make themselves felt. The theatre will most probably be the last citadel which truth will have to besiege. The public in the mass do not like to have their customs interfered with and their judgments are as brutal as the death sentence. But there comes a time when the public themselves unconsciously become the accomplices of the innovators. That time is when, weary with the old ways and touched by the new inspiration, they feel the imperious need for freshness and originality.

It is possible that I may be mistaken but it seems to me that the public have now arrived at that point. Historical drama is at its last gasp; only a blood transfusion can save it. It is said that operetta and fairy plays have killed historical drama. That is not true. It is dying a natural death; it is dying of magniloquence, of unreality, of platitudes. If comedy still manages to survive in the midst of this general collapse, it is because it has kept closer to real life and truth. I defy the romantics to put on a cloak and dagger drama; the medieval clanking of old iron, the secret doors, poisoned wines, and the rest of it would convince nobody. Melodrama, that middle-class offspring of the romantic drama, is even more dead and no one wants it any more. Its false sentimentality, its complications of stolen children, recovered documents, its brazen improbabilities, have all brought it into such scorn that any attempt to revive it would be met with laughter. The great works of 1830 will remain as struggles, as literary dates and as colossal attempts to overthrow the old classical traditions. But now it is all thrown overboard and the cloaks and the daggers have had their day. The time has come to produce plays of reality. To replace the classical tradition by the romantic tradition would be refusing to profit by the liberty gained for us by our elders. There must no longer be a school, a formula or a high priest of any kind. There is only life, an immense field where each can study and create in his own way.

I am not merely making out an argument for my own cause. It is my profound conviction—and I insist on this point—that the experimental and scientific spirit of the age is going to reach the theatre and that it is from this direction only that regeneration of our stage can come.

Let the critics look around and tell me any other source from which we can expect a reviving breath of life. The past, indeed, is dead. We must look to the future and the future is the human problem studied within the bounds of reality; it is the abandonment of all legendary tales; it is the living drama of characters and the environments, purged of all nursery tales, historical rag bags, magniloquence, trivialities, and conventional heroics. The rotten framework of the drama of yesterday has brought about its own downfall. There must be a clean sweep. The well-known tricks for introducing and unraveling a plot have been worked to death; what is needed now is a broad and simple portrayal of men and affairs—the kind of drama Molière might have written. Apart from certain conventions which are theatrically necessary, what is today called theatrical technique is nothing but a collection of meaningless little tricks, a sort of narrow tradition which brings the stage into contempt and a code of conventional language which no original mind would stoop to employ.

Furthermore, naturalism is already making its hesitant voice heard in the theatre. I do not want to mention any one work but among plays produced in recent years there are some which contain the germ of the movement of which I have been speaking. Leaving aside for the moment the younger writers, I am speaking especially of certain plays by dramatic authors who have grown old in their profession and who are clever enough to have some idea of the literary transformation which is taking place. Either the drama will die or it will become modern and realistic.

It is under the influence of these ideas that I have made a play of *Thérèse Raquin*. As I have said, the novel contained a subject, characters, and an environment and I considered that these provided first-class elements for my project. I could make a purely human study free of all irrelevancies and going straight to the target. The action lies not in some story or other but in the inner conflicts of the characters. It was not a matter of portraying facts but of working out feelings and attitudes of mind. The ending became the mathematical solution of a set problem. So I followed the novel step by step. I made the one damp, dark room the setting for the play so that nothing should detract from its atmosphere and sense of fate. I chose ordinary, colorless, subsidiary characters to show the banality of everyday life behind the excruciating agonies of my chief protagonists. In constructing the play I have tried to stress the ordinary occupations of my characters so that they shall not appear to be "acting" but "living" before the public. I was, I confess, counting—and with some reason—on the poignancy of the drama to make the audience accept this absence of plot and this minute attention to detail. The attempt has succeeded and it has made me even happier for my future plays than for *Thérèse Raquin*, for I am publishing this with a vague regret—with a foolish desire to change whole scenes.

There has been stormy criticism and my play has been the subject of violent discussion. I do not complain and I am even grateful for it. I have had my reward in hearing praise of the novel from which it was taken—that novel which, when it appeared, was treated so harshly. Today the novel is good; it is the play that is worthless. It is to be hoped that I can write something else which will be condemned and then perhaps the play will be acclaimed. Now in the matter of criticism one must know how to read between the lines. How, for instance, would it be possible for those old champions of the 1830 drama to be kind to *Thérèse Raquin?* All very well if my haberdasher heroine were a queen and if my murderer wore an apricot-colored jerkin! At the end, too, Thérèse and Laurent should have drunk the poison from a golden cup filled with the wine of Syracuse! Down with this shop-parlor stuff! Down with these common people who permit themselves to be the center of a drama round their oilcloth-covered table! Even if they had discovered some merit in my work, the old romantics would certainly have denied it with the noble injustice of literary passion. Then there are the critics whose beliefs are opposed to mine. These have tried quite honestly to prove me mistaken in following a path which was not theirs. I have read them carefully and I will try to profit by the fair comments which especially struck me. Finally, I have to thank those critics who were altogether sympathetic, those of my own age and with similar aspirations—for sad to relate, one rarely finds support among one's elders. We must grow up each with his own generation, impelled forward by those coming after us and finally emerging with the views and methods of our own time. And here is the final balance sheet of the criticism of *Thérèse Raquin*. Both Shakespeare and Paul de Kock have been mentioned; between these two there is room for me to dwell at ease.

It rests for me to express publicly all my gratitude to M. Hippolyte Hostein who has been so good as to give his whole artistic hospitality to my play. I found in him not merely a play producer but a friend, a colleague with a broad and original mind. But for him *Thérèse Raquin* would have remained long at the back of a drawer. To rescue it, it took an unhoped-for meeting with a manager who believed as I did in the necessity for reviving the drama by looking to the realities of the modern world. While an operetta was making one of his neighbors rich, it was magnificent to see M. Hippolyte Hostein in the height of summer, wanting to lose money with my drama. He has my eternal gratitude.

As for the artists who interpreted the play, they achieved one of the most outstanding successes ever experienced in the theatre. It gave me the greatest joy both to see what I had imagined come to life so fully and also to have given them the opportunity of employing all their wonderful resources.

Mme Marie Laurent in very truth created the part of Mme Raquin. I claim very little credit for it. It was she who discovered all that there was in that amazing character in Act IV, that towering figure of punishment, mute and relentless, those two living eyes fastened on the guilty pair, never ceasing to watch them even in the throes of death. Her simple good nature in Act I, her Mother's grief in Act II, the terrifying climax of Act III, in all she gave a magnificent performance and this part will remain as one of her most amazing creations. Mlle Dica-Petit was a Thérèse such as I had never hoped to find. She showed herself possessed of unexpected talent. Even her admirers were surprised at her interpretation of this complex character, this type of passionate woman, a whole world in herself, who goes from frantic love to fierce hatred passing through moods of hypocrisy, disgust, and terror, all the shades of passion and of normal human feelings. The reality of her screams lifted her audience from their seats. From now on, she is in the first rank of great creative actresses. Still another tremendous part to play is that of Laurent and M. Maurice Desrieux carried it off incomparably. He was in turn that great idle, cautious fellow who loves Thérèse "because she costs him nothing," then the lover whose mistress drives him so mad with love that she makes him a murderer, and then the poor creature refined by suffering and grown cowardly, his mind deranged to the point of hallucination who drifts towards a second crime which is to wipe out the first. Particular mention should be made of his ghastly stupefaction in Acts III and IV, his wild beast moans and all the signs of incipient madness hammering at a man's brain. And it was not only this terrible trio, the mother and the two murderers, who gave good performances. The production was such that the minor roles stood out as I never dared to hope. M. Grivot played the part of Camille, that sickly, spoilt, obstinate creature, with rare intelligence, bringing out the bourgeois miserliness and the sickly health remarkably well. M. Montrouge made an unforgettable type of comic reality of the old clerk Grivet, without ever overstepping the mark and with a tact and finesse just short of caricature, giving evidence of a really cultured mind for which I am infinitely grateful. M. Reykers really got into the skin of the retired police superintendent with the head, walk, and voice, even the mannerisms and the rough good humor of the profession. Finally, Mlle Blanche Dunoyer was the roguish smile of this dark drama, the music of the sixteen-year-old alternating with the solo of *Thérèse*, and her telling of the Blue Prince story was exquisite.

I say what a captain should say to his men the day after the battle. My thanks to all these great artists; it is to them alone I owe the victory.

NATURALISM IN THE THEATRE (1881)

The Sets and Props

I. I wish to discuss the naturalist movement that is taking place in the theatre solely with regard to the sets and props. As we know, there are two quite opposite opinions on this issue: one holds that the stage should be kept bare, as in the classical set, the other insists on an exact reproduction of the environment, however complicated it may be. I obviously hold the latter opinion; but I need to explain why.

Let us explore the question by reviewing the history of our nation's theatre. The ancient fairground *parade*, the mystery acted out on wooden stages, all those scenes spoken in the open air which gave rise to the perfect, harmonious tragedies and comedies of the seventeenth century, were performed between three scraps of material hanging from poles. The imagination of the public supplied the missing set. Later, with Corneille, Molière and Racine, each theatre had a public square, a salon, a forest, a temple; the forest was hardly ever used, I believe. The unity of place, which was a strictly observed rule, accounted for the lack of variety. Only one set was needed for each play; and since, in addition, all the characters had to encounter one another in that set, the authors inevitably kept using the same neutral environment, so that the same salon, the same road, the same temple kept on being adapted for every conceivable kind of action.

I emphasize this because here we are dealing with the well-spring of our tradition. We must not presume that this uniformity, this elimination of the set was due to the primitive conditions of the period or to the art of scene painting still being in its infancy. The sumptuous use of painted scenery and extraordinarily complicated machinery in the productions of certain operas and court plays of the time is proof to the contrary. Rather it was the aesthetic of the period that dictated a neutral role for the set.

One need only attend any of our own contemporary productions of a classical tragedy or comedy to realize that the set never has any effect on the development of the play. Servants sometimes bring on seats or a table and occasionally even place them right in the middle of a street. The other furniture, the mantelpieces, and all the rest, is painted on the backdrop, and it all

A new translation by Jane House © 2000.

seems quite natural. The action takes place nowhere in particular, the characters are symbols on display, and not complex personalities who live and breathe. I am not questioning the classical model here; I am simply stating that the reasoning, the character analyses, the dialogue examining the passions, which took place before the prompter's box without the environment ever playing any role, stood out all the more strongly because the background was minimized.

What we must accept as a proven truth is that the seventeenth century was indifferent to the truthfulness of the setting because natural surroundings, environments, were not then perceived as a force capable of having any influence whatsoever on the action or the characters. In the literature of that time, nature counted for little. Man alone was noble, and what is more, man stripped of his humanity, abstract man, studied for the way he functioned as a rational being and creature of passions. What was a landscape in the theatre? Real landscapes, like the open stretches we see before us in rain or shine, were never shown. Why create a fully appointed salon, with life warming it and giving it an existence of its own? The characters weren't made of flesh-and-blood, they didn't live there, they were only passing through to declaim their lines.

This is the formula from which our theatre set out. I cannot give a chronological account of the phases it has undergone. But it is easy to see that a slow but continuous movement has taken place lending more importance each day to the influence of the environment. Moreover, the evolution of literature over the past two centuries is entirely due to this invasion of nature. Man has ceased to be alone; the countryside, towns, and contrasting skies have become accepted as worthy of study and of serving as a vast framework for humankind. This was taken even further; it was maintained that it was impossible to know man well unless he was analyzed along with his clothing, his home, his native region. From that point on, abstract characters disappeared. Individual people were now presented living contemporary lives.

It was inevitable that this evolution should infiltrate the theatre. I know that certain critics see the theatre as something immutable, a sacred art that must remain inviolate. But that's simply laughable and the facts belie it every day. The setting already played a part in the tragedies of Voltaire; then came the fantastic sets and incredible scenic effects of the romantic dramas; Scribe gave us balls danced in the recesses of the salon; and finally we have seen a real cherry tree in *L'Ami Fritz*, an impressionist painter's studio in *La Cigale*, and the amazingly accurate clubhouse atmosphere in *Le Club*. Were one to undertake a thorough study, one would see all the transitional phases and become convinced that the results confronting us today were prepared for and gradually brought about by the evolution of our literature.

Let me repeat myself, the better to make myself understood. The problem, as I've said, is that the critics want to isolate the theatre, to see it as a completely separate entity. Certainly, it has its own perspective. But does it not always conform to the spirit of the times? Today, accuracy of setting is a consequence of our obsessive need for reality. The theatre was bound to submit to this impetus, once the novel had become nothing but an all-embracing inquest, a detailed report drawn up about each fact of life. Our modern, individualized characters, acting under the sway of environmental influences, living our lives on stage, would look perfectly ridiculous in a seventeenth-century setting. They sit down, so they need chairs; they write, so they need tables; they go to bed, they get dressed, they eat, they warm themselves, and they need all the furnishings. In addition, we investigate all possible worlds; our plays take us into every imaginable place; a great variety of tableaux must necessarily pass before the footlights. That is what our present-day dramatic model demands.

The theory of those critics who are irritated by such meticulous reproduction is that it is destructive of audience attention when the play is performed. I confess I do not understand. They maintain the thesis that only the furniture or objects used as props should be real; the rest should be painted on the scenery. Then, when the spectator sees an armchair, he murmurs: "Ah! ha! the character is going to sit down;" or else, when he sees a carafe on a piece of furniture: "Look! the character is going to get thirsty;" or else, if there is an embroidery basket in the foreground: "All right! the heroine is going to embroider while she listens to someone's declaration of love." I am not making any of this up; it seems some people find these childish guessing games very amusing. When the salon is completely furnished, when it is full of knickknacks, it disconcerts them, and they are tempted to cry out: "It's not theatre!"

Indeed, it is not theatre, if one persists in regarding theatre as the triumph of convention. We are told: "No matter what you do, there are conventions that are timeless." True, but that does not prevent a convention from disappearing once its hour has come. Unity of place has been put to rest once and for all; there is nothing astonishing about the fact that we are about to complete the process by making the scenery as accurate as possible. It is a continuation of the same course of evolution. The conventions that endure have nothing in common with those that disappear. One less is always a good thing.

How can one not sense the excitement that accurate scenery brings to the action? Accurate scenery, a drawing-room for example with its furniture, its flower stands, its knickknacks, immediately establishes a situation, tells us what world we are in, reveals the characters' habits. And since the actors feel at home there, how convincingly they live the life they have to live! It's a private place, a charming and natural nook. I know that, to appreciate this, one must love seeing actors live the play, instead of seeing them play it. This is a totally new model. Scribe, for example, does not need real surroundings, because his characters are cardboard cut-outs. I am only talking about accurate settings for plays with flesh-and-blood characters who bring with them the air that they breathe.

A critic very wisely said: "In the old days, real characters used to move around in sham settings; today, it is sham characters who move around in real settings." That is right, except that the types in classical tragedy and comedy are true, without being real. They possess a general truth, the great human traits summed up in beautiful verse; but they do not possess an individual truth, living and acting, as we understand it today. As I have tried to prove, the scenery of the seventeenth century was admirably suited to the characters of the theatre of the time; both lacked the particular; the scenery was of large dimensions, kept to a minimum, quite appropriate for the development of rhetoric and the depiction of superhuman heroes. Thus I think it is nonsense to restage the tragedies of Racine, for example, with a lavish display of costumes and sets.

But the critic is absolutely right when he says that today sham characters are acting in real sets. In each of my essays, I make no other complaint. The naturalist evolution in the theatre inevitably began with the material aspect, with the exact reproduction of the environment. That, really, was the most accessible approach. The audience could easily be won over. Furthermore, the evolutionary process had been at work for a long time. But sham characters are less easy to transform than wings and backdrops, because it means finding a man of genius. Although the set painters and machinists have sufficed for part of the task, the dramatic authors have yet to do anything more than grope in the dark. And it is amazing that a precisely reproduced setting has sometimes been enough to create a smash hit.

In conclusion, is this not a truly characteristic sign? One would have to be blind not to grasp where we are going. The critics who complain about this concern for accuracy in sets and props were only seeing one side of the issue. It is much more vast, it embraces the literary movement of the entire century, it is part of the irresistible current that is sweeping us all towards naturalism. M. Sardou, in *Les Merveilleuses*, wanted to use Directoire cups; Mssrs. Erckmann-Chatrian insisted on a fountain with real running water in *L'Ami Fritz*; M. Gondinet, in *Le Club*, demanded all the authentic props of a clubhouse. People may smile, shrug their shoulders, and say that it does not make the work any better. But, behind the obsessions of these meticulous authors, there runs more or less haphazardly the great idea of an art of method and analysis, advancing side by side with science. A writer will undoubtedly come who will at last put on the stage real characters in real settings, and then people will understand.

Costumes

II. [...] In fact, the great evolution of naturalism, which has occurred from the fifteenth century to our own, correlates totally with the gradual substitution of psychological man for metaphysical man. In tragedy, metaphysical man, man of dogma and logic, held absolute sway. Since the body did not count for anything, since the soul was viewed as the only interesting part of the human machine, every drama took place in the abstract, in the mind alone. Consequently, of what use was the tangible world? Why be concerned about the place where the action happened? Why be astonished at a strange costume, at a false declamatory style? Why notice that queen Dido was a boy whose sprouting beard obliged him to wear a mask? All of that was unimportant, one did not descend to such trifles, one listened to the play as if it were a school essay on a given topic. It was happening above man, in the realm of ideas, so distant from real man that any reality in a production would have been irritating.

The point of departure was a religious one in the mysteries, a philosophical one later on in tragedy. And from the beginning natural man, suffocated by rhetoric and dogma, thrashed about silently, wanted to get free, struggled long and futilely to do so, and finally established himself limb by limb. The entire history of our theatre lies in this victory of physiological man who, each century, came more into view from behind the mannequin of religious and philosophical idealism. Corneille, Molière, Racine, Voltaire, Beaumarchais, and in our time, Victor Hugo, Emile Augier, Alexandre Dumas *fils*, even Sardou, had only one goal, even though they did not clearly understand it themselves: to heighten the reality of the dramatic work, to make advances into truth, to liberate natural man more and more and bring him into the public eye. And, inevitably, this evolution will not stop with them, it will continue forever. Mankind is very young. [...]

III. Now I will deal with the present era, and respond to those critics who are amazed at our war on conventions. For them, truth has been pushed to its absolute limit on the stage; in short, everything has been done, our forebears have left us nothing to accomplish. I've already shown, I think, that the naturalist movement that has been carrying us along since the very beginning of our nation's theatre will not be able to stop for a minute; it is necessary and continuous, reflecting the very essence of our nature. But that doesn't suffice, one must always look at the facts, if one wants to be clear and conclusive.

I readily concede that we have achieved great accuracy in historical costumes. Today, when one stages a play of some importance set in France or abroad, during more or less distant times, one copies the costumes from the documents of the period, one makes a point of doing everything to obtain absolute authenticity. I am skipping over the little ways of cheating, the sloppy methods hidden behind an excessive show of zeal. There's also the issue of women's vanity; actresses still often shrink from wearing strange and uncomfortable clothes which make them look ugly; so they solve the problem by using a bit of imagination, they change the cut, add jewelry, invent a hairdo.

Despite that, the ensemble still passes muster; proof that an irresistible movement has taken place in the theatre, one determined by the past fifty years of historical research. Once researchers unearthed engravings and texts of all sorts, and once this expansion of knowledge made bygone ages more widely familiar, it was natural for the public to demand an exact reconstruction of past times on the stage. Hence, this is not just a whim or a passing fad, but the result of a logical intellectual journey.

So, if tradition still preserves some bizarre anachronisms, inexplicable flights of fancy in plays that were acted thirty years ago, it is rare today, when one produces an historical play, not to be concerned with the accuracy of the costumes. The movement will be even more focussed, and the truth complete, once the women are induced not make an historical play the excuse for wearing resplendent attire while sitting by the fireside and even when traveling; because, beyond accuracy of costume, there is appropriateness of costume, which brings me to the question of dress in our modern plays.

Here, for the men it is simple as can be. They dress like you and me. Some, such as comic actors, overdo the eccentric side, which makes them lose grasp of the character. One must see how effective an accurate costume can be in order to understand how much life it adds to the character. But the major issue is still the one regarding the women. In plays where the roles demand great simplicity of dress, achieving that simplicity is almost impossible; one runs up against willful vanity, which is all the more pervasive because here the women do not have the picturesqueness of historical or foreign costumes to cheat with. You may be able to get an actress to drape a beggar's rags over her shoulders, but you will never persuade her to dress as a simple working-class girl, if she has lost the first bloom of her beauty and knows that cheap clothes make her look ugly. For her, it is sometimes a vital question, because beside the actress there stands the woman who often experiences the need to be beautiful.

And here we have the reason why costuming in our contemporary plays is almost always false: a fear of simplicity, a refusal to accept the characters' social status when those characters tend toward the repulsive or ridiculous in dress. Moreover, there is also the mania for beautiful clothes evident even in the general public's taste. For example, during the last years of the Empire exhibitions of the designs of the great *couturiers* were seen at the Vaudeville and the Gymnase theatres and these shows continue today. A play cannot take place in a wealthy milieu without the actresses immediately vying over who has the most expensive outfit. In a pinch, these lavish costumes can be justified; but what is unfortunate is the importance they assume. Once that happens, since the public finds the clothes more exciting than the dialogue, authors are reduced to turning out plays solely as vehicles for ostentatious display of the latest fashions; and the aim becomes to increase the play's chances for success by deliberately selecting a setting which calls for a show of wealth.

The day after an opening, the press is as interested in the clothes as in the play; all Paris talks about them, a large number of male spectators and especially of the female spectators come to the theatre to look at so-and so's blue dress or so-and-so's new hat.

No great harm is done it will be said. But, I'm sorry, great harm is done! Beneath a hypocritical pretense at reality, success is sought by means of something extraneous to the works themselves. Moreover, these stunning costumes are unreal in their stately uniformity. No one dresses like that every hour of the day, people do not continuously pose like fashion plates. And this exorbitant taste for costly attire is disastrous because it compels authors to depict an artificial world, one of conventional elegance. Who would dare risk having a play take place among the drab bourgeoisie, or among petty merchants, or among the common folk, when the public insists on dresses costing five or six thousand francs! So the note is forced, provincial bourgeois ladies are dressed like duchesses, or a woman of loose morals is brought on so that there's at least one eye-catching flourish of silk and velvet. Three acts or five acts of nothing but woolen dresses would seem insane; ask a clever craftsman if he would risk five acts without the obligatory *grande toilette* or formal dress.

And so truth in the theatre continues to suffer. There is as much reluctance in choosing costumes that are too cheap as in introducing a bold innovation in staging. Not a single play by Mssrs. Augier, Dumas and Sardou has dared to pass up fashionable dress, not a single one portrays the humble who wear materials costing 18 sous per meter; so that a whole social class, the vast majority of human beings, finds itself virtually excluded from the theatre. Until now, the well-to-do bourgeoisie has been the outer limit. If the lower classes, workers and petty functionaries earning 1200 francs, have appeared in the theatre, it has been in utterly false melodramas, peopled by dukes and marquesses, lacking any literary merit or serious analysis of society. And you may be sure that the question of costume plays a large part in the exclusion of these people from the stage.

Our modern clothes, it's true, make for a poor spectacle. As soon as we leave the confines of bourgeois tragedy, circumscribed by four walls, as soon as we try to use the breadth of large stages and show crowd scenes, we find ourselves quite at a loss, put off by the monotony and uniform gloom of the extras. I think that, under the circumstances, we should make use of the variety offered by the mixture of classes and professions. Thus, to make myself clear, I can imagine an author setting one act in the square of the central market district, *Les Halles*, in Paris. The setting would be wonderful, teeming with life and bold in arrangement. Yes, surely, in this vast setting, it would be possible to create a very picturesque whole, showing the market porters with their huge hats, the tradeswomen with their white aprons and brightly colored scarves, the shoppers in silk and wool and printed calico, ranging from the ladies accompanied by their maids to the roving beggar women scrounging for peelings. Moreover, all one need do is go to *Les Halles* and look. There is nothing more colorful or interesting. All Paris would like to see this setting, if it were reproduced with the right degree of accuracy and scope.

And how many other settings for popular dramas there are for the taking! The interior of a factory, inside a mine, a gingerbread fair, a railway station, a flower market, a racetrack, etc. All the sites of modern life can be put on stage. It will be objected that these settings have already been attempted. Of course, in the fairy-tale spectaculars we have seen factories and railway stations; but they were fairy-tale factories and stations, in other words, settings hastily thrown together to produce a more or less complete illusion. What would be needed is meticulous reproduction. And that would inevitably mean costumes suited to the different professions, not lavish costumes, but costumes that would serve the truth of the tableaux and make them interesting. Since everyone laments the death of the drama, our dramatic authors should really attempt this genre of popular and contemporary drama. They could fulfill both the need for spectacle which the public experiences and the requirements of exact research which becomes more essential every day. But one would hope that the playwrights show us the real common man and not those sniveling workers who play such strange roles in boulevard melodramas.

Moreover, I shall never tire of repeating after M. Adolphe Jullien that everything is interdependent in the theatre. Truth in costuming requires truth in setting, in diction, in the plays themselves. Everything walks in step down the path of naturalism. When the costumes become more exact, it's because the settings are that way too, because the actors are freeing themselves from bombastic declamation, and finally because the plays study reality more closely and put on stage people who are more real. I could also make the same observations about settings that I've just made about costume. Here too, while we seem to have reached the total sum of truth possible, we still have great strides to make. The essential point is to increase illusion by reproducing environments more for their dramatic usefulness than for their picturesqueness. The environment should determine the character. Once a setting is studied from this point of view, so that it gives the impression of a description by Balzac come to life; once, at the curtain's rise, we get our first idea about the people in the play, about their character traits and their habits, merely by looking at the place where they live, we will perhaps understand how important an accurate setting can be. That's where we're heading, clearly; environments, the study of which has transformed the sciences and humanities, must inevitably assume an important place in the theatre; and I return here to the issue of metaphysical man, of abstract man who was satisfied with three walls in tragedy, while the physiological man of our modern works insists more and more imperiously on being determined by the setting and environment of which he is the product. One can see then that the road to progress is still long, as much for stage design as for costuming. We are onto the truth, but we are barely able to stammer it.

Another very important point is diction. Of course, we have gone beyond monotonous recitative chant and seventeenth-century plain-song. But we still use a theatrical voice, a false mode of recitation which is very obvious and very disagreeable. The trouble stems from the fact that most of the critics turn traditions into an immutable code; they found the theatre in a certain state, and instead of looking to the future, and making judgments about developments that are happening and will happen based on past developments, they stubbornly defend what remains of the old conventions, swearing that these relics are absolutely necessary. Ask them why, show them the road already traveled, they will give no logical response, they will reply with assertions based only on the state of things that is on the verge of disappearing.

As for diction, the trouble lies in the claim these critics make that the theatre has a language of its own. Their theory is that one should not speak on stage as one actually does in everyday life; and to support this point of view, they draw their examples from tradition, from what has been the case in the past and what is still the case today, without taking into account the naturalist movement, the phases of which M. Jullien established for us in his book. Please understand that there is absolutely no such thing as a language of the theatre; once there was a rhetorical style which has become progressively weaker and which is about to die out, those are the facts. If for a moment you compare the declamatory style of actors in the age of Louis XIV with Lekain's, and if you then compare Lekain's declamation with the style of artists today, you will clearly establish the phases of tragic song ultimately leading to our quest for the right tone, the natural tone, the ring of truth. Since then, the language of the theatre, that more resonant kind of language, has been disappearing. We are moving toward simplicity, toward the exact word, spoken without bombast, quite naturally. I could give endless examples if I had the space! Consider Geoffroy's power over the public, all his talent lies in his naturalness; he captivates his public because he speaks on stage as he speaks at home. When a phrase does not have the ring of everyday speech, he cannot say it, the author must find another.

There you have a sweeping condemnation of the supposed language of the theatre. Moreover, listen to the delivery of a talented actor, and watch the audience: the applause begins, the house gets excited, when a truthful inflection gives the spoken words the exact value they should have. All the great stage triumphs are victories over convention.

Alas! yes, there is a language of the theatre: it consists of those clichés, those resounding platitudes, those hollow words that roll around like empty barrels, all that unbearable rhetoric in our farces and our dramas that is beginning to make us smile. It would be interesting to study the question of style in such talented writers as Augier, Dumas and Sardou; I would have much to criticize, especially in the last two, who use a language of convention, a language of their own which they put in the mouths of all their characters, whether men, women, children, or old people, regardless of their sex or age. That seems wrong to me, because each character has his own way of talking, and if one wants to create living beings, one must present them to the public, not only in accurate costumes and in environments that determine their lives, but also with their own personal ways of thinking and of expressing themselves. I repeat that this is the clear goal toward which our theatre is moving. There is no language of the theatre regulated by a code as cadenced phrasing and as sonority; there is simply more and more accurate dialogue, which follows or rather leads the progress of sets and costumes down the path of naturalism. When plays grow more truthful, the actors' diction will inevitably gain in simplicity and naturalness.

To conclude, I will repeat that the war on conventions is far from being won and that it will probably always be with us. Today we are beginning to see clearly where we are going, but we are still wading through deep waters as rhetoric and metaphysics finally thaw.

AUGUST STRINDBERG

August STRINDBERG (1849-1912) was tall and slim, with a small chin, towering forehead, and a lion's fluffy mane streaked with gray. Delicate and gentle in manner, he loved flowers, tended to weep easily, and was subject to quick mood changes. Vain about his appearance, he took at least half an hour to get dressed in the morning and was continually straightening his moustache.

He smiled the strange smile of "a child who is headed straight into the woods of fairy land," but dressed like a Berlin dandy in a "suit of large-checkered design with large cuffs on the pants, a short yellowish-gray topcoat, a loud necktie, a cane of exaggerated size, and a well-polished silk hat."

"Once you had seen his face, you could not forget it, it was so striking," an admiring student wrote of his first impressions. "His hair, rich, brushed up, black—even if already sprinkled with silver threads—fell in soft, moist locks round his head and over his enormous, beautifully shaped forehead, which dominated his whole face. It was like the mountain in a landscape. Everything sunny and dark was reflected on those heights.

"The big, light-gray eyes with their black irises, almost like a horse's, looked round timidly and with an expression of dejection. Weary, sorrowful eyes, as if washed in tears. Everything, moreover, in Strindberg's manner testified to his shyness. His tread was noiseless, and with downcast eyes he took a seat." He was so shy that he preferred letter-writing to face-to-face contact, even with those living in the same house.

Le Figaro described another Strindberg, public and Parisian, who had "a majestic forehead crowned by anarchic locks; pale blue eyes; taciturn, tall, and lanky, acts as if he were on an apostolic mission." For his return to Sweden, Strindberg decided to transform his image by exchanging his dark Flying Dutchman cape for a flashy belted jacket. "Your old daddy," he wrote home, "has become a young sport. Got himself some new, painless teeth, a new outfit with knickerbockers and bicycle stockings, yellow shoes and gloves. No longer a chimney sweep, but a bright vision of spring."

One of the most popular subjects of his day, Strindberg was always eager to sit for painters and sculptors, and being photographed became one of his favorite pastimes. A talented photographer in his own right, he experimented with color, contemplated a professional career, and took pictures of himself for a planned documentary with self-commentaries.

For a bargain $134 Henrik Ibsen bought Christian Krogh's large portrait of Strindberg in his Flying Dutchman cape. The Norwegian playwright retitled the portrait "The Outbreak of Madness" and hung it on the wall of his study over his desk so that the madman with his demonic eyes would be staring down at him. "He is my mortal enemy, and shall hang there and watch while I write," Ibsen explained, "I think he looks so delightfully mad."

Endowed with multiple selves, the playwright suffered from alien incarnations and claimed that there were Strindberg impersonators at large. Careers as novelist, painter, photographer, musician, linguist, historian, and scientist occupied him at different times, but for Strindberg playwriting and performance were the most natural forms of expression. "I found it easiest to write plays," he avowed, claiming that he could write a drama every two weeks. Twice married to actresses, the foremost actors were his close friends, he spent his time advising performers how to play their roles, and he started a theatre in Copenhagen and, with the actor August Falck, ran the Intimate Theatre in Stockholm devoted to staging his own work. He had been a performer himself in his early days, working as a bit player in a theatre in Göteborg and singing Swedish university student songs, obscene and sad, to his own accompaniment on guitar.

Strindberg was sensitive to what was happening in the various arts and responsive to new trends, theorists, and artists, relabeling his works according to the latest movements of the day. When *The Father* was produced in Paris in the mid-1890s at the Théâtre de l'Oeuvre, Strindberg called it symbolist to bring it up to date. *Miss Julie* was in part inspired by Strindberg's correspondence with Nietzsche and his reading of the German philosopher's works, to whom he paid eloquent homage: "My spiritual being has received in its uterus a tremendous ejaculation by Friedrich Nietzsche, so that I feel as full as a pregnant bitch. That's my man."

Strindberg followed closely the program presented by André Antoine at the Théâtre Libre and took an active interest in the young Max Reinhardt, trying to adapt to the German's new directorial principles by calling four of his late dramas chamber plays after Reinhardt's Kammertheater and giving them opus numbers in homage to Beethoven (whose mask hung on his wall).

After his return to Stockholm in 1899, the playwright held regular musical soirées with a group of friends, both amateur and professional performers known familiarly as the "Beethoven boys." "Beethoven endures, everything else is transient," Strindberg declared. He read *The Art of the*

Theatre by Gordon Craig whom he met in Stockholm, but he was mistrustful of Craig's ideas about the actor and he refused to go see Isadora Duncan perform.

In his last years, Strindberg confessed, "I loathe the theatre. Pose! Superficiality, calculation." The playwright extended his antipathy to the entire breed of creators. "I have often believed deep down that artists are apes, conceited, rebels, lecherous, impudent, dishonest. Generally look like bandits."

PREFACE TO *MISS JULIE* (1888)

The theatre has long seemed to me to be, like art in general, a *Biblia pauperum*, a Bible in pictures for those who can't read what is written or printed, and the playwright a lay preacher hawking the ideas of the day in popular form, so popular that the middle classes, the theatre's primary audience, can understand the basic questions without too much effort. And so the theatre has always been a public school for the young, the half-educated, and women, who still possess that primitive capacity for deceiving themselves or letting themselves be deceived, that is to say, are receptive to the illusion, to the playwright's power of suggestion. It seems to me, therefore, in our time, when rudimentary, undeveloped, and fanciful ways of thinking seem to be evolving toward reflection, investigation, and analysis, that the theatre, like religion, is dying out, a form for whose enjoyment we lack the necessary preconditions. Supporting this assertion is the serious theatre crisis now prevailing throughout Europe, especially in those bastions of culture that produced the greatest thinkers of the age, England and Germany, where the art of drama, like most of the other fine arts, is dead.

In other countries people have believed it possible to create a new drama by filling old forms with new contents. For a number of reasons, however, this has failed: in part because there has not been sufficient time to popularize the new ideas, so that the public does not understand the basic questions; in part because partisan politics has stirred up emotions, making dispassionate enjoyment impossible—how can people be objective when their innermost beliefs are offended or when they are subjected in the confines of a theatre to the public pressure of an applauding or hissing audience?; and in part because new forms have not been found for the new contents, so that the new wine has burst the old bottles.

In the following play, instead of trying to do anything new—which is impossible—I have simply modernized the form in accordance with demands I think contemporary audiences make upon this art. Toward this end, I have chosen, or let myself be moved by, a theme that can be said to lie outside partisan politics since the problem of social climbing or falling, of higher or

From Strindberg, *Five Plays*, trans. Harry G. Carlson.
Berkeley: University of California Press, 1983.

lower, better or worse, man or woman, are, have been, and will be of lasting interest. When I took this theme from a true story I heard told some years ago, which made a strong impression on me, I found it appropriate for tragedy, for it still seems tragic to see someone favored by fortune go under, much more to see a family die out. Perhaps the time will come when we will be so advanced, so enlightened that we can witness with indifference what now seem the coarse, cynical, heartless dramas life has to offer, when we have closed down those lower, unreliable mechanisms of thought called feelings, because better developed organs of judgment will have found them superfluous and harmful. The fact that the heroine arouses compassion is because we are too weak to resist the fear that the same fate could overtake us. A hypersensitive spectator may not be satisfied with compassion alone, while a man with faith in the future may demand some positive proposals to remedy the evil, in other words, a program of some kind. But for one thing there is no absolute evil. The fall of one family can mean a chance for another family to rise, and the alternation of rising and falling fortunes is one of life's greatest delights since happiness lies only in comparison. And to the man who wants a program to remedy the unpleasant fact that the bird of prey eats the dove and the louse eats the bird of prey I ask: why should it be remedied? Life is not so idiotically mathematical that only the great eat the small; it is just as common for a bee to kill a lion or at least drive it mad.

If my tragedy depresses many people, it is their own fault. When we become as strong as the first French revolutionaries, it will afford nothing but pleasure and relief to witness the thinning out in royal parks of overage, decaying trees that have long stood in the way of others equally entitled to their time in the sun, the kind of relief we feel when we see someone incurably ill die!

Recently, my tragedy *The Father* was criticized for being too sad, as if one should expect cheerful tragedies. People clamor pretentiously for "the joy of life," and theatre managers call for farces, as if the joy of life lay in being silly and depicting people as if they were all afflicted with St. Vitus's dance or imbecility. I find the joy of life in its cruel and powerful struggles, and my enjoyment comes from being able to know something, being able to learn something. That is why I have chosen an unusual case, but one from which we can learn much—in a word an exception, but an important exception which proves the rule—though this will probably offend those who love the conventional and predictable. What will next shock simple minds is that I have not motivated the action in a simple way, nor is there a single point of view. Every event in life—and this is a rather new discovery!—is ordinarily the result of a whole series of more or less deeplying motives. The spectator, however, usually singles out the one that is either easiest for him to understand or is most advantageous to him personally. Take the case of a suicide. "Financial problems," says a businessman. "Unrequited love," says a woman. "Physical illness," says an invalid. "Dashed hopes," says a shipwrecked man. It might be that all or none of these were motives and that the deceased concealed the real motive by advancing a totally different one that would bring the most credit to his memory!

I have motivated Miss Julie's tragic fate by a great number of circumstances: her mother's primary instincts, her father raising her incorrectly, her own nature, and the influence of her fiancé on her weak and degenerate brain. Also, more particularly: the festive atmosphere of midsummer night, her father's absence, her monthly indisposition, her preoccupation with animals, the provocative effect of the dancing, the magical midsummer twilight, the powerfully aphrodisiac influence of flowers, and, finally, the chance that drives the couple together into a room alone—plus the boldness of the aroused man.

My treatment of the subject has thus been neither one-sidedly physiological nor exclusively psychological. I have not put the entire blame on what she inherited from her mother, nor on her monthly indisposition, nor on immorality. I have not even preached morality—this I left to the cook in the absence of a minister.

This multiplicity of motives, it pleases me to assert, is in keeping with the times. And if others have done it before me, then it pleases me that I have not been alone in my "paradoxes," as all discoveries are called.

As for characterization, I have made my people rather "characterless" for the following reasons: The word *character* has come to mean many things over the course of time. Originally, it must have meant the dominant trait in the soul complex and was confused with temperament. Later it became the middle-class expression for the automaton, one whose disposition was fixed once and for all or had adapted himself to a particular role in life. In a word, someone who had stopped growing was called a character. In contrast the person who continued to develop, the skillful navigator on the river of life, sailing not with sheets belayed, but veering before the wind to luff again, was called characterless—in a derogatory sense, of course—because he was so difficult to understand, classify, and keep track of. This bourgeois concept of the immobility of the soul was transferred to the stage, which the bourgeoisie has always dominated. There a character became a man who was ready-made; whenever he appeared, he was drunk or comical or sad. The only thing necessary to characterize him was to give him a physical defect—a clubfoot, a wooden leg, a red nose—or have him repeat an expression, such as "that was splendid" or "Barkis is willin'." This simplified view of human character still survives in the great Molière. Harpagon is nothing but a miser although he could have been not only a miser but an excellent financier, or splendid father and good citizen. What is worse is that his "defect" is very advantageous to his son-in-law and daughter, who are his heirs and therefore should not criticize him, even if they have to wait a bit before climbing into bed together.

Therefore, I do not believe in simple theatrical characters. And an author's summary judgments of people—this one is stupid, that one brutal, this one jealous, that one stingy—should be challenged by naturalists, who know how rich the soul-complex is and realize that "vice" has a reverse side closely resembling virtue.

As modern characters living in an age of transition more compulsively hysterical than the one that preceded it at least, I have depicted my people as more vacillating and disintegrating than their predecessors, a mixture of the old and the new. If the valet belches something modern from the depths of his ancient slave's soul, it is because I think it not improbable that through newspapers and conversations modern ideas filter down even to the level a servant lives on. There are those who find it wrong in modern drama for characters to speak Darwinism. At the same time they hold up Shakespeare as a model. I would like to remind these critics that the gravedigger in *Hamlet* speaks the fashionable philosophy of the day—Giordano Bruno's (Bacon's)—which is more improbable since there were fewer means then for the spread of ideas than there are now. Besides, "Darwinism" has existed in every age, ever since the description in Genesis of the steps in creation from lower animals to man. It is just that only now have we discovered and formulated it.

My souls (characters) are conglomerates of past and present cultural phases, bits from books and newspapers, scraps of humanity, pieces torn from fine clothes and become rags, patched together as is the human soul. I have also added a little evolutionary history by having the weaker mind steal and repeat words from the stronger. Ideas are induced through the power of suggestion: from other people, from the surroundings (the blood of the greenfinch), and from attributes (the straight razor); and I have inanimate objects (the Count's boots, the bell) serve as agents for *Gedankenübertragung* ["thought transference"]. Finally, I have used "open suggestion," a variation of sleeplike hypnosis, which is now so well known and popularized that it cannot arouse the kind of ridicule or skepticism it would have done in Mesmer's time.

Miss Julie is a modern character. Not that the man-hating half-woman has not existed in all ages but because now that she has been discovered, she has come out in the open to make herself heard. The half-woman is a type who pushes her way ahead, selling herself nowadays for power, decorations, honors, and diplomas, as formerly she used to do for money. The type implies a retrogressive step in evolution, an inferior species who cannot endure. Unfortunately, they are able to pass on their wretchedness; degenerate men seem unconsciously to choose their mates from among them. And so they breed, producing an indeterminate sex for whom life is a torture. Fortunately, the offspring go under either because they are out of harmony with reality or because their repressed instincts break out uncontrollably or because their hopes of achieving equality with men are crushed. The type is tragic, revealing the drama of a desperate struggle against Nature, tragic as the romantic heritage now being dissipated by naturalism, which has a contrary aim: happiness, and happiness belongs only to the strong and skillful species.

But Miss Julie is also: a relic of the old warrior nobility now giving way to a new nobility of nerve and intellect, a victim of her own flawed constitution, a victim of the discord caused in a family by a mother's "crime," a victim of the delusions and conditions of her age—and together these are the equivalent of the concept of Destiny, or Universal Law, of antiquity. Guilt has been abolished by the naturalist, along with God, but the consequences of an action—punishment, imprisonment or the fear of it—that he cannot erase for the simple reason that they remain, whether he pronounces acquittal or not. Those who have been injured are not as kind and understanding as an unscathed outsider can afford to be. Even if her father felt constrained not to seek revenge, his daughter would wreak vengeance upon herself, as she does here, out of an innate or acquired sense of honor, which the upper classes inherit—from where? From barbarism, from the ancient Aryan home of the race, from medieval chivalry. It is a beautiful thing, but nowadays a hindrance to the survival of the race. It is the nobleman's harikari, which compels him to slit open his own stomach when someone insults him and which survives in a modified form in the duel, that privilege of the nobility. That is why Jean, the servant, lives, while Miss Julie cannot live without honor. The slave's advantage over the nobleman is that he lacks this fatal preoccupation with honor. But in all of us Aryans there is something of the nobleman, or a Don Quixote. And so we sympathize with the suicide, whose act means a loss of honor. We are noblemen enough to be pained when we see the mighty fallen and as superfluous as a corpse, yes, even if the fallen should rise again and make amends through an honorable act. The servant Jean is a race-founder, someone in whom the process of differentiation can be detected. Born the son of a tenant farmer, he has educated himself in the things a gentleman should know. He has been quick to learn, has finely developed senses (smell, taste, sight) and a feeling for what is beautiful. He is already moving up in the world and is not embarrassed about using other people's help. He is alienated from his fellow servants, despising them as parts of a past he has already put behind him. He fears and flees them because they know his secrets, pry into his intentions, envy his rise, and look forward eagerly to his fall. Hence his dual, indecisive nature, vacillating between sympathy for people in high social positions and hatred for those who currently occupy those positions. He is an aristocrat, as he himself says, has learned the secrets of good society, is polished on the surface but coarse beneath, wears a frock coat tastefully but without any guarantee that his body is clean.

He has respect for Miss Julie, but is afraid of Kristine because she knows his dangerous secrets. He is sufficiently callous not to let the night's events disturb his plans for the future. With both a slave's brutality and a master's lack of squeamishness, he can see blood without fainting and shake off misfortune easily. Consequently, he comes through the struggle unscathed and will probably end up an innkeeper. And even if *he* does not become a Rumanian count, his son will become a university student and possibly a county police commissioner.

In any case he has important things to say about the lower classes' view of life—when he is telling the truth, that is, which he often does not do, for he is more interested in saying what is favorable to himself than in telling the truth. When Miss Julie says she assumes the lower classes feel oppressed from above, Jean naturally agrees since it is his intention to win sympathy, but he quickly changes his attitude when he realizes that it is more to his advantage to distance himself from the "rabble."

Apart from the fact that Jean is rising in the world, he is superior to Miss Julie because he is a man. Sexually, he is an aristocrat because of his masculine strength, his more keenly developed senses, and his capacity for taking the initiative. His sense of inferiority is mostly due to the social circumstances in which he happens to be living, and he can probably shed it along with his valet's jacket.

His slave mentality expresses itself in the fearful respect he has for the Count (the boots) and his religious superstition; but he respects the Count mainly as the occupant of the kind of high position to which he himself aspires; and the respect remains even after he has conquered the daughter of the house and seen how empty the lovely shell was.

I do not believe that love in any "higher" sense can exist between two people of such different natures, and so I have Miss Julie's love as something she fabricates in order to protect and excuse herself; and I have Jean suppose himself capable of loving her under other social circumstances. I think it is the same with love as with the hyacinth, which must take root in darkness *before* it can produce a sturdy flower. Here a flower shoots up, blooms, and goes to seed all at once, and that is why it dies so quickly.

Kristine, finally, is a female slave. Years standing over the stove have made her conventional and lethargic; instinctively hypocritical, she uses morality and religion as cloaks and scapegoats. A strong person would not need these because he can either bear his guilt or reason it away. Kristine goes to church as a quick and easy way to unload her household thefts on Jesus and to take on a new charge of innocence. Furthermore, she is a minor character, and I purposely simply sketched her in, as I did the minister and the doctor in *The Father*, because I wanted ordinary people, as country ministers and provincial doctors usually are. If my minor characters seem abstract to some people, it is because ordinary people are abstract to some extent in their occupations. As they carry out their duties, they lose their individuality, showing only one side of themselves, and as long as the spectator has no need to see them from several sides, my abstract depiction of them is probably correct.

As for the dialogue, I have broken with tradition somewhat by not making my characters catechists who ask stupid questions in order to elicit clever replies. I have avoided the symmetrical, mathematical, constructed dialogue of French drama and let characters' minds function irregularly, as they do in a real-life conversation, where no topic of discussion is exhausted entirely and one mind by chance finds a cog in another mind in which to engage. Consequently, the dialogue also wanders, presenting material in the opening scenes that is later taken up, reworked, repeated, expanded, and developed, like the theme in a musical composition.

The plot is serviceable enough, and since it really concerns only two people, I have concentrated on them, including only one minor character, the cook, and having the father's unhappy spirit hover over and behind the action. I have done this because I believe that people of today are most interested in the psychological process. Our inquisitive souls are not satisfied just to see something happen; we want to know how it happened. We want to see the strings, the machinery, examine the double-bottomed box, feel for the seam in the magic ring, look at the cards to see how they are marked.

In this regard I have kept in mind the monographic novels of the brothers Goncourt, which I find more appealing than anything else in contemporary literature.

As for the technical aspects of composition, I have experimented with eliminating act divisions. The reason is that I believe our dwindling capacity for accepting illusion is possibly further disturbed by intermissions, during which the spectator has time to reflect and thereby escape the suggestive influence of the author-hypnotist. My play will probably run an hour and a half, and since people can listen to a lecture, sermon, or conference discussion for just as long or longer, I imagine that a ninety-minute theatre piece will not be too tiring. I tested this concentrated form in 1872 in one of my first plays, *The Outlaw*, although with little success. The first draft was in five acts, and when I noticed the disjointed, restless effect it produced, I burned it. From the ashes rose a single, long, coherent act of fifty pages in print, with a playing time of one hour. And so the form is not new, and I seem to have a feel for it: changing tastes may make it timely. My hope for the future is to so educate audiences that they can sit through a one-act play that lasts an entire evening. But this will require experimentation. Meanwhile, in order to relax tension for the audience and the actors, without breaking the illusion for the audience, I have used three art forms traditionally associated with drama: monologue, mime, and ballet. The original association was with the tragedy of antiquity, monody having become monologue, and chorus, ballet.

Our realists today condemn the monologue as implausible, but if I motivate it, I can make it plausible and use it to advantage. It is perfectly plausible for an orator to pace the floor alone and practice his speech aloud, plausible for an actor to rehearse his lines aloud, for a servant girl to talk to her cat, a mother babble to her baby, an old maid jabber to her parrot, a sleeper talk in his sleep. And in order to give the actor a chance, for once, to work independently, free for a moment of the author's authority, I have sketched in the monologues rather than worked them out in detail. Since it is irrelevant what someone says in his sleep or to a parrot or to a cat, for this has no influence on the action, a talented actor, absorbed in the mood and the situation, perhaps can improvise the monologue more effectively than the author, who cannot determine in advance how much may be spoken, and for how long, before an audience senses that the illusion is broken.

As we know, some Italian theatres have returned to improvisation, producing actors who are creative in their own right, although in accordance with the author's intentions. This could be the beginning of a fertile new art form, something worthy of the name *creative*.

In places where a monologue would be implausible, I have resorted to mime, and here I leave the actor even greater freedom to be creative—and to win independent acclaim. But in order not to try the audience beyond its limits, I have let music—coming from the midsummer dance, and thus believably motivated—exercise its illusion evoking power during the sections of dumb show. I beg the music director to consider carefully his choice of pieces; the wrong mood may be produced if there are familiar selections from popular dances or operettas, or unusual folk melodies, no matter how ethnographically correct.

The ballet I have indicated cannot be replaced by a so-called "crowd scene" because crowd scenes are always badly acted, with a mob of grimacing idiots trying to use the occasion to appear clever and so disturb the illusion. And since uneducated people do not improvise when they wish to poke fun maliciously but use ready-made material that can take on a double meaning, I did not compose the taunting song they sing. Instead, I used a little-known dance song I discovered myself in the Stockholm area. The words are only approximately appropriate, but this is intentional, for the slyness (weakness) of the slave does not permit him to make a direct attack. And so the seriousness of the action forbids clowning; there must be no coarse sneering in a situation which closes the lid on a family coffin.

As for the scenery, I have borrowed from impressionist painting the device of making a setting appear cut off and asymmetrical, thus strengthening the illusion. When we see only part of a room and a portion of the furniture, we are left to conjecture, that is to say, our imagination goes to work and complements what is seen. I have also profited by doing away with those tiresome exits through doors because scenery doors, made of canvas, wobble at the slightest touch; they cannot even allow a father to express his anger after a bad dinner by going out and slamming the door behind him "so that the whole house shakes." (In the theatre it wobbles.) I have also confined the action to one setting, both to allow the characters more time to interact with their environment and to break with the tradition of expensive scenery. With only one setting we should be able to demand that it be realistic, but nothing is more difficult than to get a room on stage to look like a room, however easily the scene painter can produce flaming volcanoes and waterfalls. Even if the walls must be of canvas, it is surely time to stop painting shelves and kitchen utensils on them. We have so many other stage conventions in which we are asked to believe, we should not have to strain ourselves trying to believe in painted pots and pans.

I have placed the upstage wall and the table diagonally so that the actors can play facing the audience or in half-profile when they sit opposite each other at the table. I saw a diagonal backdrop in a production of *Aida*; it led the eye out into unknown vistas and did not look simply like a defiant reaction to the boredom of straight lines.

Another perhaps necessary innovation is the removal of footlights. The purpose of this lighting from below is said to be to make the actors' faces fatter, but I ask: why must all actors have fat faces? Does not this lighting obliterate many subtleties in the lower part of the face, especially the jaws, distort the shape of the nose, and cast shadows up over the eyes? Even if this were not so, one thing is certain: actors find it so painful for their eyes that they are unable to use them with full expressiveness. Footlights strike the retina in places usually protected (except in the case of seaman who have to look at the sun's reflection in the water), and so we seldom see anything but a crude rolling of the eyes, either to the side or up toward the balconies, exposing the whites. Perhaps this also accounts for the tedious habit, especially common among actresses, of blinking eyelashes. And when anyone on stage wants to speak with his eyes, he must resort to staring straight out, thus breaking the wall of the curtain line and coming into direct contact with the audience. Justly or unjustly, this unfortunate practice is called "greeting your friends."

Would not sufficiently strong side lighting (using parabolic reflectors, for example) provide the actor with a new advantage: the strengthening of mime effects through the most expressive asset in his face—the play of his eyes?

I have no illusions about getting the actor to play for the audience rather than with it, although this would be desirable. I cannot hope to see an actor play with his back to the audience throughout an entire important scene, though I wish very much that crucial scenes were staged, not next to the prompter's box, like duets intended to evoke applause, but in places more appropriate to the action. In other words, I call for no revolution, just small modifications, for to really transform the stage into a room where the fourth wall is removed, and consequently a portion of the furniture faces away from the audience, would probably, for the present, produce a disturbing effect.

When it comes to makeup, I dare not hope to be listened to by the ladies, who would rather be beautiful than believable. But the actor might consider whether it is really to his advantage when putting on makeup to fix an abstract character, like a mask, on his face. Picture an actor who has put the sharp, charcoal lines of anger of an old man between his eyes and then, with that incensed look, has to smile in response to someone else's line. What a terrible grimace there would be as a result! And how would the false forehead attached to his wig, bald as a billiard ball, wrinkle when the old man got angry?

In a modern psychological drama, where the subtlest movements of the soul must be revealed more through the face than through gesture and sound, it would probably be best to experiment with strong side lighting on a small stage, and with actors wearing no makeup, or at least a minimum of it.

If, in addition, we could avoid having the orchestra visible, its lights disturbing, and the musicians' faces turned toward the audience; if the seating in the auditorium were raised so that eye level for the spectator was higher than the hollow of the actor's knee; if we could get rid of stage boxes (behind bull's-eye openings), with their grinning late arrivals from dinners and supper parties; if we could have complete darkness during performances; and, finally, and most importantly, a *small* stage and a *small* auditorium, then perhaps we might see a new drama arise, or at the very least a theatre that was once again a place of entertainment for educated people. While waiting for this theatre, we will just have to go on writing, preparing the repertoire that will one day be needed.

Here is an attempt! If it fails, there is surely time enough for another!

MAURICE MAETERLINCK

Maurice MAETERLINCK (1862-1949) had a sturdy Flemish head, almond-shaped blue eyes, and large brow concealed beneath a rebellious forelock. He liked to run his long fingers through his thick head of hair. His complexion was pale, his lips thin, his mustache tidy. His gaze, hanging somewhere in mid air, was introspective. He spoke in a sing-song voice.

He dressed immaculately like a business man, but moved like a deer. Six foot one with broad shoulders and an athletic build, he took up boxing as a hobby and sparred with Kid McCoy and the French heavyweight champion Georges Carpentier. An apostle of silence, he rode a motorcycle and owned an early automobile, which he drove expertly at high speeds.

In 1890, at the beginning of his theatrical career, Maeterlinck argued that the accidental and human was antithetical to artistic masterpieces and maintained that it was necessary "to rid the stage of living human beings," who can speak only of the present moment, and replace them with shadows or projections of symbolic forms able "to wrest us from the power of our senses and to make the past and future prevail." Waxworks museums, he explained, revealed the extraordinary powers called forth by beings that had the appearance of life without being alive and thus were entitled to speak in the name of the myriad dead. The Belgian playwright proposed a new art of the dead and designated three of his early plays as "little dramas for marionettes."

Despite his theoretical rejection of the live actor, Maeterlinck attended rehearsals of his own plays and participated in the struggle to bring symbolism to the Parisian stage. Impressed by Ibsen's mastery of silence, stasis, and "dialogue of the second degree" (otherworldly subtext), he wrote an appreciative review of *The Master Builder* at the Théâtre de l'Oeuvre that later became "The Tragical in Daily Life."

In the years just prior to the First World War Maeterlinck and the singer Georgette Leblanc lived in Normandy at the ancient Abbey Saint Wandrille. Dressed in a short leather jacket and cap, wearing an old apron, Maeterlinck loved to work among his plants. Gardening unlocked the powers of life after death, enabling the poet to live in the past, present, and future simultaneously.

A gourmet and lover of fine wines, Maeterlinck covered the vast distances to the wine cellar across the immense stone floor of the Abbey on rollerskates. When Stanislavsky came to discuss the Moscow Art Theatre's forthcoming production, the Belgian, cap in hand, picked up his guest at the station and the Russian director, assuming the driver to be the chauffeur, climbed into the back seat and during the trip asked the servant many questions about his master—only realizing when they arrived that the driver was the author of *The Blue Bird*. In the summer, Georgette produced Maeterlinck's plays and *Macbeth* in the poet's own translation in an ambulatory theatre using natural settings and moving the audience from one ruined part of the Abbey to another.

Tone-deaf, Maeterlinck loathed music and most of all hated Debussy's operatic version of *Pelleas and Melisande*. When he learned that the composer would not cast Georgette Leblanc as Melisande for the premiere, the poet challenged Debussy to a duel and threatened to beat him with his walking stick.

An international celebrity after winning the Nobel prize in 1911, Maeterlinck was invited by Samuel Goldwyn to Hollywood to write film scenarios. He traveled across the country in a private railway car with a Chinese chef, Japanese valet, chambermaid, stenographer, and journalist dispatching daily reports. In a 1945 plagiarism suit (dropped after he returned to France), Maeterlinck claimed that one of the two scripts he wrote in Hollywood was used in Fritz Lang's *Woman in the Window*.

Maeterlinck, who was gifted with extra-sensory perception, was an early member of Psychical Research Society, and he corresponded with Sir Oliver Lodge, the British physicist who explored the possibility of communicating with the dead. Influenced by Emerson and the medieval Flemish mystic Ruysbroeck, he wrote books and essays dealing with the cosmic mysteries, reincarnation and metempsychosis, science, nature, and the animal world, including *The Life of Bees*, *The Intelligence of Flowers*, and *The Life of Termites*.

When the Catholic Church placed him on the Index Prohibitorum because of his writings on spiritualism, Maeterlinck's books were publicly burned in effigy in Ireland, Spain, and Austria.

Maeterlinck's friends and admirers included Albert Einstein, the Portuguese dictator Salazar (his late play *Father Setubal* was premiered in Lisbon in 1939), and the controversial Dr. Serge Voronoff, a rejuvenation expert who injected monkey glands into aging men to increase their sexual potency. Fleeing the Nazis, Maeterlinck arrived in New York in 1940 with an automobile, thirty pieces of luggage, two Pekinese dogs and two blue parakeets. During his exile in America, he gave lectures, but with a thin voice and an aversion to public occasions, he found lecturing distasteful. He preferred to remain silent.

THE TRAGICAL IN DAILY LIFE (1896)

There is a tragic element in the life of every day that is far more real, far more penetrating, far more akin to the true self that is in us than the tragedy that lies in great adventure. But, readily as we all may feel this, to prove it is by no means easy, inasmuch as this essential tragic element comprises more than that which is merely material or merely psychological. It goes beyond the determined struggle of man against man, and desire against desire: it goes beyond the eternal conflict of duty and passion. Its province is rather to reveal to us how truly wonderful is the mere act of living, and to throw light upon the existence of the soul, self-contained in the midst of ever-restless immensities; to hush the discourse of reason and sentiment, so that above the tumult may be heard the solemn, uninterrupted whisperings of man and his destiny. It is its province to point out to us the uncertain, dolorous footsteps of the being, as he approaches, or wanders from, his truth, his beauty, or his God. And further, to show us, and make us understand, the countless other things therewith connected, of which tragic poets have but vouchsafed us passing glimpses. And here do we come to an essential point, for could not these things, of which we have had only passing glimpses, be placed in front of the others, and shown to us first of all? The mysterious chant of the Infinite, the ominous silence of the soul and of God, the murmur of Eternity on the horizon, the destiny or fatality that we are conscious of within us, though by what tokens none can tell—do not these underlie King Lear, Macbeth, Hamlet? And would it not be possible, by some interchanging of the rôles, to bring them nearer to us, and send the actors farther off? Is it beyond the mark to say that the true tragic element, normal, deep-rooted, and universal, that the true tragic element of life only begins at the moment when so-called adventures, sorrows, and dangers have disappeared? Is the arm of happiness not longer than that of sorrow, and do not certain of its attributes draw nearer to the soul? Must we indeed roar like the Atrides, before the Eternal God will reveal Himself in our life? and is He never by our side at times when the air is calm, and the lamp burns on, unflickering? When we think of it, is it not the tranquillity that is terrible, the tranquillity watched by the stars? and

From Maurice Maeterlinck, *The Treasure of the Humble*, trans. Alfred Sutro. N.Y.: Dodd, Mead, and Co., 1903.

is it in tumult or in silence that the spirit of life quickens within us? Is it not
when we are told, at the end of the story, "They were happy," that the great
disquiet should intrude itself? What is taking place while they are happy? Are
there not elements of deeper gravity and stability in happiness, in a single
moment of repose, than in the whirlwind of passion? Is it not then that we at
last behold the march of time—ay, and of many another on-stealing besides,
more secret still—is it not then that the hours rush forward? Are not deeper
chords set vibrating by all these things than by the dagger-stroke of conventional drama? Is it not at the very moment when a man believes himself secure
from bodily death that the strange and silent tragedy of the being and the
immensities does indeed raise its curtain on the stage? Is it while I flee before
a naked sword that my existence touches its most interesting point? Is life
always at its sublimest in a kiss? Are there not other moments, when one hears
purer voices that do not fade away so soon? Does the soul only flower on
nights of storm? Hitherto, doubtless, this belief has prevailed. It is only the life
of violence, the life of bygone days, that is perceived by nearly all our tragic
writers; and truly may one say that anachronism dominates the stage, and that
dramatic art dates back as many years as the art of sculpture. Far different is it
with the other arts—with painting and music, for instance—for these have
learned to select and reproduce those obscurer phases of daily life that are not
the less deep-rooted and amazing. They know that all that life has lost, as
regards mere superficial ornament, has been more than counterbalanced by
the depth, the intimate meaning and the spiritual gravity it has acquired. The
true artist no longer chooses Marius triumphing over the Cimbrians, or the
assassination of the Duke of Guise, as fit subjects for his art; for he is well
aware that the psychology of victory or murder is but elementary and exceptional, and that the solemn voice of men and things, the voice that issues forth
so timidly and hesitatingly, cannot be heard amidst the idle uproar of acts of
violence. And therefore will he place on his canvas a house lost in the heart of
the country, an open door at the end of a passage, a face or hands at rest, and
by these simple images will he add to our consciousness of life, which is a possession that it is no longer possible to lose.

But to the tragic author, as to the mediocre painter who still lingers
over historical pictures, it is only the violence of the anecdote that appeals, and
in his representation thereof does the entire interest of his work consist. And
he imagines, forsooth, that we shall delight in witnessing the very same acts
that brought joy to the hearts of the barbarians, with whom murder, outrage
and treachery were matters of daily occurrence. Whereas it is far away from
bloodshed, battle-cry and sword-thrust that the lives of most of us flow on,
and men's tears are silent to-day, and invisible, and almost spiritual...

Indeed, when I go to a theatre, I feel as though I were spending a few
hours with my ancestors, who conceived life as something that was primitive,
arid and brutal; but this conception of theirs scarcely even lingers in my mem-

ory, and surely it is not one that I can share. I am shown a deceived husband killing his wife, a woman poisoning her lover, a son avenging his father, a father slaughtering his children, children putting their father to death, murdered kings, ravished virgins, imprisoned citizens—in a word, all the sublimity of tradition, but alas, how superficial and material! Blood, surface-tears and death! What can I learn from creatures who have but one fixed idea, and who have no time to live, for that there is a rival, or a mistress, whom it behooves them to put to death?

I had hoped to be shown some act of life, traced back to its sources and to its mystery by connecting links, that my daily occupations afford me neither power nor occasion to study. I had gone thither hoping that the beauty, the grandeur and the earnestness of my humble day by day existence would, for one instant, be revealed to me, that I would be shown the I know not what presence, power or God that is ever with me in my room. I was yearning for one of the strange moments of a higher life that flit unperceived through my dreariest hours; whereas, almost invariably, all that I beheld was but a man who would tell me, at wearisome length, why he was jealous, why he poisoned, or why he killed.

I admire Othello, but he does not appear to me to live the august daily life of a Hamlet, who has the time to live, inasmuch as he does not act. Othello is admirably jealous. But is it not perhaps an ancient error to imagine that it is at the moments when this passion, or others of equal violence, possesses us, that we live our truest lives? I have grown to believe that an old man, seated in his armchair, waiting patiently, with his lamp beside him; giving unconscious ear to all the eternal laws that reign about his house, interpreting, without comprehending, the silence of doors and windows and the quivering voice of the light, submitting with bent head to the presence of his soul and his destiny—an old man, who conceives not that all the powers of this world, like so many heedful servants, are mingling and keeping vigil in his room, who suspects not that the very sun itself is supporting in space the little table against which he leans, or that every star in heaven and every fiber of the soul are directly concerned in the movement of an eyelid that closes, or a thought that springs to birth—I have grown to believe that he, motionless as he is, does yet live in reality a deeper, more human and more universal life than the lover who strangles his mistress, the captain who conquers in battle, or "the husband who avenges his honor."

I shall be told, perhaps, that a motionless life would be invisible, that therefore animation must be conferred upon it, and movement, and that such varied movement as would be acceptable is to be found only in the few passions of which use has hitherto been made. I do not know whether it be true that a static theatre is impossible. Indeed, to me it seems to exist already. Most of the tragedies of Aeschylus are tragedies without movement. In both the *Prometheus* and the *Suppliants*, events are lacking; and the entire tragedy of the

Choephorae—surely the most terrible drama of antiquity—does but cling, nightmare-like, around the tomb of Agamemnon, till murder darts forth, as a lightning flash, from the accumulation of prayers, ever falling back upon themselves. Consider, from this point of view, a few more of the finest tragedies of the ancients: *The Eumenides, Antigone, Electra, Oedipus at Colonus.* "They have admired," said Racine in his preface to *Bernice*, "they have admired the *Ajax* of Sophocles, wherein there is nothing but Ajax killing himself with regret for the fury into which he fell after the arms of Achilles were denied him. They have admired *Philoctetes*, whose entire subject is but the coming of Ulysses with intent to seize the arrows of Hercules. Even the *Oedipus*, through full of recognitions, contains less subject-matter than the simplest tragedy of our days."

What have we here but life that is almost motionless? In most cases, indeed, you will find that psychological action—infinitely loftier in itself than mere material action, and truly, one might think, well-nigh indispensable—that psychological action even has been suppressed, or at least vastly diminished, in a truly marvelous fashion, with the result that the interest centers solely and entirely in the individual, face to face with the universe. Here we are no longer with the barbarians, nor is man now fretting himself in the midst of elementary passions, as though, forsooth, these were the only things worthy of note: he is at rest, and we have time to observe him. It is no longer a violent, exceptional moment of life that passes before our eyes—it is life itself. Thousands and thousands of laws there are, mightier and more venerable than those of passion; but, in common with all that is endowed with resistless force, these laws are silent, and discreet, and slow-moving; and hence it is only in the twilight that they can be seen and heard, in the meditation that comes to us at the tranquil moments of life.

When Ulysses and Neoptolemus come to Philoctetes and demand of him the arms of Hercules, their action is in itself as simple and ordinary as that of a man of our day who goes into a house to visit an invalid, of a traveler who knocks at the door of an inn, or of a mother who, by the fireside, awaits the return of her child. Sophocles indicates the character of his heroes by means of the lightest and quickest of touches. But it may safely be said that the chief interest of the tragedy does not lie in the struggle we witness between cunning and loyalty, between love of country, rancor, and headstrong pride. There is more beyond: for it is man's loftier existence that is laid bare to us. The poet adds to ordinary life something, I know not what, which is the poet's secret: and there comes to us a sudden revelation of life in its stupendous grandeur, in its submissiveness to the unknown powers, in its endless affinities, in its awe-inspiring misery. Let but the chemist pour a few mysterious drops into a vessel that seems to contain the purest water, and at once masses of crystals will rise to the surface, thus revealing to us all that lay in abeyance there where nothing was visible before to our incomplete eyes. And even thus is it in *Philoctetes*; the primitive psychology of the three leading characters would seem to be merely the sides of the vessel containing the clear water; and this itself is our ordinary life, into which the poet is about to let fall the revelation-bearing drops of his genius. ...

Indeed, it is not in the actions but in the words that are found the beauty and greatness of tragedies that are truly beautiful and great; and this not solely in the words that accompany and explain the action, for there must perforce be another dialogue besides the one which is superficially necessary. And indeed the only words that count in the play are those that at first seemed useless, for it is therein that the essence lies. Side by side with the necessary dialogue will you almost always find another dialogue that seems superfluous; but examine it carefully, and it will be borne home to you that this is the only one that the soul can listen to profoundly, for here alone is it the soul that is being addressed. You will see, too, that it is the quality and the scope of this unnecessary dialogue that determine the quality and the immeasurable range of the work. Certain it is that, in the ordinary drama, the indispensable dialogue by no means corresponds to reality; and it is just those words that are spoken by the side of the rigid, apparent truth, that constitute the mysterious beauty of the most beautiful tragedies, inasmuch as these are words that conform to a deeper truth, and one that lies incomparably nearer to the invisible soul by which the poem is upheld. One may even affirm that a poem draws the nearer to beauty and loftier truth in the measure that it eliminates words that merely explain the action, and substitutes for them others that reveal, not the so-called 'soul-state,' but I know not what intangible and unceasing striving of the soul towards its own beauty and truth. And so much the nearer, also, does it draw to the true life. To every man does it happen, in his work-a-day existence, that some situation of deep seriousness has to be unraveled by means of words. Reflect for an instant. At moments such as those—nay, at the most commonplace of times—is it the thing you say or the reply you receive that has the most value? Are not other forces, other words one cannot hear, brought into being, and do not these determine the event? What I say often counts for so little; but my presence, the attitude of my soul, my future and my past, that which will take birth in me and that which is dead, a secret thought, the stars that approve, my destiny, the thousands of mysteries which surround me and float about yourself—all this it is that speaks to you at that tragic moment, all this it is that brings to me your answer. There is all this beneath every one of my words, and each one of yours; it is this, above all, that we see, it is this, above all, that we hear, ourselves notwithstanding. If you have come, you the "outraged husband," the "deceived lover," the "forsaken wife," intending to kill me, your arm will not be stayed by my most moving entreaty; but it may be that there will come towards you, at that moment, one of these unexpected forces; and my soul, knowing of their vigil near to me, may whisper a secret word whereby, haply, you shall be disarmed. These are the spheres wherein adventures come to issue, this is the dialogue whose echo should be

heard. And it is this echo that one does hear—extremely attenuated and variable, it is true—in some of the great works mentioned above. But might we
not try to draw nearer to the spheres where it is "in reality" that everything
comes to pass?

It would seem as though the endeavor were being made. Some time
ago, when dealing with *The Master Builder*, which is one of Ibsen's dramas
wherein this dialogue of the "second degree" attains the deepest tragedy, I
endeavored, unskillfully enough, to fix its secrets. For indeed they are kindred
handmarks traced on the same wall by the same sightless being, groping for
the same light. "What is it," I asked, "what is it that, in the *Master Builder*, the
poet has added to life, thereby making it appear so strange, so profound and
so disquieting beneath its trivial surface?" The discovery is not easy, and the
old master hides from us more than one secret. It would even seem as though
what he has wished to say were but little by the side of what he has been compelled to say. He has freed certain powers of the soul that have never yet been
free, and it may well be that these have held him in thrall. "Look you, Hilda,"
exclaims Solness, "look you! There is sorcery in you, too, as there is in me. It
is this sorcery that imposes action on the powers of the beyond. And we *have*
to yield to it. Whether we want to or not, we *must*."

There is sorcery in them, as in us all. Hilda and Solness are, I believe,
the first characters in drama who feel, for an instant, that they are living in the
atmosphere of the soul; and the discovery of the essential life that exists in
them, beyond the life of every day, comes fraught with terror. Hilda and
Solness are two souls to whom a flash has revealed their situation in the true
life. Diverse ways there are by which knowledge of our fellows may come to
us. Two or three men, perhaps, are seen by me almost daily. For a long time
it is merely by their gestures that I distinguish them, by their habits, be these
of mind or body, by the manner in which they feel, act or think. But, in the
course of every friendship of some duration, there comes to us a mysterious
moment when we seem to perceive the exact relationship of our friend to the
unknown that surrounds him, when we discover the attitude destiny has
assumed towards him. And it is from this moment that he truly belongs to us.
We have seen, once and for all, the treatment held in store for him by events.
We know that however such a one may seclude himself in the recesses of his
dwelling, in dread lest his slightest movement stir up that which lies in the
great reservoirs of the future, his forethought will avail him nothing, and the
innumerable events that destiny holds in reserve will discover him wherever
he hide, and will knock one after another at his door. And even so do we know
that this other will sally forth in vain in pursuit of adventure. He will ever
return empty-handed. No sooner are our eyes thus opened than unerring
knowledge would seem to spring to life, self-created, within our soul; and we
know with absolute conviction that the event that seems to be impending over
the head of a certain man will nevertheless most assuredly not reach him.

From this moment a special part of the soul reigns over the friendship of even the most unintelligent, the obscurest of men. Life has become, as it were, transposed. And when it happens that we meet one of the men who are thus known to us, though we do but speak of the snow that is falling or the women that pass by, something there is in each of us which nods to the other, which examines and asks its questions without our knowledge, which interests itself in contingencies and hints at events that it is impossible for us to understand. ...

Thus do I conceive it to be with Hilda and Solness; it is thus surely that they regard each other. Their conversation resembles nothing that we have ever heard, inasmuch as the poet has endeavored to blend in one expression both the inner and the outer dialogue. A new, indescribable power dominates this somnambulistic drama. All that is said therein at once hides and reveals the sources of an unknown life. And if we are bewildered at times, let us not forget that our soul often appears to our feeble eyes to be but the maddest of forces, and that there are in man many regions more fertile, more profound and more interesting than those of his reason or his intelligence. ...

GORDON CRAIG

Gordon CRAIG (1872-1966) was tall and handsome with broad square shoulders, large hands and feet, a cherubic mouth, and level eyebrows. His hair, straw-like in tone and texture, was straight, not curly, and draped itself around his massive head. He had droopy eyelids like a hooded hawk that made him appear arrogant. Quite shortsighted, he saw very little without glasses, his myopia contributing to his preference for browns and grays and his choice of structural design unencumbered with details.

The son of the Victorian leading lady, Ellen Terry, whom he resembled, Craig had the theatre in his blood. "I looked like an actor," he confessed uneasily, ambivalent about a profession he quickly abandoned. As a young man, Craig found his face "far too pretty; it might be the face of a girl." Had he lived in Elizabethan times, he felt sure he would have been cast to play Shakespeare's heroines. When he left off acting at twenty-five, he lost the girlish face and soft looks he so disliked. The aging Craig became instantly recognizable by his great white mane and signature accoutrements: broad-brimmed hat and pilgrim's staff.

Theatre for Craig was always a performance, not a play to be read. In his days actors received only their cued parts, not a full text. An engaged and observant actor-spectator, Craig experienced the theatre as a privileged insider, equally at home on either side of the footlights. He grew up in the world of the Lyceum theatre as the protégé of Henry Irving, whom he studied closely from the auditorium, from backstage, and from the stage itself. Craig considered Irving the greatest actor in Europe and the ideal stage director.

When he was eight, Teddy was taken by his mother to Boucicault's *Corsican Brothers* at the Lyceum, first below the stage to see the trap being prepared, and then back to stage level to watch the ghost rising up in a blue light. Enchanted with the trick, the boy wanted to return again and again.

"I am a first-rate spectator in a theatre," Craig said of his ability to be thrilled by the magic of the stage. He grew up loving the late Victorian repertory of farces, melodramas, and "mutilated" Shakespeare that Bernard Shaw attacked as hopelessly retrograde. He frequented the rowdy London music-halls whose "fun and power" challenged the legitimate playhouses, and he applauded Bernhardt for performing there, insisting that the "variety stage is the sole remaining link connecting us with the stupendous achievement of the sixteenth century known as the *commedia dell'arte*."

Craig considered himself "one of the impossibles," a member of the clan of independents and rebels to which Hamlet belonged—dreamers devoid of practical business sense who suspect foul play everywhere. "We impossibles see ghosts," he avowed.

In fact, the key to Craig's life and art was *Hamlet*, which he played twice in his early twenties (the second time wearing Irving's old costume and sword), staged at the Moscow Art Theatre, and illustrated many times. "I somehow or other lived Hamlet day by day," Craig allowed, haunted by the ghost of his absent father, an architect and stage designer. "Always I have been Hamlet." In his eighties he declared, "Today I am an aged Hamlet."

A passionate but erratic and willful reader, Craig could not get more than half way through *Richard II*, but read Dumas's *Le Vicomte de Bradelonne* fifteen or sixteen times and was a lifelong peruser of Blake and Montaigne. Penniless as he was, he became an obsessive collector of rare and beautiful theatre books.

Having ceased to believe that acting was an art, Craig abandoned the stage to become a *metteur-en-scène* and creator of bookplates, wood-engravings, blockprints, designs, drawings, and sketches. He wrote under some 60 or 70 different pseudonyms. Although he lived abroad much of his later life, he never learned any foreign language properly.

In his unpublished "Über-Marions" notebooks, Craig recorded his secret plans for the Über-Marionette International Theatre which was to open in Dresden in May 1906. The large marionettes, ranging from four and half to six and half feet, made of wood, and padded, were to be instruments of salvation capable of expressing "unseen forces," reviving "ancient Ceremony," and restoring "Belief."

Soon after meeting Isadora Duncan, Craig began reading on ancient Egypt and studying the ritual funeral statues with movable limbs. He started collecting marionettes, assembling in Florence a museum of puppetry. Later Craig seemed to retract his radical position by suggesting that the über-marionette was only a metaphor for the ideal actor, but at the same he continued constructing large dolls moved on grooves and manipulated by pedals from below.

During his visit to the USSR in 1935 Craig saw Mikhoels's *King Lear* at the State Jewish Theatre four times, a production he found so "exalted and shattering" that he hoped to bring it to Europe. He met Meyerhold as well as Brecht and Piscator, but was most impressed with Eisenstein. Ever suspicious, Craig was not taken in by the illusions of Soviet utopia.

An admirer of the Italian dialect theatre, Craig was an outspoken critic of the Fascists' anti-dialect program. He considered the dialect actors supermarionettes and defended them in a twenty-minute private meeting with Mussolini, at which Craig was struck by the doltishness and vacuity of the dictator's facial expression. Il Duce was no true über-marionette.

At the end of his life, he made the following avowal: "I was born an actor and the son of a great actress. I still consider myself an actor and am passionately fond of the Theatre and the Theatrical."

THE ACTOR AND
THE ÜBER-MARIONETTE (1907)

"*To save the theatre, the theatre must be destroyed, the actors and
actresses must all die of the plague...They make art impossible.*"
Eleanora Duse: *Studies in the Seven Arts,*
Arthur Symons. (Constable, 1900.)

Acting is not an art. It is therefore incorrect to speak of the actor as
an artist. Art is the exact antithesis of pandemonium, and pandemonium is
created by the tumbling together of many accidents. Art arrives only by
design. Therefore in order to make any work of art it is clear we may only
work in those materials with which we can calculate. Man is not one of these
materials.

The whole nature of man tends towards freedom; he therefore carries
the proof in his own person that as *material* for the Theatre he is useless. In
the modern theatre, owing to the use of the bodies of men and women *as their
material*, all which is presented there is of an accidental nature. The actions of
the actor's body, the expression of his face, the sounds of his voice, all are at
the mercy of the winds of his emotions: these winds, which must blow for ever
round the artist, moving without unbalancing him. But with the actor, emotion *possesses* him; it seizes upon his limbs, moving them whither it will. He is
at its beck and call, he moves as one in a frantic dream or as one distraught,
swaying here and there; his head, his arms, his feet, if not utterly beyond control, are so weak to stand against the torrent of his passions, that they are ready
to play him false at any moment. It is useless for him to attempt to reason with
himself. Hamlet's calm directions (the dreamer's, not the logician's directions,
by the way) are thrown to the winds. His limbs refuse, and refuse again to obey
his mind the instant emotion warms, while the mind is all the time creating
the heat which shall set these emotions afire. As with his movement, so is it
with the expression of his face. The mind struggling and succeeding for a
moment, in moving the eyes, or the muscles of the face whither it will; the
mind bringing the face for a few moments into thorough subjection, is suddenly swept aside by the emotion which has grown hot through the action of

From E. Gordon Craig, *The Art of the Theatre.*
London: Heinemann, 1911.

the mind. Instantly, like lightning, and before the mind has time to cry out and protest, the hot passion has mastered the actor's expression. It shifts and changes, sways and turns, it is chased by emotion from the actor's forehead between his eyes and down to his mouth; now he is entirely at the mercy of emotion, and crying out to it: "Do with me what you will!" His expression runs a mad riot hither and thither, and lo! "Nothing is coming of nothing." It is the same with his voice as it is with his movements. Emotion cracks the voice of the actor. It sways his voice to join in the conspiracy against his mind. Emotion works upon the voice of the actor, and he produces the impression of discordant emotion. It is of no avail to say that emotion is the spirit of the gods, and is precisely what the artist aims to produce; first of all this is not true, and even if it were quite true, every stray emotion, every casual feeling, cannot be of value. Therefore the mind of the actor, we see, is less powerful than his emotion, for emotion is able to win over the mind to assist in the destruction of that which the mind would produce; and as the mind becomes the slave of the emotion it follows that accident upon accident must be continually occurring. So then, we have arrived at this point: that emotion is the cause which first of all creates, and secondly destroys. Art, as we have said, can admit of no accidents. That, then, which the actor gives us, is not a work of art; it is a series of accidental confessions. In the beginning the human body was not used as material in the Art of the Theatre. In the beginning the emotions of men and women were not considered as a fit exhibition for the multitude. An elephant and a tiger in an arena suited the taste better, when the desire was to excite. [...]

   Therefore, the body of man, for the reason which I have given, is *by nature* utterly useless as a material for an art. I am fully aware of the sweeping character of this statement; and as it concerns men and women who are alive, and who as a class are ever to be loved, more must be said lest I give unintentional offence. I know perfectly well that what I have said here is not yet going to create an exodus of all the actors from all the theatres in the world, driving them into sad monasteries where they will laugh out the rest of their lives, with the Art of the Theatre as the main topic for amusing conversation. As I have written elsewhere, the Theatre will continue its growth and actors will continue for some years to hinder its development. But I see a loophole by which in time the actors can escape from the bondage they are in. They must create for themselves a new form of acting, consisting for the main part of symbolical gesture. Today they *impersonate* and interpret; tomorrow they must *represent* and interpret; and the third day they must create. By this means style may return. Today the actor impersonates a certain being. He cries to the audience: "Watch me; I am now pretending to be so and so, and I am now pretending to do so and so;" and then he proceeds to *imitate* as exactly as possible, that which he has announced he will *indicate*. [...]

   The actor looks upon life as a photo-machine looks upon life; and he attempts to make a picture to rival a photograph. He never dreams of his art as being an art such for instance as music. He tries to reproduce Nature; he seldom thinks to invent with the aid of Nature, and he never dreams of *creating*. As I have said, the best he can do when he wants to catch and convey the poetry of a kiss, the heat of a fight, or the calm of death, is to copy slavishly, photographically—he kisses—he fights—he lies back and mimics death—and, when you think of it, is not all this dreadfully stupid? Is it not a poor art and a poor cleverness, which cannot convey the spirit and essence of an idea to an audience, but can only show an artless copy, a facsimile of the thing itself? This is to be an imitator, not an artist. This is to claim kinship with the ventriloquist.

There is a stage expression of the actor "getting under the skin of the part." A better one would be getting "*out* of the skin of the part altogether." "What, then," cries the red-blooded and flashing actor, "is there to be no flesh and blood in this same art of the theatre of yours? No life?" It depends what you call life, signor, when you use the word in relation with the idea of art. The painter means something rather different to actuality when he speaks of life in his art, and the other artists generally mean something essentially spiritual; it is only the actor, the ventriloquist, or the animal-stuffer who, when they speak of putting life into their work, mean some actual and lifelike reproduction, something blatant in its appeal, that it is for this reason I say that it would be better if the actor should get out of the skin of the part altogether. If there is any actor who is reading this, is there not some way by which I can make him realize the preposterous absurdity of this delusion of his, this belief that he should aim to make an actual copy, a reproduction? [...]

My pleasure shall not be to compete with this strenuous photographer, and I shall ever aim to get something entirely opposed to life as we see it. This flesh-and-blood life, lovely as it is to us all, is for me not a thing made to search into, or to give out again to the world, even conventionalized. I think that my aim shall rather be to catch some far-off glimpse of that spirit which we call Death—to recall beautiful things from the imaginary world; they say they are cold, these dead things, I do not know—they often seem warmer and more living than that which parades as life. Shades—spirits seem to me to be more beautiful, and filled with more vitality than men and women; cities of men and women packed with pettiness, creatures inhuman, secret, coldest cold, hardest humanity. For, looking too long upon life, may one not find all this to be not the beautiful, nor the mysterious, nor the tragic, but the dull, the melodramatic, and the silly: the conspiracy against vitality—against both red heat and white heat? And from such things which lack the sun of life it is not possible to draw inspiration. But from that mysterious, joyous, and superbly complete life which is called Death—that life of shadow and of unknown shapes, where all cannot be blackness and fog as is supposed, but vivid color, vivid light, sharp-cut form; and which one finds peopled with strange, fierce and solemn figures, pretty figures and calm figures, and those figures impelled to some wondrous harmony of movement—all this is something more than a mere matter of fact. From this idea of death, which seems a kind of spring, a blossoming—from this land and from this idea can come so vast an inspiration, that with unhesitating exultation I leap forward to it; and behold, in an instant, I find my arms full of flowers. I advance but a pace or two and again plenty is around me. I pass at ease on a sea of beauty, I sail whither the winds take me—*there*, there is no danger. So much for my own personal wish; but the entire Theatre of the world is not represented in me, nor in a hundred artists or actors, but in something far different. Therefore what my personal aim may be is of very little importance. Yet the aim of the Theatre as a whole is to restore its art, and it should commence by banishing from the Theatre this idea of impersonation, this idea of reproducing Nature; for, while impersonation is in the Theatre, the Theatre can never become free. [...]

Do away with the actor, and you do away with the means by which a debased stage-realism is produced and flourishes. No longer would there be a living figure to confuse us into connecting actuality and art; no longer a living figure in which the weakness and tremors of the flesh were perceptible.

The actor must go, and in his place comes the inanimate figure—the Über-marionette we may call him, until he has won for himself a better name. Much has been written about the puppet, or marionette. There are some excellent volumes upon him, and he has also inspired several works of art. Today in his least happy period many people come to regard him as rather a superior doll—and to think he has developed from the doll. This is incorrect. He is a descendant of the stone images of the old temples—he is today a rather degenerate form of a god. Always the close friend of children, he still knows how to select and attract his devotees.

When any one designs a puppet on paper, he draws a stiff and comic-looking thing. Such an one has not even perceived what is contained in the idea which we now call the marionette. He mistakes gravity of face and calmness of body for blank stupidity and angular deformity. Yet even modern puppets are extraordinary things. The applause may thunder or dribble, their hearts beat no faster, no slower, their signals do not grow hurried or confused; and, though drenched in a torrent of bouquets and love, the face of the leading lady remains as solemn, as beautiful and as remote as ever. There is something more than a flash of genius in the marionette, and there is something in him more than the flashiness of displayed personality. The marionette appears to me to be the last echo of some noble and beautiful art of a past civilization. But as with all art which has passed into fat or vulgar hands, the puppet has become a reproach. All puppets are now but low comedians.

They imitate the comedians of the larger and fuller blooded stage. They enter only to fall on their back. They drink only to reel, and make love only to raise a laugh. They have forgotten the counsel of their mother the Sphinx. Their bodies have lost their grave grace, they have become stiff. Their eyes have lost that infinite subtlety of seeming to see; now they only stare. They display and jingle their wires and are cocksure in their wooden wisdom. They have failed to remember that their art should carry on it the same stamp of reserve that we see at times on the work of other artists, and that the highest art is that which conceals the craft and forgets the craftsman. [...]

May we not look forward with hope to that day which shall bring back to us once more the figure, or symbolic creature, made also by the cunning of the artist, so that we can gain once more the "noble artificiality" which the old writer speaks of? Then shall we no longer be under the cruel influence of the emotional confessions of weakness which are nightly witnessed by the people and which in their turn create in the beholders the very weaknesses which are exhibited. To that end we must study to remake these images—no longer content with a puppet, we must create an über-marionette. The über-marionette will not compete with life—rather will it go beyond it. Its ideal will not be the flesh and blood but rather the body in trance—it will aim to clothe itself with a death-like beauty while exhaling a living spirit. Several times in the course of this essay has a word or two about Death found its way on to the paper— called there by the incessant clamoring of "Life! Life! Life!" which the realists keep up. And this might be easily mistaken for an affectation, especially by those who have no sympathy or delight in the power and the mysterious joyousness which is in all passionless works of art. [...]

In America we can picture these brothers of that family of masters, living in their superb ancient cities, colossal cities, which I ever think of as able to be moved in a single day; cities of spacious tents of silk and canopies of gold under which dwelt their gods; dwellings which contained all the requirements of the most fastidious; those moving cities which, as they traveled from height to plain, over rivers and down valleys, seemed like some vast advancing army of peace. And in each city not one or two men called "artists" whom the rest of the city looked upon as ne'er-do-well idlers, but many men chosen by the community because of their higher powers of perception—artists. For that is what the title of artist means: one who perceives more than his fellows, and who records more than he has seen. And not the least among those artists was the artist of the ceremonies, the creator of the visions, the minister whose duty it was to celebrate their guiding spirit—the spirit of Motion.

In Asia, too, the forgotten masters of the temples and all that those temples contained have permeated every thought, every mark, in their work with this sense of calm motion resembling death—glorifying and greeting it. In Africa (which some of us think we are but now to civilize) this spirit dwelt, the essence of the perfect civilization. There, too, dwelt the great masters, not individuals obsessed with the idea of each asserting his personality as if it were a valuable and mighty thing, but content because of a kind of holy patience to move their brains and their fingers only in that direction permitted by the law—in the service of the simple truths.

How stern the law was, and how little the artist of that day permitted himself to make an exhibition of his personal feelings, can be discovered by looking at any example of Egyptian art. [...]

In Asia lay his first kingdom. On the banks of the Ganges they built him his home, a vast palace springing from column to column into the air and pouring from column to column down again into the water. Surrounded by gardens spread warm and rich with flowers and cooled by fountains; gardens into which no sounds entered, in which hardly anything stirred. Only in the cool and private chambers of this palace the swift minds of his attendants stirred incessantly. Something they were making which should become him, something to honor the spirit which had given him birth. And then, one day, the ceremony.

In this ceremony he took part; a celebration once more in praise of the Creation; the old thanksgiving, the hurrah for existence, and with it the stern-er hurrah for the privilege of the existence to come, which is veiled by the word Death. And during this ceremony there appeared before the eyes of the brown worshipers the symbols of all things on earth and in Nirvana. The symbol of the beautiful tree, the symbol of the hills, the symbols of those rich ores which the hills contained; the symbol of the cloud, of the wind, and of all swift moving things; the symbol of the quickest of moving things, of thought, of remembrance; the symbol of the animal, the symbol of Buddha and of Man— and here he comes, the figure, the puppet at whom you all laugh so much. You laugh at him today because none but his weaknesses are left to him. He reflects these from you; but you would not have laughed had you seen him in his prime, in that age when he was called upon to be the symbol of man in the great ceremony, and, stepping forward, was the beautiful figure of our heart's delight. If we should laugh at and insult the memory of the puppet, we should be laughing at the fall that we have brought about in ourselves—laughing at the beliefs and images we have broken. [...]

I pray earnestly for the return of the image—the über-marionette to the Theatre; and when he comes again and is but seen, he will be loved so well that once more will it be possible for the people to return to their ancient joy in ceremonies—once more will Creation be celebrated—homage rendered to existence—and divine and happy intercession made to Death.

WILLIAM BUTLER YEATS

William Butler YEATS (1865-1939) was a tall, frail, delicate young man who knew how to create a striking silhouette in his black sombrero, black velvet jacket, flowing black silk tie, baggy black trousers, and black cloak, "his wing of raven black hair swinging across his forehead" (in the words of his friend Bernard Shaw).

Kept from school by his middleclass lawyer-turned-portrait-painter father, who read him Shakespeare, Yeats grew up in an Irish countryside steeped in folklore and the supernatural. A self-educated dreamer, the poet was poor at languages, had wretched handwriting, and could scarcely spell, but he created his own legendary biography by associating himself with the landed aristocracy and an idealized version of Ireland's hierarchical past. At the Dublin School of Art which he attended for a few years, he acquired a taste for the Pre-Raphelites, whom he subsequently met in London.

When he read his poetry, Yeats swayed like a Druid, his face grew tremulous, his lips became a dark cherry red, and his small lizard eyes glowed black. His jaw was clear-cut and firm, his mouth beautifully modeled, his nose aquiline, his eyes set far apart, the right conspicuously lower than left. He saw little enough with either of them, being extremely shortsighted and out of contact with the world of nature. He had a curious way of not looking at his interlocutor during a conversation. Although tone-deaf, he read his verse in a rich mellow voice with a subtle Irish accent. His long hair had life of its own, swaying as he spoke, but in a different rhythm from the words, while he ran his fingers through the great lock that fell over his forehead. A signet ring with an enormous stone shone on his little finger.

His first play to be produced was *The Land of Heart's Desire* in 1894 as a curtain raiser to Shaw's *Arms and the Man*, a comedy that Yeats found repellent in its cool rationality. After the production he dreamed of Shaw as a sewing-machine.

In Paris Yeats attended two of the most important avant-garde premieres of the 1890s: the proto-symbolist *Axel* by Villiers-de-l'Ile-Adam and the proto-absurdist *Ubu Roi* by Alfred Jarry. Understanding very little of the

French dialogue, the Irish poet recognized the Wagnerian architectonics of the former and the willful barbarity of the latter, noting apocalyptically, "After us the savage god."

By 1904 Yeats had transformed himself from a pre-Raphaelite aesthete into a man of action, member of the Irish National Brotherhood, Abbey Theatre partisan and strong-willed impresario—the first of many anti-selves. He held that all happiness depended on assuming the mask of some other self and that "all joyous or creative life is a rebirth as something not oneself."

Yeats and Lady Gregory began planning for an Irish national theatre in 1897. From 1899 to 1910 Yeats headed the group, first called the Irish Literary Theatre, then the Irish National Theatre Company, which in 1904 moved into the Abbey Theatre. No theatre theoretician since Goethe had as complete an experience of all aspects of the stage as Yeats, but his struggles as theatre manager left him bitter and disillusioned. At first rejecting the idea of an urban bourgeois audience, the poet dreamed of creating a lofty and remote theatre that would speak of eternal things to the true Irish people. But the ideal peasant or working class spectator craving communion with Ireland's mythic past failed to appear at the box office, and Yeats finally despaired of establishing a genuine people's theatre. On the contrary, he now hoped "to create an unpopular theatre and an audience like a secret society." He yearned for the time when the theatre director would be "as free as a modern painter."

Yeats's long involvement with the occult—in the Dublin Hermetic Society, Blavatsky Lodge of the Theosophical Society, and the Hermetic Order of the Golden Dawn—ran parallel to his life in the theatre and was another manifestation of his histrionic temperament. Acknowledging that "millions ... have substituted the séance room for the church," Yeats saw spiritualism as a modern religion and devoted years to psychic research, consulting many mediums and automatic writers in the hope that the dead could manifest themselves to the living. For Yeats, the principle of creativity derived from the world-soul or Anima Mundi. Knowledge is simply a recollection of what is stored in the Great Memory.

It was Yeats's friendship with the playwright Synge and, as manager of the Abbey Theatre, his promotion of Synge's plays in the face of ugly audience hostility that brought the poet into closer contact with all that was opposite to his dreams of the noble and regenerating Celtic Twilight. When he met Synge in Paris, Yeats advised the younger writer to go to the desolate Aran Islands in the west of Ireland and live as one of the people. From Synge, who was sick, gentle, and shy, but created a poetic art that revealed life in all its brutality and violence, Yeats derived his theory of the mask, the anti-self, and double soul.

At sixty, Yeats was an acclaimed public figure, a Nobel Prize winner, an Irish Free State senator, and a popular and well paid lecturer (touring in America three times). His mane of raven blue hair now turned white blue, the poet put on weight and appeared at the lectern smiling, immaculately clean and precisely shaved, elegantly dressed in suits of soft corn or brown tweeds, with bright blue or dark green shirt, and matching handkerchief, silver-buckled shoes, wide black ribbon attached to tortoiseshell glasses, and large gold ring. He had become an anti-self.

THE TRAGIC THEATRE (1910)

I did not find a word in the printed criticism of Synge's *Deirdre of the Sorrows* about the qualities that made certain moments seem to me the noblest tragedy, and the play was judged by what seemed to me but wheels and pulleys necessary to the effect, but in themselves nothing.

Upon the other hand, those who spoke to me of the play never spoke of these wheels and pulleys, but if they cared at all for the play, cared for the things I cared for. One's own world of painters, of poets, or good talkers, of ladies who delight in Ricard's portraits or Debussy's music, all those whose senses feel instantly every change in our mother the moon, saw the stage in one way; and those others who look at plays every night, who tell the general playgoer whether this play or that play is to his taste, saw it in a way so different that there is certainly some body of dogma—whether in the instincts or in the memory—pushing the ways apart. A printed criticism, for instance, found but one dramatic moment, that when Deirdre in the second act overhears her lover say that he may grow weary of her; and not one—if I remember rightly—chose for praise or explanation the third act which alone had satisfied the author, or contained in any abundance those sentences that were quoted at the fall of the curtain and for days after.

Deirdre and her lover, as Synge tells the tale, returned to Ireland, though it was nearly certain they would die there, because death was better than broken love, and at the side of the open grave that had been dug for one and would serve for both, quarreled, losing all they had given their life to keep. "Is it not a hard thing that we should miss the safety of the grave and we trampling the edge?" That is Deirdre's cry at the outset of a reverie of passion that mounts and mounts till grief itself has carried her beyond grief into pure contemplation. Up to this the play had been a Master's unfinished work, monotonous and melancholy, ill-arranged, little more than a sketch of what it would have grown to, but now I listened breathless to sentences that may never pass away, and as they filled or dwindled in their civility of sorrow, the player, whose art had seemed clumsy and incomplete, like the writing itself, ascended into that tragic ecstasy which is the best that art—perhaps that life—can give. And at last when Deirdre, in the paroxysm before she took her life,

From *The Mask*, October, 1910.

touched with compassionate fingers him that had killed her lover, we knew that the player had become, if but for a moment, the creature of that noble mind which had gathered its art in waste islands, and we too were carried beyond time and persons to where passion, living through its thousand purgatorial years, as in the wink of an eye, becomes wisdom; and it was as though we too had touched and felt and seen a disembodied thing.

One dogma of the printed criticism is that if a play does not contain definite character, its constitution is not strong enough for the stage, and that the dramatic moment is always the contest of character with character.

In poetical drama there is, it is held, an antithesis between character and lyric poetry, for lyric poetry—however much it moves you when read out of a book—can, as these critics think, but encumber the action. Yet when we go back a few centuries and enter the great periods of drama, character grows less and sometimes disappears, and there is much lyric feeling, and at times a lyric measure will be wrought into the dialogue, a flowing measure that had well befitted music, or that more lumbering one of the sonnet. Suddenly it strikes us that character is continuously present in comedy alone, and that there is much tragedy, that of Corneille, that of Racine, that of Greece and Rome, where its place is taken by passions and motives, one person being jealous, another full of love or remorse or pride or anger. In writers of tragi-comedy (and Shakespeare is always a writer of tragi-comedy) there is indeed character, but we notice that it is in the moments of comedy that character is defined, in Hamlet's gaiety, let us say; while amid the great moments, when Timon orders his tomb, when Hamlet cries to Horatio "Absent thee from felicity awhile," while Antony names "Of many thousand kisses the poor last," all is lyricism, unmixed passion, "the integrity of fire." Nor does character ever attain to complete definition in these lamps ready for the taper, no matter how circumstantial and gradual the opening of events, as it does in Falstaff, who has no passionate purpose to fulfill, or as it does in Henry V, whose poetry, never touched by lyric heat, is oratorical; nor when the tragic reverie is at its height do we say, "How well that man is realized! I should know him were I to meet him in the street," for it is always ourselves that we see upon the stage, and should it be a tragedy of love, we renew, it may be, some loyalty of our youth, and go from the theatre with our eyes dim for an old love's sake.

I think it was while rehearsing a translation of *Les Fourberies de Scapin* in Dublin, and noticing how passionless it all was, that I saw what should have been plain from the first line I had written, that tragedy must always be a drowning and breaking of the dykes that separate man from man, and that it is upon these dykes comedy keeps house. But I was not certain of the site of that house (one always hesitates when there is not testimony but one's own) till somebody told me of a certain letter of Congreve's. He describes the external and superficial expressions of "humor" on which farce is founded and then defines "humor" itself—the foundation of comedy—as a "singular and unavoidable way of doing anything peculiar to one man only by which his speech and actions are distinguished from all other men," and adds to it that "passions are too powerful in the sex to let humor have its course," or, as I would rather put it, that you can find but little of what we call character in unspoiled youth, whatever be the sex, for, as he indeed shows in another sentence, it grows with time like the ash of a burning stick, and strengthens towards middle life till there is little else at seventy years.

Since then I have discovered an antagonism between all the old art and our new art of comedy and understand why I hated at nineteen years Thackeray's novels and the new French painting. A big picture of *cocottes* sitting at little tables outside a café, by some follower of Manet, was exhibited at the Royal Hibernian Academy while I was a student at a life class there, and I was miserable for days. I found no desirable place, no man I could have wished to be, no woman I could have loved, no Golden Age, no lure for secret hope, no adventure with myself for theme out of the endless tale I told myself all day long. Years after, I saw the *Olympia* of Manet at the Luxembourg and watched it without hostility indeed, but as I might some incomparable talker whose precision of gesture gave me pleasure, though I did not understand his language. I returned to it again and again at intervals of years, saying to myself, "Some day I will understand"; and yet it was not until Sir Hugh Lane brought the *Eva Gonzales* to Dublin, and I had said to myself, "How perfectly that woman is realized as distinct from all other women that have lived or shall live," that I understood I was carrying on in my own mind that quarrel between a tragedian and a comedian which the Devil on Two Sticks in Le Sage showed to the young man who had climbed through the window.

There is an art of the flood, the art of Titian when his *Ariosto*, and his *Bacchus and Ariadne*, give new images to the dreams of youth, and of Shakespeare when he shows us Hamlet broken away from life by the passionate hesitations of his reverie. And we call this art poetical, because we must bring more to it than our daily mood if we would take our pleasure; and because it takes delight in the moment of exaltation, of excitement, of dreaming (or in the capacity for it, as in that still face of Ariosto's that is like some vessel soon to be full of wine). And there is an art that we call real, because character can only express itself perfectly in a real world, being that world's creature, and because we understand it best through a delicate discrimination of the senses which is but entire wakefulness, the daily mood grown cold and crystalline.

We may not find either mood in its purity, but in mainly tragic art one distinguishes devices to exclude or lessen character, to diminish the power of that daily mood, to cheat or blind its too clear perception. If the real world is not altogether rejected, it is but touched here and there, and into the places we have left empty we summon rhythm, balance, patter, images that remind us of vast passions, the vagueness of past times, all the chimeras that haunt the edge of trance; and if we are painters, we shall express personal emotion through ideal form, a symbolism handled by the generations, a mask from whose eyes the disembodied looks, a style that remembers many masters that it may escape contemporary suggestion; or we shall leave out some element of reality as in Byzantine painting, where there is no mass, nothing in relief; and so it is that in the supreme moment of tragic art there comes upon one that strange sensation as though the hair of one's head stood up. And when we love, if it be in the excitement of youth, do we not also, that the flood may find no stone to convulse, no wall to narrow it, exclude character or the signs of it by choosing that beauty which seems unearthly because the individual woman is lost amid the labyrinth of its lines as though life were trembling into stillness and silence, or at last folding itself away? Some little irrelevance of line, some promise of character to come, may indeed put us at our ease, "give more inter-est" as the humor of the old man with the basket does to Cleopatra's dying; but should it come, as we had dreamed in love's frenzy, to our dying for that woman's sake, we would find that the discord had its value from the tune. Nor have we chosen illusion in choosing the outward sign of that moral genius that lives among the subtlety of the passions, and can for her moment make her of the one mind with great artists and poets. In the studio we may indeed say to one another, "Character is the only beauty," but when we choose a wife, as when we go to the gymnasium to be shaped for woman's eyes, we remember academic form, even though we enlarge a little the point of interest and choose "a painter's beauty," finding it the more easy to believe in the fire because it has made ashes.

When we look at the faces of the old tragic paintings, whether it is in Titian or in some painter of mediaeval China, we find there sadness and grav-ity, a certain emptiness even, as of a mind that waited the supreme crisis (and indeed it seems at times as if the graphic art, unlike poetry which sings the cri-sis itself, were the celebration of waiting). Whereas in modern art, whether in Japan or Europe, "vitality" (is not that the great word of the studios?), the energy, that is to say, which is under the command of our common moments, sings, laughs, chatters or looks its busy thoughts.

Certainly we have here the Tree of Life and that of the Knowledge of Good and Evil which is rooted in our interests, and if we have forgotten their differing virtues it is surely because we have taken delight in a confusion of crossing branches. Tragic art, passionate art, the drowner of dykes, the con-founder of understanding, moves us by setting us to reverie, by alluring us almost to the intensity of trance. The persons upon the stage, let us say, great-en till they are humanity itself. We feel our minds expand convulsively or spread out slowly like some moon-brightened image-crowded sea. That which is before our eyes perpetually vanishes and returns again in the midst of the excitement it creates, and the more enthralling it is, the more do we forget it.

VSEVOLOD MEYERHOLD

Vsevolod MEYERHOLD (1874-1942) had features that lent themselves to caricature: soaring gray mane, shock of gray hair jutting out from under a cap pulled low over the eyes, huge Cyrano nose protruding from behind a raised collar, firmly molded lips, shoulders curved, and head thrown back. At five foot, seven inches, he appeared short and lithe, his movements quick, his voice slightly hoarse. Both externally and internally, he was angular, sharp, and unexpected.

His defining character trait was a constant striving for the new in himself, in his life, in his art. He loved all sorts of poses. Rancorous, mistrustful, and prickly, Meyerhold had a paranoic fear of others stealing his ideas. His epitaph, he said, should be: "Here lies an actor and director who never played and never staged Hamlet"—even though it was his favorite play.

He read voraciously in a study crammed with books, pencil in hand, scribbling notes in the margins. Versed in many languages (including sign language), he went through all of Wagner in German. His second vocation was as a writer, but although he planned eight volumes, he completed only *On the Theatre*, a collection of essays dealing with his directorial work from 1905 to 1912. An excellent rhetorician, he relished speaking in public, but soon became too busy to write and let his assistants compose his articles for him.

As a youngster, Meyerhold drank in the lively artistic culture of his native Penza, a city 350 miles southeast of Moscow. He saw the great actors of the day at the local theatre where his family had a box. He also attended the circus and watched the jesters and barkers, jugglers and acrobats, and trained bears at the fairground booths in the market place. As a child, he dreamed of becoming an actor—ever since failing to win a competition dashed his hopes of becoming a violinist. After his amateur debut at eighteen, he asserted, "I have talent, I know I could become a good actor."

As a law student in Moscow in the mid-1890s, Meyerhold spent almost every evening in the top balcony at the Maly Theatre watching the great tragic actress Maria Ermolova—before embarking on his own career and eventually joining the Moscow Art Theatre, where he would remain four years.

A regular at concerts, Meyerhold believed that actors must be trained in music, which alone gives performance a precise rhythmic score. Although intimate with the greatest actors and directors, both Russian and foreign, Meyerhold avoided the closed professional circle of the theatre, choosing his friends from among writers, musicians, and artists. Because associative images and parallels are more powerful than the text of any play, the director should study the compositional laws of painting, music, and literature, he argued. On his travels around the world Meyerhold collected art reproductions; "Look at pictures" was his slogan.

As an actor, Meyerhold played a broad range of roles both comic and tragic, his favorite being the young writer Treplev in *The Seagull*, whose views on the necessity of new forms he and his generation shared. Although he abandoned his career as a performer by the time of the revolution, finding it impossible to act and direct simultaneously, in rehearsals Meyerhold still climbed up on stage and played all the roles in his shabby old overcoat. A genius at improvisation, he insisted on the actor's obligation to improvise.

Of all world literature Meyerhold preferred *Boris Godunov* (which he rehearsed for a year and a half but never fully staged) by his favorite playwright and theatrical theorist Pushkin. Except for Mayakovsky, contemporary Soviet plays, he felt, were inferior and schooled actors in bad acting.

He loved the old Spanish theatre, admired the Kabuki actors he saw in Paris, and was a fan of Chaplin and Keaton. When he first saw Isadora Duncan in 1908, he was moved to tears, but by 1915 reacted against "saccharine barefoot dancing à la Duncan." After seeing Jaques-Dalcroze, he declared eurythmics unnecessary.

Meyerhold disliked artistic shamanism and disavowed "Meyerholdism," which was critical shorthand for modernistic formal experimentation for its own sake without any ideas behind it. "Without self-restriction," he insisted, "there is no craftmanship."

For Meyerhold, the great theme in art was the confrontation of past with future, which in his own work became the leitmotif of a generation doomed by history. The Russian director discovered too late that he belonged to that generation. His theatre was closed by the authorities in January 1938, and he was arrested in June 1939. After seven months of interrogation and torture, Meyerhold confessed to being a foreign agent and incriminated others, among them Eisenstein and Pasternak, but later denied these accusations. He was executed by firing squad on February 2, 1940, then rehabilitated in the 1960s, but the full truth about the circumstances of his death was not made known until 1989.

THE FAIRGROUND BOOTH (1912)

II. *Two Puppet Theatres*

[...] When man appeared on the stage, why did he submit blindly to the director who wanted to transform the actor into a puppet of the naturalistic school? Man has yet to feel the urge to create *the art of man* on the stage.

The actor of today will not understand that the duty of the comedian and the mime is to transport the spectator to a world of make-believe, entertaining him on the way there with the brilliance of his technical skill.

The imaginary gesture valid only in the theatre, the stylized theatrical movement, the measured tones of theatrical declamation: they are all condemned by public and critics simply because the concept of "theatricality" still bears the traces of the style of acting which was developed by the so-called "inspirational actors."

The inspirational actor is content to rely exclusively on his own mood. He refuses to bend his will to the discipline of technique. The inspirational actor proudly claims to have rekindled the flame of improvisation in the theatre. In his naïveté he imagines that his improvisations have something in common with the improvisations of traditional Italian comedy. He does not realize that the improvisations of the *commedia dell' arte* had a firm basis of faultless technique. The inspirational actor totally rejects technique of any kind. "Technique hinders creative freedom" is what he always says. For him the only valid moment is the moment of unconscious creativity born of the emotions. If such a moment comes, he succeeds; if not, he fails.

Does the display of emotion really diminish the self-discipline of the actor? Real live men danced in plastic movements around the altar of Dionysus; their emotions seemed to burn uncontrollably, inflamed to extreme ecstasy by the fire on the altar. Yet the ritual in honor of the god of wine was composed of predetermined rhythms, steps and gestures. That is one example of the actor's self-discipline unaffected by the display of emotion. In the dance the Greek was bound by a whole series of traditional rules, yet he was at liberty to introduce as much personal invention as he wished.

From *Meyerhold on Theatre*, ed. and trans. Edward Braun.
London: Methuen Drama, 1991.

It is not just that the modern actor has no comprehension of the rules governing the art of comedy (art being, after all, that which is subject to laws or as Voltaire said: "the dance is art because it is bound by laws"); he has reduced his art to the most alarming chaos. As if that were not enough, he considers it his bounden duty to introduce chaos into all the other art forms as soon as he lays hands on them. He takes music and violates its fundamental principles by inventing "melodeclamation." When he reads poetry from the stage he heeds only the content of the verse, rearranging the logical stresses and ignoring completely every consideration of meter, rhythm, caesura, pause and musical intonation.

In his search for verisimilitude the actor of today concentrates on eliminating his "self" and tries to create an illusion of life on the stage. Why do they bother to write actors' names on the playbills? In its production of Gorky's *Lower Depths*, the Moscow Art Theatre brought a real tramp on to the stage in place of an actor. The pursuit of verisimilitude reached such a point that it was considered better to free the actor from the impossible task of creating a total illusion of life. Why did they print the name of the man playing Teterev on the posters? Can a man who plays *himself* on the stage really be called a "performer"? Why mislead the public?

The public comes to the theatre to see the art of man, but what art is there in walking about the stage as oneself? The public expects invention, play-acting and skill. But what it gets is either life or a slavish imitation of life. Surely the art of man on the stage consists in shedding all traces of environment, carefully choosing a mask, donning a decorative costume, and showing off one's brilliant tricks to the public—now as a dancer, now as the intrigant at some masquerade, now as the fool of old Italian comedy, now as a juggler.

If you examine the dog-eared pages of old scenarios such as Flaminio Scala's anthology, you will discover the magical power of the mask.

Arlecchino, a native of Bergamo and the servant of the miserly Doctor, is forced to wear a coat with multicolored patches because of his master's meanness. Arlecchino is a foolish buffoon, a roguish servant who seems always to wear a cheerful grin. But look closer! What is hidden behind the mask? Arlecchino, the all-powerful wizard, the enchanter, the magician; Arlecchino, the emissary of the infernal powers. [...]

The mask enables the spectator to see not only the actual Arlecchino before him but all the Arlecchinos who live in his memory. Through the mask the spectator sees every person who bears the merest resemblance to the character. But is it the mask alone which serves as the mainspring for all the enchanting plots of the theatre?

No, it takes the actor with his art of gesture and movement to transport the spectator to the fairy-tale kingdom where the blue-bird flies, where wild beasts talk, where Arlecchino, the loafer and knave sprung from subterranean forces, is reborn as a clown who performs the most astonishing tricks.

Arlecchino is an equilibrist, almost a tightrope-walker. He can leap with amazing agility. His improvised pranks astonish the spectator with a hyperbolical improbability beyond even our satirists' dreams. The actor is a dancer who can dance a graceful monferrina as well as a hearty English jig. The actor can turn tears to laughter in a few seconds. He bears the fat Doctor on his shoulders, yet prances about the stage with no apparent effort. Now he is soft and malleable, now he is awkward and inflexible. The actor can command a thousand different intonations, yet he never employs them to impersonate definite characters, preferring to use them merely to embellish his range of gestures and movements. The actor can speak quickly when playing a rogue, slowly and sing-song when playing a pedant. With his body he can describe geometrical figures on the stage, then sometimes he leaps, happy and free as a bird in the sky. The actor's face may be a death mask, yet he is able to distort it and bend his body to such a pose that the death mask comes to life.

Since the appearance of Isadora Duncan, and now even more with the Jaques-Dalcroze's theory of eurhythmics, the contemporary actor has begun gradually to concede the importance of gesture and movement on the stage. Yet still the mask holds little interest for him. No sooner is the question of the mask raised than the actor inquires whether it is seriously proposed to restore the masks and buskins of the antique theatre. The actor always visualizes the mask as an accessory; to him it is merely that which once helped to establish the character of the role and to overcome acoustical difficulties.

The time has yet to come when the appearance of an actor without a mask will once again bring cries of disapproval from the audiences such as happened in the reign of Louis XIV when the dancer Gardel first dared to appear without a mask. For the present the actor will not concede the mask as a symbol of the theatre at any price—and in this he is not alone.

I tried to interpret the character of Don Juan according to the principles of the theatre of the mask. But the mask on the face of the actor playing Don Juan went undetected, even by a critic like Benois.

"Molière loves Don Juan; Don Juan is his hero, and like every hero, he is something of a portrait of his author. So to substitute a satirical type for the hero ... is far worse than just a mistake." That is how Benois sees Molière's Don Juan. He would like to see him as the "seducer of Seville" of Tirso de Molina, Byron and Pushkin.

In his wanderings from one poet to another Don Juan preserved the basic features of his character, but like a mirror he reflected the different nature of each poet, the different way of life of each one's country, and the moral precepts of each one's society.

Benois has completely forgotten that Molière treated the figure of Don Juan not as an end but purely as a means to an end. He wrote *Don Juan* after *Tartuffe* had raised a storm of indignation amongst the clergy and the nobility. He was charged with a whole list of malicious crimes, and his enemies lost no time in recommending suitable punishments. Molière had only his own weapons to combat this injustice. In order to ridicule the bigotry of the clergy and the hypocrisy of the nobility which he so detested, he clutched at Don Juan like a drowning man at a straw. Many of the scenes and isolated phrases which cut across the mood of the main action and the character of the hero were inserted into the play by Molière simply to gain suitable revenge on those who obstructed the success of *Tartuffe*. Molière intentionally exposes "this leaping, dancing, posturing Lovelace" to scorn and derision in order to make him a target for his own attacks on the pride and vanity which he abhorred. But then he puts into the mouth of the same shallow cavalier whom he has just ridiculed a brilliant account of the prevailing vices of the period, hypocrisy and bigotry.

Furthermore, one must not overlook the marital drama which engulfed Molière just before his anguish at the banning of *Tartuffe*. "His wife, lacking the perception to appreciate the genius and integrity of her husband, rejected him in favor of the most unworthy rivals; she became enamored of salon prattlers whose sole advantage was their noble descent. Molière had not shirked earlier opportunities to hurl gibes at these marquis ridicules." Now he employed the person of Don Juan to renew his attacks on his rivals.

Molière needed comic scenes like the one with the peasant-women, not so much to characterize Don Juan as to drown his sorrows in the stupefying wine of comedy, the sorrows of a man robbed of domestic bliss by those shallow egotistical "devourers of women's hearts."

It is only too clear that Don Juan is a puppet whom Molière employs to square accounts with his innumerable enemies. For Molière, Don Juan is no more than a wearer of masks. At one moment we see on his face a mask which embodies all the dissoluteness, unbelief, cynicism and pretensions of a gallant of the court of Le Roi-Soleil; then we see the mask of the author-accuser; then the nightmarish mask which stifled the author himself, the agonizing mask he was forced to wear at court performances and in front of his perfidious wife. Not until the very end does he hand his puppet the mask of *El Burlador de Sevilla*, which he borrowed from the touring Italians.

The greatest compliment that the designer and the director of Molière's *Don Juan* (Alexander Golovin and the author) could possibly imagine was paid to them by Benois when he described their production as "a dressed-up fairground booth."

The theatre of the mask has always been a fairground show, and the idea of acting based on the apotheosis of the mask, gesture and movement is indivisible from the idea of the traveling show. Those concerned in reforming the contemporary theatre dream of introducing the principles of the fairground booth into the theatre. However, the skeptics believe that the revival of the principles of the fairground booth is being obstructed by the cinematograph.

Whenever the question of the rebirth of the fairground booth is raised there are people who either completely reject its advantages or who extol the cinematograph and call for its enlistment in the service of the theatre.

Far too much importance is attached to the cinematograph, that idol of the modern city, by its supporters. The cinematograph is of undoubted importance to science as a means of visual demonstration; it can serve as an illustrated newspaper depicting "the events of the day;" for some people it might even replace travel (horror of horrors!). But there is no place for the cinematograph in the world of art, even in a purely auxiliary capacity. And if for some reason or other the cinematograph is called a theatre, it is simply because during the period of total obsession with naturalism (an obsession which has already cooled off considerably) everything mechanical was enrolled in the service of the theatre.

This extreme obsession with naturalism, so characteristic of the general public at the end of the nineteenth and the beginning of the twentieth century was one of the original reasons for the extraordinary success of the cinematograph.

The romantics' vague dreams of the past excluded the strict limits of classical tragedy. In its turn, romanticism was forced to yield to the proponents of naturalistic drama. The naturalists proclaimed the slogan "depict life as it really is," thereby confusing the two separate artistic concepts of form and content.

Whilst reproaching the classicists and the romantics with their obsession with form, the naturalists themselves set about perfecting form and in so doing transformed art into photography. Electricity came to the aid of the naturalists, and the result—a touching union of photography and technology—was the cinematograph.

Having once banished imagination from the theatre, naturalism, to be consistent, should have banished paint as well, not to mention the unnatural diction of actors. After all, the cinematograph took advantage of the development of verisimilitude, whilst replacing painted costumes and sets with the colorless screen and dispensing with the spoken word.

The cinematograph, that dream-come-true of those who strive for the photographic representation of life, is a shining example of the obsession with quasi-verisimilitude.

The cinematograph is of undoubted importance to science, but when it is put to the service of art, it senses its own inadequacy and tries in vain to justify the label of "art." Hence its attempts to free itself from the basic principle of photography: it realizes the need to vindicate the first half of its dual appellation "the theatre-cinematograph." But the theatre is art and photography is non-art. So the cinematograph, in its hasty efforts to incorporate colors, music, declamation and singing, is pursuing elements which are totally alien to its mechanical nature.

Just as all the theatres which are still trying to propagate naturalistic drama and plays fit only for reading cannot stay the growth of truly theatrical and totally non-naturalistic plays, so the cinematograph cannot stifle the spirit of the fairground booth.

At the present time, when the cinematograph is in the ascendant, the absence of the fairground booth is only apparent. The fairground booth is eternal. Its heroes do not die; they simply change their aspects and assume new forms. The heroes of the ancient Atellanae, the foolish Maccus and the simple Pappus, were resurrected almost twenty centuries later in the figures of Arlecchino and Pantalone, the principal characters of the *commedia dell' arte*, the traveling theatre of the late Renaissance. Their audience came not so much to listen to dialogue as to watch the wealth of movement, club blows, dizzy leaps, and all the whole range of tricks native to the theatre.

The fairground booth is eternal. Even though its principles have been banished temporarily from within the walls of the theatre, we know that they remain firmly embedded in the lines of all true theatrical writers.

Molière, France's greatest comic and *grand divertisseur du Roi-Soleil*, depicted many times in his ballet-comedies what he had seen as a child in the booth of Gaultier-Garguille and his famous *collaborateurs*, Turlupin and Gros-Guillaume, and in the other booths of the fair at Saint-Germain.

The crowd there was entertained by puppets. "Judging by the puppet plays which survive (regrettably few) and by the numerous contemporary eye-witness accounts, the humble puppet theatre was remarkable for the boldness of its attacks and the universality of its satire; France's political reverses, the squalid intrigues of the court, the ugly contortions of high society, the rigid stratification of the caste system, the manners of the nobility and the tradespeople, were all exposed to the ridicule of the nimble marionettes." (Alexei Veselovsky.)

It was here that Molière acquired the power of denunciation which he later employed to fight authority and the nobility.

At the fair of Saint-Germain, Molière watched full-blooded performances of popular farce under a canvas awning, acrobats twirling to a cacophony of drums and tambourines, the itinerant surgeon, the conjurer and the quack, all competing for the attention of the thronging crowd.

Molière studied with the players of the Italian strolling troupes. Whilst with them he encountered the figure of Tartuffe in the comedies of Aretino and borrowed the character of Sganarelle from the Italian buffoni. *Le Dépit amoureux* is all outright imitation of the Italians. *Le Malade imaginaire* and *Monsieur de Pourceaugnac* are based on all those scenarios of the Italian traveling theatre featuring doctors (*Arlecchino, medico volante*, etc.).

Banished from the contemporary theatre, the principles of the fairground booth found a temporary refuge in the French cabarets, the German

Überbrettl, the English music halls and the ubiquitous "variétés." If you read Ernst von Wolzogen's Überbrettl manifesto, you will find that in essence it is an apologia for the principles of the fairground booth.

The manifesto stresses the significance of the art of the variétés, whose roots extend far below the surface of our age, and which it is wrong to regard as "a temporary aberration of taste." We prefer variétés, continues von Wolzogen, "to the bigger theatres where the play takes up a whole evening with its ponderous, bombastic exposition of depressing events. We prefer them not because our spirit has grown barren, as certain pseudo-Catonians and *laudatores temporis acti* allege. On the contrary, we aim for conciseness and profundity for clarity and the vigorous extract.

"The great discoveries and the many changes in the spiritual and technological life of our age have led to a quickening of the universal pulse; we are short of time. For this reason we seek conciseness and precision in everything. We oppose decadence and its inherent diffuseness and obsession with detail, with brevity, clarity and depth. And always in everything we seek broad dimensions.

"It is not true that we don't know how to laugh. Granted, we no longer laugh the meaningless, *amorphous* laugh of the cretin; we have replaced it with the brief, precise laugh of the cultured man who knows how to view things from all angles.

"Depth and extract, brevity and contrast! No sooner has the pale, lanky Pierrot crept across the stage, no sooner has the spectator sensed in his movements the eternal tragedy of mutely suffering mankind, than the apparition is succeeded by the merry Harlequinade. The tragic gives way to the comic, harsh satire replaces the sentimental ballad."

Wolzogen's manifesto contains an apologia for the favorite device of the fairground booth—*the grotesque.*

"Grotesque (Italian—*grottesca*) is the title of a genre of low comedy in literature, music and the plastic arts. Grotesque usually implies something hideous and strange, a humorous work which with no apparent logic combines the most dissimilar elements by *ignoring their details and relying on its own orig- inality, borrowing from every source anything which satisfies its* joie de vivre *and its capricious, mocking attitude to life.*" [*Great Encyclopedia*, 1902.]

This is the style which reveals the most wonderful horizons to the cre- ative artist. "I," my personal attitude to life, precedes all else. Everything which I take as material for my art corresponds not to the truth of reality but to the truth of *my* personal artistic whim.

"Art is incapable of conveying the sum of reality, that is, all concepts as they succeed one another in time. Art dismantles reality, depicting it now spatially, now temporally. For this reason, art consists either in images or in the alternation of images: the first yields the spatial forms of art, the second— the temporal forms. *The impossibility of embracing the totality of reality justifies the schematization of the real (in particular by means of stylization)."* [Andrei Bely, *Symbolism*, 1910.]

Stylization involves a certain degree of verisimilitude. In consequence, the stylizer remains an analyst *par excellence.*

"Schematization"—the very word seems to imply a certain impoverishment of reality, as though it somehow entailed the reduction of its totality. The grotesque is the second stage in the process of stylization, when the final link with analysis has been severed. Its method is strictly synthetical. Without compromise, the grotesque ignores all minor details and creates a totality of life "in stylized improbability" (to borrow Pushkin's phrase). Stylization impoverishes life to the extent that it reduces empirical abundance to typical unity. The grotesque does not recognize the *purely* debased or the *purely* exalted. The grotesque mixes opposites, consciously creating harsh incongruity and *relying solely on its own originality.*

In Hoffmann, ghosts take stomach pills, a bunch of flaming lilies turns into the gaudy dressing-gown of Lindhorst, the student Anselmus is fitted into a glass bottle. In Tirso de Molina, the hero's monologue has no sooner attuned the spectator to an air of solemnity—as though with the majestic chords of a church organ—than it is followed by a monologue *gracioso* whose comic twists instantly wipe the devout smile from his face and make him guffaw like some medieval barbarian.

On a rainy autumn day a funeral procession crawls through the streets; the gait of the pall-bearers conveys profound grief. Then the wind snatches a hat from the head of one of the mourners, he bends down to pick it up, but the wind begins to chase it from puddle to puddle. Each jump of the staid gentleman chasing his hat lends his face such comic grimaces that the gloomy funeral procession is suddenly transformed by some devilish hand into a bustling holiday crowd. If only one could achieve an effect like that on the stage!

Contrast. Surely the grotesque is not intended simply as a means of creating or heightening contrasts! Is the grotesque not an end in itself? Like Gothic architecture, for example, in which the soaring bell-tower expresses the fervor of the worshiper whilst its projections decorated with fearsome distorted figures direct one's thoughts back towards hell. The lusts of the flesh, the sin of lasciviousness, the insurmountable bestiality of life: all these seem to be designed to prevent excessive idealism from turning into asceticism. Just as in Gothic architecture a miraculous balance is preserved between affirmation and denial, the celestial and the terrestrial, the beautiful and the ugly, so the grotesque parades ugliness in order to prevent beauty from lapsing into sentimentality (in Schiller's sense).

The grotesque has its own attitude towards the outward appearance of life. The grotesque deepens life's outward appearance to the point where it ceases to appear merely natural.

Beneath what we see of life there are vast unfathomed depths. In its search for the supernatural, the grotesque synthesizes opposites, creates a picture of the incredible, and invites the spectator to solve the riddle of the inscrutable.

Blok (in Acts One and Three of *The Unknown Woman*), Fyodor Sologub (*Vanka the Butler, and Jean the Page*), and Wedekind (*The Earth Spirit, Pandora's Box, Spring's Awakening*) have all succeeded in remaining within the bounds of realistic drama whilst adopting a new approach to the portrayal of life. They have achieved unusual effects within the bounds of realistic drama by resorting to the grotesque.

The realism of these dramatists in the plays mentioned is such that it forces the spectator to adopt an ambivalent attitude towards the stage action. Is it not the task of the grotesque in the theatre to preserve this ambivalent attitude in the spectator by switching the course of the action with strokes of contrast? The basis of the grotesque is the artist's constant desire to switch the spectator from the plane he has just reached to another which is totally unforeseen.

"Grotesque is the title of a genre of low comedy in literature, music and the plastic arts." Why "*low* comedy"? And why only "comic"? It is not only humorous artists who for no apparent reason have synthesized the most diverse natural phenomena in their works. The grotesque need not necessarily be comic (the aspect examined by Flögel in his *Geschichte des Groteskkomischen*); it can as easily be tragic as we know from the drawings of Goya, the horrific tales of Edgar Allen Poe, and above all, of course, from E. T. A. Hoffmann.

Our own Blok in his lyrical dramas has followed the path of the grotesque in the spirit of these masters.

> Greetings world! You're with me again!
> So long your soul has been close to me!
> And now once more I shall breathe your spring
> Through your window of gold!

Thus, cries Arlecchino to the cold starry sky of Petersburg and leaps through the window. But "the distance seen through the window turns out to be painted on paper." The injured clown with his convulsed body hanging across the footlights cries to the audience that he is bleeding cranberry juice.

The ornamentation employed in the fifteenth century by the artists of the Renaissance was based on examples found in the catacombs (*grotti*), baths and palaces of Ancient Rome, shaped into symmetrical garlands of stylized plants with animals and imaginary figures like satyrs, centaurs and other mythological beasts, with masks and garlands of fruit, birds, insects, weapons and vessels.

Was it not this particular form of grotesque which was reflected in Sapunov's costume designs for the pantomime, *Columbine's Scarf* by Schnitzler-Dapertutto? For the sake of a grotesque effect, Sapunov transformed Gigolo into a parrot by combing his wig from back to front to resemble feathers and by arranging the tails of his frock-coat in the form of a real tail.

In Pushkin's short play set in the age of chivalry the mowers flail with their scythes at the legs of the knights' horses: "some horses fall injured and others run wild." Pushkin who drew particular attention "to the ancients with their tragic masks and their dualistic portrayal of character," who welcomed such "stylized improbability," is hardly likely to have expected real horses, previously schooled to fall injured and run wild, to be brought on to the stage.

In writing this stage direction Pushkin might almost have foreseen the actor of the twentieth century riding on to the stage on a wooden steed, as was the case in Adam de la Halle's pastorale, *Robin and Marion*, or on the caparisoned wooden frames with paper-maché horses' heads on which the Prince and his entourage embarked on their long journey in Znosko-Borovsky's *Transfigured Prince*. The designer gave the horses' necks deep curves and stuck prancing ostrich feathers into their heads, which alone sufficed to make the clumsy frames covered with caparisons look like horses lightly prancing and proudly rearing on their hind legs.

In the same play the youthful prince returns from his journey to learn that his father, the king, has died. The courtiers proclaim the prince king, place a gray wig on his head, and attach a long gray beard to his chin. In full view of the audience the youthful prince is transformed into the venerable old man which a king in the realm of fairy-tales is supposed to be.

In the first scene of Blok's *Fairground Booth* there is a long table covered with a black cloth reaching to the floor and parallel to the footlights. Behind the table sit the "mystics," the top halves of their bodies visible to the audience. Frightened by some rejoinder, they duck their heads, and suddenly all that remains at the table is a row of torsos minus heads and hands. It transpires that the figures are cut out of *cardboard* with frock-coats, shirt-fronts, collars and cuffs drawn on with soot and chalk. The actors' hands are thrust through openings in the cardboard torsos, and their heads simply rest on the cardboard collars.

Hoffmann's doll complains that she has a clockwork mechanism instead of a heart. The element of deception is important in the dramatic grotesque just as it is in Hoffmann. The same is true of Jacques Callot. Hoffmann writes of this astonishing graphic artist: "Even in his drawings; from life (processions, battles) there is something in the appearance of the life-like figures which makes them at once *familiar yet strange*. Through the medium of the grotesque the comic figures of Callot yield *mysterious allusions* to the perceptive observer."

The art of the grotesque is based on the conflict between form and content. The grotesque aims to subordinate psychologism to a decorative task. [...]

FILIPPO TOMMASO MARINETTI

Filippo Tommaso MARINETTI (1876-1944) was rather short in stature, with irregular features and a dark olive complexion. He sported an upturned moustache in the Prussian style and dressed impeccably in the requisite Futurist uniform: black bowler and black topcoat over black suit and black bow tie.

Born in Alexandria, son of a millionaire, "Tom" was educated in French by the Jesuits and began his literary career writing symbolist poetry in that language. As a student in Milan, he became a passionate spectator, frequenting the popular café-concert and variety theatre as well as attending the great theatrical premieres for which Milan, with its rich cultured bourgeoisie, was famous. There he watched the celebrated actors and actresses of the day—Duse, Rossi, Salvini—and saw the plays of Rovetta, Praga, Giacosa, Bracco, Hauptmann, Ibsen, Ferrari, and D'Annunzio. At La Scala he became acquainted with the operatic repertory.

From 1898 to 1902 Marinetti wrote about theatre as the Italian correspondent for the Parisian *Revue d'art dramatique*. As an aggressive young critic, he attacked the theatre of the older generation, rejecting verist realism in favor of the mythic figures of Wagnerian music drama and the legendary heroes of D'Annunzio, whose *The Dead City* he defended when it was given in Milan.

Drawing upon his knowledge of symphony and opera, Marinetti advocated polyphonic stagecraft and pursued parallels between theatre and music, discovering an underlying kinship between Wagnerian leitmotif and Maeterlinckian repetition. A proponent of the decadent esthetic, he believed in Schopenhauer's liberation through art, which, more effectively than alcohol or love, enabled humans to forget reality through immersion in the dream. Standing above the multitude, the artist had limitless power to express the inexpressible, reveal the unknown, and escape the mediocrity of life.

But with "The Founding Manifesto of Futurism," published in the Parisian *Figaro* in 1908, Marinetti turned his back on the past, abandoning D'Annunzio and the "sickly nostalgic poetry of distance and memory" for the modern sights and sounds of the noisy, mechanical metropolis with its electrical culture.

Starting in 1910, public declamation of their manifestoes became the Futurists' most innovative form of performance. Blending art and technology with American promotional techniques, Marinetti and his band of poets, painters, and musicians traveled by motorcade throughout Italy, bringing their grand Futurist evenings to towns both large and small. The galvanic maestro, who worshiped speed and danger, made a cult of cars (theorized as "automobilism"). The aim of the evenings was to incite the paying bourgeois public to a howling frenzy of indignation and outrage. "Art, in fact," Marinetti declared, "can be nothing but violence, cruelty, and injustice." Success was measured by the hail of potatoes, tomatoes, and chestnuts with which he was pelted. A polished brawler, Tom fought back with insults and blows.

The group provocations were staged only within Italy where they invariably pricked the right cultural nerves. To export the principles of Futurism, Marinetti went to France, England, Russia, and other European countries as a one-man show on lecture-demonstration tours.

Simultaneously polemical and histrionic, Marinetti was a virtuoso performer of unusual oratorical and declamatory skills. "Everything of any value is theatrical" was his credo. He delivered his lectures rapid-fire, the sweat pouring down his face in streaks. In an almost shamanistic trance, he produced an astounding array of onomatopoeic whirring, buzzing, popping, and zooming sounds, while moving about with the jerky animation of a speeded-up film. He whinnied and yelled at the top of his lungs, said to be the most powerful in Europe. *Fisicofollia* or body-madness was central to his aesthetic of astonishment. His arms shot out to the side or straight up in the air. He pounded the podium with his fist, bared his teeth, rolled and flashed his eyes, gulping down glass after glass of water without ever stopping once to catch his breath.

Marinetti made converts among the younger generation by his attacks on authority. The Futurists made commando raids on revered cultural institutions, stopping performances at La Scala and interrupting the lectures of professors of aesthetics like Benedetto Croce. When the police intervened, young anarchists and militant members of the labor movement rallied to the support of Marinetti, who adopted the agitational techniques of the radical political left and made them part of his artistic program.

THE VARIETY THEATRE (1913)

We are deeply disgusted with the contemporary theatre (verse, prose, and musical) because it vacillates stupidly between historical reconstruction (pastiche or plagiarism) and photographic reproduction of our daily life; a finicking, slow, analytic, and diluted theatre worthy, all in all, of the age of the oil lamp.

FUTURISM EXALTS THE VARIETY THEATRE because:

1. The Variety Theatre, born as we are from electricity, is lucky in having no tradition, no masters, no dogma, and it is fed by swift actuality.
2. The Variety Theatre is absolutely practical, because it proposes to distract and amuse the public with comic effects, erotic stimulation, or imaginative astonishment.
3. The authors, actors, and technicians of the Variety Theatre have only one reason for existing and triumphing: incessantly to invent new elements of astonishment. Hence the absolute impossibility of arresting or repeating oneself, hence an excited competition of brains and muscles to conquer the various records of agility, speed, force, complication, and elegance.
4. The Variety Theatre is unique today in its use of the cinema, which enriches it with an incalculable number of visions and otherwise unrealizable spectacles (battles, riots, horse races, automobile and aeroplane meets, trips, voyages, depths of the city, the countryside, oceans, and skies).
5. The Variety Theatre, being a profitable show window for countless inventive forces, naturally generates what I call "the Futurist marvelous," produced by modern mechanics. Here are some of the elements of this "marvelous": (a) powerful caricatures; (b) abysses of the ridiculous; (c) delicious, impalpable ironies; (d) all-embracing, definitive symbols; (e) cascades of uncontrollable hilarity; (f) profound analogies between humanity, the animal, vegetable, and mechanical worlds; (g) flashes of revealing cynicism; (h) plots full of the wit, repartee, and conundrums that aerate the intelligence; (i) the whole gamut of laughter and smiles, to flex the nerves; (j) the whole gamut of stupidity, imbecility, doltishness, and absurdity, insensibly pushing the intelligence to the

From Marinetti, *Selected Writings*, ed. and trans. R.W. Flint.
N.Y.: Farrar, Straus and Giroux, 1972.

very border of madness; (k) all the new significations of light, sound, noise, and language, with their mysterious and inexplicable extension into the least-explored part of our sensibility; (l) a cumulus of events unfolded at great speed, of stage characters pushed from right to left in two minutes ("and now let's have a look at the Balkans": King Nicholas, Enver-Bey, Daneff, Venizelos belly-blows and fistfights between Serbs and Bulgars, a *couplet*, and everything vanishes); (m) instructive, satirical pantomimes; (n) caricatures of suffering and nostalgia, strongly impressed on the sensibility through gestures exasperating in their spasmodic, hesitant, weary slowness; grave words made ridiculous by funny gestures, bizarre disguises, mutilated words, ugly faces, pratfalls.
6. Today the Variety Theatre is the crucible in which the elements of an emergent new sensibility are seething. Here you find an ironic decomposition of all the worn-out prototypes of the Beautiful, the Grand, the Solemn, the Religious, the Ferocious, the Seductive, and the Terrifying, and also the abstract elaboration of the new prototypes that will succeed these.

The Variety Theatre is thus the synthesis of everything that humanity has up to now refined in its nerves to divert itself by laughing at material and moral grief; it is also the bubbling fusion of all the laughter, all the smiles, all the mocking grins, all the contortions and grimaces of future humanity. Here you sample the joy that will shake men for another century, their poetry, painting, philosophy, and the leaps of their architecture.
7. The Variety Theatre offers the healthiest of all spectacles in its dynamism of form and color (simultaneous movement of jugglers, ballerinas, gymnasts, colorful riding masters, spiral cyclones of dancers spinning on the points of their feet). In its swift, overpowering dance rhythms the Variety Theatre forcibly drags the slowest souls out of their torpor and forces them to run and jump.
8. The Variety Theatre is alone in seeking the audience's collaboration. It doesn't remain static like a stupid voyeur, but joins noisily in the action, in the singing, accompanying the orchestra, communicating with the actors in surprising actions and bizarre dialogues. And the actors bicker clownishly with the musicians.

The Variety Theatre uses the smoke of cigars and cigarettes to join the atmosphere of the theatre to that of the stage. And because the audience cooperates in this way with the actors' fantasy, the action develops simultaneously on the stage, in the boxes, and in the orchestra. It continues to the end of the performance, among the battalions of fans, the honeyed dandies who crowd the stage door to fight over the star; double final victory: chic dinner and bed.
9. The Variety Theatre is a school of sincerity for man because it exalts his rapacious instincts and snatches every veil from woman, all the phrases, all the sighs, all the romantic sobs that mask and deform her. On the other hand it brings to light all woman's marvelous animal qualities, her grasp, her powers

of seduction, her faithlessness, and her resistance.

10. The Variety Theatre is a school of heroism in the difficulty of setting records and conquering resistances, and it creates on the stage the strong, sane atmosphere of danger. (E.g., death-diving, "Looping the loop" on bicycles, in cars, and on horseback.)

11. The Variety Theatre is a school of subtlety, complication, and mental synthesis, in its clowns, magicians, mind readers, brilliant calculators, writers of skits, imitators and parodists, its musical jugglers and eccentric Americans, its fantastic pregnancies that give birth to objects and weird mechanisms.

12. The Variety Theatre is the only school that one can recommend to adolescents and to talented young men, because it explains, quickly and incisively, the most abstruse problems and most complicated political events. Example: A year ago at the Folies-Bergère, two dancers were acting out the meandering discussions between Cambon and Kinderlen-Watcher on the question of Morocco and the Congo in a revealing symbolic dance that was equivalent to at least three years' study of foreign affairs. Facing the audience, their arms entwined, glued together, they kept making mutual territorial concessions, jumping back and forth, to left and right, never separating, neither of them ever losing sight of his goal, which was to become more and more entangled. They gave an impression of extreme courtesy, of skillful, flawlessly diplomatic vacillation, ferocity, diffidence, stubbornness, meticulousness.

Furthermore the Variety Theatre luminously explains the governing laws of life:

(a) the necessity of complication and varying rhythms;

(b) the fatality of the lie and the contradiction (e.g., two-faced English *danseuses* : little shepherd girl and fearful soldier);

(c) the omnipotence of a methodical will that modifies human powers;

(d) a synthesis of speed + transformations.

13. The Variety Theatre systematically disparages ideal love and its romantic obsession that repeats the nostalgic languors of passion to satiety, with the robot-like monotony of a daily profession. It whimsically mechanizes sentiment, disparages and healthily tramples down the compulsion towards carnal possession, lowers lust to the natural function of coitus, deprives it of every mystery, every crippling anxiety, every unhealthy idealism.

Instead, the Variety Theatre gives a feeling and a taste for easy, light and ironic loves. Café-concert performances in the open air on the terraces of casinos offer a most amusing battle between spasmodic moonlight, tormented by infinite desperations, and the electric light that bounces off the false jewelry, painted flesh, multicolored petticoats, velvets, tinsel, the counterfeit color of lips. Naturally the energetic electric light triumphs and the soft decadent moonlight is defeated.

14. The Variety Theatre is naturally anti-academic, primitive, and naive, hence the more significant for the unexpectedness of its discoveries and the

simplicity of its means. (E.g., the systematic tour of the stage that the *chanteuses* make, like caged animals, at the end of every *couplet*.)

15. The Variety Theatre destroys the Solemn, the Sacred, the Serious, and the Sublime in Art with a capital "*A.*" It cooperates in the Futurist destruction of immortal masterworks, plagiarizing them, parodying them, making them look commonplace by stripping them of their solemn apparatus as if they were mere *attractions*. So we unconditionally endorse the performance of *Parsifal* in forty minutes, now in rehearsal in a great London music-hall.

16. The Variety Theatre destroys all our conceptions of perspective, proportion, time, and space. (E.g., a little doorway and gate, thirty centimeters high, alone in the middle of the stage, which certain eccentric Americans open and close as they pass and repass, very seriously as if they couldn't do otherwise.)

17. The Variety Theatre offers us all the records so far attained: the greatest speed and the finest gymnastics and acrobatics of the Japanese, the greatest muscular frenzy of the Negroes, the greatest development of animal intelligence (horses, elephants, seals, dogs, trained birds), the finest melodic inspiration of the Gulf of Naples and the Russian steppes, the best Parisian wit, the greatest competitive force of different races (boxing and wrestling), the greatest anatomical monstrosity, the greatest female beauty.

18. The conventional theatre exalts the inner life, professorial meditation, libraries, museums, monotonous crises of conscience, stupid analyses of feelings, in other words (dirty thing and dirty word), *psychology*, whereas, on the other hand, the Variety Theatre exalts action, heroism, life in the open air, dexterity, the authority of instinct and intuition. To psychology it opposes what I call "body-madness" *(fisicofollia)*.

19. Finally, the Variety Theatre offers to every country (like Italy) that has no great single capital city a brilliant résumé of Paris considered as the one magnetic center of luxury and ultrarefined pleasure.

FUTURISM WANTS TO TRANSFORM THE VARIETY THEATRE INTO A THEATRE OF AMAZEMENT, RECORD-SETTING, AND BODY-MADNESS.

1. One must completely destroy all logic in Variety Theatre performances, exaggerate their luxuriousness in strange ways, multiply contrasts and make the absurd and the unlifelike complete masters of the stage. (Example: Oblige the *chanteuses* to dye their décolletage, their arms and especially their hair, in all the colors hitherto neglected as means of seduction. Green hair, violet arms, blue décolletage, orange chignon, etc. Interrupt a song and continue with a revolutionary speech. Spew out a *romanza* of insults and profanity, etc.).

2. Prevent a set of traditions from establishing itself in the Variety Theatre. Therefore oppose and abolish the stupid Parisian "Revues," as tedious as Greek tragedy with their *Compère* and *Commère* playing the part of the ancient

chorus, their parade of political personalities and events set off by wisecracks in a most irritating logical sequence. The Variety Theatre, in fact, must not be what it unfortunately still is today, nearly always a more or less amusing newspaper.

3. Introduce surprise and the need to move among the spectators of the orchestra, boxes, and balcony. Some random suggestions: spread a powerful glue on some of the seats, so that the male or female spectator will stay glued down and make everyone laugh (the damaged frock coat or toilette will naturally be paid for at the door)—sell the same ticket to ten people: traffic jam, bickering, and wrangling—offer free tickets to gentlemen or ladies who are notoriously unbalanced, irritable, or eccentric and likely to provoke uproars with obscene gestures, pinching women, or other freakishness. Sprinkle the seats with dust to make people itch and sneeze, etc.

4. Systematically prostitute all of classic art on the stage, performing for example all the Greek, French, and Italian tragedies, condensed and comically mixed up, in a single evening—put life into the works of Beethoven, Wagner, Bach, Bellini, Chopin, introducing them with Neapolitan songs—put Duse, Sarah Bernhardt, Zacconi, Mayot and Fregoli side by side on the stage—play a Beethoven symphony backwards, beginning with the last note—boil all of Shakespeare down to a single act—do the same with all the most venerated actors—have actors recite *Hernani* tied in sacks up to their necks—soap the floorboards to cause amusing tumbles at the most tragic moments.

5. In every way encourage the *type* of the eccentric American, the impression he gives of exciting grotesquerie, of frightening dynamism; his crude jokes, his enormous brutalities, his trick weskits and pants as deep as a ship's hold out of which, with a thousand other things, will come the great Futurist hilarity that should make the world's face young again.

Because, and don't forget it, we Futurists are YOUNG ARTILLERYMEN ON A TOOT as we proclaimed in our manifesto, "Let's Murder the Moonshine," fire + fire + light against moonshine and against old firmaments war every night great cities to blaze with electric signs Immense black face (30 meters high + 150 meters height of the building = 180 meters) open close open close a golden eye 3 meters high SMOKE SMOKE MANOLI SMOKE MANOLI CIGARETTES woman in a blouse (50 meters + 120 meters of building = 170 meters) stretch relax a violet rosy lilac blue bust froth of electric light in a champagne glass (30 meters) sizzle evaporate in a mouthful of darkness electric signs dim die under a dark stiff hand come to life again continue stretch out in the night the human day's activity courage + folly never to die or cease or sleep electric signs = formation and disaggregation of mineral and vegetable center of the earth circulation of blood in the ferrous faces of Futurist houses increases, empurples (joy anger more more still stronger) as soon as the negative pessimist sentimental nostalgic shadows besiege the city

0brilliant revival of streets that channel a smoky swarm of workers by day two horses (30 meters tall) rolling golden balls with their hoofs GIOCONDA PURGATIVE WATERS crisscross of *trrrr trrrrr* Elevated *trrrr trrrrr* overhead trrrombone whissstle ambulance sirens and firetrucks transformation of the streets into splendid corridors to guide push logic necessity the crowd towards trepidation + laughter + music-hall uproar FOLIES-BERGÈRE EMPIRE CRÈME-ÉCLIPSE tubes of mercury red red red blue violet huge letter-eels of gold purple diamond fire Futurist defiance to the weepy night the stars' defeat warmth enthusiasm faith conviction will power penetration of an electric sign into the house across the street *yellow slaps* for that gouty, dozy bibliophile in slippers 3 mirrors watch him the sign plunges to 3 redgold abysses open close open close 3 thousand meters deep horror quirk go out out hat stick steps taximeter push shove *zuu zuoeu* here we are dazzle of the promenade solemnity of the panther-cocottes in their comic-opera tropics fat warm smell of music-hall gaiety = tireless ventilation of the world's Futurist brain.

BERNARD SHAW

Bernard SHAW (1856-1950) constructed his own "devilish" appearance with brushes and comb, forcing his Satanic red beard to jut out and giving a dramatic upsweep to his moustaches and Mephistophelean eyebrows (modeled after the demonic tempter in Gounod's *Faust)*. Almost six feet tall, the young art-music-theatre critic was lean and thin, with long legs and a bony, bearded face. His body was taut, his movements abrupt, as he walked at high speed, with a light springy step.

For his costume, Shaw chose a reddish-brown hygienic suit made of knitted natural wool with matching knee-breeches; it looked "as if it were a sort of reddish brown fur," his friend G.K. Chesterton said, "like the hair and the eyebrows, a part of the animal." When his red hair turned white, the diabolically impertinent upstart Bernard Shaw became transformed into the white-maned, white-bearded sage and patriarch G.B.S. who had private audiences with heads of state (including Stalin) and made self-assured comments about everything under the sun.

No modern artist has been more thoroughly represented in different media than Shaw, and none has been as inventive in striking dramatic poses, or as obliging in arranging sittings and giving commissions, designed, he claimed, to promote unrecognized talent. Sculptors, painters, and photographers vied for the right to represent him. H.G.Wells complained that it was impossible to move about Europe without being confronted by replicas of Shaw. When Shaw's wife commissioned Rodin to do a bust of her husband, audiences assembled daily at the artist's estate to watch the show, admiring Shaw's performance as model quite as much as Rodin's work as sculptor.

Shaw himself was sardonically aware that all the endless theatrical poses were only the masks of his great reputation, not the man himself. In G.B.S. the playwright had created a super persona, but contained within this gesticulating übermarionette there lurked an impish double who debunked the very idea of his public self. "I have never pretended that G.B.S. was real: I have over and over again taken him to pieces before the audience to shew the trick of him."

A great exposer of the illusions by which his Victorian and Edwardian contemporaries lived, Shaw was a master illusionist himself, so cunning that his disclosure of his own tricks made them all the more dazzling. Only Jacob Epstein's commissioned bust revealed a savage Shaw beneath the mask. The playwright called it "Neanderthal Shaw" and yielded to his wife's refusal to have it in the house.

At the writer's death, except for one portrait of Samuel Butler, one of Gandhi, and two of Stalin, all the many pictures in the house were of Shaw; even the door-knocker was an image of G.B.S. During the course of a long career, Shaw himself became the primary spectacle, but he had begun his work in the theatre as a super spectator.

As the theatre critic for *The Saturday Review* from January 1895 to May 1898, Shaw wrote 151 weekly articles and frequented the major London theatres as well as Grein's Independent Theatre and other experimental stages. Shaw was superbly qualified for the job and made a formidable critic-theorist, expert in the related arts of music and painting, highly knowledge-able about the sociology and economics of theatre, a perceptive interpreter of audience psychology, and above all a brilliant student of acting. He grew up with Shakespeare and before coming to England in 1876 regularly attended Dublin's Theatre Royal, a stock company (featuring touring stars of the old school such as Barry Sullivan and Adelaide Ristori) where he was nurtured on heroic acting and opera.

Shaw made no pretense of neutrality or objectivity. His powerful crit-ical intelligence was put entirely at the service of his program for transform-ing the British theatre and its public: "I do my best to be partial, to hit out at remediable abuses rather than at accidental shortcomings, and at strong and responsible people rather than weak and helpless ones."

Shaw knew exactly what was wrong with the theatre of his day (it was 200 years behind the times), what it should become (a realistic theatre of ideas), and how the change could be effected (through Ibsen and the new drama represented by plays like his own).

A historian of changes in sensibility, the critic for *The Saturday Review* chronicled—and promoted—the Ibsen movement in England. After Ibsen, he argued, it was impossible to read or perform Shakespeare in the old way; even those who hated the Norwegian playwright or had never seen his work would eventually have their vision of the world changed.

Resolutely for the moderns in their perennial quarrel with the ancients, Shaw was, by his own admission, a deliberately malicious spectator when confronted with "retrogressive art and wasted or unworthily used tal-ent." The critic waged a relentless campaign against Henry Irving and his Lyceum theatre for wasting his own talent and that of Ellen Terry on an old-fashioned repertory of melodrama and mutilated Shakespeare. Shaw had first hoped that Irving would create the new theatre, but totally wrapped up in his own acting, the director of the Lyceum had no time to listen to Shaw or to stage his plays. Through his correspondence with Ellen Terry, Shaw exacted his revenge, eventually converting Irving's leading lady who then left the Lyceum. "I have destroyed her belief in him," Shaw gloated theatrically.

By attacking the institution of commercial theatre, Shaw took a revolutionary stand, but the solution he proposed—to infiltrate West End theatres and gradually replace the fashionable repertory with plays from the experimental stages—was a strategic compromise that made G.B.S.'s colossal triumph possible.

TOLSTOY:
TRAGEDIAN OR COMEDIAN? (1921)

[...] Was Tolstoy tragedian or comedian? The popular definition of tragedy is heavy drama in which everyone is killed in the last act, comedy being light drama in which everyone is married in the last act. The classical definition is, of tragedy, drama that purges the soul by pity and terror, and, of comedy, drama that chastens morals by ridicule. These classical definitions, illustrated by Aeschylus-Sophocles-Euripides *versus* Aristophanes in the ancient Greek theatre, and Corneille-Racine *versus* Molière in the French theatre are still much the best the critic can work with. But the British school has always scandalized classic scholarship and French taste by defying them: nothing will prevent the English playwright from mixing comedy, and even tomfoolery, with tragedy. *Lear* may pass for pure tragedy; for even the fool in *Lear* is tragic; but Shakespeare could not keep the porter out of *Macbeth* nor the clown out of *Antony and Cleopatra*. We are incorrigible in this respect, and may as well make a merit of it.

We must therefore recognize and examine a third variety of drama. It begins as tragedy with scraps of fun in it, like *Macbeth*, and ends as comedy without mirth in it, the place of mirth being taken by a more or less bitter and critical irony. We do not call the result melodrama, because that term has come to mean drama in which crude emotions are helped to expression by musical accompaniment. Besides, there is at first no true new species: the incongruous elements do not combine: there is simply frank juxtaposition of fun with terror in tragedy and of gravity with levity in comedy. You have *Macbeth*; and you have *Le Misanthrope, Le Festin de Pierre, All's Well That Ends Well, Troilus and Cressida*: all of them, from the Aristotelian and Voltairean point of view, neither fish, fowl, nor good red herring.

When the censorship killed serious drama in England, and the dramatists had to express themselves in novels, the mixture became more lawless than ever: it was practiced by Fielding and culminated in Dickens, whose extravagances would have been severely curbed if he had had to submit his Micawbers and Mrs. Wilfers to the test of representation on the stage, when it would have been discovered at once that their parts are mere repetitions of

From *International Magazine Company*, November 30, 1921.

the same joke, and have none of that faculty of developing and advancing matters which constitutes stage action. Dickens would have been forced to make
something better than Aunt Sallies of them. Since Dickens one can think of
no great writer who has produced the same salad of comedy and tragedy
except Anatole France. He remains incorrigible: even in his most earnest
attempts to observe the modesties of nature and the proprieties of art in his
autobiographical *Le Petit Pierre* he breaks down and launches into chapters of
wild harlequinade (think of the servant Radegond and the Chaplinesque
invention of Simon of Nantua and the *papegai)* and then returns ashamed and
sobered to the true story of his life, knowing that he has lost every right to
appear before the Judgment Seat with *Le Petit Pierre* in his hand as the truth,
the whole truth, and nothing but the truth, so help him Rousseau. On his
comic side Anatole France is Dickens's French double, disguised by culture. In
one of his earliest stories, *Jocaste*, the heroine's father is a more perfect Dickens
comic personage than Dickens himself ever succeeded in putting on paper.

After Dickens, Comedy completed its development into the new
species, which has been called tragi-comedy when any attempt has been made
to define it. Tragedy itself never developed: it was simple, sublime, and overwhelming from the first: it either failed and was not tragedy at all or else it got
there so utterly that no need was felt for going any further. The only need felt
was for relief; and therefore, though tragedy remains unchanged from
Aeschylus to Richard Wagner (Europe's last great tragic poet), the reaction to
a moment of fun which we associate with Shakespeare got the upper hand
even of Aeschylus, and produced his comic sentinels who, afraid to go to the
rescue of Agamemnon, pretend that nothing is happening, just as it got the
better of Victor Hugo, with his Don Caesar de Bazan tumbling down the
chimney, and his Rustighello playing Wamba to the Duke of Ferrara's Cedric
the Saxon. But in the main Tragedy remained on its summit, simple, unmixed,
and heroic, from Sophocles to Verdi.

Not so Comedy. When *The Merry Wives of Windsor* gave way to
Marriage à la Mode, Romeo to Hamlet, Punch to Don Juan, Petruchio to
Almaviva, and generally, horseplay and fun for fun's sake to serious chastening
of morals less and less by ridicule and more and more by irony, the comic poet
becoming less and less a fellow of infinite jest and more and more a satirical
rogue and a discloser of essentially tragic ironies, the road was open to a sort
of comedy as much more tragic than a catastrophic tragedy as an unhappy
marriage, or even a happy one, is more tragic than a railway accident.
Shakespeare's bitter play with a bitter title, *All's Well That Ends Well*, anticipates Ibsen: the happy ending at which the title sneers is less comforting than
the end of *Romeo and Juliet*. And Ibsen was the dramatic poet who firmly established tragi-comedy as a much deeper and grimmer entertainment than
tragedy. His heroes dying without hope or honor, his dead, forgotten, super-
seded men walking and talking with the ghosts of the past, are all heroes of

comedy: their existence and their downfall are not soul-purifying convulsions of pity and horror, but reproaches, challenges, criticisms addressed to society and to the spectator as a voting constituent of society. They are miserable and yet not hopeless; for they are mostly criticisms of false intellectual positions which, being intellectual, are remediable by better thinking.

Thus Comedy has become the higher form. The element of accident in Tragedy has always been its weak spot; for though an accident may be sensational, nothing can make it interesting or save it from being irritating. *Othello* is spoilt by a handkerchief, as Shakespeare found out afterwards when he wrote *A Winter's Tale*. The curtain falls on *The School for Scandal* just when the relations between the dishonorable Joseph Surface and the much more dishonorable Lady Teazle have become interesting for the first moment in the play. In its tragedy and comedy alike, the modern tragi-comedy begins where the old tragedies and comedies left off; and we have actually had plays made and produced dealing with what happened to Ibsen's *dramatis personae* before the first act began. [...]

ANTONIN ARTAUD

Antonin ARTAUD (1896-1948), when he first appeared on the Parisian stage in 1921, was a soulfully handsome young actor who scarcely looked twenty, with a pale face, blue-green eyes, chestnut hair, and a frail, nervous body and expressive hands. Two decades later he had become an ancient martyr, his ravaged body gnarled with pain, his gaunt face wrinkled and toothless, his deep-set eyes burning with the inner fire of a visionary. As his friend Jean-Louis Barrault observed, Artaud "made himself into a theatre—a theatre that did not lie."

Artaud's appearance, transformed by a lifetime of suffering, is the most eloquent expression of his view of art as self-revelation. "Where others want to produce works of art," he declared, "I aspire to no more than to display my own spirit." As a theoretician of theatre, Artaud insisted on the body's concrete reality as the sole means by which the material can attain the metaphysical. Rejecting the concept of imitation for an absolute identity of art and life, Artaud asserted, "I cannot conceive of a work of art as distinct from life."

Artaud's physical appearance has been more fully documented than that of any other theatre theorist except for Shaw. A film actor, Artaud left behind a unique cinematic record of his image and voice, and as a compulsive self-portraitist during his period of psychiatric confinement, the artist produced hundreds of shattered and dismembered pictures of himself, while friends and co-workers have produced poetic verbal descriptions of the crucified figure of the *poète maudit.*

"He had an extraordinary forehead that he always thrust in front of him as if to light his path," Barrault wrote of his friend. "From this magnificent brow sheaves of hair sprouted. His piercing blue eyes sank into their sockets as if in that way they could scrutinize further. The eyes of a rapacious bird—an eagle."

"His mouth, like the whole of Artaud, preyed upon itself," Barrault explained. "His teeth seemed to wear themselves out biting his lips. His skull developed monstrously as if from the pressure of the brain. His eye-sockets seemed all the more huge because his glance carried a long way—like a laser beam. He had been particularly handsome, but his inner fire was calcining him."

Artaud had hoped to play Roderick in a silent film version of *The Fall of the House of Usher.* He carried with him, according to André Breton, "the landscape of a Gothic novel, torn by flashes of lightning."

As an actor playing small supporting roles, Artaud worked with the best directors in Paris in the early 1920s. For Dullin, he played the King of Poland in Calderón's *Life Is a Dream* and Tiresias in Cocteau's *Antigone*; for the Pitoëffs, the first mystic in Blok's *Fairground Booth*, the prompter in Pirandello's *Six Characters*, a robot in Capek's *R.U.R.*, and a detective and a policeman in Molnár's *Liliom.*

Artaud hated the theatre of his own day. He either refused to attend or went with a bottle of red wine and a chunk of salami and ate ostentatiously in the first row. A career in cinema had been his goal from the start, and in 1924 Artaud turned to film acting (despised by the Surrealists for its crass commercialism) as a source of steady income, traveling to Italy and Germany to make films on location (Pabst's *Threepenny Opera* and Fritz Lang's *Liliom*).

As a lecturer, Artaud had a frightening and hypnotic power that stemmed from his uncontrollable rages. Unwashed and bad smelling, he challenged the respectability of the stage and its position as a cultural institution by his violent and vituperative assaults on his audience. In 1933 Artaud read his essay, "The Theatre and the Plague" in a lecture at the Sorbonne in which he enacted with his own body "the experience itself, the plague itself." An eyewitness, Anaïs Nin described his performance: "His face was contorted with anguish, one could see the perspiration dampening his hair. His eyes dilated, his muscles became cramped, his fingers struggled to retain their flexibility. He made one feel the parched and burning throat, the pains, the fever, the fire in the guts. He was in agony. He was screaming. He was delirious." The spectators hissed and jeered as the lecturer lay on the floor writhing.

At his January 13, 1947 reading at the Vieux Colombier, sold out in advance, listeners fled in horror as Artaud could not hold onto his lecture notes and lapsed into anguished incoherence.

For Artaud, incompleteness was the reigning modality of art and thought. Both the poet and his art were deliberately fragmentary and self-canceling. At the same time Artaud, who was influenced by the Marx brothers' films, practiced a deadpan humor akin to Buster Keaton's.

Called upon to diagnose Artaud at the Sainte-Anne asylum, the noted psychiatrist Jacques Lacan told Roger Blin that poet's case did not interest him and that even if he lived to be eighty, he would never write another line. As it happened, Artaud lived to be only fifty, but the last ten years of his life were the most creative and productive of his career.

THE THEATER AND ITS DOUBLE (1938)

The Theater and Cruelty

An idea of the theater has been lost. And as long as the theater limits itself to showing us intimate scenes from the lives of a few puppets, transforming the public into Peeping Toms, it is no wonder the elite abandon it and the great public looks to the movies, the music hall or the circus for violent satisfactions, whose intentions do not deceive them.

At the point of deterioration which our sensibility has reached, it is certain that we need above all a theater that wakes us up: nerves and heart.

The misdeeds of the psychological theater descended from Racine have unaccustomed us to that immediate and violent action which the theater should possess. Movies in their turn, murdering us with second-hand reproductions which, filtered through machines, cannot *unite with* our sensibility, have maintained us for ten years in an ineffectual torpor, in which all our faculties appear to be foundering.

In the anguished, catastrophic period we live in, we feel an urgent need for a theater which events do not exceed, whose resonance is deep within us, dominating the instability of the times.

Our long habit of seeking diversion has made us forget the idea of a serious theater, which, overturning all our preconceptions, inspires us with the fiery magnetism of its images and acts upon us like a spiritual therapeutics whose touch can never be forgotten.

Everything that acts is a cruelty. It is upon this idea of extreme action, pushed beyond all limits, that theater must be rebuilt.

Imbued with the idea that the public thinks first of all with its senses and that to address oneself first to its understanding as the ordinary psychological theater does is absurd, the Theater of Cruelty proposes to resort to a mass spectacle; to seek in the agitation of tremendous masses, convulsed and hurled against each other, a little of that poetry of festivals and crowds when, all too rarely nowadays, the people pour out into the streets.

The theater must give us everything that is in crime, love, war, or

From Antonin Artaud, *The Theater and Its Double*, trans. Mary Caroline Richards. N.Y.: Grove Press, 1958.

madness, if it wants to recover its necessity.

Everyday love, personal ambition, struggles for status, all have value only in proportion to their relation to the terrible lyricism of the Myths to which the great mass of men have assented.

This is why we shall try to concentrate, around famous personages, atrocious crimes, superhuman devotions, a drama which, without resorting to the defunct images of the old Myths, shows that it can extract the forces which struggle within them.

In a word, we believe that there are living forces in what is called poetry and that the image of a crime presented in the requisite theatrical conditions is something infinitely more terrible for the spirit than that same crime when actually committed.

We want to make out of the theater a believable reality which gives the heart and the senses that kind of concrete bite which all true sensation requires. In the same way that our dreams have an effect upon us and reality has an effect upon our dreams, so we believe that the images of thought can be identified with a dream which will be efficacious to the degree that it can be projected with the necessary violence. And the public will believe in the theater's dreams on condition that it take them for true dreams and not for a servile copy of reality; on condition that they allow the public to liberate within itself the magical liberties of dreams which it can only recognize when they are imprinted with terror and cruelty.

Hence this appeal to cruelty and terror, though on a vast scale, whose range probes our entire vitality, confronts us with all our possibilities.

It is in order to attack the spectator's sensibility on all sides that we advocate a revolving spectacle which, instead of making the stage and auditorium two closed worlds, without possible communication, spreads its visual and sonorous outbursts over the entire mass of the spectators.

Also, departing from the sphere of analyzable passions, we intend to make use of the actor's lyric qualities to manifest external forces, and by this means to cause the whole of nature to re-enter the theater in its restored form.

However vast this program may be, it does not exceed the theater itself, which appears to us, all in all, to identify itself with the forces of ancient magic.

Practically speaking, we want to resuscitate an idea of total spectacle by which the theater would recover from the cinema, the music hall, the circus, and from life itself what has always belonged to it. The separation between the analytic theater and the plastic world seems to us a stupidity. One does not separate the mind from the body nor the senses from the intelligence, especially in a domain where the endlessly renewed fatigue of the organs requires intense and sudden shocks to revive our understanding.

Thus, on the one hand, the mass and extent of a spectacle addressed to the entire organism; on the other, an intensive mobilization of objects, gestures, and signs, used in a new spirit. The reduced role given to the understanding leads to an energetic compression of the text; the active role given to obscure poetic emotion necessitates concrete signs. Words say little to the mind; extent and objects speak; new images speak, even new images made with words. But space thundering with images and crammed with sounds speaks too, if one knows how to intersperse from time to time a sufficient extent of space stocked with silence and immobility.

On this principle we envisage producing a spectacle where these means of direct action are used in their totality; a spectacle unafraid of going as far as necessary in the exploration of our nervous sensibility, of which the rhythms, sounds, words, resonances, and twitterings, and their united quality and surprising mixtures belong to a technique which must not be divulged.

The images in certain paintings by Grünewald or Hieronymus Bosch tell enough about what a spectacle can be in which, as in the brain of some saint, the objects of external nature will appear as temptations.

It is in this spectacle of a temptation from which life has everything to lose and the mind everything to gain that the theater must recover its true signification.

Elsewhere we have given a program which will allow the means of pure staging, found on the spot, to be organized around historic or cosmic themes, familiar to all.

And we insist on the fact that the first spectacle of the Theater of Cruelty will turn upon the preoccupations of the great mass of men, preoccupations much more pressing and disquieting than those of any individual whatsoever.

It is a matter of knowing whether now, in Paris, before the cataclysms which are at our door descend upon us, sufficient means of production, financial or otherwise, can be found to permit such a theater to be brought to life— it is bound to in any case, because it is the future. Or whether a little real blood will be needed, right away, in order to manifest this cruelty.

May 1933.

THE THEATER OF CRUELTY

(*First Manifesto*)

We cannot go on prostituting the idea of theater whose only value is in its excruciating, magical relation to reality and danger.

Put in this way, the question of the theater ought to arouse general attention, the implication being that theater, through its physical aspect, since it requires *expression in space* (the only real expression, in fact), allows the magical means of art and speech to be exercised organically and altogether, like renewed exorcisms. The upshot of all this is that theater will not be given its specific powers of action until it is given its language.

That is to say: instead of continuing to rely upon texts considered definitive and sacred, it is essential to put an end to the subjugation of the theater to the text, and to recover the notion of a kind of unique language halfway between gesture and thought.

This language cannot be defined except by its possibilities for dynamic expression in space as opposed to the expressive possibilities of spoken dialogue. And what the theater can still take over from speech are its possibilities for extension beyond words, for development in space, for dissociative and vibratory action upon the sensibility. This is the hour of intonations, of a word's particular pronunciation. Here too intervenes (besides the auditory language of sounds) the visual language of objects, movements, attitudes, and gestures, but on condition that their meanings, their physiognomies, their combinations be carried to the point of becoming signs, making a kind of alphabet out of these signs. Once aware of this language in space, language of sounds, cries, lights, onomatopoeia, the theater must organize it into veritable hieroglyphs, with the help of characters and objects, and make use of their symbolism and interconnections in relation to all organs and on all levels.

The question, then, for the theater, is to create a metaphysics of speech, gesture, and expression, in order to rescue it from its servitude to psychology and "human interest." But all this can be of no use unless behind such an effort there is some kind of real metaphysical inclination, an appeal to certain unhabitual ideas, which by their very nature cannot be limited or even formally depicted. These ideas which touch on Creation, Becoming, and Chaos, are all of a cosmic order and furnish a primary notion of a domain from which the theater is now entirely alien. They are able to create a kind of passionate equation between Man, Society, Nature, and Objects.

It is not, moreover, a question of bringing metaphysical ideas directly onto the stage, but of creating what you might call temptations, indraughts of air around these ideas. And humor with its anarchy, poetry with its symbolism and its images, furnish a basic notion of ways to channel the temptation of these ideas.

We must speak now about the uniquely material side of this language—that is, about all the ways and means it has of acting upon the sensibility.

It would be meaningless to say that it includes music, dance, pantomime, or mimicry. Obviously it uses movement, harmonies, rhythms, but only to the point that they can concur in a sort of central expression without advantage for any one particular art. This does not at all mean that it does not use ordinary actions, ordinary passions, but like a springboard uses them in the same way that HUMOR AS DESTRUCTION can serve to reconcile the corrosive nature of laughter to the habits of reason.

But by an altogether Oriental means of expression, this objective and concrete language of the theater can fascinate and ensnare the organs. It flows into the sensibility. Abandoning Occidental usages of speech, it turns words into incantations. It extends the voice. It utilizes the vibrations and qualities of the voice. It wildly tramples rhythms underfoot. It pile-drives sounds. It seeks to exalt, to benumb, to charm, to arrest the sensibility. It liberates a new lyricism of gesture which, by its precipitation or its amplitude in the air, ends by surpassing the lyricism of words. It ultimately breaks away from the intellectual subjugation of the language, by conveying the sense of a new and deeper intellectuality which hides itself beneath the gestures and signs, raised to the dignity of particular exorcisms.

For all this magnetism, all this poetry, and all these direct means of spellbinding would be nothing if they were not used to put the spirit physically on the track of something else, if the true theater could not give us the sense of a creation of which we possess only one face, but which is completed on other levels.

And it is of little importance whether these other levels are really conquered by the mind or not, i.e., by the intelligence; it would diminish them, and that has neither interest nor sense. What is important is that, by positive means, the sensitivity is put in a state of deepened and keener perception, and this is the very object of the magic and the rites of which the theater is only a reflection.

Technique

It is a question then of making the theater, in the proper sense of the word, a function; something as localized and as precise as the circulation of the blood in the arteries or the apparently chaotic development of dream images in the brain, and this is to be accomplished by a thorough involvement, a genuine enslavement of the attention.

The theater will never find itself again—i.e., constitute a means of true illusion—except by furnishing the spectator with the truthful precipitates of dreams, in which his taste for crime, his erotic obsessions, his savagery, his chimeras, his utopian sense of life and matter, even his cannibalism, pour out, on a level not counterfeit and illusory, but interior.

In other terms, the theater must pursue by all its means a reassertion not only of all the aspects of the objective and descriptive external world, but of the internal world, that is, of man considered metaphysically. It is only thus, we believe, that we shall be able to speak again in the theater about the rights of the imagination. Neither humor, nor poetry, nor imagination means anything unless, by an anarchistic destruction generating a prodigious flight of forms which will constitute the whole spectacle, they succeed in organically reinvolving man, his ideas about reality, and his poetic place in reality.

To consider the theater as a second-hand psychological or moral function, and to believe that dreams themselves have only a substitute function, is to diminish the profound poetic bearing of dreams as well as of the theater. If the theater, like dreams, is bloody and inhuman, it is, more than just that, to manifest and unforgettably root within us the idea of a perpetual conflict, a spasm in which life is continually lacerated, in which everything in creation rises up and exerts itself against our appointed rank; it is in order to perpetuate in a concrete and immediate way the metaphysical ideas of certain Fables whose very atrocity and energy suffice to show their origin and continuity in essential principles.

This being so, one sees that, by its proximity to principles which transfer their energy to it poetically, this naked language of the theater (not a virtual but a real language) must permit, by its use of man's nervous magnetism, the transgression of the ordinary limits of art and speech, in order to realize actively, that is to say magically, *in real terms*, a kind of total creation in which man must reassume his place between dream and events.

Letters on Language
Fourth Letter

To J. P.   Paris, May 28, 1933

Dear friend,

I did not say that I wanted to act directly upon our times; I said that the theater I wanted to create assumed, in order to be possible, in order to be permitted by the times to exist, another form of civilization.

But without representing its times, the theater can impel the ideas, customs, beliefs, and principles from which the spirit of the time derives to a profound transformation. In any case it does not prevent me from doing what I want to do and doing it rigorously. I will do what I have dreamed or I will do nothing.

In the matter of the spectacle it is not possible for me to give supplementary particulars. And for two reasons:

1. the first is that for once what I want to do is easier to do than to say.

2. the second is that I do not want to risk being plagiarized, which has happened to me several times.

In my view no one has the right to call himself author, that is to say creator, except the person who controls the direct handling of the stage. And exactly here is the vulnerable point of the theater as it is thought of not only in France but in Europe and even in the Occident as a whole: Occidental theater recognizes as language, assigns the faculties and powers of a language, permits to be called language (with that particular intellectual dignity generally ascribed to this word) only articulated language, grammatically articulated language, i.e., the language of speech, and of written speech, speech which, pronounced or unpronounced, has no greater value than if it is merely written.

In the theater as we conceive it, the text is everything. It is understood and definitely admitted, and has passed into our habits and thinking, it is an established spiritual value that the language of words is *the* major language. But it must be admitted even from the Occidental point of view that speech becomes ossified and that words, all words, are frozen and cramped in their meanings, in a restricted schematic terminology. For the theater as it is practiced here, a written word has as much value as the same word spoken. To certain theatrical amateurs this means that a play read affords just as definite and as great a satisfaction as the same play performed. Everything concerning the particular enunciation of a word and the vibration it can set up in space escapes them, and consequently, everything that it is capable of adding to the thought. A word thus understood has little more than a discursive, i.e., elucidative, value. And it is not an exaggeration to say that in view of its very definite and limited terminology the word is used only to sidestep thought; it encircles it, but terminates it; it is only a conclusion.

Obviously it is not without cause that poetry has abandoned the theater. It is not merely an accident that for a very long time now every dramatic poet has ceased to produce. The language of speech has its laws. We have become too well accustomed, for more than four hundred years, especially in France, to employing words in the theater in a single defined sense. We have made the action turn too exclusively on psychological themes whose essential combinations are not infinite, far from it. We have overaccustomed the theater to a lack of curiosity and above all of imagination.

Theater, like speech, needs to be set free.

This obstinacy in making characters talk about feelings, passions, desires, and impulses of a strictly psychological order, in which a single word is to compensate for innumerable gestures, is the reason, since we are in the domain of precision, the theater has lost its true *raison d'être* and why we have come to long for a silence in it in which we could listen more closely to life. Occidental psychology is expressed in dialogue; and the obsession with the defined word which says everything ends in the withering of words.

Oriental theater has been able to preserve a certain expansive value in words, since the defined sense of a word is not everything, for there is its music, which speaks directly to the unconscious. That is why in the Oriental theater there is no spoken language, but a language of gestures, attitudes, and signs which from the point of view of thought in action have as much expansive and revelational value as the other. And since in the Orient this sign language is valued more than the other, immediate magic powers are attributed to it. It is called upon to address not only the mind but the senses, and through the senses to attain still richer and more fecund regions of the sensibility at full tide.

If, then, the author is the man who arranges the language of speech and the director is his slave, there is merely a question of words. There is here a confusion over terms, stemming from the fact that, for us, and according to the sense generally attributed to the word *director*, this man is merely an artisan, an adapter, a kind of translator eternally devoted to making a dramatic work pass from one language into another; this confusion will be possible and the director will be forced to play second fiddle to the author only so long as there is a tacit agreement that the language of words is superior to others and that the theater admits none other than this one language.

But let there be the least return to the active, plastic, respiratory sources of language, let words be joined again to the physical motions that gave them birth, and let the discursive, logical aspect of speech disappear beneath its affective, physical side, i.e., let words be heard in their sonority rather than be exclusively taken for what they mean grammatically, let them be perceived as movements, and let these movements themselves turn into other simple, direct movements as occurs in all the circumstances of life but not sufficiently with actors on the stage, and behold! the language of literature is reconstituted, revivified, and furthermore—as in the canvasses of certain painters of the past—objects themselves begin to speak. Light, instead of decorating, assumes the qualities of an actual language, and the stage effects, all humming with significations, take on an order, reveal patterns. And this immediate and physical language is entirely at the director's disposal. This is the occasion for him to create in complete autonomy.

It would be quite singular if the person who rules a domain closer to life than the author's, i.e., the director, had on every occasion to yield precedence to the author, who by definition works in the abstract, i.e., on paper. Even if the *mise en scène* did not have to its credit the language of gestures which equals and surpasses that of words, any mute *mise en scène*, with its movement, its many characters, lighting, and set, should rival all that is most profound in paintings such as van den Leyden's *Daughters of Lot*, certain *Sabbaths* of Goya, certain *Resurrections* and *Transfigurations* of Greco, the *Temptation of Saint Anthony* by Hieronymus Bosch, and the disquieting and mysterious *Dulle Griet* by the elder Breughel, in which a torrential red light, though localized in certain parts of the canvas, seems to surge up from all sides and, through some unknown technical process, glue the spectator's staring eyes while still yards away from the canvas: the theater swarms in all directions. The turmoil of life, confined by a ring of white light, runs suddenly aground on nameless shallows. A screeching, livid noise rises from this bacchanal of grubs of which even the bruises on human skin can never approach the color. Real life is moving and white; the hidden life is livid and fixed, possessing every possible attitude of incalculable immobility. This is mute theater, but one that tells more than if it had received a language in which to express itself. Each of these paintings has a double sense, and beyond its purely pictorial qualities discloses a message and reveals mysterious or terrible aspects of nature and mind alike.

But happily for the theater, the *mise en scène* is much more than that. For besides creating a performance with palpable material means, the pure *mise en scène* contains, in gestures, facial expressions and mobile attitudes, through a concrete use of music, everything that speech contains and has speech at its disposal as well. Rhythmic repetitions of syllables and particular modulations of the voice, swathing the precise sense of words, arouse swarms of images in the brain, producing a more or less hallucinatory state and impelling the sensibility and mind alike to a kind of organic alteration which helps to strip from the written poetry the gratuitousness that commonly characterizes it. And it is around this gratuitousness that the whole problem of theater is centered.

BERTOLT BRECHT

Bertolt BRECHT (1898-1956), as a young poet-playwright, was spider-thin with sloping shoulders, a long face, dark button eyes behind steel-rimmed glasses, hair combed straight down over his forehead and a three-days growth of beard. Artists and memoirist delighted in trying to capture the paradoxes of his expression which was at once monastic and crafty.

On first meeting Brecht in Berlin in October 1928, Harry Kessler, Gordon Craig's friend and patron, wrote in his diary: "Strikingly degenerate look, almost a criminal physiognomy, black hair and eyes, dark-skinned, a peculiarly suspicious expression; very nearly a typical twister."

A genius at visual self-representation (as were Rousseau and Shaw), Brecht devised a striking pose for the Marxist intellectual and then played the role to perfection himself, even developing his own sartorial style: belted leather jacket and cap, leather tie and vest with cloth sleeves. The playwright Karl Zuckmayer described Brecht as "a cross between a truck-driver and a Jesuit seminarist." After World War II Brecht created a new uniform for himself: a carefully tailored gray worker's suit with gray cloth cap. Gray was his official color. He wrote on gray paper, published his works in progress in gray paperbacks, and his open sports car (which he got free by writing advertising jingles for the maker) was gray.

At the age of thirty, Brecht "looked not as though he had aged prematurely but as though he had always been old," according to Elias Canetti. "He had the profile of a Jesuit," wrote a friend, "the steel-rimmed glasses of a schoolmaster, the close-cropped hair of a convict and the tattered leather jacket of an old member of the Bolshevik party."

Much of the time Brecht seemed to be playing a role. The unkempt proletarian garb and unshaven stubble that he adopted as a mask created its own alienation effect that paralleled the A-effect he sought in the theatre.

A delicate mother's boy with a heart condition, Brecht had discovered the world of the stage with a marionette theatre when he was fifteen. As a theatre critic in 1919, the arrogant twenty-one-year-old attacked the older generation in the person of the Nobel-prize-winner Gerhart Hauptmann. He admired the music hall artist Karl Valentin and the playwright Frank

Wedekind who played and sang his own songs in cabarets.

Brecht was such a performer himself. Accompanying himself on his guitar, he sang his street songs in a thin, high-pitched reedy voice that grated and mesmerized.

Like Byron, Brecht enjoyed the company of professional boxers, although he never donned gloves and entered the ring himself, unlike Shaw and Maeterlinck. He wanted the stage to have the atmosphere of a sports arena, and he proposed instituting an "Epic Smoking Theatre" in which the audience would be allowed to drink and smoke, as they do in cabarets and at boxing matches, somehow imagining that this smoke-filled alcoholic environment would promote the attitude of detachment integral to his epic theatre.

The magical effect of stage illusion, Brecht argued, hypnotized spectators and put them into a state of trance. By leading the audience to identify with the characters and accept their fate rather than calling it into question, what Brecht called Aristotelian drama served to perpetuate passivity and reinforce the status quo.

Brecht is buried in the cemetery at Charlottenburg in a plot adjacent to Hegel. Two dialecticians have come to a common resting point.

THE MODERN THEATRE
IS THE EPIC THEATRE (1930)

(*Notes to the opera* AUFSTIEG UND FALL DER STADT MAHAGONNY)

OPERA—WITH INNOVATIONS!

For some time past there has been a move to renovate the opera. Opera is to have its form modernized and its content brought up to date, but without its culinary character being changed. Since it is precisely for its backwardness that the opera-going public adores opera, an influx of new types of listener with new appetites has to be reckoned with; and so it is. The intention is to democratize but not to alter democracy's character, which consists in giving the people new rights, but no chance to appreciate them. Ultimately it is all the same to the waiter whom he serves, so long as he serves the food. Thus the *avant-garde* are demanding or supporting innovations which are supposedly going to lead to a renovation of opera; but nobody demands a fundamental discussion of opera (i.e. of its function), and probably such a discussion would not find much support.

The modesty of the *avant-garde*'s demands has economic grounds of whose existence they themselves are only part aware. Great apparati like the opera, the stage, the press, etc., impose their views as it were incognito. For a long time now they have taken the handiwork (music, writing, criticism, etc.) of intellectuals who share in their profits—that is, of men who are economically committed to the prevailing system but are socially near-proletarian—and processed it to make fodder for their public entertainment machine, judging it by their own standards and guiding it into their own channels; meanwhile the intellectuals themselves have gone on supposing that the whole business is concerned only with the presentation of their work, is a secondary process which has no influence over their work but merely wins influence for it. This muddled thinking which overtakes musicians, writers and critics as soon as they consider their own situation has tremendous consequences to which far too little attention is paid. For by imagining that they have got hold

From *Brecht on Theatre*, ed. and trans. John Willett.
N.Y.: Hill and Wang, 1964.

of an apparatus which in fact has got hold of them they are supporting an apparatus which is out of their control, which is no longer (as they believe) a means of furthering output but has become an obstacle to output, and specifically to their own output as soon as it follows a new and original course which the apparatus finds awkward or opposed to its own aims. Their output then becomes a matter of delivering the goods. Values evolve which are based on the fodder principle. And this leads to a general habit of judging works of art by their suitability for the apparatus without ever judging the apparatus by its suitability for the work. People say, this or that is a good work; and they mean (but do not say) good for the apparatus. Yet this apparatus is conditioned by the society of the day and only accepts what can keep it going in that society. We are free to discuss any innovation which doesn't threaten its social function—that of providing an evening's entertainment. We are not free to discuss those which threaten to change its function, possibly by fusing it with the educational system or with the organs of mass communication. Society absorbs via the apparatus whatever it needs in order to reproduce itself. This means that an innovation will pass if it is calculated to rejuvenate existing society, but not if it is going to change it—irrespective whether the form of the society in question is good or bad.

The *avant-garde* don't think of changing the apparatus, because they fancy that they have at their disposal an apparatus which will serve up whatever they freely invent, transforming itself spontaneously to match their ideas. But they are not in fact free inventors; the apparatus goes on fulfilling its function with or without them; the theatres play every night; the papers come out so many times a day; and they absorb what they need; and all they need is a given amount of stuff.

You might think that to show up this situation (the creative artist's utter dependence on the apparatus) would be to condemn it. Its concealment is such a disgrace.

And yet to restrict the individual's freedom of invention is in itself a progressive act. The individual becomes increasingly drawn into enormous events that are going to change the world. No longer can he simply "express himself." He is brought up short and put into a position where he can fulfill more general tasks. The trouble, however, is that at present the apparati do not work for the general good; the means of production do not belong to the producer; and as a result his work amounts to so much merchandise, and is governed by the normal laws of mercantile trade. Art is merchandise, only to be manufactured by the means of production (apparati). An opera can only be written for the opera. (One can't just think up an opera like one of Böcklin's fantastic sea-beasts, then hope to exhibit it publicly after having seized power—let alone try to smuggle it into our dear old zoo …)

OPERA

Even if one wanted to start a discussion of the opera as such (i.e. of its function), an opera would have to be written.

Our existing opera is a culinary opera. It was a means of pleasure long before it turned into merchandise. It furthers pleasure even where it requires, or promotes, a certain degree of education, for the education in question is an education in taste. To every object it adopts a hedonistic approach. It "experiences," and it ranks as an "experience."

Why is *Mahagonny* an opera? Because its basic attitude is that of an opera: that is to say, culinary. Does *Mahagonny* adopt a hedonistic approach? It does. Is *Mahagonny* an experience? It is an experience. For... *Mahagonny* is a piece of fun.

The opera *Mahagonny* pays conscious tribute to the senselessness of the operatic form. The irrationality of opera lies in the fact that rational elements are employed, solid reality is aimed at, but at the same time it is all washed out by the music. A dying man is real. If at the same time he sings we are translated to the sphere of the irrational. (If the audience sang at the sight of him the case would be different.) The more unreal and unclear the music can make the reality—though there is of course, a third, highly complex and in itself quite real element which can have quite real effects but is utterly remote from the reality of which it treats—the more pleasurable the whole process becomes: the pleasure grows in proportion to the degree of unreality.

The term "opera"—far be it from us to profane it—leads, in *Mahagonny*'s case, to all the rest. The intention was that a certain unreality, irrationality and lack of seriousness should be introduced at the right moment, and so strike with a double meaning.

The irrationality which makes its appearance in this way only fits the occasion on which it appears. It is a purely hedonistic approach. As for the content of this opera, *its content is pleasure*. Fun, in other words, not only as form but as subject-matter. At least, enjoyment was meant to be the object of the inquiry even if the inquiry was intended to be an object of enjoyment. Enjoyment here appears in its current historical role: as merchandise.

It is undeniable that at present this content must have a provocative effect. In the thirteenth section, for example, where the glutton stuffs himself to death; because hunger is the rule. We never even hinted that others were going hungry while he stuffed, but the effect was provocative all the same. It is not everyone who is in a position to stuff himself full that dies of it, yet many are dying of hunger because this man stuffs himself to death. His pleasure provokes, because it implies so much.

In contexts like these the use of opera as a means of pleasure must have provocative effects today. Though not of course on the handful of operagoers. Its power to provoke introduces reality once more. *Mahagonny* may not taste particularly agreeable; it may even (thanks to guilty conscience) make a point of not doing so. But it is culinary through and through.

Mahagonny is nothing more or less than an opera.

WITH INNOVATIONS!

Opera had to be brought up to the technical level of the modern theatre. The modern theatre is the epic theatre. The following table shows certain changes of emphasis as between the dramatic and the epic theatre.

DRAMATIC THEATRE	EPIC THEATRE
plot	narrative
implicates the spectator in a stage situation	turns the spectator into an observer but
wears down his capacity for action	arouses his capacity for action
provides him with sensations	forces him to take decisions
experience	picture of the world
the spectator is involved in something	he is made to face something
suggestion	argument
instinctive feelings are preserved	brought to the point of recognition
the spectator is in the thick of it, shares the experience	the spectator stands outside, studies
the human being is taken for granted	the human being is the object of the inquiry
he is unalterable	he is alterable and able to alter
eyes on the finish	eyes on the course
one scene makes another	each scene for itself
growth	montage
linear development	in curves
evolutionary determinism	jumps
man as a fixed point	man as a process
thought determines being	social being determines thought
feeling	reason

When the epic theatre's methods begin to penetrate the opera the first result is a radical *separation of elements*. The great struggle for supremacy between words, music and production—which always brings up the question "which is the pretext for what?": is the music the pretext for the events on the stage, or are these the pretext for the music? etc.—can simply be by-passed by radically separating the elements. So long as the expression "Gesamtkunstwerk" (or "integrated work of art") means that the integration is a muddle, so long as the arts are supposed to be "fused" together, the various elements will be equally degraded, and each will act as a mere "feed" to the rest. The process of fusion extends to the spectator, who gets thrown into the melting pot too and becomes a passive (suffering) part of the total work of art. Witchcraft of this sort must of course be fought against. Whatever is intended to produce hypnosis, is likely to induce sordid intoxication, or creates fog, has got to be given up.

Words, music and setting must become more independent of one another.

(a) MUSIC
For the music, the change of emphasis proved to be as follows:

DRAMATIC OPERA	EPIC OPERA
The music dishes up	The music communicates
music which heightens the text	music which sets forth the text
music which proclaims the text	music which takes the text for granted
music which illustrates	which takes up a position
music which paints the psychological situation	which gives the attitude

Music plays the chief part in our thesis.

(b) TEXT

We had to make something straightforward and instructive of our fun, if it was not to be irrational and nothing more. The form employed was that of the moral tableau. The tableau is performed by the characters in the play. The text had to be neither moralizing nor sentimental, but to put morals and sentimentality on view. Equally important was the spoken word and the written word (of the titles). Reading seems to encourage the audience to adopt the most natural attitude towards the work.

(c) SETTING

Showing independent works of art as part of a theatrical performance is a new departure. Neher's projections adopt an attitude towards the events

on the stage, as when the real glutton sits in front of the glutton whom Neher has drawn. In the same way the stage unreels the events that are fixed on the screen. The projections of Neher's are quite as much an independent component of the opera as are Weill's music and the text.
They provide its visual aids.

Of course such innovations also demand a new attitude on the part of the audiences who frequent opera houses.

EFFECT OF THE INNOVATIONS: *A Threat to Opera?*

It is true that the audience had certain desires which were easily satisfied by the old opera but are no longer taken into account by the new. What is the audience's attitude during an opera; and is there any chance that it will change?

Bursting out of the underground stations, eager to become as wax in the magicians' hands, grown-up men, their resolution proved in the struggle for existence, rush to the box office. They hand in their hat at the cloakroom, and with it they hand their normal behavior: the attitudes of "everyday life." Once out of the cloakroom they take their seats with the bearing of kings. How can we blame them? You may think a grocer's bearing better than a king's and still find this ridiculous. For the attitude that these people adopt in the opera is unworthy of them. Is there any possibility that they may change it? Can we persuade them to get out their cigars?

Once the content becomes, technically speaking, an independent component, to which text, music and setting "adopt attitudes;" once illusion is sacrificed to free discussions, and once the spectator, instead of being enabled to have an experience, is forced as it were to cast his vote; then a change has been launched which goes far beyond formal matters and begins for the first time to affect the theatre's social function.

In the old operas all discussions of the content is rigidly excluded. If a member of the audience had happened to see a particular set of circumstances portrayed and had taken up a position *vis-à-vis* them, then the old opera would have lost its battle: the "spell would have been broken." Of course there were elements in the old opera which were not purely culinary: one has to distinguish between the period of its development and that of its decline. *The Magic Flute*, *Fidelio*, *Figaro* all included elements that were philosophical, dynamic. And yet the element of philosophy, almost of daring, in these operas was so subordinated to the culinary principle that their *sense* was in effect tottering and was soon absorbed in sensual satisfaction. Once its original "sense" had died away the opera was by no means left bereft of sense, but had simply acquired another one—a sense *qua* opera. The content had been smothered in the opera. Our Wagnerites are now pleased to remember that the original Wagnerites posited a sense of which they were presumably aware. Those composers who stem from Wagner still insist on posing as philosophers. A philosophy which is of no use to man or beast, and can only be disposed of as a means of sensual satisfaction. (*Elektra, Jonny spielt auf.*) We still maintain the whole highly-developed technique which made this pose possible: the vulgarian strikes a philosophical attitude from which to conduct his hackneyed ruminations. It is only from this point, from the death of the sense (and it is understood that this sense *could* die), that we can start to understand the further innovations which are now plaguing opera: to see them as desperate attempts to supply this art with a posthumous sense, a "new" sense, by which the sense comes ultimately to lie in the music itself, so that the sequence of musical forms acquires a sense simply *qua* sequence, and certain proportions, changes, etc. from being a means are promoted to become an end. Progress which has neither roots nor result; which does not spring from new requirements but satisfies the old ones with new titillations, thus furthering a purely conservative aim. New material is absorbed which is unfamiliar "in this context," because at the time when "this context" was evolved it was not known in any context at all. (Railway engines, factories, aeroplanes, bathrooms, etc. act as a diversion. Better composers chose instead to deny all content by performing—or rather smothering—it in the Latin tongue). This sort of progress only indicates that something has been left behind. It is achieved without the overall function being changed; or rather, with a view to stopping any such change from taking place. And what about *Gebrauchsmusik* ?

At the very moment when neo-classicism, in other word stark Art for Art's sake, took the field (it came as a reaction against the emotional element in musical impressionism) the idea of utilitarian music, or *Gebrauchsmusik*, emerged like Venus from the waves: music was to make use of the amateur. The amateur was used as a woman is "used." Innovation upon innovation. The punch-drunk listener suddenly wants to play. The struggle against idle listening turned into a struggle for keen listening, then for keen playing. The cellist in the orchestra, father of a numerous family, now began to play not from philosophical conviction but for pleasure. The culinary principle was saved.

What is the point, we wonder, of chasing one's own tail like this? Why this obstinate clinging to the pleasure element? This addiction to drugs? Why so little concern with one's own interests as soon as one steps outside one's own home? Why this refusal to discuss? Answer: nothing can come of discussion. To discuss the present form of our society, or even of one of its least important parts, would lead inevitably and at once to an outright threat to our society's form as such.

We have seen that opera is sold as evening entertainment, and that this puts definite bounds to all attempts to transform it. We see that this entertainment has to be devoted to illusion, and must be of a ceremonial kind. Why?

In our present society the old opera cannot be just "wished away." Its illusions have an important social function. The drug is irreplaceable; it cannot be done without.

Only in the opera does the human being have a chance to be human. His entire mental capacities have long since been ground down to a timid mistrustfulness, and envy of others, a selfish calculation. The old opera survives not just because it is old, but chiefly because the situation which it is able to meet is still the old one. This is not wholly so. And there lies the hope for the new opera. Today we can begin to ask whether opera hasn't come to such a pass that further innovations, instead of leading to the renovation of this whole form, will bring about its destruction.

Perhaps *Mahagonny* is a culinary as ever—just as culinary as an opera ought to be—but one of its functions is to change society; it brings the culinary principle under discussion, it attacks the society that needs operas of such a sort; it still perches happily on the old bough, perhaps, but at least it has started (out of absent-mindedness or bad conscience) to saw it through ... And here you have the effect of the innovations and the song they sing.

Real innovations attack the roots.

FOR INNOVATIONS—AGAINST RENOVATION!

The opera *Mahagonny* was written three years ago, in 1927. In subsequent works attempts were made to emphasize the didactic more and more at the expense of the culinary element. And so to develop the means of pleasure into an object of instruction, and to convert certain institutions from places of entertainment into organs of mass communication.

ALIENATION EFFECTS
IN CHINESE ACTING (1935)

The following is intended to refer briefly to the use of the alienation effect in traditional Chinese acting. This method was most recently used in Germany for plays of a non-aristotelian (not dependent on empathy) type as part of the attempts being made to evolve an epic theatre. The efforts in question were directed to playing in such a way that the audience was hindered from simply identifying itself with the characters in the play. Acceptance or rejection of their actions and utterances was meant to take place on a conscious plane, instead of, as hitherto, in the audience's subconscious.

This effort to make the incidents represented appear strange to the public can be seen in a primitive form in the theatrical and pictorial displays at the old popular fairs. The way the clowns speak and the way the panoramas are painted both embody an act of alienation. The method of painting used to reproduce the picture of "Charles the Bold's flight after the Battle of Murten," as shown at many German fairs, is certainly mediocre; yet the act of alienation which is achieved here (not by the original) is in no wise due to the mediocrity of the copyist. The fleeing commander, his horse, his retinue and the landscape are all quite consciously painted in such a way as to create the impression of an abnormal event, an astonishing disaster. In spite of his inadequacy the painter succeeds brilliantly in bringing out the unexpected. Amazement guides his brush.

Traditional Chinese acting also knows the alienation effect, and applies it most subtly. It is well known that the Chinese theatre uses a lot of symbols. Thus a general will carry little pennants on his shoulder, corresponding to the number of regiments under his command. Poverty is shown by patching the silken costumes with irregular shapes of different colors, likewise silken, to indicate that they have been mended. Characters are distinguished by particular masks, i.e. simply by painting. Certain gestures of the two hands signify the forcible opening of a door, etc. The stage itself remains the same, but articles of furniture are carried in during the action. All this has long been known, and cannot very well be exported.

It is not all that simple to break with the habit of assimilating a work

From *Brecht on Theatre*, ed. and trans. John Willett
N.Y.: Hill and Wang, 1964.

of art as a whole. But this has to be done if just one of a large number of effects is to be singled out and studied. The alienation effect is achieved in the Chinese theatre in the following way.

Above all, the Chinese artist never acts as if there were a fourth wall besides the three surrounding him. He expresses his awareness of being watched. This immediately removes one of the European stage's characteristic illusions. The audience can no longer have the illusion of being the unseen spectator at an event which is really taking place. A whole elaborate European stage technique, which helps to conceal the fact that the scenes are so arranged that the audience can view them in the easiest way, is thereby made unnecessary. The actors openly choose those positions which will best show them off to the audience, just as if they were *acrobats*. A further means is that the artist observes himself. Thus if he is representing a cloud, perhaps, showing its unexpected appearance, its soft and strong growth, its rapid yet gradual transformation, he will occasionally look at the audience as if to say: isn't it just like that? At the same time he also observes his own arms and legs, adducing them, testing them and perhaps finally approving them. An obvious glance at the floor, so as to judge the space available to him for his act, does not strike him as liable to break the illusion. In this way the artist separates mime (showing observation) from gesture (showing a cloud), but without detracting from the latter, since the body's attitude is reflected in the face and is wholly responsible for its expression. At one moment the expression is of well-managed restraint; at another, of utter triumph. The artist has been using his countenance as a blank sheet, to be inscribed by the gest of the body.

The artist's object is to appear strange and even surprising to the audience. He achieves this by looking strangely at himself and his work. As a result everything put forward by him has a touch of the amazing. Everyday things are thereby raised above the level of the obvious and automatic. A young woman, a fisherman's wife, is shown paddling a boat. She stands steering a non-existent boat with a paddle that barely reaches to her knees. Now the current is swifter, and she is finding it harder to keep her balance; now she is in a pool and paddling more easily. Right: that is how one manages a boat. But this journey in the boat is apparently historic, celebrated in many songs, an exceptional journey about which everybody knows. Each of this famous girl's movements has probably been recorded in pictures; each bend in the river was a well-known adventure story, it is even known which particular bend it was. This feeling on the audience's part is induced by the artist's attitude; it is this that makes the journey famous. The scene reminded us of the march to Budejovice in Piscator's production of *The Good Soldier Schweik*. Schweik's three-day-and-night march to a front which he oddly enough never gets to was seen from a completely historic point of view, as no less noteworthy a phenomenon than, for instance, Napoleon's Russian expedition of 1812. The performer's self-observation, an artful and artistic act of self-alienation, stopped the spectator from losing himself in the character completely, i.e. to the point of giving up his own identity, and lent a splendid remoteness to the events. Yet the spectator's empathy was not entirely rejected. The audience identifies itself with the actor as being an observer, and accordingly develops his attitude of observing or looking on.

The Chinese artist's performance often strikes the Western actor as cold. That does not mean that the Chinese theatre rejects all representation of feelings. The performer portrays incidents of utmost passion, but without his delivery becoming heated. At those points where the character portrayed is deeply excited the performer takes a lock of hair between his lips and chews it. But this is like a ritual, there is nothing eruptive about it. It is quite clearly somebody else's repetition of the incident: a representation, even though an artistic one. The performer shows that this man is not in control of himself, and he points to the outward signs. And so lack of control is decorously expressed, or if not decorously, at any rate decorously for the stage. Among all the possible signs certain particular ones are picked out, with careful and visible consideration. Anger is naturally different from sulkiness, hatred from distaste, love from liking; but the corresponding fluctuations of feeling are portrayed economically. The coldness comes from the actor's holding himself remote from the character portrayed, along the lines described. He is careful not to make its sensations into those of the spectator. Nobody gets raped by the individual he portrays; this individual is not the spectator himself but his neighbor.

The Western actor does all he can to bring his spectator into the closest proximity to the events and the character he has to portray. To this end he persuades him to identify himself with him (the actor) and uses every energy to convert himself as completely as possible into a different type, that of the character in question. If this complete conversion succeeds, then his art has been more or less expended. Once he has become the bank-clerk, doctor or general concerned, he will need no more art than any of these people need "in real life."

This complete conversion operation is extremely exhausting. Stanislavsky puts forward a series of means—a complete system—by which what he calls "creative mood" can repeatedly be manufactured afresh at every performance. For the actor cannot usually manage to feel for very long on end that he really is the other person; he soon gets exhausted and begins just to copy various superficialities of the other person's speech and hearing, whereupon the effect on the public drops off alarmingly. This is certainly due to the fact that the other person has been created by an "intuitive" and accordingly murky process which takes place in the subconscious. The subconscious is not at all responsive to guidance; it has as it were a bad memory.

These problems are unknown to the Chinese performer, for he rejects complete conversion. He limits himself from the start to simply quoting the character played. But with what art he does this! He only needs a minimum of illusion. What he has to show is worth seeing even for a man in his right mind. What Western actor of the old sort (apart from one or two comedians) could demonstrate the elements of his art like the Chinese actor Mei Lan-fang, without special lighting and wearing a dinner jacket in an ordinary room full of specialists? It would be like the magician at a fair giving away his tricks, so that nobody ever wanted to see the act again. He would just be showing how to disguise oneself; the hypnotism would vanish and all that would be left would be a few pounds of ill-blended imitation, a quickly-mixed product for selling in the dark to hurried customers. Of course no Western actor would stage such a demonstration. What about the sanctity of Art? The mysteries of metamorphosis? To the Westerner what matters is that his actions should be unconscious; otherwise they would be degraded. By comparison with Asiatic acting our own art still seems hopelessly parsonical. None the less it is becoming increasingly difficult for our actors to bring off the mystery of complete conversion; their subconscious's memory is getting weaker and weaker, and it almost impossible to extract the truth from the uncensored intuitions of any member of our class society even when the man is a genius.

For the actor it is difficult and taxing to conjure up particular inner moods or emotions night after night; it is simpler to exhibit the outer signs which accompany these emotions and identify them. In this case, however, there is not the same automatic transfer of emotions to the spectator, the same emotional infection. The alienation effect intervenes, not in the form of absence of emotion, but in the form of emotions which need not correspond to those of the character portrayed. On seeing worry the spectator may feel a sensation of joy; on seeing anger, one of disgust. When we speak of exhibiting the outer signs of emotion we do not mean such an exhibition and such a choice of signs that the emotional transference does in fact take place because the actor has managed to infect himself with the emotions portrayed, by exhibiting the outer signs; thus, by letting his voice rise, holding his breath and tightening his neck muscles so that the blood shoots to his head, the actor can easily conjure up a rage. In such a case of course the effect does not occur. But it does occur if the actor at a particular point unexpectedly shows a completely white face, which he has produced mechanically by holding his face in his hands with some white make-up on them. If the actor at the same time displays an apparently composed character, then his terror at this point (as a result of this message, or that discovery) will give rise to an alienation effect. Acting like this is healthier and in our view less unworthy of a thinking being; it demands a considerable knowledge of humanity and worldly wisdom, and a keen eye for what is socially important. In this case too there is of course a creative process at work; but it is a higher one, because it is raised to the conscious level.

The alienation effect does not in any way demand an unnatural way of acting. It has nothing whatever to do with ordinary stylization. On the contrary, the achievement of an A-effect absolutely depends on lightness and naturalness of performance. But when the actor checks the truth of his performance (a necessary operation, which Stanislavsky is much concerned with in his system) he is not just thrown back on his "natural sensibilities," but can always be corrected by a comparison with reality (is that how an angry man really speaks? is that how an offended man sits down?) and so from outside, by other people. He acts in such a way that nearly every sentence could be followed by a verdict of the audience and practically every gesture is submitted for the public's approval.

The Chinese performer is in no trance. He can be interrupted at any moment. He won't have to "come round." After an interruption he will go on with his exposition from that point. We are not disturbing him at the "mystic moment of creation," when he steps on to the stage before us the process of creation is already over. He does not mind if the setting is changed around him as he plays. Busy hands quite openly pass him what he needs for his performance. When Mei Lang-fang was playing a death scene a spectator sitting next to me exclaimed with astonishment at one of his gestures. One or two people sitting in front of us turned round indignantly and sshhh'd. They behaved as if they were present at the real death of a real girl. Possibly their attitude would have been all right for a European production, but for a Chinese it was unspeakably ridiculous. In their case the A-effect had misfired.

It is not entirely easy to realize that the Chinese actor's A-effect is a transportable piece of technique: a conception that can be pried loose from the Chinese theatre. We see this theatre as uncommonly precious, its portrayal of human passions as schematized, its idea of society as rigid and wrongheaded; at first sight this superb art seems to offer nothing applicable to a realistic and revolutionary theatre. Against that, the motives and objects of the A-effect strike us as odd and suspicious.

When one sees the Chinese acting it is at first very hard to discount the feeling of estrangement which they produce in us as Europeans. One has to be able to imagine them achieving an A-effect among their Chinese spectators too. What is still harder is that one must accept the fact that when the Chinese performer conjures up an impression of mystery he seems uninterested in disclosing a mystery to us. He makes his own mystery from the mysteries of nature (especially human nature): he allows nobody to examine how he produces the natural phenomenon, nor does nature allow him to understand as he produces it. We have here the artistic counterpart of a primitive technology, a rudimentary science. The Chinese performer gets his A-effect by association with magic. "How it's done" remains hidden; knowledge is a matter of knowing the tricks and is in the hands of a few men who guard it jealously and profit from their secrets. And yet there is already an attempt here to interfere with the course of nature; the capacity to do so leads to questioning; and the future explorer, with his anxiety to make nature's course intelligible, controllable and down-to-earth, will always start by adopting a standpoint from which it seems mysterious, incomprehensible and beyond control. He will take up the attitude of somebody wondering, will apply the A-effect. Nobody can be a mathematician who takes it for granted that "two and two makes four"; nor is anybody one who fails to understand it. The man who first looked with astonishment at a swinging lantern and instead of taking it for granted found it highly remarkable that it should swing, and swing in that particular way rather than any other, was brought close to understanding the phenomenon by this observation, and so to mastering it. Nor must it simply be exclaimed that the attitude here proposed is all right for science but not for art. Why shouldn't art try, by its *own* means of course, to further the great social task of mastering life?

In point of fact the only people who can profitably study a piece of technique like Chinese acting's A-effect are those who need such a technique for quite definite social purposes.

The experiments conducted by the modern German theatre led to a wholly independent development of the A-effect. So far Asiatic acting has exerted no influence.

The A-effect was achieved in the German epic theatre not only by the actor, but also by the music (choruses, songs) and the setting (placards, film etc.). It was principally designed to historicize the incidents portrayed. By this is meant the following:

The bourgeois theatre emphasized the timelessness of its objects. Its representation of people is bound by the alleged "eternally human." Its story is arranged in such a way as to create "universal" situations that allow Man with a capital M to express himself: man of every period and every color. All its incidents are just one enormous cue, and this cue is followed by the "eternal" response: the inevitable, usual, natural, purely human response. An example: a black man falls in love in the same way as a white man: the story forces him to react with the same expression as the white man (in theory this formula works as well the other way round); and with that the sphere of art is attained. The cue can take account of what is special, different; the response is shared, there is no element of difference in it. This notion may allow that such a thing as history exists, but is none the less unhistorical. A few circumstances vary, the environments are altered, but Man remains unchanged. History applies to the environment, not to Man. The environment is remarkably unimportant, is treated simply as a pretext; it is a variable quantity and something remarkably inhuman; it exists in fact apart from Man, confronting him as a coherent whole, whereas he is a fixed quantity, eternally unchanged. The idea of man as a function of the environment and the environment as a function of man, i.e. the breaking up of environment into relationships between men, corresponds to a new way of thinking, the historical way. Rather than be sidetracked into the philosophy of history, let us give an example. Suppose the following is to be shown on the stage: a girl leaves home in order to take a job in a fair-sized city (Piscator's *American Tragedy*). For the bourgeois theatre this is an insignificant affair, clearly the beginning of a story; it is what one has to have been told in order to understand what comes after, or to be keyed up for. The actor's imagination will hardly be greatly fired by it. In a sense the incident is universal: girls take jobs (in the case in question one can be keyed up to see what in particular is going to happen to her). Only in one way is it particular: this girl goes away (if she had remained what comes after would not have happened). The fact that her family lets her go is not the object of the inquiry; it is understandable (the motives are understandable). But for the historicizing theatre everything is different. The theatre concentrates entirely on whatever in this perfectly everyday event is remarkable, particular and demanding inquiry. What! A family letting one of its members leave the nest to earn her future living independently and without help? Is she up to it? Will what she has learnt here as a member of the family help her to earn her living? Can't families keep a grip on their children any longer? Have they become (or remained) a burden? Is it like that with every family? Was it always like that? Is this the way of the world, something that can't be affected? The fruit falls off the tree when ripe: does this sentence apply here? Do children always make themselves independent? Did they do so in every age? If so, and if it's something biological, does it always happen in the same way, for the same reasons and with the same results? These are the questions (or a few of them) that the actors must answer if they want to show the incident as a unique, historical one: if they want to demonstrate a custom which leads to conclusions about the entire structure of a society at a particular (transient) time. But how is such an incident to be represented if its historic character is to be brought out? How can the confusion of our unfortunate epoch be striking? When the mother, in between warnings and moral injunctions, packs her daughter's case—a very small one—how is the following to be shown: So many injunctions and so few clothes? Moral injunctions for a lifetime and bread for five hours? How is the actress to speak the mother's sentence as she hands over such a very small case—"There, I guess that ought to do you"—in such way that it is understood as a historic dictum? This can only be achieved if the A-effect is brought out. The actress must not make the sentence her own affair, she must hand it over to criticism, she must help us to understand its causes and protest. The effect can only be got by long training. In the New York Yiddish Theatre, a highly progressive theatre, I saw a play by S. Ornitz showing the rise of an East Side boy to be a big crooked attorney. The theatre could not perform the play. And yet there were scenes like this in it: the young attorney sits in the street outside his house giving cheap legal advice. A young woman arrives and complains that her leg has been hurt in a traffic accident. But the case has been bungled and her compensation has not yet been paid. In desperation she points to her leg and says: "It's started to heal up." Working without the A-effect, the theatre was unable to make use of this exceptional scene to show the horror of a bloody epoch. Few people in the audience noticed it; hardly anyone who reads it will remember that cry. The actress spoke the cry as if it were something perfectly natural. But is it exactly this—the fact that this poor creature finds such a complaint natural—that she should have reported to the public like a horrified messenger returning from the lowest of all hells. To that end she would of course have needed a special technique which would have allowed her to underline the historical aspect of a specific social condition. Only the A-effect makes this possible. Without it all she can do is to observe how she is not forced to go over entirely into the character on the stage.

In setting up new artistic principles and working out new methods of representation we must start with the compelling demands of a changing epoch; the necessity and the possibility of remodeling society loom ahead. All incidents between men must be noted, and everything must be seen from a social point of view. Among other effects that a new theatre will need for its social criticism and its historical reporting of completed transformations is the A-effect.

AUGUSTO BOAL

Augusto BOAL (b.1931), of medium height and build, with a long torso and short legs, moves with an easy loping gait. His long wavy salt-and-pepper hair frames a face with strongly pronounced features: a large nose and bright, twinkling hazel-brown eyes full of mischief and intelligence. When he talks, his hands touch his face and head, more as nervous tick than as gestural illustration. His soft, lilting voice is Brazilian accented in English or Spanish. He dresses casually in jeans and short-sleeves or sweater over shirt. His manner is direct, opinionated, ideological, thoughtful, analytical.

Boal has always considered the theatre a pedagogical instrument for social change. The first period of his career was Marxist in ideology and national in its orientation. As artistic director of the Arena Theatre in São Paulo for fifteen years (at first working closely with Gianfrancesco Guarnieri), he first sought to free the Brazilian theatre from its overdependence on European models by staging the work of twelve new Brazilian playwrights and then adapting such classics as Machiavelli's *La Mandragola*, Lope de Vega's *The King is the Best Justice*, and Molière's *Tartuffe*. At the same time Boal traveled throughout the countryside without remuneration, visiting outlying towns and villages where he organized cultural centers and "people's theatres." Inspired by the popular tradition of Brazilian carnival, circus, and music, Boal acknowledged that he has also been influenced by "all intelligent and creative people," including Shakespeare, Cervantes, and Brecht.

The interaction of theatre and politics served as the stimulus for Boal's experiments with dramatic form. A 1968 coup d'etat and military dictatorship in Brazil led him to develop new genres and techniques of radical theatre, such as "Newspaper Theatre," documentary drama based on current events, and "Invisible Theatre," staged performances in public places before unsuspecting audiences. Resistant to detection by the police, these hidden theatrical events, joining fiction to reality, were presented in cafes, restaurants, markets, metro stations, and trains to spectators, who unaware they were watching a play, could easily be provoked to discussion or action.

After being imprisoned for three months and tortured (experiences treated in his first novel, *The Miracle in Brazil* and in his play *Torquemada* of 1971), Boal was freed because of international protests and forced to leave Brazil for exile in Argentina, Venezuela, Mexico, and Peru (where in 1973 the director worked to eliminate illiteracy).

It was as an exile in 1973 that Boal wrote *The Theatre of the Oppressed*, the first part consisting of essays that examine the European tradition of dramatic theory from Aristotle to Brecht. Here the playwright-theoretician attacks Aristotelian catharsis as a coercive device by means of which society can purge its members of anti-conformist tendencies so as to maintain the status quo.

The second part of *The Theatre of the Oppressed* describes the director's actual stage practices showing how theatre can become a rehearsal for social change. Rejecting a passive role for the audience, Boal proposes an "aesthetics of the oppressed" that transforms the spectator into a spect-actor ready at every moment to replace the protagonist and act out alternative scenarios.

In "Forum Theatre," the audience is asked to study the protagonist's problem, consider all available choices, and discuss possible solutions with the actors, stopping the action to influence the train of events and change the given "real-life" situation. The "joker" figure served both as a narrator who addressed audience directly and also as a "wild card" actor able to jump in and out of character and take on any role in the play. By undermining easy judgments, the joker's function was not to simplify, but to render more complex the audience's comprehension.

In the second period of his career starting in the later 1970s, Boal has directed plays and presented "Forum Theatre" for bourgeois audiences in Europe and America, extending his definition of the "oppressed" beyond the socially and economically deprived lower classes. His work as an artist, teacher, and lecturer is now psycho-therapeutic as well as political in its orientation and impact. The new techniques, exercises, and games that he devises for his experimental workshops can be applied to different countries, cultures and situations all over the world. Boal's method has become international in scope, practiced in varied contexts and taught by disciples of diverse national backgrounds. He has been elected a state legislator in modern Brazil.

In "The Rainbow of Desire," Boal's new formulation of his educational program, catharsis undergoes redefinition. Individuals and the groups they constitute can be transformed by a catharsis that releases desires which have been constrained by social stereotypes.

THEATER OF THE OPPRESSED (1974)

How Aristotle's Coercive System of Tragedy Functions

The spectacle begins. The tragic hero appears. The public establishes a kind of empathy with him.

The action starts. Surprisingly, the hero shows a flaw in his behavior, a *hamartia*; and even more surprising, one learns that it is by virtue of this same hamartia that the hero has come to his present state of happiness

Through empathy, the same hamartia that the spectator may possess is stimulated, developed, activated.

Suddenly, something happens that changes everything. (Oedipus, for example, is informed by Teiresias that the murderer he seeks is Oedipus himself.) The character, who because of a hamartia had climbed so high, runs the risk of falling from those heights. This is what the *Poetics* classifies as *peripeteia*, a radical change in the character's destiny. The spectator, who up to then had his own hamartia stimulated, starts to feel a growing fear. The character is now on the way to misfortune. Creon is informed of the death of his son and his wife; Hippolytus cannot convince his father of his innocence, and the latter impels his son, unintentionally, to death.

Peripeteia is important because it lengthens the road from happiness to misfortune. The taller the palm tree, the greater the fall, says a popular Brazilian song. That way creates more impact.

The peripeteia suffered by the character is reproduced in the spectator as well. But it could happen that the spectator would follow the character emphatically until the moment of the peripeteia and then detach himself at that point. In order to avoid that, the tragic character must also pass through what Aristotle calls *anagnorisis* —that is, through the recognition of his flaw as such and, by means of reasoning, the explanation of it. The hero accepts his error, hoping that, emphatically, the spectator will also accept as bad his own hamartia. But the spectator has the great advantage of having erred only vicariously: he does not really pay for it.

Finally, so that the spectator will keep in mind the terrible consequences of committing the error not just vicariously but in actuality, Aristotle

From Augusto Boal, *Theater of the Oppressed*,
trans. Charles A. and Maria-Odilia Leal McBride. N.Y.: Urzen Books, 1979.

demands that tragedy have a terrible end, which he calls *catastrophe*. The happy end is not permitted, though the character's physical destruction is not absolutely required. Some die; others see their loved ones die. In any case, the catastrophe is always such that not to die is worse than death.

Those three interdependent elements (peripeteia, anagnorisis, catastrophe) have the ultimate goal of provoking catharsis in the spectator (as much or more than in the character); that is, their purpose is to produce a purgation of the hamartia, passing through three clearly defined stages:

First stage: Stimulation of the hamartia; the character follows an ascending path toward happiness, accompanied emphatically by the spectator. Then comes a moment of reversal: the character, with the spectator, starts to move from happiness toward misfortune; fall of the hero.

Second stage: The character recognizes his error—*anagnorisis*. Through the empathic relationship *dianoia-reason*, the spectator recognizes his own error, his own hamartia, his own anticonstitutional flaw.

Third stage: Catastrophe; the character suffers the consequences of his error, in a violent form, with his own death or with the death of loved ones.

Catharsis: The spectator, terrified by the spectacle of the catastrophe, is purified of his hamartia.

[...] The words *"Amicus Plato, sed magis amicus veritas"* ("I am Plato's friend, but I am more of a friend of truth") are attributed to Aristotle. In this we agree entirely with Aristotle: we are his friends, but we are much better friends of truth. He tells us that poetry, tragedy, theater have nothing to do with politics. But reality tells us something else. His own *Poetics* tells us it is not so. We have to be better friends of reality: all of man's activities—including, of course, all the arts, especially theater—are political. And theater is the most perfect artistic form of coercion.

DIFFERENT TYPES OF CONFLICT: HAMARTIA AND SOCIAL ETHOS

[...] Aristotle's coercive system of tragedy requires:

a. the creation of a conflict between the character's ethos and the ethos of the society in which he lives; something is not right!

b. the establishment of a relationship called empathy, which consists in allowing the spectator to be guided by the character through his experiences; the spectator—feeling as if he himself is acting—enjoys the pleasures and suffers the misfortunes of the character, to the extreme of thinking his thoughts.

c. that the spectator experience three changes of a rigorous nature: *peripeteia*, *anagnorisis*, and *catharsis*; he *suffers a blow* with regard to his fate (the action of the play), *recognizes the error* vicariously committed and is *purified of the antisocial characteristic* which he sees in himself.

This is the essence of the coercive system of tragedy. [...] In its essence, the system survived and has continued to be utilized down to our own time, with various modifications introduced by new societies. Let us analyze some of these modifications.

First Type: Hamartia Versus the Perfect Social Ethos (classical type).

This is the most classical case studied by Aristotle. Consider again the example of Oedipus. The perfect social ethos is presented through the Chorus or through Teiresias in his long speech. The collision is head-on. Even after Teiresias has declared that the criminal is Oedipus himself, the latter does not accept it and continues the investigation on his own. Oedipus—the perfect man, the obedient son, the loving husband, the model father, the statesman without equal, intelligent, handsome, and sensitive—has nevertheless a tragic flaw: his pride! Through it he climbs to the peak of his glory, and through it he is destroyed. The balance is re-established with the catastrophe, with the terrifying vision of the protagonist's hanged mother-wife and his eyes torn out.

Second Type: Hamartia Versus Hamartia Versus the Perfect Social Ethos.

The tragedy presents two characters who meet, two tragic heroes, each one with his flaw, who destroy each other before an ethically perfect society. This is the typical case of Antigone and Creon, both very fine persons in every way with the exception of their respective flaws. In these cases, the spectator must necessarily *empathize with both characters*, not only one, since the tragic process must purify him of two hamartias. A spectator who empathizes only with Antigone can be led to think that Creon possesses the truth, and vice versa. The spectator must purify himself of the "excess," whatever direction it takes—whether excess of love of the State to the detriment of the Family, or excess of love of the Family to the detriment of the good of the State.

Often, when the anagnorisis of the character is perhaps not enough to convince the spectator, the tragic author utilizes the direct reasoning of the Chorus, possessor of common sense, moderation, and other qualities.

In this case also the catastrophe is necessary in order to produce, through fear, the catharsis, the purification of evil.

Third Type: Negative Hamartia Versus the Perfect Social Ethos.

This type is completely different from the two presented before. Here the ethos of the character is presented in a negative form; that is, he has all the faults and only a single virtue, and not as was taught by Aristotle, all the virtues and only one fault, flaw or mistake of judgement. Precisely because he possesses that small and solitary virtue the character is saved, the catastrophe is avoided, and instead a happy end occurs.

It is important to note that Aristotle clearly objected to the happy end, but we should note, too, that the coercive character of his whole system is the true essence of his political *Poetics*; therefore, in changing a characteristic as important as the composition of the ethos of the character, the structural mechanism of the end of the work is inevitably changed also, in order to maintain the purgative effect.

This type of catharsis, produced by the "negative hamartia versus the perfect social ethos," was often used in the Middle Ages. Perhaps the best known medieval drama is *Everyman.*

It tells the story of the character named Everyman, who when it comes time to die, tries to save himself, has a dialogue with Death, and analyzes all his past actions. Before Everyman and Death passes a whole series of characters who accuse Everyman and reveal the sins committed by him: the material goods, the pleasures, etc. Everyman finally recognizes all the sins he has committed, admits the complete absence of any virtue in his actions, but at the same time trusts in divine mercy. This faith is his only virtue. This faith and his repentance save him, for the greater glory of God. ...

The anagnorisis (recognition of his sins) is practically accompanied by the birth of a new character, and the latter is saved. In tragedy, the acts of the character are irremediable; but in this type of drama, the acts of the character can be forgiven provided he decides to change his life completely and become a "new" character.

The idea of a new life (and this one is the forgiven life, since the sinning character ceases to be a sinner) can be seen clearly in *Condemned for Faithlessness (El condenado por desconfiado)* by Tirso de Molina. The hero, Enrique, has all the worst faults to be found in a person: he is a drunkard, murderer, thief, scoundrel—no defect, crime, or vice is alien to him. Wickedness that the Devil himself might envy. He has the most perverted ethos that dramatic art has ever invented. At his side is Pablo, the pure one, incapable of committing the slightest, most forgivable little sin, an immaculate spirit, insipid, empty, the image of perfection!

But something very strange happens to this pair which will cause their fate to be exactly opposite of what one would expect. Enrique, the bad one, knows himself to be evil and a sinner, and never doubts that divine justice will condemn him to burn in the flames of the deepest and darkest corner of hell. And he accepts the divine wisdom and its justice. On the other hand, Pablo sins by wanting himself to be pure. At every instant he wonders if God will truly realize that his life has been one of sacrifice and want. He ardently wishes to die and move immediately to heaven, so that he can possibly begin there a more pleasant life.

The two of them die, and to surprise of some, the divine verdict is as follows: Enrique, in spite of all crimes, robberies, drunkenness, treasons, etc., goes to heaven, because of his firm belief in his punishment glorified God; Pablo, on the other hand, did not truly believe in God, since he doubted his salvation; therefore, he goes to hell with all his virtues.

That, in rough outline, is the play. Observed from the point of view of Enrique, it is clearly a case of a thoroughly evil ethos, possessing a single virtue. The exemplary effect is obtained through the happy end and not through the catastrophe. Observed from the point of view of Pablo, it is a conventional, classical, Aristotelian scheme. Everything in Pablo was virtue, with the exception of his tragic flaw—doubting God. For him there is indeed a catastrophe!

Fourth Type: Negative Hamartia Versus Negative Social Ethos.

The word "negative" is employed here in the sense of referring to a model that is the exact opposite of the original positive model—without reference to any moral quality. As, for instance, in a photographic negative, where all that is white shows up black and vice versa.

This type of ethical conflict is the essence of "romantic drama," and *Camille* (*La Dame aux camélias*) is the best example. The hamartia of the protagonist, as in the preceding case, displays an impressive collection of negative qualities, sins, errors, etc. On the other hand, the social ethos (that is, the moral tendencies, ethics) of the society—contrary to the preceding example (third type)—is here entirely in agreement with the character. All her vices are perfectly acceptable, and she would suffer nothing for having them.

In *Camille* we see a corrupted society, which accepts prostitution, and Marguerite Gautier is the best prostitute—individual vice is defended and accepted by the vicious society. Her profession is perfectly acceptable, her house frequented by society's most respected men (considering that it is a society whose principal value is money, her house is frequented by financiers) ... Marguerite's life is full of happiness! But, poor girl, all her faults are accepted, though not her only virtue. Marguerite falls in love. Indeed, she truly loves someone. Ah, no, not that. Society cannot permit it; it is a tragic flaw and must be punished.

Here, from the ethical point of view, a sort of triangle is established. Up to now we have analyzed conflicts in which the "social ethics" was the same for the characters as for the spectators; now a dichotomy is presented: the author wishes to show a social ethics accepted by the society portrayed on stage, but he himself, the author, does not share that ethics, and proposes another. The universe of the work is one, and our universe, or at least our momentary position during the spectacle, is another. Alexander Dumas (*fils*) says in effect: here you see what this society is like, and it is bad, but we are not like that, or we are not like that in our innermost being. Thus, Marguerite has all the virtues that society believes to be virtues; a prostitute must practice her profession of prostitute with dignity and efficiency. But Marguerite has a flaw which prevents her from practising her profession well—she falls in love. How can a woman in love with *one* man serve with equal fidelity *all* men (all those who can pay)? Impossible. Therefore, falling in love, is not a virtue but a vice.

But we, the spectators, who do not belong to the universe of the work, can say the exact opposite: a society which allows and encourages prostitution is a society which must be changed. Thus the triangle is established: to love, for us is a virtue, but in the universe of the work, it is a vice. And Marguerite Gautier is destroyed precisely because of that vice (virtue).

And in this kind of romantic drama, the catastrophe is inevitable. And the romantic author hopes that the spectator will be purified not of the tragic flaw of the hero, but rather of the whole ethos of society.

The same modification of the Aristotelian scheme is found in another romantic drama, *An Enemy of the People*, by Ibsen. Here again, the character, Dr. Stockman, embodies an ethos identical to that of the society in which he lives, a society based on profit, on money; but he also possesses a flaw: he is an honest man! This the society cannot tolerate. The powerful impact this work usually has stems from the fact that Ibsen shows (whether intentionally or not) that societies based on profit find it impossible to foster an "elevated" morality.

Capitalism is fundamentally immoral because the search for profit, which is its essence, is incompatible with its official morality, which preaches superior human values, justice, etc.

Dr. Stockman is destroyed (that is, he loses his position in society, as does his daughter, who becomes an outcast in a competitive society) precisely because of his basic virtue, which is here considered vice, error, or tragic flaw.

Fifth Type: Anachronistic Individual Ethos Versus Contemporary Social Ethos.

This is the typical case of Don Quixote: his social ethos is perfectly synchronized with the ethos of a society that no longer exists. This past society, now nonexistent, enters into a confrontation with the contemporary society and the resultant conflicts are inevitable. The anachronistic ethos of Don Quixote, knight errant and lordly Spanish hidalgo, cannot live peacefully in a time when the bourgeoisie is developing—the bourgeoisie which changes all values and for whom all things become money, as money comes to equal all things.

A variation of the "anachronistic ethos" is that of the "diachronic ethos": the character lives in a moral world made up of values which society honors in word but not in deed. In *José, from Birth to Grave*, the character, José da Silva, embodies all the values that the bourgeoisie claims as its own, and his misfortune comes precisely because he believes in those values and rules his life by them: a "self-made man," he works more than he has to, is devoted to his employers, avoids causing labor troubles, etc. In short, a character who follows *The Laws of Success* of Napoleon Hill, or *How to Win Friends and Influence People* of Dale Carnegie. That is tragedy! And what a tragedy!

Conclusion

Aristotle's coercive system of tragedy survives to this day, thanks to its great efficacy. It is, in effect, a powerful system of intimidation. The structure of the system may vary in a thousand ways, making it difficult at times to find all the elements of its structure, but the system will nevertheless be there, working to carry out its basic task: the purgation of all antisocial elements. Precisely for that reason, the system cannot be utilized by revolutionary groups *during* revolutionary periods. That is, while the social ethos is not clearly defined, the tragic scheme cannot be used, for the simple reason that the character's ethos will not find a clear social ethos that it can confront.

The coercive system of tragedy can be used before or after the revolution ... but never during it!

In fact, only more or less stable societies, ethically defined, can offer a scale of values which would make it possible for the system to function. During a "cultural revolution," in which all values are being formed or questioned, the system cannot be applied. That is to say that the system, insofar as it structures certain elements which produce a determined effect, can be utilized by any society as long as it possesses a definite social ethos; for it to function, technically whether the society is feudal, capitalist, or socialist does not matter; what matters is that it have a universe of definite, accepted values.

On the other hand, an understanding of how the system functions often becomes difficult because one places himself in a false perspective. For example: the stories of "Western" movies are Aristotelian (at least, all the ones I have seen). But to analyze them it is necessary to regard them from the perspective of the bad man rather than from that of the "good guy," from the viewpoint not of the hero but of the villain.

A "Western" story begins with a presentation of a villain (bandit, horse thief, murderer, or whatever) who, precisely because of his vice or tragic flaw, is the uncontested boss, the richest and the most feared man of the neighborhood or city. He does all the evil he possibly can, and we empathize with him and vicariously we do the same evil—we kill, steal horses and chickens, rape young heroines, etc. Until, after our own hamartia has also been stimulated, the moment of the *peripeteia*: the hero gains advantage in the fist fight or through endless shoot-outs and re-establishes order (social ethos), morality, and honest business relationships, after destroying (*catastrophe*) the bad citizen. What is left out here is *anagnorisis*, and the villain is allowed to die without feeling regrets; in short, they finish him off with gunshots and bury him, while the townspeople celebrate with square dances ...

How often—remember?—our sympathy has been (in a certain way, empathy) more with the bad guy than with the good one! The "Westerns," like children's games, serve the Aristotelian purpose of purging all the spectator's aggressive tendencies.

This system functions to diminish, placate, satisfy, eliminate all that can break the balance—all, including the revolutionary, transforming impetus.

Let there be no doubt: Aristotle formulated a very powerful purgative system, the objective of which is to eliminate all that is not commonly accepted, including the revolution, before it takes place. His system appears in disguised form on television, in the movies, in the circus, in the theatres. It appears in many and varied shapes and media. But its essence does not change: it is designed to bridle the individual, to adjust him to what pre-exists. If this is what we want, the Aristotelian system serves the purpose better than any other; if, on the contrary, we want to stimulate the spectator to transform his society, to engage in revolutionary action, in that case we will have to seek another poetics! [...]

Poetics of the Oppressed

In the beginning the theater was the dithyrambic song: free people singing in the open air. The carnival. The feast.

Later, the ruling classes took possession of the theater and built their dividing walls. First, they divided the people, separating actors from spectators: people who act and people who watch—the party is over! Secondly, among the actors, they separated the protagonists from the mass. The coercive indoctrination began!

Now the oppressed people are liberated themselves and, once more, are making the theater their own. The walls must be torn down. First, the spectator starts acting again: invisible theater, forum theater, image theater, etc. Secondly, it is necessary to eliminate the private property of the characters by the individual actors: the "Joker" System. [...] The people reassume their protagonistic function in the theater and in society. [...]

Experiments with the People's Theater in Peru

In the forum theater no idea is imposed: the audience, the people, have the opportunity to try out all their ideas, to rehearse all the possibilities, and to verify them in practice, that is, in theatrical practice. If the audience had come to the conclusion that it was necessary to dynamite all the fish meal factories in Chimbote, this would also be right from their point of view. It is not the place of the theater to show the correct path, but only to offer the means by which all possible paths may be examined.

Maybe the theater in itself is not revolutionary, but these theatrical forms are without a doubt a *rehearsal of revolution*. The truth of the matter is that the spectator-actor practices a real act even though he does it in a fictional manner. While he *rehearses* throwing a bomb on stage, he is concretely rehearsing the way a bomb is thrown; acting out his attempt to organize a strike, he is concretely organizing a strike. Within its fictitious limits, the experience is a concrete one.

Here the cathartical effect is entirely avoided. We are used to plays in which the characters make the revolution on stage and the spectators in their seats feel themselves to be triumphant revolutionaries. Why make a revolution in reality if we have already made it in the theater? But that does not happen here: the rehearsal stimulates the practice of the act in reality. Forum theater, as well as these other forms of a people's theater, instead of taking something away from the spectator, evoke in him a desire to practice in reality the act he has rehearsed in the theater. The practice of these theatrical forms creates a sort of uneasy sense of incompleteness that seeks fulfillment through real action. [...]

The bourgeois theater is the finished theater. The bourgeoisie knows what the world is like, their world, and is able to present images of this complete, finished world. The bourgeoisie presents this spectacle. On the other hand, the proletariat and the oppressed classes do not know yet what their world will be like; consequently their theater will be the rehearsal, not the finished spectacle. This is quite true, though it is equally true that the theater can present images of transition.

I have been able to observe the truth of this view during all my activities in the people's theater of so many and such different countries of Latin America. Popular audiences are interested in experimenting, in rehearsing, and they abhor the "closed" spectacles. In those cases they try to enter into a dialogue with the actors, to interrupt the action, to ask for explanations without waiting politely for the end of the play. Contrary to the bourgeois code of manners, the people's code allows and encourages the spectator to ask questions, to dialogue, to participate.

All the methods that I have discussed are forms of a rehearsal-theater, and not a spectacle-theater. One knows how these experiments will begin but not how they will end, because the spectator is freed from his chains, finally acts, and becomes a protagonist. Because they respond to the real needs of a popular audience they are practiced with joy and success. [...]

Invisible theater: It consists of the presentation of a scene in an environment other than the theater before people who are not spectators. The place can be a restaurant, a sidewalk, a market, a train, a line of people, etc.

The people who witness the scene are those who are there by chance. During the spectacle, these people must not have the slightest idea that it is a "spectacle," for this would make them "spectators."

The invisible theater calls for the detailed preparation of a skit with a complete text or a simple script; but it is necessary to rehearse the scene sufficiently so that the actors are able to incorporate into their acting and their actions the intervention of the spectators. During the rehearsal it is also necessary to include every imaginable intervention from the spectators; these possibilities will form a kind of optional text.

The invisible theater erupts in a location chosen as a place where the public congregates. All the people who are near become involved in the eruption and the effects of it last long after the skit is ended. [...]

Conclusion: "Spectator," A Bad Word!

"Spectator" is a bad word! The spectator is less than a man and it is necessary to humanize him, to restore to him his capacity of action in all its fullness. He too must be a subject, an actor on an equal plane with those generally accepted as actors, who must also be spectators. All these experiments of a people's theater have the same objective—the liberation of the spectator, on whom the theater has imposed finished visions of the world. And since those responsible for theatrical performances are in general people who belong directly or indirectly to the ruling classes, obviously their finished images will be reflections of themselves. The spectators in the people's theater (i.e. the people themselves) cannot go on being the passive victims of those images.

As we have seen in the first essay of this book, the poetics of Aristotle is the *poetics of oppression*: the world is known, perfect or about to be perfected, and all its values are imposed on the spectators, who passively delegate power to the characters to act and think in their place. In so doing the spectators purge themselves of their tragic flaw—that is, of something capable of changing society. A catharsis of the revolutionary impetus is produced! Dramatic action substitutes for real action.

Brecht's poetics is that of the enlightened vanguard: the world is revealed as subject to change, and the change starts in the theater itself, for the spectator does not delegate power to the characters to think in his place, although he continues to delegate power to them to act in his place. The experience is revealing on the level of consciousness, but not globally on the level of the action. Dramatic action throws light upon real action. The spectacle is preparation for action.

The *poetics of the oppressed* is essentially the poetics of liberation: the spectator no longer delegates power to the characters either to think or act in his place. The spectator frees himself; he thinks and acts for himself! Theater is action!

Perhaps the theater is not revolutionary in itself; but have no doubts, it is a rehearsal of revolution!

WOLE SOYINKA

Wole SOYINKA (b. 1934), tall, trim, casually dapper in his distinctive collarless shirts, holds his head tilted slightly back with a look of mischievous defiance. His mask-like, apple-cheeked face is rendered impressive by a great halo-shaped crown of white hair, grizzled mustache and protruding goatee. A full-throated baritone, he speaks rhythmically and mellifluously, the vowels long and mellow. When he reads poetry, delivers political addresses, or mimics adversaries, his deeply resonant voice becomes an expressive weapon. Witty and mocking, he is sometimes angry, always uncompromising.

Whether playing himself or others, Soyinka is a consummate performer—on the political platform and in the lecture hall as well as on stage and in film. Down-and-out in Paris as a young student, he performed in bars for drinks, while dreaming of a career as a cabaret singer-guitarist. With his Guerilla Theatre in his native Nigeria he performed in the streets, shantytowns, and market places. Gun in hand, he made a raid on a government radio station and, instead of the premier's speech scheduled for broadcast, put on a subversive tape in the name of the people telling the renegades to clear out.

Soyinka has been a proponent and practitioner of two seemingly incompatible tendencies in modern theatre: mythopoetic drama and revolutionary agit-prop. A social activist as well as a multi-talented artist, he combines the roles of playwright, actor, director, producer, and manager with those of poet and novelist. An advocate of joining the old and new, Soyinka has brought the techniques of traditional folk theatre to late twentieth-century mass media—radio, television, and cinema—issuing an album of satirical songs and producing a film, *Blues for a Prodigal* (1985), banned in Nigeria for its attacks on corruption in high places.

In confronting the problem of national identity in post-colonial Africa, the playwright unmasks the mechanisms of power that operate according to their own laws regardless of ideology or "the color of the foot" that wears "the oppressive boot." For opposing the state during the Nigerian (Biafran) civil war, Soyinka was arrested, tried, and acquitted, then re-arrested and held without a trial for more than two years—twenty-one months in solitary confinement. On his release in 1969 he went into exile in Europe and America, but after returning to Nigeria in 1976, the playwright soon took up political theatre again, organizing a Guerilla Theatre company that satirized corrupt state power and the abuse of civil rights.

Attacked as inauthentic and Euro-assimilationist by purist African ideologues seeking to decolonize African literature by purging it of all Euromodernist elements, Soyinka has responded aggressively, ridiculing myths of cultural superiority and labeling his opponents Neo-Tarzanists and Leftocrats. Refusing to have his role as an African writer narrowly defined by others, he has chosen to remain complex, modern, and cosmopolitan.

From his student days Soyinka had been theatre-obsessed and actively involved in the life of the stage. In his teens he wrote sketches for his college drama group and played leading roles at the Ibadan university theatre. During his term as play-reader at London's Royal Court Theatre in 1959-60, when it was the center of the English dramatic revival, Soyinka became acquainted with the plays of Osborne, Wesker, Pinter, and Bond, observed the latest trends in direction and stage management, put on an evening of his own poetry and songs, and directed a Nigerian group in a production of his *Swamp Dwellers*.

On returning home the playwright pioneered Nigerian radio drama in Lagos. He founded the Nineteen-Sixty Masks, a semi-professional acting company, in order to stage his *Dance of Forests* at the University theatre in Ibadan, when the play, which had won a competition for the Independence celebrations, proved too subversive, cynical, and iconoclastic for official presentation. Then he organized the Orisun Theatre, a younger, full-time company whose actors he trained personally for the complex physical performance style he required. He wrote scripts for a popular weekly radio serial, *Broke-Time Bar*, while appearing as Yang Sun in a university production of Brecht's *Good Person of Setzuan*.

Following the established practice of fashioning new African works out of well-known European dramas, Soyinka created a Nigerian version of Gay's *Beggar's Opera* and Brecht's *Threepenny Opera* that targeted local dictators and their supporters. His own *Play of Giants* parodying tyrants takes Genet's *Balcony* as its source.

Soyinka's model for tragedy is not European, but the Yoruba ritual theatre. After several years at Leeds University, the playwright received a Rockefeller scholarship to study traditional African theatre, enabling him to travel throughout Nigeria and other Western African countries, recording festivals, rituals, seasonal ceremonies, and masquerades.

After the military coup in 1994 which he denounced as a betrayal of democracy, the playwright and Nobel Prize winner had to flee his native country to avoid arrest. Soyinka found himself a marked man, accused of being a traitor to his country and subject to death threats. In Nigeria his works were banned, his name could not be mentioned, and he risked possible execution if he were to return home. Until 1998 Soyinka was forced to live in permanent exile in the West, going under aliases and disguises and constantly changing his place of residence in fear of assassination by death squads.

Although he rejects the notion that all art is only an organ of class rule, the playwright recognizes that for the most part the artist in modern society "is an innately regulated being" with a deep-seated craving for conformity, enslaved to seductive ideologies and dictated fashions. But art, Soyinka argues, by its very nature "will try to contain and control power," making it something always feared by despots.

DRAMA AND THE
AFRICAN WORLD-VIEW (1976)

[...] Let us, by way of a paradigmatic example, take a common theme in traditional mask-drama: a symbolic struggle with chthonic presences, the goal of the conflict being a harmonious resolution for plenitude and the well-being of the community. Any individual within the "audience" knows better than to add his voice *arbitrarily* even to the most seductive passages of an invocatory song, or to contribute a refrain to the familiar sequence of liturgical exchanges among the protagonists. The moment for choric participation is well-defined, but this does not imply that until such a moment, participation ceases. The so-called audience is itself an integral part of that arena of conflict; it contributes spiritual strength to the protagonist through its choric reality which must first be conjured up and established, defining and investing the arena through offerings and incantations. The drama would be non-existent except within and against this symbolic representation of earth and cosmos, except within this communal compact whose choric essence supplies the collective energy for the challenger of chthonic realms. Overt participation when it comes is channeled through a formalized repertoire of gestures and liturgical responses. The "spontaneous" participant from within the audience does not permit himself to give vent to a bare impulse or a euphoria which might bring him out as a dissociated entity from within the choric mass. If it does happen, as of course it can, the event is an aberration which may imperil the eudaemonic goals of that representation. The interjector—whose balance of mind is regarded as being temporarily disturbed—is quietly led out and the appropriate (usually unobtrusive) spells are cast to counter the risks of the abnormal event.

I would like to go a little deeper into this ritualistic sense of space since it is so intimately linked with the comprehensive world-view of the society that gave it birth. We shall treat it first as a medium in the communicative sense and, like any other medium, it is one that is best defined through the process of interruption. In theatrical terms, this interruption is effected principally by the human apparatus. Sound, light, motion, even smell, can all be used just as validly to define space, and ritual theatre uses all these instruments

From Wole Soyinka, *Myth, Literature and the African World.*
Cambridge: Cambridge University Press, 1976.

of definition to control and render concrete, to parallel (this is perhaps the best description of the process) the experiences or intuitions of man in that far more disturbing environment which he defines variously as void, emptiness or infinity. The concern of ritual theatre in this process of spatial definition which precedes, as we shall discover, the actual enactment must therefore be seen as an integral part of man's constant efforts to master the immensity of the cosmos with his minuscule self. The actual events which make up the enactment are themselves, in ritual theatre, a materialization of this basic adventure of man's metaphysical self.

Theatre then is one arena, one of the earliest that we know of, in which man has attempted to come to terms with the spatial phenomenon of his being. Again, in speaking of space, let us recognize first of all that with the advancement of technology and the evolution—some would prefer to call it a counter-evolution—of the technical sensibility, the spatial vision of theatre has become steadily contracted into purely physical acting areas on a stage as opposed to a symbolic arena for metaphysical contests. The pagan beginnings of Greek theatre retained their symbolic validity to dramaturgists for centuries after the event, so that the relative positions of suppliant, tyrant or *deus ex machina*, as well as the offertory or altar, were constantly impressed on their audience and created immediate emotional overtones both when they were used and by their very act of being. (I do not, for the purpose of this essay, wish to debate whether the fixity of these positions did not, contrasted with the fluid approach of African ritual space, detract from the audience's experience of cosmic relations.) Medieval European theatre in its turn, corresponding to the religious mythology of its period, created a constant *microcosmos* by its spatial correspondences of good and evil, angels and demons, paradise, purgatory and hell. The protagonists of earth, heaven and hell enacted their various trials and conflicts in relation to these traditional positions, and the automatic recognition of three hierarchical situations of man created spiritual anxieties and hopes in the breasts of the audience. But observe, the apprehended territory of man has already begun to contract! Cosmic representation has shrunk into a purely moral one, a summation in terms of penalties and rewards. The process continued through successive periods of European partial explorations of what was once a medium of totality, achieving such analytical aberrations as in this sample of compartmentalization which claims that the right (actor's) wing of the stage is "stronger" than the left. We shall not encounter any proofs of this ludicrous assertion in the beginnings of theatre, Greek or African.

Ritual theatre, let it be recalled, establishes the spatial medium not merely as a physical area for simulated events but as a manageable contraction of the cosmic envelope within which man—no matter how deeply buried such a consciousness has latterly become—fearfully exists. And this attempt to manage the immensity of his spatial awareness makes every manifestation in ritual theatre a paradigm for the cosmic human condition. There are transient parallels, brief visual moments of this experience in modern European theatre. The spectacle of a lone human figure under a spotlight on a darkened stage is, unlike a painting, a breathing, living, pulsating, threateningly fragile example of this paradigm. It is threatening because, unlike a similar parable on canvas, its fragility is experienced both at the level of its symbolism and in terms of sympathetic concern for the well-being of that immediate human medium. Let us say he is a tragic character: at the first sign of a check in the momentum of a tragic declamation, his audience becomes nervous for him, wondering—has he forgotten his line? has he blacked out? Or in the case of opera—will she make that upper register? Well, ritual theatre has an additional, far more fundamental anxiety. Indeed, it is correct to say that the technical anxiety even where it exists—after all it does exist; the element of creative form is never absent even in the most so-called primitive consciousness—so, where it does exist, it is never so profoundly engaged as with a modern manifestation. The real unvoiced fear is: will this protagonist survive confrontation with forces that exist within the dangerous area of transformation? Entering that *microcosmos* involves a loss of individuation, a self-submergence in universal essence. It is an act undertaken on behalf of the community, and the welfare of that protagonist is inseparable from that of the total community.

This ritual understanding is essential to a profound participation in the cathartic processes of the great tragedies. To attempt to define it even more clearly I would like to refer once again to painting, that essentially individualistic art. In surmounting the challenge of space and cosmos, a Turner, a Wyeth or a van Gogh utilizes endless permutations of color, shapes and lines to extract truly harrowing or consoling metaphysical statements from natural phenomena. There is, however, no engagement of the communal experience in this particular medium. The transmission is individual. It is no less essential to the sum of human experience but it is, even when viewed by a thousand people simultaneously, a mere sum of fragmented experiences, individual and vicarious. The singularity of theatre is its simultaneity in the forging of a single human experience—at its most successful. That it does not often succeed is true enough, but that does not invalidate the truth that, at the very roots of the dramatic phenomenon, this affirmation of the communal self was the experiential goal. The search, even by modern European dramatists for ritualist roots from which to draw out visions of modern experience, is a clue to the deep-seated need of creative man to recover this archetypal consciousness in the origins of the dramatic medium.

Ritual theatre, viewed from the spatial perspective, aims to reflect through physical and symbolic means the archetypal struggle of the mortal being against exterior forces. A tragic view of the theatre goes further and suggests that even the so-called realistic or literary drama can be interpreted as a mundane reflection of this essential struggle. Poetic drama especially may be regarded as a repository of this essential aspect of theatre; being largely

metaphorical, it expands the immediate meaning and action of the protagonists into a world of nature forces and metaphysical conceptions. Or, to put it
the other way round, powerful natural or cosmic influences are internalized
within the protagonists and this implosive factor creates the titanic scale of
their passions even when the basis of the conflict seems hardly to warrant it.
(Shakespeare's *Lear* is the greatest exemplar of this.) Indeed, this view of theatre sees the stage as a constant battleground for forces larger than the petty
infractions of habitual communal norms or patterns of human relationships
and expectations, beyond the actual twists and incidents of action and their
resolutions. The stage is created for the purpose of that communal presence
which alone defines it (and this is the fundamental defining concept, that the
stage is brought into being by a communal presence); so, for this purpose, the
stage becomes the affective, rational and intuitive milieu of the total communal experience, historic, race-formative, cosmogonic. Where such theatre is
encountered in its purest form, not as re-created metaphors for the later tragic stage, we will find no compass points, no horizontal or vertical definitions.
There are no reserved spaces for the protagonists, for his very act of representational being is defined in turn by nothing less than the infinite cosmos
within which the origin of the community and its contemporaneous experience of being is firmly embedded. Drama, however, exists on the boards; in
the improvised space among stalls in the deserted or teeming market, on the
raised platform in a school or community hall, in the secretive recesses of a
nature-fringed shrine, among the push-buttons of the modern European stage
or its equivalents in Africa—those elegant monstrosities raised to enshrine the
spirit of misconceived prestigiousness. It is necessary always to look for the
essence of the play among these roofs and spaces, not confine it to the printed text as an autonomous entity. [...]

Appendix

[...] Tragedy, in Yoruba traditional drama, is the anguish of this severance, the fragmentation of essence from self. Its music is the stricken cry of
man's blind soul as he flounders in the void and crashes through a deep abyss
of a-spirituality and cosmic rejection. Tragic music is an echo from that void;
the celebrant speaks, sings and dances in authentic archetypal images from
within the abyss. All understand and respond, for it is the language of the
world.

It is necessary to emphasize that the gods were coming down to be
reunited with man, for this tragedy could not be, the anguish of severance
would not attain such tragic proportions, if the gods' position on earth (i.e. in
man's conception) was to be one of divine remoteness. This is again testified
to by the form of worship, which is marked by camaraderie and irreverence
just as departure to ancestorhood is marked by bawdiness in the midst of grief.

The anthropomorphic origin of uncountable deities is one more leveler of divine class-consciousness but, finally, it is the innate humanity of the gods themselves, their bond with man through a common animist relation with nature and phenomena. Continuity for the Yoruba operates both through the cyclic concept of time and the animist interfusion of all matter and consciousness.

The first actor—for he led the others—was Ogun, first suffering deity, first creative energy, the first challenger, and conqueror of transition. And his, the first art, was tragic art, for the complementary drama of the syncretic successor to Orisa-nla, Obatala's "Passion" play, is only the plastic resolution of Ogun's tragic engagement. The Yoruba metaphysics of accommodation and resolution could only come after the passage of the gods through the transitional gulf, after the demonic test of the self-will of Ogun the explorer-god in the creative cauldron of cosmic powers. Only after such testing could the harmonious Yoruba world be born, a harmonious will which accommodates every alien material or abstract phenomenon within its infinitely stressed spirituality. The artifact of Ogun's conquest of separation, the "fetish" was iron ore, symbol of earth's womb-energies, cleaver and welder of life. Ogun, through his redemptive action, became the first symbol of the alliance of disparities when, from earth itself, he extracted elements for the subjugation of chthonic chaos. In tragic consciousness the votary's psyche reaches out beyond the realm of nothingness (or spiritual chaos) which is potentially destructive of human awareness, through areas of terror and blind energies into a ritual empathy with the gods, the eternal presence, who once preceded him in parallel awareness of their own incompletion. Ritual anguish is therefore experienced as that primal transmission of the god's despair—vast, numinous, always incomprehensible. In vain we seek to capture it in words; there is only for the protagonist the certainty of the experience of this abyss—the tragic victim plunges into it in spite of ritualistic earthing and is redeemed only by action. Without acting, and yet in spite of it he is forever lost in the maul of tragic tyranny.

Acting is therefore a contradiction of the tragic spirit, yet it is also its natural complement. To act, the Promethean instinct of rebellion channels anguish into a creative purpose which releases man from a totally destructive despair, releasing from within him the most energetic, deeply combative inventions which, without usurping the territory of the infernal gulf, bridges it with visionary hopes. Only the battle of the will is thus primally creative; from its spiritual stress springs the soul's despairing cry which proves its own solace, which alone reverberating within the cosmic vaults usurps (at least, and however briefly) the powers of the abyss. At the charged climactic moments of the tragic rites we understand how music came to be the sole art form which can contain tragic reality. The votary is led by no other guide into the pristine heart of tragedy. Music as the embodiment of the tragic spirit has been more than perceptively exhausted in the philosophy of Europe; there is little to add, much to qualify. And the function and nature of music in Yoruba tragedy is peculiarly revealing of the shortcomings of long accepted conclusions of European intuition. [...]

VÁCLAV HAVEL

Václav HAVEL (b. 1936) as a beginning playwright and dramaturg—short, chubby with light, curly hair, clear blue eyes full of innocence, and a boyish smile—looked like a cherub or a koala bear. Dressed in his preferred costume of sweater and jeans, he moved at a jogger's pace, a "gentle clumsiness" in all his gestures. Because of his capacity for wonder and his concentration on all that lay outside himself, he seemed perfectly impersonal and impartial.

At first the histrionic appears entirely absent from Havel's persona, but his was a theatricality of ironic and systematic understatement. His mask lay in modesty and methodicalness, which he used to great effect against interrogators, captors, and persecutors. Stepping back from himself, Havel applied the theatre metaphor to his victimization by the state. He saw the State Security agents who came to arrest him as characters in a play.

Fascinated with actors, Havel studied the role of the self in play-acting and based his own performance as a dissent on the politics of living in truth. Authenticity was central to playing the part for which he had been cast. Like Mickiewicz, he belonged to the Eastern European tradition of the writer as the conscience of his nation.

From a prosperous bourgeois family, Havel had been dispossessed by the communists and excluded from higher education because of his class background. For his work as human rights advocate, he had his writings cut out of anthologies and removed from libraries. He was publicly vilified, forbidden to enter theatres, and repeatedly sent to prison. Simply being Havel's friend could bring ostracism. His favorite authors, forbidden by the regime, were those like Kafka and later Beckett and Ionesco, who portrayed the experience of alienation. In his plays and essays, the writer analyzed the loss of identity suffered by individuals caught in society's anonymous mechanisms of control.

Active spectatorship was the antidote proposed by Havel. Identity could be regained through the communal experience of theatre and its "interexistentiality"—not in the large playhouses that moralized and gave the official picture, but in the small experimental studios where the conspiracy of togetherness between actors and audience led to social self-awareness and collective liberation from fear. In the clandestine performances that took place in apartments to circumvent the censor, the action shifted from stage to audience. The director Jan Grossman said that the hero of Havel's plays is the spectator.

"Drama is a favorite realm of demystification," the Czech playwright-theorist maintained, demythologizing mimesis, realism and the Brechtian Marxist model. Havel objected to self-styled Brecht disciples and pseudo-philosophical directors who wanted to transform plays into sociological theses. Each play had its own secrets, and the theatre must remain a strange and mysterious realm.

Havel knew the stage in all its aspects: he built sets and made props, served as dramaturg and assistant director, and wrote plays for specific actors at the theatres where he worked. At twenty-one an army conscript and model soldier following the regulations to the letter, Havel got his first practical experience as general stagehand and actor-writer in two productions dealing with army life: playing the villain in Pavel Kohout's *September Nights* and writing and performing *Life Ahead*, inspired by Hašek's *Good Soldier Schweik*.

In 1959-60 Havel began his professional career in the theatre as a scene shifter and stagehand at the ABC Theatre, thanks to its director, Jan Werich, who in 1930s with Jiří Voskovec had run the famous Liberated Theatre. Here Havel discovered the tradition of free humor, poetic shorthand, and clown shows that came from the Czech avant-garde of the interwar years, and he learned that the theatre can be "a seismograph of the times, an area of freedom, an instrument of human liberation."

At this point Havel wrote his first absurdist play, *An Evening with the Family*, an unperformed one-act in the manner of Ionesco. Starting in 1961, Havel began contributing theoretical articles to the journal *Divadlo* (*Theatre*) about the aesthetics and conventions of theatre, codes of acting and stage design, and the qualities of theatrical space. His letters to his wife from prison, published as *Letters to Olga*, are full of theoretical reflections about the nature and function of the stage. Like his later interviews and commentary on the politics of theatre, all these speculations are grounded in Havel's firsthand experience as a spectator and playwright.

WRITING FOR THE STAGE (1986)

[...] This invasion of "nonideological art" occurred against the background of an accelerating emancipation in the social sciences, and at the same time, it inspired this emancipation and helped to accelerate it even more. Philosophy, historiography, and other scholarly disciplines extricated themselves from their rigid, dogmatic straitjackets. And there was some thing else. Theatre is always a sensitive seismograph of an era, perhaps the most sensitive one there is; it's a sponge that quickly soaks up important ingredients in the atmosphere around it. These movements in the theatre have to be seen against the wider background of the general climate of those times. Life in Prague was different then. Today, on National Street on a Saturday evening, you will meet five cops, five moneychangers, and three drunks. Back then the streets were full. People knew how to entertain themselves spontaneously. They didn't just sit at home watching television, they went out. In the little bars and wine rooms you could find actors, painters, writers; wherever you went there was someone you knew. Life was somehow more relaxed, freer; it was as though there was more humor, ingenuousness, hope. People could get involved in something, go after something, take trouble with things; Prague had not yet been buried under a landslide of general apathy and turned stiff and corpselike under its weight. In other words—paradoxically—it made sense to deal with the absurdity of being, because things still mattered. And, in their own way, the small theatres reflected all that, gave expression to it, helped to create it. They were one of the important manifestations and mediators of this intellectual and spiritual process in which the society became aware of itself, and liberated itself; and which inevitably led to the familiar political changes in 1968.

What basic differences were there between the aesthetics of the small theatres of the time and traditional theatre ?

I've already mentioned one of the differences: the divergence, the nonideological nature of those theatres. We didn't try to explain the world; we

From Václav Havel, *Disturbing the Peace: A Conversation with Karel Hvízdala*, trans. Paul Wilson. N.Y.: Vintage, 1991.

weren't interested in theses, and we had no intention of instructing anybody. It was more like a game—except that the "game" somehow mysteriously touched the deepest nerves of human existence and social life, and if it didn't always do this, at least it did so in its happier moments. The humor was described as pure, as an example of *l'art pour l'art*, as dadaistic, as being an end in itself, but, oddly enough, this humor, which apparently had no connections with "burning events" of the time, as that phrase is conventionally understood, gave expression—strangely and indirectly—to the most urgent matter of all: what man really is. And without necessarily being intellectuals, perceptive members of the audience felt that even the most grotesque escapade by Vyskočil touched something essential in them, the genuine drama and the genuine ineffability of life, things as fundamental as despair, empty hope, bad luck, misfortune, groundless joy.

Another important characteristic of these theatres was the way they worked against illusion. The theatre no longer pretended that it was an "image of life." Psychologically detailed types, characters represented in the kind of relationship they would allegedly find themselves in real life, disappeared from the stage. The small theatres simply wanted to show something, so they showed it; they showed it in all kinds of ways, as it occurred to them, randomly, according to the law of ideas. People were on the stage in their own right; they played with each other and they played with the audience; they did not present stories but, rather, posed questions or opened up themes. And — something I considered the most important thing of all—they manifested the experience of absurdity.

What exactly is absurd theatre? How would you define it?

Personally, I think it's the most significant theatrical phenomenon of the twentieth century, because it demonstrates modern humanity in a "state of crisis," as it were. That is, it shows man having lost his fundamental metaphysical certainty, the experience of the absolute, his relationship to eternity, the sensation of meaning—in other words, having lost the ground under his feet. This is a man for whom everything is coming apart, whose world is collapsing, who senses that he has irrevocably lost something but is unable to admit this to himself and therefore hides from it. He waits, unable to understand that he is waiting in vain: *Waiting for Godot*. He is plagued by the need to communicate the main thing, but he has nothing to communicate: Ionesco's *The Chairs*. He seeks a firm point in recollection, not knowing that there is nothing to recollect: Beckett's *Happy Days*. He lies to himself and those around him by saying he's going somewhere to find something that will give him back his identity: Pinter's *The Caretaker*. He thinks he knows those closest to him and himself, and it turns out that he doesn't know anyone: Pinter's *The Homecoming*. Obviously these are model situations of man in decline. These plays are often inspired by quite trivial everyday situations, such as a visit to friends (Ionesco's *The Bald Soprano*), pedagogical tyranny *(The Lesson)*, a woman burying herself in sand at the beach *(Happy Days)*. These are not scenes from life but theatrical images of the basic modalities of humanity in a state of collapse. There is no philosophizing in these plays as there is in Sartre, for example. On the contrary, what is expressed tends to be banal. In their meaning, however, they are always philosophical. They cannot be taken literally; they illustrate nothing. They merely point to the final horizon of our common general theme. They are not overblown, highly impassioned, or didactic. They tend, rather, to be decadently joking in tone. They know the phenomenon of endless embarrassment. Often the characters are silent; often they run off at the mouth in stupid ways. They can be seen as outright comedies. The plays are not—and this is important—nihilistic. They are merely a warning. In a very shocking way, they throw us into the question of meaning by manifesting its absence. Absurd theatre does not offer us consolation or hope. It merely reminds us of how we are living: without hope. And that is the essence of its warning. Absurd theatre, in its particular (and easily describable) way, makes the fundamental questions of the modern human dimension of Being its themes. Absurd theatre is not here to explain how things are. It does not have that kind of arrogance; it leaves the instructing to Brecht. The absurd playwright does not have the key to anything. He does not consider himself any better informed or any more aware than his audience. He sees his role in giving a form to something we all suffer from, and in reminding us, in suggestive ways, of the mystery before which we all stand equally helpless.

I've already written elsewhere about absurd theatre, and I don't want to repeat myself here. I should perhaps say, though, that absurd theatre as such—that is, as a tendency in dramatic literature—was not an explicit part of the artistic program of any of the small theatres in Prague in the 1960s, not even in the Theatre on the Balustrade, which came the closest to it of any. And yet the experience of absurdity did exist somewhere in the bowels of all those theatres. It was not merely transmitted through particular artistic influences; it was, above all, something that was "in the air." That's what I value most in absurd theatre: it was able to capture what was "in the air." And I can't resist a provocative quip here: I have the feeling that, if absurd theatre had not existed before me, I would have had to invent it.

If you compare the small theatres in the 1960's with what can be seen in Czechoslovakia in the eighties, what conclusions would you come to?

The Theatre on a String, the Hana Theatre, the Theatre on the Fringe, the Činoherní Klub, and several amateur groups that have appeared in recent years—all of that is immensely important and in many ways akin to what existed in the 1960s. Once again there is that unplanned movement from below, that departure from the norm, the deliberate avoidance of ideology, the lively and understanding audiences. Again they are a symptom of a wider social awakening, a sign of activity under the surface. Theatre has always been the first to alert us to this. I follow these theatres, and I rejoice in them. I often find myself being less critical toward them than their own young audiences, which is obviously better than if it were the other way around.

If I were to say how this movement today differs from the movement I once took part in, I would have to mention a certain predominance of "how" over "what." The cultivation of acting skills, the cinematographic and directorial fantasy, the so-called theatrical techniques, all seem to me far more refined than they were in our time. From that point of view, I suppose that our performances would seem rather clumsy today. On the other hand, I think the theatre said more in our time; it burrowed more deeply into the consciousness of the time; it was more analytical, more direct, more transparent, and more emphatic in what it communicated

There are a number of reasons for this. The main one is probably that one can do far less today; the censors and the bureaucrats are far more on the alert than they were in our time, and therefore it is far more difficult to get to the heart of the matter. This has led the small theatres to adopt an increasingly sophisticated set of ciphers, suggestions, indirect references, and vague parallels. Sometimes they are so refined and so convoluted that even someone as open to everything as I am can scarcely understand them.

The second reason is deeper and clearly relates to a subtle shift in the human sensibility, a shift that reaches far beyond the borders of Czechoslovakia. The 1980s are simply different from the disingenuous and transparent 1960s. Today's small theatre here is far more a theatre of situation, action, movement, metaphor, suggestion, association, feeling, than it is a theatre of ideas. The plays that these theatres mount are strange poetic collages, highly ambiguous fantasies that attempt to set the nerves tingling and evoke feelings. They appeal to the intellect far less.

The influence of these subtle shifts in the world's cultural atmosphere (or is it stratosphere?) combines, in Czechoslovakia with the need to face up to the barbaric limitations of the country's cultural policies. The overdevelopment of external elements in theatrical expression sometimes goes hand in hand with a lack of irony towards the self, a certain seriousness, an emptiness, even a gloominess in the way things are conveyed that are far less weighty or serious than the things we once tried to convey in a deliberately light, superficial way. I'm fond of one of Jan Grossman's sayings: theatre should be done well, he used to say, but it mustn't take itself too seriously. The main problem of Czech theatre is that it takes itself insanely seriously, yet at the same time it is not particularly well done. I don't mean that today's small theatres are not doing a good job; on the contrary, their performances are sometimes polished and honed to the precision of calligraphy. But for my taste, they sometimes take themselves too seriously. If you read some of their program notes, or the theoretical writings of their creators, the erudition in them (frequently more imitation than invention), is enough to make your head spin. And I can't help feeling there is something ridiculous about it. Anyone who takes himself too seriously runs the risk of looking ridiculous; anyone who can consistently laugh at himself does not. I don't think we took ourselves that seriously. We didn't theorize and philosophize nearly as much about our work. Perhaps it was because we were more deeply immersed in the experience of absurdity; that may somehow have saved us. Reflecting on our general ridiculousness in the world, on our unfitness to be in the world, on our misery, our isolation, the grotesqueness of our illusions: these were agents of self–control that made it impossible for anyone to become unintentionally ridiculous. The brutality, the aggressivity, the exaggerations which some of the creators in today's small theatres use to try to break through the vicious circle of alienated human existence, to touch something authentic, can very easily push them right to the threshold of the ridiculous, simply because they are the result of a "short circuit." But no phase can just be skipped over; modern man must descend the spiral of his own absurdity to the lowest point; only then can he look beyond it. It is obviously impossible to get around it, jump over it, or simply avoid it. [...]

The Politics of Hope

[...] And a final thing. Most people don't know how to read plays. (And why should they? Wouldn't this render theatre redundant?) Among other things they can't drop their private reader's experience and imagine the radically different collective experience of theatre. When you are in an audience, your experience is different from what it would be at home in an easy chair. When I was supervising performances of my own plays at the Theatre on the Balustrade, I could watch audiences' reactions very closely. Each time I did, I was reminded of how being in an audience gives everything another dimension. If you read a play in which evil is named, in which everything turns out badly, and in which there isn't a single positive character, you can easily be depressed by it, and little else. But if you see the play performed in a theatre, in that exciting atmosphere of common understanding, you suddenly feel completely different about it. Even the toughest truth expressed publicly, in front of everyone else, suddenly becomes liberating. In the beautiful ambivalence that is proper only to the theatre, the horror of that truth (and why hide it—it looks worse onstage than it does when it does when we read it) is wedded to something new and unfamiliar, at least from our reading: to delight (which can only be experienced collectively), because it was finally said, it's out of the bag, the truth has finally been articulated out loud and in public.

In the ambivalence of this experience there is something that has been a part of theatre from the beginning: catharsis. Jan Grossman once wrote of my plays that their positive hero is the audience. This doesn't just mean that a viewer who is moved by what he has seen may start looking for a real solution (not a generally transferable solution, like the answer to a crossword puzzle, but an untransferable act: his own existential awakening). It also means that he becomes this "positive hero" while he's still in the audience, as one who participates and cocreates the catharsis, sharing with others the liberating delight in evil exposed. Through the demonstration of the misery of the world, an experience is evoked that is—paradoxically—profoundly edifying. Somewhere in here is the beginning of hope—real hope, not hope for a happy ending. But if the play is truly to evoke this, it must somehow be internally disposed to do so. Horror per se, or just any kind of horror, doesn't automatically lead to catharsis. Some secret enzymes must be at work in the tissue of the play. But how to do it is my problem; let me be judged only by the results. The theatrical results, of course.

A BRIEF BIBLIOGRAPHY

Anthologies and Books in English about Theatrical Theory

Adams, Henry Hitch and Baxter Hathaway, eds. *Dramatic Essays of the Neoclassic Age*. N.Y.; Benjamin Blom, 1965.

Barish, Jonas. *The Antitheatrical Prejudice*. Berkeley: University of California Press, 1981.

Bentley, Eric, ed. *Theory of the Modern Stage*. N.Y.: Applause, 1997.

Carlson, Marvin. *Theories of the Theatre: a historical and critical survey from the Greeks to the present*, expanded ed. Ithaca: Cornell University Press, 1993.

Clark, Barrett H., ed. *European Theories of the Drama*. N.Y.: Crown, 1965.

Dukore, Bernard F., ed. *Dramatic Theory and Criticism*. N.Y.: Holt, Rinehart and Winston, 1974.

Herzfeld-Sander, Margaret, ed. *Essays on German Theater*. N.Y.: Continuum, 1985.

Sidnell, Michael J., ed. *Sources of Dramatic Theory*, Vols. 1 and 2. Cambridge: Cambridge University Press, 1991.

ACKNOWLEDGMENTS

Bharata, *Natyasastra*, selections. Translated by Adya Rangacharya. Reprinted by permission of Adya Rangacharya and Munshiram Manoharlal Publishers Ltd. Copyright © 1986.

Zeami, *On the Art of the No Drama: The Major Treatises of Zeami*, selections, trans. J. Thomas Rimer and Yamazaki Masakazu. Reprinted by permission of Princeton University Press. Copyright © 1984 by Princeton University Press.

Castelvetro, "The Poetics of Aristotle." Reprinted by permission of Wayne State University from *Literary Criticism: Plato to Dryden*, ed. and trans. by Allan H. Gilbert. Copyright © 1962 Wayne State University Press.

Guarini, Giambattista, "The Compendium of Tragicomic Poetry." Reprinted by permission of Wayne State University from *Literary Criticism: Plato to Dryden*, ed. and trans. by Allan H. Gilbert. Copyright © 1962 Wayne State University Press.

Lope de Vega, "The New Art of Writing Plays," translation by Marvin Carlson. Copyright © 2000 Marvin Carlson.

Corneille, Pierre, "Of the Three Unities of Action, Time, and Place," translated by Donald Schier. Reprinted by permission from *The Continental Model*, ed. by Scott Elledge and Donald Schier Copyright © 1960 University of Minnesota.

Li Yu, "Casual Expressions of Idle Feelings," translation by Faye C. Fei and William H. Sun. Copyright © 2000 Faye C. Fei and William H. Sun.

Diderot, Denis, "Conversations on *The Natural Son*," selections. Reprinted by permission of Macmillan, a Division of Simon & Schuster from *Diderot: Selected Writings*, ed. Lester G. Crocker, trans. Derek Coltman. Copyright © 1966 Lester G. Crocker.

Schiller, Friedrich, "On the Use of Chorus in Tragedy." From *The Bride of Messina, William Tell, Demetrius*. Translated by Charles E. Passage. Reprinted by permission of the Continuum Publishing Company. Copyright © 1967.

Goethe, Wolfgang von, "Shakespeare Once Again." From *Essays on Art and Literature*, ed. John Gearey, trans. Ellen von Nardroff and Ernest H. von Nardroff. Reprinted by permission of Suhrkamp Verlag. Copyright © 1986.

Hugo, Victor, "Preface to *Cromwell*" from *Revolution in the Theatre: French Romantic Theories of Drama*, ed. and trans. Barry V. Daniels. Reprinted by permission of Greenwood Publishing Group, Inc., Westport, CT. Copyright © 1983.

Zola, Emile, "Preface to *Therese Raquin*," trans. by Kathleen Boutall, from *From the Modern Repertoire, Series Three*, ed. by Eric Bentley, Indiana Univerity Press. Copyright © 1966.

Zola, Emile, "Naturalism in the Theatre," translated by Jane House. Copyright © by Jane House.

Strindberg, August, "Preface to *Miss Julie*." From *Strindberg: Five Plays*, ed. and trans. by Harry G. Carlson. Reprinted by permission of The Regents of the University of California. Copyright © 1983

Meyerhold, Vsevold, "The Fairground Booth." From *Meyerhold on Theatre*, ed. and trans. by Edward Braun. Reprinted by permission of Methuen Drama. Copyright © 1991.

Marinetti, F. T., "The Variety Theatre." From *Selected Writings* by F. T. Marinetti, translated by R.W. Flint and Arthur A. Coppotelli. Copyright © 1972 by Farrar, Straus & Giroux, Inc. Reprinted by permission of Farrar, Straus & Giroux, Inc.

Artaud, Antonin, *The Theater and Its Double*, trans. by Mary Caroline Richards. Reprinted by permission of Grove/Atlantic, Inc. Copyright © 1958 by Grove Press.

Brecht, Bertolt, "The Modern Theatre is the Epic Theatre" and "Alienation Effect in Chinese Acting." From *Brecht on Theatre*, ed. and trans. by John Willet. Translation copyright © 1964 and copyright renewed © 1992 by John Willet. Reprinted by permission of Hill and Wang, a division of Farrar, Straus & Giroux, Inc.

Boal, Augusto, *Theatre of the Oppressed*, selections, trans. by Charles A. and Maria-Odilia Leal McBride. Reprinted by permission of Theatre Communications Group, Inc. Copyright © 1979.

Soyinka, Wole, "Drama and the African World-view." From *Myth, Literature and the African World* by Wole Soyinka. Reprinted by permission of Cambridge University Press. Copyright © 1976 Cambridge University Press.

Havel, Václav, "Writing for the Stage." From *Disturbing the Peace: A Conversation with Karel Hvízdala*, trans. Paul Wilson. Reprinted by permission of Alfred A. Knopf. Inc. Copyright © 1990 by Vaclav Havel.

THE COLLECTED
WORKS OF
HAROLD CLURMAN

Six Decades of Commentary on
Theatre, Dance, Music, Film, Arts,
Letters and Politics

edited by Marjorie Loggia and Glenn Young

"...RUSH OUT AND BUY *THE COLLECTED WORKS OF HAROLD CLURMAN*...Editors Marjorie Loggia and Glenn Young have assembled a monumental helping of his work... **THIS IS A BOOK TO LIVE WITH;** picking it up at random is like going to the theater with Clurman and then sitting down with him in a good bistro for some exhilarating talk. This is a very big book, but Clurman was a very big figure."

JACK KROLL, *Newsweek*

"**THE BOOK SWEEPS ACROSS THE 20TH CENTURY,** offering a panoply of theater in Clurman's time...IT RESONATES WITH PASSION."

MEL GUSSOW, *The New York Times*

CLOTH •ISBN 1-55783-132-7 PAPER • ISBN 1-55783-264-1

IN SEARCH OF THEATER

by ERIC BENTLEY

FIRST published in 1953, *In Search of Theater* is widely regarded as the standard portrait of the European and American theatre in the turbulent and seminal years following World War II. The book's influence contributed substantially to the rising reputations of such artists as Bertolt Brecht, Charles Chaplin and Martha Graham.

"The most erudite and intelligent living writer on the theatre."

—Ronald Bryden, *The New Statesman*

"CERTAINLY AMERICA'S FOREMOST THEATRE CRITIC…"

—Irving Wardle, *The Times*

ISBN: 1-55783-111-4

TWO COLLECTIONS BY
STANISLAW IGNACY WITKIEWICZ

THE MADMAN AND THE NUN &
THE CRAZY LOCOMOTIVE

Three plays (including The Water Hen)

Edited, translated and with an introduction by Daniel
Gerould and C. S. Durer.
Foreword by Jan Kott

paper • ISBN: 0-936839-83-X

AND

THE MOTHER AND OTHER UNSAVORY PLAYS

Including The Shoemakers and They

Edited and Translated by Daniel Gerould and C .S.
Durer

paper • ISBN: 0-936839-139-4

Before Solidarity, before Walesa, before the cold war, before
Sartre and Camus, there was Polish dramatist (and painter and
philosopher and dandy and...) S.I. Witkiewicz. He not only
anticipated it all, he was already howling his head off about it in
the intense, explosive plays he wrote in Cracow between 1918
and 1925. In his extravagant persona and outrageous dramas he
was, as many have called him, turly the Polish Oscar Wilde.

**"It is high time that this major playwright should become
better known in the English-speaking world."**

— **Martin Esslin**

THE LIFE OF THE DRAMA
by Eric Bentley

". . . Eric Bentley's radical new look at the grammar of theatre . . . is a work of exceptional virtue, and readers who find more in it to disagree with than I do will still, I think, want to call it central, indispensable . . . The book justifies its title by being precisely about the ways in which life manifests itself in the theatre. If you see any crucial interest in such topics as the death of Cordelia, Godot's non-arrival . . . This is a book to be read and read again."

— **Frank Kermode**
THE NEW YORK REVIEW OF BOOKS

"*The Life of the Drama* . . . is a remarkable exploration of the roots and bases of dramatic art, the most far reaching and revelatory we have had."

— **Richard Gilman**
BOOK WEEK

"*The Life of the Drama* is Eric Bentley's magnum opus or the put it more modestly his best book. I might call it an aesthetic of the drama, but this again sounds ponderous; the book is eminently lucid and often helpfully epigrammatic. Everyone genuinely interested in the theatre should read it. It is full of remarkable insights into many of the most important plays ever written."

— **Harold Clurman**

paper • ISBN: 1-55783-110-6